D0360218

The Dynamics of
American Politics

TRANSFORMING AMERICAN POLITICS
Lawrence C. Dodd, Series Editor

Dramatic changes in political institutions and behavior over the past three decades have underscored the dynamic nature of American politics, confronting political scientists with a new and pressing intellectual agenda. The pioneering work of early postwar scholars, while laying a firm empirical foundation for contemporary scholarship, failed to consider how American politics might change or to recognize the forces that would make fundamental change inevitable. In reassessing the static interpretations fostered by these classic studies, political scientists are now examining the underlying dynamics that generate transformational change.

Transforming American Politics brings together texts and monographs that address four closely related aspects of change. A first concern is documenting and explaining recent changes in American politics—in institutions, processes, behavior, and policymaking. A second is reinterpreting classic studies and theories to provide a more accurate perspective on postwar politics. The series looks at historical change to identify recurring patterns of political transformation within and across the distinctive eras of American politics. Last and perhaps most importantly, the series presents new theories and interpretations that explain the dynamic processes at work and thus clarify the direction of contemporary politics. All of the books focus on the central theme of transformation—transformation in both the conduct of American politics and in the way we study and understand its many aspects.

FORTHCOMING TITLES

The Semi-Sovereign Presidency: The Bush Administration's Strategy for Governing Without Congress, Charles Tiefer

The Year of the Woman: Myths and Realities, edited by Elizabeth Adell Cook, Sue Thomas, and Clyde Wilcox

Congress and the Administrative State, Second Edition, Lawrence C. Dodd and Richard L. Schott

The New American Politics, edited by Bryan D. Jones

Young Versus Old: Generational Gaps in Political Participation and Policy Preferences, Susan MacManus and Suzanne L. Parker

The Parties Respond: Changes in American Parties and Campaigns, Second Edition, edited by L. Sandy Maisel

Campaigns and Elections, edited by James A. Thurber and Candice J. Nelson

Cold War Politics, John Kenneth White

Bureaucratic Dynamics: The Role of the Bureaucracy in a Democracy, B. Dan Wood and Richard W. Waterman

The Dynamics of American Politics

APPROACHES AND INTERPRETATIONS

EDITED BY

Lawrence C. Dodd
Calvin Jillson

University of Colorado–Boulder

Westview Press

BOULDER • *SAN FRANCISCO* • *OXFORD*

Transforming American Politics

Portions of Chapter 8 appeared in the introduction to *Protecting Soldiers and Mothers: The Political Origins of Social Policy in the United States* by Theda Skocpol (Cambridge, Mass.: The Belknap Press of Harvard University Press, 1992). Copyright © 1992 by the President and Fellows of Harvard College. Reprinted by permission of the publisher.

Published in 1994 in the United States of America by Westview Press, Inc., 5500 Central Avenue, Boulder, Colorado 80301-2877, and in the United Kingdom by Westview Press, 36 Lonsdale Road, Summertown, Oxford OX2 7EW

Library of Congress Cataloging-in-Publication Data
The Dynamics of American politics : approaches and interpretations /
    edited by Lawrence C. Dodd, Calvin Jillson.
        p.   cm. — (Transforming American Politics series)
    Includes bibliographical references and index.
    ISBN 0-8133-1711-8—ISBN 0-8133-1712-6 (pbk.)
    1. United States—Politics and government.   2. Political
development.   I. Dodd, Lawrence C., 1946–   II. Jillson, Calvin
C., 1949–   III. Series.
JK21.D96   1994
320.973—dc20   93-15604
                                                                                           CIP

Printed and bound in the United States of America

The paper used in this publication meets the requirements
of the American National Standard for Permanence of Paper
for Printed Library Materials Z39.48-1984.

10   9   8   7   6   5   4   3   2

Contents

Foreword

THEODORE J. LOWI

POLITICAL HISTORY AND POLITICAL SCIENCE

In setting the tone for this volume, I aim to be provocative about political history and its relation to political science. Political history can actually cover a very large part of the entire field of political science, because history means sequence, and there can be no conception of causation and explanation without sequence, even if the time elapsed is only a few seconds. Empirical political science is replete with association, interaction, and correlation—yet the authors of such empirical studies obviously have to assume their independent variables come prior in time to dependent variables. Political history only insists that the time frame be extended, not only to do justice to the dependent variables but also to pick up the, let us say, intervening variables, such as institutions, policies, and social structures that could never be gotten directly from cross-sectional data themselves.[1]

When we are not doing history for its own sake but rather for a purpose, history means evolution, or development. The terms are almost synonymous, and in any case there is no point quibbling over the difference. Evolution refers to the emergence or "unrolling" to full maturity of something that already exists in rudimentary form, that is, where all the parts of the eventual thing are already present and await pronouncement (Williams, 1976:103–105). We in the social sciences are developmental by instinct. We speak of developed and underdeveloped societies and economies. We refer to the development of bureaucratic states, the evolution of the constitution or of human rights. Our vocabulary includes a large number of "-tion" words that imply development; "-tion" as a suffix means "in the process of" or "a condition of being or becoming," as in bureaucratization, centralization, or nationalization.

I favor an historical as well as a developmental political science because it requires, above all else, the skill and craft of description. The evolution of a party system, the institutionalization of the House of Representatives, or the concentration of modern presidential power need not require causation; yet not even the first causal hypothesis can be formulated without a very thorough description of the phenomenon in question—including the history of its becoming what it is described to be. One of the most unfortunate developments in the evolution, as it were, of the scientific study of politics is the proliferation of independent variables. With only the most primitive accounting given for the dependent variable (that is, the phenomenon to be explained), we confront an enormous apparatus of independent variables, which do not represent an improved science but merely a shift of focus away from the initial problem—as defined by the dependent variable. In contrast, when the dependent variable has been thoroughly described and its salient features have been identified, then the relevant independent variables almost present themselves. A good case in point is the phenomenon of critical elections and realignment. This is no more and no less than a description of what is alleged to be a recurring phenomenon, yet it energized the study of parties and elections for many years and was instrumental in bringing history to contemporary political science. It may now be energizing the field once again, with a new description. What else can Walter Dean Burnham mean by "pattern recognition" in Chapter 3 of this volume?

My affinity for political history and the study of the evolution and development of political institutions and practices is thus based upon their commitment to description as the most sophisticated thing we are called upon to do in political science. Description requires theory, because to render a complex whole into its essential parts demands the use of standards and criteria, which must come from somewhere. Description also requires theory because it involves categorization and classification—in a word, taxonomy—according to structure and function and according to time or sequence: periodization, in fact. This is what analysis is all about: breaking a thing down into its parts. But what parts? *Any* parts, as long as the logic imposed upon the breakdown permits you to put the parts back together again in a more meaningful way. That is definitely theory, and it is a lot of theory, even if implicit, before ever getting to questions of causation. I do not want to be misunderstood about causation: Causation is okay, so long as it knows its place. Description comes first. Development is little more than description of a particular state of affairs at more than one point in time. And causation involves the description of one thing in terms of something that precedes it.

All this may qualify me for formal affiliation with political history and the new institutionalism. But that also makes me a bit uncomfortable. To quote Groucho Marx, I generally don't like to belong to any club that would have me as a member. As I see it, the main weakness of history, as evolution or development, is that it fails to recognize its own limitations. Specifically, development is inconceivable without nondevelopment; development without nondevelopment makes development virtually an ideology. Some phenomena have a time line but are not developmental. Others are cyclical, that is, patterned but not developmental. Still others are better understood not historically at all but as systems that once having developed move more or less cyclically from equilibrium to disequilibrium and back. (Is *system* "the end of history"?) Then there are other phenomena that indeed have a history but either persist essentially without change, or move from stable nondevelopment to abrupt and discontinuous, mutational change, far from anything resembling the emergence of inherent tendencies or the successive rolling out to maturity of features that were already possessed in embryo. All these seem to me to be cases of nondevelopment. They interest me because recognition of these possibilities will actually strengthen history as method in political science.

To that end, I have picked three cases to illustrate what I consider to be nondevelopment in politics: phenomena without evolution, without change over long stretches of time, or with long durability interrupted by sudden and discontinuous change. The cases are familiar ones and require little detailing: (1) the American city as a collective entity, (2) the American presidency, and (3) the American state and the state interest.

Case One: The American City as a Collective Entity

Many things about American cities are developmental, but the American city as a corporate, governmental entity (as a state in microcosm) is not a developmental phenomenon. Its institutions and policies have always worked in a conservative direction to preserve the social order and to defend property. Cities can be pluralist or elitist or combinations thereof, just as they can be developmental in a number of respects. But they operate within a rigidly narrow range of essential constitutional or constitutive values: to keep classes and races in their places; to keep the poor invisible; to protect property from those who have none; and to rely upon institutions of church, party, and education as well as upon police and other governmental agencies to maintain and to reproduce order—order, essentially, by segregation. Maybe the nondevelopmental values are coextensive with "non-decisions." It is ironic how much we were able to learn about a developmental political science from Robert Merton's theory of the latent functions of institutions, especially of local political machines, without perceiving the nondevelopmental reality of the political context of these very same institutions, at least in cities. Back in the 1960s, functionalism was attacked as conservative. Wrong. The conservatism was not in the functionalism *or* the functionalists; it was in the functions themselves.

A false impression about the liberality as well as the development of American cities has been conveyed during the past half-century because of federal urban and urban-oriented policies. From 1939 on, and particularly since 1949, there has been a dramatic and fundamental increase in federal categoric grants-in-aid for cities; direct aid amounted to over 20 percent of city revenues, and federal aid to states came closer to 40 percent of state revenues, with much of that aimed at the cities. This artificially freed cities from their tax base (essentially a property tax base) and gave them the opportunity and the incentive, indeed the mandate, to engage in such liberal policies and programs as welfare policies for wealth redistribution; health delivery policies to integrate, rather than disease control through segregation (called quarantine); housing and civil rights policies to weaken class and racial segregation, and so on (Peterson, 1981). Yet this was artificial, and exogenous, and created a false and probably temporary impression. My favorite example is New Haven, Connecticut, where the engine of its famous redevelopment was not its pluralist local power structure—though that may have made a difference in the form and scale and speed. The real engine was the federal government, with its introduction of a highway interchange off the New England Thruway right through the Oak Street slum, in addition to a disproportionate amount of federal urban redevelopment money. Another manifestation of cities as nondevelopmentally conservative is Ed Koch, who was transformed from a crusading Fair Deal member of Congress into a profoundly reactionary mayor of New York.

Case Two: The American Presidency

No political phenomenon has received more developmental treatment than the U.S. presidency. Yet, if presidential supremacy were already in embryo in Article 2, and if the presidency had developed in the bumpy but linear pattern attributed to it, what a gigantic office it would have been for Franklin Roosevelt in 1933. Thomas Jefferson, says one biographer, gave the presidency a leadership based on mass consent, "to use the power of government on behalf of the public good."[2] But, according to many other historians as well as political scientists, Andrew Jackson was the real revolutionary and "the first modern president."[3] If so, then who or what had dismantled Jefferson's legacy? And if Jackson left the presidency more modern than it had been, and if Abraham Lincoln somehow built upon a Jackson legacy, then what happened by 1900 that left us with what Woodrow Wilson called "congressional government" and with what Lord Bryce characterized as a dreary parade of weak presidents? Conditions (that is, independent variables) favoring growth of executive power in a "new American state" were all in place, but they did not sustain so much as a memory trace, much less a legacy, from Lincoln's record.

This is the kind of trouble that comes from starting first with a set of independent variables. Do they make a development inevitable just because they could explain it if it happened? An epigram attributed to Barrington Moore is appropriate here: "The inevitable is seldom what anybody expected." The fact is that the presidency inherited by Roosevelt was still impoverished, in at least three ways: It lacked constitutional authority, it lacked management capacity, and it lacked a mass public constituency. We *can* see development after 1933—but that only serves to emphasize the lack of development prior to 1933. We impose a developmental pattern on the presidency largely for ideological reasons.

Case Three: The American State and the State Interest

The so-called American state itself has been a nondevelopmental phenomenon for most of its history. Brush aside all the factors that would help explain a developmental state, if it had been developmental, and you have, at best, a two-phase phenomenon: a nondevelopmental epoch from 1789 and a developmental epoch, perhaps since 1937.

I am aware of various periodizations of American history that suggest development from start to finish. But, as with the presidency, the state itself was so nondevelopmental that a tracing of its functions by a stranger to our history would hardly reveal that there had been a civil war or an industrial revolution. A few facts about the major eras of development will help bring the developmental aspect into serious question.

The first epoch, usually defined as the period from 1789 to the Civil War, was, of course, rich in social, economic, and political events, but these events do not produce a sustained development in the American state. During that epoch, the American state was, and steadfastly remained, a patronage state. All the serious governing was done by the state governments, using the "police power" reserved to the states by Article 1 and the Tenth Amendment. States were not even limited by the Bill of Rights.[4] This was genuine "dual federalism," in which the national government, what there was of the so-called American state, provided internal improvements, land grants, other claims, and tariffs. The Supreme Court actually tried to change nation-state relations in a way that might have given the nation and the presidency a developmental impulse. The famous case of *McCulloch v. Maryland* was an open invitation to expand and be positive about national powers through what came to be called "the elastic clause."[5] From *Gibbons* to *Dred Scott*, the Court proved more than ready to approve not only an expansive and positive national government but also one not particularly limited by prior state government actions or commitments.[6] Yet, Congress simply did not choose to act in ways that would erode the states' powers. As for the presidents of that epoch, they were actually against "developing" the nation-state's interest.

The ultra-strong "first modern" President Jackson used his own powers to reduce, not to expand, the nation-state's powers and interest. He did not expand the Bank of the United States or try to make monetary policy (in the modern sense) with it. He vetoed its renewal and closed it down. Even the internal improvements program, which comprised most of the national government's functional reality not only in this epoch but also during the entire nineteenth century, was emaciated by Jackson's vetoes, including his veto of the famous Maysville Road turnpike. By the end of the 1830s, the national government had withdrawn almost entirely from internal improvements. James Polk, the other reputedly powerful nationally oriented president, put the quietus on the rest of internal improvements until after the Civil War with the 1846 veto of federal money for rivers and harbors projects. And he did so for the constitutional reason that the national government possessed no power in this sphere. Likewise, Jackson devolved decisions on Indian policies to the states. All this is to say that the stronger presidents used their energies to negate or stop the development of national power.

The only significant congressional action asserting national power was the Force Act of 1833, authorizing the president to close ports, to directly collect customs revenues, and to intervene if South Carolina and other states attempted nullification or secession in order to avoid obeying the tariff acts. But this was a reaction to an attack on the very essence of national sovereignty and was not a precedent for, or a step toward, any kind of development beyond what Jefferson would have done under the same conditions thirty years earlier. In other words, there was never a time when a direct threat to the national sovereignty would have been accepted. The Civil War is another reaction of exactly the same sort to a threat to the national sovereignty itself, and it, too, was a single action, albeit an important one, that set no precedent for later state developments in the nineteenth century.

Although there is ample evidence that the Confederacy as well as the Union governments were advanced state-centered systems, further evidence shows that both were demobilized within a decade or so afterwards (Bensel, 1990). By 1880, the American state, at least as manifested by the functions of the national government, was back almost to the *status quo ante bellum*. The Fourteenth Amendment, adopted in 1868, was also almost certainly intended to revolutionize federalism, shrinking the power of state governments over their citizens (reversing *Barron v. Baltimore*) and enhancing the power of the national government, at least to the extent of making certain aspects of the Bill of Rights national rights, which did not vary from state to state. The constitutional cases, however, negated that effect and basically reaffirmed the system that had existed prior to the Civil War. Not only did the cases maintain the relative autonomy of the state governments, they shrank the public realm still further by recognizing the corporation as a person for purposes of protection under the Bill of Rights.[7] This opened the way in 1897 for the only case incorporating any provision of the Bill of Rights into the Fourteenth Amendment, until the incorporation of the First Amendment in 1925–1931 and the rest of the Bill of Rights only in the 1960s.[8] These cases, important as they are in and of themselves, are even more significant as indicators of the lack of development of state power until well into the twentieth century. Stephen Skowronek makes creative use of what I have called a two-phase pattern, with state development beginning for him in the 1880s. But a close look at Skowronek's cases of efforts to "build a new American state" will show that they were precursors at best, leaving little more than a few foundation stones in place for what was to begin only forty or fifty years later (Skowronek, 1982).

Even after the 1930s, when state development became a recognizable fact, it was still not a simple fact, because as our new state followed form and became more powerful, it also became more vulnerable. This particular contradiction may be a nondevelopmental feature of all states, particularly of democratic states.

The best insight into this phenomenon of nondevelopment within development may come from the reactions of the U.S. government to social movements—in other words, to nascent, emergent, "developing" social forces. I devoted the better part of a book to capturing from the social movement literature a clear developmental pattern among nascent interests (Lowi, 1979). But the point here is that although social movements can be shown to move quite predictably through certain phases of development (I identified four in my developmental theory), the government's response to such developments is distinctly nondevelopmental. When a movement is just emerging, it is also in its most radical phase; consequently, responsible agents of the state tend to see the emergent interest as a threat to public order. If ever there was a "state interest," it is this—and it points back to the conservatism of cities. Relevant government agencies respond with repression, then with cooptation. Repression is not biased against any particular orthodoxy; it is strictly oriented toward order. For example, the Federal Bureau of Investigation made no distinction whatsoever between the domestic racial Right (Ku Klux Klan), the domestic Left (including the civil rights movement), and the international far Right and far Left. *All* were put under surveillance, *all* were subject to infiltration and blackmail (Keller, 1990).

As long as an interest remains nascent and radical, government policy remains repressive. As the emergent interest matures (toward phases two and three in my scheme), its relation with government develops accordingly, toward cooptation. Thus, if a nascent movement is to fully realize and maintain its influence, it must articulate its internal organization sufficiently to routinize its politics and deal with the relevant offices in terms of the required routines and procedures. However, such a movement loses its original character as a movement. Most movements in America succeed, if success is measured by a positive governmental response. But as the movement develops, succeeds, and then cools into a mainstream group, the needs of the state to restore order are met. The state structure did not develop. The *group* did.

CONCLUSION

Reflecting back over my text, I am disappointed with its moderation. By denying the status of development to three familiar phenomena—American cities, the American presidency, and the American state—I have committed the rather minor heresy of suggesting a different kind of narrative to impose upon their histories. Whether my own narrative is convincing or not, I have demonstrated merely that since institutions and states are, like systems and power structures, useful fictions and nothing more, we are left with a lot of choice about what they are, where they come from, and what kind of narrative to impose upon them. This means that the test of the value of a narrative or an explanation is not its truth but whether it is good political science; and the test of that is how far into the data and through how much of the narrative we can sustain our argument. If we cut through all the forms and formalities, I will bet this is what theory is all about for most of us.

A second minor heresy arises out of my contention that description comes before explanation and that description of a complex whole calls upon the most important faculties we possess as observers and analysts. I refuse to allow anyone to belittle this contention by referring to a Norman Rockwell painting or the journalistic account of the man biting the dog. We describe for a serious purpose and not for the sake of description alone. We use narrative as a serious novelist would, on two levels. The first level, of course, is the level of the story itself, and it should be told in rich detail. But there is a second level, the purpose of which is to construct the narrative in such a way as to convey character, meaning, and argument.

A third minor heresy is related to the other two, and the three together may very well tip the scale toward one major heresy. It is that there is a lot of ideology in development, just as there is in causation. For the relation between causation and ideology, I recommend Stephen Jay Gould's *The Mismeasure of Man*. As for the connection between ideology and development, I will not try to argue the case further here but would end on an appeal: In each instance where we attempt to construct a developmental narrative, we should ask the question, Of what use is development to its author? For example, a developmental presidency was once a major ideological fulcrum for the New Deal liberals. Now the fulcrum *and* the lever seem to be securely in the hands of the Right. But the really unhappy news is that most everyone, Left or Right, is in agreement on the developmental presidency because each seems to need it to justify a heroic presidency to fulfill its own social program. That is the ideology of the innocents.

The new institutionalism and the revived use of history and development make for a much more powerful, more interesting, and more *political* political science. But let us be sure that the added power is analytic and not ideological. Let us not be guilty of innocently contributing to *any* ideology—whether it be in the service of order, or rationality, or of some particular party's program. Our job is to expose ideologies in all their contradictions, not to give them the stamp of science.

Heresies having been identified, let the inquisition begin.

NOTES

1. Two clarifying comments. First, I could also add the term "state," but it is a term of art whose standards are adequately met by the other terms, especially "institution." Second, some scholars search through history to locate a large number of cases for purposes of comparison. Whatever its virtues, this is not really history, since time is not a relevant factor in the analysis.

2. Ralph Ketcham, "The Jefferson Presidency and Constitutional Beginnings," in Martin Fausold and Alan Shank (eds.), *The Constitution and the American Presidency* (Albany, NY: SUNY Press, 1991), p. 6.

3. Robert V. Remini, "The Constitution and the Presidencies: The Jackson Era," in ibid., p. 30.

4. *Barron v. Baltimore*, 7 Pet. 243 (1833).

5. *McCulloch v. Maryland*, 4 Wheat. 316 (1819).

6. *Gibbons v. Ogden*, 9 Wheat. 1 (1824); *Dred Scott v. Sandford*, 60 U.S. 393 (1857).

7. *Santa Clara County v. Southern Pacific Railroad*, 118 U.S. 394 (1886).

8. *Chicago, Burlington & Quincy Railroad v. Chicago*, 166 U.S. 226 (1897).

1

Conversations on the Study of American Politics: An Introduction

LAWRENCE C. DODD
CALVIN JILLSON

The study of American politics resembles nothing perhaps more closely than the American political system itself. Students of American politics almost universally point to the fragmentation of American governmental processes, the inadequate dialogue among our political actors and institutions, and the incoherence of American public policy. And so it is with American politics as a field of academic study, wherein we find a vast assortment of differing schools of thought and scholarly approaches, scholars of differing traditions who seldom converse with one another or listen to competing interpretations, and an incoherent body of knowledge that often appears in fundamental contradiction. As Theodore Lowi (1992) has remarked so astutely, we do truly become what we study.

And yet, just as the political system is capable of change, so too is the study of American politics. Thus, in the past several decades scholars have embraced sophisticated methods for the measurement and modeling of political behavior. Today virtually every conceivable aspect of our politics is weighed and measured, sifted and culled—all with an eye to those statistical patterns and logical theorems that may give contemporary scholars a special insight into political processes denied their predecessors in a less technological age. Likewise, scholars have extended the scope of their inquiry, looking not only at contemporary politics but also increasingly at historical patterns, searching for dynamic regularities that may clarify contemporary politics and provide a broader understanding of political life. No longer are the founding era, antebellum politics, the progressive movement, or New Deal machinations solely the province of historians. Political scientists also see in earlier eras, and in patterns across eras, a unique opportunity for empirical discovery and theoretical learning.

As political scientists have looked back across history, teasing out the statistical regularities and analytical stories that an historical awareness unveils, they have discovered how dynamic American politics can be. Political patterns thought to be universal truths because of their predominance in the contemporary period—for example, the electoral security and low turnover of members of Congress—suddenly appear to be momentary truths at best, subject to change and transformation in response to new historical contexts (Polsby, 1968; Dodd, 1981). With this awareness has dawned the realization that our understanding of politics must be dynamic as well—that it must account for development and change in institutions, behavior, and policy processes across time, much as biologists must understand the evolution of species across time. And as political scientists seek to understand development and change, as Lowi reminds us in the Foreword, they must be careful to describe phenomena accurately, to distinguish between development and nondevelopment, between evolution and discontinuous mutation, so that they truly focus on the critical issues of political change.

The embrace of political history by political science has also led to a heightened sensitivity to the multiplicity of factors—the state, partisan realignments, cultural beliefs, institutional norms—that account for political behavior, thereby fueling a proliferation of approaches to political analysis not unlike the expanding hyperpluralism of group politics in American society. With this sensitivity has come a very special awareness of the distinctive interplay of two levels of analysis—macro context and micro behavior—that scholars who focus solely on contemporary politics often fail to acknowledge. It is increasingly recognized that just as individuals and groups shape society through their individual and collective choices, so too does society, in its cultural, geopolitical, economic, and institutional manifestations, shape individual and group choice. It is the interplay between individual and societal forces that gives rise to the distinctive politics of an age. Our understanding of politics depends on discerning the nature of this interplay between macro and micro phenomena (Eulau, 1969). Yet the search for understanding tends to become lost amidst the vast array of distinctive analytic approaches, the inherent difficulties of grasping the interactive role of macro and micro factors, and the absence of systematic dialogue among adherents of the different approaches and levels of analysis.

The study of American politics, then, is in a quandary. We realize more and more that explanations of political phenomena require a dynamic, diachronic perspective (Cooper and Brady, 1981; Lowi, 1969; Polsby, 1982; Harris and Milkis, 1989). As we focus on patterns of change, we also realize that the forces that produce them are complex. In seeking to understand this complexity, American political science has fragmented into separate schools or "sects" looking at distinct aspects of the dynamics of American politics. This specialization has generated a growing body of literature marshaling evidence to support the role of a wide range of causal factors. But we have specialized so extensively that we are in the process of losing our focus on the central issue facing our field of study—our collective ability to generate a theoretically coherent understanding of American politics (Almond, 1990).

In light of this state of affairs, the time has come for a fundamental rethinking of how we study American politics: The time has come for a self-conscious and integrative dialogue among scholars—a collective conversation—exploring the different explanatory approaches to politics and identifying the foundations for theoretical convergence. The purpose of this book is to help stimulate such a dialogue.

It is, of course, difficult to engender dialogue amidst the specialization and career pressures of modern academia. As Hugh Heclo notes in Chapter 16 of this volume, "Particular approaches often seem to be developed and maintained, not for the contribution they make to further understanding but as vehicles for career advancement, ideological proselytizing, intellectual one-upsmanship and other benighted purposes. Moreover, since publication résumés grow on dissension, academics often develop a vested interest in not agreeing or in dwelling on minor differences contained within the larger body of unspoken, non-career-enhancing agreement." How can common ground be found amidst such pressures? How can movement toward theoretical coherence and collective inquiry be fostered amidst the divisions and disincentives of modern social science?

We believe that the movement toward dialogue must start, quite literally, with an organized conversation among scholars from differing approaches and schools of thought. To that end, we invited several dozen scholars to meet together in February 1992 in Boulder, Colorado, to discuss the study of American political change. We asked the participants—who are from contrasting intellectual orientations and do not normally meet and interact at disciplinary conferences—to prepare statements on their distinctive approaches to American politics and political change, to read all statements beforehand, to listen to and critique one another's ideas during three days of meetings, and then to return home to prepare final essays in light of these discussions. From this process has come, we believe, a set of essays that are unique in the study of American politics. Together they provide a broad explication of the major analytic approaches to American politics and political change—one which considers both the major perspectives that stress macro context and those that emphasize micro dynamics in their explanations of development and change. Across the essays, we believe, a conscious effort is reflected among disparate scholars to engage in a sustained and genuine conversation about how best to conceptualize and understand political change in America.

We have organized these essays into five parts. The book opens with an overview in Part One of the patterns of change and development that characterize American political history and the patterns of inquiry that characterize the study of these changes. The purpose here is to establish the historical and intellectual context for the conversation among approaches that constitutes the core of the book. Parts Two and Three look, respectively, at the predominant macro and micro approaches used in the study of political change, with focus on key debates or conversations among these approaches. Part Four presents three efforts to develop broader interpretations of politics and political change—interpretations that can serve to bridge and integrate various approaches presented in Parts Two and Three. Finally, Part Five provides a reflective assessment of the overarching conversation that exists across the essays and points to emerging convergences that could provide broader common ground for political inquiry. This common ground emerges, it should be stressed, not as a result of preexisting analytic agreement among these scholars but through the commitment of a diverse group of scholars to engage in a collective conversation about their differing analytic strategies.

PART ONE: PATTERNS OF CHANGE AND INQUIRY

Our search for common understanding begins, in Part One, with Calvin Jillson's historical overview of the patterns of change and continuity that have characterized American politics. Jillson's task in Chapter 2, in a sense, is the reverse of Theodore Lowi's effort in the Foreword: Lowi seeks to identify shifting patterns of nondevelopment that we often mistake for evolutionary sequence, thereby admonishing us to use precision in our descriptions of political change; Jillson seeks to identify reliable developmental patterns of American history amidst Lowi's discontinuities and paths of nondevelopment. Looking across the sweep of American history, Jillson identifies three distinct developmental or constitutional eras: These include the era of democratization that produced the American Revolution and culminated in the election of Andrew Jackson in 1828; the era of partisan competition of the mid- to late nineteenth century that ended with the McKinley election in 1896; and the era of interest group liberalism of the twentieth century that began to fade with the elections of Jimmy Carter and then of Ronald Reagan in the late twentieth century. Within these broad historical eras, Jillson then identifies periods of stable partisan loyalties, systematic adjustments in party alignments, and recurring mood swings in voter attachments to parties and policies; such periodic shifts occur within all three historical eras, and do so with a broadly common temporal patterning. While various authors throughout the book emphasize somewhat different categorizations of dominant historical eras, Jillson's comprehensive periodization illustrates the dynamic shifts that occur in American politics across time and thus highlights the need for students of politics to be attentive to the existence and explanation of political change.

In Chapter 3, Walter Dean Burnham asks whether the patterns that we see in political history have the stature of empirical phenomena that deserve our systematic attention. Is history "just one damn thing after another" or does it hold a scientifically valid meaning and significance? Building particularly on evolutionary biologists such as Stephen Jay Gould, Burnham argues that when we see many different types of phenomena converge to create the appearance of similitude during an historical era, we are observing a *consilience* of phenomena that together allow us to induce the empirical existence of an abstract patterning within history. Under such conditions, historical events such as "partisan realignments" are scientifically credible occurrences that we should seek to explain and from which we should seek to learn. In doing so, we must beware of the problem of *presentism*—of seeing the past solely in terms of the present and thereby missing the true character and meaning of historical phenomena. Likewise, we must avoid the problem of historical *anachronism*, of overlooking critical historical details in ways that distort our understanding of historical patterns and processes. Yet insofar as we can bring to our awareness of patterns a respect for the distinctiveness, richness, and integrity of historical experience, we can identify a meaningful historical periodicity.

The periodicity of history, Burnham argues, suggests that deep and long-lasting processes are at work in a society. Such processes, illustrated by partisan realignments, do not necessarily recur in identical ways across time; they may nevertheless generate analogous patterns of political change and development that we can identify through attentiveness to empirical consilience. Awareness of such periodic patterns may then sensitize us to a dynamic understanding of our own era and thereby help us to identify and interpret contemporary developments that we would otherwise overlook. To Burnham, then, history is more than "one damn thing after another"; it is a key to understanding the nature and meaning of contemporary politics.

Given that history is characterized by an appearance of periodicity, as Jillson demonstrates, and that such appearances can have both a scientifically valid standing and a contemporaneous relevance, as Burnham argues, how are we as a discipline to study and understand these historical processes? Will continued attentiveness to history only multiply interpretations and further obfuscate our understanding of politics? In Chapter 4, Elaine Swift and David Brady maintain that an attentiveness to history, while increasing the range of empirical phenomena we study, may actually provide the basis for some analytic common ground across the disparate perspectives on contemporary politics. As they argue, contemporaneous studies may focus on an unrepresentative or uncharacteristic slice of political life and magnify its importance, whereas an historical perspective can more nearly identify the range of variables, conditions, and outcomes that are truly representative of politics—and that all practitioners must address. Practitioners from different traditions may still accent distinctive factors, but they should do so with more concern for the interplay of such factors with other historical forces.

The common ground that Swift and Brady seek for scholars of political history is, actually, a common appreciation of the combined and interactive influence that various macro and micro factors may have on political development and change. They illustrate their arguments about the necessity and possibility of such common awareness by examining the intellectual developments in statist, organizational, and rational choice studies of political history. Parts Two and Three of this book seek to facilitate such awareness through extensive discussions of a range of macro and micro perspectives.

PART TWO: APPROACHES TO MACROANALYSIS

Part Two focuses on macrolevel approaches to the study of political development and change, particularly on two major conversations within the scholarly literature about macrolevel influences on American politics. The first conversation revolves around the issue of American exceptionalism: Is the distinctiveness of the American experience, as contrasted to European nations, for example, a result of our political institutions, or a result of a peculiar American culture, so that one or the other should be given special emphasis in explanations of American political development? This scholarly debate is addressed in Chapter 5 by Sven Steinmo and in Chapter 6 by Russell Hanson. The second conversation revolves around the issue of state autonomy: Does economic structure drive politics, or is there a distinctive truth to be derived from an understanding of the nation's general political processes and governing institutions, separate from the influence of economics? This question is addressed in Chapter 7 by Edward Greenberg and in Chapter 8 by Theda Skocpol.

In Chapter 5, Steinmo argues forcefully against the predominant influence of culture in American politics, as found in the liberal exceptionalist arguments of Hartz (1955) and Huntington (1981), and emphasizes instead the influence of American political institutions. Steinmo's argument is that institutional power in America is fragmented so extensively that, irrespective of the citizenry's ideologies or values, the immobilism inherent in the American constitutional system would inhibit the public's ability to achieve those policy goals and thereby teach people to doubt the efficiency of government. This fragmentation has created such weak parties, labor movements, and governments that the American welfare state is necessarily more limited than that of any other Western industrialized nation. These developments have occurred, moreover, despite American popular support for a welfare state akin to levels of public support found in European nations. Even worse, American institutional arrangements have also fostered a hyperpluralist system of interest groups, which reinforces institutional fragmentation by serving particularized interests rather than the common good, so that when government acts, it does so in response to particularized demands that overburden the fiscal resources of the state without providing for the general welfare of the citizens. Such policy results convince the citizenry that the government is not simply inefficient, but is counterproductive, and thus their belief in limited government is reinforced.

In contrast to Steinmo, Hanson asserts in Chapter 6 that culture does matter in quite significant ways, but that it does so in a different manner from the globalist and liberal exceptionalist arguments of Hartz and Huntington. Following Elazar (1970), Wildavsky (1990), and others, Hanson emphasizes the tripartite cultural diversity of American society, with the nation divided into regions dominated by individualist, moralist, and traditionalist values. Despite locally fragmented political systems, Hanson suggests, states with individualist or moralist values during the early to mid-twentieth century did develop social welfare programs that approximated the welfare commitments of European nations; it was the traditionalist states, concentrated in the South, that were most opposed to such programs. The refusal of the traditionalist states to enact expansive social welfare programs—and their ability to use their power within Congress to protect the rights of states to determine the specifics of local welfare programs—eventually threatened to make the moralist and individualist states into "welfare havens" for poor citizens from the South; this prospect thereby led moralist and individualist states to restrain the further development of their social welfare programs. The result was a limited American state. Without the local dominance of traditional values in the South, Hanson suggests, and regardless of our fragmented institutional arrangements, the nation probably would have developed a welfare state similar to (or at least more similar to) European nations. With the predominance of values in the South that opposed a welfare state, and with a fragmented institutional system that provided southern politicians with veto power that they could use to slow and decentralize the move to a welfare state, the nation was left with an exceptionally limited commitment to social welfare.

The conversation between Steinmo and Hanson generates an intriguing perspective on the American exceptionalism debate and on the relative role of institutions and culture. Both authors acknowledge an exceptional quality to American politics and public policy, both believe that this exceptionalism results from the macro context of American politics, and both acknowledge a role for institutions and for culture, but with different emphases. To Steinmo, the fragmented and thus inefficient institutional arrangements of American politics have forced citizens, irrespective of their initial values, to learn an antistatist value orientation across generations; this antistatist culture then reinforces the limited welfare state produced as a result of institutional fragmentation. Had the nation possessed a less fragmented institutional system, Steinmo implies, it would not have developed such a strong antistatist culture and would therefore be less exceptional. To Hanson, the key to American exceptionalism is the cultural diversity of the nation, particularly the existence of traditional cultural values in the South; it is the existence and peculiar regional patterning of cultural diversity that activates the obstructive potentialities of institutional fragmentation. Had the nation truly been homogeneous and liberal in its values, he suggests, institutional fragmentation would not have mattered as much and America would have been less exceptional; but with cultural diversity, institutional fragmentation then comes forcefully into play and together culture and institutions generate an exceptionally conservative social welfare policy. Interestingly, while differing in their stress on the precedence to be given to institutions or culture, both authors emphasize that some form of systemic heterogeneity—whether institutional or cultural—induced a learning process that produced American exceptionalism.

The second macrolevel conversation focuses on the contrasting roles of economics and political processes in shaping American political development. Edward Greenberg initiates this dialogue in Chapter 7 with his forceful argument that it is change in the macroeconomic structure of society that drives political change in America, thereby producing a succession of "policy regimes" shaped by the nation's changing macroeconomic structure. According to Greenberg, macroeconomic change shapes and constrains political processes and institutions by playing a central role both in the determination of the political agendas for individuals, groups, classes, and state actors in an historical period, and in the determination of the distribution of politically relevant resources in society. This combined shaping of political agendas and resource distribution thereby serves to generate the rise and fall of policy regimes. Such policy regimes rise and fall largely in rhythm with the coming and passing of economic problems for which a regime is or is not appropriate. Within such regimes, the state and the dominant class will tend to form a partnership based on their mutual need for one another, with state actors needing economic resources and the dominant economic class needing influence on governing decisions. Strains necessarily exist in these partnerships, with the state being particularly sensitive to highly united and mobilized class struggles that could topple the political elites through mass democratic uprisings. Despite such strains, the protection of the capitalist state tends to be the ultimate and overriding goal of the partnership and thereby shapes the character of American political development.

Greenberg's argument, while acknowledging a role for politics and for state actors separate from the dominant economic class, clearly stresses the dominance of macroeconomics and economic change in shaping public policy across time. In so doing, Greenberg raises the classic issue posed by neo-Marxists throughout much of the century: Must public policy and political choice be interpreted largely as a reflection of the economic conditions of an era, or is there a distinct and significant political component to government actions that thereby requires a distinctly political analysis in order to understand public policy and political development? This is the issue addressed by Theda Skocpol.

In Chapter 8, Skocpol challenges the notion that politics and policy are a direct and simple outgrowth of macroeconomic forces and argues instead for a "polity-centered" approach to understanding political development and policy change. Rejecting the notion that there exists such a thing as a "capitalist state," Skocpol insists that politicians and administrators are social actors in their own right who make contributions to the development of a nation's social policies quite independently of economic or social groups. They do so because the "state" of which they are a part is an authoritative and resourceful organization—a collector of revenues, a center of cultural authority, a hoarder of the means of coercion—that can and does act quite autonomously from other societal forces. Perhaps most critically, the character of the state —whether it is centralized or decentralized, federal or unitary, democratic or authoritarian—will have enormous consequences for political actors and public policy quite distinct from economic and social factors in society. In particular, the political and policy success of different political groups in society may have more to do with how well their organizational structures and strategies "fit" with the existing state apparatus than with their economic and social power. Thus veterans' groups and women's groups in the late nineteenth and early twentieth centuries were organized—perhaps serendipitously—along federated lines that meshed well with the structure of the federal American state and thereby allowed them to exert meaningful pressure and enact social policies nationwide that served their policy interests, despite their lack of economic dominance in society. By contrast, trade unions, corporations, and big business associations were not organized along federated lines that meshed with the structure of the American state, and they proved less successful in pursuing their policy strategies during the same time period. As this comparative illustration makes clear, the state and its political processes must be seen as quite separate from the economic forces in society.

Neither Greenberg nor Skocpol, it must be emphasized, claim total dominance for their economic and polity-centered perspectives. Greenberg sees the state as having some potential independence, but believes macroeconomic structure must necessarily be at the center of any study of political change and public policy. Skocpol acknowledges that the state may be responding to broad socioeconomic developments, but sees the state as the central actor in policy choice and argues that economic and social forces will win or lose in some large measure, not simply as a result of economic resources but according to how well they fit with state structures and political processes. In acknowledging the relevance of both economics and state structures, Greenberg and Skocpol raise the possibility that a dynamic interactive process exists between the two factors that produces a more equal influence between economic and state forces than either author acknowledges. Seen across time, perhaps state structures mediate economic forces, which in turn change state structures to fit new economic conditions, setting in motion a continuous and reciprocal process that requires roughly equal roles for both factors in order to proceed.

Wherever the truth lies in terms of the appropriate predominance of one perspective or another, these two conversations on state autonomy and American exceptionalism serve both to highlight distinctive macro-level approaches to political development and also to demonstrate how practitioners of macroanalysis think about understanding politics. All four macro-oriented scholars identify broad systemic features of American politics and focus on how these features shape political behavior and policy outcomes. The interests and actions of individuals and groups are essentially shaped by the systemic context in which participants are situated, so that to understand politics and political change one must primarily understand macro context. Macroanalysts differ among themselves about which aspects of context to highlight, so that different analysts may tilt toward institutions, culture, economics, or political process, while giving some credence to other perspectives. Yet they all agree that the logic of politics is shaped by the context of politics, so that the major tasks of students of politics is to identify, characterize, and explain the macro outlines of politics—constitutional and institutional arrangements, cultural value systems, macroeconomic structure, and distinctive political processes. Standing in contrast to this predominant focus on macro factors is the microlevel emphasis on the motives and behavior of individuals and groups.

PART THREE: APPROACHES TO MICROANALYSIS

Part Three focuses on microlevel approaches to the study of political change and development, again with special attention given to two conversations. The first conversation concerns the issue of individual motives and actions: Are we to understand politics and political change primarily as a result of rational choice by political actors, or as an outgrowth of social psychology? This debate is addressed in Chapter 9 by John Aldrich and in Chapter 10 by Murray Edelman. The second conversation revolves around the issue of group behavior: Does the effect of groups on politics primarily result from interpersonal associations and informational networks of their members, or from shared discrete interests and organized activity? This debate is addressed in Chapter 11 by Robert Huckfeldt and Paul Allen Beck, and in Chapter 12 by Clarence Stone.

Aldrich initiates the conversation over individual motives and behavior by presenting a systematic introduction to contemporary rational choice theory and its relationship to politics and political change. The fundamental premise of rational choice, he argues, is that political outcomes are the product of goal-seeking behavior by actors, with such actors making choices within a set of institutional arrangements and a particular historical context. Such actors, perhaps politicians motivated by a common concern for re-election, shape their institutions to accord with their goals and respond to the shifting historical context in ways designed to realize their goals. Utilizing this simple premise or "equation," one can then explain a broad range of contemporary and historical phenomena, including mass political behavior (such as the retrospective character of voting), and the structure of institutions (as, for example, the decentralized nature of Congress). The key to understanding political development and change, then, is to understand the preferences of historical actors, the common principles of rationality (particularly the maximization or cost-benefit principles) by which they pursue these preferences, the consequent actions that they take in pursuit of preferences, and finally, the outcomes that their actions necessarily produce. At the heart of political history thus lies a relatively simple, straightforward, and self-interested set of rational calculations by political actors that can be modeled in analogous ways across historical context and from which a process understanding of history can be derived.

In Chapter 10, Murray Edelman issues a strong challenge to rational choice theory and proposes, in its place, a social psychology of politics. From Edelman's perspective, it is language that creates politics, because we experience political events or actions not directly, but only through the symbols that we use to describe them and to give them meaning. Because language is inherently plastic and reflects our shifting psychological needs, we necessarily create multiple interpretations of reality. As a result, no simple and uncontested interpretation of a political event, political interests, political preferences, or rational action is possible. Therefore, all closed systems of analysis are, inherently, rationalizations of the ideologies of their creators, with modern rational choice (with its materialist emphasis on cost-benefit analysis) being perhaps the primary example of such tendencies. In truth, politics and political change, to Edelman, result from continuing and extraordinarily complex struggles among elites and masses over the resources and value commitments of society—struggles fought through the creation and manipulation of language systems. In this struggle, the control of language and symbols becomes the most potent weapon that a group can command, so that the creation of mass communications and its control by government elites in the past century or so constitutes the great story line of modern history. Recognizing the socially constructed nature of reality, and the possibility that elites can use particular constructions of reality to subjugate a citizenry, scholars must therefore value rich and contested ambiguity rather than simplicity in their political interpretations of politics and history.

Aldrich and Edelman thus offer starkly contrasting perspectives on microlevel motives and political analysis. Both writers see individuals acting in pursuit of interests, and both acknowledge that such action corresponds to personal understanding of political reality. The authors differ markedly, however, in their conceptualization of these processes. For Aldrich, interests are relatively clear-cut and obvious to the individual; preferences can be ordered and shared by individuals in a relatively forthright manner; and consequent actions can be calculated and modeled in a parsimonious way that provides a deterministic account of collective action. For Edelman, interests are embedded in complex social contexts that individuals (particularly powerless individuals) may fail to fully see and comprehend; understandings of the world are subject to multiple and shifting interpretations that allow for self-delusional distortion, rationalization, and elite manipulations—all of which means that political scientists can hope to gain an understanding of politics and political change only through an appreciation of ambiguity, irony, and multiple realities, and then only with great sensitivity paid to each scholar's ideological biases, language systems, and rationalizations. Neither writer explores the possibility that his own description of the world may be context-specific, with some contexts yielding relatively clear-cut interests, preferences, and rational calculations whereas others generate a more contested, ambiguous, and manipulable understanding. At issue between these two conceptions of micropolitics, then, is not simply whether one is right and the other is wrong, but whether, across historical contexts, these two perspectives provide a more complete guide to individual behavior than either one would offer separately. This issue is addressed by the second conversation among microanalysts, which debates the character of group behavior in politics.

Huckfeldt and Beck argue that to understand political behavior and its variable consequences for political change we must systematically assess the distinctive settings in which individuals are embedded and through which they understand and shape their political actions. According to these authors, individual behavior is decidedly contextual in nature—shaped neither by the isolated characteristics of an individual nor solely by formal group affiliations, but rather by the personal associations and informational mediums of daily life through which they obtain political information. Because of the vast array of such informational sources or "intermediaries," individuals do confront multiple interpretations of the meaning of contemporary politics. Such multiple levels of meaning may reinforce each other if individuals live and associate in a relatively homogeneous political environment and can thereby arrive at a clarity of meaning that allows, in Aldrich's terms, for simple preferences and rational purposive action. By contrast, if individuals live and associate in relatively heterogeneous and diffuse political environments, they may experience confusion about preferences and demonstrate a less engaged sense of political purpose. Echoing Edelman, Huckfeldt and Beck see the rise of the national mass media over the past century as having created a heterogeneous context for political behavior that makes simple preferences and purposive behavior more difficult. In contrast to Edelman, they see the rise of the national media as important not because it has become a vehicle of elite manipulation for partisan advantage but because the professionalization of national news organizations has produced a nonpartisan (or even anti-partisan) information system; this nonpartisan system deprives citizens of the clear-cut informational cues that existed in earlier times, when news was localized and dominated by community mores and partisan affiliations. The growth of neutral national sources of information, ironically, is producing a public that is less sure of its political preferences and more vulnerable to momentary political forces and events.

In contrast to Huckfeldt and Beck, in Chapter 12 Clarence Stone focuses less on the broad informational context in which citizens are embedded and looks more directly at the organized groups to which they belong. Such groups may differ considerably in the intensity of their preferences and in the capacities of the groups to act on their preferences; therein lies the key, from Stone's perspective, to the tendency of the nation's political economy to shape and sustain the groups that dominate American politi-

cal life. To Stone, the essential shape of political development does not reflect the rise of a national media that influences the diffuse daily information available to citizens, but rather demonstrates the existence of private
control of national investment—and this gives business a privileged position in our society, makes private economic decisions an immediate concern to citizens and to governmental officials alike, and thereby shapes the
organization and agendas that are most likely to have influence on political life. Countervailing group movements concerned with broad social
and moral issues, as in the 1960s, can arise to challenge the dominant
forces of the political economy; such countervailing movements will almost certainly fail, however, or fall far short of the intended agenda, because they lack the sustained resources and daily immediacy of economic
forces. In addition, they will fail because the American institutional system is so fragmented that only organized economic groups are likely to
have the resources and incentives to sustain the institutional involvement
that will produce broadly based and viable policy outcomes.

Taken together, the essays by Huckfeldt and Beck and by Stone provide
a powerful analysis of the group dynamics driving American politics;
they also present a troubling assessment of the direction of contemporary
politics. Clearly, the authors differ in their primary focus, with the former
stressing informational context and the latter stressing organizational resources and capacities. Seen together, however, these separate emphases
create a picture of American society in which individuals have decreasing
contextual and group guidance in their political actions, are susceptible to
short-term forces, and may be particularly influenced by business forces
that could ignore fundamental moral and social concerns of the citizenry.
Whereas clear-cut preferences and rational choice may more nearly have
fit the informational context of an earlier America, wherein citizens could
derive clear informational cues from their local communities and personal
associations, today the realm of clear preferences and rational choice, in
Aldrich's terms, has been narrowed to the very limited area of business
policies; faced with confusion in their broader arena of social policymaking, citizens may in fact be increasingly susceptible, in Edelman's terms, to
elite manipulation. The ability of the nation to avoid such dire outcomes
depends, according to Huckfeldt and Beck, on the emergence of new social intermediaries that help citizens clarify their political preferences and,
according to Stone, depend as well on the creation of a less fragmented institutional system that is more responsive to countervailing group influence. As such developments occur, the ability of citizens to engage in rational, purposive behavior may be enhanced. Left unclear, unfortunately,
is how such change occurs. How is it that individuals and groups, heavily
embedded in existing social and institutional arrangements that shape

and constrain their preferences, actually change the fundamental nature of politics?

The micro approaches to politics thus generate some heated debate over the appropriate way to conceptualize individual and group behavior and also present some provocative and surprisingly congruent interpretations of the broad development and direction of American politics. Most important, they illustrate the essential nature of microanalysis—the belief that political analysts must primarily focus on the beliefs and actions of individuals and groups. These individual and group beliefs may well derive from the broader context of which such actors are a part. But the consequence of action, from a purely micro perspective, can be traced and understood only by understanding the individual and group logic of action, not by observing the broad outlines of macro context. What is at contest among scholars of microlevel phenomena is the exact nature of that microlevel action—is it a rational individual calculation in a world of simple preferences or a confused process of individual grappling in a world of multiple realities; likewise, is it an outgrowth of informational context or of shared economic preferences and organized effort?

Left unaddressed by these microanalysts is the issue of individual autonomy and change: Is it possible for actors, whether rational or irrational, whether shaped by informational contexts or group interests, to change the nature of the societal and institutional forces that confront them? Are they ultimately shaped solely by those forces, or are there ways in which they are truly autonomous actors? This is, of course, only the reverse side of what is perhaps the central question facing macroanalysts—whether macro forces are merely the reflection of aggregated individual choices, or have some separate autonomous being. Addressing these questions requires that we look beyond the classic approaches contained in Parts Two and Three and consider new ways of interpreting politics that help us see more clearly the linkage between micro- and macropolitics and help us understand more completely the true nature of political change.

PART FOUR: GENERAL INTERPRETATIONS OF CHANGE

As scholars stand back from the approaches discussed in Parts Two and Three and attempt to understand political change in a more integrated manner, they face a challenging task: to specify more clearly the general nature of the political world that they see; to clarify why it is that the political world changes; and to specify how it is that political actors can influence the nature of that change. The three essays in Part Four take up this challenge from very distinctive theoretical orientations: In Chapter 13 Jane Mansbridge introduces a revisionist game-theoretic model of the political world that seeks to broaden our conception of self-interest to include moral concerns such as love and duty; in Chapter 14 Karen Orren and Stephen Skowronek present a "new institutionalism" approach that treats historical tensions among institutions as the driving force of political change; and in Chapter 15 Lawrence Dodd proposes that we see the political world from an evolutionary learning perspective that highlights the role of ideas and shifting world views. As with the other essays in the book, these essays should be seen as an open conversation among scholars who are attempting both to identify the broad outlines of an interpretation that they find convincing and to stimulate a broader dialogue among professional colleagues on how best to conceptualize and understand political change.

Jane Mansbridge introduces Part Four with an innovative discussion of politics as persuasion. Mansbridge approaches the political world within the confines of game theory, seeing the world ordered roughly as a prisoner's dilemma game; at issue in the game is the ability of citizens to produce outcomes that serve their collective interests when rational self-interested behavior on the part of each individual would seem to erode the collective good and destroy the political order. Political analysts have generally agreed that the solution to the collective goods problem is some form of the use of power and coercion, a solution illustrated most vividly by Thomas Hobbes's *Leviathan* (1986). In contrast, Mansbridge proposes that we see citizens as moral individuals who not only pursue material self-interest but also respond to feelings of empathy, love, altruism, and duty. Confronted with collective goods problems, individuals can be persuaded to cooperate for the common good through an emphasis on love and duty, without the use of material coercion and state power; power and coercion may, of course, be used as a fallback or as fail-safe mechanisms to ensure full cooperation among citizens, but need not be the primary focus of politics and public policy. In point of fact, an emphasis on public-spirited concerns such as love and duty is actually cheaper, requires less monitoring, and is more adapted to changing situations than an emphasis on material sanctions. Mansbridge thus suggests blending the game-theoretic vision of an ordered politics adopted by rational choice scholars with a moral vision of citizens suggested by such political sociologists as Huckfeldt and Beck. Political change and development across time therefore flow at the micro level from a combination of public spirited persuasion supported by the potential for material coercion. This strategy allows Mansbridge to link her microlevel analysis to macrolevel concerns with the role and power of the state, since the state is a primary arena for deliberative persuasion in politics, a primary locus of public-spirited feelings and attachments, and a primary source of legitimate force and the threat of sanctions.

In contrast to Mansbridge, Orren and Skowronek challenge the utility both of game theory and of "order" itself as a useful characterization of politics. For Orren and Skowronek, the central unit of politics is not the individual actor or the general game but the political institution. Whereas scholars have traditionally seen institutions as the basis of order in society—as heavily static rule structures that freeze politics into long-lasting and organized political games—Orren and Skowronek see institutions as the basis of a seamless pattern of disorder across history. Institutions inherently generate political disorder because their nonsimultaneity of institutional origin produces institutional interests and processes that are in perpetual conflict, with differing institutions continually seeking to dominate each other. Because institutions are characterized by a nonsimultaneity of origin, and thus are engaged in perpetual struggle with one another, it makes no sense to see them as sharing common periods of rule making or game playing. Rather, history is driven by the collisions of institutions always in conflict, with politics best characterized as a world of patterned anarchy. In this view, there is no political "system" or system "equilibrium"; there is no synchronization among institutions in their operation or effects; there are no time lags, institutional catch-ups, or shared principles of ordering across institutions. Politics is inherently a process of dissonance rather than fit, of tension and contradiction rather than agreement and compatibility. Whereas Mansbridge can envision an ordered world of public-spirited empathy and persuasion across individuals, Orren and Skowronek envision an anarchical world of unending conflict and of tensions across institutions.

In the concluding essay of Part Four, Lawrence Dodd presents yet a third interpretation of politics and political change. For Dodd, politics is best conceived as a process of evolutionary learning across time. From Dodd's perspective, political participants create a sense of order and meaning by developing a shared understanding of how it is that groups, institutions, and processes fit together in a particular era to facilitate collective governance; participants develop such shared understanding by experimenting with different ways of conceptualizing politics until they find a strategy that gains broad acceptance, by virtue of providing some degree of mutual empowerment across individuals, groups, and institutions; order and meaning are thus neither inherent qualities of politics nor inherent impossibilities, but are instead the temporary and transient products of human creation through experimentation and learning. As times change, preexisting understandings of politics cease to operate effectively in new historical conditions; tension, confusion, and disarray mount; participants lose their sense of meaning and order, yet resist the embrace of new worldviews as a result of habit and fear; deep political crises then engulf society that can be resolved only by a cathartic and experimental learning of a new shared understanding appropriate to the new historical conditions. Success in such experimental learning processes will be shaped, in part at least, by the severity of the learning tasks a society faces and by the character of its learning conditions, both of which are influenced by a nation's macro context. But in Dodd's view the key to understanding politics and political change lies in recognizing the creative learning capacities of political participants and their abilities through experimental learning to develop an orderly and meaningful understanding of politics appropriate to the historical conditions of their age.

The essays by Mansbridge, Orren and Skowronek, and Dodd thus provide three distinctive conceptions of political change and actor autonomy, each with a distinctly new analytical slant. Mansbridge stresses, in a sense, the rationality of love and duty in politics and the capacity of participants who stress such moral concerns to solve collective dilemmas that an emphasis on power may only poorly address; individuals can have an autonomous impact in changing politics, separate from the power structures and incentive systems in which they are embedded, insofar as they respond to feelings of love and duty toward fellow citizens. Understanding political change therefore requires attention to the persuasive role that love and duty can play in sustaining and shaping the collective game of politics. Orren and Skowronek ask us to look beyond the vision of politics as an ordered game and see the institutional tensions and contradictions that pervade politics; institutions have an autonomous impact on history, separate from individuals, because of the disparate historical meanings that institutions reflect through their distinctive origins, rules, and processes. Understanding political change in this case requires the recognition that the resulting conflicts among institutions are the continuous driving forces of history, with a pattern of unfolding anarchy being history's chief characteristic. Finally, Dodd directs our attention to the processes of political learning and evolutionary reconstruction through which participants periodically generate a meaningful and orderly pattern to politics amidst history's complexity and disarray; individuals, groups, and institutions have an autonomous influence on politics via the separate and collective processes of learning through which they recognize shared interests, compatibilities, and possibilities. Here, understanding political change and development requires a critical appreciation of the learning capacities of political participants as well as a recognition of their deep-seated tendencies to hold to preexisting mindsets and thus to induce disarray.

Taken together, these three perspectives challenge scholars to confront their own broader vision of politics. They challenge us, in particular, to grapple with central issues of politics and political change that we often ignore:

- Our predilection to stress material constraints and power over public-spirited concerns and persuasion.
- Our presumption of a world of order despite plentiful evidence of institutional conflict, tensions, and disorder.
- Our tendency to magnify and reify one pattern of politics (whether that be power or persuasion, order or disorder, learning or resistance to learning) in a world of shifting and evolving patterns.
- Our inclination to see a nation's institutions and governing principles as sharing simultaneous origins and therefore as having a natural compatibility, when in fact institutions and principles often arise in very different historical conditions that may generate a natural antipathy between them.
- Our propensity to treat individuals and institutions as inherently hostile and perpetually resistant, despite evidence of their capacities for empathetic understanding and evolutionary learning.

Addressing such issues requires scholars to look beyond their separate approaches and engage in a broad conversation about the more fundamental nature of politics and political change as seen across levels and dimensions of analysis. This overarching conversation is addressed in the concluding section of the book.

PART FIVE: CONCLUDING REFLECTIONS

Our concern in this book is to facilitate a broad and integrative dialogue on the study of political change in America. The issue is quite simple: We believe that amidst the disparate approaches and "sects" of American politics a common ground exists that scholars can find allowing them to talk with one another about the broad and enduring questions of American political change that no one approach seems capable of adequately addressing. To foster that dialogue, we have brought together a broad range of scholars—first in a conference format and now in this book—to discuss the historical patterns of American politics and political inquiry, to assess the macro and micro approaches to inquiry, and to consider alternative interpretations of the general nature of political change. The conversations across these essays, we believe, have been rich and stimulating—but is there a broad common ground among the essays upon which scholars can build a more coherent and shared understanding of American political change? This is the topic of Hugh Heclo's concluding essay.

Heclo's task in Chapter 16 is necessarily a difficult one—to be true to the diversity and divergences of positions and approaches present in this book, and yet to identify the convergences that may exist among them. Clearly, Heclo acknowledges the distinctiveness of the scholarly approaches and positions, noting that the essays of this book offer no one "system" of thinking, but rather a complexity of perspective. Nevertheless, based on listening to the dialogue in Boulder, reading the essays, and almost a year of reflection, Heclo identifies three convergences among these scholars that would seem to provide common ground for a broader professional conversation about American politics and political change.

The first common area of approximate agreement, Heclo argues, concerns the nature of the knowledge that students of American politics can realistically seek. This knowledge, as evidenced in the conversations in this book and the preliminary discussions, must encompass an awareness of both micro and macro levels of analysis, must relate to historical context, and yet should also speak to general process and historical types. Although such knowledge will necessarily yield no universal and unalterable scientific laws, at least at the current stage of the development of political science, it can help guide us to an appreciative understanding of patterns of American political change as well as sustain an attentiveness to the necessary limits of such understanding.

The second area of convergence is a general agreement on the basic elements that are absolutely central to our common understanding. The three common building blocks of analysis across these essays, Heclo argues, are ideas, interests, and institutions. The most central characteristic of these basic building blocks of politics, moreover, is their interrelatedness and inseparability, indicating that political analysis must move among all three; as Heclo concludes, "Interests tell institutions what to do; institutions tell ideas how to survive; ideas tell interests what to mean." An adequate understanding of American politics must reflect this interplay, so that an emphasis on one building block to the exclusion of the others will necessarily yield misleading conclusions and a false sense of intellectual closure. By contrast, insofar as scholars look to the interplay of these three essential components of politics, as the authors in this volume seem willing to do, an approximate and sensitive understanding of historical processes can begin to emerge.

Finally, Heclo sees the essays and broader conversations converging on an evolutionary learning perspective of political change and development. As he puts it, "evolutionary learning is exactly what is happening when things happen. Particular codependencies of actions among ideas, interests, and institutions are selected, due to demonstration of their adaptability to a changing environment, which is itself conditioned partly by the prior choices participants made and by the characteristics they have acquired." Such evolutionary processes are made possible by the distinctly human capacity for language, with humans using language to create and evolve distinctive interrelations among ideas, interests, and institutions across time. Cautioning against the misperception that such learning follows a single master plan of evolution or that it necessarily connotes "getting smarter," Heclo sees the convergence toward an evolutionary narrative of political learning as a scientifically liberating process that accents the centrality of movement and openness in politics, rather than equilibrium and prediction, thereby inducing an intrinsic humility in political inquiry.

To Heclo's three convergences we would add, in conclusion, a fourth: a willingness among the authors, even an anxiousness, to engage in a mutual conversation. As Heclo notes in the introduction to his essay, disciplinary specializations often become barriers—even "barricades"—to an open-minded and affirmative discussion of the subjects that scholars share in common and that inspired each of us to study politics in the first place. Certainly scholarship on American politics—probably as much as any field of inquiry in the social sciences—is characterized by specialization and by the competitive academic conflicts that arise amidst such specialization. And yet there also appears to be a desire among "Americanists" today to reach beyond their specialized barriers and see the broader picture of politics. Thus, of the several dozen scholars whom we invited to Boulder to discuss the state of American politics, only two declined, and they did so owing to prior engagements. And the authors in this volume have willingly contributed their essays to an enterprise the very nature of which is designed to challenge the adequacy of their career commitments, and to activate a search for broader conceptual approaches that could move the profession beyond their analytic specialties.

Why this willingness to converse across specialties, when academic incentives so often reinforce separation? We have no clear and general answer. Our own motivation stems from the troubling doubts that arise as we privately sense the limits of our singular explanations of politics; from the frustration that arises as we look outward for broader intellectual guidance and see only the barricades; from an apprehension that American politics in the late twentieth century may momentarily shift under our feet in ways that our separate approaches can neither foresee nor explain; from the hope that in dialogue with others we may gain a broader insight that helps us make sense out of the political world of which we are a part, and which so fascinates and yet eludes us.

Whatever the source, the broad willingness to converse evident in these pages augurs well for the future of a science of American politics. It suggests a maturing recognition that we can approximate a satisfactory understanding of politics only by lowering the barricades that separate us, listening to one another, and looking together at the broad patterning of politics across time that we only partially see from within the boundaries of our separate analytic prejudices. As we listen to one another, we give ourselves the chance to learn—to see the broad, shifting, and dynamic patterns of politics that our obsession with one approach, institution, or historical era might miss; to recognize the importance both of macrohistorical conditions and of microhistorical actions in shaping the dynamics of politics; to sense an interconnection across approaches that may help us make sense out of history's unfolding complexities. Perhaps most important, as we engage across the barricades we give ourselves and our students the opportunity to embrace the passionate joy of discussing politics, in all of its complexities and elusiveness, wherever that discussion may lead, whatever barriers it may lead us to cross, whatever certainties we are forced to relinquish, and whatever academic heresies we must reluctantly embrace. It is our hope that the conversations begun in these pages will both stimulate a renewed appreciation of the dynamic and complex character of American politics and help activate a broader and impassioned conversation among students of American politics.

PART I

Patterns of Political Change and Inquiry

2

Patterns and Periodicity in American National Politics

CALVIN JILLSON

Students of republican government have long been concerned that the powers allocated to governments and the programs and policies that governments pursue may affect the very nature of the polity. James Madison, following Thucydides, Cicero, Machiavelli, and Hume, warned the founding generation that "measures can mold governments" and that new "systems of policy" can redefine the character of a regime (Madison, 1900, 6:338–340, 407). Like Montesquieu, Madison thought that every regime radiated a distinctive "spirit" and that some governmental activities were incompatible with the "spirit" of republican government. For example, both Montesquieu and Madison were convinced that when a republican regime turned its attention to war or to preparations for war it encouraged an imperious and overbearing officialdom and an aggressive martial spirit among its citizens—both of which were destructive of republican aims and institutions. Further, the passage of two centuries has not altered the importance of Madison's recognition that what government does affects what it is or may become. Theodore Lowi's contention that "policies determine politics" serves to remind us of the continuing relevance of Madison's warning that "measures can mold governments" (Lowi, 1972:299).

THE FOUNDERS' READING
OF THE REPUBLICAN TRADITION

Cicero defined a "commonwealth" for the republican tradition as "the coming together of a considerable number of men who are united by a common agreement about law and rights and by the desire to participate in mutual advantages" (Cicero, 1929:129). Nonetheless, this same republican tradition encouraged the conviction that just and efficient government, even once established, could never be maintained, given the inevitable stress and strain of social development (Pocock, 1975:viii). History, in fact, indicated to the founding generation that "agreement about law and rights" deteriorated over time as changing circumstances rendered the social distribution of "advantages" less clearly "mutual." The cyclical view of history shared by Cicero, Machiavelli, and many of the American founders promised social and political degeneration, which could be forestalled, but never wholly evaded (Adair, 1957:347).

Yet the last half of the eighteenth century saw new and hopeful elements entering the republican tradition, holding the promise that the human material of which society and government were composed was uniform and predictable (Middlekauff, 1987:661). David Hume, whose influence on the American founders has been demonstrated by Douglass Adair, Garry Wills, and other authors, echoed Machiavelli in arguing that "there is a great uniformity among the actions of men, in all nations and ages, and that human nature remains still the same in its principles and operations" (Hume, 1955:92–93). Since history seemed to show that human nature was constant, political structure was left as the critical determinant of social and economic order. Hume (1970:296) assured the founders that "so great is the force of ... particular forms of government ... that consequences almost as general and certain may sometimes be deduced from them as any which the mathematical sciences afford us."

The founding generation concluded that the object of political craftsmanship was to design institutions that would forestall—not just initially, but into the distant future—that degree of concentrated power that provided the very definition of tyranny for Cicero, Montesquieu, and Madison. The founders' confidence that such a goal might be achieved was expressed by Alexander Hamilton in *Federalist* No. 9. Hamilton explained that "the efficacy of various principles is now well understood, which were either not known at all, or imperfectly known to the ancients. The regular distribution of powers into distinct departments; the introduction of legislative balances and checks; the institution of courts composed of judges holding their offices during good behavior; the representation of the people in the legislature by deputies of their own election: these are wholly new discoveries, or have made their principal progress toward perfection in modern times" (Madison, Hamilton, and Jay, 1937:48).

However, even these new republican principles did not promise that the effects of social change could be restrained forever: As late as 1829 Madison was advising his colleagues at the Virginia Constitutional Convention to conduct their deliberations with an eye toward "the changes which time is rapidly producing." He reasoned, much as he had over forty years earlier at the federal Constitutional Convention in 1787, that if "we are to prepare a system of Govt. for a period which it is hoped will be a long one, we must look to the prospective changes in the condition and composition of the society on which it is to act." Madison warned that it was "to the effect of these changes, intellectual, moral, and social, [that] the institutions and laws of the Country must be adapted" (Madison, 1900, 11:360).

The founding generation was clearly correct to consider that social and economic changes would bring great stress to bear upon American national life. Not only would the population and the productive capacity of the nation expand, but perhaps more important, population and industry would also be redistributed from rural to urban settings, from the Atlantic coast to the inland regions, from the Northeast to the South and West, and from the industrial center to the industrializing periphery. Changes in the social and economic structure of American life have, as the founders anticipated, forced compensatory political changes, and not surprisingly, citizens, scholars, and statesmen have struggled to understand both the pace and the pattern of political change in America.

SOCIOECONOMIC DEVELOPMENT AND PATTERNS OF POLITICAL CHANGE IN AMERICA

Economic and social development have constantly posed new challenges to the American political system—challenges that have engendered meaningful response on at least three distinct levels of American political life. These interrelated patterns of political change constitute macrolevel, middle-range, and microlevel adjustments to the pressures generated by socioeconomic development. I believe that the following description of interrelated patterns of political change in America is important because one of the most prominent patterns—the simplest version of the realignment synthesis—has been called into serious question. Simultaneously, however, both broader and narrower descriptions of periodicity in American political history have attracted a positive response. There are a number of ways in which these patterns provide support and context for one another, as will be explored in this essay.

First, socioeconomic change has led to broad adjustments at the macro level in what Lowi calls the "public philosophy" and Walter Dean Burnham refers to as the "political universe" (Burnham, 1965:1; Lowi, 1967:1). At this *constitutional* level, the structure, tone, and character of political life are set within the context of a shared understanding of the nature and purpose of politics in America. Samuel Huntington suggests that four periods of dramatic adjustment at the constitutional level "stand out in American history: the Revolutionary, Jacksonian, and Progressive eras and the years of protest, exposure, and reform of the 1960s and early 1970s" (Huntington, 1981:85). In each instance socioeconomic change had so reconstituted American society that its political structures no longer promoted the fundamental principles of equity and justice that were supposed to provide their foundation; in response, Americans demanded thoroughgoing reform.

Second, within each constitutional era, ongoing struggles for control of America's political institutions have produced sharp adjustments. I will call this the *governmental* level of American political life. Governing coalitions at the national level have adjusted—sometimes successfully, sometimes not—as new social and economic groups have gained national prominence and sought to push new "systems of policy" through government. In addition to the periods Huntington highlights (the 1770s, 1820s, 1890s, and 1960s), one immediately thinks of Thomas Jefferson's revolution of 1800, Abraham Lincoln's prosecution of the Civil War, and Franklin Roosevelt's New Deal, as other periods of momentous change. Interestingly, V. O. Key, Jr., Lawrence Dodd, and Bruce Ackerman consider precisely the periods that Huntington omits—especially the two "catastrophic" events, the Civil War and the Great Depression—as triggers to fundamental change in American political life (Key, 1952:161–165; Dodd, 1981:394–396; Ackerman, 1991:40–41).

What distinguishes change at the constitutional level from that at the governmental level? I follow Huntington and others in arguing that transformations from one constitutional era to another produce dramatic changes in the structure and character of the political system itself. Challenges are posed not just to the opposition party and its program, but to the political system itself, as then constituted. Major institutions within the political system rise and fall in status, role, and power. During partisan realignments within constitutional eras, on the other hand, change is restricted to a struggle for control over a political system in which institutional structures and relationships are broadly accepted (Huntington, 1981:112–113).

Allan Lichtman, Stephen Skowronek, Burnham, and many others touch upon, but do not develop, this distinction. Lichtman calls for a reexamination "of the American past, searching not only for transitions that shuffle voter coalitions and shift the balance of party power, but also for transitions that qualitatively change the prevailing system of electoral politics ... movement across the American political universe may not only recast voter loyalties but may also modify the causal forces underlying voter decisions" (Lichtman, 1976:347–348; see also Marquette, 1974:1,059; and Converse, 1972:266). Thus, modification of the "causal forces" driving American politics marks the transition from one constitutional era to the next. For example, Lichtman suggests that "the 1890s could be seen as a critical point, not in the traditional sense of the [realignment] theory, but in the sense of introducing a qualitatively different era of electoral politics" (Lichtman, 1976:347; see also Skowronek, 1982:30–32, 55). Burnham makes precisely the same point in distinguishing between the reform content of the 1890s and the more limited realignment character of the 1930s (Burnham, 1974:106). Although the American political system has undergone significant adjustments about every thirty-five years, some of those adjustments have been deeper and more thoroughgoing (those of the 1770s, 1820s, 1890s, and 1960s) than others (those of the 1800s, 1860s, 1930s, and 1980s).

Interestingly, whether a new party system begins with a period of complete institutional reform or a realignment of political forces within familiar institutional structures, a regular pattern of "mid-sequence readjustments" is evident. In each case, about fifteen years of majority party dominance has been followed by fifteen to twenty years of competitive politics in which the major parties alternate in power, third parties rise to contest new issues, and divided government is common (Burnham, 1991:118–120).

The political importance of these fifteen-year periods of dominance by the majority party and of the periods of close partisan competition that follow should be evident. The realignment that sets a new party system in place occurs when the electorate concludes that one of the nation's parties is more capable, intellectually and politically, of confronting the nation's most pressing problems (Hurley, 1991:4–5). The favored party must then act on the opportunity presented to it by addressing the nation's problems in a way that the voters find credible. If successful, the majority party retains political control long enough to initiate, adjust, and eventually lock in its policy agenda (Sinclair, 1977:940).

As the period of majority party dominance proceeds, new problems arise, spawning new political issues, which may not relate directly to the established policy agenda. These new issues provide opportunities for dissident elements of the majority party, new third parties, and the established minority party to capture or regain competitive status by effectively addressing the new issues (Riker, 1982a:198–212). These new problems may anticipate issues that will be central to the next realignment, and although they send shivers through the electorate, they do not realign it (Carmines and Stimson, 1981:108–109). Further, as the realignment cycle plays itself out, neither major political party enjoys the kind of stable control of national political institutions that would allow the party to implement a program even if it had one (Skowronek, 1986:293).

Finally, at the third level, social and economic changes produce *psychological* tensions, which affect the patterns of association in which individuals embed themselves (Beck, 1974b:200; Elazar, 1976:207; Schlesinger, 1986:29; Mayhew, 1991:144–145). Paul Allen Beck's "Socialization Theory of Partisan Realignment" suggests that the characteristic realignment pattern—realignment, stable alignment, dealignment—"is explicable when change is conceptualized in terms of the movement through the electorate of the realignment generation, the children of realignment, and the children of normal politics" (Beck, 1974a:207, see also 1979:129; Carmines and Stimson, 1981:108). Beck's "socialization thesis" gives us a plausible microlevel explanation for the mid-level phenomenon of partisan realignment, mid-sequence adjustments and all. The logic behind Beck's insight, using the Civil War generation as an example, is that the generation that came of political and military age in the 1850s and 1860s as the nation plunged into conflagration had its partisanship made permanent by those life experiences. Beck calls these fierce partisans "the realignment generation." The children of the realignment generation were socialized around the dinner table in the immediate aftermath of the war by parents who had lived through that war, even if they had not been on the battlefield. While the children's partisanship would not be as unshakable as their parents', it would be firm.

The next generation, which Beck calls "the children of normal politics," were socialized during the period of competitive party politics lasting from 1874 to 1894, by parents who had not reached adulthood at the time of the previous realignment. The children of normal politics—young adults who began entering the electorate approximately twenty years after the conclusion of the Civil War—were witnesses to the Liberal and Mugwump splits from the Republican party, the Greenback, Farmers' Alliance, and Populist splits from the Democratic party, and had observed the general timidity of both parties in confronting the critical issues of the 1880s and the early 1890s. This generation was, therefore, available for realignment when the panic of 1893 struck down the Grover Cleveland administration and set the stage for William McKinley's destruction of William Jennings Bryan in the election of 1896.

Shortly after Beck introduced the generational thesis as a basis for realignment theory, Daniel Elazar (1976:23–46) took up the argument, specifying and elaborating it in very useful ways. More recently, and in light of the demise of political parties as vehicles capable of reflecting this underlying generational rhythm, analysts as diverse as James Stimson and David Mayhew have been drawn to Arthur Schlesinger, Jr.'s (1986:27) attempt to describe an individual-level psychological dynamic which produces "a continuing shift in national involvement between public purposes and private interest." Schlesinger contends that the eventual result of "sustained public action" is that it becomes "emotionally exhausting. … So public action, passion, idealism and reform recede. Public problems are turned over to the invisible hand of the market." Yet, "epochs of private interest breed contradictions too. … Segments of the population fall behind in the acquisitive race. Intellectuals are estranged. Problems neglected become acute" (Schlesinger, 1986:28; and see Weir, Orloff, and

Skocpol, 1988:15, 23). As these problems are increasingly interpreted as major threats to persons, institutions, and principles, the national mood swings back to concern for public, as opposed to narrower or more exclusively private, problems, issues, and concerns. This alternating pattern of activism and introspection, like the realignment cycle, averages roughly thirty to thirty-five years, but is differently motivated and more complex (Mayhew, 1991:144–145; Stimson, 1991:31).

Finally, Schlesinger (1986:29) also ties his understanding of cycles in the national mood to the passage of generations through the electorate. He draws explicit attention to this aspect of the phenomenon by noting that "in basic respects it is the generational experience that serves as the mainspring of the political cycle." Like Beck and Elazar, Schlesinger is careful to say that it is not so much birth rates as "epochal historical events [which] establish boundaries between generations. Common experience precipitates common perceptions and outlooks" (Schlesinger, 1986:29; see Mannheim, 1936:270). Depending upon the skill of the key actors and the vulnerability of the political system to change, these ephocal events send ripples of varying depth and dimension through the social system.

I began by arguing that economic development and social change engender political responses of different types and at different levels of the American political system. In fact, I agree with James Morone who comments in his recent book, *The Democratic Wish*, that "the periodicity of American democratic reform is hard to miss" (1990:19). The question is not whether one can uncover distinctive patterns of political response to socioeconomic change in American political history; clearly, one can, and several of the most important attempts have been laid out above. The problem is not one of paucity, but of surfeit; we are awash in interesting and suggestive descriptions of and explanations for the patterns that are evident in American political history. The question to be addressed in this essay is whether these patterns relate to each other in some sensible way. I believe that they do, as shown in Figure 2.1.

THE FIRST CONSTITUTIONAL ERA:
POLITICS OF DEMOCRATIZATION, 1765–1828

Many members of the founding generation understood quite clearly that the American Revolution neither began with nor ended in the clash of arms. For John Adams, the American revolution was an intellectual and emotional phenomenon, which occurred between 1765 and 1776. Near the end of his life, after more than forty years of reflection, Adams concluded that a "radical change in the principles, opinions, sentiments and affections of the people was the real American revolution" (Adams, 1856, 10:283). Even more important, Benjamin Rush understood that the suc-

FIGURE 2.1 Patterns of Change in American National Politics

Year	Constitutional Eras	Party Systems	Realignment Phases	Mood Cycles
1765	**Politics of Democratization 1765–1828**	Preparty System of Notables 1765–1800	Preparty Phase	Resistance and Revolution 1765–1787
				Federalists 1788–1800
1800		Jeffersonian Democracy 1801–1828	Stable 1800–1815	Jeffersonians 1801–1815
			Dealignment 1816–1828	Era of Good Feeling 1816–1828
	Era Transformation	1828–1836		
	Politics of Party Competition 1836–1896	Jacksonian Democracy 1829–1860	Stable 1829–1840	Jacksonian Democrats 1829–1840
1850			Dealignment 1841–1860	Whigs and Doughface Democrats 1841–1860
		Lincoln and the Republicans 1861–1896	Stable 1861–1874	Lincoln/Radicals 1861–1869
			Dealignment 1875–1895	Post-Reconstruction 1870–1882
				Populist Turmoil 1883–1896
	Era Transformation	1896–1901		
	Politics of Interest-Group Liberalism 1902–1968	McKinley and the Republicans 1896–1932	Stable 1897–1910	McKinley 1896–1901
1900			Dealignment 1911–1932	Progressive Reforms 1902–1917
				Republican Restoration 1918–1932
		Roosevelt and the Democrats 1933–1968	Stable 1933–1945	Roosevelt and the New Deal 1933–1945
1950			Dealignment 1946–1967	Eisenhower and the 1950s 1946–1960
				Johnson and The Great Society 1961–1968
	Era Transformation	1968–1980		
	Post-Partisan Hyper-Pluralism	Divided Government 1968–1992	Continuing Dealignment	The Reagan/ Bush Agenda 1980–1992
2000				

cessful revolution provided little more than an initial opportunity for the American people and their leaders to build their new ideas into equally new and untried political institutions. Rush observes that "there is nothing more common than to confound the terms American Revolution with those of the late American War. The American War is over, but this is far from being the case with the American Revolution. On the contrary, but the first act of the great drama is closed" (as quoted in Morris, 1967:84–85). The slow movement from a deferential to an aggressively democratic polity defined the first constitutional era in American political history (Formisano, 1974:473; Wood, 1992:6, 125, 229).

The American Revolution

Both Rush and Adams were part of a generation just coming of age as the Revolution approached. Rush was barely thirty and Adams just forty when each signed the Declaration of Independence in the summer of 1776. The Declaration itself was, of course, the work of thirty-three-year-old Thomas Jefferson. Not yet perched atop the political structure of their individual colonies or embedded within the imperial relations of their society, these "young men of the Revolution" were prepared to consider independence while older and more established leaders, Thomas Hutchinson of Massachusetts and Joseph Galloway of Pennsylvania, simply were not so inclined (Elkins and McKitrick, 1961; Bailyn, 1973:16–17). South Carolina's David Ramsay, another young man of the Revolution, noted this generational difference, explaining that "the age and temperament of individuals had often an influence in fixing their political character. Old men were seldom warm Whigs: they could not relish the great changes which were daily taking place; attached to ancient forms and habits, they could not readily accommodate themselves to new systems" (quoted in Martin, 1973:152).

The revolutionary transformation of American politics that occurred in the 1760s and 1770s began with rebellion against an imperial elite and moved to a reconfiguration of American politics around its more popular institutional components. In this period of intense institutional innovation, governors and upper houses lost power to lower houses, and lower houses lost the initiative to local governments and publics operating "out-of-doors." The Pennsylvania Constitution of 1776, with its weak executive, its unicameral legislature, and its espousal of popular ratification in which all adult white males were eligible to participate, epitomized the political tendencies of the revolutionary era.

Nonetheless, by 1786 a conservative reaction had taken hold and many thoughtful Americans had concluded that overly democratic state governments and a pitifully weak Confederation had spawned the critical problems facing the new nation. James Madison's detailed analysis of the

American political experience under the Articles of Confederation resulted in April 1787 in a short essay entitled, "Vices of the Political System of the United States." Madison's fundamental concern was that volatile and frequently misdirected state governments were abusing their own citizens, each other, and the weak Confederation government. Madison believed, as did George Washington, Hamilton, and many others, that nothing less than a continental republic with a national government strong enough to control volatile local authorities would provide the requisite stability to the new nation.

The Federal Convention and Federalist Rule

The federal Constitutional Convention that sat in Philadelphia throughout the summer of 1787 was determined to constrain the democratic instability of the previous decade. Virginia's Governor Edmund Randolph opened the convention on May 25 with a speech in which he warned of "the prospect of anarchy from the laxity of government every where" (Farrand, 1937, 1:19). Few members were surprised when the first motion passed on the first day of substantive debate resolved "that a national government ought to be established consisting of a supreme legislative, judiciary and executive" (Farrand, 1937, 1:30; see also Madison, Hamilton, and Jay, 1937, *Federalist No. 26*). While the common people were not barred from politics, the constitution's system of large electoral districts, indirect appointments, and expanded national powers moved many important political decisions out of their reach.

Under the new constitution, elites—increasingly broad, but elites nonetheless—dominated every level of government in America. Many scholars have noted that this control was secured by structural devices such as "restrictions on the franchise, large electoral districts, the absence of a 'top of the ticket' as a focus for popular enthusiasm and, of course, the absence of an organized opposition, [which] together limited the size of the active electorate" (Shefter, 1978:219; Burnham, 1987:32–37). These rules and structures helped the conservative, northern, commercial elite which gathered around Hamilton to dominate American politics through both of Washington's administrations and through that of Adams (Hofstadter, 1954:33; Kelley, 1977:539). The Federalist party politics of the 1790s produced policies in the interest of the Middle Atlantic and New England states—the bank, the tariff, and Hamilton's funding program—policies that seemed to cut against the interests of the South—the tariff in particular—and the West—most notably the tax on whiskey. Following Washington's withdrawal in 1796, Federalist control began to slip, leading Adams to enact and enforce the Alien and Sedition Acts of 1798 and 1799. In 1800 Thomas Jefferson swept the Federalists from power.

The Jeffersonian Revolution of 1800

Realignments within constitutional eras, as opposed to the more thoroughgoing reform periods that mark the end of one constitutional era and the beginning of another, involve capture and control of the political system rather than any broad change in the character or structure of the system. The basic relationships that pertain to the society and its political institutions do not change even though the identity and character of the interests that control the institutions may. Martin Shefter (1978:217) makes just this point in noting that both the Federalists and the Jeffersonians were coteries of elites. Moreover, many have agreed with Dodd and Richard Schott's observation (1979:18) that "the Jeffersonians, who captured the reins of power from the Federalists in 1801 and held them until the election of Andrew Jackson in 1828, kept the administrative structure they inherited largely intact" (see also McCoy, 1980:186; and Morone, 1990:71).

Jefferson understood quite clearly that his presidency did not begin from scratch; rather, he took over a system already in operation. Soon after his inauguration, Jefferson wrote: "When this government was first established, it was possible to have kept it going on true principles, but the contracted, English, half-lettered ideas of Hamilton destroyed that hope in the bud. We can pay off his debts in 15 years; but we can never get rid of his financial system. ... What is practicable must often control what is pure theory" (Hofstadter, 1954:35). Jefferson believed that by displacing the Federalists he had won the opportunity to reconsider and revise, though not to replace wholesale, the policies and programs of his predecessors.

Nonetheless, the Jeffersonian displacement of Hamiltonian intentions was important to the future development of the American state. Consider three issues: the bank, the debt, and the navy. Hamilton's vision was state-centered mercantilism: The bank would provide the state with the capacity to manage currency, credit, and the economy; the debt would tie the interest of the wealthy to the state; and the navy would, as in Britain, enhance state power and the national defense. Naturally, the state's ability to extract wealth from the society would have to be substantial in order to support Hamiltonian ambitions.

Jefferson, of course, rejected root and branch this desire for enhanced state capacity. He allowed the charter of the First Bank of the United States to lapse, paid off the national debt, and agreed to fund only the tiniest military establishment. Jefferson thus minimized national state capacity in favor of states' rights and local control of virtually all domestic policy. He first articulated this position in a letter of December 16, 1786, to James Madison. And almost forty years later, following six terms in which he, Madison, and Monroe had filled the president's chair, Jefferson reiterated this point in a letter of April 4, 1824, to Edward Livingston. Jefferson wrote that "the radical idea ... which I have adopted ... is that the whole field of government is divided into two departments, domestic and foreign ... that the former department is reserved exclusively to the respective States within their own limits" (Jefferson, 1955:132, 149). American politics has, to this day, adapted its sense of the possible to this Jeffersonian matrix of state sovereignty and local control (Weir, Orloff, and Skocpol, 1988:21).

Madison, Monroe, Adams, and the Federalization of Jeffersonian Democracy

Jeffersonian presidents of the old school held sway from 1800 through about 1815. Though they were challenged by the Federalists, they increasingly restricted these enemies to their New England strongholds. Nonetheless, the commercial development of New England and the Middle Atlantic states, combined with the conservative control of the judiciary that John Adams had assured with his appointment of John Marshall to be Chief Justice of the Supreme Court, began to bear increasing fruit after 1815 (Current, 1955: x, 28–34). In 1816, President James Madison, Jefferson's chosen successor, chartered the Second Bank of the United States, endorsed a protective tariff, and recommended a constitutional amendment to permit federal support of internal improvements. In 1819 Chief Justice Marshall, writing in *McCulloch v. Maryland*, struck a fierce blow against Jeffersonian localism by denying Maryland's claim to control federal entities, in this case a branch of the Bank of the United States, operating within its boundaries (Schlesinger, 1945:18–19).

The partisan realignment of 1800, during which the Jeffersonian Republicans, representing a broader and more agriculturally oriented segment of the aristocracy, displaced the narrower and more commercially oriented Federalist coalition of notables, occurred within a constitutional era whose defining characteristic was the cautious democratization of American politics (Burnham, 1991:118). As the territories of the West filled up and began to seek admission to the Union, they adopted constitutions mandating universal, white, male suffrage. In addition, five of the original thirteen states amended their constitutions prior to 1820 to permit all white males to vote. Nonetheless, much of politics remained beyond the effective reach of the common man.

ERA TRANSFORMATION: BIRTH OF THE PARTY SYSTEM, 1828–1836

Transformations that introduce new constitutional eras involve broad adjustments in the way society relates to the political system and in social expectations of the political system, as well as adjustments in the way power is located and distributed within the political system. In the American case, the rise to dominance of mass-based, professionally organized, political parties steadily displaced the loosely organized coalitions of notables that had dominated early American politics (McCormick, 1966:3; Shefter, 1978:218; Skowronek, 1982:25). For this reason, Joel Silbey (1991b:9) recently referred to the decade following the election of 1828 as a "transforming political moment" in the development of the American political system.

The construction of mass-based political parties in the United States brought a new political class to power with new connections to the nation's broader social classes. As Martin Van Buren and the first generation of party managers attempted to pull together the disparate interests that had begun to coalesce around Andrew Jackson, they faced a political situation that they understood only partially. New forces were changing the shape of American politics: "The people, the propertyless masses, were beginning, at first quietly and almost unobtrusively, to enter politics. ... As poor farmers and workers gained the ballot, there developed a new type of politician ... the technician of mass leadership, the caterer to mass sentiment. ... They ... spread the conviction that politics and administration must be taken from the hands of the social elite ... and opened to mass participation" (Hofstadter, 1954:50–51).

The Whigs followed closely on the heels of the Jacksonians as both plunged into this era of rapid transformation from deferential democratic to partisan politics (Formisano, 1974:473; Watson, 1990:4–6). Moreover, party leaders proposed and passed a series of electoral and bureaucratic reforms which fastened down their control of this newly configured political system. Shefter (1978:219) and others have explained how "the electoral reforms of the Jacksonian Era—white manhood suffrage; the paper ballot; small polling districts; direct election of governors, presidential electors, heads of state executive departments, and local government officials; and short terms of office—swamped the older, elite-dominated mechanisms of election management and political recruitment."

As Richard Hofstadter observes in his classic, *The Idea of a Party System* (1969), this reorientation and recasting of the American political system was the work of a new generation of political leaders only tenuously connected to the founding generation (Hofstadter, 1969:212; see also Wood, 1992:298–299). Hofstadter describes the generational movement of these new party men from political nonage to political dominance in terms that are so fully consonant with the arguments of Beck, Elazar, and Schlesinger, that they deserve to be quoted at some length.

The new apologia for partisan politics was in some considerable measure the work of a generation and a type. Its leading exponents were men who, in the main ... like Van Buren himself, came of age during Jefferson's presidency and took the first Republican President as their model of a political hero. As children they were raised on hero tales of the Revolution. As youths they saw an established two-party competition in action, then in decline. As young men making their own places in the civic order under different conditions, they could look back upon the years from 1790 to about 1812 with a new perspective and with at least a trace of detachment. ... They were considerably more interested than their predecessors in organization, ... less fixed in their views, ... less ideological. (Hofstadter, 1969:213)

As this new generation of party managers assumed center stage, men of the previous generation, even the giants among them, were painfully aware that their era had passed. No less a figure than Thomas Jefferson complained to an old friend in a letter of January 11, 1825: "All, all dead, and ourselves left alone amidst a new generation whom we know not, and who know not us" (Wood, 1992:368).

THE SECOND CONSTITUTIONAL ERA:
POLITICS OF PARTY COMPETITION, 1836–1896

The economic and social bases of American society changed dramatically over the course of the nineteenth century. Migration south and west, first into Kentucky and Tennessee, then into the Ohio and Mississippi valleys, and finally across the continent to the West Coast followed well-established routes by the second quarter of the new century. However, as Barrington Moore (1966:127–128) pointed out some years ago, though pioneers moved west, the goods that they produced upon settlement usually traveled downriver to supply the more specialized slave economy of the South. This economic connection spawned the Jacksonian coalition of southern and western agrarian interests, which stood against the commercial interests of New England and the Middle Atlantic states between 1825 and 1850. Nonetheless, development continued apace so that "by 1860 the United States had developed three quite different forms of society in different parts of the country: the cotton-growing South; the West, a land of free farmers; and the rapidly industrializing Northeast" (Moore, 1966:115; Agnew, 1987:43–46). Moreover, the patterns of interaction and interest among these three regions had changed so markedly by mid-century that a northern alliance in favor of tariffs, family farms, and free labor became increasingly likely.

In terms very similar to those that his father had used to describe the sea change in political sentiments that had constituted the *real* American revolution, John Quincy Adams remarked that the years immediately following his defeat by Andrew Jackson in 1828 revealed a "revolution in the habits and manners of the people" (Current, 1955:114). American national

politics increasingly came to be dominated by an intensely partisan electoral system and a national political system in which Congress held the
central role (Lowi, 1972:300). The partisan transformation of American
politics that occurred in the 1830s set the character and tone of the nation's
politics for the next sixty years (Silbey, 1991b:6; Mayhew, 1968:139).

Jacksonian Democracy and the Second Party System

Andrew Jackson and his close associates in the Democratic party, most notably Martin Van Buren and James Polk, set the political agenda for the
second quarter of the nineteenth century. Jackson and the Democrats
stood for universal, white, male suffrage and for the broad provision of
political and economic opportunity within American society. Democratic
candidates for the presidency won three elections in a row, and six out of
eight, between 1828 and 1856.

Jackson came to the presidency in 1828 determined to redefine for a
new era the Jeffersonian principles of states' rights, local control, and individual initiative. Therefore, he opposed federal expenditures for internal
improvements; a national bank advantaged by federal government de-
posits; protective as opposed to revenue-producing tariffs; high prices for
federal lands in the West; and a federal debt that might unduly interest the
monied class in the power and prestige of the national government. In
brief, he opposed the policies that Hamilton had originated, that the administrations of James Monroe and John Quincy Adams had embraced,
and that Henry Clay called "the American system." Jackson held consistently to the view that the national government's "true strength consists
in leaving individuals and States as much as possible to themselves" (as
quoted in Watson, 1990:150).

In May 1830, with the support of Van Buren in the Senate and Polk in
the House, Jackson vetoed an appropriation for the Maysville Road as
both expensive and unconstitutional (not incidentally, the road ran
through Henry Clay's Kentucky). A series of similar vetoes killed federal
support for state and even regional inland projects for most of the decade.
Moreover, Jackson's stinging defeat of Clay in the election of 1832 resolved the issue of whether the Bank of the United States would be used
as an instrument of national, fiscal, economic, and credit policy. Jackson
reproduced another of Jefferson's accomplishments by employing revenues from the brisk sale of western lands to completely pay off the national debt. Finally, when Chief Justice John Marshall died on July 6, 1835,
President Jackson nominated, and the Senate approved the president's
own close political associate, Roger Taney, to be chief justice of the United
States Supreme Court. Therefore, as Jackson approached the end of his
second term, he could feel that he had accomplished his goal of returning
the national government to solid Jeffersonian foundations. Once again,
Hamilton's "half-lettered" economic program had been turned back. The

Second Bank was dead, the tariff was lowered, the debt was liquidated, and Chief Justice Marshall, the last Federalist, had gone to his grave.

Still immensely popular as his second term drew to a close, Jackson was able to deliver the Democratic party's presidential nomination to Vice President Van Buren. Unlike the Democrats, the Whigs had no single leader around whom to rally. Their strategy in 1836 was to run several regional candidates in the hope of denying Van Buren an electoral college majority. The strategy nearly worked, though Van Buren ultimately prevailed, drawing slightly less than 51 percent of the popular vote, while William Henry Harrison (Ohio), his strongest challenger, drew 37 percent. Once the House was organized, Van Buren could look to fellow Jacksonian James Polk in the speaker's chair. Nonetheless, President Van Buren's ability to govern was almost immediately compromised by severe recessions in 1837 and 1839. Moreover, Van Buren lacked the political weight either to hold together his disparate coalition or to keep Clay, Calhoun, and Webster at bay.

Military Chieftains and Doughface Democrats

Political instability and conservative political drift reigned during the two decades preceding the Civil War. Though Van Buren was able to retain the nomination of his party in 1840, Whigs recognized his weakness and determined to run a single candidate against him. William Henry Harrison (Ohio), Henry Clay (Kentucky), and Winfield Scott (Virginia) entered the Whig convention as candidates for the nomination. Though Clay led on the first ballot, movement of Scott delegates to Harrison on later ballots eventually led to the Ohioan's nomination. The convention members then thought to balance the ticket ideologically and regionally by nominating a former Democratic senator, John Tyler of Virginia, as vice president. In recognition of the ideological divergence between their presidential and vice-presidential candidates, the Whigs declined to offer a platform.

Whig partisans cheering Harrison's victory over incumbent President Van Buren gave little thought to the presence of Tyler in the second spot. Yet, less than a month after his inauguration, Harrison was dead and John Tyler was president. Henry Clay decided to use Whig majorities in the Congress to control the new president or to break him. Clay introduced bills to charter a national bank, raise the tariff, and undertake extensive internal improvements. When Tyler vetoed the bank bill, Clay called on the cabinet to resign. All except Daniel Webster did so immediately.

Following his rejection by the Whigs in Congress, Tyler looked to former allies among the southern Democrats. But when President Tyler turned his attention to southern expansion and the possible annexation of Texas, Daniel Webster decided that he too had to leave the cabinet. His place as secretary of state was filled first by the pro-slavery Virginian, Abel Upshur, and then by John Calhoun himself. What had seemed in

1840 to be a Whig mandate to reconsider the results of the Jacksonian revolution had, following Harrison's death, become a Jacksonian administration bent on the dramatic expansion of territory open to slavery (Foner, 1980:42).

Though President Tyler sought renomination in 1844, Henry Clay was the unanimous choice of the Whig party convention. Former President Van Buren was the front-runner for the Democratic nomination until his opposition to Texas annexation eroded his already weak southern support. Van Buren's principal challenger, Senator Lewis Cass, a Democrat from Michigan, favored admission of Texas to the Union. Though Van Buren led in the early balloting, Cass eventually pulled ahead, but neither could come close to the required two-thirds. As the delegates cast about for a compromise candidate, James Polk, former speaker of the House and more recently governor of Tennessee, emerged as the consensus choice. Polk, after declaring that if elected he would serve only a single term, was nominated on the ninth ballot.

The popular vote for president was excruciatingly close in 1844. Nationwide, Polk's advantage was less than forty thousand votes out of the more than 2.7 million cast. Moreover, Polk suffered the political indignity of being defeated in his home state of Tennessee by Kentucky's Clay (Clay got 60,040 votes to Polk's 59,917). Polk immediately sought to advance the Democratic agenda of tariff reductions, an independent treasury, and opposition to internal improvements. More important for the long term, however, President Polk ordered General Zachary Taylor into disputed territory along the Rio Grande, thereby sparking war with Mexico. The result was the admission of Texas into the Union and the seizure of California and what is now the Southwest and the western mountain states.

The expansionism of the Tyler and Polk administrations changed the character of American politics in critical ways. By the end of Polk's term, Congress and the country were deeply divided over the status of slavery in the newly acquired territories. Neither national party seemed capable of addressing this critical issue. Both sought to span the chasm between their northern and southern wings by nominating men of indistinct or anomalous principles. Democrats nominated "doughface" candidates, northern men of southern principles, while Whigs looked to their "cotton" as opposed to their "conscience" wing for candidates. With the parties so badly divided no president achieved reelection between 1840 and 1860 (Morone, 1990:88). Third parties proliferated.

Lincoln and the Rise of the Republican Party

When Lincoln won the presidency in 1860, the new Republican party also took majority control of the U.S. House and Senate (Foner, 1980:53).

Most southern members had of course withdrawn. Republicans held control of the presidency and both houses of Congress until 1874 when the Democrats broke through in the House. Between 1876 and 1896 Democrats and Republicans again competed on an even basis, with Democrats, behind Grover Cleveland, winning two of five presidential elections and enjoying control of the House for sixteen of the twenty-two years between 1874 and 1896, while the Republicans held the Senate for eighteen of these twenty-two years.

The realignment of 1860 saw Lincoln and the Republican party move decisively to consolidate control over a political system bequeathed to them by its Jacksonian architects. Like Andrew Jackson, Abraham Lincoln stood for the real opportunity of the little man to rise in the scale of economic and social life. Where Lincoln differed from Jackson was in his conviction that national government policy and power should be employed to aid the economy in producing the opportunity that men might seek to grasp. Therefore, while Lincoln's party stood for generous homestead legislation and the founding of land grant universities to spur and broaden landholding, and agricultural science and education, it stood just as strongly for high tariffs, stable banks, and industrial inducement (Sundquist, 1983:90; see also Foner, 1980:32–33, 48; Brady and Stewart, 1982:338–345). Moreover, radical Republicans sought to reconstruct southern society through constitutional amendments and legislation intended to insure equal rights for freedmen in the post–Civil War polity.

Nonetheless, coming to power in the middle of the second constitutional era, the Republicans sought to capture and use to their advantage, rather than to change or reform, the basic structures and processes of the political system within which they operated. Skowronek (1982:30–31) notes that "if new institutional forms are to constitute a new state, they must alter the procedural bonds that tie the governmental institutions together and define their relationship to society. The Civil War did not do this. The constituent party machine reigned supreme in governmental operations before, during, and after the crisis." While the victory of the Union armies changed America fundamentally and forever, this change took the form of demanding that the South conform to established northern principles of social and economic organization. The Republican party held sway throughout the nation—in the North and South.

Lincoln's assassination in 1865 brought Tennessee's Union Democrat, Vice President Andrew Johnson, to the presidency. Once again, the person filling the bottom half of a fusion ticket had ascended unexpectedly to the presidency at a critical time. Johnson's sympathy for the defeated southerners led him to work for their rapid reintroduction into the political life of the nation with their traditional white elites still securely in place. Radical Republicans, described by C. Vann Woodward as "frankly revolutionary in mood," responded by impeaching President Johnson in the House, falling one vote short of conviction in the Senate (Woodward, 1966:15). Moreover, the 1866 elections brought radical Republican majorities to both houses of the Congress. Though Senator Thaddeus Stevens's plan to reconstruct southern society by expropriating all rebel holdings over 200 acres and redistributing them to freedmen in lots of "forty acres and a mule" was defeated, the South was subjected to military occupation and political reconstruction. Republican administrations throughout the South held conventions to rewrite constitutions to include full legal and political rights for freedmen. Southern electorates were expanded to include 700,000 new black voters, while exclusion of former rebels reduced the white electorate to about 625,000. While political reconstruction was carried on in the South, President Grant and the Republican Congress turned their attention to rebuilding the northern economy and reorienting it to civilian production.

The presidential election of 1876 brought Republican ascendancy into fundamental question. Republican candidate Rutherford Hayes appeared to lose both the popular and electoral college votes to the Democrat Samuel Tilden. However, electoral votes in several southern states were contested. In the end, a 'bargain' was struck in which all of the contested electoral votes went to Hayes, providing the narrowest of victory margins, in exchange for the abandonment of the remaining Republican governments in the South, the withdrawal of Union occupation troops, and favorable consideration of southern projects in the rivers and harbors legislation then pending in the Congress.

This bargain was struck, as Woodward explains, because the mood of the country and its leaders had become decidedly conservative following the fervor of the war and reconstruction. Woodward writes that "if the Men of 1787 made the *Thermidor* of the First American Revolution, the Men of 1877 fulfilled a corresponding part in The Second American Revolution. They were the new men who come at the end of periods of revolutionary upheaval, when the hopes and soaring ideals have lagged and failed, and the fervors have burned themselves out" (Woodward, 1966:215). Reconstruction ended ignobly as a conservative tide flowed through the land, pushing both Cleveland Democrats and Harrison Republicans before it.

The Era of Post-Reconstruction Industrialization

Not surprisingly, those who built the post-reconstruction party system, did so in order to address their most fundamental interests. As a result, "the national party system of the late nineteenth century organized into the political process issues that were highly salient to northeastern, industrial, commercial, and financial interests, and organized out of politics issues that might have led to a coalition between southern and western agrarian radicals" (Shefter, 1983:481; see also Bensel, 1984:137–139). As rural populists and urban progressives seethed over the blatant corruption and narrow partisanship of Republican programs for industrial development, the U.S. economy grew rapidly, becoming the largest industrial economy in the world in the nineteenth century's last decade (Agnew, 1987:22).

During the last quarter of the nineteenth century, the far-flung nation became bound together by transportation and communication links that facilitated the rapid expansion of commercial and manufacturing enterprises into regional and national scale systems (Jahnige, 1971:494). The nationalization, industrialization, and urbanization of American life, particularly in the North, put an end to what analysts have quite aptly called "island communities"; small, isolated, social outposts that revolved around local issues and local personalities while remaining quite ignorant of, and therefore impermeable to, outside influences (Clubb, Flanigan, and Zingale, 1980:284). As Samuel Hays (1975:166) explains, "Urban, industrial society involved a fundamental reordering of human relationships which permeated not only economic and social life but political life as well." The ability to move information and goods rapidly and efficiently over long distances "gave rise to new forms of social organization ... involving human relationships over broad geographical areas" (Hays, 1975:167–171; see also Olson, 1965:84; Huntington, 1973:7).

These technological developments seemed to demand two fundamental changes in the way Americans thought about how to organize national politics. First, the arrival of new technologies in transportation and communication—principally railroads and telegraph—allowed commercial and industrial enterprises to expand to national dimensions. Businesses, formerly limited to local and, at most, regional markets by constraints on their ability to send and receive information and materials over long distances were, in the years from the end of Reconstruction to the arrival of the new century, released from these constraints. These developments in transportation and communication technologies seemed to undermine Madison's case for an "extended republic." Extensive territory no longer guaranteed that persons sharing narrow interests could not come together, pool their power, and press their interests on government. With startling rapidity, national trusts and monopolies appeared in banking, railroads, oil, sugar, tobacco, and countless other product lines. Farmers, wage laborers, and small business owners, helpless before these economic giants, demanded protection. Second, the complexity and scope of these enterprises seemed to demand that government abandon the idea of "separation of powers." Hence, the Interstate Commerce Commission, chartered in 1887 to regulate the railroads, was given a broad mandate to develop, implement, and adjudicate "fair" and "reasonable" freight rates.

The development of national communication and transportation systems provided the basis for an explosion of trade and professional organizations beginning in the early 1880s. These developments also insured that stories about the transgressions of corrupt business enterprises could be transmitted quickly to a nation increasingly eager for political, economic, and social reform.

ERA TRANSFORMATION:
ASSAULT ON THE PARTY SYSTEM, 1896–1901

In the closing years of the nineteenth century, corporate, progressive, and partisan interests all challenged the structure and character of the existing party system (Clubb, Flanigan, and Zingale, 1980:283). Once again, as in the Revolutionary and Jacksonian eras, the impetus behind the fundamental political changes that produced the era of interest-group liberalism was the widespread feeling that social and economic developments had outrun the capacity of American political institutions to cope effectively with them (Skowronek, 1982:17, 39). Nonetheless, scholars disagree over exactly which social and economic interests brought about the institutional changes of the new constitutional era, for what purposes these changes were made, and what the implications of the changes were for American political development in the twentieth century.

E. E. Schattschneider, Walter Dean Burnham, and David Brady offer a menacing picture of the dismantling of America's democratic political institutions by conservative corporate interests (Schattschneider, 1960:78–79; Burnham, 1965:23–25; Brady, 1988:52–53). Others, including Philip Converse and Stephen Skowronek, argue that urban, progressive elites, determined to clean up the corruption of traditional partisan politics, successfully advocated a series of reforms designed to weaken parties in favor of direct citizen involvement in electoral politics and governance (Converse, 1972:297; Skowronek, 1982:53, 287). A third interpretation, offered by historians such as Richard Jensen and Samuel McSeveney, mediates between the progressive reform and corporate capture theses in a way that views Republican party leaders around William McKinley, as well as corporate and progressive interests (for different reasons), actively initiating the changes that led directly to the era of interest-group liberalism (Jensen, 1971:10, 58; McSeveney, 1972:6).This disparate coalition advanced a set of institutional and electoral reforms that was specifically designed to deflate partisanship in the electorate, break party dominance of congressional politics, and enhance the presidency in its ability to set the course and purpose of national policy (Orloff, 1988:56–59). Each of these changes was designed to disperse the power of political parties operating through the Congress and to enhance the president's "capacity to intervene far more actively in the economy and society. ... and to implement 'reforms' in the areas of public health, education, welfare, and morals, and in the management of the public domain" (Shefter, 1978:235–236; see also Lichtman, 1976:347; and Clubb, Flanigan, and Zingale, 1980:286). The transformation era, which began with McKinley's "System of 1896," laid the groundwork for the era of interest-group liberalism. The impact of organized interests on the conduct of American politics has broadened and deepened throughout most of the twentieth century.

THE THIRD CONSTITUTIONAL ERA:
INTEREST-GROUP POLITICS, 1902–1976

Scholars have for some time been relatively united on the question of how McKinley's "System of 1896," interacting with determined calls for corporate order and efficiency and progressive demands for openness and honesty in the conduct of government, affected the institutional core of American political life: Coherence and order gave way to incoherence and disorder. As the national political parties lost their role as meaningful vehicles for contesting the control of government, the electorate steadily cut its ties with them. Unfortunately, state administrative capacity, or bureaucracy, could not replace mass-based, militaristically organized political parties as devices for ordering, mobilizing, and informing the American voting public. Skowronek concludes that "modern American state building progressed by replacing courts and parties with a national bureaucracy, and this dynamic yielded a hapless confusion of institutional purposes, authoritative controls, and governmental boundaries" (Skowronek, 1982:287).

McKinley and the Politics of Interest

In 1890 the Democrats captured the House and in 1892, backing Grover Cleveland, they unseated President Harrison and took control of the Senate. Against this strong Democratic tide, William McKinley won reelection to the House in 1890 and then election to the governorship of Ohio in 1891 and 1893. As McKinley and other Republican leaders contemplated the massive losses suffered by their party during the early 1890s, they concluded that "the basic weakness of the GOP was its shelter for the pietistic reformers who harped on divisive cultural issues" (Jensen, 1971:153; see also McSeveney, 1972:20, 185). These issues, including prohibition, Sunday-closing laws, mandatory support for public schools, and English-only laws, alienated large blocs of immigrant voters, including many who traditionally had been staunch Republicans. Party professionals came to view the party system of the late nineteenth century as too emotionally charged and too volatile to be able to operate successfully in a political setting in which "less than two percentage points separated the total Democratic and Republican vote for congressmen in the elections of 1878, 1880, 1884, 1886, and 1888" (Jensen, 1971:10, 58; see also McSeveney, 1972:6).

Meanwhile, the broad Democratic victory of 1892, won behind the moderate Cleveland wing of the party, was followed by the devastating economic collapse of 1893 and the capture of the Democratic party by its most hard-pressed elements—the farmers of the South and West, who united behind 36-year-old William Jennings Bryan (Schattschneider, 1960:78–79; Brady, 1988:52–53). Bryan's alienation of the urban working classes of the industrial Midwest and Northeast in the campaign of 1896 created "an alignment which eventually separated the Southern and Western agrarians and transformed the most industrially advanced region of the country into a bulwark of industrialist Republicanism" (Burnham, 1965:25). One-party politics—Republican in the metropole and Democrat in the periphery—became the rule in most states. As elections became less meaningful, usually involving nothing more than intramural squabbles within the monopoly party, voter interest waned and turnout fell (Burnham, 1965:10, 23).

This "system of 1896" was the work of a new generation of politicians. Michael King and Lester Seligman demonstrate that "many of the congressmen who lost in 1896 ... were defeated by younger men ... the average age of the defeated congressmen was fifty-eight, while the new congressmen averaged forty-one years" (King and Seligman, 1976:282, 287). Just as a new generation of politicians around Jackson and Van Buren had been forced to reform the Democratic party in the wake of its defeat by John Quincy Adams, so the Republican party under Mark Hanna and William McKinley, in the wake Cleveland's defeat of Harrison, had to reform the party to make it relevant to the new century. New men with new ideas came together around McKinley to restructure the basic connections between American society and its national political institutions.

McKinley's famous front porch campaign eschewed narrow partisanship and, in its place, promised "pluralism to the American people. ... Every occupation, every religion, every industry, every section would receive fair treatment. ... Cooperation and compromise, within the framework of sound economics" would return unity and prosperity to the nation (Jensen, 1971:291). While McKinley spoke of unity and prosperity, Bryan raged against the Republican dominated "metropole" of New England and the upper Midwest, calling these areas "the enemy's country." Jensen concludes (1971:308) that "McKinley's new spirit of pluralism ... carried its champion to the White House and set the tone for national and midwestern politics" (see also Rusk, 1974:1,038). The Democrats, unable to adapt to these new realities, nominated Bryan again in 1900 and yet again in 1908.

Though parties weakened steadily, competitive party dynamics during the period from 1896 to 1932 were remarkably similar to those of earlier party systems: a fourteen-year period of majority party dominance, followed by a period of conservatism and drift, leading up to the next realignment. When McKinley and the Republicans won the presidency in 1896 they also took the House and Senate, holding all three until the congressional elections of 1910 when the Democrats again broke through in the House. The Democrats, with Woodrow Wilson as the new standard-bearer, won two of the next five presidential elections. This time, however, Democratic inroads into the House and Senate were restricted almost exclusively to the first six years of the Wilson presidency. Following World War I, the Republicans held sway until the Democrats again broke through in the House elections of 1930.

Wilson and Progressivism

As increasing numbers of producer and consumer groups organized to press their claims on state and national governments it became clear that many of their interests were incompatible. Moreover, numerous exposés by muckraking journalists during the first decade of the new century reported to national audiences the effects of large-scale campaign contributions and of politicians being lobbied by business. A pattern of national corruption seemed apparent. Attempts to address these problems were largely the work of a new generation of Republican and Democrat politicians. James Sundquist has noted that "the displacement of conservatives by progressive party leaders was to a large extent a generational phenomenon. The typical conservative leader was of the generation that had come to political maturity in a simpler age, before the Industrial Revolution and the exploding urbanization had transformed America. ... The typical progressive was of a newer generation, drawn into politics by concern about problems arising from industrialization and urbanization. He was young and issue-oriented" (Sundquist, 1983:176).

The composite result of the next decade's efforts was that campaign contributions, lobbying, and gratuities to politicians were regulated. Regulatory agencies were established to oversee key sectors of business and industry. For example, following Charles Evans Hughes's investigation of corruption in the life insurance industry in New York, "forty-two state legislatures met; thirty considered life insurance legislation; twenty-nine passed laws" (McCormick, 1981:268). Similar spasms of state and national regulatory activity occurred, targeting one major commercial or industrial sector after another. In addition, progressives in both parties successfully pursued a broad range of partisan and governmental reforms during the years preceding World War I. The Australian ballot, initiated in the 1880s, anticipated many similar reforms, including effective formal registration of individual voters, the primary election, initiative, referendum, recall, and female suffrage. Similarly, the long ballot and nonpartisan municipal elections were designed to return control of local politics to the voters. The intent was to break the hold of corrupt politicians and their party machines over the election of officeholders and the making and implementation of public policy.

In the wake of World War I, ideas of "trust-busting" and regulation gave way to a decade of unprecedented growth—the Roaring Twenties— and to a boisterous celebration of America's military and economic might. "Social reformers recognized that the 1920s were a remarkably unpropitious time for advocating public solutions to the problems of industrial capitalism" (Orloff, 1988:63). Progressivism faded into the background as processes of economic development and concentration driven forward by the war played themselves out. During the 1920s the American economy, in which businessmen and industrialists had a free hand, seemed capable of producing wealth and opportunity in abundance, even if its distribution proved to be increasingly asymmetrical. Those least well off could look, as President Hoover noted, to welfare capitalism, voluntarism, and private charity in difficult times.

Roosevelt and the New Deal

The depression "shattered the ideas that businessmen could guarantee the economic and social well-being of Americans, and that limited private and local charity and corporate welfare programs could serve as a substitute for public social provision in times of economic downturn. ... Popular and expert interest again turned to *public* policy solutions to economic and social problems" (Orloff, 1988:65). Following the stock market crash of October 1929, the onset of the depression, and Hoover's ineffective response to it, Franklin Roosevelt and the Democrats swept into power in 1932. Not surprisingly, the reformers with whom Roosevelt surrounded himself in his first administration were from a generation new to national politics. Orloff (1988:70) notes that "Roosevelt and the people he chose to be architects of the Social Security Act came of age politically in the Progressive Era; as products of the progressive movement, they shared its concerns with 'good government' and fiscal 'responsibility'." Similarly, King and Seligman (1976:286–287) document that a new generation came to Congress in 1932. They observe that "the losers averaged seventy-two years, while the newly elected had an average age of fifty."

The Democrats held the presidency and both houses of Congress from 1932 until the Republicans took both the House and the Senate in the 1946 congressional elections. Although the Democrats narrowly won back both the presidency and the Congress in the 1948 elections, the Republicans surged back to win both the presidency and the Congress in 1952. Eisenhower did hold the presidency for the Republicans in 1956, but the Democrats won both houses of Congress and have rarely relinquished them since.

Richard Jensen describes Roosevelt's impact on the development of American political life in terms that are fully appropriate to a realignment occurring within a constitutional era. Jensen (1971:308) contends that "Franklin Roosevelt perfected McKinley's strategy of inclusive pluralism by giving practically every major economic, ethnic, cultural, and regional interest group in the country the recognition and legislation it wanted." Stephen Skowronek (1982:289) agrees that "the major constructive contribution of the New Deal to the operations of the new American state lay in the sheer expansion of bureaucratic services and supports. ... Like party patronage in the old order, bureaucratic goods and services came to provide the fuel and the cement of the new institutional politics." Roosevelt's "New Deal" developed, elaborated, and extended the institutional logic of McKinley's "System of 1896."

The problems that the American people faced during the 1930s were enormous, and Roosevelt's response was both broad and energetic. For example, unemployment had fluctuated at between 3 and 5 percent between 1900 and 1925. By 1935, in the depths of the depression, it was over 20 percent and as late as 1940 it was still over 14 percent. The gross national product (GNP) fell by nearly half between 1929 and 1933, from $103 billion to only $55 billion. Simultaneously, deflation resulted in wholesale prices falling by fully 40 percent between 1929 and 1938. In fact, wholesale prices did not regain their 1920 levels until after World War II.

Roosevelt attacked this economic catastrophe in all of its manifestations. To combat unemployment, Roosevelt made the national government the employer of last resort. Both the Civilian Conservation Corps and the Works Progress Administration employed at their height hundreds of thousands of young men. To combat poverty, both among displaced workers and the elderly, in 1935 Roosevelt implemented both the Unemployment Compensation and Social Security programs. New programs followed soon thereafter—Public Housing (1936), Urban Renewal (1937), and many others. Roosevelt also created or expanded dramatically a set of economic agencies charged with regulating the economy in ways designed to avoid another depression. The Federal Reserve (1913) was supplemented by the Securities and Exchange Commission (1935), the

Federal Deposit Insurance Corporation (1935), and the Banking Act of 1935.

Fifteen years of economic dislocation and world war left the American people longing for the private pleasures of peace and prosperity. With much of the rest of the industrialized world lying in ruin, the American economy was adapted to the twin post-war needs of international security and domestic consumption. Average annual growth rates in GNP of 3.2 percent between 1948 and 1965 seemed to suggest that both needs could be served simultaneously. Median family income in the United States increased by 37.6 percent during the 1950s. Most of this new wealth, and a great deal more, was expended in personal consumption. John Agnew (1987:78) notes that "urban mortgage debt increased nine-fold from 1945 to 1962. Installment debt for the purchase of automobiles, furniture, household appliances, boats, and recreational vehicles increased at similar rates, particularly in the 1950s." Eisenhower's limited sense of the public purposes that government might serve left Americans free to concentrate on the private concerns of jobs and family.

ERA TRANSFORMATION: HYPERPLURALISM
AND THE PUBLIC INTEREST MOVEMENT

If the "System of 1896" began a steady dissociation of the electorate from parties and from the political system more generally, where has this process stood in the post–World War II period? The answer is very well known and can be summed up in a few brief phrases—the rise of independents, decline in voter turnout, split-ticket voting, an alienated electorate, divided government, and policy deadlock. Processes set in motion in the mid-1890s continued to develop through the Roosevelt realignment of 1932 and seemingly have culminated in the breakdown of political institutions, processes, and expectations over the past two decades.

Skowronek and Burnham join Huntington in arguing that the turbulence and upheaval of the 1960s and 1970s involved a fundamental reconsideration and rejection of the "System of 1896" as it had become institutionalized in American political life over the intervening sixty to seventy years. Skowronek (1982:290) very clearly states that "the economic and international changes of the past decade [1970s] have thrown the administrative expansion of twentieth-century state building into serious question. A new governing impasse has been exposed, and a reform challenge unprecedented since the late nineteenth century has emerged. Once again, the organization of state power itself has been made a major political issue." Burnham (1974:1,055) states the case in equally dramatic terms, saying that "an astonishingly large part of the profound political and constitutional crisis through which we are now living [mid-1970s] can be traced directly back to this [1896] deformation and its subsequent evolution." (see also Jensen, 1971:xv).

Who brought about the reforms and changes of the 1960s and 1970s and who gained power and influence most directly as a result? I argued earlier that Progressives could not have displaced the party elites unless these elites cooperated in the changes for reasons of their own. Similarly, in this case it is necessary to know how the political elites—bureaucratic, congressional, group, and partisan—benefited from the political reforms and changes of the 1960s and 1970s. And more important, why did the "new politics" of the 1960s and 1970s fail to produce a new political dispensation, whether partisan or postpartisan (that is, beyond partisan), capable of dealing with the critical social, economic, and political issues of the last third of the twentieth century.

Johnson, Interest-Group Liberalism, and the Great Society

John F. Kennedy opened the decade of the 1960s with a clarion call to public service for those who could afford to give of their time and talent and with a promise of help to those still in need. The American economy, growing at an average of more than 3 percent a year for the first half of the decade, seemed capable of supporting regional development programs for America's Appalachian and urban poor, as well as Peace Corps and Alliance for Progress programs for the poor in other parts of the world. Moreover, median family income expanded by 33.9 percent during the decade of the 1960s, suggesting to many Americans that helping others might be done without great discomfort to the tax-paying middle and upper classes. By the early 1970s expanding national government obligations began to collide with declining patterns of economic growth and real income expansion in ways that brought the assumptions of the previous decade into question.

By far the best extended description of the structure and dynamics of the modern American political system has been provided by Theodore Lowi. Lowi opens *The End of Liberalism* with the declaration that "this book is dedicated to the proposition that the most fundamental political problem of our time *is* our politics" (Lowi, 1979:xiii). Lowi's argument, in very general outline, is that while the character, structure, and operation of American politics had undergone dramatic change, a consonant and parallel change in the "public philosophy" by which citizens understood and approved the broad thrust of their politics had failed to develop. A massive readjustment of the basic connections of American politics had begun with McKinley, gained scope and speed with Roosevelt's New Deal, and culminated in Lyndon Johnson's Great Society. But increasingly it became clear that Americans could not look upon the results of these changes and pronounce them to be good.

Lowi (1967:12) defines the nexus of public bureaucracy and the organized group structure of society as "interest-group liberalism." Interest group liberalism simply assumes that the policy agenda and the public interest can be defined in terms of the organized interests of society. Depending upon the input of organized groups seemed to insure the representation of those who had a clear stake in the issue. Moreover, interest-group liberalism created few losers among organized interests. Organized interests were welcome to participate directly in their own governance and regulation; politicians sought to deliver an ever-wider range of services to an appreciative electorate; and bureaucrats administered more programs through larger and better funded bureaucracies (Huntington, 1973:32; see also Fiorina, 1977:82; Moe, 1984:768). Despite the obvious benefits to closed sets of participants, the politics of interest-group liberalism exacted a heavy toll on broader publics and on the structure and performance of the political system as a whole.

In a political system that had increasingly come to revolve around the delivery of services to organized interests, one would expect to find established groups adjusting to maximize their effectiveness and find the unorganized seeking new ways to organize. In fact, one of the key thrusts of Johnson's Great Society program was to organize the unorganized—most particularly the racial minorities, and more generally, the poor—to better press their claims on government. As a result, the massive expansion of the federal role in addressing poverty, education, housing, health care, civil rights, and many other issues, not only increased programmatic coverage and spending, but also required that recipient groups be included in program design and service delivery (Edsall and Edsall, 1992:36–39). Many programs included "outreach" provisions requiring agencies to actively go out into the community to identify, register, and involve potential recipients (Broder, 1980:232).

Other new actors also entered American politics in large numbers during the 1960s. Robert Salisbury (1984:66) directs attention to the fact that there are "several modes of 'interested activity'." Beyond the membership groups that chiefly concern Lowi, "the American political universe, in fact, contains ... individual corporations, state and local governments, universities, think tanks, and most other *institutions* of the private sector. Likewise unnoticed are the multitudes of Washington representatives, freestanding and for hire, including lawyers, public relations firms, and diverse other counsellors" (Salisbury, 1984:64). While a few of each of these categories of "interested" actors had been around for a long time, their numbers, activity, and influence increased dramatically during the 1960s and 1970s.

Clearly, the growth of bureaucratic regulatory responsibility, the self-management assumptions of interest-group liberalism, and the dramatic increase in the numbers of "Washington representatives" available to intervene with government on a fee-for-services basis are the key self-enhancing dynamics of modern American politics. The principal impact of the operation of these tight policy networks, each concentrating on a narrow set of policy concerns, was to intensify the fragmenting, disaggregating tendencies in the American public policymaking process. The fundamental dynamics of interest-group liberalism serve to insure that policy domains are separate and independent, involving distinct and largely non-overlapping sets of actors and interests.

Finally, American politics was further changed during the 1960s and 1970s by the public-interest movement. Jack Walker (1983:394) shows that "citizen groups multiplied at twice the rate of all types of occupationally based groups" during these years. The public-interest movement, epitomized from its inception in the 1960s by Ralph Nader and in the 1970s by John Gardner's Common Cause, had dramatic effects on American politics—effects that were both substantive and procedural. The animating idea was to supplement the link between narrow, private-interest groups and their bureaucratic and political allies by establishing new organizations that would represent the broad public interest. Substantively, "the public interest movement forced through sweeping changes in areas of law from the environment to public health to the penal code": procedurally, the public-interest movement "helped change federal laws on campaign financing, income disclosure for elected and appointed officials, secret meetings, recorded votes, lobbying … not only in Washington but, literally, in one or more respects, in every state and many of the cities" (Broder, 1980:226, 234).

Toward the end of the 1970s, American governments at all levels were committed to a wider range of services and higher levels of spending than at any earlier point in peacetime history. They were also open to a wider range of organized interests, both public and private, and were required to conduct business more publicly than ever before. Simultaneously, changes in the domestic and international economies (stagflation and oil price shocks among them) forced growth in family income down to a mere 6.7 percent for the entire decade. Per capita productivity actually declined from 1978 to 1980 (Agnew, 1987:131, 138). Citizens more often begrudged the government its required resources. Government was perceived as inefficient and expensive, and confidence in it waned.

Reagan-Bush and the Vulnerability of the
Public Interest Movement

Budgetary constraints and resultant program reductions in the 1980s struck hard at public-interest groups and the programs they supported. Mancur Olson (1965) and others have explained that voluntary associations will form and operate only with great difficulty because rational calculations among potential beneficiaries concerning the cost of organizing and maintaining such a group will result in a crippling number of "free riders." Outside sources of support are almost always required. During the relatively prosperous years between 1965 and the late 1970s, such support came both from private philanthropic sources and from government. As budgets tightened, support declined inexorably. First, during the late 1970s, foundations—most prominently the Ford Foundation, but others as well—sought to wean their public-interest clients from funding by reducing and then canceling their grant support. In addition, the courts and Congress made clear by limiting fees and denying direct support for public-interest representation that government would not underwrite their activities.

A second flurry of even heavier blows came in the wake of Ronald Reagan's victory in 1980. Moving to fulfill his pledge to "get the government off the backs of the people," Reagan sought both to shift income from the less productive to the more productive and to limit opportunities for government to interfere with competition and innovation among the more productive. Economic growth was to be restored through a program of tax cuts, entrepreneurship, privatization, and enterprise zones in a rejuvenated society unimpeded by government. The conservative-dominated "decade of the 1980s produced one of the most dramatic redistributions of income in the nation's history. ... The income of families in the bottom decile fell by 10.4 percent, ... while the income of those in the top one percent rose by 87.1 percent" (Edsall and Edsall, 1992:23).

Moreover, policies designed to increase competitiveness through tax cuts, program reductions, and deregulation undermined or eliminated regulations and programs that public-interest groups concerned with consumer and worker safety, air and water pollution, and government services thought critical to their continued influence, perhaps even to their continued survival. More broadly, Reagan moved to "defund the Left" by reducing supports for a wide range of social and cultural programs—from legal aid to the poor to federal support for the National Endowment for the Arts. In general, "discretionary domestic spending as a share of gross national product was cut by 33.9 percent" during the eight years of the Reagan presidency (Edsall and Edsall, 1992:23).

Bill Clinton: What Good Is Unified Government in the Absence of Strong Parties?

Bill Clinton's victory was a rejection of George Bush and the private-interest politics of the 1980s. Prominent pre-election polls showed a precipitous decline in the public's confidence in Republican domestic policy, particularly economic policy, but no great increase in confidence in the ability of the Democrats to manage the economy. At most, the Democrats in Congress and Bill Clinton have been given an opportunity by a very frustrated public to do better than, or at least to take a different approach than the Republicans did during the previous twelve years. Nonetheless, Clinton has a rare opportunity to act decisively; if successful, he might reestablish the Democrats as the governing majority going into the next century. The key to his future success will be continued improvement in the domestic and world economies. Promises may suffice for a time, but in the end only prosperity will provide the political slack necessary to enact a coherent set of policies. Prospects for success are mixed.

First, at the level of the individual voter, it is clear that many Americans concluded in 1991 and 1992 that the greed and selfishness of the 1980s had done substantial damage to the country and to large numbers of its citizens. Clinton convinced voters that sustained public attention needed to be given to various forms of public investment in the nation's physical infrastructure and in the education and health of the work force. Moreover, Clinton sought to address the emotional scars that the 1980s left on many Americans, and not only on the most vulnerable, by explicitly acknowledging the fears of those struggling to make ends meet in a rapidly changing society and economy. Clinton's focus on public service and personal accessibility spoke directly to these concerns in the electorate. His bus trips, excursions into McDonald's, his walking tour of minority small businesses along Massachusetts Avenue during his first post-election trip to Washington, D.C., and his public inaugural were all designed to reconnect the government and the president to the public and its concerns.

At the governmental level, Clinton and the Democrats have been given an opportunity to govern. For the first time since 1980, Democrats control the presidency and both houses of Congress. Moreover, many analysts, including David Broder of the *Washington Post*, have noted that Clinton's election is not merely a change of presidents or parties—it is a change of generations that spans the whole national government, not the White House alone. Fully half of the 121 new members of Congress are younger than the forty-five-year-old president. Like Clinton, these young legislators were shaped by Vietnam and the 1960s, rather than by the experiences of World War II and the Cold War that shaped every previous president from Kennedy through Bush.

These new members of the House and Senate, the largest freshman class since 1948, will have an impact on Congress well beyond their numbers. They represent disruption of old relationships, in committees, on the floor, and between members and established interests. New members, not yet embedded in Congress's tight networks of power, politics, and interest, are likely to be more amenable to new initiatives than older, more entrenched members. On the other hand, the new members are diverse and impatient. Many represent groups and interests previously underrepresented and no longer willing to wait patiently for politics-as-usual to deliver on promises made long ago. Membership in the new House will include thirty-nine blacks, nineteen Hispanics, and forty-eight women—all large increases from the previous Congress. The Senate will contain six women (up from two) one of whom is black. Colorado's Ben Nighthorse Campbell, a Native American, will move from the House to the Senate in 1993. These members, as well as more senior members frustrated by twelve years of Republican vetoes, may prove difficult for the new president to organize and lead.

Finally, there are powerful long-term reasons to be skeptical that Clinton's victory will translate into a stable period of Democratic governance for the 1990s and beyond. At least to date, nothing but the vaguest outlines of a new "public philosophy," a new, effective, and widely shared sense of the role of government in American public life, has been offered. Nonetheless, some positive steps have been taken, including the campaign focus on public service and the campaign and transition focus on keeping organized interests at arm's length. During the campaign, Clinton's distant relationship with Jesse Jackson drew much comment, as has his vocal complaining about the narrow demands for more cabinet positions by women's and minority groups. Clinton clearly wishes to demonstrate that he is pushing traditional organized interests away from the critical decisions of government to clear a space where the public interest might be addressed. However, all of nature, including politics, abhors a vacuum. What will fill the space left by organized interests in the unlikely event that Clinton is able to hold them at arm's length for a time?

Clinton seems not to believe that he needs to place an institutional screen—the Democratic party—between the interests and government, lest the interests rush right back into the space he has sought to clear. Without a rejuvenated Democratic party Clinton will find the American political system too diffuse to govern. Yet there is little to suggest that Clinton and his team will be able to gather the disparate reins of power together. Although many of the broad contextual dynamics are positive for the new administration (a rising economy may help for a time), most of his efforts seem ad hoc, tentative, and probably insufficient to defeat the forces and dynamics that will soon array against him.

CONCLUSION

I have argued that American political development has been characterized by patterns of adjustment and change that have assumed several characteristic forms. At the most general level, which Burnham calls the "political universe," the ways in which the key components of the American political system (Congress, the president and his bureaucracy, the courts, parties, and interest groups, and the lower levels of the federal system) have fit together and interacted show rapid change during certain periods, that is, during the Revolution, the era of Jacksonian democracy, the Progressive Era, and the 1960s and 1970s. These periods of dramatic political reform, in Allan Lichtman's words (1976:348), "modify the causal forces" which shape American politics. The direction in which the causal forces underlying American politics have most commonly been reformed has been toward the inclusion of new groups and new interests in the political universe.

Yet, describing American politics as progressively inclusionary is too simple. While the politics of inclusion and absorption describe the nineteenth century quite well, with the expansion of suffrage to most adult white males during the era of democratization, the rise of political parties to organize and mobilize this broad electorate, and the astounding participation rates of the 1870s and 1880s, this type of politics describes the twentieth century much less well. Even acknowledging the inclusion of women in the 1920s, of blacks and other minorities in the 1960s, and the entry of eighteen- to twenty-one-year-olds in the 1970s, one must focus most intently on the precipitous drop in participation rates among eligible voters, which began in the final years of the nineteenth century and has continued through the twentieth century. What should we make of a political system that has come to represent the interests of citizens through a nexus between interest group and bureaucracy rather than between political party and elected official?

I think we must conclude that interest-group liberalism and its extension to hyperliberalism and the public-interest movement is fraught with danger. This is not because all interest groups, and particularly all public-interest groups, are dangerous, but rather because they are inadequate replacements for political parties. This is chiefly because interest groups, especially the "voluntary" and "public-interest" groups, are peculiarly vulnerable to changes in the political climate. It seems very likely that the access to start-up and operating funds that voluntary and public-interest groups enjoyed in the late 1960s and the 1970s was a function of the dramatic growth of both the public and the private sectors in the post–World War II period. However, due to changes in the position of the United States in the world economy, wages, profits, and revenues to government have grown more slowly and, on a real basis, have actually declined in some cases. As public and private budgets tighten, it becomes less likely, I believe, that business and government will continue to fund their natural opponents—public-interest groups. For reasons that Mancur Olson, Jack Walker, and David Broder explain, public-interest groups are unlikely to form unless outside funds are available.

The vulnerability of that part of the group structure not organized around economic activity should refocus our attention on the importance of political parties in articulating and defending lower class and community interests. Schattschneider (1960:35) stated over thirty years ago that interest-group liberalism is fatally flawed by the fact that society's needs cannot be served by organizing policy formulation and implementation around private demands—that "the flaw in the pluralist heaven is that the heavenly chorus sings with a strong upper-class accent." To change the accent with which society's heavenly chorus sings was the overriding purpose of Kennedy's New Frontier and Johnson's Great Society, and of the hyperpluralist politics that sought to organize and include the traditionally unorganized and excluded. To the extent that the politics of interest-group liberalism and hyperpluralism accomplished these most basic purposes, they gained a voice for the previously mute, but only at the cost of gravely aggravating the problems of policy coordination and integration. These problems have created what Lowi, Dodd, Huntington, and many others see as a crisis in American governance and governability.

Madison would have recognized at first glance the causes of our dilemma. Groups should be organized, they should be heard, and they should be encouraged to confront and check one another; but they should not, and cannot, govern directly. For Madison, the great benefit of interests checking interests outside of government was that the resulting clash and clamor would leave the people's elected representatives fully informed and free to exercise their judgment in the public interest.

3

Pattern Recognition and "Doing" Political History: Art, Science, or Bootless Enterprise?

WALTER DEAN BURNHAM

Not too long ago, I was a participant in an American Political Science Association panel. Its papers saw the light of day in a 1991 volume that bore the catchy title *The End of Realignment?* (Shafer, 1991a). Opinion among the initial paper givers was divided on the subject. One person thought that, whatever its uses may have been for studying the past, the once-promising "critical-realignment framework" was irrelevant to the present. Another scholar observed that it didn't explain the past well either. Still others on the panel professed one or another form of agnosticism. So strongly negative was the overall sentiment that it was only at my insistence that the question mark was added to the title of the book. I found the whole experience sufficiently thought-provoking to make an effort to deal with the general issues raised by my colleagues (Burnham, 1991:101–138). This in turn led to some reflections on "doing" political history, and hence to this chapter, which is, in a sense, a continuation of that earlier discussion.

OF CONSILIENCE AND PERIODIZATION

In thinking about pattern recognition in history, we necessarily touch upon some very deep issues. Oswald Spengler, Arnold Toynbee, and Pitirim Sorokin all advanced models claiming striking regularity at the highest imaginable levels of integration—whole civilizations across the entire span of recorded history. The mainstream of the historical profession responded over time by thoroughly shooting them down for their pains: In the majority view, such attempted syntheses went vastly beyond what data and reasonable inference therefrom could support. Indeed, H.A.L. Fisher, and other critics, argued that there was no definable pattern at all: History was to all intents and purposes one damned thing after another. The Metatheoreticians assert the existence in one form or another of inexplorable *laws* that overdetermine all the myriad details of time-linked experience. Those who reject all pattern, on the other hand, say in effect that *contingency* is all there is in history. Both are probably wrong, though for different reasons and in different ways.

In *Wonderful Life* (1989b), his recent study of very early multicellular life forms, the paleontologist Stephen Jay Gould has offered some fertile insights into historical process. These insights center on a conviction he shares with the historian Martin Sklar (whose ideas we discuss below) and myself: History is a legitimately scientific enterprise in its own right, as much so as the "ahistorical," model-building natural (and social) sciences. Of all natural sciences, the evolutionary biology in which Gould works is, along with geology, the most "historical." For obvious reasons, he is thus at great pains to refuse the slighting comments made by pure physicists like Luis Alvarez that work in such areas of science is no more intellectually elevated than stamp collecting.

Perhaps the most important point Gould raises is derived directly from his hero, Charles Darwin, and it is this: There is a cardinal distinction between *laws in the background* and *contingency in the* (often vitally important) *details*. The universe runs by law, in this formulation, "with details, whether good or bad, left to the working out of what we may call chance (Gould, 1989b:290). In human affairs, the role of contingency in determining what happens is notoriously huge. For example, suppose that Guiseppe Zangara had in fact achieved his goal of assassinating president-elect Franklin Roosevelt on February 15, 1933—what would have happened to the New Deal, not to mention to the global struggle of World War II? Obviously quite a lot; yet even so, one could well doubt whether it would have been possible to return to the laissez-faire state of the "System of 1896" on the one hand, or whether Hitler would have won the war, on the other. Both regularity *and* contingency exist in history. The historian's task, ideally, is to provide an account of causalities and sequences of events that strikes the most accurate possible balance between the two.

To be credible, explanations for states of affairs must be more than private visions, no matter how vital the role of individual imagination is in shaping the intellectual enterprise. They should also be more than merely plausible, taking their place with equally plausible alternative explanations. There are guides in such a quest, several of which we will examine in this chapter. The first, discussed at length by Gould, is *consilience*. As he notes:

> We search for repeated pattern, shown by evidence so abundant and so diverse that no other coordinating interpretation could stand, even though any of them, taken separately, would not provide conclusive proof.

The great nineteenth-century philosopher of science William Whewell devised the word consilience, meaning "jumping together," to designate the
confidence gained when many independent sources "conspire" to indicate a
particular historical pattern. He called the strategy of coordinating disparate
results from multifarious sources consilience of induction. (Gould,
1989b:282)

Real-world systemic identity (or major systemic change processes) in
society may be thought of as a syndrome of interrelated and specifiable
characteristics, which can be analytically subdivided into interrelated but
discrete segments (or, pursuing the biomedical metaphor further, into
"symptoms"). It follows that, assuming that a system operates as a system, opportunities for an effective pursuit of a "strategy of coordinating
disparate results from multifarious sources" should be rather plentiful—
so much so that consilience of induction becomes, or should become, an
essential part of scientific enterprise in this domain of inquiry. A prime
function of consilience is that, at least ideally, it should systematically reduce the scope for heteronomy in explaining what is going on. One can
expand the idea a bit by noting that consilience has both positive and negative aspects. The positive side is set forth concisely in Gould's discussion.
On the other side lies a negative check on proposed alternative explanations. If a consilience-yielding demonstration for a particular historical
pattern is empirically substantiated, to that extent the burden of proof
shifts decisively to those who propose alternative arguments.

Limitations of space do not allow more than a very brief development
of examples of consilience as it applies to the critical-realignment or
punctuational-change model of American political history. We begin with
some well-known "history of history" on the subject. As long ago as 1949,
the eminent American historian Arthur M. Schlesinger, Sr., first clearly
presented the argument that certain presidential elections—those of 1800,
1828, 1860, 1896, and 1932—stood out far above all others as marking cardinal turning points in the flow of our political history. Since then, and notably since V. O. Key, Jr.'s, seminal 1955 extension of the idea in his paper,
"A Theory of Critical Elections," a great many historians have found the
periodizations implicit in this model to be useful and credible organizers
of the data with which they have to deal—so much so, indeed, that the
term "realignment synthesis" has been rather commonly employed to describe the field situation.

And yet, as we have noted, this suggested synthesis has come under attack to such an extent that many scholars insist that it is now overripe for
burial. Consilience, as discussed below, may give us some purchase for
evaluating these claims. We may begin with three summary points that
are discussed more extensively in my 1991 essay. First, the field today is
marked by rival explanations and associated methodological approaches.

These lead to starkly divergent findings, to the extent that it is clear that all of these approaches cannot be adequate to the tasks their authors have set for them. Second, there can be no doubt that one chief reason for this condition lies in the very substantial conceptual weaknesses linked to the research mainstream of first-generation work on the subject. Third, as the historian Paul Kleppner (1987) has recently insisted, despite all its defects the "realignment synthesis" has survived as long as it has because in a number of vital respects, and despite all, it remains the only game in town.

If one rejects such an elaborated structure of pattern recognition outright, two choices remain. One can propose another model, for example the "political eras" construct advanced by the distinguished student of nineteenth-century American politics, the historian Joel Silbey (1991b). The other choice is to reject the notion of pattern recognition altogether, as some of the authors in *The End of Realignment?* seem to have done; or, alternatively, to reject it for one level of systemic action (voting behavior) but retain it for another (elite activities). In turn, such a latter choice is exposed to evaluation by the strength and adequacy of consilience as asserted (or more usually, implied) by "realignment-synthesis" scholars.

One may note, for example, that many critics of this "synthesis" have based their claims for its irrelevance to contemporary history on the ground that it "predicted" a critical realignment for the years 1968–1972 and was falsified when no such realignment materialized.[1] Yet a recent paper by John Aldrich and Richard Niemi (1990) finds, to the contrary, that survey evidence for just such a basic realigning change occurring at exactly this point in the flow of events is very strong. If it was not found at the time or for long after, this was to no small degree because people working with the assumptions of the first-generation model looked for realignment in the wrong places, and thus of course did not find it. One may likewise note that it is from 1968 on, and not before, that divided government (a Republican presidency and continuing Democratic control of at least one house of Congress for twenty of the twenty-four years between 1968 and 1992) becomes a *normal* political condition for the first time in American political history. Yet old-style critical realignment requires old-style political parties as channelers and mobilizers of mass political action. The realignment of the late 1960s, on the other hand, pivoted on a decisive shift away from such parties and toward the candidate-dominated politics—capital-intensive rather than as once labor-intensive—of the "permanent campaign." If old-style Type I realignments required the existence of institutions that now no longer dominate the political landscape in the old way, such punctuational-change mechanisms may in fact have become extinct. If so, however, this does not necessarily mean that all possible types of critical realignment have ceased to exist—a point I discuss at some length in the 1991 essay.

Silbey's (1991b) "political eras" construct has, on the other hand, a good deal to recommend it. It explains an important part of reality—the vast comparative differences between the partisan-optimum political world of the nineteenth century and the very different ordering of politics which evolved over the twentieth. Nor, it should be needless to add, has any serious claim ever been made that periodically recurring bursts of punctuational change have been the *only* processes through which major change has developed in our political history. Yet Silbey's formulation seems essentially to minimize the empirical significance of the realignment of the 1850s, out of which came the Civil War and the characteristic party system of that era. Moreover, to the extent that everything after about 1893 is more or less lumped together in a "postpartisan era," such a periodizing procedure leaves us with no real clue for evaluating the very large-scale and decidedly partisan-focused changes which produced the New Deal realignment and the creation of the modern American state.

As for the argument that there is no pattern at all, there is a certain point beyond which one cannot go in efforts at refutation. If people *will* dismiss large but inconvenient ranges of data that, taken together, point to the existence of such a pattern, there is certainly no way to stop them. Appeal, if any, can only be made to the larger court of professional judgment. All that can be said is that refusal to come to terms with large masses of evidence bearing on the subject does not seem compatible with the logic of scientific enterprise.

We broaden our consilience search further now, only to narrow it again to focus on certain aspects of electoral behavior later on. One extremely interesting effort is the work of the sociologist J. Zvi Namenwirth on a large-scale historical change in American political value preoccupations (Namenwirth and Weber, 1987). Utilizing the Yale-Lasswell propositional dictionary to code American party platforms from the first in 1844 to recent times via content analysis, Namenwirth constructs a search routine for evaluating movement and maxima in each of four major types of long-term preoccupations: from Expressive to Adaptive, Instrumental, Integrative, and back to Expressive again in a long-term cycle that, he asserts, takes 152 years to complete. Maximum value-preoccupation points fall at 1856 (E), 1894 (A), 1932 (Inst.) and 1970 (Int.). The methods used produce sine waves, not sharp semi-discontinuous cutting points of the sort found in the analysis of electoral data, for example. Yet despite this and other differences in method and analytic focus, the result produced is chronologically identical with the realignment peaks produced using other data and methods (especially if we argue that "1970" should be read in realignment terms too). Namenwirth's discussion of the substantive content of his categories also casts useful light on the substance, particularly the symbolic-value substance, of these upheavals.

We now turn our attention to two scholars, one a political scientist and the other a legal scholar. The first of these, Stephen Skowronek, has recently attempted a preliminary outline of a major program for reconstructing the history of the American presidency in "political time" (Skowronek, 1986:286–302). There is at all times an interaction between the personal attributes of particular presidents and the "opportunity spaces" available to them in structural-political terms. At any given time, a given regime order exists, and it is relatively resilient (R) or relatively vulnerable (V) to stress. A president coming to power at any given moment, either by election or succession, is affiliated (A) to this regime order and its commitments, or he is opposed (O) to them. This creates a fourfold array of cases, listed in regime-president order: (1) R-A; (2) R-O; (3) V-A; (4) V-O. The first cell, as could be expected in normal-state conditions, includes the large majority of presidents and most "political time" across American history. The second cell is a rather bizarre mixture of mostly "guerrilla-raid" cases, all ending badly and depending particularly for their accession on a mixture of chance and political miscalculation by their party.

The last two cases very often form chronologically continuous pairs: structurally repudiated presidents followed by "great" or near-great presidents. The first hapless set is given no acceptable action options at all (repudiate one's commitments or go down with the ship), while the second set is dominated by men who are architects of the overthrow of the previous (failed) regime order and, equally, of the new order which takes its place. Certain obvious pairs present themselves: John Adams-Jefferson; John Q. Adams-Jackson; Buchanan-Lincoln; Cleveland-McKinley; Hoover-Roosevelt (and some might have thought Carter-Reagan). Literature on the vulnerable-affiliated group presents this major theme: the active—though for their own interests negative—part adherents to the group have played in accelerating the crisis processes works to sweep away the regime order to which they are affiliated. While Skowronek nowhere mentions the point in his argument, my own belief is that critical realignment in the electorate is the dominant process affecting each man in each pair of these presidents operating in quite exceptional "political time," closing doors on the first of these presidents and opening up more or less unlimited action possibilities for the second.

We now turn to the very recent work of the distinguished constitutional analyst, Bruce Ackerman. As I have explained elsewhere, my first awareness that there might well be a recurrent systemwide cycle based on punctuational change in American history came, not from electoral analysis, but from work done in my youth on the history of the United States Supreme Court and its relationship to the rest of the political order. I have long hoped that the realignment connection would one day be made by a constitutional scholar whose integrative powers were up to the task. Ackerman's project was first set forth in two extensive articles (1984, 1989), and has now borne fruit in the first volume of a proposed trilogy, *We the People: Foundations* (1991). He seems to have already gone far toward closing this ring.

Ackerman's argument is much too richly textured to be captured in these few comments, which concern only what he calls "constitutional moments." As Ackerman sees the matter, the Constitution we have today is the product not of just one of these "moments," the creation period of 1787–1791, but of three. The other two, periods short in duration but of fundamental redefining significance, occurred in the 1860s and the 1930s. The first of these two, the Reconstruction "moment," profoundly modified the structure of the Union: It not only formally abolished slavery, but also at least set forth the constitutional precedent for establishing full citizenship rights for black Americans. The "radical impulse" worked very substantially, but not exclusively, through the formal amendment procedures established in Article 5. (Thaddeus Stevens commented on the carving out of West Virginia from Virginia and its admission to the Union in 1863: "I will not stultify myself by supposing that we have any warrant in the Constitution for this proceeding." Randall and Donald, 1961:241) The second of the two, the New Deal transformation, Ackerman believes to be of as fundamental consequence as the others, and he develops a massive case for his view. Here it is noteworthy that formal amendment under Article 5 was not involved at all.

A central part of Ackerman's argument about "constitutional moments" is that the American public itself becomes a central player in the enterprise, mobilizing to debate and act on fundamental matters of principle. In his view, these are "great exercises in popular sovereignty"— genuinely constituent acts associated with the Federalists of the 1780s, the Republicans of the 1860s, and the Democrats of the 1930s. Nor is this meant metaphorically, despite the vastly smaller relative size of the politically relevant public in the 1780s than in subsequent "constitutional moments." This would imply a situation in which, rarely but decisively, this popular sovereignty is exercised by a public which plays a proactive, autonomous, and central role quite at variance with the models of passivity and indifference projected by modern survey research. This, it should be noted, is precisely the argument made by Paul Kleppner, who perceives this to be one important singularity of mass political behavior in critical-realignment crises (Kleppner, 1987: especially 11–15). It is very much what "critical-realignment theory" would lead us to expect: Business as usual is not necessarily business as always.

But we should also candidly note that consilience in this case goes just so far and no further. To be sure, Ackerman does recognize transformational impulses at other points in time, notably those of the Jacksonians. Still, neither the quite consequential reorganizations of American politics in the 1830s nor those, at least equally large, of the 1890s qualify for his "constitutional moment" shortlist. The first of these episodes involved at least one very important and sharply defined constitutional change—the democratization of the presidency (which involved, with very much else, a substantive transformation in the use and incidence of the veto power.) The second episode, and the regime order which emerged from it, pivoted around a metapolitical ascendancy of the Supreme Court in the American political order lasting from 1895 to 1937, and had neither precedent nor sequel.

Ackerman's focus on the "big three" is certainly warranted. And yet these other two "moments" impress me as having considerable significance in their own right. Perhaps we may in time develop some "hard" measures of the criticality of critical realignments. Perhaps we can even begin to ask whether there might not be a major-minor-major-minor-major time dimension to the process of "exceptional" constitution-remaking. To my mind, there is certainly now enough "jumping together" in this sector of the front to anticipate that analysts of the American past, including but not confined to those who work on realignment issues, will find substantial enrichment from the work of legal scholars like Bruce Ackerman. It seems reasonable to surmise that, conversely, the constitutionalists' intellectual perspectives may be enriched in their turn as they tap into the literature on American political development, including the realignment literature. This is just the sort of thing that consilience stimulates.

Let us now turn to that most central of historical enterprises, *periodization*. As everyone knows, centuries ago historians began making the effort to give shape to the data flow of their field by positing the existence of three vast periods of Western history: Ancient, Medieval, and Modern. Marxists, of course, have advanced their own metaperiodization scheme, with its transitions from ancient slave-holding, to feudal-manorial, to capitalist, and thence (as they thought) finally to socialist modes of production, and the social, political, and cultural systems generated by each. American historians have regularly employed such macro terms as the "Age of Jackson," the "Progressive Era," and the "New Deal Era." By doing so they work with the essential ordering assumption that the object of inquiry is an interrelated set of symptomatic phenomena that in their totality define a relatively bounded system of human action in politics, economics, culture, and other relevant dimensions. It is for them to show that the posited system decisively differs, at least in the areas with which they are primarily concerned, from anything that comes before or after. But periodization seems much more often to be practiced than analyzed very thoroughly by the practitioners. What is it? Surely, at the very least, it is an organized prioritization of a vast and otherwise unmanageable flow of raw data. The impulse to periodize is stimulated and controlled by the enormous volume of information; it is as essential to historical enterprise as the construction of models is to the natural, and to some social, sciences. As a prioritization mechanism, a periodization scheme asserts that certain facts are at the core of what is going on, while others are more or less subsidiary to them. Such an assertion, of course, must be defended.

One can go further, and the historian Martin Sklar has recently done so. He makes what are probably the most advanced claims ever made for the centrality of periodization to historical analysis as a scientific enterprise. His discussion is worth quoting, even at very great length.

What general and special theories are to the meaning and indeed the very designation of facts in the physical sciences, so periodization is to their meaning and designation in history. ...

The requirements and capabilities of a society include not only their geophysical, technoeconomic, and other "material" conditions, but also their manifestations in social consciousness, both secular and religious, including theories, ideologies, outlooks, or world views of those who exercise authority, whether governmental or nongovernmental, as well as in subordinate position in society. As this implies, there is some causal connection between a society's requirements and capacities as a social system and its pattern of authority and structure of power.

As theory that postulates society type and its state of evolution in this way, periodization establishes not only the ground of permissible deductive reasoning about a society's prevalent modes of behavior and thought, and how they interrelate, but also the essential foundation for fashioning the inductive framework of inquiry into them and their interrelations, into their genesis, their development, and their transformations. Periodization also thereby informs the range and limits of reflective generalization respecting the society's actualities and potentialities in the political, economic, social, intellectual and cultural spheres. As a method of study, or theory of history, periodization imposes a discipline upon inquiry that acts as a control against the presuppositions, the fashionable interpretations as well as the compellingly irrelevant ones, the personal intuitions, the current political persuasions, or the professional infighting of the inquirers and their critical audience.

Understood in this way, periodization fosters vigilance against the arbitrary adoption of a tight interpretive grid, on the one hand, or the loose invocation of dissociated concepts, principles, sentiments, or axioms, on the other, not well founded in evidence, logic, or reason. Made explicit, it invites constant testing of interpretation, by both deductive and inductive reasoning, against rules of coherence and empirical inquiry. Periodization also subjects to such critical assessment the range and limits of its own corresponding mode of reflective generalization. Periodization, or theory, in this sense, yields historical knowledge whose meaning is subject to objective verification, or more precisely to falsification, and establishes at the same time the ground of its own validation, alteration or discard. As and when its set of premises or its range falls short of comprehending pertinent materials in a manner consistent with its discipline, it signals the limits beyond which it is unable to proceed, and therefore its impending modification or demise and displacement by a theory, or periodization, that is more sufficient. In this sense, periodization, or theory, in history is no different in general principle from theory in the physical sciences. (Sklar, 1991:173–213)[2]

Sklar's substantive preoccupation is with the "corporate restructuring of America," the central national activity of the period extending from the 1890s to 1916. There are, he attempts to show, quite clear boundaries separating this particular period from what came before and after it. Its emergence presupposes what could be described as a functionally congruent set of adaptations of cultural expectations, mentalities, norms, and attitudes—no less than systemic transformations in the material order. The emergence also involved myriad conflicts, themselves capable of clear specification within this framework. Many of the more decisive of these conflicts pivoted on the social consequences of this massive transition from a proprietary-competitive stage of capitalist development to an increasingly dominant corporate organization both of the political economy and the society at large.

Associated with periodization is the use of counterfactual hypotheses. In the specific case here, this essential tool of historical analysis is based on *comparative* knowledge about the different paths which corporate reorganization of society took in other advanced capitalist societies at about the same time. (As many dissenters from mainstream orthodoxy then and later insisted, developmental paths other than the one actually taken were theoretical and even practical possibilities at various points along the way). The specifically American variant among these cases was "corporate *liberalism*," rather than the statist, *dirigiste*, or corporate variants common enough elsewhere. By confronting clearly what might have been (and often enough what actually was in other comparable societies), the analyst gains boundedness and clarity when dealing with what actually did unfold. As Sklar (1991:205) aptly remarks, in the United States "corporate capitalism came into the world, grew, and developed with continual, heavy, lasting and habit forming doses of both populism and socialism." In this milieu, a consensus emerged that the state's primary role in dealing with the new configuration of power was to be regulatory rather than indicative. This constituent decision, as a penetrating essay by Ira Katznelson and Bruce Pietrykowski (1991) has recently demonstrated, was reaffirmed under real "statist" challenge in the 1940s. At this precise juncture there was sufficient fluidity in the policy to make serious debate and its resolution possible, as had not been the case since the Progressive era and as was not to be the case at any later point in our history.[3]

Sklar likewise stresses the significance to the task of constructing adequate periodization of conceptualizations centering on the phenomenon of modernization. Marx, Mill, and Weber—the last of whom died as long ago as 1920!—provided many or most of the basic foundations. One could well part company with Sklar's dismissive view of the potential of more recent work on modernization and political development, but it is evident that the intellectual effort to construct better periodization in Sklar's sense can only be enriched by incorporating the insights and some of the models developed in this literature.

If it has tried to do anything at all, the critical-realignment synthesis has been from the first preoccupied not just with the identification of moments of punctuational change in American political history, but also—and inevitably—with the specific periodization which is involved in these processes. Works by historians on the second (Jacksonian) and third (Civil War) party systems abound, not to mention studies of the "System of 1896" and the rise and fall of the New Deal order. The realignments presuppose the systems or regime orders lying between them, and a major reason for the considerable success the realignment framework has had lies in the fact that it has permitted scholars, and especially historians, to achieve a parsimonious, credible, and useful periodization of the subjects with which they have to deal. But for the most part this first-generation work lacked clear inputs from sources such as the political development and modernization literature. With the robust and much more recent development of the professional genre of historically and comparatively grounded, state-centered analysis of American politics, conceptualization is likely to be substantially enriched in this field— naturally involving, as it will, modification and perhaps abandonment of propositions and hypotheses advanced by first-generation scholars. To take one obvious case in point, we may mention the so-called "first party system" era of the early Federal period. Even now, at the level of electoral analysis, this pre-1824 period remains very largely a "lost Atlantis" of research, despite a remarkably voluminous record of available data. We may expect that this situation is likely to change in the years ahead. As it does, the striking peculiarities of this system, in comparison with any that followed it, will come into sharp and precise view. As this occurs, understanding is likely to be considerably enriched by the incorporation of models developed by contemporary political modernization literature concerning colonial dependency relations and "colonial situations," which frequently last for decades after formal political independence is achieved.

SOME ISSUES OF METHOD AND SUBSTANCE

Let us attempt to bring some of the foregoing discussion to bear on a narrower range of subjects: voting behavior and its links to elites and their activities. In places the argument is very close to that developed by Kleppner in "Realignment Theory After Key," which is an admirable and quite recent summary of the interaction between substantive assumptions about the "real nature" of the subject and the methodologies chosen to analyze it (Kleppner, 1987:239–249).

One perspective on the subject (which I favor) argues that a critical realignment produces a change in universe state. The net transfer of previously durable partisan loyalties among minorities of voters at such a time produces a new state of affairs, which is not only different from the old but is durably so. This perspective is followed through a longitudinal (or time-series) search across the electoral data file to identify not merely the timing, but the territorially (and thus sociologically) defined differential impact of such events. Characteristic patterns sharply distinctive from the norm duly appear when iterative longitudinal analysis of electoral data is performed. The foci of such exercises are universe-level rather than individual-level in their primary orientation, though it is obvious that in any realignment an exceptional number of individuals must have undergone durable change in their habitual behavior (voting for party $a, b, \ldots, n$, or nonvoting, as the case may be) to bring about the aggregate results that we see.

In their influential study *Partisan Realignment* (1980), Jerome Clubb, William Flanigan, and Nancy Zingale utilize a realignment-search technique based on two-way analysis of variance of geographical units across a large number of elections. Such an $i \times j$ matrix will have point-unit entries (X_{ij} might be, say, the Democratic percentage of the vote or the potential electorate in Hillsborough County, New Hampshire, in the 1868 election), column means of county percentages in any given election, row means of percentages in a given county across all elections, and a grand mean derived from all county and election data points in the matrix. From these compilations residuals are derived for each unit and then analyzed. Use of the ANOVA technique results in a classification not of types of elections, but of types of electoral change pivoting on two dimensions: durability and internal distributional pattern. The former permits the identification of deviating (temporary) and realigning (more permanent). The latter distinguishes between across-the-board "surges" and "interactive" change involving substantial cross-movement among units.

As Kleppner observes, Clubb, Flanigan, and Zingale seem more concerned with identifying individual level change than are the authors working within the first perspective discussed above. Yet using a territorial grid with an ANOVA residual-evaluation technique involves major levels-of-analysis problems that seem not far removed from those found in correlation analysis of territorial units, as in the classic critique of 1950 by the statistician W. S. Robinson. One can easily imagine situations, for instance, in which bidirectional movements of voters *within* units could produce uniform change *across* them; and, conversely, cases in which unidirectional change at the individual level could result in differential or "interactive" change at the territorial level. The search for individual-level movement requires a technique appropriate to it. So far as I know, the only one which has thus far been successfully employed is ecological regression estimation, which involves estimating the cell entries within a table by transitional probability from the information contained in the marginals. Using ANOVA for this purpose seems to muddy the waters. In addition, the authors leave us with little or no clear sense of the amount of change that must appear to confirm the existence of partisan realignment.

The most striking feature of this study's findings is what might be called "the strange case of the missing realignments." The only such sequence which this technique finds, in fact, is the massive "surge" realignment of the 1930s. The other two cases, on which virtually everyone else agrees as to their realigning character—the 1850s and the 1890s—essentially disappear from view. Assuming the validity of the methodology employed in this work, the conclusion logically follows that *electoral* change as a sign of nationwide partisan or policy realignment must be very heavily discounted, if not rejected altogether. What then emerges is the "extended perspective" proposed by Clubb, Flanigan, and Zingale. This perspective is based on the model of a nearly purely reactive mass public found in the canon of Michigan survey research analysis. It particularly stresses the activities of political elites in reshaping political reality with the power given them, once they have acquired it. Thus electoral change, such as it is, is just the first stage of a critical-realignment process. Such change often involves nothing more than the desire under what might actually be transitory stress to reject the party in power. Once the opposing party is given unified control of the agencies of government, realignment then follows, *if* these two conditions are met: (1) the new majority enacts policies dealing with the dominant crisis issues; and (2) these appear to ease the situation. In that case, following the pure-reactive assumptions about the public that are at the core of this analysis, public perception of this responsiveness works to shape a durable change in the distribution of the "normal vote," and presumably, in the structure of party identification at the individual level on which such a vote is largely based.

Now if many others, using other methods, have converged on agreement that electoral realignment also occurred in the 1850s and 1890s crises, and this study finds no such thing, we are probably on the trail of negative consilience. Either something is very wrong with that substantial corpus of research, or the methods employed here are inappropriate to the discovery of electoral realignments. There seems to be no middle ground on this. My own assessment is that if we wish to determine whether lasting change first manifested in a particular election had large, medium, or small effect on the ongoing electoral system, time-series analysis of some description is a more appropriate tool of inquiry. If individual-level change estimates are sought, one is better advised to look for them with ecological-regression methods.

There is no doubt that first-generation work on critical realignment paid far too little attention for far too long to developing analyses of elites, elite activities, and policy changes. As Skowronek's model (1986) also suggests, presidents taking office in a realignment upheaval (the "vulnerable-opposed" group) are much more often than not masters of creative destruction; they and other key actors in the new coalition play a vital and sometimes constitution-redefining role in constructing a new regime order on the ruins of the old. At the least, one can say that *Partisan Realignment* has forcefully called on the research community to redress this analytic imbalance. One of the most hopeful signs of progress in the years since 1980 is that in fact the imbalance has become increasingly redressed.[4] The electoral side of the authors' analysis ultimately fails to persuade, however, because its underlying conceptualization of the electorate is steeped in the assumptions of the Michigan Survey Research Center/Center for Political Studies (SRC/CPS) school of survey research. To the extent that it does, it shares in the fallacy of presentism, which we shall discuss below. But, Charles Lyell and many others to the contrary, present states of affairs and inferences derived therefrom are not always infallible, or even necessarily accurate, guides to the past.

The null finding of *Partisan Realignment* about the realigning character of elections in the 1850s or 1890s is neither consistent with the voluminous testimony of people who lived through these times and set their reactions down in writing, nor with the conclusions of historians who incorporate such evidence, and far more besides, into their accounts. Consider just four examples of this: one from the 1850s and three from the 1890s. In the first example, reflecting on the 1858 Senate race in Illinois between incumbent Democratic Senator Stephen Douglas and his Republican challenger, Abraham Lincoln, one of Douglas's party workers commented: "It was no ordinary contest, in which political opponents skirmished for the amusement of an indifferent audience, but it was a great uprising of the people, in which the masses were politically, and in a considerable extent socially, divided against each other. In fact, it was a fierce and angry struggle, approximating the character of a revolution" (Quoted in Jaffa, 1959:23). The second and third examples come from the prefaces by the editor to each annual edition of the *Chicago Daily News Almanac* (1894, 1895, 1896, 1897). Normally anodyne summaries of major events of the preceding year, the prefaces dealing with the years 1894 and 1896 strike a considerably more urgent tone.[5]

> Few years in times of profound peace have been so crowded with stirring political and social events as 1894. The year opened with serious and disastrous labor troubles, which continued, with almost unabated intensity, until the middle of July. Political disturbances of the tariff controversy in congress created as much interest as any legislative action in our national history, while the November elections were a surprise to all parties. ... Add to these disturbances the financial panic which caused so much distress during the whole year up to the first of October, and the year 1894 becomes the most interesting of any in our history since the close of the war.

> From a political standpoint the year 1896 has been the most remarkable in our history. It has witnessed the partial disruption of one of the great parties, the formation of the free-silver party, the union of one wing of the democratic with the people's party and the harmonious action of the other wing with the republicans to compass the defeat of the regular nominee of the democratic party. How permanent any one of these changes may be no one can tell, but the election in November, 1896, will always be one of those points of departure from which political reckonings must be taken in the future.

And finally, the historian J. Rogers Hollingsworth gives us a sense of the unusual but recurrent phenomenon of "masses in motion" which, according to realignment theory, accompanies such abnormal moments in American political history.

> With the nation's press leading the way, silver and gold became more exaggerated than ever as symbols of justice and injustice, democracy and plutocracy. Party loyalties, once so important, lost their meaning as the central issue of the campaign took on moral overtones. Mammoth torch-light parades wound through the streets of cities and towns, with captains of industry as well as farmers and laborers marching in line. Men grew angry at the very sound of the names of McKinley, Cleveland and Bryan. (Hollingsworth, 1963:72)

Obviously, exaggeration may well be detected in such accounts; they can hardly be taken uncritically, but require (as all data does) sifting and evaluation. But there is far too much of this sort of evidence to dismiss. Kleppner, Ackerman, and I believe such evidence is very strong—in realignment situations particularly, the public is highly *proactive*, not merely reactive. Not infrequently, it is then the task of leadership to catch up with the situation, as in the sentiment attributed to a French political leader caught up in one of the revolutions in that country's history: "There go my people. I must follow them, for I am their leader." Needless to say, evidence of the sort just cited fits easily with time-series, system-state-oriented realignment analysis. It does not fit easily with an analysis whose methods fail to identify such moments of upheaval.

Still another set of issues raised along somewhat similar lines can be found in David Brady's important study, *Critical Elections and Congressional Policy-Making* (1988). Like Clubb, Flanigan, and Zingale, Brady is deeply impressed with the very limited net movements that occurred in the 1850s and the 1890s at the electoral level. The explanation he offers for the much more substantial change in the partisan composition of the U.S. House of Representatives is a structural one. Swing ratios, that is, the proportional seat increases for a given party for each increment of increases in its share of the two-party vote, were extremely high in much of the nineteenth century, particularly in its last quarter. This was associated with a sharply peaked distribution of congressional-district outcomes, with a two-party mode very close to 50–50. In the context of the 1890s realignment in particular, when 7–10 percent incremental seat gains for a party accompany a single percentage-point increase in its popular vote, vast turnover can be secured on very small margins—exactly what classically happened in the 1888–1894 congressional-election sequence. After 1896, however, these ratios were dramatically damped down, falling to 3:1 or 4:1. This, coupled with a limited but durable pro-Republican shift away from the 50–50 mode of earlier times, led to a stabilization which (until 1910 and again after 1916) left control of the House consistently in Republican hands—though usually not by very large margins.

It should go without saying that no realigning event has ever produced anything remotely approximating a *total* transformation of partisan distributions in American elections. On the other hand, there is no doubt that earlier analyses often explicitly or implicitly exaggerated the magnitude of durable electoral change that was produced on such occasions. The crucial universe-level criterion for realignment is in fact that of the movement of *decisive minorities* of voters. This adds up on a net basis to a displacement of the normal vote that has lasting consequences for the distribution of power in the political system. There is no doubt that the realignments of the 1850s and the 1890s were strikingly "interactive" rather than "surge" events, as with the 1930s. Necessarily, *net* shifts were smaller by far in these nineteenth-century situations than in the 1930s event, which was in a class by itself.[6] But the *gross* displacements seem far more substantial when, with the use of ecological regression, movements by voters among parties—and from nonvoting to voting—are compared in realigning "moments" with those found in stable-phase or "normal" elections.[7]

Brady's analysis of the transformations in congressional power balances and policy activities is first-rate, original, and a major contribution to the literature. The electoral side of the analysis is rather less satisfactory, for Brady accepts, essentially uncritically, the election-analysis framework given by Clubb, Flanigan, and Zingale. Accordingly, there needs to be a more detailed inquiry into the underlying structure of congressional-district outcomes, and changes in them, during these earlier phases of our electoral history.

In doing this, the first point to observe is that partisan House majorities from 1854 through at least 1964 were very heavily influenced by the South's peculiar position in the national system. When it was entirely out of that system, hegemonic Republican majorities in what was left of the Union made possible the political base for the Civil War Reconstruction "constitutional moment" that Ackerman identifies. When the South returned, it passed through several stages of "solidification" en route to an eventually normal 100-seat Democratic regional majority. This imposed a requirement for *any* national Republican majority in the House at any time between 1874 (when Reconstruction began to collapse) and the early 1960s. The "core" areas of the Union, the North and West, occupied about two-thirds of the total seats in the House. To gain a majority in that chamber, Republicans had to win *at least 70 percent* of seats in this "core." This figure is only somewhat less than the share of seats they did in fact receive (with the South out of the picture) in the decisively "constituent" 1864 and 1866 elections. It is also noteworthy that this requirement remains remarkably stable across four periods extending from 1874 to 1950, with regression estimation of the Republican share of seats in the North and West necessary to produce a bare House majority yielding a minimum result of 70.0 percent and a maximum of 71.4 percent.

Naturally, these extremely unbalanced conditions at the district level in the "core" did not normally exist between 1874 and 1892—hence the usual Democratic control of the house during this second phase of the Civil War party system. But they did normally exist from 1894 to 1930, only to disappear for good from 1932 on (except for the "deviating elections" of 1946 and 1952). The "interactivity" of the 1890s realignment existed as well at this gross regional level of analysis. If Republicans could normally count on ten or a dozen seats from the South before 1900 (even without manipulating election contests as in 1888 or 1894), the post-1912 pattern had reduced these to a "norm" of four seats with a larger total base, equivalent to three in the late nineteenth century. This movement was, of course, counter-cyclical to the pro-Republican displacement in congressional outcomes that occurred elsewhere at about the same time. If one were confined to looking only at global results, the extent of critical realignment "where it mattered," and where electoral conditions remained more or less (if decliningly) competitive, would be significantly underestimated.

Let us therefore turn to a review of certain aspects of electoral dynamics in these "core" areas of the Civil War's Union—areas a very large part of which were to become the metropole in the society, economics, and politics of the era of corporate-capitalist organization of the country. We begin with a periodized summary of the Democratic percentage of the two-party vote—itself a summary of congressional district-level outcomes—and its relationship to the Democratic percentage of seats actually won. We then add, as an heuristic device, the seat "projection" to be expected from applying the so-called cube law.[8]

Assuming that the cube law gives us a generally unbiased estimate or model of the relationship between vote and seat percentages, then the first finding of note is that there was a substantial and persistent pro-Republican bias in the "delivery" of seats for the whole period from 1854 to 1914. This was a mirror-image of the pro-Democratic bias that prevailed during the second or Jacksonian party-system era. The second point to observe is that, while the net vote displacement involved in the Civil War realignment was just 4.8 percent, this translated into a partisan vote *lead* of very nearly 10 percent, or, to normal near landslide conditions. As is evident from Table 3.1, considerably more pro-Republican displacement was produced during the first phase of the "System of 1896" which followed. This indeed led to a balance of seats in the North and West fully comparable to the vast margins produced in 1864 and 1866, and was further aided by the persistent pro-Republican bias in vote-seat relationships.

As we have said, there is absolutely no doubt that Brady is right in holding that the swing ratio declined very substantially after the realignment of the 1890s. This does not, however, necessarily imply that the volatility of district-level partisan swing from election to election also decreased. In fact, it would appear that the opposite happened: longitudinal volatility increased rather substantially. To show this, we have selected six states that remained generally competitive after the 1896 realignment, and have evaluated district-level outcomes in them during two apportionment eras, 1882–1890 (pre-realignment) and 1902–1910 (post-realignment). These states are Connecticut, Illinois, Indiana, Iowa, New Jersey, and West Virginia, which had 59 seats in the first period and 69 in the second. In aggregate, the mean district-level Democratic share of the two-party vote was 49.6 percent in 1882–1890, falling to 45.1 percent in the 1902–1910 period. The swing ratio in the first period was 7.27 and 4.12 (a reduction of 43 percent) in the second. Yet while this was going on, the mean absolute two-party swings in these districts rose very substantially, from 3.0 percent in the pre-realignment period to 5.4 percent in the post-

TABLE 3.1   Partisan Balance in U.S. House Elections, 1832–1940: North and West

	Mean Dem. % of 2-Party Vote	Mean Dem. Partisan Lead	Mean Dem. % of 2-Party Seats	Cube Law Projection	Deviation of CL Projection from Actual Seat %
1832–1852	49.6	−0.8	54.6	48.8	+5.8
1856–1872	45.2	−9.6	28.5	36.2	−7.7
1874–1892	48.7	−2.6	38.5	45.8	−7.3
1896–1914	42.8	−14.4	23.3	29.8	−6.5
1916–1930	39.4	−21.2	21.4	21.5	−0.1
1940	49.3	−1.4	45.6	48.0	−2.4

realignment period. Moreover, the district-level variances increased as well, from 5.40 to 8.01.

The mean district-level Republican vote margin in these states increased from 0.8 percent in 1882–1890 to 8.9 percent in 1902–1910. If in the first period this resulted in Democrats winning 51.4 percent of the 292 contests in these states, they were able to win only 26.4 percent of the 345 contests in the second period, 1902–1910. What this shows is the decisive marginal effect of a bodily displacement toward a less competitive balance in the underlying vote that was particularly substantial, given the tightly structured partisanship of that era. This bodily shift was large enough not to be compensated for by increases in district-level volatility. As the results of the 1910 election demonstrated under two-party conditions (not to mention those of 1912 or 1914, when the Republican party was divided), Democratic congressional victories remained possible. But 1910 and 1916 were the only two-party contests between 1896 and 1930 where this occurred, and as that fact reveals, this could happen only under quite exceptional conditions.

How much is a "lot" of system-transforming electoral change? Unfortunately, there is no agreed-upon definitional standard to tell us. But consider the general story of Table 3.1 again. In the North and West, the 1850s replaced a virtual dead heat in the popular vote with a near landslide Republican ascendancy *as a normal state of affairs*. The second phase of this Civil War system, separated from the first by the "midlife crisis" of 1874–1878, produced enough Democratic resilience so that the average Republican lead in the "core" was cut from 9.6 percent to 2.6 percent, which of course implied Democratic control of the House in all but four of the twenty years from 1875 to 1895. The realignment of the 1890s, reinforced by subsequent developments like the first-of-its-kind landslide of 1904, saw this average Republican vote margin widen from 2.6 percent to 14.4 percent. Taken as a whole, congressional elections in the North and West now remained barely within the competitive range; and they fell quite out of that range during the second half of the "System of 1896" (1918–1930), when this mean lead widened to 21.2 percent. We cannot unequivocally answer questions such as How much is enough evidence? but I would argue that the shift in the constitutionally decisive 1856–1872 period fully qualifies as convincing, and that the post-1892 displacement more than fully qualifies, by any reasonable definition. The evidence for such a view is only strengthened, as Brady's footnote 24 explains, when some sense of gross movements, and comparison of them in realigning and normal phases of the electoral cycle, is obtained. The basic problem with Brady's electoral analysis lies in a dismissive, minimizing approach to the role of electoral inputs in system transformation, which he derived from Clubb, Flanigan, and Zingale, and thus from conceptualizations which lie at the core of the Michigan survey-research program. To repeat, such conceptualizations may very well be of questionable utility when applied to historical states of society (including electorates) other than those prevailing when the conceptualizations were generated.

Finally, let us turn to another issue one too often encounters in work which employs historical materials, but which may be defective in its understanding of historical method. This is the issue of *anachronism*. At its simplest, anachronism involves a blunder on the part of an author whose grasp of the details of the time dimension has slipped for some reason. One small case in point seems to have occurred in Francis Fukuyama's recently published book, *The End of History and the Last Man*. According to the eminent historian William MacNeill's review, Fukuyama claims that Isaac Newton had a great influence on Thomas Hobbes, though in fact, Newton was only eleven years old when *Leviathan* was published.[9] This sort of thing crops up surprisingly often, but ordinary quality-control techniques used by historians—including reviews—probably catch many or most of the more egregious cases.

There is, however, another form of anachronistic fallacy to which researchers with behavioral-science backgrounds may be particularly susceptible. This, alluded to more than once in the preceding discussion, is the fallacy of *presentism*: of assuming that what we see and derive inferences from in the here and now adequately describes reality at other times and in other places. Essentially, this is the foundation of Gould's critique of the dogmas of substantive uniformitarianism developed by Charles Lyell and maintained over the decades by the professional mainstream in those "historical" natural sciences—geology and evolutionary biology. This critique could be extended to not a few social-science treatments of historical materials. Space constraints preclude any extensive discussion of presentist fallacy in political science. Readers should be assured, however, that it is far too common a failing in this literature, extending, for example, from behavioral retrodictive efforts to the attempts of some public-choice scholars to buttress their arguments by including what they think to be empirical examples derived from past states of affairs.[10] One hopes that presentist fallacy will over time come to be a less acute professional problem as it comes to be more widely recognized that history has its own integrity and that periodization implies that states of affairs constituting one period cannot simply be translated bodily into states of affairs constituting another. At every step along the way, consonance between the relevant patterns and data of one era and those of another cannot be merely assumed; it has to be demonstrated.

CONCLUSION: PATTERN RECOGNITION

Let us attempt now to draw the threads of this discussion of pattern recognition together. A generation after V. O. Key, Jr., first provided a modern definition and some criteria for recognizing the existence of critical elections, this field of inquiry remains in thoroughly unsatisfactory condition. Many things, not least the deficiencies of first-generation work on the subject, have contributed to this situation. We have attempted here to analyze some dimensions which this disarray has displayed. The strange case of the missing realignment of 1968, which we think is not missing after all, has, for example, contributed to a sentiment among political scientists that realignment is at best a phenomenon of an unrecoverable past.

Reflection on this situation has prompted me to propose two arguments. First, the systemic propensity toward intense and cyclically recurrent bursts of punctuational change remains permanently embedded. It arises out of a singularly American pattern of relationship between form of state and political culture on one hand, and the sociopolitical effects of untrammeled modernizing transformation of economy and society on the other. As such, they are apparently permanent and important features of the subject of inquiry, the political and electoral history of the United States. But, second, the historically concrete ways in which these bursts of punctuational change are processed through the system will differ over time. They will differ not only across the long, but historically limited, lifetime of partisan domination over the electoral system, but also—even more important—they will differ depending on whether the bulk of the citizenry is effectively incorporated and mobilized into it or not. This has led me to propose a distinction between Type I and Type II realignments. Critics may very well regard this as only a desperate effort to save a failing model; but I think not. Debate cannot even be hinted at here: I believe that over time, further work by people in a number of diverse fields will support my judgment.

This essay has been an attempt to think through some of the issues involving this particular corner of research into history, and thus to think through some aspects of the historical enterprise itself. "Ways of knowing" include working hard on developing the specific implications of "laws in the background, contingency in the details," and striking the best attainable balance between the two. They also include the vital role of consilience in minimizing heteronomy in the field (i.e., believing just what one pleases), and the equally vital role played in this respect by periodization.

Without a doubt, a major contributing factor to the lack-of-resolution problems we have been discussing is that there has tended to be only one research community organized as scientific research communities typically are—the one constructed with such brilliant results as the Michigan survey-research group. Otherwise, we have only the cottage industry, coupled with the professional blinders that arise from the division of scholarly labor across more than one discipline. This has been a mighty brake on progress, but my ultimate sensation is not one of complaint but of steadily growing optimism. In recent years especially, there has been a considerable growth of opportunities for consilience to manifest itself more effectively as workers in previously partitioned research communities have come to be aware of each other. And there is a genuine desire for this: A few years ago, for instance, Terry Moe issued a call for people doing "positive theory of institutions" and scholars in the field of historically grounded, state-centered studies to move into interaction, to the benefit of both communities (Moe, 1987:236–299). This call is clearly evoking a response, and it is easy to predict that it will grow in size and payoffs over time.

We seem to be at a threshold: An era of creative integration across these and other fields lies just ahead as people with convergent research problematics begin to find and react to each other. Much wheat will be winnowed along the way from a much larger supply of chaff. If, in this process, we learn enough to come to an agreement that critical-realignment theory should now be given a decent burial—that would be progress, however unlikely I think such an outcome will be. In the meantime, this chapter, like Chapter 2, is an effort to point out why the supposed death of realignment has been prematurely announced. It is also an effort to suggest why and how generally better work with historical data in our field might be performed than has been the case hitherto.

NOTES

1. For further information, see Lichtman (1976:317–350; and 1982:170–188). This program has eventuated in a book (Lichtman and DeCell, 1990), the subtitle of which, "The Revolutionary System that Reveals How Presidential Elections Really Work from the Civil War to the 21st Century," makes broad claims, as does the work itself.

2. Sklar's full treatment of the Progressive Era is found in his remarkable book (1988).

3. Katznelson and Pietrykowski (1991:301–339) observe that there were two quite discrete and coherent models of the state's role that grew out of the Great Depression, the New Deal, and World War II. The first was planning-*dirigiste* in perspective. It failed politically with the great intensification of the Conservative Coalition's strength in Congress after the 1942 election (compare the abolition in 1943 of the National Resources Planning Board). The second, which eventually prevailed, was the fiscalist model, which was to become a cardinal given of policymaking for the next generation and more. It involved indirect rather than indicative public-sector involvement with the private-sector economy. As the authors are at pains to point out, two quite different (but not necessarily unequally "strong") articulations of the state were involved in an initially fluid transitional situation, during which serious alternatives and serious debates over them were yet possible. The triumph and institutionalization of fiscalism strikes me as reaffirming—note, in *period-specific* terms—the constituent character of the Progressive-era regulatory consensus which Sklar sets forth.

4. We have little space to dwell here on the fascinating, counterfactual might-have-beens concerning leadership's role in consolidating the policy, public-philosophy, and coalitional terms of the emergent regime order that it begins to install in the wake of critical realignment. The authors of *Partisan Realignment*, in stressing the central importance of this leadership in defining what happens next, also imply the counterfactual. This is an "incompetent" leadership that fails in its task, with the result that a "potential" realignment followed by a new stable regime order fails to be actualized. A discussion with somewhat similar overtones is also found in Sundquist (1983).

Such outcomes are obviously theoretically possible. It is striking, however, that there has been no empirical trace of them thus far throughout two centuries of national political existence. The leadership situation described by Skowronek for that group of presidents coming to power in opposition to a collapsing regime order is, as he says, optimal for creating and entrenching its successor through a process of "creative destruction." As he and others have also observed, it very often happens that the crises producing these rare leadership opportunities are not "resolved" in any clear-cut way by the winners, least of all in terms of the rhetoric of critique employed by them in the critical election which brings them to power. "Laws in the background," connected with the nature of "political-time" circumstance and purposive action by the new chief and his elites and allies, seem to have produced a pattern in which post-realignment leadership has never yet failed to construct a new and durable regime order.

5. See *Chicago Daily News Almanac for 1895*, and *Chicago Daily News Almanac for 1897*.

6. The sheer size and robustness, for example, of the Democratic opposition in the Union states during the Civil-War era has long been noted by historians. See, for example, Silbey (1977).

7. Some concreteness can be lent to this discussion by consulting, for example, the tabular ecological-regression data in Gienapp (1987:482–551) and especially the ecological regressions of voter transitions in Baum (1984).

Baum's study covers only the single state of Massachusetts, but over an exceptionally long time span (1848–1876) and with an unusually fine territorial grid of more than 300 units for each pair of elections. Including not only movements in partisan choice but between abstention and voting, Baum finds that in the last "normal-phase" presidential election pair of the Jacksonian party system (1848–1852), 13 percent in the potential electorate were switchers. But, beginning with the regression pair 1852–1854, and then proceeding through a sequence of four other elections ending in 1860, the percentage of switchers nearly tripled to a mean of 34 (a range of 30 to 39). Beginning with the 1856 presidential election—the first to be contested by the Republican party in this state—the percentage of switchers then abruptly fell almost to the vanishing point. Across fourteen elections ending in 1875, the switcher mean was now 6, with a range of 0 to 11. The switcher component in the potential electorate was cut by nearly five-sixths from the levels found during the realignment crisis. Such available information as we have would thus suggest that, in general, during the "interactive" realignments such as those of the 1850s and the 1890s, gross movement in the electorate is at least three times as large as the net levels revealed by aggregate data analysis, and can well be even more than this in certain local electoral environments.

8. These data are compiled and analyzed from election returns in the public domain. In the search for a rough approximation of a two-party aggregate indicator of the "normal vote," we have made one exception to the two-party format. In 1912 and 1914 the Progressive vote was overwhelmingly derived from Republican voting streams. We have thus employed the Democratic percentage of the three-party vote for these years. Similarly, we have employed seat percentages for these two elections based on the share of congressional districts won by Democrats with an absolute majority of the three-party vote.

9. See MacNeill (1992) for the review of Fukuyama's book.

10. One concrete case in point is the interesting study by Anderson (1979), much of which argument is also included as chapter 5 of Nie, Verba, and Petrocik (1979). Much of the analysis hangs upon a posited and very large group of "potential Democrats" in the nonvoting half of the potential electorate in the 1920s; their subsequent mobilization was chiefly, or almost entirely, responsible for the changed partisan balance associated with the critical realignment of the 1930s. Detailed analysis of aggregate data, however, makes it clear that in the religiocultural contest of 1928—the highest stimulus election by far in that decade—there was *both* a Smith and a Hoover surge in working-class environments, with the relative density or scarcity of Roman Catholics in the electorate making a decisive difference between the two surges. Only the Smith surge has been widely discussed in the literature. It thus seems clear that classifying such people as "potential Democrats" in the 1920s creates a false picture of their latent partisan allegiance *at the time*. It refers back to pre-realignment era conditions, which came to exist only during and following realignment, and draws on the Michigan survey-research studies.

4

Common Ground: History and Theories of American Politics

ELAINE K. SWIFT
DAVID W. BRADY

Never before have political scientists been more interested in history, a fact made plain by the dramatic increase in the number of historically oriented books and articles over the last decade. Not only does this interest show no sign of abating, but it has also begun to institutionalize itself with the establishment of historically oriented political science journals, *Studies in American Political Development* and *Journal of Policy History*; the initiation series of books by Princeton University Press, Stanford University Press, and Westview Press; and the formation of the History and Politics Section within the American Political Science Association (Robertson, 1993). This turn to the past is only in small part due to the discipline's increased interest in history for its own sake. Rather, many political scientists have come to believe that history is an essential ingredient in building dynamic, generalizable, and accurate theory. Because a longer time line confronts scholars with conditions of stability and instability, thereby challenging them to account for both, historically informed theory is more likely to be dynamic, that is, better able to account for both continuity and change. A longer perspective also prompts attention beyond a particular phenomenon in a particular context to a phenomenon in its various manifestations and contexts over time, thereby encouraging the formulation of theory broad enough to capture that phenomenon's variegated nature over time. In addition, historically based research is more likely to be accurate. Any contemporary study is likely to draw upon a small sample in comparison to an historical study and therefore be less suited for formulating or testing theory than historical approaches, whose range of variables, conditions, and outcomes is more likely to be representative of the true nature of political phenomena.

These and other advantages that history offers to political scientists are well-known and explored in depth elsewhere (Cooper and Brady, 1981; Gottschalk, 1963; Mills, 1959; Polsby, 1968; Potter, 1969; Robertson, 1993; Swift and Brady, 1991). In the following pages, we wish to present another important contribution history can make: the provision of a common ground of knowledge whose special nature could help scholars communicate with and learn from each other, thus enhancing the prospects for a richer understanding of politics. This kind of communication is in increasingly short supply. Although political scientists might focus on many of the same phenomena—public policy, political institutions, political behavior, and political economy, among others—they divide more and more along theoretic lines, with each theory's particular epistemology, respective methods, and pertinent vocabulary drawing its adherents inward, leaving them mainly to communicate with each other. Specialization certainly has its benefits, creating the possibility that scholars will pursue distinctly different kinds of research that might nonetheless complement each other and yield a deeper and more rigorous comprehension of political phenomena than if they had all adopted the same approach. However, it can also exact steep costs, the most serious of which is the tendency toward autarky. Like a protectionist nation closing down its economic borders, a scholarly autarky inhibits intellectual imports, expediting its own stagnation and obsolescence. To arrest the development of overspecialization, political scientists could benefit from a mutual and thoughtful exploration of the various theories' strengths and weaknesses, differences and similarities; however, they engage far more in what Thomas Kuhn (1970) has called "paradigmatic misunderstandings," in which the adherents of separate approaches fruitlessly and frustratingly talk past each other.

We will argue that history as common ground offers one possibility that could help us to preserve the benefits of specialization while limiting some of its drawbacks. To develop this argument, we will explore how it applies to research on American national institutions, the chosen subject because its theory-based divisions and growing historical orientation typify other areas of political scholarship. The conclusions we draw can therefore be generalized. In the first section of this chapter, we examine a growing topic: the ways in which three dominant approaches—state, organization, and rational choice theories—use history to explain U.S. national political institutions. To make this task more manageable, our survey focuses on how history explains two key institutional dynamics: behavior and change. In the second section, we consider the strengths and weaknesses of these theories by exploring the different ways each uses history. Inductive approaches, such as state and organization theory, use history to formulate theory, and deductive approaches, such as rational choice, use history to test theory. History has parallel effects on all three approaches—it can enhance their strengths or weaknesses, and reveal how their epistemologies could be refined in order to retain their strengths and minimize their weaknesses.

STATE, ORGANIZATION, AND RATIONAL CHOICE THEORIES OF AMERICAN NATIONAL POLITICAL INSTITUTIONS

While political scientists frequently apply a blend of theories to the study of American national political institutions, three major approaches increasingly dominate this area of research: state, organization, and rational choice theories. Each approach is complex, containing different and often vigorously contending schools of thought. Divisions notwithstanding, adherents to each approach agree more often than not.

State Theory

Theorists of the state probe why and how "the public sector—what we call here the State—has grown increasingly important in every society, from every advanced industrial to Third World primary-good exporter, and in every aspect of society—not just politics" (Carnoy, 1984:3). Much of the research on the U.S. has a strong focus on those institutions that scholars commonly believe "further[s] the autonomy and discretionary authority of the central state." These primarily include nonlegislative bodies, particularly the federal bureaucracy (Bensel, 1990:108).[1]

How does America's federal bureaucracy behave and how does that behavior change over time? No matter what conception of the state is favored—pure or synthetic versions of Weber, Tocqueville, Marx, or others—bureaucracies are viewed as necessary, albeit insufficient, components since laws, policies, ideologies, and other elements are also part of a state. Consequently, scholarship on the state is seldom focused solely on institutions. Instead, examinations of institutional behavior and change most often occur within the larger analytical context of state dynamics and development. In studies of the American state, institutional dynamics receive their most sustained treatment in analyses of state autonomy and state capacity. State autonomy is part and parcel of any state-centered approach. As Theda Skocpol explains, "States conceived as organizations claiming control over territories and people may formulate and pursue goals that are not simply reflective of the demands or interests of social groups, classes, or society. ... Unless such independent goal formulation occurs, there is little need to talk about states as important actors" (Skocpol, 1985:9). If students of the state are to build more than a functionalist understanding of autonomy, they must better understand the concept of state capacity, defined as its ability to formulate and implement action (Skocpol, 1980).

Institutions are the primary means of achieving both autonomy and capacity. According to J. P. Nettl, states exercise autonomy by developing "in a functional sense a distinct sector or arena of society." Thus it is "that a relatively autonomous state tends to proliferate specific institutions both for the adequate fulfillment of functional tasks of primacy within society and for replicating various internal functional requirements" (Nettl, 1968:564–565). These institutions are usually characterized by insulation from external, particularly societal, influences, coupled with a clear mission and strong dedication to fulfillment of that mission. What elements compose institutional capacity? As Skocpol (1985:16) puts it, "Obviously, sheer sovereign integrity and the stable administrative-military control of a given territory are preconditions for any state's ability to implement policies. ... Beyond this, loyal and skilled officials and plentiful financial resources are basic to state effectiveness in attaining all sorts of goals." It should also be noted that since autonomy and capacity are logically and practically separable, an institution may possess autonomy, but not capacity, and vice versa. In the event of the first condition, however, an institution would have limited potential to carry out its mission and maintain its autonomy. If the second condition prevailed, it would likely be penetrated and controlled by dominant societal forces.

In the United States, where federalism, a strong legislature, and other factors constrain the central bureaucracy, the coincidence of autonomy and capacity in any one institution or institutional sector is far from common. However, students of the American state have uncovered important exceptions, with the New Deal's Agricultural Adjustment Agency (AAA) being one of the best known historical examples (Skocpol and Feingold, 1982; Hooks, 1990; Gilbert and Howe, 1991). To exercise its autonomy, an institution requires capacity. According to Skocpol and Kenneth Feingold, capacity in the AAA primarily came in the form of its numerous, technically expert, and politically seasoned staff. Stephen Skowronek (1982), analyzing the development of state capacities in American administrative, military, and regulatory institutions around the turn of the twentieth century, likewise observes the importance of capacity, as evident in such qualities as consolidation, centralization, professionalization, and information.

Most scholars suggest that although, in general, nonlegislative political institutions have acquired significant capacity over time, who or what influences the ends that capacity is directed toward depends on the degree of autonomy an institution enjoys. According to scholarly consensus, because the U.S. remains a weak state, most of its nonlegislative national political institutions are not autonomous. Therefore, exogenous forces, specifically dominant societal groups, greatly shape both institutional means and ends. Where and when U.S. national political institutions have enjoyed autonomy, endogenous elements assume primary influence over institutional capacity.

How nonlegislative American political institutions change has been most fully explored in another line of inquiry: state development. In his study of the development of national administrative capacities in civil administration, business regulation, and the army, Skowronek contends that "environmental stimuli, official responses, and new forms of government are the basic elements of the state-building process" (Skowronek, 1982:10). While environmental factors including crisis, the economy, and social trends and forces can "singly or in some combination" act as powerful catalysts, they "are only the stimuli for institutional development," and instead, "the intervention of government officials is the critical factor in the state-building process" (Skowronek, 1982:12). With these officials aiming to address environmental challenges as well as enhance, or at least not undermine "the particular arrangements" that sustain them, their responses are in turn "mediated by the institutional and political arrangements that define their positions and support their prerogatives with the state apparatus." The result around the turn of the twentieth century was significant institutional change in the form of the "reconstruction of institutional relationships and the establishment of a bureaucratic mode of governmental operations" (Skowronek, 1982:13).

In *Yankee Leviathan: The Origins of Central State Authority in America, 1859–1877*, Richard Bensel argues that sectionally based domestic political economy had a fundamental impact on American state development and institutional change in both wartime and peacetime. Before the Civil War, the South attempted to protect its slave-based plantation system by acting to limit the powers of a national government that threatened that system's continued existence. When faced with the challenge of opposing a wealthier, more populous adversary, "the agrarian, economically underdeveloped South" ironically instituted "all-encompassing economic and social controls ... so extensive they call in question standard interpretations of southern opposition to the expansion of federal power in both the antebellum and post-Reconstruction periods" (Bensel, 1990:95). Political economy also conditioned the North's statist response to war. Dependent upon "unregulated capitalist markets and industrial production," the "northern war effort left the industrial and agricultural sectors almost untouched by central state controls and only skimmed the surface of northern labor pools" (Bensel, 1990:94). Following the war, sectional political economies continued to influence state development as "American state formation assumed the form of a northern, industrial program"; the North tolerated "incomplete political integration" in return for "national markets and corporate consolidation" (Bensel, 1990:17).

Within Bensel's approach, not only the state, but implicitly its political institutions are significantly, though not solely, shaped by the dynamics of domestic political economies. He explains that "only when efforts to harness existing productive potential are not sufficient to meet the challenge presented by the enemy do states attempt to innovate or go beyond the prewar forms of societal production." The Union "[i]n terms of material capacity and manpower potential ... did not face such a challenge." Therefore, its "war effort became a more-or-less capitalist, market-oriented response to the requirements of mobilization, well within the potential of northern society and well molded into its forms and structures." For the Confederacy, with a very different political economy, the opposite held true; its "war effort far outstripped the productive capabilities of the prewar economy and compelled a much more innovative, almost futuristic mobilization of resources." So it was that "southern mobilization was far more state-centered and coordinated than its northern counterpart" (Bensel, 1990:98).

Organization Theory

How institutions behave and change is, of course, a central concern of organization theory. Although institutions are only a subset of the subfield's larger focus on all organizations, and American national political institutions a still smaller subset of that focus, nonetheless organization theory has long made significant contributions to understanding institutions (March, 1965; Jackson, 1990). For the most part, organization theory has traditionally studied institutions ahistorically, often relying on empirical observation in the form of case studies or controlled social scientific experiments and developing abstract explanations of a wide variety of institutional phenomena.

Yet within the past few years, James March and Johan Olsen (1984, 1989) have identified a significant strand of organization theory of particular relevance to the historical dynamics of America's national administrative institutions. The authors call this strand "the new institutionalism," which at present is "neither a theory nor a coherent critique of one" (1984:747). Nonetheless, it calls into question what March and Olsen (1989:3) see as the dominant modes of institutional analysis since 1950, including contextualism, or the predisposition to see politics as an "integral" rather than a separate sphere of society; reductionism, meaning the view that "political phenomena" are "the aggregate consequences of individual behavior"; utilitarianism, or the inclination "to see action as a response to obligations and duties"; and functionalism, that is, the interpretation of "history as an efficient mechanism for reaching uniquely appropriate equilibria."

According to March and Olsen's characterization of the new institutionalism (1984:742), how institutions behave has much in common with, and in many ways complements, state theory. Like statist accounts of institutional autonomy, the new institutionalism holds that although environmental factors can have a significant impact, "[i]nstitutions seem to be neither neutral reflections of exogenous environmental forces nor neutral arenas for the performances of individuals driven by exogenous preferences and expectations." Further, new institutionalism "posits a more independent role for political institutions," an "argument" that is "a claim of institutional coherence and autonomy" (March and Olsen, 1989:17). To understand how institutions behave, the new institutionalism therefore looks inward to endogenous factors, of which rules are among the most important. These authors define rules as "the routines, procedures, conventions, roles, strategies, organizational forms, and technologies around which political activity is constructed. We also mean the beliefs, paradigms, codes, cultures, and knowledge that surround, support, elaborate, and contradict those roles and routines." As they explain, "[i]t is a commonplace observation in empirical social science that behavior is constrained or dictated by such cultural dicta and social norms," including the behavior of American political institutions. Indeed, "[a]ction is often based more on identifying the normatively appropriate behavior than on calculating the return expected from alternative choices" (March and Olsen, 1989:22).

Individuals are also essential, but not primarily causal, factors. Therefore, institutional behavior cannot be reductively explained by the sum of individual behavior. As March and Olsen (1989:23) observe, rules "are independent of the individual actors who execute them and are capable of surviving considerable turnover in individuals," compelling the actors to conform even though it may not be in their "narrow self-interest" to do so. How? Although some conformity with rules may be coerced, to a greater extent adherence to rules comes about as the product of education and other forms of socialization. So it is that "[r]ules, including those of various professions, are learned as catechisms of expectations. They are constructed and elaborated through an exploration of the nature of things, of self-conceptions, and of institutional and personal images."

Although "political institutions are sources of order and stability in an interactive world that might otherwise appear quite chaotic," they nonetheless change (March and Olsen, 1989:53). To explain how political institutions change, most contemporary social science theory "emphasizes the efficiency of historical processes, the ways in which history moves quickly and inexorably to a unique outcome, normally in some sense an optimum" (March and Olsen, 1984:743). The new institutionalism challenges this position, contending that in general institutions change neither readily nor functionally. Stephen Krasner (1988:74) notes that with "the tendency of patterns of behavior, norms, or formal structures to persist through time," institutional change "can never be easy, fluid, or continuous." At those junctures when change does occur, internal dynamics can figure more significantly than environmental pressure. But when environmental pressure is the primary stimulus, "the institutional bases of routines and meaning tend to limit the efficiency of history," producing "adjustments that are slower or faster than are appropriate, or are misguided" (March and Olsen, 1989:53).

How then do institutions change? The new institutionalism offers no specific, testable theories. It does, however, advance certain considerations that theories of change should incorporate. Krasner (1988:72) argues for the importance of carefully delineating "the nature of particular institutional arrangements because such arrangements are both a dependent variable at time *t* and an independent variable at time *t+1*" and for the need to explain "how institutional arrangements perpetuate themselves across time, even in situations where utilitarian calculations suggest they are dysfunctional." March and Olsen outline a research agenda that includes "trying to specify the conditions under which the sequential branches of history turn back upon each other and the conditions under which they diverge"; "characterizing the role of standard operating procedures, professions, and expertise in storing and recalling history"; and calling "attention to the ways in which the preferences (interests), resources, and rules of the game of politics are not exogenous to politics but heavily influenced by institutional processes" (March and Olsen, 1989:56).

Rational Choice Theory

In American politics, rational choice theorists have focused primarily on contemporary legislatures and specifically on the U.S. Congress. Works treating change over time in Congress are thus the exception and not the rule. Below we briefly outline some major features of basic models of legislative behavior and then turn to several studies to illustrate how various rational choice perspectives have been applied to behavior and change over time.

Spatial models of legislatures are concerned with the "choice space," which is composed of the decisions legislators can make; the behavior, which is most often derived from the strategic calculi of legislators; and the amount of information legislators have about the relationship between policies and their consequences. Based on the assumptions made about each of the above features, spatial modelers identify and interpret equilibria. The main distinguishing feature of these models turns on how the researcher treats different legislative institutions, and distributional and informational properties. Distribution models emphasize who wins and who loses, given the policy outcome under a particular institutional arrangement. Information models emphasize the reduction of uncertainty over the course of the choice process. The extent to which complex arguments and assumptions about information and behavior affect the results does not concern us here; our purpose is to examine how these models can be applied to explain institutional behavior and change over time.

One explicit discussion of behavior and change over time appears in a study by Thomas Gilligan and Keith Krehbiel (1987) on the effects of restricting amendments to committee proposals on committee informational roles. The authors argue that under restrictive procedures, committees will acquire specialized information, while under unrestrictive procedures, they will not. Gilligan and Krehbiel develop a model in which the actors are initially uncertain about the consequences of alternative policies, but have common probabilistic beliefs concerning the relationship between policies and their consequences. Given this uncertainty, the committee and the parent body engage in a sequence of activities that culminates in a policy. The parent body selects restrictive or unrestrictive procedures and the final policy. Committees choose whether to specialize or not and propose a bill to the parent body. Committee specialization means acquiring information that reveals the exact consequences of policies prior to their adoption. The committee's decision to specialize is observed by the parent body, but the actual information is initially known only to the committee. In equilibrium, the behavior of the two actors maximizes their expected utilities based on their beliefs about the likely consequences of the policy alternatives.

The formal results show that under an unrestrictive procedure (open rule), where the parent body may select any alternative to the committee's proposal, informed decisionmaking is undermined in two ways. First, a rational committee makes proposals that induce the parent body to make imprecise inferences about the policies and their consequences. Second, because only limited inferences are possible, the parent body often makes decisions under conditions of uncertainty and the committee's expected rewards from specialization are limited. In short, the committee often chooses not to acquire information relevant to the policy process even though the information would benefit the parent body.

In contrast, the formal results from the restrictive procedure show that such procedures enhance the information role of the committees. This is so because under restrictive procedures the parent body's choice is between the committee proposal and the status quo. Thus, the parent body can make more precise inferences about the committee's private information and use the information in its selection of a policy. In addition, since the committee has more influence on policy under a closed rule, it has a greater incentive to specialize or obtain information. In short, under the assumption of the model, compared to unrestrictive procedures, restrictive procedures enhance the information role of the committees.

To test their model, Gilligan and Krehbiel turn to an historical analysis of House rules, focusing on the use of three classes of restrictive procedures—recognition precedents, suspension of the rules, and special orders from the Rules Committee—in the post-1870 House. The key characteristics of these procedures is that they are selective commitments by the parent chamber to limit its own ability to amend the committee proposals. The credibility of such commitments is enhanced because they are delegated to third parties—the speaker, the Rules Committee, and party leaders. Two puzzles emerge: Why did such procedures develop in the 1870s? Why would a parent chamber commit to the use of procedures that appear to limit its influence on policy?

Gilligan and Krehbiel's answer to the first question is that *ceteris paribus*, the effects of restrictive procedures ought to be most compelling in times of policy innovation because innovation, almost by definition, implies uncertainty about policies and their consequences. The formal model is driven by this uncertainty about policies and their consequences, thus one should expect that when uncertainty is high, actors will want to reduce it. The authors argue that the post–Civil War period of rapid industrial development generated enough uncertainty about policies and their consequences to prompt a desire on the part of the House to lower it. Therefore, the reason the parent body would agree to limit its power lies in the effects of restrictive procedures, which would actually enhance collective decisionmaking by providing clearer information to the parent body and maintaining the committee's incentive to specialize. The explanation is grounded in the motivation of individuals to maximize their utilities, and the equilibrium is stable. This study is, to our knowledge, the only study where a formal model is explicitly used to explain institutional change in legislatures. There are, however, historical studies of institutions and policy change which are loosely based on choice theories.

One historical period that has received attention is bounded by the years 1876 to 1922, when the House of Representatives decentralized the appropriations process so that seven committees in addition to Appropriations had the right to appropriate funds. The choice perspective in this literature falls into the "new institutionalist" school of rational choice theory, and is concerned with whether institutional structure affects policy results. Researchers in the area (Brady and Morgan, 1987; Cogan, Muris, and Schick, 1993; Stewart, 1989) make assumptions compatible with standard study of rational choice: Actors wish to maximize their budget utilities and their chance of reelection, and institutional arrangements, particularly committees, are endogenous. Using this framework, all three studies show that the change in rules, from 1876 to 1885, which decentralized the appropriations process, resulted from members' desires to increase the flow of appropriations to their constituencies. The return to a decentralized system in the 1919 to 1921 period is more problematic. John Cogan, Timothy Muris, and Allen Schick (1993) use an information model to show that over the 1870 to 1988 time period, committees with sole jurisdiction over funds, for example, Ways and Means' jurisdiction over Social Security, did not favor deficits. In contrast, those committees with jurisdiction over generally funded programs favor deficits because they do not have any incentive to balance revenues and expenditures. Thus for Cogan, equilibrium results because sole jurisdiction committees have a balanced budget; multiple jurisdiction committees in the aggregate have deficits.

Another study of committees using rational choice assumptions is Rick Wilson's (1986) analysis of what a committee seat is worth. Wilson examines the Rivers and Harbors Committee at the turn of the century and calculates the value of each of its projects. These resulting data reveal that a seat on the committee is worth a dollar amount in excess of what noncommittee members could have expected.

Rational choice scholars have recently begun to tackle historical problems and over the next decade, we can expect more historical work in this field. It is worth mentioning Calvin Jillson and Wilson's (1994) investigation of the Continental Congress; John Aldrich's (1987) study of the formation of the Republican party in the 1850s; and Barry Weingast's (1991b) use of credible commitment models to understand the South's secession from the Union. William H. Riker's (1984) work on the ratification of the U.S. Constitution is another example of the application of choice perspectives to important historical events.

The bulk of the work, extant and forthcoming, fits into the new institutionalist framework—institutional arrangements affect outcomes. Over the next few years, this view will be challenged by those who believe that institutions do not affect outcomes. Essentially, the question is: Do institutions matter or do they simply reflect bargains struck outside the institutional framework? One way to demonstrate the nature of the argument is to focus on alternative views of American parties. In their most recent book, Gary Cox and Matthew McCubbins (1993) argue that parties emerge to solve a prisoner's dilemma problem and can therefore matter in determining policy outcomes. In one chapter, they take on the traditional view that measurements of low levels of party voting show that congressional parties are weak; they argue that the proper measure is not party voting, but rather party cohesion. They show that although party voting is relatively low, party cohesion is high, and such cohesion is generated by the party members' agreement on fundamental policies. Thus, though party voting is low, party cohesion prevents minority parties from changing the status quo.

This result is in contradiction to committee-centered models where party membership plays a role (Shepsle and Weingast, 1981, 1987). In these median voter models, only individual members' preferences in policy space and the committee's *ex ante* powers determine policy outcomes. One may question whether parties are more than the sum of aggregate preferences. Does party membership induce members to vote for proposals that differ from their ideal points? If the answer is yes, as seems to be the case with European parties, then parties matter. If members do not vote for anything other than their ideal points, then parties are simply the sum of preferences of members and do not need to be modeled since aggregating the preferences of members provides a sufficient understanding.

HISTORY AS COMMON GROUND

At first glance, this survey of state, organization, and rational choice theories suggests that history is less common ground than contested territory, lending empirical support to very different conclusions about how American national political institutions behave and change. With rational choice theory, history lends support "to individual analysis and to reduction," and although "the need to take contextual factors into account is acknowledged, the role accorded these factors is simply to structure or inform individual decision making regarding the realization of underlying preferences. Moreover, ultimately the goal is to reduce contextual factors ... to explanation at the individual level" (Cooper, 1988:119). Therefore, to understand the behavior of, and change in, American national political institutions, rational choice theorists argue that we must primarily look to the self-interested goals of individual actors.

State and organization theorists use history to assert the opposite: Little can be explained "by examining atomized individuals. At the very least, individuals are confronted with a limited repertoire of social roles and values from which to choose" (Krasner, 1988:73). Explanation of how American national political institutions change and behave should instead look to the context that shapes that repertoire. According to organization theory, "enduring institutional structures [are] the building blocks of social and political life. The preferences, capabilities, and basic self-identities of individuals are conditioned by these institutional structures" (Krasner, 1988:67). To understand institutional dynamics therefore requires a better grasp of such endogenous factors as the "standard operating procedures and structures that define and defend values, norms, interests, identities, and beliefs" (March and Olsen, 1989:17). State theorists would agree, but with an important qualifier: Endogenous institutional factors are the primary contextual influence when an institution is autonomous. When it is not, exogenous contextual factors such as class structure, party regime, political culture, and dominant ideology have a greater causal impact.

How history comes to be used towards such different ends can be traced to the role that empiricism more generally plays in building state, organization, and rational choice theory. State and organization theory largely proceed inductively, pursuing "the development of ideas, concepts, and models based on empirical observations and relevant to a behavioralist understanding and prescriptive ordering of political life" (March and Olsen, 1984:742). As such, history supplies admirable raw material for building state and organization theory in at least two important ways. First, history affords a perspective on phenomena that becomes possible only after they have receded into the past. Just as it is often easier to perceive a city's plan when peering down from an airplane than when walking within its midtown, so too the historical perspective allows scholars to more comprehensively assess what dominates and what recedes from view in the larger causal picture. A history professor at one university makes the same point in a pedagogical exercise: Students are asked to compare explanations given at the time an event occurs with explanations profferred decades later. Typically, those made later draw from the perspective of history to identify contributing factors and causal interconnections either unknown or underappreciated to contemporary observers. So it is, for example, that an historical perspective allows Bensel (1990) to discount the contemporaneously inflated influence of states' rights ideology in favor of sectional political economic configurations as a primary force in American state development.

Second, and relatedly, the breadth and depth of an historical perspective suggest a host of causal factors often too subtle or inchoate for contemporary observers to adequately grasp. By using this perspective, new institutionalists have been able to draw attention to the importance of such factors as "values, norms, interests, identities, and beliefs" (March and Olsen, 1989:17). Such a perspective also suggests causal dynamics that are counterintuitive, illogical, or even disturbing to contemporary observers. Only the historical perspective could, for example, prompt scholars to challenge functionalist theories of institutional change that "see history as an efficient mechanism for reaching uniquely appropriate equilibria, and [seem] less concerned with the possibilities for maladaptation and nonuniqueness in historical development" (March and Olsen, 1989:3). In the same vein, only the historical point of view could lead scholars to advocate an institutionalist version of a punctuated equilibrium theory of evolution that posits that "change is difficult: once a particular institu-

tional structure (biological stock) is established, it tends to maintain itself—
or at the very least to channel future change"; and that "optimal adaptation is not always possible because the institutional stock is not always
available. Features selected during one point in time impose limits on future possibilities" (Krasner, 1988:79).Yet, if inductive approaches are epistemologically well-poised to utilize the perspective, the causal revelations,
and the other advantages history confers, such approaches are also well-
positioned to fall for the trap history sets. We will call it the allure of the
arcane, a downward spiral in which scholars become ever more enmeshed
in the pursuit of historical details and heated disputes over its interpretation, endangering the formulation of more general, let alone theoretical,
understandings. Clifford Geertz captured the dynamic well in his "Indian
story—at least I heard it as an Indian story—about an Englishman who,
having been told that the world rested on a platform which rested on the
back of an elephant which rested in turn on the back of a turtle, asked ...
what did the turtle rest on? Another turtle. And that turtle? 'Ah, Sahib, after that it is turtles all the way down'" (Geertz, 1973:28–29).

Historians themselves have long recognized the trap. "If the historian
has a responsibility not only to work in a context of infinite items of data
but also of an infinity of attendant circumstances for each item of data, his
only criterion of selection," David M. Potter (1973:25) observed, "must be
the significance of the points which he chooses to emphasize. But we have
no yardstick for measuring significance." New institutionalists and state
theorists are also aware of the problem. In *Rediscovering Institutions*, March
and Olsen (1989:17) declare that they wish to propose "a more independent role for political institutions. The state is not only affected by society
but also affects it." To that end, they attempt to structure induction by providing a de facto research agenda that will keep the goal of empirically
testable theory in sight (March and Olsen, 1984:747). In fact, greater communication between theories of American politics might also advance
that goal.

For the most part, rational choice proceeds deductively, having as its
starting point certain explicit and implicit assumptions about human nature, behavioral tendencies, and constraints that limit the ambit of those
tendencies. From these assumptions one deduces, by means of logic, testable propositions on the subject at hand. Empiricism is the crucial test of
whether these propositions can be confirmed or disconfirmed, which depends upon whether they do or do not correspond with the evidence at
hand or do or do not predict a future course of events. History, with its
longer range and fuller set of data, brings with it the potential of being a
source of especially rigorous empirical testing, even for the great majority
of rational choice propositions that are explicitly aimed at explaining only

contemporary institutional phenomena. For these propositions, it can supply important evidence for or against their historical assumptions that the Congress of today is very different from previous Congresses. It can also suggest that these time-bound propositions might also be formulated more generally to explain other periods of history, thereby enhancing their ability to account for a larger *n*.

Let us illustrate how rational choice theory has benefited from these and other advantages by examining historical tests of the dominant rational choice paradigm of the contemporary Congress, as exemplified in David Mayhew's (1974) elegant formulation of an electoral connection. Mayhew argues that the components of today's fragmented, individualistic House and Senate are the products of modern members' interrelated goals of congressional careers and reelection, which they pursue by engaging in certain political and institution-building behavior. Does Mayhew's formulation stand the test of time, that is, does a longer range and fuller set of data confirm or disconfirm the accuracy of its explanation of the contemporary Congress or its potential for generalizability? Many argue that it stands the test of time in both respects. For example, in their examination of diachronic electoral patterns, John Alford and David Brady (1989) lend important historical support to Mayhew's contentions that incumbents' electoral advantage is a uniquely contemporary advantage and that the electoral connection is thus a unique congressional phenomenon. In addition, Brady (1988), Charles Stewart (1989), Wilson (1986), and others contend that in a more generalized form, the fundamental assumption that members of Congress are self-interested seekers of political gain can also go far in explaining different dimensions of congressional behavior in the late nineteenth century through the twentieth century; they thereby also argue that the electoral connection formulation is far more robust than its original application would have suggested.

Of course, not all scholars agree. Some have argued that although political careerism and careerist behavior (Swift, 1987–1988) as well as high re-election rates (Huckabee, 1989) extend back to the earliest Congresses, these behavior patterns failed to foster the decentralized structure and weak partisanship the electoral connection predicts. Do these and other disagreements vitiate the importance of history as a source of empirical substantiation? Might historical disagreements also fall for the allure of the arcane, producing more and more detailed historical research with fewer and fewer historical implications? We believe not. As long as historical inquiry is pursued either through deductive approaches, such as rational choice theory, or through inductive approaches, such as state and organization theory, and is structured by a theory-generated research agenda, then disagreements of this sort can only lead to the same theoretical benefits of rigor that scholarly controversies over contemporary evidence produce.

If deductive theorists can more easily avoid the allure of the arcane, they more easily fall for the allure of the ahistorical. The nature of rational choice approaches heightens an already powerful temptation political scientists feel to perceive America's past from a largely contemporary perspective. Let us more closely examine this point by first looking at why political scientists might find it tempting to view American history ahistorically. Although the United States is a dynamic country that has undergone a significant amount of change, as noted above it has also enjoyed enormous stability. Stable political elements include national institutions more than two centuries old. The continuous existence of those institutions, many features of which have endured to the present day, tempts political scientists to believe explanations of contemporary institutions could also be extended to their very similar historical counterparts with little or no adjustment.

So, for example, a political scientist with a theory of presidential vetoes of congressional legislation might be tempted to extend that theory by beginning with Washington's administration. After all, it is certainly true that from the start, the Constitution has guaranteed presidents the veto power and throughout time presidents have used it. Such an extension would, however, be fundamentally misguided. Early presidents up to and including John Quincy Adams (1825–1829) exercised the veto only if they had constitutional objections, which was a very narrow perception of its legitimate application compared to the far more liberal view subsequent presidents have held. Beginning with Andrew Jackson (1829–1837), most exercised it on the grounds of policy objections as well. A theory of presidential vetoes ignoring this shift in philosophy would therefore have as its dependent variable a mix of apples and oranges.

Deductive theories like rational choice increase the understandable, but unfortunate, temptation political scientists feel to use American history ahistorically. As explained above, rational choice theory increasingly looks to the past to test propositions logically deduced from certain assumptions. Although these assumptions and resulting propositions are often expressed in a relatively abstract, seemingly timeless manner, they are informed by a subtle, implicit, but unmistakably modern day perspective that in turn invites the seductively easy use of American history from a modern day, in other words ahistorical, perspective.

Let us illustrate with a simple example. Suppose a rational choice theorist makes the assumption that presidents have as their goal boosting their political popularity. Moreover, as rational politicians, they act in ways to promote their goal. Our theorist then advances the proposition that presidents will try to limit their association with polarizing political issues. To test this proposition, for very good reasons the theorist selects James Monroe as one of the cases: He was an extremely popular president, who in 1820 won nearly unanimous reelection in the electoral college, and his administration (1817–1825) coincided with one of American history's most divisive issues, the Missouri controversy. From an historical perspective, this case would indeed appear to confirm the proposition. During the two years the Missouri controversy was considered in Congress, Monroe for the most part avoided public involvement and even privately played an ancillary role. With the proposition apparently confirmed, our theorist would likely stop there. However, a closer reading of history would undermine this confirmation. Many antebellum, late nineteenth, and even a few early twentieth century presidents philosophically adhered to a very narrow conception of their office that did not endorse involvement in legislation, which they believed was more properly Congress's constitutional prerogative. Monroe, perhaps the foremost champion of this limited vision of presidential prerogative, viewed even the Missouri Compromise as a congressional, not an executive, responsibility. Therefore, Monroe's role in the Missouri controversy was less a calculation aimed at boosting his political popularity than a part of a consistent pattern of limited involvement in legislating that was in turn tied to his conception of the presidency (Ketcham, 1984; Lowery, 1984).

As the above shows, history is a useful common ground, serving to underscore the very different strengths of inductive and deductive approaches to American national political institutions as well as to call attention to their particular weaknesses. State, organization, and rational choice theorists could easily leave the contributions of history at that, gaining a valuable perspective that would allow them to stop talking past each other and better understand their own, and others', approaches. But we believe that history as common ground could make still another important contribution, providing the impetus for these theories to address their respective weaknesses and incorporate the others' strengths. More specifically, theorists of the state and the new institutionalism could incorporate into their inductive approaches explicit and systematic statements of the theories that guide their analyses, indicating how and why their research does or does not confirm these theories. Doing so would clarify and strengthen the relationship between their rich historical research and the goal of theory building, and help diminish the allure of the arcane. For their part, rational choice theorists could relax deduction in order to sufficiently take into account the breadth and depth of history necessary to formulate plausible, truly generalizable propositions as well as historically appropriate tests. This would help dampen the allure of the ahistorical and encourage legitimate uses of the past.

To elaborate, this is not to suggest that inductive and deductive theorists shed their separate epistemologies and thus jeopardize their considerable contributions to the understanding of institutions and other political phenomena. Rather, it is to suggest wider recognition of the fact that, in practice, there is no such thing as a purely inductive or deductive epistemology. In a purely inductive epistemology, we would derive generalized theory from empirical observations, reasoning "from what we know to be the case in some situations to what might be the case in other situations" (Manheim and Rich, 1991:20). In practice, of course, what connections we make between the concrete and the specific to the general and more abstract are deductively shaped by ideas, assumptions, or other preconceptions based on extant social, political, economic, or other theory. A purely deductive epistemology would explain an event "as a logical consequence of certain axioms and other lawlike statements" (Leege and Francis, 1974:36). However, in practice, deductive approaches rely on empirical knowledge or induction to select those constructs more likely to yield a realistic, plausible explanation.

Although in practice inductive approaches make use of deduction and vice versa, both remain distinct. While inductive approaches such as state theory and the new institutionalism begin with a priori notions, the role played by empirical observation predominates. Theoretically deduced starting points structure research and shape conclusions, but empiricism provides the driving force behind theory building. In a fluid, back and forth manner, adherents of induction adapt theoretical formulations to empirical observations, producing a generalized understanding that is often at variance with its theoretical origins. Similarly, while induction helps rational choice theorists to select empirically realistic assumptions and otherwise construct a plausible proposition, it is deduction that provides the essential theory-building tool. Milton Friedman contends:

> Viewed as a body of substantive hypotheses, theory is to be judged by its predictive power for the class of phenomena which it is intended to 'explain'. ... [T]he only relevant test of the *validity* of a hypothesis is comparison of its predictions with experience. The hypothesis is rejected if its predictions are contradicted ('frequently' or more often than predictions from an alternative hypothesis); it is accepted if its predictions are not contradicted; great confidence is attached to it if it has survived many opportunities for contradiction. Factual evidence can never 'prove' a hypothesis; it can only fail to disprove it, which is what we generally mean when we say, somewhat inexactly, that the hypothesis has been 'confirmed' by experience. (Friedman, 1953:8–9)

CONCLUSION

If in practice epistemologies are synthetic, state theory and the new institutionalism can be more appropriately characterized as inductive-deductive, and rational choice theory as deductive-inductive. This being the case, we believe that state, new institutionalist, and rational choice theory are therefore epistemologically well-positioned to take advantage of what history as common ground reveals. To obviate the allure of the arcane and incorporate some of the strengths of more deductive approaches such as rational choice, state theorists and new institutionalists need not proceed in the classic deductive sequence of positing a priori propositions or hypotheses and then formally testing them to confirm or disconfirm. While classic scientific procedures have their place in the study of politics, they are often too constraining or otherwise ill-suited to apply to the complex phenomena state and new institutionalist theorists typically investigate.

Postfactum theory building offers greater promise in several ways. It lends itself easily to the study of complex phenomena and is also consistent with the general inductive-deductive approach that state and new institutionalist theory already employs: the implicit use of a priori notions to guide empirical research, with the resulting findings forming the base for substantively new understandings. Since the process of state and new institutionalist theory building usually stops there, it invites criticism that its explanations are historically specific or overly concrete; too detailed or inelegant; overly flexible; and nonfalsifiable. Postfactum analysis would address these criticisms by appending two more steps to the theory building process: first, the operationalization of these new understandings into the form of empirically testable claims; and second, the actual testing of such claims using replication or new data (Rosenberg, 1968:222–239). By appending these two steps, postfactum analysis could add much of the rigor of deduction to the rigor of induction that state and new institutionalist theories already offer. Because these two new steps involve the refinement of theory and therefore help underscore the ultimate objective of achieving satisfactory theory, they assist scholars in avoiding the allure of the arcane by reminding them that empirical research is the means to an end, not an end in itself.

To avoid the allure of the ahistorical and incorporate the strengths of state and new institutionalist theory, rational choice could and should use history to build more realistic, plausible propositions. What does the inductive use of history require? Certainly it presumes a command of the facts, which includes accurate identification of people, places, and events, and facility with historical sources when those facts are as yet unknown or ambiguous. Although a command of the facts can save scholars from the kind of errors that instantly call into question a theory that in other respects might be entirely satisfactory, accuracy by itself will not foreclose the possibility of ahistoricism. What is needed in addition is the quality much state and new institutionalist theory displays: an historical sensibility, or sensitivity to differences between the present and the past much like the awareness for cross-cultural variations that comparativists have learned to cultivate. As a novelist once observed, the past is a foreign country. Even in a nation as young as the United States, the span of history contains such classic cross-cultural differences as language, behavior, and thought. To begin with, take language. While Americans in the late eighteenth century also spoke English, they used such words as *faction, party, president, bicameralism, senate,* and other words to connote or mean something very different than they do today. Thus, for example, only ahistorical rational choice theorists would mistakenly generalize from the founders' understanding of political parties to political parties today. While the term remains the same, by political parties the framers of the Constitution meant evil, divisive factions that could destroy the unity a republic required. This is very different than conceiving of parties as political organizations whose competition preserves democracy, which is the far more favorable meaning that Martin Van Buren formulated, and the meaning Americans still continue to favor (Hofstadter, 1969).

Not only words, but actions can have a very different meaning. For example, although political bargaining of the past can resemble bargaining of the present, opportunities for bargaining and the bargain itself were structured by very different circumstances and norms. To illustrate, in 1825 Speaker Henry Clay was widely believed by contemporaries to have thrown his support in the U.S. House of Representatives' presidential election to candidate John Quincy Adams in exchange for a cabinet seat. Today we would see that as a shrewd quid pro quo on Clay's part. However, given the circumstances of the 1820s—barely ten years following one war with Great Britain and within a generation of the American Revolution—it was popularly viewed as a "corrupt bargain" that violated the separation of powers, reminiscent of British political "corruption" in which the ministry interfered with the legislature by attempting to directly influence the parliamentary rank and file. The "corrupt bargain" helped to keep Clay out of the White House for the rest of his life.

In the past, people also thought differently, with direct implications for rational choice theory, which assumes that egoistic individuals rationally maximize self-interest, conceived either narrowly or broadly enough to encompass even altruism (Downs, 1957:27–28). How do egoistic individuals decide where their-self interest lies? Rational choice is largely silent on the subject, although Jon Elster has observed that individuals do not decide either autonomously or atomistically (Elster, 1986:23; see also England, 1989). A look back to the past does not supply a definitive source either, but it does underscore how historically contingent or contextual goals have been over time. Political scientists, for instance, have long noted the changing contours of congressional careers: In the late eighteenth and most of the nineteenth century, the majority of members of Congress voluntarily chose to leave office, often to pursue other political offices on the state or national levels. They were, in other words, nonspecialists. By the late nineteenth and early twentieth centuries, the pattern of nonspecialization reversed itself. Increasingly, members were opting to stay put in Congress in significant numbers (Price, 1971, 1975).

If the basic impulse of self-interest can be assumed to be intrinsic to human nature, how did politicians come to concomitantly recalculate their self-interest along the same lines? Some scholars have pointed to what they view as increasingly obliging environmental factors, including a newly important national government, weakening party competition and discipline, and even improving living conditions in Washington, D.C. These factors, they observe, allowed members of Congress to entertain the possibility of making congressional office a career in ways they never could before. Closer to the target, others have pointed to the late nineteenth century development of growing careerism in a host of other pursuits, including the law, architecture, medicine, and the ministry (Hofstadter, 1955; Larson, 1977; Wiebe, 1967). They suggest that larger socioeconomic forces of specialization and professionalization may have played an important, and perhaps primary, role in the reformulation of members' goals as well (Kernell, 1977; Swift and Brady, 1991). Whether the impetus for congressional careerism lies in socioeconomic patterns of specialization as well as in other factors, the larger point remains that individuals do not act in a vacuum. They, and their goals, are very much shaped by their times.[2]

The deductive approach of rational choice can only be strengthened by incorporating these and other inductive insights on the uses of history into the process of theory building. To ignore historical differences in how people spoke, behaved, and thought, and to treat the past as if it were the present, is ahistorical, that is to say, inaccurate and artificial. Ahistorical scholarship should not and cannot be used to formulate or confirm useful social science theory.

History as common ground, of course, will never erase differences among approaches. Even as state, new institutionalist, and rational choice theories turn to the past, sharp distinctions remain. Nonetheless, their increasing use of history provides a valuable opportunity for institutionalists to start talking to adherents of other approaches, as opposed to talking past them. As we have argued in this chapter, this dialogue could provide the comparative basis for a fresh examination of the respective strengths and weaknesses of state, new institutionalist, and rational choice theory, and of efforts to improve each theory. Ultimately, we believe our understanding of American national political institutions past, present, and future would be better for it.

NOTES

1. For a critique of state theory's treatment of legislatures, see McDonagh (1990).

2. For the same conclusion derived from the study of other institutions, see March and Olsen (1989, chap. 9) and Mather (1990).

PART II

Macroanalysis

5

American Exceptionalism Reconsidered: Culture or Institutions?

SVEN H. STEINMO

America is one of the world's richest nations, yet its government takes a smaller percentage of this wealth than does any other democratic government in the world. I believe that the most obvious and common explanation for America's exceptionally small state—that we have a uniquely individualistic political culture—is wrong. It is clearly true that the rhetoric and symbolism of individualism is particularly strong in America. And it is also true that Americans are increasingly skeptical of their public institutions. I do not think, however, that these values and attitudes explain the size and structure of America's welfare state.

This chapter will present an institutionalist explanation for this country's small welfare state. I will suggest that the fragmentation of political power in America biases the political system in favor of certain kinds of interests and strategies, while it disadvantages others. This fragmentation profoundly shapes who can effectively participate in politics, how they must be organized, and what is possible to achieve— *irrespective of our ideologies or values*. I argue further that the fragmentation of power and authority has stripped our political system of efficacy. When American governments do act, they too often act badly. In short, Americans have come to distrust their government because it doesn't work very well.

POLITICAL CULTURE
AS AN EXPLANATORY VARIABLE

The cultural explanation for American exceptionalism is both plausible and logical: America is a country founded by immigrants who sought to escape oppressive governments. These people, moreover, were the most individualistic and entrepreneurial members of the societies they left. Thus America was built on antistatist beliefs and attitudes, on an unwillingness to defer to authority, and with emphasis on liberal freedoms and values. Due to these political-cultural assumptions, Americans are simply more individualistic, resistant to accepting state intervention in their society, and unwilling to let the government step in the way of the private market. In fact, "the state plays a more limited role in America than elsewhere because Americans, more than other people, want it to play a limited role" (King, 1973b:418).

I believe, however, that using political culture as an explanatory variable poses several thorny analytic issues. Generally, political cultural explanations tend to be highly static. The power of this theory, for example, lies in large part in its elegance: America is different because it has always been different. Although this simplicity makes an intuitively appealing proposition, it also leaves much to be explained. First, the liberal traditions explanation fails to either explain or account for political change. Secondly, in that political cultures consist of a mix of often contradictory or competing ideas and values, culturalists fail to provide a convincing explanation for why certain parts of the political culture become dominant in certain times or policy arenas, while others are more prominent elsewhere. Finally, proponents of this approach tend to be quite vague about the causal mechanisms at work when evoking political culture as an independent variable. It is not enough to know that Americans hold different beliefs or world views than other peoples; we also need to understand how these beliefs are translated into real policy choices. Given all these problems, perhaps we should not be surprised that political culture can be used to explain an enormous variety of different outcomes (Elkins and Simeon, 1979).

These flaws, when added together, force us to reject political culture as an explanation for American exceptionalism. I will instead suggest that the institutionalist approach provides a more compelling account for the exceptional character of American politics and policies. I will not argue that American political culture is the same as that of other industrialized democracies; rather, I suggest that cultural differences do not provide an adequate explanation of political differences between nations. An institutional account, in contrast, can explain both how and why particular policies are chosen at particular moments in political history as well as show why certain patterns tend to persist within nations over time.

Cultural Change

The static quality of the liberal exceptionalism explanation is in some ways quite surprising given the historical emphasis and analytic traditions of the central proponents of this argument. Still, as it is normally conceived, the liberal traditions argument is profoundly ahistorical. The argument is essentially that the United States began with a liberal political culture and that the ideas ensconced at that time continue to shape political debate and public policy today. Again, this explanation can be intuitively quite appealing. But if we begin to think through the analytic logic of this explanation we are forced to question the mechanisms supposedly at work here. What is the mechanism for the transmission and continuation of a political culture? Culturalists do not, of course, simply argue that each generation simply passes a set of fixed beliefs down to the next; their argument is substantially more sophisticated. In one of the most interesting attempts to defend culturalist theory against charges that it is too static,[1] Harry Ekstein tells us:

> Culturalists proceed from a *postulate of "cumulative" socialization*. This means two things. First, although learning is regarded as continuous throughout life (which is not likely to be questioned) early learning—all prior learning— is regarded as a sort of filter for later learning: early learning conditions later learning and is harder to undo. Second, a tendency is assumed toward making the bits and pieces of cognitive, affective, and evaluative learning form a coherent (consistent, consonant) whole. (1988:791)

In short, what we learn from our family and in our early years growing up profoundly shapes our perceptions of the world and our understanding of our experiences in later life. Thus, basic values and attitudes about things like self-reliance, individuality, and respect for and deference to authority are learned early in life and can act as filters through which we interpret our world as adults. Precisely because these cultural values are general and not specific interpretations they can be handed down from one generation to the next.

Although the continuity suggested in this explanation is appealing, it also engenders suspicion. Is it reasonable to expect that these basic interpretive filters are handed down through multiple generations without being adapted, changed, or even fundamentally altered over the course of history?[2] Explicitly recognizing this weakness in cultural theory, Ronald Inglehart, in his most recent book, *Cultural Shift in Advanced Industrial Societies*, examines changes in political culture in postindustrial society. Not only does he discover that cultures do change, but he also suggests a mechanism which should make us rethink the static quality of the liberal exceptionalism argument. He tells us that while generational learning is clearly important, "a people's world view does not depend solely on what their elders teach them; rather it is shaped by their entire life experience, and sometimes the formative experiences of a younger generation differ profoundly from those of previous generations" (Inglehart, 1989:4).

The point here is that values, culture, and attitudes *change with experience*. Thus, it cannot be enough to say that America is a nation founded on a set of liberal values and *therefore* we hold those values today (and therefore we have a small welfare state). To the extent that we find strong liberal and individualistic tenets in American political culture in the late twentieth century one needs to explain more than their origins. We need to also understand what it is about the American experience that has encouraged Americans to reinterpret these general values into antistatist policy preferences.

Which Values? Whose Values?

Any nation's political culture obviously contains a mix of different values, beliefs, attitudes, and so on. Seymour Martin Lipset, one of this country's most astute students of American political culture, depicts this culture as follows: "The United States is organized around an ideology which includes a set of dogmas about the nature of a good society. ... That ideology can be subsumed in four words: anti-statism, individualism, populism, and egalitarianism" (Lipset, 1991:16). The conflicts between the constituent parts of American political culture present several problems for culturalist explanation. First, as Russell Hanson points out in Chapter 6, in a country as large and diverse as the United States, different values can appear dominant in different parts of the country at different points in history. Hanson's essay very convincingly shows us that American Social Security policy was not the product of the predominance of liberal values in the United States, but instead was more reflective of traditionalist values of a particular segment of American society. By citing Piven and Cloward —"The South was nothing less than triumphant in shaping the nation's social welfare policy"—Hanson reminds us to ask the question, Whose values? even if we accept the power of values in an explanatory model (cited in Hanson, 1993:35).

In my view, this problem represents the tip of an intellectual iceberg for culturalist theory. As Hanson shows, all complex polities consist of different people with different values, orientations, and ways of interpreting the world. The United States in particular presents a confusing and complex conglomeration of cultures. Even to the extent that it is now true, as Michael Thompson, Richard Ellis, and Aaron Wildavsky (1990) have recently suggested, that the American polity is dominated by "individualists" and those who hold the competing hierarchical or communitarian cultures are subordinate, we can still wonder why. If there are competing cultural interpretations of the world even within the United States, what explains the fact that one culture is dominant? In other words one could agree that values are important for politics but still question why a particular set of values appears to be winning.

The majority of those analysts who have examined American political culture have specifically argued that ours is a mixed bag. In their superb empirical examination of American public values, *The American Ethos*, Herbert McClosky and John Zaller argue that it is precisely the conflict between liberal and egalitarian values that defines American political culture. It is worth citing at length from their book:

However vital the roles of democracy and capitalism have been in American life, not all of the values incorporated into the ethos are mutually consistent and harmonious. Value conflicts, after all, are endemic to all complex societies, including the United States. Among the most important of these, as we have suggested, are the conflicts that arise from the differing perspectives of the two traditions. Capitalism is primarily concerned with maximizing private profit, while democracy aims at maximizing freedom, equality, and the public good. From this difference, others follow. Capitalism tends to value each individual according to the scarcity of his talents and his contribution to production; democracy attributes unique but roughly equivalent value to *all* people. Capitalism stresses the need for a reward system that encourages the most talented and industrious individuals to earn and amass as much wealth as possible; democracy tries to ensure that all people, even those who lack outstanding talents and initiative, can at least have a decent livelihood. Capitalism holds that the free market is not only the most efficient but also the fairest mechanism for distributing goods and services; democracy upholds the rights of popular majorities to override market mechanisms when necessary to alleviate social and economic distress. (McClosky and Zaller, 1984:7)

It is simply not the case that all Americans have always shared a common liberal antistate orientation. Indeed much of American history can be and has been interpreted as a conflict over which set of values would hold force. To the extent that liberal or antistate values or ideologies appear dominant at any point in time, we need to understand these as the products of powerful political struggles, not as if there were some massive, consistent, and overwhelming consensus dictating these values and attitudes.[3]

In a fascinating recent article, Richard Ellis (1992:827) shows that even the teachings of John Locke can and have been interpreted in radically different ways throughout American history. He tells us, for example: "Locke's notion that laws should secure to each man the fruits of his labor can be harnessed to competing cultural visions. It can be used by individualists to justify the right of each man to keep what he has acquired, but it can also be employed by egalitarians to attack large concentrations of wealth on the grounds that such holdings are not derived from productive labor."

Thus, even if Lockean liberalism has held some kind of special place in the hearts and minds of Americans, the substantive implications of these beliefs remain far from clear. Indeed, radical egalitarians from Thomas Paine to the Populists either echoed or directly borrowed from Locke's ideas on private property: "A Lockean consensus on private property does not, in short, translate into a consensus on a competitive individualist way of life. That egalitarians in the United States only infrequently reject private property in favor of collective ownership should not obscure the strength of egalitarianism in this country nor the often thoroughgoing nature of their critique of competitive capitalism" (Ellis, 1992:844).

Can Culture Explain Policy?

Most culturalists readily agree that cultural predispositions are not clear or unambiguous guides to public policy.[4] Indeed, quite the contrary: "The values of the ethos, however, are not in themselves sufficient to determine policy. The values of capitalism and democracy, as usually stated, are too general and abstract, and too often in conflict with one another, to provide more than general guidance on specific issues" (McClosky and Zaller, 1984:12).

Early in the century national health insurance (NHI), for example, was widely defended with an argument quite similar to that used to support the extension of free public education, that is, that it supported the vaunted American value of equal opportunity. The failure of the early versions of NHI had more to do with interstate competition, the medical industry's opposition, Congressional deadlock, and financial constraints, than with public preferences or values (Poen, 1979; Brown, 1979; Marmor, 1970). Only after an enormous public relations campaign financed by the American Medical Association in the 1940s and 1950s, did NHI become tagged with the un-American label "socialized medicine." This massively funded public relations campaign worked. Since the late 1940s, those who have labored for NHI have, in effect, been saddled with defending an "un-American" program, albeit one which is "necessary anyway" (Marmor, 1970). In short, free public education succeeded and became as American as apple pie, while health care became associated with an intrusive state—but not because of fundamental differences in these two types of policies. Instead, private education did not have a wealthy and powerful organized interest group that could use the checks and balances of the American political system to veto this legislation.

If the ethos, ideology, values, or political culture are vague and even contradictory guides to particular public policy outcomes, is it reasonable to argue that these are independent variables which can explain the peculiar nature and structure of the American welfare state as a whole? I think not. In sum, while the liberal traditions argument is intuitively appealing, closer examination proves it inadequate. In the following sections of this chapter I will present an explanation for American exceptionalism, which in my view is substantially more convincing.

HOW EXCEPTIONAL IS AMERICA?

The first thing that we have to understand about the modern American welfare state is that it is not all that different from its European counterparts. We need to be conscious of this point or our explanations may go afield by explaining too much. It is not the case that other democracies have created massive social welfare programs that have never been attempted or considered in the United States. It is not the case that other democratic governments intervene in the society or the economy in ways fundamentally different than the American government does. Nor is it the case that other democratic states address problems that American governments simply ignore. It is instead the case that American governments (I mean to emphasize the plurality of governments in the United States) have taken somewhat different approaches to public policy problems than have most European governments. American governments tend to spend somewhat less, and do somewhat less, to address the social and economic problems faced in all advanced industrial nations.[5] American governments do provide public housing, public health, public education, and direct financial assistance to the poor, the aged, the disabled, and the unemployed, but these programs tend to be less well-funded[6] and less comprehensive than those typical in European countries.

It is also easy to overstate and oversimplify the differences between European and American public attitudes and preferences. While it is quite clear that Americans today hold a general distrust of their government, it is far from clear that this distrust has been consistent over time or that this distrust has always been greater in America than elsewhere. The Progressive Era, the New Deal, and the 1960s are each examples of periods when great masses of Americans rose demanding state intervention in the society and the economy. Moreover, it is far from clear that citizens of other democracies have an abiding and enduring trust in their states as is often implied by American scholars. Indeed, as recently as the 1960s Americans showed they trusted their government to do the right thing more often than citizens in most other democracies.

While Americans do hold more negative attitudes toward "welfare" as a general survey category than is typical in most European states (Coughlin, 1980), it not true that they oppose specific social welfare programs. On the contrary, as Table 5.1 demonstrates, when asked about specific social welfare programs, the majority of Americans wants to see them expanded or maintained and does not favor cutting them back.

Interestingly, as Table 5.2 indicates, the proposition that citizens generally want to maintain, but not massively expand, the particular social welfare programs they have at any given time holds for Swedes as well as Americans.

We might question whether Americans have opposed the introduction or expansion of social welfare programs in the past, when Europeans have historically demanded them. Once again, the data do not support this assumption. As Hugh Heclo's (1974) detailed analysis of the development of social welfare programs in Britain and Sweden has shown, these programs have been introduced in Europe by political and administrative

TABLE 5.1   Public Support for Increasing, Maintaining, or Decreasing Benefits for Seven Social Welfare Programs in the United States, 1986

	Percent of Respondents Who Say Program Benefits Should Be		
	Increased	*Maintained*	*Decreased*
Medicare	67.6	29.9	2.5
Supplemental security income	57.3	40.0	2.7
Social Security	56.7	40.0	3.3
Medicaid	47.1	46.3	6.6
Unemployment compensation	31.5	55.5	13.0
Aid to families with dependent children	32.6	51.9	15.5
Food stamps	24.6	51.0	24.4

Source: Adapted from Fay Lomax Cook, "Congress and the Public: Convergent and Divergent Opinions on Social Security," in Henry Aaron, ed., *Social Security and the Budget* (Lanham, Md.: University Press of America, 1988), p. 86.

TABLE 5.2   Attitudes Toward Social Program Expenditure, Sweden, 1982

Revenues from taxation are used for different purposes. Do you consider that the amount of money used for the purposes mentioned on this card should be increased, remain unaltered, or decreased?

	Increased	*Remain Unaltered*	*Decreased*	*Don't Know/ Won't Answer*
Medical and health care	45	50	3	2
Support for the elderly	30	67	1	2
Support for families with children	31	55	12	2
Social assistance	16	58	21	5
Housing allowances	13	46	36	5

Source: Adapted from Axel Hadenius, *A Crisis of the Welfare State? Opinions About Taxes and Public Expenditure in Sweden* (Stockholm: MiniMedia AB, 1986), p. 85.

elites in their efforts to solve particular public problems and were not the product of specific demands for particular programs or solutions.

Table 5.3 illustrates another dimension of this issue. It shows that for most of the past two decades the majority of Swedish citizens has been opposed to the expansion of social assistance. In this period, however, the Swedish welfare state has exploded—to the point where it is widely regarded as the most generous welfare state in the entire world. During this period, public spending rose from less than 30 percent of gross domestic product (GDP) to more than 50 percent of GDP.

TABLE 5.3   Support for Social Assistance in Sweden, 1960–1979

Social reforms have gone so far in this country that in the future the government ought to reduce rather than increase allowances and social assistance.

	1960	1964	1968	1970	1973	1976	1979
Agree	60	66	46	62	65	65	71
Disagree	40	34	54	39	35	35	29

Source: Walter Korpi, *The Democratic Class Struggle* (London: Routledge and Kegan Paul, 1983), p. 203. Reprinted by permission.

The liberal traditions argument *assumes* that the difference in public output between the European and the American welfare state is a product of the fact that Americans want different policies than Europeans. But in reality there seems to be very little linkage between public attitudes toward specific programs and program development. Some culturalists even admit that: "[T]he American mass public seems to differ hardly at all in this connection from mass publics of other countries. The evidence on this point is, for once, abundant. … the state's comparatively limited provision of social services in the U.S. is not readily attributable to differences in public opinion" (King, 1974b:412–413).

In sum, the American welfare state varies somewhat from most of its European counterparts, but it is very difficult to attribute the variation to clear and consistent differences in public attitudes or preferences. Indeed, as many scholars have shown, there is only a weak connection between public attitudes and specific policy outputs. What then, can explain the differences in policy outputs?

My argument is that the unique constitutional structure established over two hundred years ago pushed the United States toward a polity in which it has been exceedingly difficult to develop and maintain strong political parties, a mass Socialist, Labor, or leftist political movement, and comprehensive, universalistic social welfare policies typical in European welfare states. The result of this institutional fragmentation has been the fragmentation of political authority and responsibility on the one hand, and the proliferation of special interest politics on the other. America has developed a pluralist—even hyperpluralist—system of policymaking. This fragmented pluralist system and the enormous political power it yields interest groups is the reason we have a relatively underdeveloped welfare state.

THE CONSTITUTIONAL FOUNDATIONS
OF AMERICAN EXCEPTIONALISM

It is impossible to understand American society without seeing the formative influence of the Constitution upon it.

—Martin Diamond, *The Founding of the Democratic Republic*

The delegates from the twelve ex-colonies represented at the Constitutional Convention in Philadelphia in 1787 were institutionalists. They believed that the institutional arrangements of a new union (if there was to be a union) would determine more than what kinds of interests would be advantaged or disadvantaged—decisions about these institutions would ultimately also determine what kind of society America would become. Diamond's eloquent analysis of the thinking behind the construction of the United States Constitution reveals the following:

[The word "constitution"] derives from the Latin *statuere* which means to "set up" in the sense of giving a thing its essential and peculiar nature. ... In the ancient tradition, a constitution establishes the fundamental nature or genius of a political system; that is, a constitution is a people's way of life. Thus it consists in the human ends towards which a particular system strives, both by virtue of its positive arrangements as well as by virtue of limits placed upon its rulers. ... And in these ways it shapes the very being of the society and forms the kinds of human beings who live there. (Diamond, 1981:99)

The elites who finally (albeit narrowly) agreed to the particular structure of the United States Constitution were thus ultimately agreeing to a vision of future citizens as well as to a certain design for our political institutions. Drawing from the writings of Montesquieu and Locke, these writers viewed the good society as one with a limited state that would promote liberal values. Montesquieu was particularly interested in the formative capacity of institutions on human nature. Both Locke and Montesquieu believed that limited government was an ideal to be strived for because only limited government could secure the maximum degree of individual freedom, "which was viewed as the highest human possibility" (Diamond, 1981:99).

Not all participants in the Convention, or for that matter, activists in the subsequent debates over ratification, held identical philosophical positions. Quite the contrary, as many constitutional scholars have shown, there was very dramatic conflict over what kinds of institutions should be constructed—in other words, there was deep conflict over what kind of society should be built (Main, 1962; Jillson, 1988; Beard, 1913; J. Smith, 1965). It is widely accepted, moreover, that the particular institutional structures finally agreed to were compromises between various interests (farmers versus industrialists, big states versus small states, and so on) as well as compromises over fundamental ideas about what type of society America should become (liberal versus communitarian, egalitarian versus hierarchical, and so forth). It should be stressed, however, that irrespective of the hallowed position the Constitution now holds in the hearts of Americans, it was not a tablet handed America from heaven and agreed to with acclamation by the whole of society.

Through a long series of hard-fought compromises, the framers of the Constitution finally agreed to a system, which was in James Madison's words, "in strictness neither a national nor a federal constitution, but rather a composition of both" (Madison, Hamilton, and Jay, 1937, *Federalist No. 39*). The key compromise for the new republic was that it was to have a large nation with free trade between states, but at the same time political sovereignty would be constitutionally divided and national power would be severely limited. These basic compromises were not what either the Federalists or the Anti-Federalists had hoped for, but this was the best compromise that these men could achieve, given the very large divisions between them at the time. These compromises, however, had enormous implications for how this nation would adapt to the challenges of a modernizing society and economy more than a century later.

Adapting the Constitution to the Modern World

Nothing could have prepared either European or American political elites at the end of the eighteenth century for the huge social and economic changes that their countries would undergo in the next century and a half. During this period, modernizing countries changed from being mostly rural and agricultural to becoming increasingly urban and industrial societies. Modernization brought with it new demands for the expanded involvement of the state in society *in all modernizing countries* (Ashford, 1986; Rimlinger, 1971; Flora and Heidenheimer, 1977; Rueschmeyer, Stephens, and Stephens, 1992; Wilensky, 1975).[7] In each case, these countries witnessed the growth of new ideas on the one hand, and the reconfiguration of the balance of power between economic classes on the other. "In each of these countries surveyed, there was a similar conflict, and each has its own way of managing the tensions created" (Rimlinger, 1971:85). In both Europe and America, middle- and working-class reformers demanded both more responsive political institutions and more efficient government. Political reform was necessary, reformers believed, in order for government to be transformed into a tool of social and economic progress.

To achieve these common ends, however, the specific reform strategies developed in radically different ways. In Europe, where national power was much more centralized and the right to vote had yet to be won, reformers organized themselves into strong programmatic political parties on the one hand, and large, politicized unions on the other—the aim was to gain the right to vote and then seize the reins of national power.[8] In the United States, with its large national economy, its federal division of sovereignty, and its male suffrage, reformers' political strategies took quite a different turn. In this case, democratic reform meant undermining the power of democratic political elites. The following sections will examine exactly why these strategies differed in the ways they did.

Weak Parties

Few would argue with the proposition that one of the central explanations for the laggardly development of the American welfare state is the fact that political parties in America are relatively nonprogrammatic, non-ideological, and internally divided. In the absence of strong political parties, elected officials must cater to local or highly particularistic constituency interests to an extent that is truly unique in the democratic world. Accommodating these interests often means going against the party, its elites, and even its stated goals and ideology. Indeed, even when a single political party nominally controls the Senate, the House, the presidency, and the majority of state legislatures and governorships across the county, there is almost no hope that the party will be able to legislate more than a fraction of its political commitments.

The question, of course, is why the United States does not have strong programmatic political parties, and why in particular a Socialist party never developed in the late nineteenth century here. Certainly, there were Socialist parties and no small measure of mass support for the Left in America in the later decades of the century (Hofstadter, 1963; Bell, 1967; Greenstone, 1969), but for some reason these movements floundered on American shores, while succeeding throughout Europe.

The liberal traditions theorists argue that these movements failed in America because they ran counter to basic American ideology: Communism and socialism offered a vision of the good society that conflicted with American's vision of and for itself. The historical evidence, however, leads us to question this assertion. Indeed, historians who study this era have shown that it was far from the case that liberal ideology was hegemonic in this era (Hattam, 1992; Ross, 1991). Some have even argued that the weakness of socialism in the United States was due to the powerful socialistic tendencies already present in American political culture, that is, "[t]he country's image of itself contained so many socialist elements that one did not have to go to a separate movement opposed to the status quo in order to give vent to socialist emotions" (Harrington, 1972:118). Others have argued that it was America's fantastic wealth that limited the appeal of socialism (Sombart, 1905), whereas still others suggest that ethnic diversity and racism undermined class consciousness (Korpi and Shalev, 1979).

In my view, each of these may have played some role, but a more convincing explanation for the weakness of United States Socialist political parties looks to the institutional context in which the new political demands were filtered and shows how this context shaped both political organization and reform strategies.

In both Europe and the United States, the end of the nineteenth century marked an era spent in intense political conflict, culminating in demands for democratic reform. In Europe, where the franchise had still to be extended beyond the landholding elite, middle- and working-class activists built strong political parties and mobilized around them in order to demand access and representation for the unenfranchised. European democratic reformers wanted to seize the reins of power from the ruling elite, and the best mechanism for doing this was to mobilize the workers and the middle class to form coherent politicized organizations—political parties and labor unions (Rueschemeyer, Stephens, and Stephens, 1992).

The democratic puzzle was different in the United States, in part because of the "free gift of suffrage" (Perlman, 1949, quoted in Lipset 1991:9), which meant there was less to get working class people to mobilize around—to get them angry about.[9] It is equally important, though, that the constitutional structure had given local elites a power base quite apart from the national center. The early extension of the franchise allowed local elites to use the patronage system to control their constituencies and control their members of Congress. Local elites were thus both well-entrenched in democratic and electoral politics and were major stalwarts against progressive reform and governmental activism.[10] This radically altered the task of democratic reformers, who "hoped that people ... would be filled with the desire to do something about corrupt bosses, sweated labor, civic decay, monopolistic extortion. If the people were sufficiently aroused, they would wrest power away from city and state bosses, millionaire senators, and other minions of invisible government and take it back into their own hands" (Hofstadter, 1963:5). Because of this basic decentralization of authority in nineteenth century America, local elites and their party machines were seen as the central obstacles to reform.

In Europe, political parties were perceived quite differently by democratic reformers. Instead of being obstacles to democracy and governmental activism, mass political parties were perceived as the major instruments to bring about democratic reform—a means for making the national government more responsive to reformers' demands and interests.[11] It is also important to recognize that in both Europe and America, governmental reform was intimately tied to the belief that government should be used as an instrument of social and economic progress. Reformers believed that as long as the current elite held power, progress would be stifled. In short, these reformers believed that government could, would, and should become "activist." As Richard Hofstadter (1963:4–5) notes, "They believed that the people of the country should be stimulated to work enthusiastically to bring about social progress, that the positive powers of government must be used to achieve this end." The debate and strategies in America and Europe, then, were quite different, but the goals were not. "Conservatives generally believed in time and nature to bring about progress; Progressives believed in energy and governmental action."[12]

In America, reformers pushed for and eventually won a large set of institutional reforms specifically designed to take power away from the current political elite and the parties that they controlled. In the decades surrounding the turn of the twentieth century, several attempts were made at organizing new political parties, but the Democrats and Republicans proved to be adept at adopting many of the reformers' policy platforms and thus undermining their electoral appeal.[13] We must remember that the localization of power in the United States allowed the two standing parties to be malleable enough to adopt new reform positions—and the consequence was that the two parties were colonized by reformers, and in the end the parties were used as vehicles for undermining their own elites. Among the most important institutional reforms introduced were the direct primary, the Australian ballot, recall elections, citizen initiatives on state ballots, voter registration reform, and the direct election of U.S. Senators (cf. Burnham, 1970).

In Europe, the democratic impulse had quite different effects. Rather than attempting to break the link between parties and government, reformers worked to mobilize the unenfranchised into newly formed political parties that could then take over government. Since the vast majority of the public was excluded from the right to vote, the traditional parties could less easily absorb working- and middle-class interests and demands into their platforms. Democratic reformers, at the same time, saw the political potential in organizing separately from the small ruling elite then in power. Why join the enemy when you outnumber him ten to one? As working-class parties grew and as the pressures for broadening the franchise mounted, it quickly became obvious that these parties would one day run the government.[14] In these cases reformers had no incentive to neuter political parties—quite the contrary, they could easily see that they would soon be able to use this power to effect social and economic change.

In sum, democratic reformers in Europe sought political reforms that could enable and strengthen mass-based political parties, hoping to make their political systems more democratic and responsive. Democratic reformers in the United States, in contrast, sought policies that would weaken political parties in order to achieve precisely the same goals.

Weak Labor

Another distinctive feature of twentieth century American politics has been both the weakness of trade unions and the antipolitical strategy they adopted late in the nineteenth century. European unions tend to be much larger and stronger than their American counterparts; moreover, they have been active forces in supporting Socialist political parties, and in pushing for welfare state programs. The weakness and timid political strategy adopted by American unions is often seen as a critical variable that helps explain why American politics has not been pushed further to the left.

The liberal traditions argument posits that the size and strategy of American unions is a result of our cultural individualism as well of our belief in the market as opposed to the state; in short, Americanism conflicted with politicized unionism. Once again, the historical evidence tells a somewhat different story. The structure and strategy of American unions is instead best understood as a rational adaptation to the institutional realities within which they were forced to operate.

In this case it was the decision of the Founding Fathers to create a large federal nation—a country with divided sovereignty and structural limits on national political authority—that altered the strategic choices of working-class organizers as America industrialized. The unique American federalist structure directly impinges upon the ability to organize unions because this system creates a discrepancy between political and economic power. Size, of course, is often presented as a major explanation of America's exceptionalism, but we must remember that to have a large federal union was an explicit institutional choice. Madison, arguing for the adoption of the Constitution in *Federalist No. 10*, put the issue most bluntly:

> The smaller the society, the fewer will be the distinct parties and interests composing it; the fewer the distinct parties and interests, the more frequently will a majority be found of the same party; and the smaller the number of individuals composing a majority, and the smaller the compass within which they are placed, the more easily they will concert and execute their plans of oppression. Extend the sphere and you take in a greater variety of parties and interests; you make it less probable that a majority of the whole will have a common motive to invade the rights of other citizens; or if such a common motive exists, it will be more difficult for all who feel it to discover their own strength and to act in unison with each other. (Madison, Hamilton, and Jay, (1937), Federalist No. 10:83)

With the Connecticut Compromise, the Founders specifically agreed to a large national economy in which the national government would still have relatively limited powers. They built, in short, a polity in which commerce, trade, industry, and employers could travel across state boundaries, but state laws could not. As Theodore Lowi (1984:46) points out, "[e]ven a cursory review of the policies of state governments in the nineteenth century quickly demonstrates that the 'reserve powers' amounted to virtually all of the important government in the United States. ... Those features of capitalism about which a proletarian consciousness presumably develops—such as the laws against trespass and obstruction, laws against any interference with individual contract, laws against conspiracies to organize to control labor against subsistence wages—were state laws. Laws justifying legal violence were state laws."

In other industrializing nations the political battles were for worker protection and the right to organize, and they were national battles. In the United States these were state battles. This difference sets up radically different political and economic constraints and incentives. In the United States, as soon as a state would consider the interests and demands of working-class reformers, capital would threaten to leave the state for other states with a "more favorable" environment. Thus, this form of federalism dramatically enhanced the "exit" option for capital, and in so doing dramatically biased the game against strong working-class organization. American unions developed the peculiarly 'voluntaristic' strategy late in the last century as a conscious response to these political realities.

There were, of course, several quite militant working organizations that attempted to organize in the United States despite the institutional obstacles. But in each case these unions were repeatedly beaten back by either private or public armies representing the interests of employers who routinely used new immigrants to replace organized workers (Greenstone, 1969; Shalev and Korpi, 1980). But much more important than the violent opposition unions had to overcome were the institutional obstacles they faced.[15] The most important of these was the power of the Federal courts to overrule state legislation. Victoria Hattam (1992), for example, shows that it was only after the courts had overruled legislative victories in several industrial states that labor organizers decided to adopt the voluntarist approach. Adolf Strasser, one of the early union advocates for the voluntarist approach, explicitly argued that legislation was futile in the American political context:

> "There is one fact that cannot be overlooked" he exhorted during a debate over the demand for an eight-hour work day at the A.F of L.'s 1894 convention. "You cannot pass a general eight-hour day without changing the constitution of the United States and the constitution of every State of the Union. ... I hold that we cannot propose to wait with the eight-hour movement until we secure it by law. ... I am opposed to wasting our time declaring for legislation being enacted for a time possibly after we are dead. I want to see something we can secure while we are alive." (cited in Hattam, 1992:164)

Indeed even noted voluntarist American Federation of Labor (AFL) chairman Samuel Gompers was an "economic determinist" who was profoundly class-conscious.[16] But Gompers was a pragmatist and not an individualist ideologue. This pragmatism grew out of rational calculation of what he believed was possible within the political and economic context he saw in America in the late 1800s. From his experiences he concluded that "the concentration of economic power is an inevitable fact of industrial capitalism. Labor could try to hedge in, but not challenge, the power of the rising new class" (Bell, 1967:37).

By the 1890s Gompers, once an advocate of political unionism, had resorted to voluntarism in response to the past failures of a more political strategy (Hattam, 1992). "[The AFL] is guided by the history of the past," Gompers replied, when questioned by Socialist Congressman, Morris Hillquit, "drawing its lessons from history, to know of the conditions by which the working people are surrounded and confronted; to work along the lines of least resistance; to accomplish the best results in improving the condition of the working people."[17] He saw these experiences as evidence that a political strategy could not work in this country. Why? The necessary political alliances with farmers, greenbackers, small businessmen, intellectuals, and others "merely sucked the worker into the vortex of a swiftly rising political whirlwind, lifted him high, and dumped him unceremoniously when its force was spent" (Bell, 1967:37).

In short, the dominant American unions' commitment to voluntarism was pragmatic, not ideological. The decision was not based on a belief in liberal ideas or individualism, or on a commitment to market principles, but instead grew out of deep skepticism about the possibilities for a successful political strategy, given the American political and economic context. Hattam, in a superb comparison of early British and American union strategies, argues similarly: "After almost a century of parallel development, the English and American labor movements began to adopt quite different strategies, largely in response to the pattern of frustrations and rewards that flowed from the political systems within which they organized" (Hattam, 1992:178).

Weak Government

The final key feature of American politics that is necessary to explain the relative underdevelopment of this county's welfare state is the fragmentation of political power within national decisionmaking institutions. Clearly, weakness of the political parties is part of this story, but it is equally important to recognize that inside the halls of Congress power is institutionally fragmented and decentralized. American political history is brimming with cases in which there was widespread majority agreement in Congress that a particular reform was desirable, but recalcitrant key members—who clearly did not represent the majority view—were able to radically slow the process down, reshape the proposals in important and meaningful ways, and even sometimes prevent reform from becoming law.[18] The institutional fragmentation of power inside the halls of Congress yields a degree of political power to individual members that would be unthinkable in any other democratic system in the world.

How and why did we develop these kinds of decisionmaking institutions in the United States, while European democracies became more centralized and elitist? In this case the culturalists would argue that America's liberal ideology does not provide the best explanation, rather, it is the egalitarianism of our political culture which is to blame. I argue instead that the constitutional separation of powers provides the foundation for an explanation, but we must also examine the ways in which Congress and the executive branch adapted during the eighteenth century to the new needs and demands of an increasingly complex industrial democracy.

Premodern legislatures throughout the world were loosely structured, decentralized, and relatively unspecialized, and decisionmaking tended to be informal, which allowed the institutions to be adapted to the particular needs of the time. But as Stephen Skowronek (1982:13) suggests, these institutions were insufficient for the challenges of the modernizing nation. In his study of the modernization of the American state he tells us, "Industrialism, in all its dimensions, exposed severe limitations in the mode of governmental operations that had evolved over the nineteenth century and that supported the powers and prerogatives of those in office."

Whereas the legislature could claim that it was more democratic (and could increasingly open itself up to broader segments of the public in order to demonstrate this point), the executive branch could claim that it alone was capable of managing the turbulence of the times. Once again, all modernizing democracies in the late 1800s were caught between the demand for a more responsive political system on the one hand, and the demand for more efficient decisionmaking institutions on the other. In most countries this dilemma evolved into an institutional battle between the executive and the legislature. European polities eventually addressed this dilemma through the centralization of political authority. By the turn of the century, the balance of power was shifting to parliament. In some cases this process was incremental, and in other cases quite dramatic, but in each case European parliaments demanded greater and greater participation and eventually gained control over the executive functions of government. They specifically demanded and won control over their respective cabinets. The result was that with the growth of increasingly powerful mass-based political parties, a single set of elites could now dominate both the legislative and executive functions of government; in fact, they developed "cabinet government." In this context, then, the demands for more efficient government and for more democratic government could both be accommodated through the centralization of political power.

In the United States, of course, the battle between the executive and the legislature was structured quite differently, largely because the executive and legislative branches of government were constitutionally separated and democratically legitimate. The executive in America was therefore better able to fight off the encroachment of its power by the legislature than were its European counterparts. But this institutional battle only complicated the demand for more efficient government. Congress, we should note, was not populated by strong ideologically united political parties, but instead continued to be fragmented into a multiplicity of regional interests (Sundquist, 1973). Certainly one option would have been that Congress yield authority over substantive policy to the president. But, as Nelson W. Polsby has shown, Congress instead chose to protect its institutional prerogatives, creating an elaborate committee system that devolved political authority for particular policy decisions to individual committees and subcommittees (Polsby, 1968; Polsby, Gallagher, and Rundquist, 1969); they created "committee government."

I have tried to show in the preceding discussion how the basic constitutional structure, the early extension of suffrage, federalism, and the separation of powers shaped the ways in which American political reformers structured responded to the enormous changes witnessed in all modernizing nations at roughly the turn of the last century. Europeans developed strong union movements that could be used as political support for policy activists in their attempts to build welfare state programs. American unions, instead, had much weaker links to the state and sometimes even opposed specific welfare state programs. The United States developed institutional barriers to strong national political parties, but European nations developed coherent ideological parties broadly representing different classes in society. Whereas power within national government became fragmented in the United States, European nations developed cabinet government. As will be discussed, these basic institutional decision-making structures have contributed to the development of different welfare state institutions, and this has contributed to the antistatism so easily observed in America.

THE MODERN AMERICAN WELFARE STATE

In parliamentary terms, one might say that under the U.S. Constitution it is not now feasible to 'form a Government' one formed of an elected majority that is able to carry out an overall program, and is held accountable for its success or failure.
—Lloyd Cutler, "To Form a Government"

The fragmentation of institutional power and responsibility in American politics has had fundamental consequences for the development of the character of American policymaking throughout the twentieth century.[19] Fragmentation weakens political elites' ability to govern effectively. Lloyd Cutter observes: Each member of Congress gains access to his or her own base of institutional power and therefore is less dependent upon those higher up the institutional hierarchy for support. This has meant that it is exceptionally difficult and sometimes impossible for those in leadership positions to push or pull Congress into policy positions— even when a majority of the citizenry and a majority of the political elite desire change.

In more centralized parliamentary systems, individual legislators are bound to support their party's position. This institutional fact gives these same legislators the 'political cover' to support measures that they may find politically distasteful in the short run but that could either strengthen the party or help solve national problems in the long run. The fragmentation of authority in the United States, in contrast, leaves members of Congress individually accountable for their actions. They thus face powerful incentives to pay closer attention to the short-term electoral consequences of their votes than to the long-term policy effects of their actions (cf. Mayhew, 1974; Fiorina, 1977).

> The consequent destruction of the structures, rules, and norms that facilitate broad-gauged deliberative dialogue produced a Congress unable to engage in a reasoned and collective consideration of emerging national problems. In other words, Congress so "adapted" its organizational structures and procedures to the strategic processing of an industrial-era agenda that it weakened or lost those institutional mechanisms necessary for a broad discussion of the problems and governing principles. Lacking such mechanisms, Congress now finds it difficult to discover a new logic of politics that would enable its members to break out of the politics of interest representation and embrace collective solutions to postindustrial policy dilemmas. (Dodd, 1993:429)

Studies of American welfare state development are, in effect, studies of how policy activists have attempted to get around America's uniquely fragmented political institutions in their effort to bring about reform. Any student of American political history knows the essential story line well. Even in cases where the president and both houses of Congress have been controlled by the same political party, the fragmentation of political authority has either entirely prevented reform, or has forced reformers to dramatically scale back their reform ambitions. In every single public policy arena, whether it might be health, housing, or employment policy, or social security, taxation, or whatever, political history tells a common story: Political and administrative reformers design a plan which is radically altered, watered down, or rejected as it moves through the legislative branch. Reformers can be quite persistent and eventually, usually only after many failed attempts and significant alteration of the original plan, they are able to push a bill through both houses.

In the process of bringing in the required congressional support, however, reformers are forced to not only water down the program, but also to provide particular incentives or sweeteners to a huge number of particular constituencies or interests. If the president signs onto the new plan (if he signs it and if the courts don't overturn it), the final program is generally a shadow of the original program. So many compromises and concessions are required along the way that many of the original sponsors are left wondering whether what they got is better than nothing at all—too often, it is not.[20]

In sum, the further fragmentation of Madison's system of checks and balances has contributed to a polity replete with veto points.[21] This has meant a political structure that encourages interests to mobilize in small and narrow interest groups and that disadvantages broad coalitions of interest. This system also gives huge power to interests wishing to stop, alter, or modify governmental action. And this, in turn, has meant that if and when public policies do make it through the labyrinth, they have to accommodate a large number of very specific interests, therefore tending to be far less coherent or efficient than they would have been had they not had to wheedle their way through the labyrinth and past so many veto points. Martha Derthick's study of the development of the American Social Security system demonstrates the ways program activists have had to manipulate and adapt their vision to the political realities caused by the fragmented nature of American politics.

> If they were to build the structure of social protection they believed the nation needed, they had to adapt to their environment without sacrificing essential objectives, and they had to manipulate it without jeopardizing their own legitimacy.
> Their adaptations to the external environment took many forms, of which the incremental mode was probably the most important. They learned not to ask for everything at once. They asked for a piece at a time, and then trimmed the pieces. (Derthick, 1979:206)

The contrasting histories of the American Social Security Act and the Old Age Pension system in Britain could not be clearer. In the British case reformers cloistered themselves from the fray of parliamentary politics precisely because they did not want to have their plan diluted and compromised. Lloyd George and Winston Churchill, working separately on two different parts of the plan, were able to design their system in virtual isolation from the political fray. When the act was finally introduced, the parliament was left on the sidelines. Indeed, according to Heclo (1974:89), "Parliamentary consideration of the government's plan was perfunctory and added nothing of substance." In the American case, "parliamentary considerations," for better or worse, defined the structure of our old age pension system.

Similar contrasts could be drawn with respect to virtually all major public policy arenas. In the United States, reformers must design and adapt their policies to cater to the objections and desires of a huge number of interest groups and congressional constituencies. In parliamentary systems compromises must be made, particularly in the cases of coalition government, but when programs have been decided on by relatively small groups of elites, they can and usually are passed though their respective legislatures with very little substantive change or amendment.

Consider for a moment how different America's social welfare state would be today if Presidents Franklin Roosevelt, Harry Truman, John Kennedy, and Lyndon Johnson could have called the Democratic party leadership together, and with this small group of elites, could have designed and implemented social welfare policies, tax policies, urban renewal policies, and national health insurance policies without needing to tailor these programs to the demands or objections of particular members of Congress and the interest groups they represented. It is difficult to imagine such an outcome precisely because this kind of decisionmaking would be inimical to the twentieth century American system of government. Such a system would undermine America's system of "checks and balances." It would also enhance the power of technocrats and social reformers. It would, quite clearly in my view, contribute to a larger and more efficient welfare state.

THE COSTS OF FRAGMENTATION

There are two deeply troubling consequences of the fragmentation of political authority in America. First, it makes government enormously inefficient. This is not simply an issue of slowing down the process, or choosing incremental decisionmaking over synoptic decisionmaking. Second, although this system of interest group and veto politics too often underfunds and poorly designs programs benefiting broad or general constituencies, it too easily yields enormous particularized benefits, programs, and tax dollars to special interests. On the one hand, citizens see their government spending hundreds of billions of their tax dollars on ineffective programs designed to combat poverty, crime, drugs, public housing, education, infrastructure, and so on. Despite this spending, these problems have not gotten any better and in many cases they have gotten worse. On the other hand, citizens see their tax dollars being spent on pork barrel and a large number of other programs that have only one real justification—the politically powerful interest groups demand them.[22] It should not be difficult to appreciate why citizens in America do not trust public officials with their money. There is simply too much evidence telling them that much—too much—of that money is being wasted and that too few problems are being solved.

In short, policies shape attitudes about public policy. As Karl Polanyi (1957:86–102) argued long ago, when a state does something badly, this becomes an argument for why the state should do less. Or, as Francis Castles (1978) remarks, when a state does something well, this becomes an excellent argument for allowing the state to engage in further activity. Over time these types of historical experiences will shape political culture.

Thus, the more inept and inefficient state policies are over time, the more antistate values are reinforced.

As Inglehart has shown, ideas about politics are learned—they are not genetically inherited, or otherwise passed down unaltered from one generation to the next. Each generation develops its ideas about what is true, what is good, and what is possible by interpreting what they see through what they value. And when we have inherited competing values, such as equality and liberty, or responsibility and liberty, experience helps us decide which values more accurately reflect the reality we experience, and thus, which values we should choose to guide our actions, our behaviors, and our public policies.

Even in the late twentieth century Americans hold conflicted values. But our experience with government increasingly teaches us that these institutions are not trustworthy and that collective solutions do not solve social or economic problems. Americans widely believe that politicians only listen to powerful interest groups and that citizens' general interests are not represented. A multitude of academic studies has confirmed this basic proposition (see typical data in Table 5.4). As a consequence, Americans believe that they don't get what they pay for, and—increasingly—they distrust their state (Ladd et al., 1979; Hochschild, 1981; Eismeier, 1982; McClosky and Zaller, 1984; Crocker, 1981).

CONCLUSION

We rather naively tend to think of a democratic republic as a political system in which the government does what the citizens want it to do.[23] This assumption is too naive for many reasons. First of all, citizens only rarely are clear about what they want; more often their preferences, opinions, and even their values are multiple, conflictual, and vague. Democratic governments must then translate and interpret what their citizens want, and sometimes democratic government must do things that citizens clearly do not want (like raising taxes). A naive understanding of democracy also fails to recognize the substantial power that elites have in evoking and shaping the preferences of ordinary citizens. Governments do not simply wait for citizens to demand public policies; they also set the agenda. Finally, what citizens believe about politics, and what they think is possible and desirable is fundamentally shaped by what government does for them. In other words, what citizens want is in part determined by what they have seen and experienced. Thus if a government is disorganized, inefficient, and ineffective citizens will want it to do different things than they will if their experience tells them that it is efficacious.

The new president, Bill Clinton, entered office on a rising tide of optimism. Much of the nation shares the hope that governmental power can now be harnessed to manage the difficult transition this country will

TABLE 5.4   Public Confidence in Government

Do you think that people in government waste a lot of money we pay in taxes, waste some of it, or don't waste very much of it?

Year	% Replying Wastes a Lot
1964	47
1968	59
1970	69
1972	66
1974	74
1976	74
1978	77
1980	78

Source: Margaret Weir, *Politics and Jobs: The Boundaries of Employment Politics in the United States* (Princeton: Princeton University Press, 1992), p. 159. Reprinted by permission.

have to make as it enters the twenty-first century. However, he faces enormous obstacles to his success. The problems of institutional fragmentation have only gotten worse in the most recent decades, and thus the president's power to move a legislative agenda through Congress is unfortunately limited. Clinton also confronts a nation which, although hopeful, has become increasingly skeptical of its government's ability to govern.

If the president is successful and his administration is able to overcome the institutional sclerosis we have constructed in this country, he can contribute to the reconstruction of the American political culture. He can tap into that part of our culture that is deeply egalitarian and that has an abiding belief in a common good for all Americans. If, however, his initiatives flounder in the legislative maze and the programs enacted are half-hearted and ineffective, the new evidence will reconfirm Americans' distrust of government and will build on their individualism, their egocentrism, and their suspicion of all things collective. My institutional analysis suggests that the later outcome is most likely—I hope that it is wrong.

NOTES

1. See Ronald Rogowski (1974) for very solid critique of culturalist theory on this point.

2. As Ekstein (1988) admits in a spirited defense of the concept: "The basic reason why a culturalist account of change is intrinsically difficult to construct (hence, why culturalists have in fact tended to waffle in explaining change) is simple: the postulates of the approach all lead to the expectation of political continuity."

3. Historians have long fought over whether American political history is best characterized as consensual or conflictual. Richard Hofstadter (1974:xxviii, xxx), whose book, *The American Political Tradition*, is one of the most widely regarded analyses in the "consensus" tradition recants on the consensus view in the following way: "It has been awkward for me, in the sense that it [*The American Political Tradition*] has linked me with other historians with whom I have significant misgivings, and because I have misgivings of my own about what is known as consen-

sus history ... I was less interested in the art of exercise of power than I was in the art of acquiring it, and this I suppose to some extent sets limits upon the value of what I had to say about several members of my cast of characters." For explicit critiques of consensus theory see Ross (1991).

4. Ekstein (1988:790), for example, tells us: "'Orientations to action' [the "touchstone of culturalist theory"] are general dispositions of actors to act in certain ways ... We may call them, as did Bentley, soul-stuff or mind-stuff ... Orientations are not 'attitudes': the latter are specific, the former *general*, dispositions."

5. In the United States, taxes consumed 30.1 percent of GDP in 1989. British taxes were 36.5 percent of GDP. Swedish taxes, however, took a shocking 56.1 percent of GDP. Most European countries fall closer to the United Kingdom than to Sweden.

6. There are, however, important exceptions to these general tendencies. The United States has historically spent more on public education and old age security than have most other democracies.

7. The basic observation that modernization brought new demands with it is uncontroversial. Some scholars, however, have argued that we can essentially reduce differences in welfare state output to differences in the timing of industrialization and levels of economic development. In so doing, the "logic of industrialism" school has simply taken the basic observation about the relationship between modernization and the social welfare state too far. See for example, Wilensky and Lebeaux (1958) and Wilensky (1975). For a more elaborate critique of this argument see, Flora and Alber (1977).

8. Space limitations prevent a discussion of the differing institutional reforms adopted within Europe. For example, whereas Britain adopted a single member district electoral system and stripped the House of Lords of its budgetary authority, most continental countries adopted one form or another of proportional representation and several retained bicameral legislatures. These differences are important and should not be ignored. For a further discussion of these issues, see Carstairs (1980) and Steinmo (1993).

9. Lenin himself noted this problem, arguing that there was no big nationwide democratic task facing the proletariat in America, and that therefore it was difficult to mobilize the proletariat to revolt.

10. The literature covering this era in American history is particularly fascinating. For example see, Shefter (1977), Burnham (1970), Sundquist (1973), Hofstadter (1963), Skowronek (1982), Hays (1957).

11. The literature on this and on reform in Europe is also abundant (for cross-country comparisons in English see, Rueschemeyer, Stephens, and Stephens, 1992; Moore, 1966; Bendix, 1964; Rimlinger, 1971; Ashford, 1986; Heclo, 1974; and Flora and Heidenheimer, 1977).

12. Compare the analyses of this era in the writings of Bagehot (1977), Beer (1969), Dodd (1977), Shefter (1978), Ashford (1986), Fraser (1973), Rueschemeyer, Stephens, and Stephens, (1992), Skocpol and Ikenberry (1983), Sundquist (1973), Wilensky and Lebeaux (1958), Flora and Alber (1977).

13. We should not lose sight of the impressive electoral gains achieved by both Socialists and Progressives in this era despite the large disincentives faced by third parties, given the decentralized, first-past-the-post, single-member-district elec-

toral system for House elections and the winner-take-all electoral college system for the country's only national election.

14. It was the ruling elite that attempted to fragment political power in Europe at the turn of century. The introduction of proportional representation, for example, was a last-ditch attempt to undermine the growing power of working class organizations.

15. Unions faced violent opposition in Europe as well. Most European states, however, did not experience a huge influx of immigrant workers who could be used to replace striking workers.

16. Gompers wrote in his autobiography, "Economic power is the basis upon which may be developed power in all other fields. It is the foundation of organized society." But, Bell tells us, these philosophical beliefs did not turn Gompers into a socialist activist precisely because of his belief that labor could not win in the struggle over state power. "This conviction underlay Gompers' philosophy of 'voluntarism,' which consisted essentially, in a fear of the state. Since the state was a reflection of dominant economic pressure groups, any state intervention could only lead to domination by big business" (Bell, 1967:38).

17. Cited in Litwack (1962:40). See also Greenstone (1969).

18. Recall the case of national health insurance discussed above. It is interesting to consider the fact that if the U.S. Congress had passed a national health insurance plan, as has been favored by strong majorities of American citizens since the mid-1940s (Coughlin, 1980; Free and Cantril, 1967; Marmor, 1970), and if we spent as much on health care through this system as we do through the private health care system (a dubious assumption, I agree), the United States would not have an exceptionally small social welfare state. In fact, if American government paid for all health care now paid for privately, the United States would have very close to the average Organization for Economic Cooperation and Development tax burden (37 percent as compared to the 38.4 percent average.)

19. For a similar argument see Dodd (1977). See also Schattschneider (1942, 1960).

20. I can think of no major policy issue which has not followed some approximation of this general pattern in the United States. There are some examples of good political histories on particular policy issues that tell this basic story (Marmor, 1970; Witte, 1985; Weir, 1992; Derthick, 1979; Weir, Orloff, and Skocpol, 1988; Skocpol and Ikenberry, 1983; Manley, 1970; McConnell, 1966; Light, 1985; Birnbaum and Murray, 1987; and Steinmo, 1993).

21. I borrow this phrase from Immergut (1992).

22. See Downs (1957, 1960) for an examination of the rational basis of these perceptions.

23. This is why the culturalist explanation for America's relatively smaller welfare state is so appealing.

6

Liberalism and the Course of American Social Welfare Policy

RUSSELL L. HANSON

For the past decade policymakers and scholars alike have been keenly interested in the development of welfare states, albeit for different reasons. In many industrialized countries, policymakers are struggling to contain the growth of social welfare policy; some are even trying to reduce its size out of concern for economic vitality. For their part, scholars are trying to understand the functions and limits of social welfare policy in different settings, and at different times. Interestingly, both groups have focused their attention on the United States, which has an "exceptional" welfare state regarded by some policymakers as a model for the future, and by many scholars as an anachronism in a postindustrial age (Bell, 1989).

Indeed, the U.S. welfare state is exceptional in many respects, including its rather late appearance on the scene. Although its lineage may be traced to pension programs for Civil War veterans, the welfare state in this country really did not take shape until passage of the Social Security Act in 1935, which established Old Age Insurance (OAI), unemployment compensation (UC), and three forms of public assistance: Old Age Assistance (OAA), Aid to Dependent Children (ADC), and Aid to the Blind (AB). By then equivalent programs existed in Western Europe, Scandinavia, and even Canada, so the development of social welfare policy in the United States was slow in comparison with other industrialized nations in the West.[1]

Furthermore, programs enacted in this country were far from universal. A broad spectrum of the population was entitled to support in many European countries, but not in the United States. The public assistance programs addressed only certain categories of dependency, and they were means-tested. OAI covered a fairly narrow segment of the work force, until it was extended in the 1950s to include the self-employed. Also, OAI was a contributory program funded by workers and their employers (although most economists believe the payroll tax merely constituted a subtraction from potential wages). Thus, social welfare policy in the United States was narrowly defined, and lacked a strong redistributive thrust.

Finally, only a restricted range of social services was provided in the United States. Medical insurance (Medicare) and medical assistance (Medicaid) were not made available until 1965. Other services, including disability pay and leave, still are not publicly guaranteed by national legislation; they are left to private negotiations with employers, union insurance plans, and so forth. And public housing is much less extensive in the United States than it is in most European countries, where housing is an important aspect of social welfare policy.

Many explanations have been offered to account for American exceptionalism in social welfare policy. "Society-centered" explanations cite the imbalance of social forces in the United States as the principal reason for its backward policies. For example, Jill Quadagno (1984) stresses the power of capitalists from the monopoly sector who shaped welfare policy according to their own economic interests. A host of others point to the weakness of organized labor and the absence of a working-class party capable of ruling in the interests of its constituency, as European labor parties did.

"State-centered" explanations of American exceptionalism focus less on social forces and more on the effects of political institutions and the behavior of party elites. Thus, Theda Skocpol and John Ikenberry (1983) and Skocpol and Edwin Amenta (1985) stress congressional deference to existing laws and administrative arrangements at the state and local level, while Frances Fox Piven and Richard Cloward (1971, 1981) emphasize elites' opposition to welfare policy, except when it proves useful for reestablishing social control. These explanations find the origins of American exceptionalism in the peculiarities of federalism and party politics, not the imbalance of social forces.

State- and society-centered explanations of American exceptionalism are not mutually exclusive (though they are often presented as if they were). A complete account of the origin and development of social welfare policy in the United States must include elements of both types of explanation, as the leading participants in the debate concede, once they are removed from the heat of battle over claims and interpretations specific to their own theories. A judicious synthesis of state- and society-centered explanations could provide a fuller understanding of the late, and comparatively incomplete, development of a welfare state in the America.

However, a synthetic explanation would not adequately account for the unusual shape of the American welfare state, according to Gary Klass (1985) and Charles Lockhart (1991). For them, the federal organization of public assistance and the attendant bifurcation of social welfare policy is the most exceptional aspect of the American welfare state. This should not

be understood as a case of arrested development, but as a sui generis political phenomenon rooted deeply in the nation's political values. Klass
(1985:430) refers to this cultural tendency as "decentralized social altruism," that is, "a preference for collectivist social action and public policies
that extract and distribute resources within rather than between social
groups." This preference stems from the isolation of different socioeconomic and racial groups—an isolation that works against national conceptions of citizenship, and in favor of culturally distinct understandings of
citizenship and its entitlements.

The reliance on values to explain policy development may seem regres-
sive to those who believe that cultural explanations have finally been left
behind by recent advances in our understanding of the development of
welfare states. That is an illusion, for both state-centered and society-centered explanations ultimately obtain much of their power of persuasion
by referring to values. This is most obvious where society-centered explanations are concerned, since they describe the mobilization of competing
interests, for example, capitalists and the working class. These interests
seldom understand and present themselves politically as interests; rather,
they employ rhetorical strategies designed to appeal to values widely
held in the culture. Only in this way can interests hope to legitimate their
cause in the eyes of potential supporters and escape opponents' efforts to
castigate them as "special" or "vested" interests opposed to the common
good. In short, an exceedingly important aspect of interest-based struggles is the mobilization of values, as the mountain of work inspired by An-
tonio Gramsci's theory of cultural hegemony demonstrates.

Values are no less important in state-centered explanations, which
draw attention to the sense in which policies represent choices made by
actors constrained by the institutional settings in which they operate.
Values enter into the choices that actors make in the performance of their
institutional roles, sometimes quite consciously, it is clear. But the importance of values goes much farther. The roles played by individuals, and
the institutions which comprise these roles, are themselves political
choices. This is particularly true of formally defined institutions, for instance, legislatures, which spring from constitutions and operate under
well-defined rules of order and clearly understood norms of political conduct. None of these features of legislative politics is a given; or rather, they
are all objects of political negotiation. That is why mathematically inclined
advocates of the "new institutionalism" are willing to use them as congealed values or preferences, pointing to the sense in which institutions
are mobilized values.

Thus, institutional explanations of policy development require some
account of prevailing values and their distribution. On the other hand,
cultural explanations of policy development cannot be reductive. Values

are deeply embedded in cultural practices and institutions that shape human conduct. The relationship between values and behavior is heavily mediated by these institutions and practices. Thus, if we want to understand how culture works, we must explore this process of mediation. We must approach it directly, examining the institutionalization of values in order to see how certain values come to play a dominant role in the life of political communities.

A focus on the institutionalization of values is particularly important where diverse communities are concerned. There, many values are in play, so to speak, yet one value or set of values may exercise a decisive influence on collective decisionmaking. That value or set of values becomes hegemonic, often as a result of the winnowing of demands by institutions that are far from neutral in the contest of values. Sometimes the institutional bias is overt, but an overarching need for accommodation may also privilege one set of values over others. If consensus is a condition for collective action, groups that hold veto power may be able to extract enormous concessions in exchange for their cooperation. Their values may dominate, even if the groups are relatively small, so long as they occupy key positions in public councils.

Social welfare policy in the United States fits this pattern, I argue. American exceptionalism is the product of a federal system of decisionmaking. Under this arrangement, distinct cultural enclaves enjoy political autonomy at the local level, but exponents of conservative values exert a disproportionate influence at the national level by virtue of their position in the Democratic party and their power in Congress. The imperatives of coalition-building lead to policies that respect local differences, and even reinforce them. The arrangement works against the adoption of progressive entitlement programs because policymakers do not want to exceed the efforts of conservative policymakers, for fear of becoming a haven for welfare recipients seeking better benefits. Thus, conservative policymakers act as a drag upon the development of welfare throughout the country, not just in their own enclaves.

I develop this argument at greater length toward the end of this chapter, after criticizing a more conventional interpretation of American exceptionalism. That interpretation assumes the hegemony of liberal values in U.S. politics, and traces any peculiarities in social welfare policy to the power of individualism in our culture. My own view is that welfare policy in the United States would be less exceptional if it were more thoroughly liberal in orientation. Liberalism is capable of sustaining more robust policies in support of the poor, but the dominance of conservative values prevents policymakers from exploring this potential. Thus, it is not the hegemony of liberalism, but its secondary role in social welfare policymaking, that is the starting point for my cultural analysis of American exceptionalism.

LIBERALISM AND AMERICAN EXCEPTIONALISM

A sharp-eyed English observer has produced one of the better-known arguments in favor of a cultural explanation for American exceptionalism in social welfare policy. Anthony King (1973b:423) claims that "the pattern of American policy is what it is, not because America is dominated by an elite (though it may be); not because demands made on government are different from those made on governments in other countries; not because American interest groups have greater resources than those in other countries; not because American institutions are more resistant to change than those in other countries (though they probably are); but rather because Americans believe things that other people do not believe and make assumptions that other people do not make."

The beliefs King has in mind are those described by Louis Hartz in *The Liberal Tradition in America.*[2] According to King, these liberal values are particularly strong among national policymakers. Citing opinion surveys showing that American citizens favor expansion of (some) social welfare policies, King suspects that "the role of the State in America is limited, not because all Americans believe it should be and are prepared to act on that belief, but because those who make policy in America—ultimately the politicians—believe it should be" (1973b:424). Thus, the American welfare state is exceptional because that is the way national elites want it.

This is not a recent development. Skocpol (1983) highlights the constraining effects of liberalism on the development of social welfare policy in the United States in the late 1930s. She condemns the political shortcomings of the New Dealers, who abandoned their early and "essentially social democratic" aspirations in favor of a more practical approach to policymaking. The New Dealers stopped using the rhetoric of collective solidarity, with its implicit critique of the excessive individualism of liberalism. Increasingly, they turned toward policies that were conceived and legitimated in terms of their contribution to self-sufficiency and individual responsibility. As a result, social welfare policy never came to be seen as an important and permanent part of public life; its value was always open to challenge by those who blamed welfare for eroding liberal values, instead of serving them.

The subsequent development of the Social Security Act seems to confirm its liberal underpinnings. Lockhart (1991:526) argues that old-age insurance "attained thorough and lasting acceptance primarily because its design was purposely crafted so as to appeal to the prevalence of individualistic cultural biases among Americans." By contrast, public assistance programs never enjoyed much support, and came to be seen as thoroughly illegitimate in the late 1960s and early 1970s, when welfare rights organizations demanded more egalitarian policies, for example, guaranteed incomes. Such demands aroused resistance from elites in Congress, who found the proposals too much at variance with individualist values, or "biases," to use Lockhart's (1991:522) term.

This whole line of interpretation might be called a theory of liberal exceptionalism, insofar as it attributes American exceptionalism to the ideological outlook of national elites. The theory has a certain amount of plausibility, although it raises a number of thorny questions about the characterization of elite values. For example, how can the values of relevant elites be uncovered, and what marks them as being truly "liberal"? And who are the relevant elites, anyway: Are they the leaders of interest groups, who make policy demands upon decisionmakers? Are they civil servants, who shape proposals for Congress's consideration? Are they members of Congress, who ultimately choose among policy alternatives? Are they administrators, to whom Congress delegates authority for implementing programs? Or if, as seems likely, all these elites are relevant actors, how should their different viewpoints be summed or combined in a way that adequately describes the value or values that inform social welfare policymaking in the United States?

Important though these questions are, I will not address them here, as I want to focus on the underlying explanatory premise of the theory of liberal exceptionalism. That premise, which is somewhat obscured by the attention to liberalism, is that social welfare policy in the United States is ultimately determined by national elites—an assumption that is difficult to sustain where public assistance and unemployment insurance are concerned. These programs are characterized by a high degree of fragmentation and an extraordinary amount of decentralization, not only in the administration of policies, but in their definition as well. Indeed, it would be better to describe the programs as noncentralized, insofar as decentralization implies a devolution of authority that Congress and national administrators never had, practically speaking.

The general features of federally organized social welfare programs are too well-known to repeat here. What must be stressed is the extent to which state policymakers control the determination of eligibility and the establishment of benefit levels in public assistance and unemployment insurance programs. The federal organization of public assistance and unemployment insurance permits a wide variation in programs, if state policymakers choose to go in different directions. That they will do so is assured by the fact that states differ enormously in their need for social welfare policy, in their ability to finance welfare, and in the strength of policymakers' (and citizens') inclination to provide public assistance. In fact, states have different economies and political cultures, and these differences are manifested in federal policies that allow for the expression of local values in policy formation and implementation.

Aaron Wildavsky (1990) suggests a way of appreciating this cultural diversity and its impact on policymaking. In his view, three strains of values compose American political culture. One is collectivist in orientation and emphasizes equality of result in policymaking. The second is individualist and stresses policies that promote equal opportunity (where policies are required at all). And the third is hierarchical and oriented toward the preservation of morally and socially distinct ways of life. The individualist strain may be dominant, but the existence of the other two strains means that "competitive individualism cannot be the only American way" (Wildavsky, 1990:264).

The three orientations identified by Wildavsky correspond with the moralist, individualist, and traditionalist American political subcultures described and analyzed by Daniel Elazar (1970, 1984).[3] According to Elazar, the three subcultures originate in streams of migration by groups with different religious and ethnic backgrounds. When these groups came to the United States, they brought their values with them and created distinctive cultural enclaves wherever they settled. In turn, moralist, individualist, and traditionalist enclaves gave rise to distinctive political institutions, practices, and policies, as many researchers have shown (Kincaid, 1982; Wirt, 1991).

Given the federal (that is to say, permissive) organization of public assistance, different welfare policies ought to be associated with the three political subcultures. For example, Elazar's theory implies that moralist subcultures support social welfare policies out of a sense of collective responsibility for needy members of a polity, and also out of an incipient commitment to equality among a polity's members. In this subculture, income support is treated as a matter of right, and payments tend to be higher than elsewhere. Also, policies are not threatened by changes in control of government, since social welfare orientations transcend party lines. For the same reason, assistance is typically administered by a neutral, professional bureaucracy without regard for clients' political affiliation.

States with individualist subcultures should produce very different welfare policies, if Elazar is right. Assistance for the poor in individualist subcultures is not a matter of right, so much as it is a partisan affair; control over policy is one of the spoils of victory. Parties that do not depend on "have nots" for electoral support will be hostile to welfare fraud (though not to welfare per se, as we shall see). Parties that need the votes of poor people are likely to pursue progressive policies, so long as that does not alienate other important constituencies. Even then, the delivery of assistance will often be politicized, with pressures on bureaucracies to convert aid into a form of patronage for supporters of the relevant party.

Still another kind of welfare policy is suggested by the traditionalist subculture, where policies tend to be underdeveloped or nonexistent because they disrupt existing patterns of power. Entitlements are inconsistent with a hierarchical vision of society in which subordinates enjoy few rights and may not even expect much in the way of private charity. That is so because public assistance and unemployment insurance weaken elites' control over labor markets by providing an alternative to the incredibly low wages usually found in agrarian economies. Not surprisingly, ruling classes oppose policies that diminish control and do everything in their power to prevent the enactment and implementation of entitlement programs, which are condemned as immoral and unwarranted intrusions on the natural order of things.

The existence of such wide variation is virtually impossible to comprehend within an explanatory framework that rests on a Hartzian foundation. In fact, quantitative analyses of welfare policy expenditures support predictions of interstate variation consistent with Elazar's theory (Kincaid, 1982; Wirt, 1991). However, studies of expenditure patterns do not provide direct evidence about the values that inform elites' policy choices. It is therefore necessary to explore other types of evidence in order to gauge the impact of different cultural values on the development of social welfare policy in the United States. Case studies are particularly helpful in this regard, since they shed light on the substantive content of policy and the values that inform those policies on the one hand, and the values that affect their acceptance by citizens, on the other.

Thus, I illustrate further on the impact of different values on American social welfare policy by examining outcomes in three states, each representing a distinct political subculture. Policymaking in the moralist culture is represented in a case study of Washington; Indiana and Georgia represent the individualist and traditionalist styles of policymaking, respectively. A comparison of these cases should provide useful information about the validity of Elazar's scheme, and by implication, the extent to which liberalism, in the Hartzian sense, is sufficiently pervasive to account for American exceptionalism.[4]

To show how distinct cultural values sustain different types of social welfare policy, I shall focus on these three states' transition from mothers' aid to Aid to Dependent Children, once the Social Security Act was passed in 1935. The time of transition offers a particularly good glimpse of values in action, since most states struggled to adapt existing mothers' aid programs to meet the requirements of ADC. In that sense, they tried to maintain policies that were consistent with underlying values, embodied in choices made in years when the national government exerted little or no influence. Thus, the transition allows us to see cultural differences before they were softened by legal requirements and administrative regulations associated with the long-term implementation of the Social Security Act.

For similar reasons, I focus on the transition to ADC rather than the other public assistance or unemployment insurance programs. Only two states had unemployment insurance programs before passage of the Social Security Act; it was the attraction of matching funds from the national government that led to their proliferation after 1935. This makes it hard to isolate and compare the effects of cultural values on the definition and administration of policy, since nearly all of the examples were created under federal regulations that restrict variation, however loosely and permissively. Hence, values had ample room to influence decisions about assisting poor women with children; accordingly, that is a good place to look for differences across political subcultures.

MORALIST VALUES IN WASHINGTON

In his desire to criticize the hegemony of liberalism in America, Louis Hartz (1955) exaggerated the pervasive hold of individualist values, especially outside the South. Consequently, Hartz and those who follow him have played down the importance of politics rooted in collectivist values found in some of the Union states. The occasional eruption of progressive waves of reform is mentioned, of course, but only to show that it seldom dominated the national scene, where liberalism reigned triumphant. What remains unclear from this account is how liberalism absorbed progressive impulses, and why progressive waves of reform persisted in spite of liberalism's putative hegemony.

Both problems can be solved by admitting the existence of a moralist political subculture, and explaining how the influence of that culture is submerged in the confluence of values that shapes social welfare policy at the national level. The state of Washington provides a good locus for exploring the moralist style of policymaking during the transition from mothers' aid to ADC. The story begins with the state's historic commitment to progressive welfare policies. As in other Pacific Slope and Rocky Mountain states, a successful, albeit modest, program of mothers' aid provided the foundation for Washington's ADC system. Mothers' aid became available early, in 1913, when the state legislature enacted a law permitting counties to assist women with dependent children. Although they were not required to provide this aid, most counties did so by 1921. And by 1931, every county assisted indigent mothers, and still more impressively, they continued to do so throughout the Depression.[5] Left to itself, Washington was developing social welfare policies that reflected the collectivist values of the moralist culture, not the individualist values of liberalism.

State government in Washington played no role in financing or administering mothers' aid. That should have made it more difficult to establish ADC, since the Social Security Board expected state agencies to oversee the local administration of public assistance. But no such problems were encountered in Washington, primarily because the impetus (and a precedent) for centralization had been supplied by a powerful old-age pension movement,[6] which produced a mandatory old-age pension program. Boards of county commissioners throughout the state were compelled to distribute pensions to qualified applicants; they could not abstain or withdraw from the program.

The demand for pensions grew quickly, and soon forced counties to the verge of bankruptcy. The ensuing crisis led Governor Clarence Martin, a Democrat, but no friend of the New Deal, to propose a state takeover of relief and welfare functions (Patterson, 1969:155). Early in 1935 the legislature assumed full financial responsibility for Old-Age Assistance, and began making payments in July 1935—one month before passage of the Social Security Act, and eight months before matching funds were first authorized by the Social Security Board. OAA was administered directly by the state Department of Public Welfare, with no involvement of county commissioners. This configuration was designed to minimize the role of local officials, who sometimes obstructed the relief effort or converted it into political patronage (Blumell, 1973, chap. 4).

Aid to Dependent Children was a beneficiary of this arrangement. The new laws allowed the state welfare department to establish a more uniform system of public assistance for needy children and the aged in Washington. Central intake facilities were established in each county and were assigned responsibility for accepting applications for all of the new public assistance programs, as well as for the old poor-law operations. Trained professionals were recruited to staff these facilities, and representatives from the local offices of the state Department of Public Welfare encouraged further training and staff development. They also relayed information and policy directives from the state agency to local administrators (Blumell, 1973:365–366).

Central intake at the local level was an advanced form of functional integration and reflected state leaders' broad conception of social welfare policy in the modern era. This approach was warmly received by the Social Security Board, the national agency charged with implementing the various titles of the Social Security Act. Washington earned a reputation as one of the most progressive administrators of public assistance in the nation (Blumell, 1973:355). Indeed, state officials claimed to be assisting 95 percent of the families eligible for ADC and AB, and 75 percent of those who qualified for OAA (Blumell, 1973:354). The far-reaching aid included both money and services; the department's leader was a firm believer in prevention and rehabilitation, for which services were indispensable. Medical and dental care for public assistance recipients was urged on the counties in 1937, and the overall pattern was more European than liberal (in the Hartzian sense).

Charles Ernst, the director of the state Department of Public Welfare, was not satisfied with this successful beginning. He advocated a further "decentralization of service and centralization of operations" (Blumell, 1973:385). The system of state administration was replaced by an arrangement in which public assistance was administered by boards of county supervisors, through county departments of welfare. However, county operations were closely supervised by the state Department of Social Security, as the welfare department came to be called. A plan for equalization was also approved, whereby each county's share of assistance costs was fixed at three mills of assessed value. The state furnished the rest, paying more in poor counties.

Supervision by the state Department of Social Security was both elaborate and vigorous. County commissioners were required to submit detailed quarterly budgets for public assistance to the Department of Social Security for prior approval; in addition, all payments to recipients were disbursed by the state. Even more important, all county welfare department employees with authority to spend money or make policy had to be hired from a list of qualified candidates supplied by the Department of Social Security. The hiring was done by the county commissioners, but the possibilities for making patronage appointments were radically constrained by the listing requirement. Reinforcing this requirement was a 1937 law requiring the use of a merit system and job classification scheme for all state and local employees in the area public assistance. (This was two years before the Social Security Board persuaded Congress to impose this requirement on all states; Washington was in the vanguard of states on the vital issue of professionalization.)

Supervision also had a constructive side. The Department of Social Security developed a capable field staff, whose members regularly visited the county departments of public welfare and held regional conferences. The staff explained the intent of state laws and regulations and helped local administrators and caseworkers interpret rules and bulletins in light of these underlying objectives. The Department of Social Security compiled a staff manual on policies and procedures, which was designed to promote greater efficiency and uniformity in the provision of public assistance. The state also provided a broad array of consulting services to all counties that requested help.

After a visit in November 1938, officials in the Bureau of Public Assistance, an operating agency of the Social Security Board, concluded that Washington had "built up an unusually well qualified staff in the counties" by hiring people with professional training and experience in social welfare. The state had even established training centers for employees in Seattle and Spokane, satisfying the bureau's emphasis on aggressive "in-service training" of state and local employees.[7] Just as important, the department backed county welfare workers facing opposition from local officials who resented "interference" by the state in county affairs. In September 1940, the Department of Social Security assumed control of the Whatcom County Welfare Department, after its director was dismissed by the county commissioners in apparent violation of the merit law covering public welfare employees. The intrusion of politics threatened to undermine the state's drive to professionalize the administration of public assistance, and so Ernst moved promptly to beat back the threat. His actions reassured workers in other counties that the state meant to insist on a strong form of supervision, even if that incurred the ire of local officials.

Washington was unable to sustain momentum in the development of its social welfare policies, however. Moralist values did not flag; indeed, they flourished in continuing demands for improved programs and benefits. But national officials worried that progressive public assistance programs might jeopardize old-age insurance, and they resisted further improvements (Cates, 1983). In late 1938, Richard Neustadt, the Director of Region Twelve, reported to the capital that the state's governor was in a tough battle against "left wing groups" who wanted to liberalize OAA and ADC.[8] As a result of this communique, and in apparent disregard of evaluations from the field, William Galvin, chief of field operations, listed the condition of public assistance in Washington as "poor" in his summary to the executive director of the Social Security Board, Oscar Powell.[9] Almost overnight, the state went from being a model to a problem for national policymakers, who opposed suggestions for expanding Washington's public assistance.

The lack of support for welfare rights organizations in Washington State was compounded by the board's failure to push hard in Congress for the removal of maximums on benefits. Under the terms of the Social Security Act, the national government funded one-third of the cost of supporting dependent children, up to a monthly limit of $18 for the first child, and $12 for each additional child. States wanting to make more generous payments were forced to pay 100 percent of the cost in excess of the maximums. In effect, they were penalized for their generosity—and Washington was one of the generous states.

Effective June 1, 1940, the matching percentage for ADC was raised to 50 percent, the rate for OAA. But it was not until 1946 that the maximum payments for which matching funds were available were increased to $27 for the first child and $18 for each additional child. By then progressive states such as Washington had learned that national policymakers were willing to tolerate less generous policies enacted by other states, and they began to regress in the face of worries about becoming "welfare havens," with correspondingly heavy tax burdens that inhibited economic development. The underlying moralist values lost some of their force, once public assistance was institutionalized on a federal basis under cautious national leadership. But for a while at least, a decidedly progressive program existed in Washington—the theory of liberal exceptionalism to the contrary notwithstanding.

INDIVIDUALIST VALUES IN INDIANA

The values of liberalism, understood in the Hartzian sense, are best realized in what Elazar calls the individualist political subculture. The individualist subculture emphasizes a marketplace conception of the democratic order, and social welfare policy is seen as a partisan affair; its development depends on which party dominates. In this country, Democrats may use social welfare policy to broaden their electoral constituency (Mollenkopf, 1983; Jennings, 1979; Piven and Cloward, 1971, 1981). For them, entitlements are not just a matter of right, they are part of the spoils of victory: Recipients get what is coming to them by virtue of their contributions to the party's success. For their part, Republicans generally pursue more restrictive policies. They are not opposed to social welfare in principle; they support assistance for the deserving poor, meaning those who find themselves in need through no fault of their own. However, Republicans worry about aiding the undeserving poor, who ought to be responsible for righting themselves. Political attacks on programs that coddle the undeserving poor are effective ways of mobilizing electoral support, especially where liberal values prevail, making it possible to tap the energy of rugged individualism and the work ethic, which are central to Hartz's conception of liberalism in America.

This pattern is nicely illustrated in Indiana, where mothers' aid legislation was first proposed in 1913, only to be defeated because of opposition from the operators of orphanages and foster homes (Abbott, 1935:202). Counties were finally authorized to provide mothers' aid in 1919, and this authorization was expanded in 1923. The law was not mandatory, but about two-thirds of the counties in the state regularly made payments to the mothers of eligible children, once enabling legislation was passed. The result was a dramatic alteration in the mode of assisting families with dependent children. The traditional forms of assistance—poor farms, asylums, and so on—gave way to mothers' aid and other forms of home care, including boarding houses (or paid foster care).

The operators of private child-care facilities were a powerful force in the Republican party, which dominated Indiana politics and government until the Depression. Consistent with individualist mores, mothers' pensions were never allowed to undermine the position of orphanages or boarding homes: in all three cases the rate of payment from public funds was 75 cents per day. However, that changed with the enactment of a "little New Deal" in the state under Paul McNutt, a Democrat whose public assistance programs were broadly conceived and vigorously implemented.

Indiana had been a Republican stronghold until McNutt, who was the dean of the Law School at Indiana University, and past state and national commander of the American Legion, was elected governor of Indiana in 1932. He out-polled Roosevelt and helped elect 91 (out of 100) Democratic members of the general assembly's House, and 43 (out of 50) members of the Senate (Madison, 1982). McNutt used his enormous personal popularity and legislative majority, in addition to his control of a considerable amount of patronage, to reorganize state government and restructure its revenue base. By adopting a gross income tax, McNutt and his supporters dramatically improved the fiscal condition of the state's government, making possible the swift adoption of liberal laws for public assistance under the Social Security Act.

Indeed, the American Public Welfare Association considered Indiana's welfare code a model for other states (White, 1936). Under the law, eligibility for ADC was liberally construed and benefits were relatively generous. In 1936, Indiana made average monthly payments of $30.51 per ADC family, which made participation financially attractive to those who were otherwise eligible. Moreover, the state established a means test that was less restrictive than those in other states, inviting widespread participation.

Increased enrollment in ADC was also a result of a vigorous campaign to publicize the new assistance programs. In January 1937, a new division of information and public relations was established in the state Department of Public Welfare in order to better "interpret" public assistance in light of growing public curiosity and misunderstanding. The division employed two welfare extension agents, and created a bureau of thirty-two speakers who would address civic, professional, and religious organizations. Exhibits were held at county fairs, in courthouses and public schools, and at political conventions to "clarify the general conception of public welfare responsibility." News releases were made available to the papers, and weekly radio broadcasts presented discussions of welfare in Indiana (Shackelford, 1939).

Most of the work of the welfare extension agents in the new division was aimed at cultivating popular support for public assistance in Indiana, but the agents also recruited recipients to ADC and OAA. Additionally, Indiana worked assiduously to absorb recipients from general relief and women who had been employed by the Works Progress Administration and to relieve the burden on private agencies (State Survey of Public Assistance in Indiana, 1938). The results were impressive. In 1936 Indiana had the twelfth largest population in the country, but had the third largest ADC program (after New York and Pennsylvania). Coverage of the eligible population was one of the best in the nation, and benefits were well above average (Bucklin and Lynch, 1939:30).

These accomplishments proved short-lived, however. McNutt became high commissioner of the Philippines, and with his departure Indiana Democrats were in trouble. They lost control of the lower chamber of the general assembly in 1938. A resurgent Republican party gained a 2:1 control over both chambers of the legislature in 1940, and very narrowly missed capturing the governor's office—something they did accomplish in 1944. Throughout most of the 1940s, then, the Democrats had little success in Indiana politics (McClure, 1969).

Once in power, the Republicans wasted no time attacking public welfare, or more precisely, the alleged abuses of public welfare. In 1943 the general assembly created a Welfare Investigation Commission to review the administration of public welfare in Indiana. After holding numerous hearings throughout the state, the commission conceded that "public decency demands that those in need must, in some reasonable fashion, be assisted," but complained that "we consider it both dangerous and unsound to even attempt, much less accomplish an irrevocable shift from old-fashioned conceptions of thrift, industry and self-help to any so called modern concept of need regardless of anything else as a basis for public assistance" (Indiana Welfare Investigation Commission, 1944:5).

Blame for promoting a "modern concept of need" was fixed on the Democratic administration of Franklin D. Roosevelt. The commission was particularly incensed that the Social Security Board and hence the state Welfare Board as well were unduly influenced by social workers' conceptions of need and social obligation. In support of its interpretation, the commission cited evidence "that many of the actions of the State Welfare Board are largely governed by dictatorial instructions received from the Social Security Board, and that the Social Security Board continually stretches its authority, thus bewildering, restricting and confusing local county welfare boards" (Indiana Welfare Investigation Commission, 1944:6–7).

The state Board of Welfare, whose members were appointed by the Democratic governor, took the highly unusual step of circulating a statement in response to the commission's report, praising the improvements brought about by the involvement of the Social Security Board and emphasizing the extent to which county boards participated in the formulation of welfare policies. A point-by-point rebuttal of the commission's reform recommendations, which aimed to increase the authority of local boards, was made—and was successful, as it turned out, as the legislature declined to act on the recommendations (probably because of pressure from national authorities). Thus, public assistance became deeply embroiled in partisan warfare.

Republican resentment over "federal dictation" broke out again in 1947, when the legislature adopted the "Anti-Federal Aid Resolution" (Ori, 1961). The resolution, which was circulated among the states and in Congress, was an announcement by officials stating: "We are fed up with subsidies, doles and paternalism" embodied in federal grants-in-aid for a host of domestic purposes, including public assistance. Of course, being "fed up with paternalism" did not mean that Indiana Republicans were prepared to refuse monies from the national government; they simply wanted to return policymaking authority to the state and local levels, where their party was firmly in control.

More control over public assistance by subnational actors in Indiana meant greater freedom to attack alleged instances of waste and fraud, that is, the dispensation of benefits to the undeserving poor. The latter included "welfare chiselers," "reds," "foreigners," and unwed mothers living off the stipends of their illegitimate children (Ori, 1961). However, the truly deserving poor, for instance, widows with children, would still be supported; the Republicans were not inclined to challenge public assistance per se, only its abuse by constituencies linked to the Democratic party (immigrants, radicals, and the like).

The assertion of state's rights and the invocation of personal responsibility (which underlay the distinction between deserving and undeserving poor) went hand in glove for Indiana Republicans. It was a popular theme in a liberal or individualist subculture, and the party was handsomely rewarded at the polls. Republican legislators responded accordingly. Indiana openly defied the Social Security Administration in 1951 when the legislature enacted (over the veto of the governor) a law declaring ADC rosters a matter of public record. The measure was designed to bring social and legal pressure on welfare recipients who were ostensibly abusing public assistance under the cover of confidentiality of records.

Passage of the law meant that public assistance in Indiana was no longer in conformity with national requirements. At the recommendation of the Bureau of Public Assistance, the Social Security Administration temporarily withheld matching funds, until such time as the state came into conformity. Unbowed by the pressure, Indiana Senator William

Jenner (R) succeeded in 1952 in attaching a rider to a congressional appropriations bill that permitted states to make rolls public for certain purposes. This opened the floodgates, as twenty-one states began publicizing
ADC rolls in 1953 (though this had little effect on the size of caseloads,
much to the disappointment of the proponents of publication).

Gilbert Steiner (1966:97) suggests that the Jenner amendment demonstrated the efficacy of political appeals for a reversal of policy made by the
Social Security Administration. Such incidents probably made the Bureau
of Public Assistance more cautious in dealing with recalcitrant states, out
of fear that congressional retaliation might undo years of quiet diplomacy
in many individual states. In fact, that caution, not liberalism, was a hallmark of national policymakers charged with the implementation of public
assistance, and it permitted very conservative values to play a disproportionately large role in the development of social welfare policy in the
United States, as the next section shows.

TRADITIONALIST VALUES IN GEORGIA

Indiana Republicans' commitment to "states' rights" and the administration of welfare according to local mores was hardly unique. In fact, resistance to oversight by the Social Security Board was even stiffer in the
South, where state officials were neither willing nor able to supervise local
activities in a satisfactory manner. In no other region of the country were
state governments so ill-prepared to oversee the local administration of
public assistance and obtain compliance with minimal standards of administrative performance. Consequently, the board—and by extension its
Bureau of Public Assistance—was generally not able to rely on state officials' supervision of public assistance. This seriously weakened the
board's political position, since it had no direct authority over local administrators (Burns, 1942:400).

The strength of local politicos vis-à-vis state legislatures and executives
was especially great where social welfare policy was concerned. Southern
traditions of local relief were very strong, and generally worked against
the provision of aid in all but the most rudimentary forms. Mainly, this reflected concern over the deleterious impact of relief on the availability of
cheap labor, the mainstay of local agricultural economies (Cash, 1941). Social welfare policies threatened to diminish the supply of cheap labor on
which the new South depended, and should be avoided for that reason,
opponents alleged. Their control over the machinery of party politics allowed them to enlist state legislators and chief executives in a battle to defend the prerogatives of local elites (Lancaster, 1937:366).

The power of local elites was justified in terms of traditionalist values.
In this subculture, politics was regarded as a privileged form of activity,

which reflected an older, precommercial attitude that accepted "a substantially hierarchical society as part of the ordered nature of things, authorizing and expecting those at the top of the social structure to take a special and dominant role in government" (Elazar et al., 1986:85). Government had an important role to play in communal affairs, as it did in moralist subcultures, but it was dominated by members of an elite social stratum that used the powers of government to preserve its position in the social hierarchy. Political competition tended to be quite limited in scope, and centered on personal factions, rather than on parties or interest groups. Political participation also tended to be low and confined to those who "inherit their 'right' to govern through family ties or social position" (Elazar, et al., 1986:85). Since politics was of the face-to-face variety in traditionalist subcultures, impersonal bureaucracies were avoided.

This pattern was evident in Georgia, where opposition to the New Deal in general, and to its public assistance programs in particular, was very pronounced. The Peach State was dominated by a Democratic party that was an assemblage of personal factions motivated by a desire to control the spoils of office (Fossett, 1960). Since the governor's office was the center of political patronage in Georgia, the struggle between factions was played out in Democratic primary elections. But a statewide primary election in Georgia was in truth no more than the summation of county results, and candidates were forced to seek support from the "courthouse gangs" that existed in each of the state's 159 counties (Fossett, 1960:27).

The political power of the courthouse gangs was rooted in the county unit system, an indirect method of nomination for statewide office. Under this method, the person winning a majority of unit votes became the Democratic nominee for governor. The unit votes were allocated by county. The eight most populous counties in Georgia, representing one-third of the adult white population, cast six unit votes each. The next thirty most populous counties cast four unit votes each. The smallest 121 counties cast two unit votes each. Thus, the smallest counties, with 40 percent of the adult white population, controlled 59 percent of the unit votes in Democratic primary elections in Georgia (Key, 1949:119).

The effects of the county-unit system were plain to all: "Only those candidates for state office who can win pluralities in the small, rural, two-unit-vote counties have a reasonable expectation of success." The rural counties were dominated by planters, and so in Georgia "there is not only the positive need to be an effective rural campaigner but there is the absence of need to be solicitous of city voters. It then becomes possible to use the cities as whipping boys, to inflate rural pride and prejudices, including that against the Negroes who vote most frequently in the cities, and to perpetuate the frictions between county and city" (Key, 1949:121–122).

In short, the system favored demagogues like Eugene Talmadge, the "wild man from Sugar Creek," who was best remembered for obstructing New Deal legislation that infringed on state prerogatives by substituting the advice of "foreign" social workers for the traditional wisdom of local politicians. In the spring of 1935 Talmadge vetoed enabling legislation to create a "little New Deal" in Georgia, boasting that he "threw every New Deal bill in the trash can without ever reading it," no matter how popular it was in the legislature (Anderson, 1975:119). In his veto message Talmadge explained: "I am opposed to all kinds of pensions except a soldier's pension. ... I do not want to see the incentive of the American people to work and lay up something for their old age destroyed. ... It is not the purpose of the state to support its people" (Lemmon, 1954:230).

Seeking a national pulpit for his preaching, Talmadge chose to contest the senate seat then held by Richard Russell, the "boy wonder of Georgia politics" (Meade 1981). During his campaign against Russell, Talmadge repeatedly attacked the Social Security Act by claiming it would destroy the supply of Negro labor. As he later said, "The Federal [Social Security] Board in Washington is going to make them add on nearly every Negro of a certain age in the county to this pauper's list. What will become of your farm labor—your washwoman, your cooks, your plowhands?" (Fossett, 1960:233).

Talmadge also condemned the centralizing tendencies of New Deal programs. In typically hyperbolic language, he asserted that programs in areas such as public assistance would effectively abolish "practically every county in the state of Georgia" (Fossett, 1960:233). The requirements of state supervision would lead to the centralization of power in Atlanta; in turn, state government would have to follow the dictates of boards and bureaus in Washington. Thus, traditions of local autonomy, and the power of courthouse gangs which enjoyed that autonomy, were in danger.

These were heavy charges, but Russell weathered the challenge, and Talmadge's personally endorsed candidate for governor, Charles Redwine, lost to New Dealer Eurith D. Rivers. Rivers' call for a "little New Deal" in Georgia was not easily redeemed, however. At that time the constitution of Georgia made no provision for using state tax revenues for social welfare programs; the new governor was obliged to seek amendments that would allow the state legislature to appropriate money for public assistance. The necessary amendments were approved by a two-thirds majority in each chamber of the legislature, and then by voters on June 8, 1937, who by a very wide margin agreed to permit state and county governments to use tax levies for assisting the aged and dependent children.

Even so, the new public assistance programs were grossly underfinanced and subject to cutbacks occasioned by revenue shortfalls. A little more than $3 million in state funds had been appropriated for OAA, AB, and ADC during fiscal year 1939, but in the second quarter of the fiscal year the state Department of Public Welfare notified counties that only 55 percent of that appropriation could be made available for public assistance. Naturally, this made local officials reluctant to take on new cases, and a huge backlog of applications accumulated, constituting an informal waiting list. As a result, aid was actually provided to less than one-third of those who were thought to be eligible for public assistance in Georgia (Georgia State Department of Public Welfare, 1939:8–9).

The situation was aggravated by Talmadge's return to the governor's office in 1940. He moved quickly to reduce the state's deficit; many jobs in state government were eliminated, and salaries for others were reduced. The state welfare department was virtually gutted: When Talmadge assumed office in January 1941, the department employed 176 people, many of them involved in public assistance and unemployment compensation. Only 36 of these individuals were still with the department as of November 20, 1942, near the end of Talmadge's term in office. Most of the others had resigned, usually to accept better paying positions elsewhere.

Talmadge's assault on the state welfare department was made possible by passage in March 1941 of Act No. 373, which gave him the power to suspend, evaluate, and fire (with "good cause") any employee of the state Department of Public Welfare, any member of the county boards of public welfare, or any county director of public welfare. Since the governor was also empowered to evaluate an employee's performance and weigh the value of an employee's response to suspension or termination, Georgia's "merit system" was reduced to nothing more than a patronage arrangement for the convenience of the governor.

Talmadge's use of Act No. 373 was challenged by the Social Security Board, which threatened to withhold matching funds. The situation was not finally rectified until February 4, 1943, when a new governor, Ellis Arnall, sought and obtained approval for a state merit system covering the employees of state and county departments of health, public welfare, and bureaus of unemployment compensation. The subsequent professionalization of welfare administration helped reduce the huge backlog of applications. Interestingly, this did not lead to massive caseload increases; the ADC rolls actually declined during Arnall's tenure. Closings increased in number, and so did denials of aid. Most significantly, pending applications were disposed of for "other reasons," meaning the death of an applicant, the voluntary withdrawal of applications for assistance, or the department's inability to locate an applicant.

Perhaps this was a clever strategy of bureaucratic disentitlement, or perhaps it really was a matter of catching up on paperwork. In either case, A. J. Hartley, Arnall's director of the state Department of Public Welfare, was surely exaggerating when he claimed: "The abolition of these waiting lists was an epoch-making achievement and relieved the heart-breaking situation which had existed for years in which the people who needed the old-age assistance, aid to the blind and aid to dependent children were able to get prompt action on their applications for the first time in the history of the department" (Georgia State Department of Public Welfare, 1944:7).

In fact, public assistance remained quite undeveloped in Georgia and elsewhere in the South, even after men like Talmadge passed from the scene. As Michael Holmes (1975:12) explains, these programs promised to free poor people from their condition of economic dependency, and this could only be done by altering the South's distinctive social system. That system pitted poor whites against poor blacks and kept both subordinate to white landowners, manufacturing interests, and railroad companies. The New Deal's "color-blind" programs of relief and public assistance struck at the heart of this social system, and Southern elites refused to allow the programs to develop beyond what was minimally required to remain eligible for matching funds.

DYNAMICS OF FEDERALISM

The existence of moralist, individualist, and traditionalist subcultures casts strong doubt on Hartz's characterization of the pervasive hold of liberalism in America. It also makes it difficult to accept accounts of American exceptionalism that rely on liberal values to explain the course of social welfare development in this country. Such accounts ignore profound differences between policies enacted by individualist subcultures, on the one hand, and policies found in moralist or traditionalist cultures, on the other. These differences suggest that a mixture of values informs the most exceptional aspect of the American welfare state, the public assistance programs (and perhaps unemployment insurance, as well). Liberal values, which are best realized in individualist subcultures, are evidently only one part of that mixture.

Of course, there is another way in which the hegemony of liberalism might be understood. Devotees of the theory of liberal exceptionalism could argue that liberal values dominate the policymaking process even though they are not pervasive. The theory of liberal exceptionalism might be usefully reformulated to admit the inevitability of interstate differences in welfare policymaking and to allow for the possibility that some states pursue policies that do not fit the mold of liberal individualism. Under the reformulation, such states would be treated as exceptions to the pattern of American exceptionalism. They would not be regarded as typical examples of social welfare policy, nor would they be assigned much of a role in shaping the overall pattern of choices that constitutes the American way.

Instead, the claim would be that liberal states dominate the process, producing the general effect of exceptionalism.

This is an attractive reformulation of the theory of liberal exceptionalism, not least because it allows for its own falsification. After all, it is distinctly possible that a dynamic process of competition could establish the hegemony of values that are not liberal in the Hartzian sense. For example, traditionalist values may dominate policymaking in a federal system, compelling policymakers in moralist and individualist states alike to constrain the development of social welfare policies that are not consistent with their values. In that case, federalism supports a set of values that is most definitely not liberal, and may even be opposed to liberalism, insofar as traditionalist cultures favor ascription over achievement, and privileges of station over statutory entitlements.

Which values, then, dominate American social welfare policy, those of the individualist (or liberal) subculture, or those of the traditionalist subculture? It is hard to know for certain, but there is little evidence to suggest that federalism favors liberalism in the competition of values (or conversely, that liberalism is naturally inclined toward federally organized welfare programs). In fact, the weight of opinion runs against claims of liberal hegemony. Thus, Klass (1985:430) explains the exceptional character of the American welfare state in terms of a different value, which he calls "decentralized social altruism," that is, "a preference for collectivist social action and public policies that extract and distribute resources within rather than between social groups."

This preference stems from the isolation of different socioeconomic and racial groups—an isolation that works against national conceptions of citizenship, and in favor of culturally distinct understandings of citizenship and its entitlements. Consequently, federally organized programs are the rule, since they do not disturb existing patterns of isolation; nationally organized programs emerge only when, and to the extent that, cultural and social isolation is overcome, as it was during the broad-based movement for retirement security in the New Deal.

The absence of similar movements explains the New Dealers' choice of federally organized programs of public assistance and unemployment. In both cases, national programs were discussed, but then dismissed in favor of federal designs, out of concern for the prerogatives of state politicians (Skocpol and Ikenberry, 1983; Skocpol and Amenta, 1985). This deference was partly rooted in an electoral and party system that kept members of Congress accountable to local interests. However, this general tendency was reinforced by the existence of state pension programs for the aged and for widows, and in a handful of states, by unemployment insurance programs. Skocpol, Ikenberry, and Amenta argue that these programs gave state and local policymakers a vested interest in federal programs that built upon existing administrative foundations, thereby preserving state and local control over policies already in place. The system of representation insured that Congress would accede to this demand for local control, which, it should be noted, spared some state policymakers the pain of abandoning programs that were more progressive than national standards then being debated.

Quadagno (1984, 1985) disputes this explanation. She observes that states with pensions did not vociferously oppose proposals for national programs, probably because the expense of maintaining pensions was becoming prohibitive. Instead, the staunchest opposition to national programs came from Southern members of Congress, who represented states that either had no pension programs, or had programs that were pitifully underdeveloped and underfunded. Quadagno concludes that the deference of Congress cannot be attributed to pressure from the beneficiaries, administrators, and supporters of existing state pension systems.

Rather, the Congressional preference for federal arrangements was a concession to southerners, who feared that national programs would undermine the plantation economy and the caste system spawned by it (Quadagno, 1988; Bensel, 1984). The importance of the southern wing of the Democratic party was only slightly diluted by Roosevelt's massive popular majorities, and in any event southerners filled the chairmanships of key congressional committees by virtue of their seniority. This enabled them to delay public assistance and unemployment insurance, and when that was no longer possible, southerners were able to insist on federal programs that were very permissive. That is, the programs delegated an enormous amount of policymaking discretion to state politicians, whose careers were determined by electoral arrangements expressly designed to magnify the influence of economic elites at the expense of disenfranchised blacks and poor whites. Thus, the legislative organization of the American welfare state was dictated primarily by southern elites, in Quadagno's view.

The subsequent implementation of the Social Security Act by the Social Security Board was similarly distorted by deference to southern sensibilities. The board was unable to establish sound programs of public assistance in many states because it was committed to a fairly conservative plan for old-age insurance, as Cates (1983) shows. This plan faced competition from progressive proposals of the sort advocated by Abraham Epstein and Isaac Rubinow. It also faced competition from flat-grant pension schemes, for example, the Townsend Plan, which remained popular long after the Social Security Act was passed in 1935. The success of OAI was even threatened by OAA, the public assistance program administered by the states. Political support for liberal OAA programs might have made them more attractive to citizens and businesses than OAI, and it was therefore necessary to stifle the development of OAA in order for OAI to survive, or so Cates argues.

The fact that the board set policy for both programs made this easy, and Cates presents interesting and fairly persuasive evidence of a systematic campaign to portray public assistance as a degrading form of support, in contrast with the meritorious entitlement of contributory insurance—a distinction promoted by the board itself. Thus, it was Chairman Altmeyer and other top executives at the agency who conveyed the message that OAI was a matter of right and a sign of thrift, whereas OAA (and other forms of public assistance) was only for those who were "down and out" and beholden to the polity for their support (Cates, 1983:28-49). Naturally, some states (especially those in the traditionalist South) were disinclined to assist those who where "down and out," and the board's commitment to old-age insurance prevented it from demanding better assistance programs.

Other states, as Skocpol and Amenta (1985) insist, and as the example of moralist Washington shows, were interested in pursuing a more progressive line. An uneven pattern of institutionalization was predictable, especially since the Social Security Board chose to build on existing administrative foundations, instead of razing the structure and starting from clear ground. This strategy permitted quick delivery of assistance that was desperately needed in the spring of 1936, but it perpetuated historic differences in states' capacity for assisting the poor. States with sturdy foundations in relief, for example, Washington, built even stronger programs of public assistance, whereas those with weak traditions of relieving the poor, for example, Georgia, established only modest OAA, ADC, and AB programs. The gap between leading and lagging states remained and in fact grew larger with the passage of time.

Concerned with this trend, the Social Security Board dedicated itself to closing the gap between leading and lagging states. As the agency in charge of implementing public assistance, the board assumed responsibility for boosting the capacity of states with a poor record of implementation. The board's strategy seemed to work. An analysis of benefit changes between 1940 and 1950 reported a 29 percent national increase in average ADC payment per child, after adjusting for inflation, but changes in poor southern states were much larger (Perkins, 1951). Percentage changes in benefits grossly overstated progress in the southern states, however. In spite of liberalization, payments remained abysmally low throughout the South in 1950. Payments in Oklahoma, for example, averaged $10.43 per child in June 1950—less than half the amount available in many northern states. Georgia's average payment was $10.72, compared to Washington's $24.35 and Indiana's $16.18 (Perkins, 1951). Payments were even lower in

North and South Carolina, Alabama, Florida, Mississippi, and Arkansas. In absolute terms, the advances were almost negligible.

A similar illusion of progress was created by the expanded coverage of ADC between 1940 and 1950. By one estimate, the proportion of eligible families receiving assistance quintupled in Florida. It quadrupled in Georgia and Arkansas and almost trebled in Alabama. Rates of coverage were twice as high in Virginia and South Carolina as previously. And they more than doubled in North Carolina, Louisiana, and Tennessee (Perkins, 1951:15). Such increases dwarfed the changes that occurred in wealthy, industrialized states. But in absolute terms, access to ADC was still highly restricted in the South, where poverty was endemic. After quadrupling, Georgia's ADC recipient rate (per 1,000 population) was 35 in December 1950—but Washington's was 41. And of course recipients in Washington received far more generous benefits; the low payments in Georgia insured that recipients newly admitted to ADC would never escape from their condition of deprivation.

Thus, the gains in the South were not very impressive, and they were obtained at considerable cost. The leading programs of 1940 were still exemplary in 1950, but they were beginning to stagnate: payments had not improved dramatically since 1940, and rates of coverage were not much higher either (Perkins, 1951). In fact, the Bureau of Public Assistance found itself struggling to prevent backsliding on the part of states that had been leaders. Perkins (1951:15) reports significant contractions in eligibility for ADC in New Jersey, where the rate of coverage in 1950 was less than half what it had been in 1940. Wisconsin's coverage was smaller by one-fourth. Similar reductions occurred in four western states—Idaho, Colorado, Utah, and Wyoming—and in Indiana.

One important reason for the regression was that leading states recognized national officials' willingness to tolerate inadequate programs of public assistance. The Bureau of Public Assistance was unable to generate substantial progress in traditionalist states, and yet it continued to authorize the release of matching funds for inferior programs. Policymakers in individualist and moralist states observed the permissive attitude of national officials, which was rooted in concern for the recipients of public assistance, as well as the fear of retaliation in Congress by state delegations angered by the withdrawal of matching funds. The lesson was not lost on policymakers in state capitals outside the South, who concluded that they, too, might offer less public assistance and not be challenged.

Very often, the result was stagnation in moralist states, which did not want to become "welfare havens" by virtue of their comparative generosity. In individualist states, stagnation was often punctuated by periods of retrenchment upon the ascendance of Republicans to power. Thus, in Indiana the recipient rate for ADC actually fell from 35 to 22 per 1,000 between 1940 and 1950. And payments increased by an average of only $2.31, after adjusting for inflation. Neither moralist nor individualist values were able to flourish in a federal context dominated by Southern values.

CONCLUSION

The terms of the Social Security Act and the history of its implementation both suggest that the importance of traditionalist values extends far beyond the borders of the old Confederacy, their natural home. Indeed, Piven and Cloward (1991:737) go so far as to say that "the South was nothing less than triumphant in shaping the nation's social welfare policy" by virtue of its power in Congress. This allowed the South to defeat progressive and liberal proposals for securing the incomes of vulnerable populations and to hold out for decentralized programs that preserved the autonomy of state and local policymakers. And it was these policymakers, not only, but perhaps especially, in the South who made the decisions that constituted the pattern of American exceptionalism.

The fact that traditional values are in many respects antithetical to liberal individualism makes it necessary to reject the theory of liberal exceptionalism, even in its amended form. However, there is much to be learned from this rejection. In particular, the rejection raises the possibility that American social welfare policy might have been much less exceptional had it not been rooted so deeply in deference to Southern mores.

For example, if moralist values dominated social welfare policymaking, states like Washington would have been the norm, and the American welfare state would not have been very exceptional at all. This outcome might have been accomplished by financing the full cost of public assistance out of the national treasury, while retaining a federal organization for administrative purposes. That would have reduced competition between the states and allowed moralist values to survive in fuller form. But it seems unlikely that moralist values would ever have been influential enough to bring about this type of financing, so the counterfactual scenario must be dismissed as unrealistic.

Dominance by states with individualist or liberal cultures is easier to imagine, as Skocpol (1983) shows. In that case, states like Indiana would have been the norm in public assistance. That is, the idea of public assistance would have been widely accepted, but its implementation would vary, depending on whether the party of the haves or have-nots enjoyed control of state policymaking institutions. This scenario follows the pattern described by Piven and Cloward (1971), for whom the creation of income support programs was a politically acceptable and electorally attractive response by elites concerned with the social unrest that accompanied the Depression. Once the crisis passed and the need for cheap labor increased, assistance programs became more restrictive, according to Piven and Cloward, who go on to characterize relief-giving as a countercyclical process that next erupted during the War on Poverty.

However, the cycle of expansion and contraction can be interrupted, as Piven and Cloward explain in *The New Class War*. If these authors are right, the development of public assistance is cumulative. Entitlements become permanent by virtue of the political support they enjoy, and attempts to bring about a contraction will fail. If—and it is a big if—the same process applies at the state level, then the history of public assistance in states with individualist political subcultures ought to follow a similar path. However slowly and fitfully, ADC and other forms of social welfare policy should continue expanding over time, breaking the cyclical pattern of relief—unless fears of becoming "welfare magnets" become too strong, and prevent further liberalization.

Such fears may be set aside in counterfactual analyses by theorists who wonder what the course of social welfare policy in the United States might have been if individualist, and not traditionalist, states set the pace of development. A pattern of cumulative development or expansion, such as that implied in Piven and Cloward's revised thesis, suggests that public assistance would be more generous than it is, albeit less generous that it might have been under a regime of moralist values. That is, it seems very likely that the American welfare state would be less exceptional, if only it were more thoroughly liberal in character.

NOTES

I thank Larry Dodd and Cal Jillson for their support and encouragement, and for their editorial suggestions.

1. Old-age pensions were introduced in Germany in 1889, in Britain in 1908, in Canada in 1927, and in France in 1930. Unemployment insurance was introduced in Britain in 1911, in France in 1914, in Germany in 1927, and in Canada in 1935 (though the law was declared unconstitutional and was replaced by another in 1940). Compare King (1973a:300, table 3).

2. Hartz is only the best-known exponent of liberalism's hegemony in America. For a more recent statement of the position, see Huntington (1981), whose description of a prevalent "American Creed" parallels Hartz's characterization of "Lockean liberalism." A more subtle description of the American culture of liberal individualism is given by Merelman (1991), who mentions countervailing tendencies, but goes on to assert their weakness, compared to similar tendencies in other liberal cultures, for example, in Canada and, especially, in Great Britain.

3. The correlation is imperfect, as may be seen in Thompson, Ellis, and Wildavsky (1990), but the differences between Wildavsky and Elazar need not detain us here. Ellis (1991a) provides an incisive evaluation of Elazar's theory of political culture and criticism of his choice of descriptive labels.

4. The choice of cases is strategic. The connection between values and policy will naturally be strongest in states where a single subculture predominates. According to Sharkansky's (1969) revision of Elazar's cultural classification of states, moralist values are most pronounced in Minnesota, which has a score of 1, but Washington is the next closest, with a score of 1.66. Traditionalist values are most strongly developed in Arkansas and Mississippi, each of which has a score of 9. Georgia is nearly as traditionalist, with a score of 8.80. Indiana is in the middle, with a score of 6.33.

For comparative purposes, Minnesota and either Arkansas or Mississippi are too small; Washington, Indiana, and Georgia constitute a more useful set of "medium-size" states. Each is culturally homogenous, allowing for a good assessment of the impact of the three different value strains on policy. Also, other differences between the states are relatively minor; the three have similar populations, and their economies depend heavily on agriculture (though heavy manufacturing is also significant in each state's economy).

5. Abbott (1933:9) reports that twenty-three of Washington's thirty-nine counties made mothers' aid payments in 1921. See Abbott (1933) and Bucklin and Lynch (1939) for data on the scope of mothers' aid during the Depression. In Washington, mothers' aid provided broad coverage, but few benefits. As of 1931, the average monthly grant per family was $19.66, which ranked twenty-ninth among the forty-three states with mothers' aid. Sixteen families per 10,000 population were served, which ranked eighth (Abbott 1933:17; 19).

6. See Blumell (1973:430), and Laws of Washington, 1933, Chapter 29.

7. See National Archives, 1938a.

8. See National Archives, 1935–1940.

9. See National Archives, 1938b.

7

Macroeconomic Change and Political Transformation in the United States

EDWARD S. GREENBERG

I argue in this chapter that economic change, broadly understood, is the basic generator of political change in American politics. To understand the historical transformation of government institutions, political processes, and public policies in the United States, one must first understand the nature of economic transformations and how they are linked to the political. While I no longer believe that Marxism provides the only tool, or perhaps even the best tool, for illuminating these complex transformations and interactions, I continue to believe that specific insights from the Marxian tradition remain extremely useful in such an effort.

In this chapter, I want to speculate about the nature of the complex linkages that connect economic and political change, but I want to do so in a way that neither depends on Marxian foundations nor abandons them entirely—my aim is to transcend the conventional dichotomy in the social sciences in which the economic is either everything or nothing. For most Marxian scholars, the economy is determinative and explains all that needs explaining. For most mainstream scholars, the economy is taken as given, or otherwise ignored. Neither approach is very useful for understanding the state, political change, or public policy. The former gives the economic factor far too much credit, the latter not enough. The former is unacceptably deterministic; the latter is scientifically untenable. I will make the case for the primacy of macroeconomic change in explaining macropolitical change, even while I abandon much in the Marxian intellectual tradition.

More specifically, I will suggest that American post–Civil War political history can be periodized into a succession of what I call "policy regimes" that co-vary with and are substantially explained by macroeconomic change. While I believe that macroeconomic change is the most important factor in this story, I reject the idea that the economy is determinative, either in the first or the last instance (Althusser, 1969:111; Poulantzas,

1976:72). The particulars of the anatomy and physiology of "policy regimes," that is, cannot be automatically or directly derived from an analysis of the economy. Instead, regimes are the outcomes of the complex interplay of class and group conflict and cooperation, political alliances, party activities, the calculations of political actors, the weight of precedent and traditions, and the effects of governmental institutions.

THE ECONOMY AND ECONOMIC CHANGE

I hope to conceptualize the macroeconomy in a way that is broad enough to capture the many relationships between the economic and the political, yet that is precise enough for investigators to know what to look for in the course of their empirical investigations. In order to accomplish this specification, I draw on both Marxian and mainstream literatures in the belief that, at the taxonomic level of analysis at least (that is, at the level of formulating and naming categories or classes of things), the two are not contradictory. I suggest that we think about the macroeconomic as containing five main components. Macroeconomic change, it follows, refers to changes in any one, or any combination, of these components:

The Forces of Production

As defined by Marx, the forces of production[1] are those things used by agents to produce commodities; they are those things that contribute directly and materially within and to production. The productive forces conventionally include the instruments of production (such as tools, machines, factories, and the like), raw materials used in production, and labor power, understood as faculties and capacities (for example, strength, skill, inventiveness, and knowledge, including scientific knowledge). Technological advances in transportation and communications are examples of changes in the forces of production that continuously affect American politics.

The Social Relations of Production

Again, following Marx, social relations of production may be defined as the characteristic patterns of social interaction and social relationships under which and by which production is set into motion and controlled. They are, more simply, the prevailing patterns of control of production in a society. Social relations of production for Marx are class relations, meaning the distribution of and effective ownership rights over persons and productive forces (Cohen, 1978:35). For Marx and many others, the identification of the prevailing pattern of social relations of production remains the best way to differentiate and classify societies. A basic change in the social relations of production would mean a change in the fundamental nature of society—a transition, let us say, from feudalism to capitalism, or from capitalism to socialism. One example of this kind of change during our history was the transformation of the South from a slave-based economy to a wage-labor-based economy after the Civil War.

Patterns of Production Concentration

For workers, for people who use the goods produced by workers, and for the politics of the society in which they are located, it matters whether production takes place in a small enterprise or in a very large one and whether enterprises, no matter their size, are relatively autonomous from other enterprises or substantially linked together. Although I do not have the space to spell out all of the implications, it is clear that production size and concentration matters for economics and politics, if only at the simple level where concentrated economic power almost always translates into power in other spheres, whether social, cultural, or political. Size and concentration also matter for the typical patterns of work that exist in a society, the character of worker-management relations, and the kinds of problems that require the attention of public officials. Two periods of enterprise consolidation stand out during our history: the years on either side of the turn of the century, and the late 1970s and 1980s. Each of these periods of business consolidation is associated with significant political change.

Location in the World Economy

To describe an economy properly, that economy must be situated in the set of production, distribution, and financial networks in which it is imbedded. Failure to do so not only gives an incomplete picture of a national economy but leaves out of the equation a set of economic relations whose changing character cannot help but have political repercussions. Our own history in this regard is the story, first, of the transition from colony to industrial, commercial, and financial giant, and second, of our recent relative decline in the global economy. The rise of Reaganism took place in the midst of this last development.

Performance

Mainstream economists understand macroeconomic change as change in an economy's level of prices, money, production of goods and services, productivity, and the like. I include this element in my understanding of the macroeconomic not only because it seems to be a self-evidently useful way to describe an economy, but because changes in the overall economic performance of a society are almost always politically consequential. Deterioration in overall U.S. economic performance in the 1970s was an important part of the story of the election of Ronald Reagan; continued deterioration in the 1990s is at the root of the fundamental rethinking on competitiveness that is going on today.

Macroeconomic change, then, refers to change in any one of these five components, or to change in some combination of them. No one component has primacy over the others in explanations of political and policy change.[2] The linkages between components of economic change and political and policy change, moreover, are historically contingent, and must be examined empirically, rather than taken as given or predetermined. One cannot "read off" the particulars of political change from the particulars of macroeconomic change, whether such changes occur in technology, class relations, or location in the world economy. The effects of each must be traced and demonstrated.[3]

CAPITALISM

The United States is a capitalist society. It makes sense, then, if we want to understand the relationship between macroeconomic and political change in the United States to grasp some of the essentials of the organization and operation of capitalist economies.

Capitalism (like any other economic system), at any particular moment in its history and in any particular society, may be described in terms of its forces of production, its degree of concentration, its overall performance, and its place in the world economy. It is distinguished from other economies, however, by its characteristic social relations of production, namely by the prevalence of free wage labor (nonslave, nonfeudal labor), private ownership of the means of production, and coordination of production and distribution through markets. This definition remains useful even if one does not accept the Marxian conception of the "laws of motion" of capitalism. That is to say, classification of economies in terms of their dominant social relations of production remains useful even if one does not accept Marx's claims about the historical trajectory of capitalist societies and its transformation into socialism (Heilbroner, 1985).

Though the scientific status of the laws of motion is unclear, it is undeniably the case that capitalism is a uniquely dynamic and ever-changing form of economic society in which the productive forces are constantly being expanded and periodically being revolutionized (Cohen, 1978; Wright, 1979:94–96). All economies undergo change, of course, but constant change is especially characteristic of capitalism; it has never been and cannot be a steady-state system, as many precapitalist and feudal systems have been (Heilbroner, 1985: chaps. 2, 3; Kuznets, 1953; Smith, [1776] 1965, book 1, chaps. 1–3). As Robert Gilpin puts it, "In the absence of social, physical, and other constraints, a market economy has an expansive and dynamic quality. It tends to cause economic growth, to expand territorially, and to bring all segments of society into its embrace"(Gilpin, 1987:19). It also continuously transforms the division of labor, reshapes the forms of work, and refashions how enterprises are organized and how they operate.

Gilpin suggests that the dynamism of market capitalism is caused by the centrality of competition as a determinant of individual and institutional behavior and the importance of efficiency in determining the survivability of economic actors in a competitive environment (Gilpin, 1987:19; also see Heilbroner, 1985, chap. 3). Marxists would substantially agree with this formulation, but add to it the centrality of the struggle of social classes over the division of the surplus: For example, workers push for higher wages; owners mechanize and automate to escape wage pressures on profits; competitors must match or surpass this level of mechanization and automation as the price of survival (Block, 1987:63–65; Cohen, 1978; DuBoff, 1989:8–9; Greenberg, 1985:36–38; Heilbroner, 1985, 1980; Wright 1979, chap. 3). Whether capitalism has an unfolding logic or historical trajectory (other than the expansion of the productive forces, as in Cohen, 1978) is unknown and unproved; all that is known is that capitalism is ever-changing and uniquely dynamic.

Persistent change in capitalism may also be seen in the phenomemon of "long waves," rhythmic upturns and downturns in prices and economic growth. Empirically, the existence of long waves, whether of the Kondratiev price variety or the Simon Kuznets growth variety, are reasonably well-established, though the causal mechanisms that generate such waves are matters of intense scholarly dispute.[4] While the causal linkages in the story of "long waves" are not yet established, the phenomenon of long waves of expansion and contraction adds another element of change and transformation to the economy that is politically consequential, in the sense that these elements provide the context within which political and economic actors operate. Public policy and corporate strategy are likely to be different, for instance, in a period of rapid economic expansion than in a period of long-term contraction.

Some scholars working within the Marxist tradition believe that capitalism has experienced a series of historical transformations that, without changing the capitalist character of society (that is, without changing its fundamental social relations of production), create stages characterized by contrasting institutional forms, class relations, trade and intercourse with other societies, and crisis tendencies. Erik Olin Wright, for instance, posits six such stages: primitive accumulation, manufacture, machinofacture, monopoly capitalism, advanced monopoly capitalism, and state-directed monopoly capitalism, each with a unique set of crisis tendencies, class relations, and state forms and policies (Wright, 1979). Economic historian Robert Heilbroner, following closely on the pioneering work of Ernst Mandel (1975) identifies four major stages in the history of capitalism, with transformation points in the world system around 1848, 1893, 1941, and 1973, roughly corresponding to long-wave transition points indentified by Brian Berry (1991). Sociologists Robert Ross and Kent Trachte periodize capitalism into competitive and monopoly stages, adding a relatively new global capitalist one (Ross and Trachte, 1990). It is the struggle to come to grips with this last transformation that, in my view, accounts for much of the sense of policy drift in our own time, and for the failure to create a new "policy regime" during the Reagan years.

WHY ECONOMIC CHANGE IS POLITICALLY CONSEQUENTIAL

I have suggested that macroeconomic change involves changes in the forces and relations of production, in patterns of enterprise concentration, in performance, and in location in the world economy. I have added that while change characterizes all forms of economic society, it is particularly dramatic in its scale, extent, and pace in capitalism. I have further suggested that change in capitalism does not follow a smooth line but progresses, instead, through stages that are analogous to what has been called "punctuated equilibrium" in the biological sciences.[5] I have offered the thought, finally, that economic change of the sort I have described is politically consequential. Let me propose several reasons why this may be the case before I take up the issue of the relationship between political and economic stages.

In the first place, overall economic performance in a society, particularly the capacity of the economy to produce a surplus, sets the parameters of the standard of living of the population and determines the level of resources available to people in society to pursue their private and collective goals. The size of the surplus represents a fundamental constraint on what is possible in any society.

Economies are mechanisms not only of production but of distribution; they distribute the surplus among individuals, groups, and regions in particular ways. Economic change tends to alter these distributions among classes, regions, economic sectors, and social groups. And this change process almost always creates new winners and losers, with winners often turning to politics for protection of their gains and the losers doing likewise to rectify their declining fortunes.

The nature of the distribution of the surplus is politically consequential, moreover, because control of wealth and income is always an important ingredient in the mix of factors that determines the distribution of social and political power. To the extent that macroeconomic change alters the nature of this distribution or the places of individuals and groups in the income and wealth stratification systems, so too does it alter social and political power.

Long-term economic change—whether it involves growth, shifts in the location of production, technological change, changes in the prevailing forms of business organization or in the balance between the agricultural, industrial, and service sectors—tends to disrupt established ways of life and prevailing social arrangements and institutions. Short-term economic change, in business cycles in capitalist societies, is often severe enough to cause social pain and disruption. Such disruptions in the fabric of social and personal life are among the most powerful spurs to political mobilization and involvement and, in a democracy, in particular, something that political leaders must attend to on pain of being turned out of office (McAdams, 1982; Smelser, 1962; Truman, 1951).

In summary, then, macroeconomic change in all of its complexity shapes and constrains political processes and institutions by playing a central role in the determination of the *political agenda* for individuals, groups, classes, and state actors, and the *distribution of politically relevant resources* in society. The combination of agenda setting and resource distribution is a key ingredient, I will suggest below, in the story of the rise and fall of policy regimes in American politics.

In making these claims, I do not propose that influence is unidirectional, only that it tends to be weighted, in probabilistic terms, from the economic to the political. Lines of influence can and do sometimes move in the other direction. Thus, it is the state that determines the nature and distribution of property rights as well as many of the rules governing economic behavior (Gilpin, 1987:10). States have even been known to alter the composition of social classes (Richards and Waterbury, 1990:38–39) and the basic structures of the economy, as in Ataturk's Turkey, Meiji Japan, and post–World War II Taiwan. I suggest the existence, then, of an interdependency between the economic and the political, with stickiness in one direction: from the economic to the societal and political.

I have discussed capitalism thus far as an economic system in which change is endemic, and have observed that the pattern of change is one of stages, or punctuated equilibrium, and that economic change is strongly linked to political change. Is there reason to believe that there is a relationship between capitalist economic stages and political stages over the course of American history? Clearly, this is so. For one thing, strong evidence exists that American political history may be fruitfully understood in stage-specific terms. In this volume Jillson (Chapter 2) reviews the literature on this question quite exhaustively, so I will not present an extended discussion of the issue. Suffice it to say that eras of various lengths and characteristics have been identified. Samuel Huntington has identified sixty- to seventy-year periods of creedal passion (Huntington, 1981), while Lichtman (1976), McCloskey (1960), Skowronek (1982), and Ackerman (1991), among others, have identified similar broad constitutional-political periods in American history that differ from each other in terms of prevailing ideas, institutional arrangements, party systems, popular opinion, and constitutional interpretation. Within these broad constitutional-political eras, an abundant research literature demonstrates the existence of distinctive party systems, linked to institutional and policy transformations (Brady, 1988; Burnham, 1970; Beck, 1974a, 1979; Carmines and Stimson, 1981; Clubb, Flanigan, and Zingale, 1980; Key, 1955; Sundquist, 1983). Shorter mood-swing periods, which alternate between public purpose and private interests, have also been identified by historian Arthur Schlesinger, Jr. (1986).

The key issue remains: Do these cycles coincide with the periodization in the economy? The evidence remains somewhat ambiguous, to be sure, but there is some reason to believe that, at the least, a clear link exists between critical elections and economic turning points. As Brian Berry demonstrates, every critical election in American history—1800, 1828, 1860, 1896, and 1932—is associated either with a Kuznets growth peak or a Kondratiev price trough (Berry, 1991, chap.8). It is still too early in the research on this question to accept Berry's conclusion as the final word on the link between critical elections and economic long-wave turning points, but there is suggestive evidence that links economic and political stages in American history. The links between economic turning points and other periodizations—mood swings, constitutional periods, and the like—are less persuasive.

Though this literature is copious, I believe that it remains deficient in several important respects. The focus in the economic literature has been primarily on price movements and growth, though attention has also been paid to stock market price movements. The focus in the political science literature, for its part, has been primarily on voters and their shifting party loyalties, though some impressive stabs have been made at linking institutional and policy changes to party eras as well (Brady, 1988; Skowronek, 1982; Sundquist, 1983). However, most of the major conceptualizations do not consider changes in prototypical forms of production in society, business strategies, and business organization. Economic stages and party periods are important, but they must also be tied to underlying structural changes in the economy and to the role of business groups in dominant political coalitions. I try to bring all these factors together in my conceptualization of policy regimes (Greenberg, 1985).

POLICY REGIME

By "policy regime" I mean a relatively stable period in democratic capitalist societies when a dominant political coalition, generally organized by a
fraction of the dominant economic class, is able to agree upon and institute a set of public policies that (for a time) address the fundamental problems that are posed by a dynamic and ever-changing economy.[6] The key
operational indicators for a policy regime are (1) a dominant political coalition, (2) an identifiable consensus among dominant political actors
(public and private) on the main outlines of public policy, and (3) public
policies that work reasonably well to address the problems that called
forth the "policy regime" in the first place. Because they "work," in some
sense, policy regimes also tend to be characterized by the presence of a
widespread sense of legitimacy about the regime within the population,
and self-confidence among political leaders.

Policy regimes have similar forms, though they differ in content. Each
has a period of gradual formation in which a dominant political coalition
and a policy consensus is fashioned and policies favored by that coalition
are implemented; then, a temporary period of stabilization ensues as the
problems to which policy is directed are temporarily managed; and, finally, a period of unravelling of the political coalition and the policy consensus occurs, as new and largely unanticipated problems emerge, which
are usually economic in origin, and for which the prevailing policy regime
is either inappropriate or counterproductive. The periods between regimes tend to be periods of confusion and dissension, as society drifts
without benefit of a dominant political coalition or policy consensus, as in
the periods following the Era of Good Feelings and the collapse of corporate liberalism in the early 1970s in the United States (which I will review
in some detail below).

Economic change and transformation are the primary factors underlying this process, though, as mentioned above, the specific nature of the
policy regime is not determined by the nature of the economy. Rather, the
economic represents the ground of the political; as the ground shifts, political actors must respond to the problems and prospects of changing economic conditions. Because capitalism has been the prevailing mode of
production in the United States since the end of the Civil War, what Marx
called the social relations of production (or the dominant system of class
relations) have remained relatively constant. However, as the American
economy changed from an agriculturally based, relatively insulated, and
competitive economy in the beginning into a concentrated, industrial, and
service economy of worldwide scope, everything else has been in flux: the
forces of production, forms of business organization and the degree of
economic concentration, the place of the United States in the world econ-

omy, and overall performance. As I have suggested elsewhere, moreover, these various economic changes have come in clusters, giving a particular character to different periods of our economic history (Greenberg, 1985) and are associated with both the undermining of existing policy regimes and the rise of new ones.

Though there are some surface similarities, my conceptualization of the dynamics of policy regimes is not coterminous with the concepts, "regime of accumulation" (Aglietta, 1979; Boyer, 1979), or "social structures of accumulation" (Gordon, Edwards, and Reich, 1982), both of which I find to be too deterministic (that is, both argue that particular forms of production and particular stages of capitalist development *require* particular and determinate kinds of state policies and institutional arrangements)—they are too closely tied to the traditional and not terribly useful base-superstructure relationship in which state policies are automatically and directly derived from the social relations of production. My conceptualization of policy regimes is more historically contingent, with the policy options more open than is allowed for in "regulationist" accounts. Rather than saying, as regulationists tend to do, that given a particular dominant form of production, a particular stage in the development of an economy, and x problem, y policies, and z institutions must follow, I say that y policies and z institutions are among several that might be adopted, depending on a variety of factors, including existing institutional arrangements, lines of political conflict, and class conflict and cooperation. Policy regimes, therefore, are not capitalistically preordained, or stage-determined, though (as in "biased pluralism" accounts like those of Lindblom, 1977 and Schattschneider, 1960) we can make reasonable probability statements about the identity of those who are most likely to be members of the dominant coalitions and those who are not.

POLICY REGIMES AND THEORIES OF THE STATE

Before I turn my attention to specific cases of policy regimes and their linkages to economic change, it is important that I first clarify my general approach to the state, as implied in the statement above about the identity of individuals, groups, and classes in the dominant coalition of a policy regime. My central point will be that none of the major approaches to the state in capitalist society are convincing, including the several Marxian variants, and that a synthetic approach that incorporates the most convincing features of each, yet reserves a special place for the role of the business corporation in general and vanguard capitalist fractions in particular, is required. Let me elaborate.

I have identified elsewhere what I consider to be the three major approaches to the state in capitalist society and their major shortcomings

(Greenberg, 1990). The "citizen-responsive" state model locates the sources of state action in the articulated demands of popular majorities or intense minorities, and in the need for public officials to respond to such demands as the price for their retention of political power. Here I am mainly thinking about the pluralist and voter-centered literature in the social sciences that pertains to formally democratic societies (Alford and Friedland, 1985; Bentley, 1935; Carnoy, 1984; Downs, 1957; Dahl, 1961; Dahl and Lindblom, 1953; Fiorina, 1981; Pomper, 1968; and Truman, 1951). The state-centric approach, calling for "bringing the state back in" (Evans, Rueschemeyer, and Skocpol, 1985), rejects what it considers to be the overly society-centered emphasis in alternative approaches, arguing instead that state behavior and policy must be explained by factors internal to the state itself: the interests of elected and bureaucratic officials, the effects of law and institutions, the momentum of existing policies, and the overall capacities of states relative to competing centers of power (Evans, Rueschemeyer, and Skocpol, 1985; Katznelson, 1985; Katzenstein, 1978; Krasner, 1978; Levi, 1981; Nettl, 1968; Nordlinger, 1981; Trimberger, 1978; Stepan, 1978). The capitalist state approach of Marxists and neo-Marxists asks why states in capitalist societies are necessarily capitalist states. There are basically three schools of thought on this question. Instrumentalists answer that capitalist states behave in ways that favor capital because the dominant capitalist class has both the need and the resources to directly influence the state to do its bidding (Domhoff, 1971; Greenberg, 1985; Kolko, 1965; Miliband, 1969; Weinstein, 1968). Structuralists counter that state action and policy are explained by the systematic and inescapable need of the state to maintain capitalism in the face of persistent crisis. In this conceptualization, it is the need to reproduce capitalism and its social relations of production that forces the state to do what it does; the state is the effect rather than the cause (Cohen, 1978; Habermas, 1975; O'Connor, 1973; Offe, 1975; Poulantzas, 1973; Wright, 1979). Those who counter with a class struggle approach typically argue that whereas the state in a capitalist society tends to reflect the interests of the capitalist class in the long run, the state is constrained in this role by the waxing and waning of the political power of the working class. Thus, state policy is not uniformly favorable to capitalist interests, but often must accomodate the working class to the benefit of that class (Block, 1977, 1987; Esping-Andersen, 1985; Korpi, 1983; O'Connor, 1973; Przeworski, 1985; Stephens, 1979; Wright, 1979).

Each of these approaches represents a powerful yet flawed and limited approach to an understanding of the state and how it relates to macroeconomic change. Each of these state theoretic traditions has, in John Alford and Roger Friedland's (1985) terms, a "home domain" where it is most comfortable and convincing in an explanatory sense, and a foreign terrain where it ignores essential issues and leaves others untheorized. The citizen-responsive state approach, for instance, nicely highlights the everyday dynamics of the actions of state actors, groups, and citizens, but almost completely misses the boat on the importance of the economy, the political consequences of unequal economic power, the role of the large corporation, the sometimes relatively autonomous power of public officials, and the influence of state institutions. The state-centric approach nicely highlights the important role of independent politicians, political leadership, the rules of the game, policy traditions, and governmental institutions, but almost entirely ignores or fails to incorporate structural influences like the economy, the culture, and society. What is unacceptable in this approach are arguments that state autonomy is axiomatic and unproblematic, and that influences which arise from group, class, and political conflict in society, or from the contradictions and tensions created by change in the economy, must take a backseat to factors internal to the state itself. Finally, the capitalist state approach nicely illuminates many of what might be called the preconditions of American political life—how a changing capitalist economy fashions much of the agenda of politics and helps determine the distribution of politically relevant resources—but fails to incorporate the important insights about politics and the state made by the other two approaches discussed above. The capitalist state approach, that is to say, does not properly theorize either politics or the state as a set of institutions and practices. Each of the conceptual paths within the capitalist state approach, moreover, is problematic in its own right (van den Berg, 1988): Instrumentalist accounts, modern versions of the simple class theory of Marx's *The Communist Manifesto* and Lenin's *State and Revolution*, are wrong empirically; structuralist accounts are unacceptably functionalist; class struggle accounts, though more convincing at the empirical level, do not differ much from the biased pluralism approaches of the later Dahl and Lindblom (Dahl, 1989; Lindblom, 1977), or the earlier Grant McConnell (McConnell, 1966) and E. E. Schattschneider (Schattschneider, 1960), and have no reasonable claim to being Marxist.

I believe that the best approach to the state in a capitalist society is one that brings these approaches together in such a way that the strengths of each are preserved and their shortcomings compensated for (Greenberg and Page, 1988). What is needed, in my view, is a conceptualization that places economic change and the disproportionate political power of dominant economic power at the center of analysis, namely, a conceptualization that recognizes the constraints on what is politically possible in every economic system, yet one that also recognizes the independent interests and capacities of state actors, the structuring influences of institutions, and group and popular pressures on political decision makers. While a totally acceptable formulation has not yet been advanced, Ralph Miliband has gone some distance in solving the problem (Miliband, 1983).

In his article, "State Power and Class Interests," Miliband proposes that the "relationship between the dominant class in advanced capitalist societies and the state is one of *partnership between two different, separate forces*, linked to each other by many threads, yet each having its own separate sphere of concerns" and capacities (Miliband, 1983:65). In his formulation, state actors have broad areas of autonomy and pursue a set of goals that are their own; they seek to protect their own power and realize their own conception of the national interest. In his formulation, moreover, capital does not enjoy uncontested hegemony but is frequently forced to make concessions against its wishes, especially if there is strong popular and group pressure on political decisionmakers. For the most part, however, the state and capital are partners; most of the time, the interests and goals of state actors and capital are compatible. Though their interests are not fused, an alliance between them is usually both possible and helpful to both.

These interests, although compatible, are almost never identical. Miliband (1983) suggests that a permanent tension necessarily exists between the two. Each reads the current situation and what must be done from different angles. Each has separate spheres of competence, power, and concerns. The terms of their relationship are not fixed. Most important, according to Miliband, state actors tend to increase their distance from capital the more fully the working classes are united and mobilized. To use his terms, the strains on the partnership are most evident in historical periods when the class struggle is most marked. The partnership becomes closer when popular and group pressures from below are weak, a description that fits the United States for most, but not all, of its history.

In the end, however, as Miliband notes, the state is a capitalist state in the sense that protection of the capitalist system becomes its overriding goal. It is not difficult to see why this might be so. According to Miliband and others (Block, 1977), the ability of elected state actors to retain their popularity and thus stay in power, and the revenues necessary for them to enact their policy goals, depends on a healthy, expanding capitalist economy, and forces them to be particularly attentive to the investment climate and the needs of large investors. It is also the case that economic power translates rather easily into political power in modern polyarchies (Dahl, 1989; McConnell, 1966; Miliband, 1969; Schattschneider, 1960). Charles Lindblom's classic discussion of the privileged position of the large corporation and the phenomenon of "circularity" (business advantages in the interest group system, in access to political decisionmakers, in shaping campaign choices, and in molding and mobilizing volitions) in modern democracies like the United States provides most of the raw material for a microfoundational explanation of Miliband's broad claim, though I suspect that Lindblom would say that the state in a capitalist society *tends* to favor large scale capital, rather than *must* do so. I would agree.

The main problem with this structural power of capital account, in both its Marxian and non-Marxian forms (Block, 1977; Lindblom, 1977; Miliband, 1969), in which the special advantages enjoyed by business put it in a privileged position relative to the state, is that its proponents fail to take proper note of the internal divisions within the capitalist class (or big business in Lindblom's formulation) and within the state, never investigating how these divisions affect state action and direction, particularly during crises and periods of rapid transition. Hugh Ward has formulated a promising approach to these issues in his paper "Evolution and Regulation: A Defense of Weak Economism" (Ward, 1989). Ward suggests that in periods of crisis neither capital as a whole nor the state as a whole has a purchase on the proper strategies to transcend prevailing difficulties; the state is not automatically able to make the proper response to economic difficulties. What happens, instead, according to Ward, is that the market tends to select the most successful adapters to crisis to insure that those businesses that adapt most effectively will enjoy the highest rates of return. These businesses, in turn, eventually become the leading fraction of the capitalist class as their approach becomes widely emulated, as they prove most effective in attracting financial capital, and as they come to enjoy broad legitimacy within their class and beyond. Successful adapters also have more resources to put into the political arena when they attempt, as most do at some point, to seek government policies favorable to their interests. State officials, for their part, casting about for a road out of economic difficulties, tend to be attracted, according to Ward, to the most successful adapters, both because of the potential support of such adapters for the political careers of helpful officials and the promise that the strategies of the successful adapters might work as a model for the entire economy. While there is much to be worked out in Ward's approach, it offers a promising beginning, recognizing the internal divisions within the dominant economic class, how public officials are pulled within the orbit of its leading fractions, and how new political alliances and public policies emerge out of economic crisis and transformation. Most important, he has provided a microfoundational basis for the close ties of leading capitalist fractions and state officials during periods of crisis and transformation.

CORPORATE CAPITALISM: A SHORT CASE STUDY
OF THE RISE AND FALL OF A POLICY REGIME

Let me review what I have tried to establish up to this point. First, I have suggested that the history of the United States may be conceptualized as a series of punctuated equilibriums within an overall pattern of dynamic capitalist change. I have proposed, moreover, that American political history can be conceptualized as a series of policy regimes whose rise and fall are tied closely to these economic transformations. Further, the policy regimes that appear in response to crisis are not random but are created by a dominant coalition made up of private and public actors and groups, in which the leading fraction of the capitalist class plays a particularly prominent role.

Because of space limitations, I will not review previously published material that establishes, at least in a provisional sense, the existence of a series of policy regimes in American history (Greenberg, 1985). The remainder of this chapter is devoted instead to sketching the outlines of one of the most consequential U.S. policy regimes, to show how its rise and fall was linked to macroeconomic transformations. My hope is that a short case study of the rise and fall of what I call "corporate liberalism" will help establish the utility of the general approach I call for in this analysis.

The Rise of Corporate Liberalism

The corporate liberal[7] regime spanned the years from about the end of World War II to the mid-1970s. Like all "policy regimes," it was characterized by a period of policy effectiveness, broad agreement on policies and ideology, and a stable ruling coalition. I will argue that the regime collapsed in the mid-1970s for reasons both internal and external to itself, with macroeconomic change being a primary causal factor.

The belief that steady economic growth with minimal inflation was both possible and likely in a modern corporate economy was the ideational heart of corporate liberalism. This belief was constructed during the postwar years on solid economic foundations: United States supremacy in the world trading system, an efficient and productive domestic economy, and the management tools of modern economic science. It should be recalled that two world wars had left the principal trade rivals of the United States (Britain, France, Germany, Japan, and the Netherlands) in virtual ruin, highly dependent upon American economic, financial, and military resources, and helpless to prevent American economic penetration into their former colonial empires. The United States emerged from the war as the single most dominant, industrialized capitalist country, as well as the leading trading nation—with the most powerful and productive industrial system the world had ever seen. For a time, the United States was able to provide its citizens with an unprecedented and ever-increasing standard of living. For decades, growth in gross national product, low levels of unemployment (as compared to the 1930s and 1980s), and very low rates of inflation were the norm. This industrial machine was assisted by the boost given its productive and technological infrastructure by the war itself, as well as by the general militarization of the American economy after the war.

Corporate liberalism was also characterized by a reigning public policy consensus, fashioned partly from the raw materials of previous regimes and policy agendas. The New Deal put in place the first building blocks of the regime: programs of unemployment and old-age insurance, limited public welfare and public works projects, cooperative business-labor relations through legally defined and government protected collective bargaining, the rationalized management of agriculture through programs of production control and price supports, and business self-regulation. The experience of World War II added needed lessons concerning the role that a large military establishment with a growing defense-dominated federal budget might play in a strategy to avoid economic stagnation, and about the benefits to be enjoyed by close collaboration between corporate and political leadership in Washington. The immediate postwar years also contributed, I would suggest, to a decisive move away from the isolationist tradition and a strong belief in the prospects and possibilities of controlled and perpetual economic growth.

A set of ideas and assumptions, shared by private and public elites, supported the policy consensus during corporate liberalism's period of stable equilibrium, which stretched from about the mid-1950s to the late 1960s. These included the following: government encouragement of economic growth, guided by the principles of Keynesian "demand-side" theory and stimulated primarily by the defense budget; government support of and assistance to oligopolistic corporations and open dependence on their economic, scientific, and technological contributions; government provision of the machinery for the regulation of collective bargaining in the oligopolistic sectors of the economy; government protection for and encouragement of the expansion of American business into world markets, particularly in the Third World; and provision of a full range of social insurance programs to protect against some of the harsh personal consequences of unemployment, old age, and illness. For a time, preeminence in the world market allowed government during this era to serve all of these ends and to avoid the unhappy choice between "guns and butter." Policymakers thought it possible to satisfy the requirements of the Defense Department and to significantly expand the social welfare and social insurance systems out of this "growth dividend." For a time, furthermore, there even seemed to be enough economic and political slack to allow for significant stabs against social injustice and racial discrimination.

The imperative of economic growth lay at the heart of corporate liberalism. With economic growth, it was believed, virtually all things were possible, and especially, the always difficult choice between guns and butter need no longer be faced. With economic growth, one could have both a strong military establishment and a strong social security system; one could meet the worldwide commitments of a great power while providing a safety net for the worst-off members of society. With economic growth, one could increase both private consumption and funding of the public sector, including the military; and the problems of the poor could be solved without the need for redistribution.

How was growth possible? To a surprising degree, liberal intellectuals and political leaders saw the corporation as the central institution in this economic drama.[8] The corporation became a principal location of techno-logical innovation and the fount of capital investment.[9] It was generally believed that the health and welfare of the large corporations were essential to the health and welfare of the nation, and public policies from 1945 to 1965 were largely consistent with this view,[10] and included loose anti-trust enforcement; a healthy level of defense expenditures; an exceedingly light regulatory burden; research and development support; and a wide range of subsidy arrangements (Greenberg, 1985).

Because it was able to pursue these many seemingly contradictory poli-cies beneficial to so many and diverse interests in American life, the politi-cal coalitional character of corporate liberalism proved to be strikingly comprehensive.[11] It was centered, notably, in the Democratic party, whose dominance in the American system was initially won by Franklin Roose-velt's New Deal, cemented by Democratic party leadership during World War II, and guaranteed by postwar prosperity. While Republican presi-dents were elected during this era, the country was solidly Democratic—Democrats enjoyed supremacy in the vast majority of statehouses and governorships, in the U.S. Congress, and in popular party identification. The Democratic party was a vast tent under which a tumultuous and di-verse cast of characters rested, including oligopolistic corporations and fi-nancial institutions, liberal foundations, organized labor, white ethnic groups, farmers, southern segregationists, university and urban-based lib-eral intellectuals, black Americans, the rural and urban poor, and many others. The party was able to accomplish this seemingly impossible task because the growth dividend allowed each of these interests to enjoy some piece of the policy action. In a period of sustained growth, farmers could have their subsidies, corporations their defense contracts, southern states their full complement of military bases and shipyards, university scholars their research grants, racial minorities their antidiscrimination laws, unions their place at the bargaining table and in the councils of gov-ernment, and the poor their antipoverty and community action funds. Un-der the aegis of the Democratic party, American public policy assumed a form that Theodore Lowi has termed "interest group liberalism" (Lowi, 1969) in which—given an economy whose potential growth knew no lim-its—privileges, resources, and program administration were freely and generously parceled out to virtually every organized interest group in the country, with oligopolistic corporations enjoying an especially privileged place at the table (Lindblom, 1977; Vogel, 1989).

It is an astonishing fact that this system seems to have worked in both an economic and political sense for more than two decades. It satisfied for a considerable length of time the needs of large corporations, eased some of the tensions between labor and management, and protected America's position in the world economy. The economy advanced, corporate profitability was nearly automatic, living standards rose dramatically, and the conditions of the poor and of racial minorities noticeably improved.

The Disintegration of Corporate Liberalism

The corporate liberal regime that dominated American political life in the postwar period began to unravel in the early 1970s, and was in shambles by the mid-1970s. By then, each and every one of its foundation stones had crumbled before an onslaught of developments at home and abroad; its fall was unavoidable as its supporting economic, social, cultural, and political structures proved to be transitory rather than fixed features of the American system. Most important were macroeconomic changes that drastically transformed the position of the United States in the world economy by the early 1970s; its fall from a dominant economic and political position was represented by defeat in Vietnam, the rise of the Organization of Petroleum Exporting Countries (OPEC), the slide in its position in world trade, and dollar devaluation (Gilpin, 1987; Kennedy, 1987; Magaziner and Reich, 1982).

The protracted war in Southeast Asia was played out within the context of the reemergence of the economies of Western Europe and Japan. Indeed, in one of history's recurring ironies, the war itself became an important contributory factor in the shifting positions of the major powers as the United States saw its material and financial resources drained by the war and the economies of its rivals fueled by massive war orders. The war, however, merely exaggerated tendencies already well under way, as Western Europe and Japan gradually emerged as powerful and competing trading nations (Kennedy, 1987). Although the American economy remained the single most powerful economy during the 1970s, it no longer stood unchallenged. Instead, it found itself caught in a process of gradual yet inexorable decline relative to the other advanced market economies. In the end, its position came to be characterized by an overall interdependence with the other advanced market economies and the loss of its position as the leading and guiding nation among them. Interdependence, moreover, came increasingly to tip over into intense rivalry. This renewed struggle and incipient anarchy may be observed in the abandonment of the Bretton Woods arrangements in 1971; the trade struggles with Japan involving electronics, automobiles, textiles, and steel; the international struggle over guaranteed sources of oil after the 1973 OPEC boycott; and the recurrent efforts of central banks to gain trade advantages through currency manipulations.

The decline of America's international position was further propelled by the rise of OPEC and the end of the era of cheap energy resources. To a very great extent, the impetus for the American postwar boom was provided by a seemingly inexhaustible supply of cheap petroleum products, a situation that could no longer be obtained once crude oil prices skyrocketed after the OPEC boycott and the formation of new international oil arrangements in its aftermath. These changes contributed to a decrease in investment funds for the domestic American economy; enormous deficits in the American balance of payments; and enhanced efforts by other raw material suppliers in the Third World to form cartels to try to increase the world prices for their resources.

These combined developments contributed significantly to reversals in the performance of the American economy by the early and mid-1970s. Recall that one of the basic foundation stones of corporate liberalism was steady, predictable economic growth tied to acceptable levels of inflation. Only such a base could sustain the guns-and-butter policy package and command the loyalty of a broad and varied range of interests feeding on the growth dividend. This foundation stone crumbled in the face of unprecedented levels of (combined) inflation and stagnation by the closing years of the Nixon presidency. The "capacity utilization rate" for American industry fell from an average in excess of 90 percent in the 1950s to an average of less than 80 percent by the early 1970s. The unemployment problem, kept in partial check for most of the 1960s, began to show signs of secular increase in the late 1960s and early 1970s. By the middle of the 1970s, unemployment rates of 6 and 7 percent and "underemployed" and "discouraged worker" rates of another 3 or 4 percent were considered normal, that is, relatively resistant to the normal governmental counter-stagnation tools. By 1975, the United States was suffering the worst unemployment rates since the Great Depression.

This situation of stagnation characterized by high unemployment and idle plants was exacerbated by a collapse in private investment in the early 1970s, particularly in those sectors of the economy most important to long-term recovery, namely, in plant and machine replacement, modernization, and capacity expansion (Magaziner and Reich, 1982; Thurow 1980), and by a serious decline in the rate of profit.[12] These changes made the corporate-organized labor compact impossible to sustain as the business community mounted a sustained attack on the size of the wage bill, the rising costs of the welfare state, and the regulatory threats to competitiveness and profitability (Edsall, 1984; Vogel, 1989). What was unprecedented during this same period was the existence, side-by-side with stagnation, of uncomfortably high levels of price inflation, a development at odds with the widely accepted "Philips Curve" and prevailing economic doctrine.[13]

All of these economic and political troubles for the United States were coincident with and probably a reflection of basic changes taking place in world capitalism. Berry has shown, for instance, that a fundamental long-wave turning point of the Kuznets variety occurred in 1973 (Berry, 1991). Several scholars have pointed to the early and mid-1970s as a crucial period of transformation in the organization of industrial production, corporate organizational and strategic behavior, and corporate-labor relations (Cox, 1987; Greenberg, 1985; Ross and Trachte, 1990).

The performance of the economy seems also to have contributed to a crisis of confidence in the Keynesian-derived tools for management of the economy. At the height of regime self-confidence in the mid-1960s, Walter Heller, the eminent economist and former chair of the Council of Economic Advisors, was moved to observe that "economics has come of age in the 1960s. Two presidents have recognized and drawn on modern economics as a source of national strength and presidential power. Their willingness to use, for the first time, the full range of modern economic tools underlines the unbroken U.S. expansion since early 1961" (Heller, 1966). What became increasingly self-evident within but a few years of this statement was that the degree of managerial control available to any single national government was increasingly limited, given the oligopolistic organization of the most important sectors of the economy and the resultant ability of the major industrial and financial corporations to ignore or vitiate the prodding of Keynesian managers, given endemic and permanent unemployment, given massive increase in the debt structure, and given the growing internationalization of the operations of trade, industry and finance. The promise of perpetual economic stability built upon the steering capabilities of modern economic science proved to be short-lived indeed.

By the mid-1970s this combination of a sputtering economy, international retreat, stagnant living standards, and the various disillusionments surrounding the Watergate affair had developed into what might be called a crisis of legitimacy—a deterioration in the confidence of the American people in their major institutions and leaders. Opinion polls during this period were unambiguous on this issue, consistently demonstrating distressingly low and ever-declining scores on popular confidence in political leaders, political and governmental institutions, business and labor leaders, and so on (Lipset and Schneider, 1983). Identification with and participation in the political life of the country was also at a historic nadir.

At the political level, the collapse of corporate liberalism was signalled by the disintegration of the Democratic party coalition, which had dominated American political life for over a quarter of a century. With the economic base no longer able to support federal government financing of both defense and social justice in a noninflationary manner, and as tough choices had to be made between competing group demands, elements of the coalition began to fall away from the Democratic party. The defection of the once solid South from the party ranks and the slow but steady decline in the enthusiasm (and thus in votes, contributions, and campaign work) of labor unionists, white ethnics, and Jews was notable. This tendency was first evident on a substantial scale during the two elections of Richard Nixon (1968 and 1972) and continued unabated throughout the decade. The oligopolistic corporate sector also exited the coalition. As corporate leaders began to see corporate liberal economic and social policy as a fetter on their competitive position in the global economy, they began to assault the regime's public policies (note their support of neoconservative think tanks like the American Enterprise Institute, the creation of university endowed chairs in free enterprise and sponsorship of university policy centers, the widespread use of advocacy advertising pushing the business point of view), and to increase spectacularly their funding of business Political Action Committees and the Republican party (Edsall, 1984; Vogel, 1989).

As political scientist Walter Dean Burnham has often pointed out, the disintegration of the Democratic party was very different from the classic realignment patterns of American parties, for most defectors from the Democrats during the 1970s tended not to join the ranks of the Republicans but joined instead the "party of nonvoters." The Democratic party, stripped of many of its voters and coalition partners, was in tatters; the Republican party in the early to mid-1970s was moribund, unable to create a policy alternative (Burnham, 1981). I would hypothesize that by the end of the 1970s the United States found itself devoid of a stable ruling coalition with an agreed-upon set of policy ideas able to manage and steer the system in a consistent and coherent manner. This is the context within which a triumphant Ronald Reagan tried to form a new policy regime in the 1980s. He failed, but that is a different story (Greenberg, 1990).

NOTES

1. See Cohen (1978) for the most cogent definition of Marx's conception of the forces and relations of production.

2. This is contrary to Marx's approach in which, according to Cohen (1978), the productive forces have theoretical primacy.

3. This point is also made by Stuart Hall in his analysis of the rise of what he calls the representative or interventionist state in Great Britain (Hall, 1984).

4. For the most careful and extensive review of the literature on long waves, see Berry (1991). See also Goldstein (1988).

5. See Walter Dean Burnham's discussion of pattern recognition and punctuated equilibrium in Chapter 3 of this volume.

6. This notion bears some resemblance to Poulantzas's notion of the "power bloc," though I try here to avoid some of the deterministic character of Poulantzas's formulation (Poulantzas, 1973). It bears some resemblance, as well, to the formulation of Gosta Esping-Andersen (1987), though his focus is mainly on institutional forms and arrangements, while my focus is primarily on political coalitions and policies.

7. My use of the term "corporate liberalism" differs from the way it has been used by several other scholars (Domhoff, 1971; Lustig, 1982; Kolko, 1965; Weinstein, 1968). I name this regime "corporate liberalism" because it represents a union of the New Deal, in both its policy and political coalitional character (thus, "liberalism"), with the large, capital-intensive, internationally oriented corporations, as well as large internationally oriented financial institutions (thus, "corporate"). On the corporate "core" of the postwar New Deal coalition, see Ferguson and Rogers (1981) and DuBoff (1989).

8. I say "surprising" because of the anticorporate stance of many liberals during the Great Depression and the popular image of liberal as the Left in American politics.

9. This mood is nicely captured in Galbraith (1952, 1968).

10. The one major exception was President John F. Kennedy's confrontation with U.S. Steel over its increase in steel prices. Kennedy apparently learned his lesson from this confrontation. Though he was successful in his effort to roll back, the subsequent collapse in stock prices compelled him to court the good opinion of the business and financial communities for the remainder of his time in office. For this story see Miliband (1969) and McQuaid (1982).

11. See the various contributions in Ferguson and Rogers (1981), particularly the chapter by Walter Dean Burnham, "The 1980 Earthquake: Realignment, Reaction, or What?" See also Cohen and Rogers (1983).

12. The concept of the "falling rate of profit" forms the basis of the landmark analysis, *Late Capitalism*, by Ernst Mandel (1975). For empirical evidence on the falling rate of profit during the 1970s, see Nordhaus (1974).

13. One obvious result of these developments was a steady decline in the relative standard of living of almost all Americans. In their provocative book, *Minding America's Business: The Decline and Rise of the American Economy*, economists Ira Magaziner and Robert Reich (1982) summarize the evidence on the subject and demonstrate how poorly the United States was performing by the early 1970s compared to all other Western industrialized nations on measures of economic growth, employment, security of employment income, social services, income and wealth distribution, crime victimization, health care, life expectancy, pollution, and the like.

8

The Origins of Social Policy
in the United States:
A Polity-Centered Analysis

THEDA SKOCPOL

In October of 1889, President Charles Eliot of Harvard University—a prominent Mugwump located in the very heartland of that status-conscious movement for good government reform—delivered a speech to the Bay State Club of Boston. The speech explained why he, formerly a loyal Republican, was switching his allegiance to the Democratic party. Eliot's preference for the Democratic stand on tariffs and his great respect for the efforts of Democratic President Grover Cleveland on behalf of civil service reform were cited as two reasons for the shift. The third reason was Eliot's sense that patronage-oriented Republican politicians were leading the way in "prostituting and degrading" the Civil War pension system into what was becoming, in effect, America's first large-scale nationally funded old age and disability system. Eliot explained that as "things are, Gentlemen, one cannot tell whether a pensioner of the United States received an honorable wound in battle or contracted a chronic catarrh twenty years after the war. One cannot tell whether a pensioner of the United States is a disabled soldier or sailor or a perjured pauper who has foisted himself upon the public treasury. I say that to put the pension system of the United States into this condition is a crime … against Republican Institutions" (quoted in McMurry, 1922:34–35).

Eliot knew whereof he spoke. By the time the elected politicians—especially Republicans—had finished liberalizing eligibility for Civil War pensions, over a third of all the elderly men living in the North, along with quite a few elderly men in other parts of the country and many widows and dependents across the nation, were receiving quarterly payments from the United States Pension Bureau. In terms of the large share of the federal budget spent, the hefty proportion of citizens covered, and the relative generosity of the disability and old-age benefits offered, the United

States had become a precocious social spending state! Its post–Civil War system of social provision in many respects exceeded what early programs of "workingmen's insurance" were giving needy old people or superannuated industrial wage earners in fledgling Western welfare states around the turn of the century.

Early in the twentieth century, a number of U.S. trade union officials and reformers hoped to transform Civil War pensions into more universal publicly funded benefits for all workingmen and their families. But this was not to be. From Mugwumps to progressive reformers, many elite and middle-class Americans viewed Civil War pensions as a prime example of governmental profligacy and electorally rooted political corruption. During the Progressive Era, public opinion was preoccupied with curbing the fiscal excesses of patronage-oriented political parties. In this political climate, various social reforms were enacted into law, but not those calling for new public spending on old-age pensions or other kinds of workingmen's social insurance. America's first system of public social provision for men and their dependents died with the Civil War generation, and was not to be replaced by other measures until the Great Depression and the New Deal of the 1930s.

The United States thus did not follow other Western nations on the road toward a paternalist welfare state, in which male bureaucrats would administer regulations and social insurance "for the good" of breadwinning industrial workers. Instead, America came close to forging a maternalist welfare state, with female-dominated public agencies implementing regulations and benefits for the good of women and their children. From 1900 through the early 1920s, a broad array of protective labor regulations and social benefits was enacted by state legislatures and Congress to help adult American women as mothers, or as potential mothers.

Most American women did not gain the right to vote until 1920 or a few years before, so they were outside the party politics that had fueled the expansion of Civil War benefits. Even so, nation-spanning federations of local women's clubs were the chief proponents of such maternalist policies as mothers' pensions, minimum-wage regulations, and the creation of the federal Children's Bureau. In European nations, well-established bureaucracies and programmatic political parties devised and administered workingmen's social insurance and labor regulations. But in the United States, as clubwoman Mrs. Imogen B. Oakley explained (1912:805), most men were preoccupied with partisan politics or business and "the initiative in civic matters has devolved largely upon women," organized into voluntary associations. As they took the lead in U.S. social-welfare politics during the first decades of the twentieth century, moreover, American clubwomen acted from a broadly shared, gender-based vision of a maternal public mind: "loving and generous, wanting to save and develop all" (Robertson, 1912:160). Women aimed to extend the domestic morality of the nineteenth century's "separate sphere" for women into the nation's public life. For a while, this vision was a remarkable source of moral energy and political leverage for the female instigators of the first U.S. programs of public social provision destined to endure (despite unintended transformations) through the New Deal and down to the present day.

AMERICAN SOCIAL PROVISION IN
HISTORICAL AND COMPARATIVE PERSPECTIVE

Parts of the historical sketch I have just offered will come as a surprise to many readers. Properly schooled citizens of the United States, scholars of American history, and social scientists who analyze the growth of Western "welfare states"—all take for granted certain received truths about the American past. Nineteenth and early twentieth-century America was supposedly a land of rugged individualists, profoundly distrustful of government and engaged in freewheeling market competition to gain the fruits of an expanding capitalist economy. Individual dependency was little recognized—and socially stigmatized—in this land of plenty. Such public provision as there was for the needy, the disabled, or the elderly was virtually always local, provided through poor houses, or private charity, or niggardly outdoor public assistance. State governments did little beyond setting up a few custodial institutions and, especially in the industrializing areas of the country, regulating "charities and corrections" toward the end of the nineteenth century. Above all, we have been taught that the U.S. federal government did virtually nothing about public social provision until the Great Depression and the New Deal of the 1930s. Then at last, in a "big bang" of social reforms that accompanied many extensions of federal power into the country's economic and social life, the United States enacted nationwide social insurance and public assistance policies (Leman, 1977). At that point, most scholars presume that the United States joined the evolutionary mainstream of Western social progress—as a "laggard" on the universal road to "the modern welfare state."

Despite the desire of many scholars to view the history of U.S. social policy in universal evolutionary terms, the United States has never come close to having a "modern welfare state" in the British, the Swedish, or any other positive Western sense of the phrase. It did not institute social benefits for workingmen or the elderly during the early twentieth century. The Social Security Act of 1935, still the framework for nationwide public social provision in the United States, included only one national program, contributory retirement insurance. Unemployment insurance was a federally mandated program with the states left in charge of taxes, coverage, and benefits. Public assistance programs were offered federal subsidies with the states left responsible for devising and administering policies. National health insurance was not included in the Social Security Act, and it was not enacted in the late 1940s or afterwards, either. No comprehensive American welfare state emerged from the New Deal and World War II. Nor was any such welfare state "completed" during the next "big bang" of U.S. social policy innovations, namely, the War on Poverty and the Great Society of the 1960s and early 1970s.

That the United States has never really approximated an ideal-typical Western welfare state has not prevented scholars from discussing the history of its social policymaking almost single-mindedly in relation to that model—a perspective encouraged by the assumption that national and state governments in the United States were little involved in public social provision prior to the 1930s. Social scientists debating alternative theories of welfare state development have primarily examined U.S. social provision from 1935 onward (see studies summarized in Skocpol and Amenta, 1986). They have offered a variety of hypotheses about why the United States was a "welfare laggard," that is, why it started its welfare state so late by international standards. Comparativists have also offered hypotheses about why the United States still has fewer programs, less comprehensive social coverage, and lower expenditures on social insurance than most other highly industrialized nations. To explain these things, comparative models of welfare state development draw our attention to the factors *absent* in American history compared to other national histories, or else to factors only weakly apparent.

To bring into sharper focus things distinctively *present* in the history of American social policy, we should presumably turn to historians who have looked closely at happenings before, as well as after, the 1930s. But, here too, the model of evolutionary progress toward a modern welfare state holds sway, directing our attention to some realities and away from others. Historians of American welfare politics from the nineteenth century to the 1930s paint a picture of heroic reformers endeavoring to pull the country away from local poor law practices and toward national social insurance. *The Struggle for Social Security, 1900–1935*, the title of Roy Lubove's classic book ([1968] 1986), captures this perfectly. Historical accounts such as this treat the period before the 1930s as one in which "obstacles"—such as liberal values or business power—frustrated early reformers' attempts to create an American welfare state.

My purpose is hardly to make light of scholars who note absent conditions in American history or obstacles to social insurance before the New Deal. Part of my analysis focuses on such matters. Still less do I mean to dismiss the many insights that appear in excellent histories of U.S. social policy and in cross-national studies of welfare states that include the American case. What I do wish to suggest is that received wisdom about the past of U.S. social provision—framed as a struggle to move the country along an evolutionary path from nineteenth-century local poor relief to the modern welfare state as embodied in the Social Security Act— blinds us to important patterns that need to be explained.

Inspired by fresh descriptions of what did and did not happen in the development of social policies from the 1870s through the 1920s, we can pose new questions about U.S. social provision in comparative perspective.

Why did the United States provide such generous benefits for many disabled and elderly men and their dependents under the rubric of Civil War benefits? And how did the resulting U.S. system of social benefits compare to early modern social policies in other Western nations?

Civil War benefits were offered by the federal government and by state and local governments. They cannot be set aside as mere unavoidable concomitants of the human damage inflicted by the original military conflict, for the extension of Civil War benefits came after claims directly due to wartime casualties had peaked and were in decline. From the 1880s through the 1910s, federal veterans' pensions became the keystone of an entire edifice of honorable income supplements and institutional provision for many northern Americans who were longstanding citizens. In many ways, the extent and terms of these disability and old-age benefits compared favorably to the coverage and terms of early social insurance and pension policies in other Western nations. Yet there were also crucial differences of form, coverage, and justification between U.S. policies and the programs of fledgling welfare states.

If the United States by 1900 had costly old-age and disability benefits outside the poor law, why did the nation subsequently refuse to build upon, or replace, this early system of public social provision, never transforming it into workingmen's social insurance or more general pensions for the elderly?

Inspired by European precedents, proposals for need-based old-age pensions, health and unemployment insurance covering wage earners, and labor regulations to protect all adult male workers received considerable intellectual justification and political support in the early twentieth-century United States (Skocpol, 1992: part 2). Yet even though reform ferment peaked during the Progressive Era, and even though Civil War pensioners were visibly dying off, most such proposals were defeated or deflected by the legislatures and the courts. From the overall agenda of workingmen's social provision, only laws mandating compensation for industrial accidents succeeded. Once we realize that the U.S. federal government (along with many states) was centrally involved in offering social benefits to respectable citizens long before the New Deal, then we need to wonder anew about the failure of most proposals for social benefits and labor regulations for workingmen and the elderly during the early 1900s. The failure of these proposals is obviously not simply attributable to inherent obstacles to overcoming local poor relief in industrializing America. There must be more to it than that.

If proposed social policies for workingmen were not successful during a period when all U.S. adult white males had the suffrage, then why—mostly at times and places where women could not vote—did U.S. legislatures enact, and the courts sustain, social spending for mothers and certain protective labor regulations for adult female wage earners? And why did the federal government establish the Children's Bureau and expand its mission until the middle of the 1920s?

In U.S. politics during the early decades of the twentieth century, the story is not only one of social policies that were not enacted. Beginnings were made in creating public social provision not tied to generational entitlements, even if these beginnings were later to be reworked and superseded. As Table 8.1 illustrates, social policies for women loomed much larger in early modern U.S. social provision than in the pioneering Western welfare states for workers. The pioneering paternalist welfare states might emphasize social insurance, as did Germany; or regulations to establish a "living wage," as did Australia and New Zealand; or a combination of both, as did Britain. But all of them focused on helping the breadwinning male wage earner. Although the pioneering paternalist welfare states sometimes had laws for mothers or for women workers comparable to those enacted in the United States, they invariably had many laws covering male workers that the United States did not enact during this period.

America's first publicly funded social benefits outside of military pensions and poor relief were mothers' pensions. These were laws passed in 40 states between 1911 and 1920 to enable localities to provide payments for needy widowed mothers (and occasionally others) in order to let them care for children at home. Four more states passed mothers' pensions during the 1920s (along with 2 in the early 1930s). Protective labor regulations for women wageworkers (understood as potential mothers) also proliferated during this period. New or improved limits on women's hours of work passed in 13 states between 1900 and 1909; in 39 states between 1909 and 1917; and in 2 more states prior to 1933. Minimum-wage laws for women workers were enacted by 15 states between 1912 and 1923. In addition to state-level laws for women, in 1912 the U.S. federal government established a children's bureau headed and staffed not by the usual male officials but by reformist professional women who aimed to look after the needs of all American mothers and children. Across the nation, women's groups campaigned for the creation of the Children's Bureau, just as they pressed for the enactment of mothers' pensions and protective labor regu-

TABLE 8.1 Early Modern Social Policies, 1880–1929

	Workmen's Compensation	Old Age Pensions or Insurance	Sickness Insurance	Unemployment Insurance	Labor Regulations for Men[a]	Labor Regulations for Women	Mothers' Pensions
Germany	1884	1889	1883	1927	No Industrial relations courts	1908	No
Australia	1990–1914 Laws in all 6 Australian states 1920s 2 more states	1908	No	No	Hours laws by late 19th C. Arbitration of Industrial Disputes Minimum wage from 1919		No
New Zealand	1900	1898	No	No	Hours laws by late 19th C. Arbitration of Industrial Disputes Minimum wage from 1918		1912
Britain	1906	1908 1925	1911	1911 1920	Trade Boards 1909–1918 for minimum wages	Hours laws from 19th C. Trade Boards for minimum wages	No
United States	1911–1920 42 states 1920s 2 more states	No (except 6 states in 1920s)	No	No	No	Hours Laws in 41 states by 1929 Minimum Wage Laws, 1912–1923 15 states	1911–1920 40 states 1920s 4 more states

[a]Laws applying only to special dangerous occupations do not apply here.

Source: Theda Skocpol, *Protecting Soldiers and Mothers* (Cambridge: Harvard University Press, Belknap, 1992), p. 9.

lations. In the 1910s, a national government bureau "run solely by women" was "without parallel elsewhere in the world" (Sklar, 1986:17). And by 1921 the Children's Bureau had successfully spearheaded a campaign for the first explicit federal social welfare program, one that offered grants-in-aid to the states. The Sheppard-Towner Infancy and Maternity Protection Act encouraged the creation of federally subsidized pre- and postnatal clinics to disseminate health-care advice to mothers, in the hope of reducing the high infant mortality rates that the Children's Bureau had documented for the United States compared to other industrial nations (Ladd-Taylor, 1986).

In sum, U.S. social provision in the late nineteenth and early twentieth centuries cannot be understood in the usual fashion, as a mere evolutionary backdrop to the eventual triumph of Social Security in the 1930s. Often thought to have lagged behind other countries in providing for the welfare of citizens, the United States actually pioneered certain policies to help honored groups of men and women. As other nations launched fledgling welfare states for workers between the 1870s and the 1920s, American federal and state governments created protection for veteran soldiers and for actual or potential mothers.

How can early U.S. social policies—protecting soldiers and mothers, but not workers—best be explained? In the remainder of this chapter, I shall first point to some limitations shared by a variety of theoretical perspectives on the development of modern welfare states. Then I will outline my own polity-centered approach to situating and explaining the early U.S. social policies I have described. This approach illuminates not only patterns of social policymaking in the United States between the 1870s and 1920s but many other aspects of American political development as well.

THEORIES OF THE WELFARE STATE: SHARED LIMITATIONS

Existing theories about social policies in the United States and other modern nations fall into several major schools of thought, ranging from those that stress the causal priority of industrialization or capitalist development, to those that place emphasis on national values or class politics, and those that highlight transformations of patriarchy (for overviews, see Skocpol and Amenta, 1986; Skocpol, 1992:11–40). Despite their many differences, however, all existing perspectives share a number of problematic assumptions about the evolutionary nature of "the welfare state" and the social roots of political processes. A brief look at these shared assumptions underlines why an analytical reorientation is needed.

"The modern welfare state" has been seen by scholars in all camps as unified and inherently progressive, growing in recognizable stages in all industrializing and urbanizing nations. According to particular schools of thought, either national values or balances of social strength may affect the pace and comprehensiveness of welfare state development. Nevertheless, most scholars presume that some approximation of the welfare state necessarily, progressively, and irreversibly develops in every country that undergoes industrialization or capitalist development. Ideal-typical conceptions of "the welfare state" have been abstracted from certain understandings of a few national histories, and then turned into general explanatory variables. Applied to the American case, such conceptions have been especially harmful. They have ruled Civil War pensions and maternalist policies out of the analysis altogether, and distracted attention from the disjunctures between major phases and configurations of national social provision.

An incomplete conception of long-run social change underpins progressivist visions of the welfare state. Social policies have been seen as "responses" to long-term change conceived in socioeconomic terms. The motors that transform societies are thought to be industrialization and urbanization—or if one has Marxist proclivities, capitalist development, which also involves changing class (and perhaps gendered) relations of production. Right after World War II, some British writers speculated on the possible relationships between stages of modern war and the expansion of social provision (Titmuss, 1978). But recent students of social policies have less and less to say about geopolitics and warfare. What is more, hardly anyone acknowledges that long-run processes of state formation—processes which include sequences of wars and revolutions, along with constitution-making, electoral democratization, and various forms of administrative bureaucratization—might have had as much or more impact as socioeconomic transformations on the contexts within which social policies have been fashioned. Yet only by taking processes of state formation and patterns of political organization seriously, and noticing that these intersect in varied ways with economic and social transformations, can we break with the progressivist notion of social policies as aspects of societal evolution.

Existing perspectives on social policy development not only ignore long-run processes of state formation, but they also presume that governmental activities express social conditions and straightforwardly respond to social demands. The following diagram captures typical understandings of social change and the political process:

SOCIOECONOMIC ——> CHANGING CLASS/GROUP FORMATION ——>
TRANSFORMATIONS   AND NEW SOCIAL NEEDS

——> WHAT POLITICALLY ACTIVE ——> GOVERNMENTAL
      GROUPS DEMAND   RESPONSES

According to this socially determinist frame of reference, politically active groups, including parties, are considered vehicles for the expression of demands that arise from underlying socioeconomic conditions. After groups and parties weigh in at the political arena—some perhaps more effectively than others because of class, racial, or gender advantages—then governments generate policy outputs to meet the social demands. In this view of the political process, if modern social policies do not emerge or mature, it must be because economic development has not yet created sufficient needs or resources, or because for cultural reasons the citizenry has not yet demanded new social policies, or, the industrial working class may not be sufficiently organized to have its preferences met in the face of capitalist resistance. Many puzzles about American social provision are left unresolved by arguments such as these.

A POLITY-CENTERED ANALYSIS
OF AMERICAN SOCIAL PROVISION

Without discarding the valid insights of socially determinist perspectives, we need to correct our angle of vision. State formation, political institutions, and political processes—all understood in non-economically determinist ways—must move from the penumbra or margins of analysis and toward the center. I call the framework that embodies this corrected angle of vision "polity-centered."

Some may wonder why I am using this label rather than "state-centered." The reason has to do with clarity of communication. The "polity" includes state organizations, political parties, and all politically active social groups. Just as I argued some years ago in the essay "Bringing the State Back In" (Skocpol, 1985), we must focus on the state not only as a set of organizations that may be sites of partially autonomous official action. In addition, we must examine the relationships between states and political parties, and understand the impact of state and party organizations on the outlooks and capacities of social groups that are active in the political process. This has always been (Skocpol, 1979), and still is, my theoretical position. However, the term "state-centered" can be misinterpreted and thereby given overtones of bureaucratic determinism, which subsumes the important interrelationships of states, political parties, and social groups. Consequently, I am now using the term "polity-centered" to underline the importance of looking at all of these together.

Political scientists such as Hugh Heclo (1974), Martin Shefter (1977, 1978), and Stephen Skowronek (1982); historians such as Paula Baker (1984), Richard McCormick (1979), and Richard Oestreicher (1989); and historical sociologists such as Seymour Martin Lipset (1963, 1976, 1977) and Charles Tilly (1975, 1984), all have contributed fundamental ideas to the sort of polity-centered approach I use here. Drawing upon their insights as I present my own formulations, I can sketch an analytical frame of reference that suggests hypotheses about the patterns and tempos of U.S. social provision. This framework draws our attention to four kinds of processes: (1) the establishment and transformation of state and party organizations through which politicians pursue policy initiatives, (2) the effects of political institutions and procedures on the identities, goals, and capacities of social groups that become involved in the politics of social policymaking, (3) the "fit"—or lack thereof—between the goals and capacities of various politically active groups and the historically changing points of access and leverage allowed by a nation's political institutions, and (4) the ways in which previously established social policies affect subsequent politics. Let me explore these in turn, moving from the theoretical rationale for taking each process seriously to illustrations of how it illuminates important aspects of the early history of modern U.S. social provision.

State Formation and the Initiatives of Politicians

A polity-centered perspective holds that politicians and administrators must be taken seriously. Not merely agents of other social interests, they are actors in their own right, enabled and constrained by the political organizations within which they operate. Political officials can therefore make independent contributions to the development of a nation's social policies.

Because states are authoritative and resourceful organizations—collectors of revenue, centers of cultural authority, and hoarders of the means of coercion—they are sites of autonomous action, not reducible to the demands or preferences of any social group. Both appointed and elected officials have ideas and organizational and career interests of their own, and they devise and work for policies that will further those ideas and interests, or at least not harm them. Of course, elected or appointed officials are sensitive in many ways to social preferences; and they normally want to promote the health of the economy. Yet politicians and officials are also engaged in international and domestic (including intrastate) struggles among themselves, and they must pursue those struggles by using the capacities of the organizations within which they are situated. If a given state possesses no existing (or readily adaptable) capacities for implementing given lines of policies, political leaders are not likely to pursue them. But such leaders are quite likely to take new policy initiatives—conceivably well ahead of social demands—if the capacities of state organizations can be readily adapted or reworked to do things that they expect will bring advantages to them in their struggles with political competitors, at home or on the international scene.

A state is any set of relatively differentiated organizations that claims sovereignty and coercive control over a territory and its population, defending and perhaps extending that claim in competition with other states. The core organizations that make up a state include the administrative, judicial, and policing organizations that collect and dispense revenues, enforce the constitutive rules of the state and society, and maintain some modicum of domestic order, especially to protect the state's own claims and activities. According to this definition, not all societies have had states, and states have coexisted with—and persisted across—different "modes of production." Properly speaking, there is no such thing as a generically "feudal state" or "capitalist state." Rather, there are variously organized states coexisting with various patterns of economic production and exchange. By this definition, plenty of room is left for variation across time and space, within and between types of socioeconomic systems, in the ways states are organized, and in the mix of activities they undertake. There are only some states, for example, that have institutions of representative decisionmaking linked to their core organizations. When they do, it is important to understand how their constitutional, legislative, and electoral arrangements intersect with the coercive, administrative, judicial, and policing organizations.

If the state is so defined, then certainly the United States has always had one. We can identify the distinctive and changing organizational features of the U.S. state, the resources its officials have commanded, and the ways the resources and organizational features have influenced official proclivities and abilities to shape U.S. social policies. The following relationships need to be explored:

```
STATE     ——>   POLITICAL ORGANIZATIONS   ——>   POLICY
FORMATION       WITH GIVEN CAPACITIES            CONTRIBUTIONS
                AND OPERATING NEEDS              OF OFFICIALS
```

The processes that have formed the U.S. state include the revolution and constitutional settlement that founded the nation, the wars in which it has engaged, and its adaptation to special geopolitical environments. By modern times, many continental European nations possessed centralized bureaucracies and standing armies, because their states had been built by absolute monarchs who warred constantly with one another and had to wrest the men and most of the fiscal resources for war-making from locally entrenched landlords and peasantries (Tilly, 1975). In contrast, through a loosely coordinated revolution against British colonial rule, the American colonies forged a federalist constitutional republic (Hollingsworth, 1978; Huntington, 1968; Lipset, 1963; Skowronek, 1982). After some years of continued sparring with Britain, the fledgling nation found itself facing westward toward a huge continent available for conquest from always-worrisome yet militarily unequal opponents. Wars have never had the same centralizing effects for the U.S. state as they have had for many European states, in part because America's greatest conflict was the Civil War—an introverted event. In addition, mobilization for both World War I and II in the twentieth century relied heavily on the organizational capacities of large business corporations and trade associations (Cuff, 1973; Vatter, 1985). Only after World War II, when the United States took on global functions, did a federal "military-industrial complex" emerge, nourished by the persistence into peacetime of substantial direct federal taxation (Witte, 1985, chap.7).

The U.S. state was also formed by, in comparative terms, early mass electoral democratization and late, fragmentary administrative bureaucratization within a three-tiered federal system of non-hierarchically arrayed national, state, and local governments. Nineteenth-century America developed a federal "state of courts and parties" (Skowronek, 1982, chap. 2; Skocpol, 1992, chap.1) In this polity, the patronage-oriented politicians who coordinated the workings of parties, administrative agencies, and legislatures, elaborated social and economic policies as cross-class distributions rather than as class-oriented categorical measures (McCormick, 1979). Not until the late nineteenth and early twentieth centuries—decades after the establishment of electoral democratization for males, and well after capitalist industrialization had created private corporate giants operating on a national scale—did federal, state, and local governments in the United States make much headway in the bureaucratization and professionalization of their administrative functions.

With the greatest changes coming first in certain cities and states, bureaucratic transformations occurred in piecemeal ways through reform movements spearheaded by executive officials and professionalizing elements of the American middle class (Schiesl, 1977; Wiebe, 1967). As the various levels of U.S. government were partially bureaucratically and professionally reorganized, the fragmentation of political sovereignty built into U.S. federalism, and into the divisions of decisionmaking authority among executives, legislatures, and courts, was reproduced in new ways during the twentieth century (Skowronek, 1982, part 3 and epilogue; Karl, 1983). Rather than becoming lifelong governmental civil servants, U.S. professionals, and particularly policy-oriented intellectuals among them, tended to spend but short periods in governmental agencies, while pursuing careers predominantly anchored outside of governments, in corporations, or private associations or universities. While competing with professionals and bureaucrats for control over new realms of public policymaking, twentieth-century U.S. political parties became perhaps even more decentralized in their basic operations; and in many localities and states the major parties uneasily combined patronage-oriented and interest-group-oriented modes of operation (Shefter, 1978; Mayhew, 1986).

Indeed, contrary to the image offered by some scholars that the United States became bureaucratically centralized in response to industrialism, one could argue that U.S. social politics became less centrally coordinated around the turn of the twentieth century. The federal government's Civil War pensions were no longer the major arena of social policy; and the New Deal would not arrive until the 1930s. Political parties became less nationally competitive and patronage-oriented. And the U.S. Constitution was judicially interpreted as leaving jurisdiction over industrial and social policies largely to the forty-eight state legislatures. Meanwhile, within the federal government, Congress, with its strong roots in state and local political establishments, has remained pivotal in national domestic policy-making throughout the twentieth century (Fiorina, 1977; Huntington, 1973; Grodzins, 1960). Because of its limited fiscal and bureaucratic capacities, the U.S. national government has recurrently relied for policy implementation on subsidies or activities channeled through business enterprises, state or local governments, or "private" voluntary associations.

Because the U.S. federal state was slow to develop modern administrative capacities, reformers opposing "political corruption" (that is, advocating civil service reform and nondistributive social and economic policies) had to reorganize or bypass the entrenched arrangements of nineteenth-century patronage democracy (Skowronek, 1982). At the same time, they had to wrest substantive jurisdiction from the courts. When new agencies empowered to administer social legislation were finally established, they were typically isolated islands of expertise within local, state, and federal governments, limited by ongoing jurisdictional disputes among legislatures, executives, and courts. Initially, these agencies were often limited to information-gathering and regulation. Even so, if they developed continuities of personnel and a sense of collective purpose, some of these agencies became capable of promoting social programs.

Understanding the historical formation of the U.S. state and its disjointed reorganization at the turn of the twentieth century helps us to see the ways in which different kinds of political officials have promoted social policies of particular sorts, with varying degrees of success. In nascent Western welfare states, labor regulations and social benefits for workingmen were pursued by central officials of governmental bureaucracies and by politicians in charge of governments with national administrative capacities. In the United States, by contrast, democratically elected legislators and patronage party politicians were the propellers and shapers of widespread distributive social policies—including Civil War benefits—during the nineteenth and early twentieth centuries. Thus the

Republican party, the U.S. Pensions Bureau, Congress, and state legislatures (pressured by the Grand Army of the Republic) were all central to the propelling and shaping of generous social benefits for veterans of the Civil War and their dependents (McMurry, 1922; Skocpol, 1992, chap. 2).

From the turn of the century onward, collectively oriented social insurance programs and labor regulations were promoted across the states by reformist professionals with aspirations to build new administrative agencies, as well as by established governmental agencies (such as bureaus of labor statistics) serving as relatively stable centers of professional-bureaucratic expertise. In addition, some female professional reformers eventually managed to achieve a bureaucratic beachhead within the Children's Bureau of the federal government, from which they pursued a program that would administer maternal health education services in partnership with state and local governments and voluntary groups.

Nevertheless, the efforts of turn-of-the-century U.S. reformist professionals to promote new social policies succeeded only when they were allied with popular constituents associated across many localities and legislative districts. While the major political parties were less important than they had been in the nineteenth century, Congress and state legislatures remained pivotal arbiters of social legislation. In contrast to European reformers who could work through national bureaucracies and parliamentary political parties, U.S. reformist professionals—including actual or would-be government officials—could make headway toward new social policies only if they could gain decentralized political leverage on legislatures. When this happened at all—as, for example, in the instances of the U.S. Department of Agriculture and the U.S. Children's Bureau—it happened because ongoing political alliances were formed between professionals and officials, on the one hand, and widespread local voluntary groups, on the other.

Political Institutions and Social Identities in Politics

Socially determinist theories overlook the ways in which the identities, goals, and capacities of all politically active groups are influenced by political structures and processes. Patterns of bureaucratic development influence the orientations of educated middle-class groups as well as the possibilities for all social groups to "do things" through public authority. In addition, the scope of the electorate, along with changes in rules about electoral access and voting routines, affects the popular social identities that figure in political debates at different periods. The institutional arrangements of the state and political parties affect the capabilities of various groups to achieve self-consciousness, organize, and make alliances. Thus socioeconomic theories about group consciousness and class conflicts have to be reworked to take the effects of changing governmental and party organizations into account.

The following diagram suggests the dual lines of determination that should enter into any analysis of the social identities and relations involved in political processes. Notice that socioeconomic relations and cultural patterns are important parts of the analysis. I am not trying to substitute "political determinism" for "social determinism." I propose to explore how social and political factors *combine* to affect the social identities and group capacities involved in the politics of social policy-making.

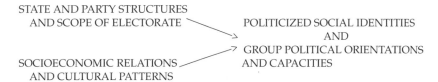

STATE AND PARTY STRUCTURES
   AND SCOPE OF ELECTORATE　　　　POLITICIZED SOCIAL IDENTITIES
                               AND
                             GROUP POLITICAL ORIENTATIONS
SOCIOECONOMIC RELATIONS　　　　AND CAPACITIES
   AND CULTURAL PATTERNS

With the aid of this frame of reference, we can make sense of a fundamentally important aspect of U.S. social politics in the early twentieth century: the relative weakness of "working-class" political consciousness, and the simultaneous prominence of middle-class women's gender consciousness and female moral determination to project domestic and maternal values into national politics.

As the comparative-historical scholarship of Martin Shefter (1977) has demonstrated, the kinds of appeals political parties have made, and the sorts of group identities they have helped to politicize, have depended on sequences and forms of state bureaucratization and electoral democratization. In certain European countries, state bureaucratization preceded the emergence of parliamentary parties, or the democratization of the male electorate, or both. When political parties emerged in such circumstances, they could not get access to the "spoils of office" and instead had to make programmatic appeals to collectively organized constituents, including organized workers. But circumstances were sharply different in the nineteenth-century United States, where no premodern centralized bureaucracy held sway, and where full democratization of the electorate for white males was virtually completed nationwide by the 1840s. The intensely competitive political parties that mobilized this mass American electorate colonized all levels of public administration and used the spoils of office to motivate party cadres. The parties also relied heavily on distributions of public jobs and publicly funded divisible benefits to appeal to locally situated constituents. What is more, since no class-defined group of American males was excluded from the democratic electorate, there was little space—much less than in continental European countries, or even nineteenth-century Britain—for old or new parties to appeal on ideologically or programmatically collectivist lines to newly mobilizable, socioeconomically defined groups of men.

It is ironic that as American workers were transformed from artisans into wageworkers, or migrated from rural into industrial and urban settings, they were discouraged from becoming politically class-conscious because of their full incorporation into democratic electoral and party routines rooted in local communities that were often ethnically defined (Katznelson, 1981). Because they were already voting, American workers did not *need* to mobilize along class lines to overcome exclusion from the suffrage. At the same time, workers' organizations *could not* call on autonomous bureaucrats for help in their struggles with capitalists. And trade unions soon learned to distrust the U.S. state, because of the increasingly vigorous efforts of one of its arms, the judiciary, to block union activities (Forbath, 1991; Hattam, 1993). Given all of these circumstances, the American trade unions that eventually become most successful on "bread-and-butter" workplace issues did not forge stable ties to labor-based political parties during the period around the turn of the century when European Social Democratic movements, linking unions and parties, were formed. As the historian Richard Oestreicher has summed up in a brilliant analysis of the disjunction between "class sentiment" and "political consciousness":

> From the 1870s until the 1930s, class sentiments were widespread among American workers, but before the 1930s the structure of political power in American society ... made it harder to mobilize class sentiments in the political arena than in the workplace. ... In an entrenched party system, with winner-take-all elections and an electorate highly mobilized on a different [i.e., non-class] basis, political mobilization around class sentiments demanded far greater resources and involved greater risks than the labor movement was able or willing to muster while workplace mobilization around work-related issues needed far fewer resources. Without a tradition of successful political mobilization, class sentiment could not be translated into an articulated political consciousness.(Oestreicher, 1989:1269)

Whereas political forces claiming to represent the industrial working class had (in cross-national perspective) relatively little presence in U.S. social politics around the turn of the twentieth century, national and local groups claiming to speak for the collective interests of women were able to mount ideologically inspired efforts on behalf of maternalist social policies. Patterns of exclusion from—and tempos of incorporation into—electoral politics shaped the possibilities for women's political consciousness, just as they influenced possibilities for working-class consciousness. But the results for women were quite different. Middle-class American women fashioned an ambitious and influential maternalist consciousness at the turn of the century (Skocpol, 1992, chap. 6), during a period when mainstream U.S. workers' organizations were eschewing class-oriented ideologies and programs.

In major European countries during the nineteenth and early twentieth centuries, either no one except monarchs, bureaucrats, and aristocrats had the right to participate in national politics, or else property ownership, education, and other class-based criteria were used to limit electoral participation by categories of men. Thus European women were not the only ones excluded from the suffrage and, at least at first, economically privileged women did not have to watch lower-class men exercise electoral rights denied to them. Class-defined political cleavages tended to proliferate and persist in Europe, and even politically active women's organizations oriented themselves to class issues. In the United States, by contrast, for almost a century the rights and routines of electoral democracy were open to all men (even to the black ex-slaves for some decades after the Civil War), whereas they were denied to all women (Baker, 1984).

By virtually universal cultural consensus, a woman's "separate sphere" in the nineteenth century was the home, the place where she sustained the highest moral values in her roles as wife and (especially) mother. Yet this did not mean that American women stayed out of public life. Through reformist and public-regarding voluntary associations American upper- and middle-class women, joined by some wives of skilled workers, claimed a mission that they felt only their gender could uniquely perform: extending the moral values and social caring of the home into the larger community. In the process, reformist women took a special interest in social policy issues that they felt touched the well-being of other women. By the Progressive Era, moreover, women's associations concluded that women must have the suffrage in order to reform all of politics, acting as "housekeepers for the nation."

Although maternalist ideas about social welfare spread across the industrializing world in the late nineteenth and early twentieth centuries (Koven and Michel, 1990), they loomed politically largest in the United States, for three major reasons. First, women's community organizations started out tied to churches in the United States, as in other Christian nations. Yet institutional religion was less of a restraint on the eventual emergence of transdenominational and autonomously female-led voluntary associations in the United States than elsewhere because America was an overwhelmingly Protestant nation with no established church. There was Catholic bureaucracy, as in France, and no established Protestant church, as in England, to channel and limit female social activism.

Second, it was critical that American women gained more and better higher education sooner than any other women in the world. This prepared a crucial minority of them for voluntary or irregularly recompensed public leadership, especially since regular elite career opportunities were limited. Widespread education also set the stage for strong alliances between higher-educated professional women and married housewives scattered across the nation, many of whom were relatively well-educated, and some of whom in every locality had been to college and worked as schoolteachers before marriage.

Finally, as I have already stressed, American women reacted more intensely, both ideologically and organizationally, against their relatively sharper exclusion from a fully democratized male democracy. Throughout the nineteenth century, no major industrializing country differentiated worlds of politics—understood in the broadest sense as patterns of participation in public affairs—so sharply *on strictly gender lines* as did the United States. Given the absence in the United States of bureaucratic and organized working-class initiatives to build a pioneering paternalist welfare state for industrial workers and their families, there was more space left for maternalism in the shaping of fledgling modern social policies. Thus the policies and new public agencies especially for women and children sponsored by American women's associations loomed especially large on the overall agenda of issues that Progressive Era politicians took seriously.

Using the same perspective we have just applied to understand the possibilities for working-class and women's political consciousness, we can also gain insights about the political outlook of U.S. capitalists. To a greater degree than business people in many other capitalist nations, U.S. capitalists (in the apt phrase of David Vogel, 1978) "distrust their state." This is, of course, somewhat ironic, given that American capitalists have not had to contend with a highly mobilized, nationally politically conscious working class, and they often get their way in governmental affairs. Yet U.S. business-owners have often had to operate in a long-democratized polity prone to throw up periodic moralistic "reform" movements, including farmers' movements and women's movements prone to challenge business prerogatives. What is more, the distrust that U.S. capitalists feel toward government reflects the frustrations that they have recurrently experienced in their dealings with a decentralized and fragmented federal state—a state that gives full play to divisions within business along industrial and geographical lines.

Conflicts within the ranks of U.S. business were (and still are) readily politicized, since losers can always "go to court"—or back to the legislatures, or to another level in the federal system, or to a new bureaucratic agency—for another round of battle in the interminable struggles that never seem to settle most public policy questions. For American capitalists, the state has seemed neither coherent nor reliable. Indeed, the uneven and inconstant effects of U.S. political structures help to explain—contrary to the expectations of the "welfare capitalism" school—why "progressive" corporate leaders have always found it difficult to inspire broad business support for national social policy initiatives, even those that might benefit the economy as a whole on terms favorable to the dominant sectors of business. With a few individual exceptions American capitalists have never seen government as a positive means to achieve classwide purposes. Various industries and smaller as well as larger businesses have concentrated on fighting one another through politics. Different sectors of business have come together only episodically, and then usually in efforts to block reformers or popularly appealing social movements that want to extend government regulation or taxation and spending for social welfare purposes.

The "Fit" Between Political Institutions and Group Capacities

As governmental institutions, political party systems, and electoral rules of the game develop, they affect not only the political consciousness and orientations of various social groups. At the same time, the overall structure of political institutions provides access and leverage to some groups and alliances, thus encouraging and rewarding their efforts to shape government policies, concurrently denying access and leverage to other groups and alliances operating in the same national polity. This means that the degree of success that any politically active group or movement achieves is influenced not just by the self-consciousness and "resource mobilization" of that social force itself (for an analysis along these lines, see Amenta and Zylan, 1991). As the following diagram suggests, degrees of success in achieving political goals—including the enactment of social legislation—depend on the relative opportunities that existing political institutions offer to the group or movement in question (and simultaneously deny to its opponents and competitors).

POLITICIZED SOCIAL IDENTITIES   GOVERNMENTAL INSTITUTIONS;
AND GROUP POLITICAL   POLITICAL PARTY SYSTEM;
ORIENTATIONS   >————<RULES OF THE GAME
AND CAPACITIES

"Fit?"
How much access?
How much leverage?

This kind of perspective has been used to explain why U.S. business interests, past and present, often successfully oppose new public social policies. Multiple points of access to legislatures, committees within legislatures, executives and agencies, and—if necessary—state or federal courts, give well-organized and resourceful groups such as business many opportunities to delay or block undesired legislation. If one point of access does not work, another often does. What is more, as David Robertson has recently emphasized, especially during the early twentieth century, business interests gained considerable negative leverage from the fact that forty-eight states, rather than one national government, were the loci for legislative struggles (Robertson, 1989; Graebner, 1977). Business groups could argue that each state's business climate and economic competitiveness would be harmed if it enacted regulations or taxes not matched by other states.

Nevertheless, we cannot treat the prominence of the states within the federal system as an absolute bar to strong legislation in individual states, still less as simply an impediment to nationwide social policy innovations. In 1911, for example, the state of Massachusetts enacted a workmen's compensation law with very broad work force coverage, overriding vociferous arguments by businessmen and other conservatives that the local business climate and the ability of Massachusetts enterprises to compete with out-of-state firms would thereby be grievously harmed (Asher, 1969). Moreover, both women's hour laws and mothers' pensions were very rapidly enacted across forty-some U.S. states during the 1910s. In these instances, most of the U.S. states engaged in what might be called competitive emulation, a process in which interstate rivalry promoted rather than retarded nationwide social policy enactments within the nonparliamentary and decentralized U.S. federal system.

In general, U.S. political structures allow unusual leverage to social groups that can, with a degree of discipline and consistency of purpose, associate across many local political districts. From the nineteenth century onward, what I call "widespread federated interests" have weighed heavily on particular issues in U.S. social politics, sometimes without regard to partisan alignments on those issues. U.S. trade unions during the early twentieth century were *not* effectively organized in this way; they were concentrated in certain urban centers rather than spread out across thousand of localities, and they were functionally organized rather than nested in local-state-national organizational hierarchies. In isolation, big corporations or associations of big businesses did not function as widespread federated interests either. Yet big and small U.S. businesses have often been allied through federated associations such as the National Association of Manufacturers. And by the 1920s, private medical doctors in the United States had created a powerful three-tier federation, the American Medical Association, that could easily rival the legislative leverage of business in opposing new public social policies such as health insurance or the 1926–1927 renewal of the federal Sheppard-Towner program.

Yet widespread federated interests have also included cross-class movements advocating the enactment or extension of major U.S. social policies. The Grand Army of the Republic was such a federated association and it fought very successfully for generous Civil war benefits. Huge women's federations that successfully promoted social legislation in the late nineteenth and early twentieth century included the Women's Christian Temperance Union, the General Federation of Womens' Clubs, and the National Congress of Mothers. Such women's federations were influential in the rapid diffusion of maternalist social legislation across many states during the 1910s (Skocpol, 1992). Tying together clubs based in local legislative districts into statewide and nationwide networks of social communication, all of these widespread associations were well-situated to promote specific kinds of social policies, especially as proposals had to make their way through many different state legislatures, or through the House of Representatives in the national Congress.

Why were maternalist forces considerably more effective in promoting social policies for mothers and women workers in U.S. politics during the early 1900s than paternalist forces that simultaneously worked for the enactment of policies targeted on male wage earners? This question can be answered in significant part through exploration of the "fit" between the organizational capacities of maternalist and paternalist forces, and the opportunities afforded by U.S. political institutions.

During the Progressive Era support for certain paternalist social policy proposals came from reform-minded public administrators and social scientists; and for certain other paternalist proposals, support came from national- or state-level trade unions. But male reformers and trade unionists often operated at ideological and organizational cross-purposes during the early twentieth century; they did not form effective political alliances on behalf of new social policies, except in a few individual states (Skocpol, 1992, part 2). What is more, neither reformist professionals nor trade unions were organized as widespread federated associations reaching into localities across the nation. Supporters of paternalist social policy proposals in the early twentieth-century United States usually found it difficult to conduct simultaneous legislative drives across many states.

By contrast, turn-of-the-century U.S. women's groups were able to form broad alliances between reformist professionals and locally rooted women's groups, to simultaneously press legislatures to enact new social policies for women workers and for mothers and children (Skocpol, 1992, part 3). U.S. unions and reformist male intellectuals could not work together cooperatively, as did female intellectuals and popular groups in early twentieth-century U.S. social politics, in ways analogous to intellectual-worker alliances in other nations' social democratic movements. In addition, American maternalist alliances achieved considerable leverage in the national polity. Because the largest women's associations of the day, especially the General Federation of Women's Clubs and the National Congress of Mothers, had been built up out of voluntary associations created by elite and middle-class women excluded from the nineteenth-century routines of U.S. electoral and party politics, they developed as autonomous federations *paralleling* the three-tier local-state-national structure of U.S. governmental federalism. This happened at a historical juncture when male-only U.S. political parties were weakened, when state legislators were more sensitive to moralistic waves of public opinion than to partisan party controls, and when U.S. courts were more willing to accept labor regulations for women than for men.

Thus U.S. women's political mobilization through nationwide federations of voluntary groups faced a receptive governmental context during the 1910s and early 1920s. For a time, the structures of U.S. politics rewarded broad maternalist alliances with many (although not invariable) legislative successes. And this happened even as the same political arrangements were quite unreceptive to the importunings of the social scientists and trade unionists who worked for paternalist social policies.

Policies Transform Politics

We need, finally, to keep in mind a fourth process—policy feedbacks—highlighted by a structured polity approach. Too often social scientists who study national systems of social provision forget that policies, once enacted, restructure subsequent political processes. Analysts typically look only for synchronic determinants of policies—for example, at the roots of policies in current social interests or in existing political alliances. In addition, however, we must examine patterns unfolding over time (and not only long-term macroscopic processes of social change and polity reorganization). We must make social policies the starting points as well as the end points of analysis: As politics creates policies, policies also remake politics.

Once instituted, policies have "feedback" effects in two main ways. In the first place, because of the official efforts made to implement new policies using new or existing administrative arrangements, policies transform or expand the capacities of the state. They therefore change the administrative possibilities for official initiatives in the future, and affect later prospects for policy implementation. In the second place, new policies affect the social identities, goals, and capabilities of groups that subsequently struggle or ally in politics. Thus, as summed up in the following diagram, social policies feed back into the processes we have already posited within the polity-centered frame of reference:

POLICIES (time 1) → TRANSFORMED STATE CAPACITIES → POLICIES (time 2)

POLICIES (time 1) → CHANGES IN SOCIAL GROUPS AND THEIR POLITICAL GOALS AND CAPABILITIES → POLICIES (time 2)

Our analysis of policy feedbacks can be taken a bit further by asking whether any given policy has effects on state capacities and politics that serve either to promote or to frustrate the further extension of that line of policymaking. This is a way of getting at the "success" of policies in terms of ongoing political processes. It contrasts with other ways of discussing the success or failure of policies, for example, by assessing their "efficiency" according to some external economic criterion, or by assessing their moral worth according to a given normative standard. According to this political-process approach, a policy is "successful" if it enhances the kinds of state capacities that can promote its future development, and especially if it stimulates groups and political alliances to defend the policy's continuation and expansion (for analyses in these terms, see Esping-Andersen, 1985; Headey, 1978). Indeed, public social or economic measures may have the effect of stimulating brand-new social identities and political capacities, sometimes for groups that have a stake in the policy's expansion, sometimes for groups that seek to repeal or reorient the policy in question. What is more, positive or negative policy feedbacks can also "spill over" from one policy to influence the fate of another policy proposal that seems analogous in the eyes of relevant officials and groups. Tracing these feedback processes is crucial for explaining the further development of social provision after initial measures are instituted. The importance of policy feedbacks is one of the best reasons why any valid explanation of the development of a nation's social policies must be genuinely historical, sensitive to processes unfolding over time (this is a central theme in Heclo, 1974).

Certainly, policy feedbacks figured in the early phases of social policymaking in the United States, especially the positive and negative feedbacks from Civil War pensions. The expansion of Civil War pensions included powerful positive feedbacks. After initial legislative liberalizations, veterans became self-consciously organized and mobilized to demand ever-improved benefits; and the Bureau of Pensions became one of the largest and most active agencies of the federal government. By the early twentieth century, moreover, many American workers and citizens appear to have wanted to extend this policy precedent into more widely available old-age pensions. Yet at the same time, Civil War pensions set in motion reactions against future public social provision along similar lines. Because the very successes of Civil War pensions were so closely tied to the workings of patronage democracy, these successes set the stage for negative feedbacks that profoundly affected the future direction of U.S. social provision. During the Progressive Era, the precedent of Civil War pensions was constantly invoked by many American elites as a reason for opposing or delaying any move toward more general old-age pensions, even though such pensions could have allowed elite reformers to build alliances with trade unions similar to those achieved by contemporary British reformers. The party-based "corruption" that many U.S. reformers associated with the implementation of Civil War pensions prompted them to argue that the United States could not administer any new social spending programs efficiently or honestly.

CONCLUSION

To understand patterns and transformations of social policies in the United States (and beyond), I have argued that we need to analyze politics as being jointly influenced by historically changing governmental institutions, political parties, and social groups. By focusing on the historical formation of the U.S. state and political parties, we can understand the policy initiatives taken by politicians, administrators, and reformist professionals. At the same time, we need to analyze how changing political institutions and social transformations have jointly influenced the relative political impact of social group actors based in identities of class, gender, and ethnicity. Such an approach can help us understand why working-class movements with Social Democratic orientations were relatively weak in the United States around the turn of the twentieth century, whereas associations of male veterans and female homemakers were remarkably strong.

We must also keep in mind that policy "outcomes" are never settled. The policies of one period in turn affect the governmental arrangements and politically active social groups that will debate and help to determine what policies come next. Politics is inextricably historical—and our theories neglect this fact only at their peril. A polity-centered framework is necessarily an historically oriented approach to asking the right questions, and arriving at valid answers, about the course of American political development—past, present, and future.

PART III

Microanalysis

9

Rational Choice Theory
and the Study of American Politics

JOHN ALDRICH

The purpose of this chapter is to assess the role that rational choice theory has already played and can hope to play in the study of American politics. Concomitant with posing a question about positive influence is posing one about negatives, specifically to investigate the current and looming limitations of this enterprise: How might rational choice theory overcome these problems and limitations, and how, if at all, does rational choice theory relate to other approaches and ways of formulating questions useful in the study of American politics. This chapter, then, is more about theorizing than about American politics per se, and leans more toward "positive," that is, scientific, than normative theory. After presenting some of the very basics of rational choice theory, we move to examination of three substantive topics: mass political behavior, institutional politics, and political history.

Rational choice theory has unquestionably assumed a very prominent place in political (and social) science generally, and this is especially true in the field of American politics. It is a theory of how individuals choose and of the consequences of those choices for political outcomes. Thus, it is quite possible, and appropriate, to develop a rational choice theory of peasant behavior applied to South Vietnam (Popkin, 1979) or a rational choice theory of political-economic outcomes in nations that have neither democratic governments nor market economies (Bates, 1981). Nonetheless, it is fair to say that rational choice theorists have made their mark in the study of liberal democracies in general and of American politics in particular, and the theory has been originally, most richly, and most fully developed in American politics.

I argue here that the importance that rational choice theory has assumed in American politics is due to the scope of its inquiry and, perhaps more important, to the dynamic character of theory development. Rational choice theory, as a theory about individual and social choices, naturally enough made its first impact in the study of individual decision-making in political settings. At essentially the same time, interactions between individuals' choices were studied with an eye toward understanding both the interdependencies among actors, notably in game theoretic settings, and in the aggregation of individual decisions, typically in voting and its general representation in social choice theory. Even within this context, theory has progressed. Most important, game theory went through a revolution in the 1970s, with great advances made in the theory of noncooperative games and of information. These advances have, in turn, yielded significant advances in formal modeling and, less quickly, in empirical applications.

Beginning in the late 1970s, however, rational choice theory in political science made a great advance by adding the rigorous treatment of institutions. Called the (rational-choice-based) "new institutionalism," work in this area tends to blend social choice and voting theory with the new directions in game theory. The basic idea is that political outcomes are the product of actors seeking to realize their preferences and are a product as well of the institutional context in which that behavior is set. In this view, an "institutional equilibrium" is sought, which may differ from an equilibrium based on preferences alone, or may not exist at all when the latter does not.

Political choices differ from other types of choices, because at least elite political actors are often able to change the rules, as well as choose the outcomes within those rules. For example, national party conventions adopt (and often change) their rules by simple majority vote shortly before choosing their primary outcomes, the platform and nominees, under those rules by the same majority procedure. In theoretical parlance, many political institutions are "endogenous." The question, therefore, is whether these endogenous institutions are, themselves, capable of being understood within, and derived from, the theory. In this view, the new institutionalism asks whether there are "equilibrium institutions" (Shepsle, 1986).

Since institutions are intended to structure relationships over time, the study of "equilibrium institutions" is necessarily dynamic. Thus, the new institutionalism of the 1980s has paved the way for a third major theoretical advance, the study of political history. This move was anticipated in what I believe to be the first use of the term "new institutionalism." David Rohde and Kenneth Shepsle (1978) outlined what I call the "fundamental equation" of rational choice theory in political science: Political outcomes are the product of goal-seeking behavior by actors, choosing within both a set of institutional arrangements and a particular historical context. The promise in this development is that proper attention to "history" will sever any remaining impression that rational choice theories of politics are little more than situations where "microeconomists study Congress." Rather, the particular characteristics of political choices, examined with a proper understanding of history, promise to make political-style rational choice theory not only a theory of and for politics, but also promise to make a genuine and unique contribution to social science generally. That is, we may at last have some original theoretical contributions to make to our sister disciplines. No longer must political scientists only borrowers be.

MODELS OF INDIVIDUAL DECISIONMAKING

Duncan Luce and Howard Raiffa (1957) discussed three categories of decisionmaking: certainty, risk, and uncertainty. There are very few interesting political circumstances for direct application of decisionmaking under certainty, since each action by an individual leads to a well-defined outcome, and thus, this setting is truly individual. Its value, therefore, is for developing the fundamental principles of rational choice. Such a theory is composed of (at least) the following: a) a well-defined set of *outcomes*, b) a well-defined set of *actions* or behaviors, c) a way of *combining the two*, meaning that each action leads to a single outcome, d) (complete, reflexive, and transitive orderings of) *preferences* over outcomes from which preferences over actions can be inferred (or "induced"), and e) a *rationality principle* that ties preferences to choices, which in this case is a simple preference maximization principle—choose that action that yields the most preferred outcome available.

Individual decisionmaking under risk concerns situations in which c does not hold. In its place is c': each action leads to a well-defined *set* of outcomes over which decisionmakers can be assumed to act as though they assign a well-defined set of probabilities for each action. Individual decisionmaking under uncertainty weakens (generalizes) part c even farther to c'': each action leads to a well-defined set of outcomes, where for at least one feasible action (and usually all actions) it *cannot* be assumed that decisionmakers act as though they assign well-defined sets of probabilities. In both cases, weakening c to either c' or c'' requires changing both parts d and e. For d, ordinal preferences alone are generally insufficient. Instead, d has to be strengthened to d' (often used as well for d''): preferences are assumed to form a *cardinal utility function*, typically in political science the cardinal utility function of John von Neumann and Oscar Morganstern (1945). As a result, the rationality principle of choosing that action that leads to the most preferred outcome is insufficient. Typically (but not invariably, i.e., it is not necessary that) the rationality principle for decision making under risk is e': decisionmakers are assumed to choose that action that yields the highest expected utility over outcomes, that is, *ex-*

pected utility maximization. For decisionmaking under uncertainty, various decision rules, e'', are possible. The most important such rules are developed for situations of strategic interaction that define the domain of game theory. The only well-known, non-game-theoretic example of decisionmaking under uncertainty in the scholarship on American politics is John Ferejohn and Morris Fiorina's use of Savage's minimax regret rule, which they apply to turnout (1974; see the various critiques and their response, 1975, for illustration of its controversial nature). Here, I will discuss only game-theoretic applications, otherwise ignoring decisionmaking under uncertainty (see Luce and Raiffa, 1957, for further discussion of non-game-theoretic rules).

While all rational choice theories of politics must build on the base of some individual decisionmaking model, all interesting models are about outcomes that depend upon the actions of more than one actor. It is for this reason that decisionmaking under certainty rarely applies. It is also for this reason that some (e.g., Ordeshook, 1986) believe that game theory, and hence decision making under uncertainty, is the core theory of politics.

There are, however, important classes of decisions, including most cases of mass political behavior, in which the strategic interaction at the heart of game theory is sufficiently remote to be ignored. These reduce to expected utility models, because the actions of one are able to be assumed to be strategically irrelevant to the actions of all others. In such cases, the projected decisions of others may define the probabilities expected utility calculations, such as the anticipated closeness of an election. It must be remembered, however, that this is an additional, simplifying assumption, which may be false without affecting the core assumptions of rational choice theory. Thus, Ferejohn and Fiorina (1974) reject that assumption for studying turnout, while Thomas Palfrey and Howard Rosenthal (1985), among others, have studied the same problem in explicitly game-theoretic terms.

William Riker (1982b) once argued that there is no law for political science akin to the law of supply and demand in economics. In its place, he continued, expected utility maximization should serve as the core building block. While others may disagree (as in Ordeshook's claim for game theory), expected utility maximization is a viable candidate for such status when strategic interaction is sufficiently remote, such as in mass political behavior. Conveniently, this area illustrates exceedingly well: (1) an important set of rational choice models applied to American politics, (2) problems that have served as two of the major criticisms of rational choice theory, and (3) some avenues that appear to me to be extremely promising for scientific advancement.

Before turning to that subject let me note that Riker may be correct in a second sense. He pointed to Bruce Bueno de Mesquita's work on war (1981) as an example of the potential power of expected utility maximization. Since then, that project shifted to a game-theoretic account—and it is much the better for it. Similarly, Gordon Black (1972) and Rohde (1979) cast Joseph Schlesinger's theory of political ambition (1966) into expected utility maximizing form, and doing so greatly advanced that theory. As I will argue later, I believe that ambition theory is one of the most important accounts in American politics. While already greatly appreciated in its current areas of application, it may well turn out to be one of the most important ways to study campaigns, elections, political parties, and elective institutions generally. There have been some recent attempts to transform it into game-theoretic terms (Aldrich and Bianco, 1992; Banks and Kiewiet, 1989), also promising to make ambition theory much the better for it. Thus expected utility maximization may be an important way to formalize many problems initially, generalizing to game-theoretic forms, when and where it turns out to be useful. Often, it becomes useful when political elites and some other set of small numbers of actors are involved, *and* when some or all of these relatively few actors are genuinely concerned about the outcome.

THEORIES OF MASS POLITICAL BEHAVIOR
IN AMERICA

The typical setting of mass political behavior differs in several crucial ways from studies of political elites. The study of mass behavior is just that—study of the behavior of a great many actors, whether in voting, in interest groups, or in political participation generally. This has the important consequence already noted that true strategic behavior is usually minor or remote, sufficiently so that expected utility maximization is one plausible model. Certainly, collective action relies on, or at least is consonant with, prisoner's dilemma or other game-theoretic representations, and "strategic voting" (Ferejohn and Fiorina, 1974; 1975; Abramowitz, 1989; Abramson, et al., 1992) is possible, albeit in terms of expected utility models.

But two other classes of attributes are also common to this distinction. First, the range of actions open to the individual is often highly circumscribed: one can vote for one of two (or some small number of) candidates or abstain; one can contribute to a group or not; one can choose to participate in one or at most a small number of ways or not. The limited range of alternatives characteristic of mass behavior means that the determination (or the inducing) of the actors' preferences for actions based on their preferences over outcomes is *relatively* straightforward. The definition of the set of feasible outcomes, over which preferences must be defined, is also frequently quite circumscribed. Indeed, if choice is between exactly two candidates, the rational choice postulate itself requires only that the voter cast a ballot for the preferred candidate. In these highly limited circumstances, therefore, the choice postulate is unproblematic, and it is widely shared by scholars regardless of theoretical orientation. (This is different from asserting that the full range of assumptions, a-e', entailed in rational choices theories of voting is unproblematic, only that e' is.) And it is the nature of most mass political settings that makes this so.

Second, while certainly not always true, political choices are often not terribly important to most such choosers. All who study electoral behavior, for example, agree that most political choices are typically remote from the ordinary lives of the public. The remoteness of outcomes from one's own actions not only eliminates true strategic interaction, but it also frequently greatly attenuates interest—and self-interest—in the decision problems in ways vividly contrasting with much of elite politics.

In most studies of elites, by contrast, at least some of them care a great deal about outcomes; there are often a broad array of actions at least potentially open to some or all of the elites (and there may be sufficient room for innovative, "heresthetical" actions, as Riker (1986) notes, and these relatively few elites are set in circumstances where their choices, or even the anticipation of their choices, may directly affect the strategies, choices, and actions of the other elite actors. Also, political elites may have the possibility of changing the rules, while mass actors generally must take the rules as given and act within (or rebel against) those constraints. In this sense, mass political actors are more like "price takers," while elite political actors may, at times, be "price setters."

MASS BEHAVIOR: INFORMATION

The first lesson taught about mass behavior is that citizens have low levels of information—both factual information and information of the sort useful for decisionmaking. Many choice-theoretic models assume some form of full information. This assumption is often the basis for criticizing rational choice theory.

By design, regular avenues of mass political participation are highly simplified, especially with respect to the range of alternative actions under serious consideration, and these further are often, to use Sidney Verba and Norman Nie's (1972) apt term for the vote, "blunt." In such circumstances, rational choice is unproblemmatic and uncontroversial. If election outcomes are defined as the election of one candidate or another, all that must be assumed is that citizens can form preferences over the candidates and vote accordingly. Henry Brady and Stephen Ansolabehare (1989) found that, even in presidential nomination campaigns with many candidates, most of whom were far from "household names," these assumptions were satisfied rather well. Much the same can be said for most other regular avenues of participation.

Nonetheless, there are regular and important circumstances in which the setting is limited and even these minimal assumptions often (apparently) fail. It is often the case, for example, that many do not even know both major candidates running for election in their congressional district (Jacobson, 1992). And many, although not all, local elections have low turnout rates because potential voters may be unaware that there even is an election, let alone aware of the candidates or issues at stake. For congressional elections, one might argue that voters know that if they do go to the polls, the partisanship of the contenders will be identified, so that voting by partisanship is both possible and at least potentially rational (see below). Still, the rise in importance of incumbency voting suggests that some base their decision on their view of the incumbent alone, without knowledge of the opponent and in spite of partisanship. If true, as most seem to accept, it is necessary to develop a theory consonant with these patterns. It may be possible to develop such an account, which (depending on the model) may provide a significant advance either into rational choice in highly limited informational settings, or into choice with effectively one "alternative" (similar perhaps to the study of presidential approval), or both. It is one thing to construct a theoretical account of a small number of empirical patterns and thus provide a rational reconstruction. It is another thing to convince scholars that the model should be taken seriously as more than rationalization. It should be considered seriously only if that account can be shown to explain other empirical regularities (either wholly new ones, yielding new, nonobvious insights, or already known regularities that were not previously seen to be related to the original patterns rationalized), or if the account can be shown to be a special case of a more general theory, new or already established.

The assumption of full information characteristic of many rational choice models is partially historic in two senses. First, the history of the development of many rational choice theories begins by modeling with highly restrictive assumptions, such as full information, followed by relaxation (generalization) of those assumptions. Thus, for example, the spatial theory of elections originally assumed that voters knew the positions of both candidates on all issues. More recently, Richard McKelvey and Peter Ordeshook (1986) developed a spatial theory in which voters inferred candidate positions from highly limited information, such as poll reports or reports of endorsements of candidates by groups. They proved that voters would choose the same candidates as if fully informed (and candidates would converge to equilibrium positions), and they demonstrated that this theory worked empirically through an extended series of experiments. James Enelow and Melvin Hinich's model of predictive dimensions (1984) is another important example of this point.

This work also illustrates the second sense of "history." Theoretical advances have made it possible to analyze limited information more rigorously. McKelvey and Ordeshook, for example, exploit rational expectations theory, especially in terms of signal extraction and its consequences for choice. This technology effectively did not exist when the original spatial model was developed. Similarly, the profound revolution in game theory included games with repeated play, asymmetric information, signaling, reputation, "cheap talk," and related topics (Fudenberg and Tirole, 1991). These advances made it possible—and desirable—to use game theory without full information assumptions.

The earlier assertion that rationality is unproblematic in, say, presidential voting might strike the reader as a very "thin" definition of rationality. What it actually means is a radical simplification of the set of outcomes to merely one or the other candidate winning. In fact, we often want to know something of the basis of those preferences, or in the jargon, what the arguments are of a citizen's utility function. Presumably, voters do not have a fundamental value based on which particular person is president, but rather have more basic preferences and values concerning what the government does. In that sense, preferences over candidates are *induced* preferences. Typically, scholars of voting would say that candidate preferences are based on evaluations of the policies of the candidates, evaluations of the two candidates' personal and professional qualifications, and evaluations of the consequences of having one party or the other in control of the White House. Seeing outcomes in these more general terms re-raises the information question.

As in so many areas of elections, Anthony Downs (1957) established the research agenda. A substantial portion of Downs's efforts went into explaining why the electorate is, rationally, little informed and explaining how an electorate would choose with limited information. As to the latter, he argued that citizens would first employ information "accidentally" (or, better, incidentally) acquired, not for the purpose of making a vote decision, per se. He further suggested that citizens would tend to rely on the judgments and evaluations of others already informed and, presumably, with a known stance or reputation, whether "opinion leaders," similar to the old two-step flow of information arguments, or "experts," consistent with the usage of McKelvey and Ordeshook. He also concluded that parties have incentives to hold fairly consistent positions over time, thereby developing a reputation. And, he developed an account of retrospective voting, whereby citizens use their experience of outcomes under incumbents (hence "incidentally" acquired information) to forecast future actions.

Fiorina (1981) expanded on this latter account, developing a systematic theory of retrospective voting and testing it extensively. He also developed a theory of partisanship based on this retrospective voting account. His analysis showed that it aligned empirical regularities that corresponded closely to those of the social-psychological approach to partisanship (Campbell et al., 1960, 1964).

Christopher Achen (1989) specified Fiorina's theory of partisanship and voting in a Bayesian framework. (Interestingly, the Downs-Fiorina-Achen progression reverses the usual development of rational choice models by moving in this case from the more general to the more precise.) From this model, Achen was able to prove a number of results that were precisely identical to many of the known empirical regularities about partisanship, such as: new voters' partisanship will be less stable than more experienced voters'; parental experience will impact positively on their children's partisanship, but at a diminishing rate over time; new political experiences will impact on partisanship at a rate that declines over time; past partisanship has an increasing impact on current partisanship over time; outside of realigning eras, only *unexpectedly* high or low experienced benefits will change partisanship; and independents will disproportionately have lower levels of information than partisans. All of these results had been empirically tested already and make up a significant proportion of the central empirical results about partisanship. He also derived conditions under which some of these patterns should not hold and some as yet untested implications, thus satisfying the conditions I posed above for making this more than a mere rationalization of known results.

Downs's explanation of why citizens ought (rationally) to be expected to be ill-informed about politics is, perhaps, even more important. Because essentially all mass political decisions are reached by the actions of a very large number of decisionmakers and because the outcomes are reasonably close to pure public goods, it follows that the benefits of reaching an informed decision are greatly outweighed by the costs of information acquisition and utilization. This is a stronger explanation than the usual reference to the "remoteness" of politics from everyday life, although it is, of course, a demonstration of what "remoteness" entails. It is also illustrative of an implicit "comparative statics" approach, yielding testable implications for differing circumstances (e.g., with smaller N, more information should be acquired intentionally, ceteris paribus, and as N approaches 1, it becomes a personal decision, equivalent to a decision about a private good, for which there is a strong incentive to acquire information intentionally). There is an implicit model of information cost expenditure here, whereby citizens simultaneously seek to minimize decision costs and maximize the accuracy of their assessments, leading to a global maximization of expected utility over actions. This model is essentially equivalent to standard profit maximization, gathering new information until the marginal cost of gathering a new datum equals the expected benefits of greater surety that the choice is correct. One could employ, for example, standard or Bayesian results on optimal sample size. What I want to emphasize here, however, is that a blending of Downsian rational information, or "rational ignorance," with new results in cognitive social psychology is both possible and desirable.

At about the same time that Downs was writing his book, Herbert Simon and others initiated the cognitive sciences, from which various notions of bounded rationality were developed that emphasized the human limitations in information-processing capabilities (see Simon, 1985, for a recent statement). Recently, the intellectual heirs of this early work have attracted attention in political and the other social sciences, both in what is sometimes called behavioral decision theory, often associated with Daniel Kahneman and Amos Tversky's "biases and heuristics" (Kahneman, Slovic, and Tversky, 1982) and in cognitive social psychology with its emphasis on such constructs as "schemas," "stereotypes," and "scripts." The latter concepts have been used to analyze partisanship (Lodge and Hamill, 1986), evaluations of presidential candidates (Kinder, 1986; Kinder and Fiske, 1986), and full models of voter choice (Lodge, McGraw, and Stroh, 1989; Rahn et al., 1990; Aldrich, Sullivan, and Borgida, 1989).

All of these models are united under an overarching assumption called: "the *cognitive miser* viewpoint. The errors and biases in people's ordinary thought processes more descriptively portray us as doing well enough (satisficing) under the circumstances of having limited brains to confront complex information environments. The best examples are the inferential heuristics ... and the schema theories. ... These cognitive shortcuts allow people to make rapid but not necessarily accurate judgments, and motivation has nothing to do with it" (Fiske, 1990:5, emphasis in original). This is sometimes referred to as a "theory-driven processing" of information, meant in the sense that schemas and the like are little "theories" in people's minds that can be used to infer with a paucity of information. This contrasts with "data-driven" processing, whereby decisionmakers gather information to reach decisions. The problem with the pure cognitive miser view is that there is an easy answer to the question these theorists ask about how much effort should go into decisionmaking: zero. That is, this is a perspective that focuses solely on costs, ignoring benefits. With nothing on the benefit side, there is no way to theorize about what "doing well enough (satisficing)" means, since there is no inclusion of goals or motivations of the decisionmaker to assess when the decisionmaker is satisfied "well enough" with the decision.

Susan Fiske calls for a new direction:

> However, the cognitive miser viewpoint tilted too far in emphasizing people's theory-driven processing over their attention to the information given. Consequently, the current generation of approaches presents a more balanced view of the social (and political) thinker as a *motivated tactician*, one with a variety of cognitive strategies available, choosing among the more effortful and complete strategies or easy and approximate ones, as the motivational situation demands. Thus, in the current view, people who are sufficiently motivated do not neglect the data in favor of their schemas; they combine their prior expectancies with the available information, making adjustments to fit. This viewpoint predicts an important role for involvement in the degree of processing exerted by the thinking person. This is not to say that effort necessarily begets accuracy, for people often think hard only to construct elaborately justified biases. This perspective does suggest that people make cognitive choices in the heat of cognitive battle to manage the barrage of information, but the choices are not so planful as to constitute a priori battle strategies; hence I have chosen the term "tactician," not "strategist." (Fiske, 1990:5–6, emphasis in original)

"Motivation" refers to the benefit side of the equation, indicating how concerned the decisionmakers are with concluding that they have reached an acceptable decision. Something very similar to Fiske's creation of the motivated tactician is clearly what Samuel Popkin (1991) had in mind in his ambitious effort to combine rational choice and social cognitive theories to understand electoral behavior.

At this point, it is too glib to say that the Downsian perspective and Fiske's motivated tactician are, or can easily be made, fully consonant. It is clear, however, that there is significant potential for these two approaches to gain from one another and work together, rather than as opposites. Much as Fiorina (1981) extended the Downsian viewpoint, there is room for work in the style of Achen's paper to translate some aspects of a "motivated tactician" into rational choice terms to see if some of the empirical regularities already produced from the "cognitive miser" perspective, can be derived (for more illustrations of empirical regularities to explain, see Fiske 1990; those in Aldrich, 1990b, 1993; and in Rahn, 1990).

There are limits to the ability to merge political science and psychology. Psychology, even social psychology, is inherently focused on getting individual decisionmaking "right," and therefore is justly concerned with specifics or particulars, such as what makes one person unique. Political science, because it is concerned with collective choices and outcomes, inherently focuses less on the "idiographics" and more on how to make sense of, or make general statements about, decisionmaking across many individuals. Thus, for example, the traditional spatial model (Davis,

Hinich, and Ordeshook, 1970) assumed that all voters agree on the positions of candidates, share weighing of dimensions, and so on. They made such assumptions not because they believed them to be empirically accurate, but because *something* must be assumed to be able to theorize about any social setting.

MASS BEHAVIOR: COLLECTIVE ACTION

Rational ignorance follows (or at least is greatly enhanced) because the political outcome is a public good, attained by the decisions made by a very large number of individual actors. The second problem usefully raised by expected utility maximization in mass publics is the collective action problem. This problem, flowing from Paul Samuelson (1954) and Mancur Olson, Jr. (1965), as well as from Downs (1957) and Riker and Ordeshook (1968, 1973) is, like the problem of information, both a very important component of rational choice theories of mass behavior and the basis for a long-standing critique of that theory (raised most famously by Barry, 1970; see also Hardin and Barry, 1982; Ferejohn and Fiorina, 1974). The collective action problem is at the heart of the calculus of voting, of Olson's work on interest groups and those who have reacted to (or against) it (such as Salisbury, 1969, 1984; Moe, 1980; Johnson, 1987; Walker, 1991) and of the many and varied impacts that the study of repeated interactions has had on this—and other—disciplines (Taylor, 1976; Hardin, 1982; Axelrod, 1984).

The critique can be easily stated whether in expected utility terms as here or in game-theoretic terms. The probability terms in expected utility refer to the impact of a chosen action on changing the outcome. In mass political actions, there are so very many individuals involved that the probability that one person's individual action has any effect, except in wildly implausible circumstances, is so remote as to be able to be ignored. Actually ignoring it means that one's action affects the collective choice literally not at all. With this radical decoupling of an individual's action from collective results, there is no purpose to, and no reason for, participating in such settings, other than to assert one's preferences (Fiorina, 1976). In no case would it be sensible to act for the purpose of affecting political outcomes.

Turnout illustrates the logic of collective action exceedingly well, and the analysis of turnout applies to virtually the full range of (ordinary) political participation. I agree that ordinary political participation is essentially similar to turnout, although there are, of course, important institutional and decision-setting differences that make letter writing different from participation in local causes, different from campaign participation, and so on. I disagree, however, that the collective action problem devastates rational choice models of turnout or other regular forms of mass participation, and I disagree that turnout is even a very good example of the genuine importance of collective action problems in politics (see Aldrich, 1993, for amplification).

While the calculus is a good example of a collective action problem, because it is so easy to understand, and it is an important one because it is so common, it is not really an important illustration. Important illustrations are ones where the stakes are high, that is to say, valued and important to the potential participants, but the costs of "cooperating," or participating, are also high. High benefits, discounted by probabilities, and high costs indicate that something important to the actors is at stake, and the inability to solve the collective action problem means that something of genuine importance to the actors risks being—and often is—lost. Contrast the struggle to find means to achieve international cooperation as extreme counterpoint to the embarrassing, but apparently not tragic, 10-point decline in turnout in presidential elections.

Put alternatively, the low-cost–low-expected benefit nature of most cases of the collective action problem in mass behavior means that the decision to participate or not is a marginal, or relatively unimportant, decision for most. This marginality has two consequences. The less important, theoretically, is that a whole host of variables affects costs and expected benefits weakly, that is, at the margin, but since that margin may be just the difference needed to swing the choice one way or the other, many variables are weakly related to such choices as turnout. Many will be systematic, many will be idiosyncratic. As a result, many independent variables will be significantly related to participation, and there will be a large unexplained part of the decision (e.g., leading to relatively low R^2 results and related measures). This, of course, is exactly what years of empirical research has found.

The theoretically more important consequence is that the marginality of such choices for most individuals permits application of a "strategic political organization" hypothesis (purposefully paralleling the Jacobson and Kernell's "strategic politicians" hypothesis, 1983). Whether the election is expected to be close or not matters little to rational citizens, making each one only marginally more likely to vote. It matters a great deal, however, to the two candidates involved, to the two parties, and to other interested groups such as Political Action Committees. Resources invested in such close elections can be used to offset the costs of voting for individuals thought likely to support the appropriate candidate, and such are certainly wiser investments in close than in one-sided races. Thus, on average, more campaign effort and resources are likely to be invested in competitive than noncompetitive races. More citizens will, therefore, receive the benefits (whether in reduction of costs of participating, enhanced benefits, or both). As a result, the marginal participant will be more likely to turn out in close contests, because of the extra efforts of candidates, parties, and other organizations. The result is that, through the rational actions of strategic electoral organizations, there will be higher turnout in elections expected to be close than in those not expected to be so, whether citizens consider the closeness of the election or not. Among other things, this may explain the otherwise curious results that show that turnout is higher at the aggregate level in close than in non-close contests, while there is only marginal support for the individual-level hypothesis that voters are more likely to turn out, the closer they perceive the election to be.

Strategic electoral organizations may also (although less surely so) help explain why there is evidence of sophisticated or strategic voting in mass elections (as found in presidential primaries by Abramson, et al., 1992; in Canada by Black, 1978; and in Britain by Cain, 1978). If individual efficacy is, indeed, very low, then *all* votes are, effectively, wasted, whether cast for a hopeless party or candidate or for one of the leading contenders. But it *is* in the interests of strategic electoral organizations to try to convince the electorate to reason strategically when doing so would redound to the benefit of that organization's preferred party or candidate. Thus, in 1980, Jimmy Carter argued that a "vote for Anderson is a vote for Reagan." The electorate responded in fine Key-like, echo-chamber fashion (Key, 1966). Anderson's support dropped precipitously, and many erstwhile Anderson supporters cited "wasted vote" reasons for their switch (Abramson, Aldrich, and Rohde, 1983).

RATIONAL CHOICE AND INSTITUTIONS

Rational choice theory has deep roots in institutional analysis. The "classic" analyses that served to launch rational choice in political science included such path-breaking books as Downs (1957), Duncan Black (1958), and James Buchanan and Gordon Tullock (1962). Each of these was an analysis of rational action in highly structured institutional settings. The first two primarily studied how candidates, parties, and voters, and how legislators, respectively, would choose, given the institutional setting in which their actions were to take place; these works were, in other words, searches for "institutional equilibria." The latter book was primarily a study of why rational actors would choose to create and maintain a democratic republic; this work was a search for an "equilibrium institution." Kenneth Arrow's theorem (1951) was also presented as, in effect, a search for an equilibrium institution (in a very general sense of the term), even if Arrow demonstrated that there was no such institutional arrangement.

The point, of course, is only that the new questions that define the "new institutionalism" of the 1980s have a longer pedigree.

Shepsle (1979) and others who figure so prominently in the new "new institutionalism," however, have made genuinely important and original contributions. Not the least of these has been the rigorous development of formal representations of significant aspects that seem to capture the flavor of real-world institutions, such as the U.S. House of Representatives. These seem to be sufficiently close renderings to convince students of those institutions, who may not have found much direct value in older rational choice theories, that the newer theory has something of real value to offer for understanding American politics.

This literature asks two major questions. The first concerns behavior of rational actors within institutional settings. This line of inquiry either seeks to find equilibria outcomes due to the interaction of actors seeking to achieve their goals within the institutional rules, when goals alone are insufficient to yield equilibria at all (Shepsle's "structure-induced-equilibria"), or seek to establish the impact of rules, in combinations with actors' preferences and goals, in altering the location and nature of equilibria from what they would be in the absence of, or under different, institutional arrangements. The latter are well-illustrated by the kinds of models Keith Krehbiel considers (1991) in enabling collective action sorts of problems to be overcome (or, in other words, in deriving conditions under which more efficient equilibria can be attained; see also Cox and McCubbins, 1993). In this sense, these models can be compared to the relatively "institution free" models of the failure of collective action, as in Olson (1965). That is, the "institution free" models yield Pareto-inferior equilibria in comparison to the conditions from which the other models (including Olson's "by product" account) derive Pareto-superior equilibrium properties. Krehbiel also contrasts his models of House-like legislatures with those in the Kenneth Shepsle-Barry Weingast (1987) tradition. In this contrast, the question is the comparison of differing equilibria, in which Krehbiel's tend to yield median voter outcomes, whereas Shepsle and Weingast's can yield more extreme, "high demand" outcomes. Typically, the analysis in all of these models is similar to prior rational choice models, searching for equilibrium outcomes, and characterizing them, given rules and goals. Typically, as well, this question is a more "static" one, holding goals, rules, and "history" constant.

The second major question is all but necessarily more dynamic. It asks, in effect, where the rules come from. It seeks to understand why rational actors would adopt and maintain the particular set of institutional rules they do, and why they change them when they do.

This question verges on, but is not yet quite fully realizing, a fundamental difference between many political and many economic outcomes.

In the classic economic setting, economic actors and agents take the rules as given. The rules are exogenous to the economic actors under question. Of course, oligopoly theory is about a few unusually powerful agents who are capable of affecting things that market agents are otherwise unable to affect as individuals, such as prices. And surely, many of the important questions asked by economic historians are about how various rules and regimes come about, although one might well argue that this subject is actually a part of political economics, and not economics, per se. That is, property rights, rules of exchange, and so on, are established and enforced by governments, quite possibly in response to demands from economic actors. The Coase and Williamson projects, however, have demonstrated that, at least in some important cases, economic rules are endogenous to economic actors and their actions.

Still, there is no gainsaying that political elites have the choice both of outcomes *and* of the rules that help determine those outcomes much more often than economic agents. Many political rules, that is, are especially endogenous. Perhaps the most famous broad claim of this sort is David Mayhew's (1974) argument that Congress looks for all the world like an institution designed to further the central goal of its members: reelection.

The theoretical concerns raised by the new institutionalism, of searching for the impact of institutions on individuals' behavior and of seeking to understand why rational actors chose the rules they did, is well-placed. The two specific questions that define "institutional equilibria," namely the study of institutional conditions under which the extended consequences of Arrow's theorem are avoided and the search for institutional conditions that solve the Samuelson-Olson collective action problem of Pareto-inferior, or inefficient, equilibria are fine, but too easily overstated. Terry Moe (1991), for example, has convincingly argued that we have all too often overlooked two critical features in our fascination with majority rule disequilibrium and failure to realize common interests in collective action. First, unlike many economic transactions, political outcomes directly make some winners and others losers. Indeed, precisely because laws are (partially) public goods, with one law or electoral victor imposed on all, some will value those outcomes as positive gains, while others will suffer losses. While politics is not really very often purely zero-sum, Riker's classic emphasis on winning and losing (1962) is not misplaced. Secondly, precisely because some win and some lose, today's winners can—and should be expected to anticipate that they very well may—lose tomorrow. In Moe's deft hands, this leads to an understanding of why elected officials create bureaucracies whose designs are otherwise bewildering and apparently ineffective. This healthy reminder of the immense political uncertainty of even the relatively near future serves as one part of the understanding of political history that will form the subject of the next section.

There are some more steps to take before turning to that topic, however. Riker (1980) raised a problem in the study of equilibrium institutions, known as the "inheritability problem." If institutional arrangements are endogenous to the actions of the same set of actors who are choosing political outcomes, and if those outcomes are infected with Arrovian-style disequilibrium, as virtually all cases of majority rule are likely to be, then the choice of rules to affect those outcomes should be expected to inherit that disequilibrium. A simple example is the vote on rules at the 1976 Republican nomination. Reagan, who had already blundered in selecting his running mate in advance of the convention, hoped to force Ford into a similar error by requiring that all candidates for presidential nomination reveal their vice-presidential choice before the nomination vote. Since both vice-presidential nominees four years earlier were forced to resign, one shortly after nomination and the other from office, careful deliberation in the selection of vice-presidential nominees had a great deal of normative appeal. But, of course, everyone knew that this rule was merely a subterfuge to try to force Ford to err and thereby lose the nomination he otherwise surely would win. As a result, delegates voted on the rule based not on their normative appraisal of the proposal but on their preferences for presidential nominee. Here, then, was a fully endogenous institution, with the rules being voted upon by exactly the same set of people as those who would choose the outcomes forty-eight hours later. And here was a case in which the preferences over the choice of rules inherited the preferences over presidential nominee.

Is inheritability a serious problem? Clearly, it can be, as the above example demonstrates. But its logical possibility does not mean that it is likely to arise often. Moreover, I believe that this problem, as genuine as it may be, illustrates a general problem with the way rational choice theory has studied institutional rules over the last decade. Rules are often seen as constraints on behavior. Perhaps they should also be seen as opportunities. Thus, rules that gave more power to the Democratic caucus in the House may best be understood as having given that majority party the opportunity to find what was in its interests and capabilities to achieve. Those rules were enacted in the 1970s, when the Democratic party was still divided, and there was no common interest to take advantage of that opportunity. These rules, however, began to be used with some effectiveness in the 1980s, when the party was less internally divided, so that the party members had sufficient common interest to exploit the opportunity those procedural changes offered.

More important, rules in places like the U.S. House rarely are truly binding constraints. Committees have a variety of "gatekeeping" powers, but there are also avenues around such rules, from discharge petitions on. Looked at alternatively, the House of 1965–1966 was able to pass massive amounts of consequential legislation because the (Great Society) Democratic majority was so powerful that no intra-House rules could stop it. Later, when the working majority was much closer to minimal winning, the ex ante rules-as-constraints were sufficient to stop that congressional majority from working its will so often.

While it may sometimes be the case that the immediate outcome is so critical that a majority will write rules for the exclusive purpose of enacting its will on that specific outcome, more often, rules are chosen to help shape the institution for some time to come, rather than "merely" determine a single outcome. Indeed, it may well be that the choice of rules is often little more than an epiphenomenon, symbolically illustrating some larger concern. Consider, once again, national party conventions. From 1832 through 1932, the Democratic party required a two-thirds rule for presidential nomination. As I have argued elsewhere, this rule was particularly important in the second party system for ensuring that any nominee would be acceptable to North and to South—effectively giving the South a veto over nominees (and underpinning a part of Weingast's (1991b) insightful analysis of the importance of "balance" in the national government, keeping slavery off the effective agenda and from dividing the nation for a generation). The problem with merely saying that the two-thirds rule gave southern Democrats a veto in the face of a northern majority, however, is that the two-thirds rule was voted in—and could be voted out—at any convention by a simple majority of delegates. In 1836, the two-thirds rule was voted on—and it lost by majority vote (231–210). Perhaps because no one expected it to lose, nor did a majority really want it to lose—it was reinstated by voice vote. In the 1844 convention, Martin Van Buren had support from a workable but small majority of the delegates for nomination. On the first ballot, he received 146 votes, well over half of the 266 total, but also well short of two-thirds. He lost support over succeeding ballots, and the convention eventually turned to a compromise candidate, the first dark horse, James Polk—a southerner. Interestingly, the two-thirds rule was debated and voted on earlier in the convention. Presumably, if inheritability had been commonplace, Van Buren's supporters would have defeated it. Instead, it remained in effect, receiving the support of 148 delegates, eerily similar to the 146 Van Buren soon received. Of course, Democrats might have argued that they were likely to win anyway. After all, the Whigs were sufficiently divided after their one stint of unified control over government that their incumbent president, John Tyler, was nominated independently for president, but withdrew in favor of Democrat Polk! However, it is harder to argue that such calculations would apply to such nominations as in 1924. In a party evenly divided between urban and rural forces, and dominated in part by differences over the Ku Klux Klan, a minority report against the Klan failed by a vote of 542.35 to 543.15 (with 12.5 abstaining). Smith and McAdoo (receiving urban and rural support, respectively) battled it out for 100 ballots, before John Davis eventually won on the 103rd ballot. Certainly such division is not calculated with an eye toward winning the subsequent election.

Something more than inheritability was at work in the decisions of the convention delegates on the two-thirds rule for the selection of the party's nominee, no matter how shortly to be chosen thereafter. Rather than the preferences for the rule simply and only inheriting their preferences over nominee, there were other "arguments" in their utility functions, such as longer-term effects of the rule on party (and national) unity by selecting only nominees who enjoyed broad support and by granting large minorities (such as the slave states) a veto that simple majority would not provide.

It should then be asked why politicians care about the long term. Two classes of answers are possible, and likely both matter simultaneously. One class is that these politicians value something other than that which can be captured by considering their own self interest. That class, in other words, concerns policy or even more fundamental outcomes, such as party or national unity. As a strategy for explanation, we must, of course, be careful to avoid ad hoc invocation of "other values." Surely, a plausible case can be made for national unity, especially in the second party system. But *party* unity is something else altogether. Especially after the Civil War, and ending only in 1932, why might Democrats care about party unity sufficiently to all but ensure, by continuation of the two-thirds rule, that the party would sometimes go down to defeat in the immediate election? This case suggests a second kind of answer: It might be in the long-term *self-interest* of the politicians. In this case, it might be in the long-term self-interest of party politicians to maintain their party as a viable, major party.

To put the argument in more general terms, I believe that revived analysis of Schlesinger's ambition theory (1966), formalizing it to address long-term career calculations (as Black, 1972, and Rohde, 1979, did for short-term calculations), would provide answers to the kinds of questions asked in equilibrium institutional analysis. Such a move could, at least in principle, tell us when it is in the self-interest of some to support rules that have short-term costs but long-term potential rewards. This would provide answers to when (and for whom) Riker's inheritability problem would apply, and when and for whom it would not. For example, long-term career ambitions were realized through the agency of political parties in the nineteenth century, so that it is explicable that Democratic convention delegates would maintain the two-thirds rule, even when not in the immediate self-interest of a majority of them. Similarly, the decline of parties as agencies for careers, a decline that led to party-centered careers being supplanted by personal, candidate-centered elections *and* "incumbent-centered" long-term careers, such as in the contemporary Congresses, might explain the failure of the two-thirds rule to have such long-term value any longer, and therefore yield to calculations of more immediate interests. One might ask: If it is indeed the case that the two-thirds rule was maintained by the Democratic party for a century due to long-term career calculations, why didn't the other major party adopt and maintain that rule? One answer is "history," that is, it was a part of Democratic party history to have given the South a veto in the party, while it was obviously not a part of the Republican party's "history." Having now put the elements needed to consider how rational choice theory might be useful for, and benefit from, serious consideration of history, it is time to turn, at last, to that subject.

RATIONAL CHOICE THEORY AND HISTORY

The "fundamental equation" of the new institutionalism is that political outcomes are the result of the interplay of actors as they seek to realize their goals, of the institutional settings in which they act and which they may help to shape, and of the historical context in which their decisions are set. The last few sections have addressed actors, how we might understand how they seek to realize their goals, and the institutional arrangements in which they act and which they shape. Roughly speaking, the history of rational choice theory in political science was first to examine actors and their goal-seeking behavior and then to analyze how that interacts with institutional arrangements. Until recently, the "historical setting" appeared in models, if at all, as merely the ex ante status quo. More recently, some initial attempts have been made to "take history seriously" and add it to the repertoire of rational choice.

There are three ways in which "history" might be employed. The first is, if you will, "history as data." In part, this means that considering earlier points in our history opens up new sources of data to test theoretically interesting propositions. At one very simple level, this is, in effect, just what we do when we test models of voter choice on National Election Study/Center for Political Studies (NES/CPS) data from 1952 to date. After all, this forty years of data is the same length of time as the period from the last year of James Madison's presidency to the first year in which the Republican party became the second major political party. "History as data" might sound trivial, but there are three important uses of it. First, some phenomena are too rare to be able to conduct "nonhistoric" systematic data analysis. There have been too few presidents, wars, and so on, to not seek to exploit what data there are. Second, scientific theories are not, often, time-bound. Thus, if people are assumed to seek to achieve their goals, this is so today; but it should be so in earlier eras, too. Richard McCormick (1960) analyzed turnout over the 1824–1844 period in ways that are quite consistent with the calculus of voting. Finding positive evidence of the impact of costs and expected benefits on turnout rates in 1828, as well as in 1988, should only add credibility to the theory. Third, broadening our scope to include historical accounts may yield conditions that permit tests of hypotheses that contemporary circumstances have not provided. For instance, I have extended McCormick's analysis to include tests of the "strategic political organizations" hypothesis described above (1994). From 1828 through 1836, the newly organizing Democratic party was the only "modern, mass party" in existence. This permitted tests of hypotheses about the order of individual states the party would choose to allocate its scarce resources to organize, based on the costs and expected benefits of doing so. Such tests are impossible today, since both parties have long-established organizations throughout the nation.

The second way in which to employ history is related to the last example, is less trivial than the first, and begins to use "history" seriously. I think of it as "history as comparative politics." Just as one might reasonably compare parliaments with legislatures in presidential systems, as Shepsle and Michael Laver (1991) have done so well in theoretically informed but otherwise "traditional" comparative analysis, so too might one compare different historical eras in the same nation. To do so well requires paying attention to the methods of comparative politics. Since much of this is likely to be comparisons of a relatively small number of different eras, serious attention to the comparative case study methodology is in order (obviously, within the confines of something close to a "most similar systems" design). In addition, careful attention to one of the other great methodological problems of comparative politics, what x means in nation one compared to nation two, is also in order. Just as party identification may mean something quite different in electoral systems that vote on candidates versus those that vote on parties, so, too, might party identification mean something different in today's candidate-centered elections compared to its meaning during eras of party-centered elections. A good illustration of this latter point is provided by Charles Stewart III in *Budget Reform Politics* (1989). He examines institutional designs in the House for making appropriations from 1865 to 1921, using rational choice arguments. Since the theory was developed for the contemporary Congress, in which Mayhew's reelection imperative guided theorizing, it was incumbent upon Stewart to show, as he carefully did, the applicability, and limits, of that assumption. History as data or as comparative method, however, is fairly conventional (if, perhaps, too little used). Moreover, there is nothing about this use, at the level discussed above, that is special to rational choice theory, or to which rational choice theory makes an unusual contribution. The same is not true for the third and most interesting sense of "taking history seriously."

The third way in which history can be employed is "history as process" (I'm tempted to refer to it as "history as history"). If the first use of history can be said to be little more than claiming that interesting political science can be done on earlier times than right now, and if the second use of history can be said to contain the warning (and opportunity) that we must pay attention to the context of the times, this third use of history can be said to be, genuinely, "taking history itself seriously." This argument is roughly that the particular sequence of events is consequential. Thus, for example, sequence mattered to understanding why the Democratic party, from the Civil War to the Depression, used the two-thirds rule for nomination. They had adopted it before the war as a means of uniting the party by giving the South a veto. Conversely, the Republican party did not have the two-thirds rule in this time period, and presumably never had an incentive to consider adopting it, because it did not have a prior history as an intersectional alliance (nor did it seek to give its southern supporters, few as they were, a veto). In the "fundamental equation," the historical context is, in this view, said to really matter in explaining the historical path, and thereby the dynamics, followed. Put alternatively, it takes as hypothesis that political outcomes are path-dependent, or at least path-dependency must be taken as a plausible hypothesis.

Rational choice theory provides us with good reasons to believe that dynamic processes are always potentially, and perhaps even likely to be, path-dependent. It is a standard teaching device to illustrate the consequences of Arrow's theorem by showing that, when an Arrovian cycle exists, the outcome is dependent upon the path followed. The nearly generic existence of Arrovian-style cycles under majority rule, such as in the chaos theorems (McKelvey, 1976; Schofield, 1978), means that path-dependence is, therefore, an ever-present possibility.

Rational choice theories of politics differ considerably from those of economies in this way. The most impressive results in economics are the general equilibrium theories, justly being a major part of several Nobel prizes. These theorems yield a global equilibrium, typically singular and attractive as well as retentive. More important for this discussion, they also yield equilibrium outcomes that are independent of the starting point. Like a Markov chain, the equilibrium result does not depend upon the starting point. Where ever one starts, one ends up at the same equilibrium.

Arrow's theorem, and its kindred results about behavior under majority voting methods, shows that there may be no equilibrium, let alone outcomes that are independent of the path chosen. Only when there are median-voter outcomes (or their even rarer multidimensional analogues) will the outcome be independent of the path followed. Moreover, suppose the general response is, in fact, to build institutional arrangements that yield structure-induced equilibria (SIE). It is, then, easy to show that different such arrangements will yield different SIEs. For example, in Shepsle's models (1979) different assignments of jurisdictions to committees (or different assignments of members to committees) will generally yield different SIE outcomes. Similarly, if parties are the institutional arrangements, they may yield SIEs as well (Aldrich, 1990b), and these will be SIEs different from the committee-induced ones. Only if Krehbiel's models apply—and only if there already exists a median-voter equilibrium—will structures not yield differing equilibrium outcomes. But, of course, the whole point of the social choice and voting theory literature is that Krehbiel's required a priori condition (a "preference-induced equilibrium," or median voter, exists) is unlikely in the extreme. It happens with mass-probability zero. Thus, what outcome occurs depends upon the historical path, that is, the set of endogenous institutional arrangements, chosen in advance of the selection of the particular outcome(s) being analyzed.

"History as process" in rational choice theory is likely to focus on the changing institutional context. Thus, Stewart's book (1989) provides a good illustration of the choice of appropriations institutions for reforming the budgetary process. This is so because of the presumption that the choice of rules, when combined with preferences, affects the outcomes. Perhaps the most extensive example of this is Weingast's current work (1991a, 1991b) on institutional arrangements that served to make credible commitments to the South, during the second party system, to ensure that the issue of slavery would not be acted upon (or, more accurately, something close to the status quo policy would be maintained). He asks, in other words, what institutional arrangements ensured to the South that they would have a veto, even though they were a minority and, therefore, could in principle simply be outvoted. Stewart and Weingast (1991) have extended Weingast's analysis, which focuses heavily on the Senate and the "balance rule" there (which kept an equal number of slave and free states in that body and, thus, a southern veto in the government) to its post–Civil War manifestation. In this period, they argue that the Republican party admitted new states to the union in strategic fashion, yielding them more votes there (and in the electoral college) than pure popular voting would have given them. The result, in this era of very close balance between the two parties in national popular voting, was that Republicans tended to hold at least the Senate and therefore commanded a veto over legislation. One important result was that Democratic House majorities, even when combined with a Democratic president, could not significantly alter the status quo of relatively high tariffs.

CONCLUSION

To return to a more theoretical theme, history as process provides a means for studying outcomes in a social choice, voting theoretical framework in spite of (or because of) Arrow's theorem and its extended consequences. Begin with actors and their goals. From the dominant perspective of Mayhew (1974), one begins analysis of congressional outcomes by examining the impact of the various choices on the reelection fortunes of incumbents in the coming election. One might add, of course, other considerations, looking at the short-term consequences of such as Richard Fenno's (1973) values of good policymaking and of seeking power within the chamber. To that, however, we should add longer-term career ambition considerations (and, perhaps, the longer-term versions of policy and power). It may be that today's candidate-centered elections mean that there will be fewer cases of trade-offs between congressional members' long- and short-term ambitions than in the more party-centered elections of the nineteenth century, but that must be shown rather than assumed. Next, behavior in seeking to affect the outcome must be seen in light of the rules shaping the institutional context as well as the goals to be sought. Here, of course, one would seek to establish how those rules would create or change the behavioral equilibrium defining the theoretical prediction of outcomes. Finally, complete analysis would ask why a potential (or actual) majority did not seek to change the rules to achieve a more desired outcome. Often, therefore, the question may be to ask why inheritability did *not* happen, rather than asking why it might undermine the study of rule selection.

All of this has been written from the social choice and voting theoretic perspective, with its emphasis on the problems that Arrow's theorem, chaos theorems, and the like, pose for the study of outcomes chosen by majority rule processes. The study of history as process may be even more useful for analysis in the other major theoretical problem posed by rational choice theory, the study of Samuelson-Olson results for public goods, collective action, and optimality. The analysis of repeated interactions, iterated games, and similar exercises, typically analyzed under the prisoner's dilemma or related problems or formulations of collective action, is, in a fairly direct sense, the study of history as process. Indeed, modern (post-1970) game theory has proven so attractive in large part because of its advances in repeated—that is to say, dynamic—games. Results produced by such as Michael Taylor (1976) and Robert Axelrod (1984) have justly generated a tremendous amount of interest and application precisely because of the demonstration that repeated interaction may, under the proper conditions, "solve" the collective action problem "naturally," that is, due to the long-term, self-interested choices of rational actors.

In a way quite comparable to the "chaos theorems," however, the various "folk theorems" in this literature have posed an extremely consequential, and often worrisome, result (see Fudenberg and Tirole, 1991). The basic thrust of these various theorems is that, although repeated interaction may be consistent with a behavioral equilibrium that "solves" the collective action problem, virtually every set of strategies is also a behavioral equilibrium, at least all of those that minimally fulfill the "always defect from collective action" strategy. Where the chaos theorems conclude that "anything can happen" in majority voting because there is no equilibrium, the folk theorems conclude that virtually "anything can happen" in collective action, because almost anything is, potentially, a behavioral equilibrium.

Thus, by parallel reasoning, virtually everything said above about path-dependence, long-term goals, and the like, applies with equal force to the study of collective action sorts of problems. Moreover, while only some things are determined by majority voting in politics, potential or actual collective action problems, which need only two people to be able to appear, are endemic to nearly all of politics. Further, the various "rules" noted above for conducting such an analysis, beginning with long-term objectives of the principal actors, become even more consequential in the study of repeated games.

Economic theory is dominated by the search for conditions that generate a single, global, path-independent equilibrium. Success in finding such equilibria effectively reduces the study of "history" to two questions. One concerns dynamics around the global equilibrium, such as speed of convergence to it initially and path of re-convergence to it, if perturbed away from it. The second concerns the study of the rules and regimes that form the context in which the global equilibrium can be shown to exist. These are, to be sure, very important questions. Their status in economics or related disciplines, however, is somewhat problematic. It is ordinarily assumed that behavior within a regime is concerned with optimization, the movement towards or remaining at that global equilibrium. Thus, the choice of rules or regimes must be studied separately from the study of behavior within regimes. In economics, that means that the study of regime formation or maintenance is distinct from the study of ordinary economic behavior, and it often means that it is study from a perspective that is nearly a different "discipline," such as history or political economy. To that extent, such studies are not at the core of economics (pun intended).

We should take from several decades of research that such a singular general equilibrium does not exist in politics. Rather, we should take from Arrovian, chaos, and folk theorems the conclusion that multiple equilibria are the ordinary course of political affairs. We should also take from them the lesson that outcomes are very often, perhaps always, path-dependent. And, we should take from them the lesson that the dynamic path, that is to say, the political history, is the central object of our theoretical inquiry.

Critical elections, major institutional reforms, and other such substantial "regime" changes may be seen as (purposeful or otherwise) attempts to change from one equilibrium path to another. These will remain, therefore, important historical moments. Of equal importance, however, is the study of historical dynamics within (or temporally between) such dramatic changes as secular realignments, dealignments, and the like.

Two more implications follow directly from this style of thinking. The first is that there is no reason to think that the various works that fall into such categories as the macrohistorical, or sociohistorical dynamics of political development are *opposite* to the study of politics via rational choice theories. They are, instead, *complements*, and perhaps it can be said that proponents of rational choice, such as Weingast, Stewart, and Aldrich are beginning to appreciate the kinds of questions—and answers—that Walter Dean Burnham, Theda Skocpol, and Stephen Skowronek have been offering. Although late to the table, rational choice theory has, I believe, something to offer to those already there, as I hope this chapter makes clear.

The second point is that the rigorous pursuit of dynamics of choice in the presence of multiple equilibria promises to make a new and genuinely important contribution to the scientific study of human behavior. The point of the new game theory when applied to economics and elsewhere is that multiple equilibria are, in fact, sustainable generally. Thus, all disciplines are likely to turn to this sort of analysis. The theory of majority voting and the theory of public goods and collective action are particularly consequential for politics and are particularly deeply affected by the existence of multiple equilibria, and therefore, by path-dependence. This puts political science in a unique position to make genuine theoretical and methodological advances of relevance to many social sciences—hence my belief that no longer must we borrowers be.

10

The Social Psychology of Politics

MURRAY EDELMAN

Psychological explanations of political phenomena focus largely on the nonrational and the irrational. It is, unfortunately, all too easy to find examples of major political actions throughout American history that illustrate the conspicuous role of nonrational factors in shaping behavior, in allocating praise and blame, and in otherwise interpreting historical events. More often than not the key dynamic in such developments is the shaping of political action and thought in order to rationalize private interests and prejudices, even while those who act and those who support them remain convinced that rationality, not rationalization, explains their behavior and their thinking (Lasswell, 1930).

The key historical examples involve precisely those beliefs that have been most strongly cherished by a large part of the population, most assiduously taught to children, and most frequently proclaimed in patriotic oratory. We are taught, for example, that the United States is a democratic and pluralistic society that provides an equitable voice for all group interests and settles conflicts through evenhanded procedures. This reassuring assumption continues to be the dominant view in spite of the fact that throughout American history minorities and dissidents have been repressed, often violently. The roster of victims has included African Americans, labor unions, strikers, Catholics, pacifists, Chinese, Japanese, the poor, all kinds of political radicals, and, not infrequently, Jews, women, and homosexuals (Zinn, 1980). Beliefs that reassure and strengthen the dominant groups persist as dogma regardless of inconvenient and contradictory facts. When political beliefs on controversial subjects do describe the world adequately, that is only incidental to their primary function: to further the interests and ideologies of those who can get them disseminated and accepted.

The riots and rebellions that have frequently broken out throughout American history offer another example of the widespread reinterpretation of events so as to conform to ideology and reinforce it. As they occur, each of these episodes is commonly interpreted as a unique and rare event because it conflicts with the premise that conventional institutions settle conflicts of interest. But popular uprisings are also conventional; they have been endemic and frequent in the United States, from Shay's Rebellion through the Civil War draft riots to the repeated uprisings in the ghettos of large cities in the twentieth century (*Report of the National Advisory Commission on Civil Disorders*, 1968).

A major reason they often occur is that they serve necessary psychological functions for both their participants and their adversaries. For the former they represent a kind of empowerment and escape valve, even if it is only temporary, against institutions that are seen as symbols of oppression. For the latter they offer further evidence that tough controls against irresponsible, subversive, or pathological people need to be even tougher.

Even the contrasting labels attached to these events reveal their ideological uses and the decisive psychological influences that shape the recounting of history. The African Americans who participated in the ghetto disturbances of the latter part of the twentieth century saw them as "rebellions." To the media and most of the white public they were "riots." The contradictory implications of these terms for responsibility, blame, and remedial action are self-evident.

Throughout this essay other historical events illustrate the important roles in political thought and action of psychological processes that have no necessary relevance to the rational or systematic solution of social problems.

Psychological explanations of political phenomena can, nonetheless, be facile, simplistic, and wrong even when they look insightful and profound at first blush. These risks flow from the dubious categorization of the individual person in a way that overlooks his or her potentiality for transcending the category as social situations change. To move from the individual person to the social situation as the unit of analysis is to escape a stilted and ahistorical mode of explanation while gaining flexibility, breadth, and richness.

That is precisely what the social psychologies of such seminal theorists as George Herbert Mead (1934) and Lev Vygotsky (1962) have done. These approaches have proven invaluable in throwing light on political tactics, maneuvers, and outcomes because they require the analyst to take full account both of the influences upon action and thought functioning at a particular time and on the potentialities for altered action and thought inherent in new opportunities, more rigid constraints, different associates, heroes, or enemies, changed incentives, or fresh horizons.

The mind, unlike the heart, the liver, or the brain, is not located inside an individual person's skin. In Mead's formulation mind becomes what it is by "taking the roles" of other people who are significant to the individual. It is a fully and unavoidably social phenomenon and a thoroughly dynamic one because it reflects a social scene that can change. If George Bush's "significant others" in the Arab world are the feudal sheikhs and the oil companies rather than the millions who are poor and powerless, that phenomenon tells a lot about social role-taking in the Washington bureaucracy and in the Middle East and very little about Bush's IQ, extroversion, or personality type. Such traits do not create the social setting but rather reflect it, just as political leaders do not create policies but rather reflect the dominant interests, social inequalities, and pressures of their times in order to survive as leaders.

Because economic interests and pressures are always a major influence on the quality of people's lives, psychological traits are partly derivative from these as well. Affluence and poverty are not irrelevant to an optimistic or a pessimistic outlook, to assertiveness or docility, or to political conservatism, liberalism, or radicalism. The stages of the business cycle are therefore major influences on the outlook and psychological dispositions of groups and individuals, though there is, of course, no neat correlation between these developments. The discussion below of the bearing of declines in well-being on political behavior and beliefs offers further analysis of this point.

Stiff competition for advancement in a corporation or government agency is likely to encourage anxiety, self-seeking, ruthlessness, and other attitudes and behaviors. There are psychological traits as well that are influenced or shaped by membership in particular occupations.

Clearly, social psychological explanations of politics have to reject simple correlations with individual traits, both because social influences are highly diverse and variable and because they can have disparate effects on behavior and attitudes. This complexity increases their explanatory power even while it decreases or destroys their predictive power.

In recent decades the efforts to understand how the mind processes and transforms stimuli into assumptions, beliefs, actions, and nonactions have been labeled "cognitive psychology." This discipline has advanced our understanding of a wide spectrum of topics applicable to political analysis. The pertinent literature ranges from the work of Charles Osgood on the semantic associations of words and phrases (Osgood, Tannenbaum, and Suci, 1957) to studies of the behavioral consequences of inconsistent beliefs (Newcomb, 1957; Festinger, 1964) to the efforts of Jerome Bruner, Nelson Goodman, and others to probe the ways in which actions, language, works of art, and other human activities construct realities (Bruner, 1986; Goodman, 1978, 1984). The complex and fascinating picture of the mind that is emerging from such studies is helping us understand both its impressive creative potentialities and its susceptibility to distortion, misperception, and bias. At the same time this work raises fundamental doubts about the utility and validity of any behaviorist psychology that treats the mind as a black box whose contents and transformations can be ignored; and it raises equally weighty doubts about any rational choice theory that assumes that rationality is the basic premise of thought. I return to this last issue below.

LANGUAGE

The ability to use language not only to name or point but also to make claims about absent entities, to reason, and to construct "realities" in particular forms is clearly the endowment that most radically distinguishes human beings from other forms of life (Langer, 1970). Through language we make our worlds, and through language we also make ways of interpreting them, living in them, and destroying them (Goodman, 1984; Edelman, 1988).

Language accomplishes these functions because the creation and dissemination of meaning through language is inherently social in character, even if mastery of syntax and of grammar are in some sense inherited individual endowments (Bickerton, 1990). It is not private, idiosyncratic worlds but public, shared worlds that we construct through the use of language; that is why they are fundamental to politics.

Language about politics is especially potent and sometimes especially controversial because it deals with matters that substantially influence the quality of life—because interests are often in conflict, and because perceptions are linked to motives and are not readily corroborated. To a peculiar degree, then, political language discloses the realm of the ambiguous and the domain in which rationalizations of self-interest become the definition of the "public interest " (Lasswell, 1930). The "security threats" of the armaments manufacturers and of the "intelligence community" are the "constructed enemies" of peace advocates and of groups that want public funds expended on social programs rather than on war and preparations for it.

Sometimes the rationalizations are so potent that they mute conflicts of interest even if the conflicts remain real. The substantial consensus, even within the American working class, during the forty-five years following World War II, that the Soviet Union posed an imminent and major threat to American security rationalized frequent and costly wars against Third World countries and the conversion of the American economy to military ends in ways that increased unemployment and decreased both real wages and the gross national product, though no shot was fired in anger between the supposed major military antagonists. The language that created and maintained this remarkable pattern of misperception and futile action in the two major powers of the time provides a striking example of the capacity of rationalizing language to construct dubious political threats even while obliterating serious conflicts of economic interest from attention.

Of all the social psychological influences on politics, language is certainly paramount, for it constructs the issues, the leaders, the enemies, the categories, and the tests of rationality on which political support and opposition are based. It does so both powerfully and inconsistently, creating issues to justify particular courses of action, constructing and dethroning leaders, creating enemies that may abruptly become allies, and defining news and governmental actions into dubious categories that emphasize some of their aspects while masking others. We do not experience political events or actions in any direct way, but always through the language used to describe them and so give them a particular meaning. Language, then, *is* political reality.

That women were treated in demeaning ways and severely limited in their professions and aspirations was not classified as a political issue through most of human history but rather was seen as part of the natural order; but in the twentieth century this phenomenon is defined as a political problem in at least part of the world, generating political conflict and support for changing the balance of power, status, and opportunity between the sexes. Practices that some people call child abuse are labeled necessary discipline or parental rights by others. Advocates of civil liberties in the abstract may also be defenders of restrictions on the freedom of expression of Communists, Fascists, homosexuals, or their own employees. A political issue and its meaning depend upon the language that constructs it, not upon how severely or extensively it benefits or damages people.

Political "leaders" are not necessarily the individuals who lead or innovate. The usual reason for bestowing the label is incumbency in a formal governmental office, though such incumbency is more often than not a signal of conformity to common or popular practices rather than deviation from them or innovativeness in any other sense. In any case, leaders serve the psychological function of becoming magnets for praise for favorable developments and for blame for unfavorable ones, although the developments are likely to be the outcome of historical, structural, economic, and social conditions that would prevail regardless of who is labeled a leader at the time. In the Freudian tradition praise and blame for political leaders is seen as a projection or displacement of the feelings of fear, envy, admiration, or hatred for the father.

Unlike leadership in the arts or sciences, where radical innovativeness is more likely to be rewarded than disparaged, and unwarranted claims more likely to be exposed and consensually recognized for what they are, however, case political leadership is more nearly dramaturgy than policy formation.

In the same way it can be shown that language and other kinds of signs frequently reconstruct the meanings of past developments and construct and reconstruct expectations of the future. By the same token language constructs political enemies (often of people who do no harm) and other kinds of subjects (Edelman, 1988; Foucault, 1971, 1976).

Language, then, is the fundamental form of political action, giving meaning to other actions. It can be highly creative, constructing subjects, issues, or enemies in ways that change the political landscape, as the Keynesian redefinition of budgetary deficits did in the 1930s and the feminist redefinition of the roles of women in society did in the 1960s. It can also be intensely distorting, as the definition of racial or religious or sexual groups as enemies typically has been and as the definition of the Cold War apparently was.

Notice, however, that adjectives like "creative" and "distorting" are themselves instances of political language that construe actions, so that their meanings inevitably depend upon ideologies, moral stances, and other language. To use political language is to enter a hall of mirrors in which it is impossible to establish which actions and images are real to the satisfaction of all observers.

MULTIPLE REALITIES

Indeed, multiple realities are inherent in politics. To phenomenologists they are inherent in all human cognition (Schutz, 1962), but in political maneuver they both express and create conflict, agreement, quiescence, and action. Affirmative action is simple fairness to many and reverse discrimination to many others. The Gulf War of 1991 was a defense of Kuwait against aggression, assurance that President Bush would never again be called a wimp, the exchange of blood for oil, preservation of the status quo in the Middle East, the establishment of a continuing American military presence in the Middle East, a noble fight against an Iraqi tyrant who threatened world peace, a diversion from recession, Iran-Contra, homelessness and other domestic American problems, and so on.

Political motives, objectives, and outcomes are all bound to be ambiguous, yet the ambiguity is often linked to sacrifices for many, large rewards for some, and clashing values and ethical standards. In that situation people are bound to read into governmental actions whatever reflects their interests, ideologies, hopes, and fears. In consequence there are not only diverse realities for different people, but often multiple realities for the same person when considering the different aspects of an issue. The defender of freedom of expression may favor curbs on expression for bigots or Communists or Fascists. The advocate of diplomacy and negotiation in foreign policy may support military action when deciding on a particularly blatant instance of aggression.

Because language and symbolism are means for creating alternative meanings, it is apparent that there is no single form of reality that everyone embraces and not even a single reality that any individual person accepts consistently, as just noted. To be alive and act is to create and encounter multiple realities in everyday life, and multiple realities are probably more readily recognizable in politics than in most activities—partly because of the constant deliberate efforts to construct them just described and partly because for most people politics is a peripheral interest and therefore readily defined in new ways that serve disparate and changing concerns.

The conspicuous place of multiple realities in political action and maneuver has some important consequences. It means that interest groups, public officials, and others for whom a political issue *is* a major concern are more likely to try to win support for their respective causes by encouraging redefinitions of reality than by finding effective ways to cope with the issue. Abortion is likely to be a troubling way of dealing with a widespread and serious social problem even for those who are willing to use it, but to define it either as murder or as liberty is to ignore the reasons it is a dilemma while constructing a "reality" that garners support or opposition.

A related and probably more cogent consequence is the often dubious relevance of rational considerations in the search for politically acceptable courses of action. But the conspicuous absence of rationality and the predominance of manufactured fears, hopes, and enthusiasms in politics are readily noticed and are frequent grounds for pessimistic evaluations of politics as a human activity.

The strategic and tactical implications for interest groups of a political world composed of multiple and shifting realities are evident enough. Every issue, problem, and development of concern to the group must be construed so as to highlight some of its aspects and mask others in order to maximize public support. The emphasis always is on constructing a picture of the issue that appeals to hopes or fears. To opponents of abortion a fetus becomes a baby. To racists a parole program means that black prisoners are allowed to commit new crimes. To those who fear or hate the poor, welfare recipients are cheaters, while to liberals, welfare recipients are victims of a world they never made.

THE DISSEMINATION OF CONSTRUCTED ISSUES

In a society in which the electronic media and literacy are widespread, the means for spreading such constructed issues (and constructed leaders and enemies as well) widely are easy enough to come by, especially for groups with substantial financial resources, including the regime itself. The exasperating consequence is that the readier access of the world's population to news reports has become a source of mystification and intellectual subjugation more than an opportunity for the intelligent exercise of choice.

Indeed, both public officials and the general public increasingly take it for granted that news originating in government agencies, the source of most domestic political news and of almost all news dealing with international politics (Segal, 1973), as well as reports provided to the media by interest groups, will be slanted to put its source in a favorable light.

The regime and the public itself increasingly see news reports as an art form, to be judged by how adroitly they maintain public support rather than by their accuracy or comprehensiveness. Ronald Reagan was widely applauded as a "great communicator" precisely because he was adept at erasing public concern over the regime's blunders and dubious actions and maximizing his popularity in spite of prevalent doubt about most of his policies. Regimes frequently boast about their ability to maintain support in spite of disastrous mistakes; they publicize phrases that point to that capability, like "damage control."

With access to the media more extensive than ever before in human history, people have paradoxically come to expect propaganda and public relations as the key features of news reports emanating from governments in both the technologically advanced countries and the Third World. This development signals a degree of public alienation from government that is genuinely profound, just as it signals a rejection by governments of democracy as an objective, even while they continue rhetorically to embrace democracy. For both officials and the general public, politics has become an arena for the practice of dramaturgy in order to best rivals in the competition for power, wealth, and other private resources, not a site for discovering and implementing the public will.

SYMBOLS, IMAGES, AND HYPERREALITIES

At the most visible level of analysis politics deals with the authoritative allocation of values, with who gets what, just as the textbooks claim it does. There are constant contests over such controversial issues as the distribution of lucrative armaments contracts and other government contracts, the level at which minimum wages are set, the prohibition of commerce in drugs and alcohol, and budgetary allocations for education, conservation, wars, roads, bridges, and other purposes.

But every law, executive or administrative action, and court decision that allocates such values carries other, less visible meanings as well, and these are often more important and more controversial for concerned groups than the self-evident meanings of such governmental acts. The ap-

parent meaning may be largely specious, so that there is no tangible benefit to the groups that have ostensibly been the victors, while the law or administrative regulation nonetheless reassures others in the same class or
group that they are being protected (Edelman, 1964). Many regulations of
business in the supposed interest of politically weak groups like consumers and workers are of this kind.

A governmental action may elevate or lower the status of a group of
people by granting or denying their ideological claims. Joseph Gusfield
has shown that the Eighteenth Amendment to the United States Constitution advanced the status of rural, fundamentalist opponents of the consumption of alcohol while diminishing the status of urban and liberal advocates of the freedom to have a drink; while the ratification of the
Twenty-first Amendment, which repealed the Eighteenth, had the opposite effect on the status of these groups (Gusfield, 1963).

An action may convey the belief that a high government official is
tough or sensitive or identified with a particular ideology. President
George Bush's decision to fight the Gulf War erased for a time the frequent
charge that Bush is a "wimp," indecisive, and unassertive. Many governmental actions are designed to convey the impression that a regime is taking steps to deal with a widely deplored condition, especially when there
is general suspicion that it is doing little or nothing. The appointment of a
study commission can be one such ploy. Failure to implement a highly
publicized law or to fund it adequately is another. Regimes may justify
new burdens on the general public on specious grounds, depicting a war
that establishes military dominance in a new part of the world or protects
oil supplies as a crusade against aggression or rationalizing failure to help
the poor and the homeless as a tactic to instill self-reliance or as evidence
of economy.

A conspicuous form of symbolic politics consistently accompanies the
decision of a regime to undertake military action when the need for war is
not clear and the action is controversial. In the second half of the twentieth
century this situation recurred repeatedly as the United States and the Soviet Union launched armed invasions of Third World countries. In each
case the regime justified resorting to war with claims that an outside
power with designs upon the country in question needed to be deterred
and, sometimes, by claims that the invaded country had already been
taken over by an illegitimate and repressive regime. The onset of military
action consistently brought overwhelming support at home. The need or
legitimacy of each of these wars was now taken for granted by many, its
actual consequences were hardly debated, and the issue became support
for the troops. A strong herd spirit demanding such support spread
quickly, fueled by censorship of disturbing news about the invasions and
also by the presence of a minority at home who continued to oppose the

war. To a striking degree, then, the facts were unknown and ignored, and myths fanned public passions. The most ardent political passions typically appear when there is little or no evidence to justify them, for sentiment then hinges upon biases that are not qualified by observations or data.

This form of redefinition of reality persisted for the duration of the invasions that ended in quick military victories, usually in a few days or a few weeks. It conspicuously did not persist in the case of the two great power invasions of Third World countries that never brought military victories and continued as indecisive or losing military actions for many years: the Soviet invasion of Afghanistan and the American invasion of Vietnam. In both cases the symbolic redefinitions became harder and harder to sustain and domestic public opinion gradually turned against the wars in question. It is vital for the continued potency of political symbolism that there be no opportunity or no incentive for the general public to verify the claims it incorporates.

In the case of one of the most common forms of political language and action the impossibility of verification and the continued potency of an incentive to believe are intrinsic to the action itself. A high proportion of political language consists of promises that current problems will be solved if the public will only support a particular candidate, official, party, interest group, or policy. Because the promised inversion of whatever plagues people currently is to appear in the indefinite future and because the definition of a solution remains ambiguous, it is not a verifiable change but the *promise* of change that maintains some measure of public support. The historical record demonstrates that such promises can remain politically potent indefinitely, as they have regarding such vague assurances as restoration of peace and prosperity and also regarding such more specific pledges as controls over industrial monopolies and oligopolies, improvement in living standards, and tax cuts. The promised future typically never arrives, and the very fact that grievances are not solved keeps promises to deal with them politically potent.

In the contemporary state a high proportion of governmental actions is symbolic in these or other respects, another way of saying that a great many publicized governmental actions accomplish something quite different from what the public is led to believe they do. They usually fail to serve the interests of large segments of the citizenry, even while claiming to do so, and often they damage those interests severely while buttressing the power, status, and income of elite groups.

There are two major and closely linked reasons for the predominance in late twentieth century government of symbolic actions of this sort. One lies in the ready access of a high proportion of the public to news accounts, making it necessary for incumbent regimes to use those accounts to rationalize its actions and inactions. This tactic can make claims "hyperreal" through careful choice of language and television pictures (Baudrillard, 1983). The second reason lies in the grossly unequal ability of different groups in the modern state to influence its policies. Those who control large amounts of money and other resources enjoy ready access, while the great majority who lack those assets can deploy only formal modes of access, such as the right to vote and petition, which rarely entail significant influence. In this sense voting and the right to petition and express opinions are also potent forms of symbolism in the contemporary state.

Symbolic reassurance of most of the population encourages a quiescent stand in the face of problems and grievances that might otherwise invite resistance. Political quiescence of most of the population is usually accepted as natural or normal, whereas the occasional eruption of protest and resistance is regarded as an abnormal phenomenon that calls for explanation and repression. That is one reason that symbolic reassurance and other explanations for quiescence in the face of deprivation and oppression have rarely been examined seriously in news accounts and academic studies, whereas resistance and rebellion are constantly "explained," often by defining those who engage in them as pathological or irrational. The psychological language that purports to tell us something about mass behavior frequently tells us more about the ideological blinders that influence social studies and media accounts.

Paradoxically, then, these observations about the role of symbolism in political life and maneuver have become more cogent as the media of mass communication have grown more sophisticated and widespread. This turn in political focus clearly constitutes a major distinction between the state in the late twentieth century, and politics and state action in the eighteenth, nineteenth, and early twentieth centuries.

THE POLITICAL USES
OF A DEPRESSED QUALITY OF LIFE

A related psychological phenomenon has been a major influence upon politics in recent years. The more disadvantaged people are and feel, the more deprivations from which they suffer, the more ready they are likely to be to support groups and governments that maintain or enlarge existing inequalities. Put another way, discontent and anxiety now lend themselves to winning wide support for the Right, including the radical Right. This phenomenon stems in large part from the ability of groups that control large resources to influence opinion by managing the news.

In the competition for scarce resources it is easier to engender resentment against the weak than against the powerful by exploiting class, racial, and gender differences and biases. People who are fearful of losing a precariously held status or job or have already lost either or both are often ready to blame those who are even worse off than they are themselves: welfare recipients, blacks, women, and advocates of affirmative action. Such targeting of a politically weak scapegoat is readily stimulated by images, rumors, and myths that offer a vivid, if deceptive, depiction of the threat posed by a group that is already a target of prejudice. Political campaigns have increasingly resorted to such depictions as it has become clear that they "work." They have also been effective in weakening the support of target groups as well as the middle class for policies designed to ameliorate social and economic inequalities.

At the same time people whose status is threatened are likely to identify with elites, whom they have been socialized to accept as role models. Indeed, discontent makes it easier to believe in political leaders who promise reforms that never arrive while demanding sacrifices of most of the population. It makes it easier as well to generate concern for "problems," such as alleged threats from despised groups, that rationalize ineffective or repressive policies; and it focuses attention upon "enemies" who do no harm but serve compellingly as scapegoats.

While these psychological effects typically buttress conservative movements and policies, they also serve in conditions of severe deprivation to muster support for persecution of the politically weak and so become generators of neo-Fascism. In recent American recessions as well as in European countries experiencing large influxes of people from the Third World and from Eastern Europe, there has been mounting demand for policies that deny jobs, civil rights, welfare, and continued residence to part of the population. Racist and anti-Semitic incidents have been increasing, as has the gap between the incomes of the poor and the minorities on the one hand, and the affluent on the other. Trade unions have been destroyed or weakened in most industries even while the real incomes of most of the population have been declining.

Perceptions of what is extreme, leftist, and right-wing, all constructed categories, have also been shifting so as to win support for, or acquiescence in, conservative policies. Unemployment levels amounting to 3 or 4 percent of the labor force were regarded through the first half of the twentieth century as high and unacceptable, but 6 percent is now accepted as normal.

It is evident that the consequences of social distress are markedly different in the late twentieth century from those that the Left has historically assumed would occur. Discontent and suffering are not winning political support for radical change in social and economic institutions to benefit the weak. The objectives of the American, French, and Russian revolutions no longer seem to be relevant for those who would have to launch and support movements for radical change. While conservatives like

Reagan, Ford, and Bush were once defined as extreme, they are now considered "moderate."

Though elites always fear it, the fact is that serious resistance to established regimes and dominant ideas has always been infrequent; and when it has occurred, it has been instigated by social groups whose conditions were improving rather than by those that were declining or powerless (Tilly, 1978; Gurr, 1970). There has to be a general perception as well that the governmental regime is evil and responsible for misery and repression, as was clearly the case in the revolts in Eastern Europe in 1989, as well as in major revolutions of the past.

For the reasons noted earlier, however, contemporary governments can take advantage of widespread public access to daily news reports to persuade large numbers of people that the regime is their ally in undoing the alleged unfair advantages enjoyed by groups that are regarded with suspicion. Political power incites prejudice and resentment against the weak to aggrandize its power still more.

RATIONAL CHOICE

In the late twentieth century many social scientists and public administrators have embraced the view that rational premises and calculation drive public policy or that it can be best evaluated by how well it conforms to such a criterion; and officials have an incentive to inculcate the same view in the general public. The premise is, of course, valid for some policy decisions; the insightful chapter in this volume by John Aldrich reviews its potentialities well. But for the reasons already outlined in this chapter, that optimistic assumption does not typically describe the motives, processes, or outcomes of governmental policy formation. My discussion of language and symbolism has called attention to the ready possibility of constructing divergent and conflicting meanings and distortions regarding controversial issues and policies.

It is hard to avoid the conclusion that the focus on rationality is largely a reaction of policymakers, and of academics who identify with them, to conspicuous evidence that public policies in the twentieth century have too often been notably *irrational*, bringing disastrous results in the form, inter alia, of needless wars, the holocaust, and other genocidal operations, and domestic policies that impoverish substantial portions of the population, increase crime and homelessness, and ruin educational institutions and other aspects of the infrastructure. A comforting response to these disturbing trends for those with a stake in the status quo is to persuade themselves and a wider public that policy choice is a rational process. Much of the rational choice literature therefore impedes fundamental change in policy or in institutions, for it deters critics and policymakers from addressing the irrational features of politics and administration with which social psychology is chiefly concerned. The words that succeed and the policies that fail help create each other.

Those who stress rational choice analysis inculcate fetishism into policy formation, for they create symbols that then dominate the thinking and actions of their creators and of a large part of the interested public; and the fetishism is effective even when the policies are not. Such displacement of failed or controversial action by reassuring language has become a central attribute of contemporary government because failures are frequent and serious, because the tests of success or failure are largely ideological, and because the likelihood of failure or ineffective action is built into the political system. The failures typically serve the economic and status interests of powerful groups of people, so that disparities in resources and the language that rationalizes the disparities construct and reinforce each other.

Like all political texts, this language offers a political weapon more often than it offers a description. It is itself a potent form of political action, for it creates a world in which biases can be erased, ideological differences objectively evaluated, the consequences of policies both predicted before the fact and rigorously appraised afterward, and costs and benefits expressed in comparable terms and their balance calculated.

CONFUSIONS ABOUT POLITICAL GOALS

The metaphor that underlies the terms "efficiency" and "rationality" clouds the nature of public policymaking in such a way as to insure that proclaimed goals will be achieved only imperfectly, even while the public is reassured. These words imply that there is an unambiguous goal to be achieved, for only in that case does it make sense to search for the least costly and most effective methods of achieving it. But by definition political goals are always either ambiguous or in conflict with other widely supported objectives. To state one's ends in language that speaks of a "public interest," "the public welfare," or a general virtue like "happiness" is to avoid conflict by maximizing ambiguity; while to state one's ends in specific terms ("make discrimination against homosexuals a crime," "double the minimum wage," "ban handguns," "cut the defense budget 20 percent") is to take it for granted that opposition and conflicting positions will also be put forward as goals. What, then, is the efficient or the rational course?

These concepts become ambiguous containers into which actors and onlookers place divergent policy proposals. And, like the term "the public interest," the words "rationality" and "efficiency" are revealed as polemical weapons for whatever policy their users favor, rather than as the scientific or technical terms they pretend to be. But because these terms rationalize different and conflicting ends, the actions they justify are certain to be compromises so as to make them politically feasible, insuring that no such proclaimed goal will be pursued resolutely or effectively achieved.

It is evident that beliefs about rationality and efficiency incorporate controversial value assumptions and that their meanings change with the values and ideologies of those who use them. These concepts are the constructions of capitalism and bureaucracy in the countries affected by the industrial revolution. More often than not they reflect the values upon which those institutions are built, notably the assumptions that human beings, natural resources, and planning are instruments for the production of profits from capital resources, and that everyone benefits to the extent that this goal is realized.

IMPLICATIONS FOR THE EXALTATION AND DEBASEMENT OF PEOPLE

The methodological and explicit emphasis of systematic policy planning is on choosing means to achieve ends at the lowest cost; but the substantive and implicit emphasis that gives this worldview its motive force is often on the definition of people as means rather than ends. More specifically, workers, consumers, and those who reproduce them are regarded as instruments for making the economy productive and profitable, a postulate that is all the more powerful because it is tacit, usually masked by some variation of Adam Smith's metaphor of the unseen hand and by discourse about helping the unfortunate. This central assumption is therefore rarely examined or criticized.

The focus upon rational choice embraces some related premises as well. It encourages a focus on leadership or, more precisely, on followership: the equation of hierarchical position with effective planning, competence, expertise, status, level of reward, and level of sacrifice; the penalizing of gratifications that divert attention from hierarchical roles; the premise that damage to groups of people defined as unworthy is irrelevant to the calculus of costs; and the assumption that inequality is a prerequisite of efficiency and rational action.

Policy planners and managers responsible for administering policies are likely to be even more susceptible to this kind of reassurance about their competence than their critics and the general public. From the perspective of involved officials systematic decisionmaking suggests that those who use it are competent and professional and that their critics are dilettantes, a posture that generates unjustified confidence in decisions and in one's own talents and that discourages self-criticism and self-reflection.

Such evocation of hubris and dogmatic self-assurance is a hallmark of a great deal of administrative decisionmaking, and it is especially pervasive and damaging in organizations operating in areas in which the pursuit of dubious policies brings severe harm to many people. As Irving Janis (1982) has shown, criticism from people defined as outsiders or dilettantes is likely to reinforce determination to pursue the very policies that evoked the criticism and the failures, as such remarkable and frequent foreign policy fiascoes as the Bay of Pigs, Vietnam, the stationing of marines in Lebanon, and the support of the Contras in Nicaragua illustrate; and domestic fiascoes illustrate the point just as well: Consider the creation of homelessness in recent decades through housing and economic policies.

Just as this kind of language augments the power and the self-assurance of officials, it encourages humility and acquiescence in deprivation among the population hurt by particular policies. It teaches these unfortunates that they are unable to understand or criticize the actions of the authorities, who are uniquely qualified to determine what is rational. They are taught that their role in society is to support competence, and the rational and patriotic course is to offer such support.

To try to calculate the ratio of benefits to costs also distorts or erases ethical priorities among benefits and among costs. Until rational choice theory became fashionable, for example, industrial health and safety laws rested on the premise that protection of workers from maiming or death in the course of their employment was self-evidently worth the costs of the administration of such laws, and the same priority of life and health over increased profits justified unemployment compensation, workmen's compensation, child labor, and other kinds of protective legislation. The emphasis in recent years, by contrast, has been upon highlighting the monetary costs of administering such laws, thereby providing a rationale for eliminating or weakening them. If the calculated benefits of treating injured workers or compensating surviving spouses are not significantly greater than the costs of administering the laws or of an arbitrary determination of the monetary value of a life, it follows that the rational course is to minimize expenditures to avoid or compensate accidents in the workplace. An arithmetic calculation based on a masked ideological premise supplants respect for life and health, an impressive tribute to the power of language to construct reality.

The conviction that quantitative calculations of benefits and costs enhance rational choice and efficiency is all the easier to sustain because the success or failure of a controversial public policy is itself not a matter of fact, but is always dependent on interpretation. When an automobile mechanic is asked to repair faulty brakes, there is an obvious empirical test of that person's success or failure; but that model is not at all applicable to judging the success or failure of governmental actions, even though the language of election campaigns and ideological arguments typically imply that it is. Advocates of a challenged policy construct tests that show success, while its opponents construct other tests that show failure, so that both are likely to persevere in their opinions regardless of experience with the policy. Many decades of experience with welfare laws, abortion laws, increases in the arms budget, economic and military interventions in Third World countries, and countless other controversial policies have failed to produce any consensus on which courses of action have succeeded and which have failed. The argument of this chapter should have made it clear why that kind of ambiguity and continued political contention is inevitable.

Many of these observations make it clear that rational choice models offer a rationalization for decisions rather than a formula for arriving at them. Their formulation flows from complex and conflicting political pressures respecting controversial policies, mutually incompatible objectives of concerned interest groups, uncertainties regarding the relative power of those groups, the sanctions at their disposal, their probable reactions to future developments, and consequent confusions and disputes regarding what concrete measures to adopt. The rational choice model assumes a polity in which these perplexing complications either do not exist or can readily be overcome. But they always exist for planners and administrators, though individuals differ widely in their sensitivity to them, as well as in their personal sympathies with particular interests, and their skill in coping with them. The least risky way of coping is to respond to the group interests that wield the strongest clout.

It is hardly surprising, then, that the hallmarks of difficult administrative decisions are vacillation, confusion, and a more sensitive regard for short-term political rewards and sanctions than for long-term consequences. In this milieu the calculation of benefit-cost ratios or some other measure of rationality or efficiency can win support for dubious past decisions from legislators and part of the public, not because the calculations themselves are persuasive, studied, or widely known, but because the claim that a decision was made rationally and the language in which the claim is couched become potent condensation symbols. As symbols they reassure people who know that policies are often misconceived, wasteful, or disastrous and who want to believe that there is a facile resolution for a disturbing dilemma.

CONCLUSION

Attention to political psychology yields conclusions that are, for the most part, discouraging. That is hardly surprising in view of the evidence that political behavior and attitudes stem less from rational calculation than from the dubious influences on political calculation of threatening social and economic conditions, the subtle associations of language, the construction of leaders, issues, and enemies to serve political interests, the inevitable presence of multiple or contradictory realities, and the marked effects of symbols and images on political beliefs.

It is important to recognize in this regard that optimism and pessimism are not only descriptions of individual psychological states but are also political constructions—highly ideological—and major influences on public opinion. Optimism, illustrated in recent years by Ronald Reagan's outlook on the political scene, is appealing because it lets us deny, or define as inconsequential, evidence of unfairness or of current and future problems. Incumbents encourage the public to look at the bright side, while challengers do the opposite. Psychological explanations, however, are not so much generators of pessimism about social conditions as pessimistic about the capacity of the political system itself to respond adequately to those conditions.

By the same token they are likely to imply that efforts to counter or overcome the aspects of the social and political scene that are troubling should not be directed mainly at psychological dispositions or traits. Because these stem, when they are widespread, from the material circumstances in which people live, it is the latter that require initial and paramount attention. Incentives to distort, to construct scapegoats, and to bypass rational calculation have grown historically when social inequalities and status threats increased, as in depressions and wars. Economic, social, and psychological measures and conditions are closely interwoven. Effective action must therefore take the form of reducing inequalities in resources, power, and status.

11

Contexts, Intermediaries, and Political Behavior

ROBERT HUCKFELDT
PAUL ALLEN BECK

This chapter is built on the premise that citizens do not experience politics directly as isolated individuals, but rather, do so indirectly as individuals who are embedded within distinctive contexts and settings. Various information sources within these settings serve as intermediaries in communicating particular interpretations of political reality, and thus politics depends on this larger social and political experience in fundamentally important ways. The environmentally contingent nature of political activity and involvement arises in part because people talk about politics with friends and relatives and associates, but also because they learn about it through the mass media and other environmentally specific intermediaries. In short, politics is environmentally contingent at its core because it is experienced by individuals as part of larger groups and collectivities—as part of a larger social and political experience.

How does the larger environment impinge upon politics and political behavior? The contingent basis of politics is far-reaching in its implications. Different citizens experience different political realities because: they read different newspapers, they are employed at different workplaces, they are exposed to different forms of partisan organization, they belong to different groups, they talk and interact with different people. Just as important, different citizens are surrounded by different populations that are radically dissimilar in terms of partisan leanings, religious beliefs, racial composition, class composition, and so on. Thus we can usefully view citizens as being located within a series of both nested and overlapping environments, each of which sustains and fosters some interpretations of politics while discouraging others.

At the same time, individual citizens also exercise important elements of control over many qualities and aspects of their own social experience.

Some people refuse to discuss politics; others may thrive on political argument. Some discuss only with Democrats, and others only talk with Republicans. Some people subscribe to the *New York Times* or the *Wall Street Journal*, whereas others make do with the local paper. Some belong to a union and attend to its political messages; others do not. In short, not only are people located within complex matrices of social and political experience, but they also make important decisions regarding where in these matrices they will reside. Thus, politics might be seen as a complex set of intersections between the individual and the environment—the points at which individual political preference confronts, and is confronted by, its political surroundings and the interpretations of political reality that these surroundings sustain (McPhee, 1963).

An ongoing challenge in the study of politics, and particularly in the study of mass political activity and involvement, is to understand individual preference within these settings. Yet the manner in which most studies are conducted ignores the context of individual behavior. Most national random probability samples, as well as many experimental methodologies, address individuals who are divorced from a particular place and time. Indeed, the frequently implicit goal of random selection and random assignment is to produce an individual citizen who is abstract from particular environmental circumstances, and for many purposes such a strategy is quite appropriate. The problem arises when we wish to move beyond the abstract citizen and confront politics as it occurs—as it is located within the particular settings that give rise to its particular shape and form.

The goal of this chapter is to address the contexts and intermediaries of political experience—to return the individual to the personal setting in an effort to assess the consequences of political intermediation. We are, in particular, concerned with several agents of intermediation: social interaction and personal networks of information, media messages and the information they convey, political parties and other secondary organizations from which citizens obtain political information. We do not pretend to provide comprehensive treatment of any of these agents. Rather, we intend to demonstrate their features as vehicles of intermediation. All of these agents can be compared profitably along a number of dimensions, and they are highly interdependent in ways we will consider below.

INDIVIDUALS AND ENVIRONMENTS

Perhaps the first systematically empirical effort aimed at demonstrating the relevance of environmentally bounded political and social experience is found in the work of Herbert Tingsten (1963). In his study of Stockholm precincts during the 1920s and 1930s, Tingsten presents evidence which suggests: (1) Swedish workers were more likely to vote if they lived among other workers, and (2) the Socialist vote depended not only upon the class membership of the individual voter, but also upon the class composition surrounding the individual voter. Tingsten's early effort may not have taken us far toward a complete mapping of the forces acting on individual citizens, but it is important for its demonstration of the multiple levels of meaning that underlie democratic politics. The role of citizens cannot be understood simply as a product of individual characteristics and predispositions—it must also be understood at the level of political and social experience. And such experience is the product of individual choice within the confines of a particular environment.

Tingsten's insight was carried into the modern age of survey research by the efforts of Paul Lazarsfeld, Bernard Berelson, and Hazel Gaudet, and their Columbia University colleagues in studies of Erie County (Lazarsfeld, Berelson, and Gaudet, 1948) and Elmira, New York (Berelson, Lazarsfeld, and McPhee, 1954). Both of the Columbia studies paid particular attention to social groups as sources of political information. Once again, the multiple levels of meaning in democratic politics emerged quite clearly. Group membership was not conceived simply as a characteristic of individuals, but rather as a factor affecting political and social experience. Being a member of the middle class was not only important as a determinant of loyalties and interest, but also because such membership affected opportunities and constraints operating on the transmission of political information.

Not only did the Columbia sociologists demonstrate the multiple levels of meaning in democratic politics, but they also showed the multiple and intersecting bases of political and social experience. For instance, working-class Protestants and middle-class Catholics were portrayed to be cross-pressured citizens of a democracy; further, these groups provided the cohesive agent which holds the system together. At the same time they also paid the individual costs of conflicting cues and information regarding appropriate political behavior—a cost frequently paid in the currency of indecision, disinterest, and withdrawal from politics. Similarly, the importance of "opinion leaders" was established in a "two-step flow" of communication that ties individual citizens to other citizens at the same time that it links citizens to the political system more generally (Katz, 1957).

The work of V. O. Key, Jr., and Frank Munger (1959) is often cited as a critique of the Columbia tradition in particular and of political sociology in general, and it certainly did serve to reemphasize the central importance of the explicitly political aspects of social experience. For our own purposes, however, Key and Munger were playing in the same band as the Columbia sociologists. Their emphasis on explicitly political experience and the "standing decision" of partisan loyalty is not an emphasis on the primacy of atomistic citizens. Their analysis is built on the implications of shared political histories and traditions within particular Indiana counties—shared histories which extend beyond the control of individual residents. The heart of their argument is lost if it is translated into individualistic terms. Similarly, there is no more dramatic statement of the importance that derives from context and environment than Key's (1949) central argument in *Southern Politics*. His thesis was that white racial hostility in particular and southern politics in general must be understood with respect to the political implications that are attendant on the racial composition of southern counties. There is no room in Key's work for an analysis that focuses solely on the importance of individual belief systems for individual attitudes regarding racial equality.

Given these auspicious beginnings, how did modern studies of mass political behavior become so tightly focused on individual characteristics and attributes as the explanations for individual political behavior? First, it is mistaken simply to lay the responsibility at the feet of Angus Campbell and his associates (1960) in *The American Voter*. Even a cursory reading indicates a very sensitive awareness of the extra-individual factors that give rise to politics and political behavior. The new age of survey research and the theoretical bias which accompanied it was more important. As Seymour Martin Lipset argues in his introduction to Raymond Boudon's (1974) book on social inequality, methodology and theory are inevitably and inseparably intertwined. Given a new survey methodology that focused on randomly sampled, environmentally independent individuals, political scientists began to theorize about individuals. The historical accident of the national election study had profound consequences for theories of democratic citizenship, and it meant that many of them would be based on individual psychology. Indeed, one legacy of this tradition is to push further toward an individualistic understanding of citizenship, and this has often meant the adoption of experimental methodologies that rely even more completely upon an individualistic abstraction of citizenship and political behavior.

At the same time that an individually centered political psychology was becoming a prosperous industry, the increased popularity of economic interpretations of democracy (Downs, 1957) meant that many other political scientists began to think in terms of individual calculation, individual utility functions, and individual trade-offs. The most straightforward way to incorporate this powerful logic was to carry on an analysis in terms of *independent* individuals. And thus the psychologists at one pole and the economists at another were providing new and compelling models of citizen behavior in democracratic politics, both of which typically focused on independent, isolated individuals.

The final nail in the coffin lid of theories stressing environments, contexts, or mediation was the discrediting of ecological analyses. The demonstration of the ecological fallacy by W. S. Robinson (1950) meant that a principal tool for the aggregate analysis of democratic elections was called into question, or at least it was called into question if one wished to study individuals. But political economists and political psychologists were persuasive in their arguments regarding the primacy of individual-level explanation. Thus, by default, analyses of context, community, environment, and the multiple levels of meaning in democratic politics were rendered problematic and separated from the mainstream individualistic focus of political research.

We do not intend to suggest that important demonstrations of the political influence due to context and environment cannot be found during the ensuing years. Warren Miller's (1956) classic statement of "one-party politics and the voter" and Robert Putnam's (1966) study of the mechanisms giving rise to community influence continue to demonstrate the value of understanding individuals within particular political settings. David Butler and Donald Stokes's (1969) demonstration of community effects on individual behavior similarly points toward the socially contingent nature of political choice. Our only point is that these studies served as exceptions to a general rule—as departures from the mainstream of political analysis. Neither do we intend to suggest that rationality or psychology has no place in the study of political behavior. Indeed, the view we adopt below is grounded explicitly in methodological individualism. Our argument is that *individuals* be viewed as interdependent rather than independent, as constrained by environmentally specific sources of information, as subject to the biases and interpretations of the intermediaries they encounter.

Where have these earlier studies taken us? What questions remain unanswered? These efforts and others have shown quite clearly that political preference is not a simple function of individual characteristics and interests, and thus citizens cannot be understood as isolated individuals—abstracted from a particular place and time. Rather, it becomes quite clear that citizens base their choices on shared understandings and shared information. The behavior of citizens is not simply a function of individual preference and calculation but a function of surrounding preferences as well.

Less well understood is the manner in which the multiple levels of political reality are tied together. How do surrounding preferences and viewpoints affect the behavior of individual citizens? What are the mechanisms of information transmission? How do citizen preference and the environmental supply of information interact in the diffusion and collection of political information among individuals? If surrounding preferences are a function of space and time, how are space and time related to the dynamics of individual preference? The essence of intermediation is the transmission of political information—information that is inevitably biased at its source—and thus we begin by considering the qualities of mediated information.

INTERMEDIARIES AND POLITICAL INFORMATION

Citizens make political choices on the basis of information that is always and inevitably biased and incomplete. In this sense, then, political choice is contingent upon a particular mix of political information. Citizens must become informed regarding both the nature of their own political interests and the most efficient steps for achieving outcomes favorable to those interests. Thus, even when citizens share identical interests in some objective sense, their choices and actions invariably depend upon the information they receive. The informationally contingent basis of political choice would not matter if citizens possessed complete information; or if citizens sampled randomly from the same information sources; or if they obtained direct and unbiased information that was untainted by any intermediary. In fact, none of these conditions hold. Citizens participate on the basis of very limited and incomplete information taken from radically different sources. Most important, the information is inherently and inevitably biased at its source—*intermediation determines the political content of information and becoming informed is thus a political activity.*

At the same time that political choice is contingent upon information, informational options and alternatives vary across environments in a systematic fashion. Thus, the study of political intermediation should focus on individual behavior within these distinctive environments of informational cues, options, and alternatives. What are the important changes that occur across such environments? Certainly the substance and reality of politics changes, but just as important is the extent to which the *interpretations* of politics change across these environments: Voters who live in Republican counties are less likely to be contacted by Democratic party organizations; newspaper readers in Manchester, New Hampshire, are unlikely to read a newspaper with a Democratic bias; Mississippi whites have a difficult time finding other Mississippi whites who argue in favor of supporting Democratic presidential candidates (Huckfeldt and Kohfeld, 1989). In short, even when the reality of politics is held constant, the perception of that reality varies as a function of received interpretations. And the interpretations that citizens receive vary systematically across contexts and environments.

Democrats who live in Republican communities might prefer to receive Democratic campaign literature, to read Democratic newspapers, to talk politics with other Democrats; but these informational preferences are not determinate. Rather, citizens choose probabilistically from a menu of choices that is inherently stochastic and subject to environmental variation. Oftentimes it is difficult to find a Democratic paper, or a Democratic discussant, or a Democratic party worker—especially for citizens who live in Republican environments. In short, an individual's control over his or her environment is incomplete, and thus studies of intermediation see citizen purpose and rationality as being circumscribed and bounded by structurally and institutionally imposed constraints.

There is a strong temptation to ignore the importance of contexts and environments. The technology of the national random survey is explicitly designed to abstract the individual from an environment in an effort to obtain a view of the average citizen. We argue that such an average citizen is a myth, at least in the atomistic terms so often used by modern political science. The truly average citizen reads a particular newspaper; talks politics with particular associates; receives phone calls from particular party organizations. All these environmentally embedded experiences are crucial to the choices that average citizens make, and a national random sample does not reduce their importance by rendering them obscure.

Our position is summarized in three interrelated arguments. The first argument is that political information is almost always mediated, and the intermediary brings along a political bias that is specific to the source. The important point is that when citizens confront the complexity and ambiguity of politics and policy they seldom go it alone. Instead, they depend upon a diverse set of information sources that vary along a number of dimensions. As a result, the citizenry is not composed of isolated and independent individuals who make political choices in a vacuum. Rather, politics and political life are best understood from the standpoint of individuals who are embedded within a range of informational environments, each of which passes along a distinctive bias and interpretation.

Our second argument is that citizens tend to be purposeful in their search for political information and political intermediaries, and thus a focus on intermediation is in no way incompatible with a rational actor view of politics. Perhaps the best support for this second argument comes from Anthony Downs's (1957:229) focus on the high costs of becoming informed and the labor-saving devices that reasonable citizens employ to reduce those costs. Once we accept the unavoidable fact that political information is costly and often comes at a steep price, it becomes entirely sensible to obtain it from trusted intermediaries. In so doing the citizen economizes in two ways. First, the careful choice of intermediaries allows an individual to exercise greater control over the topics covered by the incoming stream of information. Second, the source of the information might be selected in a manner that conforms to the citizen's own political predispositions—people might seek to obtain information from politically sympathetic intermediaries.

This second argument must be seen, however, in the context of our third argument. Each citizen is located within a particular environment, and this environment limits the citizen's range of informational alternatives. At one extreme, anyone growing up in a family of Republicans has little choice but to be confronted by political information with a Republican bias. At a somewhat less extreme level, our view of information control on the part of individuals is that it is incomplete. Everything else being equal, Democrats are more likely to choose information sources with a Democratic bias. But everything else is *not* equal, particularly the menu of information sources that serves as the basis of choice. Thus, confronted with multiple and recurring sources of information with a particular bias, reasonable citizens do the best they can, and often this means encountering information that departs from their own predispositions.

THE ROLES OF CONTEMPORARY
POLITICAL INTERMEDIARIES

The principal agents of political intermediation in the citizen's environment today are personal discussants, secondary organizations, political party organizations, and the mass media. The context in which the citizen receives political information is largely defined by his or her exposure to, and the political bias of, these types of intermediaries and their interaction, with the intermediaries' biases sometimes reinforcing one another, but other times conflicting (Chaffee, 1982).

People receive a good deal of political information through discussions of politics with others—within the family, at work, or among friends and neighbors. This information may be received through explicitly political discussion, but it may also be passed along in the offhand comments and gestures that are incidental to discourse on nonpolitical matters. The set of potential political discussants of course is large, for it may include anyone with whom one comes into contact. This discussion network may also be thought to encompass the ties of discussants to discussants of their own, as the communication of personal political information "snowballs" to connect family, friends, neighbors, and co-workers to the more remote context set by the neighborhood, workplace, city, and county (Katz and Lazarsfeld, 1955; Weatherford, 1982b). The process of personal influence involves selectivity at both ends, with "senders" choosing when and where to make politically relevant comments and potential "receivers" avoiding political subjects with certain individuals but not being reluctant to raise them with others. As Michael MacKuen (1990) and Huckfeldt and John Sprague (1987, 1991) have demonstrated, political discussion can be a complex mix of explicit and implicit give and take among a variety of partners.

It is paradoxical considering the important political role traditionally ascribed to secondary organizations, but the mechanics of organizational intermediation have largely been ignored. Politicized organizations bombard their supporters with messages, and they often reach nonmembers as well. Citizens for whom that organization is a reference group, whether positive or negative, may be especially motivated to pick its messages out of the stream of political information. When the American Federation of Labor and Congress of Industrial Organizations (AFL-CIO) endorses a candidate for president or the National Organization of Women (NOW) opposes a nominee for the Supreme Court, for example, the message provides a valuable reference point for members and nonmembers, and supporters and opponents (Carmines and Kuklinski, 1990). The political role of secondary organizations, then, is traced in intermediation analysis through the flow of political messages from them to the public.

One of the distinguishing features of modern societies is the power of the mass media as instruments of political communication. Whether viewed from their dark side as mechanisms for propaganda or from their bright side as pluralistic sources of information, there is no questioning the overwhelming presence of the media in the modern intermediation process (Kinder and Sears, 1985). For many people, perhaps even most, they are the prime conduits for political information, and for many more they are the intermediary source of the messages that are carried through a discussion network (Page, Shapiro, and Dempsey, 1987). In recent decades television has emerged as the dominant medium for political information, and there is growing evidence of its agenda-setting (Shaw and McCombs, 1977), priming (Iyengar and Kinder, 1987), and even attribution functions (Iyengar, 1991). Nonetheless, newspapers (Erbring, Goldenberg, and Miller, 1980) and radio remain important sources of political information as well.

The media differ in several important ways from the other intermediaries. For one thing, with the conspicuous exception of a few newspapers that are throwbacks to the old partisan press, for example, the Manchester, New Hampshire, *Union Leader* (Rubin, 1981), they are less likely than personal discussants or politicized secondary organizations to be purveyors of political bias (Robinson and Sheehan, 1983; Graber, 1989)—except via the editorial pages of newspapers. For another, the similarity of the national television networks (Robinson, 1977) and the growth of one-newspaper markets limits the variety of media communications even more than is accomplished for the other intermediaries by the homogeneity of personal networks or secondary organization settings.

As an empirical matter, the political information obtained by American citizens depends upon their exposure to the various agents of intermediation and the particular political bias of the messages from them, and we now turn to these two dimensions explicitly. Exposure is a function of availability and selectivity—an interaction between what the environment offers and how the individual chooses from the menu of alternatives. Bias, on the other hand, is a property of the intermediary. Once exposed to a specific source, only selective perception of messages can insulate the individual from the slant of those communications.

A clear picture of exposure and bias in the political intermediation process is difficult to obtain, in large part because the individualistic orientation of voting research has restricted the search for comprehensive information about the intermediation environment. The best that we can do right now is to piece together a mosaic by drawing pieces from different studies. The best recent data on exposure and bias in personal discussion networks comes from a study of South Bend, Indiana, during the 1984 presidential campaign. Contemporary data on exposure to the mass media are available from the most recent National Election Study (NES) survey, but complementary assessments of bias must be drawn from less systematic sources. For secondary organizations, information on organizational memberships gained from the National Opinion Research Center's General Social Survey (GSS) needs to be interpreted using the perspectives gained from more detailed investigations of organizational activities and reference-group associations in subnational studies.[1]

PERSONAL DISCUSSION NETWORKS

Where do citizens obtain socially communicated information regarding politics? Respondents to the second wave of the 1984 South Bend study were asked a series of questions regarding various life domains—neighborhoods, organizations, workplaces, recreational activities, and families. One of the questions asked how often respondents talked about politics within each life domain. As Table 11.1 shows, the extent to which people discuss politics varies across the domains. Political discussion is most likely to occur within the family and least likely to occur as part of neighboring or recreational activities. Political discussion is somewhat more frequent within organizations and at the workplace, but notice the reduced *n*-size for the workplace. While workplace discussion is more likely than neighborhood discussion, it affects relatively fewer people because many people do not work. Another approach to understanding the locus of political discussion is to ask respondents with whom they discuss politics. At the third wave of the South Bend study, after the 1984 election was over, respondents were asked to name the three people with whom they

TABLE 11.1   Frequency of Political Discussions Across Life Domains

Frequency of political discussion		Life Domains			
	Neighborhood	Secondary groups	Work place	Recreation	Family
Often	6.1	12.3	13.3	7.3	25.9
Once in a while	32.5	34.3	36.8	32.9	45.0
Rarely	37.3	29.9	29.8	38.2	22.9
Never	24.1	23.6	20.1	21.6	6.3
$N =$	1,505.0	1,460.0	900.0	1,500.0	1,504.0

Source: 1984 South Bend study.

were most likely to have discussed the events of the past election. Respondents were then asked a battery of questions regarding each discussant. The end result is rudimentary three-person political network information for more than 1,300 main respondents and more than 4,200 discussants. What does this information tell us?

Even though Table 11.1 indicates that the family is the most common life domain for political discussion, Table 11.2 shows that more than half of the discussants are not relatives of the main respondent. Moreover, nearly half of these nonrelative discussants are not intimates. This is extremely important information for the study of intermediation because it means that discussions among citizens are not restricted to friendship cliques and families. And thus, the social communication of political information does not require that the communicators be intimates. This fact, in turn, suggests several qualities of personal intermediation.

First, the social transmission of political information is not contained within closed social cells, but has the potential to disseminate information across populations. As Mark Granovetter (1973) informs us, the "strength of weak ties" is that they lead to a more widespread diffusion of information. To the extent that information flow is restricted to ties among intimates, the social flow of information is severely truncated. Political information would be socially communicated *within* families and other groups of intimates, but it would be less frequently shared *between* these circles of intimates. This is because, as Granovetter demonstrates (1973), if Tom and Dick are strongly tied, neither of them is likely to be strongly tied to Harry unless both of them are. Thus, rather than being individually atomistic, the public would be composed of small group cells that are disconnected and isolated from one another. In contrast, to the extent that political information flows across weak ties, the potential is created for a truly public opinion that is informed by the discussions of citizens. Information would be shared both within and between circles of intimates by virtue of the information that flows through weak ties.

TABLE 11.2   Selected Characteristics of Political Discussants

Percentage of discussants who are:		
Relatives	30%	
Spouses	17%	
Not relatives	53%	
$N =$	4,285	
Percentage of respondents with at least one discussant who is:		
Employed at same workplace	41%	$(n=1,367)$
A resident of same neighborhood	40%	$(n=1,366)$
Percentage of nonrelative discussants who are:		
Close friends	55%	
Friends	30%	
Just regular contacts	15%	
$N =$	2,272	

Source: 1984 South Bend study.

Second, the social diffusion of information through weak social ties also affects the way in which we think about social influence in politics. If political persuasion is limited to intimate ties, then we should focus on close friends and families. We should, in short, spend our time studying the cozy cliques and groups that are idiosyncratic to the citizen—an individualistic focus should be replaced by a small group focus. Alternatively, if political persuasion also occurs through more casual social contact, we should cast a much broader net to examine a wide range of contexts within which citizens reside. Indeed, other analyses of these data (Huckfeldt and Sprague, 1991) show that casual contacts among nonrelatives are at least as influential as intimate contacts in affecting citizen preferences.

In keeping with this second point, Table 11.2 shows that 41 percent of the respondents have at least one nonrelative discussant from the workplace, and 40 percent have at least one nonrelative discussant from the neighborhood. The workplace and the neighborhood may not be perceived by the respondents to be arenas of political discourse, but they would appear to be important reservoirs from which discussants are drawn.

Third and finally, the incorporation of weak ties within political discussion networks suggests that the bias of social communication is more likely to reflect the bias of the larger community (see also Putnam, 1966). If people only obtained socially communicated political information through family members and intimates, social communication would be divorced from the larger environment, acting to shield individuals from dominant political preferences and viewpoints. To the extent that political information is obtained through casual contacts, the bias of the information is more likely to reflect the bias of the larger community. In other words, by obtaining political information through casual social contacts, people expose themselves to the bias of the larger community.

In short, a focus on intermediation must take personal communication seriously. As William McPhee (1963) informed us thirty years ago, the opinions conveyed through social interaction have the potential for a dramatic cumulative effect. Furthermore, social interaction with political content becomes the integrating mechanism through which other political information must travel, and thus it plays a pivotal role in interpreting and transforming the messages conveyed by other intermediaries.

SECONDARY ORGANIZATIONS

The classic intermediary, well-heralded in the annals of traditional political sociology, is, of course, the secondary organization. Secondary organizations proliferate in modern societies, and many of them play important political roles. Labor unions endorse candidates for office and proselytize to support those candidates. Associational, ideological, corporate, and even labor political action committees often define their membership more loosely as mailing lists of actual and potential contributors, but in their appeals for money as well as in the usage of the funds they raise, they directly attempt to influence voters to back or oppose particular candidates. And political parties are the politicized secondary organizations par excellence, although they are not typically thought of as voluntary associations in the American context.

Measurement of exposure to the intermediation activities of secondary organizations is no simple matter, for the forms of exposure are so varied. Where organizational influence is restricted to its members, membership and degree of involvement by members in the organization may suffice. Since the reports of Alexis de Tocqueville (1946) in the 1830s, Americans have been noted for an extensive voluntary association life, and estimates from the GSS show relatively widespread involvement in recent years. According to the 1989 GSS estimates, shown in Table 11.3, only 32 percent of all adult Americans did not belong to a secondary organization, while roughly 25 percent of the population was affiliated with one, another 31 percent was affiliated with two or three, and only about 11 percent with more than three.[2] The average number of organizations associated with (including people who had no memberships) was close to 1.6. Other data from the study show that church-affiliated groups dominated organizational life, enrolling an estimated 32 percent of the population; Sports clubs (at 21 percent) were second, with labor unions (at 13 percent) a distant third.

What these figures do not show, however, is whether the organizations are politicized—that is, whether they are involved in any way in a politi-

TABLE 11.3   Involvement in Secondary Organizations

	Number of organizational memberships for each respondent (%)
0	31.8
1	25.4
2	19.3
3	11.9
4	5.6
5	3.0
6 or more	2.6
no answer	.4
N = 1,035	
mean = 1.56	

Source: General Social Survey, 1989 (Q328).

cal campaign. Many, maybe most, organizations are avowedly apolitical or at least nonpartisan, as even slight intrusions into partisan politics may threaten to divide their membership and undermine their very existence. The perceptions of organizational politicization recorded in a 1988 statewide Ohio survey (did the organization "endorse or otherwise openly support a particular candidate for president?") provide some insight into organizational partisan involvement at the height of a presidential campaign (Beck and Richardson, 1989). Fewer than 30 percent of all members saw their organizations as supporting either Bush or Dukakis. These data suggest that politicized organizations, at least in a partisan sense, are quite atypical.

Two kinds of organizations—labor unions and churches—stood out in the 1988 Ohio study as exhibiting support for a presidential candidate. Of the respondents reporting that their organization favored a candidate, a majority implicated either unions (39 percent) or union-analogue teachers' associations (13 percent). Not surprisingly, the bias of these organizations was in a Democratic direction. An additional 20 percent of those perceiving a bias reported it for their church (Beck and Richardson, 1989)—hardly a surprising result in the context of the times (Wald, Owen, and Hill, 1988) or given the history of church involvement in American politics (Kleppner, 1979; Lipset, 1968). This is only a small percentage (10 percent) of church members, but it constitutes a substantial number in the aggregate because of widespread church affiliation.

The partisanship of the politically active churches, moreover, followed an important racial divide. A majority of those reporting that their church organization favored the Democratic candidate were blacks, reaffirming the reported politicization of many black churches (Gurin, Hatchett, and Jackson, 1989). All but one reporting Republican favoritism were whites—

a sign of the increased partisanship of fundamentalist congregations. In estimating the direct intermediation influence of secondary organizations, then, focus is most fruitfully directed to labor organizations and to churches.

Organizations may also be viewed as communities of like-minded people. Even if the organization takes no official position in the campaign, and literally remains neutral in a formal sense, the prevailing sentiment of the organizational community may be an important political cue during a campaign. In our conceptualization, though, these represent "contextual" effects rather than organizational effects and are best captured through analysis of personal networks, however far-flung they may end up being.

A third avenue of organizational influence in politics comes through the organization as a reference group. For members and nonmembers alike, the positions on candidates and issues associated with different groups in the society—formal organizations as well as demographic groups, the AFL-CIO and the Moral Majority as well as blue-collar workers and fundamentalists—provide important political cues to voters. Sometimes these cues are conveyed by the organizations themselves, for example, when a union announces its endorsement of a particular candidate, in which case it is the organization that is the intermediary. In other instances, the cues about group or organizational positions are more subtly transmitted, such as when the impression arises that blacks or Catholics or Evangelicals support a candidate. Assigning the intermediation role is substantially more difficult in this situation. When the impression is a stereotypic result of generalizations from actions of related organizations (e.g., each of a number of black organizations endorses a candidate, so blacks must be for that candidate), the intermediary role should be attributed to secondary organizations. When the impression is the result of more or less independent individual political choices (e.g., most blacks decide to support a candidate), by contrast, some other institution is serving as the intermediary.

Politicized secondary organizations, those emitting partisan messages to their members (and, indirectly, to their nonmembers, especially their antagonists), then, play an uncertain role in the American electoral process. Much has been made in the study of political sociology of the organizational roots of electoral behavior (see, especially, Lipset and Rokkan, 1967; Rose and Urwin, 1969), but more is assumed than is known about the mechanisms through which organizations convey this influence or about the actual extent of their electoral effects (Sartori, 1969). We believe that one of the principal items on the agenda for studying political intermediation is the determination of how exposure to organizations interacts with the political content of their messages to produce organizational influence on voting behavior.

POLITICAL PARTIES AS INTERMEDIARIES

While we are probably more confident about the role of political parties in the American electoral process, we actually know very little regarding their influence as intermediaries. Much of the scholarly and journalistic literature regarding political parties places them on an endangered species list, but these treatments typically evaluate parties against a centralized, hierarchically organized model that was thought to exist during the golden age of political machines. Systematic treatments of contemporary party organizations suggest that they have become more active (Gibson et al., 1983), and to the extent that we include the activity of candidate-centered organizations as party activity, the case for active partisan organization becomes even more impressive. Indeed, the 1988 NES survey estimated that a third of all Americans were encouraged by party or campaign workers to vote in the upcoming election. Still others were solicited for money or were somehow active on behalf of parties or candidates in the election campaign.

An intermediation focus on parties and partisan organization isolates those activities of parties that seek to provide information (however biased) to individual citizens. Americans are not inclined to think of political parties as voluntary associations, but in many communities registration or some other voluntary but institutionalized attachment to a party triggers attempts by that party to influence the individual voter's choices in an election. In a real sense, people join the party when they register to vote or when they go on record as a voter in the party's primary. The party, in turn, makes special efforts to contact its members—those people who have gone on public record as registered Democrats, registered Republicans, voters in Republican primaries, or voters in Democratic primaries.

Numerous studies in the past that have attempted to assess the effects of these party contacts agree that they produce a marginal, albeit significant, improvement in the fortunes of the candidate on whose behalf they are made (Cutright and Rossi, 1958; Katz and Eldersveld, 1961; Kramer, 1971; Crotty, 1971; Beck, 1974b). There is disagreement, however, regarding whether the contact affects the direction of the vote or only the probability of turnout. Moreover, most of these studies—particularly the more recent ones—only ask whether people who are directly contacted vote differently than people who are not. Huckfeldt and Sprague (1992) address the problem from a somewhat different perspective, focusing instead on the cascading consequences of party contacts that produce second and third order effects within the electorate. That is, party contact might be viewed as a catalytic agent that stimulates a mobilization process. Organizational contacts with citizens are often aimed at mobilizing core supporters—organizational cadres who in turn influence the population at large. To the extent that such a view has merit, the consequences of party contact are undervalued by focusing solely on the initial contact.

A more systematic assessment of parties as intermediaries is surely in order. As one example, consider the role of bumper stickers and yard signs. Does such activity actually have any consequence? The South Bend study suggests that this influences voter expectations regarding the behavior of other voters. Respondents in the South Bend study were randomly sampled from 16 very diverse neighborhoods, and they were asked for their predictions regarding which presidential candidate would receive the most support in their neighborhoods. Table 11.4 cross-classifies their predictions by individual partisanship and by the ratio of Democratic to Republican bumper stickers and yard signs within each neighborhood.[3]

What does Table 11.4 tell us? It says that people who live in neighborhoods with more Democratic yard signs and bumper stickers are more likely to believe that the Democratic candidate will receive more support in the neighborhood, independently of their own partisan inclinations. Are these signs and stickers the only information that respondents have to use when assessing their neighbors' political leanings? Of course not, but other analyses suggest that the signs and stickers do, in fact, play an influential role (Huckfeldt and Sprague, 1992). Do these perceptions regarding neighborhood politics matter? Undoubtedly. The signs and stickers on our neighbors' cars and lawns tell us that people who are like us—people with common interests and concerns—hold particular political viewpoints. Information such as this meets at least part of the Downsian test: it is cheap to obtain, it includes the correct bias, and hence it may be extremely useful. Such information is rightfully seen as a consequence of party activity. After all, how many people put up yard signs without being asked?

THE MASS MEDIA

The data from the 1988 NES survey that demonstrate media exposure rely upon self reports (i.e., perceptions) of attention to the various media for political information. These are fragile indicators indeed, for they ignore political messages conveyed through campaign advertisements, through the increasingly popular radio and television call-in shows, or through the guise of ostensibly nonpolitical stories, songs, or shows. Moreover, they focus only upon presidential campaign information and are filtered through the receiver's perceptual screen. But, until more refined measurements are developed, they provide the best available estimates of exposure.

TABLE 11.4   Respondents' Perceptions of Which Presidential Candidate Will Receive the Most Support in the Neighborhood, by Partisan Self-identification and the Neighborhood Ratio of Democratic to Republican Yard Signs and Bumper Stickers.

	Ratio of Democratic to Republican Yard Signs and Bumper Stickers		
	Most Republican	*Intermediate*	*Most Democratic*
Democrats' Perceptions			
Mondale, easily	9.8	21.9	39.1
Mondale, close race	15.8	43.8	36.4
Reagan, close race	30.5	22.9	16.3
Reagan, easily	43.9	11.4	8.2
$N =$	82.0	105.0	184.0
Independents' Perceptions			
Mondale, easily	2.0	10.5	30.6
Mondale, close race	9.2	22.9	34.2
Reagan, close race	35.7	32.4	21.6
Reagan, easily	53.1	34.3	13.5
$N =$	98.0	105.0	111.0
Republican's Perceptions			
Mondale, easily	1.4	13.8	27.0
Mondale, close race	5.1	16.1	33.3
Reagan, close race	44.2	20.7	27.0
Reagan, easily	49.3	49.4	12.7
$N =$	138.0	87.0	63.0

Source: 1984 South Bend study.

The story these data tell is outlined in Table 11.5. As one would expect, by a wide margin more people pay attention to television news as a source of political information than any other single medium. Moreover, 26 percent of the sample was regularly exposed to only one of these media, and for almost all of them that medium was television. But the story does not end on a note of television dominance. Of all respondents, 22 percent paid attention to no medium during the 1988 campaign, leaving the field clear for influence by other intermediaries. Another 43 percent relied upon other media, with 35 percent of them using newspapers in addition to television. For them, media intermediation comes from diverse rather than single sources, which may dampen the effects of television.

An individual's exposure or attentiveness to a medium is a necessary condition for it to play a direct role in the formation of personal political orientation. The direction of a medium's influence, though, depends on the content of the communications which emanate from it—what we have referred to as its bias. Partisan bias in the media is commonly alleged; except for such deviant cases as the Manchester *Union Leader*, though, it is rarely documented.

TABLE 11.5   Exposure to Different Media, 1988 (by percent)

	Regular Attention (%)[a]
Single media	
Television news	70
Newspaper	30
News/political magazine	21
Radio news	15
Combinations	
No media	22
Any one media	32
Any two media	27
Any three media	15
All four media	5
No television news	30
Television news only	26
Television news + another medium	43
Television + newspapers	35

[a]Regular attention to the media means that the respondent is exposed to the particular medium and paid more than some attention to it (or, for radio, listened to at least several speeches or discussions on it) in getting information about the campaign for president.

Source: 1988 American National Election Study, variables V129 (TV), V135 (newspapers), V137 (magazines), V139 (radio).

Because of a legacy of federal regulation, television from its beginnings has refrained from endorsing candidates or otherwise adopting partisan political positions. Accusations of partisan favoritism in television abound, but they all too commonly come from partisans themselves rather than from scholars who have done systematic analysis of media content. This is not to say that television has no biases; there is clear evidence that the issues and themes it emphasizes shape how voters think about a campaign (Iyengar and Kinder, 1987; Patterson, 1980; Patterson and McClure, 1976) or how they attribute responsibility (Iyengar, 1991). But the professionalism of this medium and its fear of violating the norm of neutrality probably prevent it from manifesting clear partisan biases.

Newspapers, of course, have a far different history. They were born in this country as instruments of the political parties, and for much of the nineteenth century they were shrill and unabashed partisan propagandists. Few of them, however, play this role today! With the economic changes of the late nineteenth century from dependence on subscriptions to dependence on advertising, they began to cultivate a readership base that transcended a particular partisan crowd. With the professionalization of journalism in the twentieth century, journalists have struck an independent stance from the parties, laboring mightily to be objective "reporters" of the news rather than ideologues or partisan propagandists (Rubin, 1981).

While partisan bias may creep into news stories, because reporters and their editors are not political eunuchs, it is likely to be subtle in most newspapers—perhaps so subtle as to be lost on all but the most sophisticated readers. Overt partisan positions are usually restricted to the editorial page, but even there most papers attempt to provide representation for columnists of varied ideological, if not ostensibly partisan, viewpoints. It is little wonder that most content analyses of the prestige national press and the wire services find little partisan bias in them (Robinson and Sheehan, 1983; Graber, 1989)—as surely seems to be the case for the national news magazines as well. One suspects that the same findings would emerge for the majority of the nation's newspapers, but curiously little systematic attention has been paid to this matter (Graber, 1989).

Although the evidence is thin, there is good reason to believe that the American media, television and printed press alike, transmit mixed cues when it comes to partisan politics. In their attempts to be professional, to be neutral between the parties and the candidates, to be above the partisan fray, the media that provide most voters with their campaign information in the United States today present a fairly balanced partisan picture. And this is the way they fail to reinforce the one-sided views of the committed partisan. Evidence in support of this inference is found in the 1988 Ohio study. Newspapers and television were either perceived to be neutral or to support the *opposing* candidate, even when by all objective measures they did not (Beck, 1991). Thus, newspapers, too, fail to give clear direction to the uncommitted voter who is searching for reasons to vote one way or the other. The media, in sum, sow doubt and dissonance—and probably undermine partisan ties. It may be more than mere coincidence that, as the media have become more neutral and the most neutral of them, television, has become more important, partisanship and partisan fidelity have declined.

THE COMPREHENSIVE
INTERMEDIATION ENVIRONMENT

That the citizen is embedded in an intermediation environment combining personal discussion networks, mass media, and secondary organizations has long been recognized. Research on intermediaries, however, has rarely examined the interaction of any two of these environments, much less the full intermediation environment that we have described.[4] A better understanding of the mediation of political information requires extending the scope of inquiry beyond the rather insular streams of research on each type of intermediary.

Such a focus, of course, presumes that the premise of this chapter is valid—that variations in a citizen's intermediation environment have consequences for political behavior, that the sources of political information influence its content and partisan direction. Even the most committed devotee of either the rational choice or the psychological perspectives on political decisionmaking would be hard pressed to deny this assertion. Moreover, evidence abounds, albeit in piecemeal form, of the critical importance of context—of what we have called intermediaries. Huckfeldt and Sprague's (1987, 1991) study of personal networks in South Bend demonstrates significant discussant effects. Shanto Iyengar and Donald Kinder's (1987) experiments on television agenda-setting show how it primes evaluations of political leaders. Adam Przeworski and John Sprague's (1986) ecological analysis links the strategic decisions of particular Social Democratic parties and the internal class-based conflicts within these parties' coalitions to the electoral successes and failures of the parties. And so on. Nevertheless, we still lack a systematic analysis of intermediation environments that can begin to estimate the contingent and interactive effects of discussion, media, and organizations—an analysis that might well take inspiration from William McPhee's (1963) model of political information-processing. Such analysis heads the agenda for future research on intermediation.

CONCLUSION: INTERMEDIATION ENVIRONMENTS AND THE DYNAMICS OF AMERICAN POLITICS

How people receive political information is indeed consequential for their political behavior and for the nature of politics. At any one time, there is substantial variation within one nation as well as across nations in the intermediation environments in which citizens reside. And across time, changes in the character of these environments have had profound effects on patterns of American politics. In concluding our discussion of intermediation, we turn to a consideration of a few of these changes and their consequences.

We have already identified one important change in the intermediation process in the United States. The mass media have become more nonpartisan (some might even say antipartisan) as their professionalization and national penetration have steadily grown over the last century, especially with the rise of television in recent decades.[5] As the media have become less partisan, they (especially television, the most nonpartisan of them) have emerged as the dominant source of political information in voters' eyes.

The changing content and role of the mass media produce, we think, three important consequences for the behavior of the American electorate. First, increasing reliance on a partisan-neutral source of information makes voting choices more difficult. Presentation of messages that are not skewed markedly in favor of a single candidate or party undermines the certainty of partisan convictions. Because voters are exposed to information that may challenge their predispositions, reliance on the media increases cross-pressures on the vote (Beck and Crone, 1990). In short, partisan-neutral messages undermine partisan commitments within the electorate, and thus it may not be at all coincidental that the emergence of television as a dominant information source was soon followed by a declining role for party identifications.

Second, by their very nature, the media (especially television, in which messages are conveyed largely in video) focus on candidates more than on parties, institutions, or issues. By "personalizing" politics, they transform the battle for electoral supremacy into a contest of competing personal images. Much has been made of the increasing personalization of politics in democracies worldwide. This change is often more apparent in the parliamentary democracies, where the vote creates party legislative majorities whose leaders then become chief executive, than in the American presidential system in which the character of the candidate has always been of great importance (Bean and Mughan, 1989). But it seems undeniable that the "persona" of the presidential candidates affects American voters more today, when it is conveyed nationwide to an attentive television audience, than it did a century ago, when it was carried to voters by local party activists and the loyal partisan press.

Third, the nationwide penetration of the media is a significant new element in American politics. Not too long ago, candidates for the presidency could tailor their political messages to suit numerous different constituencies. Today these messages, at least as conveyed through the media, are much more uniform across the nation. The domination of television by national networks, which have grown in number through the medium of cable, has contributed the most to this trend. Reliance by newspapers on national news services and national syndicates of columnists has extended this effect to the press as well. Where a presidential campaign is concerned, moreover, most news emanates from that traveling band of campaign reporters, who exchange reactions and thoughts in covering their beat. The effect of these various forces is to homogenize the presentation of presidential candidates to the audience of voters nationwide—voters in Peoria, Mobile, and Santa Monica are exposed to the same candidates and virtually the same messages. In the face of this homogeneous political signal, it becomes important to reconsider the role of the localized and heterogeneous environments where voters reside, and through which they interpret these messages.

The changing role and impact of the mass media have been accompanied by considerable alteration in the intermediation role of secondary organizations. Although one must be careful of exaggeration in the absence of systematic longitudinal evidence, there seems to have been a decay throughout the Western world in the traditional organizations that long guided political choice. In the United States, labor unions enroll a much smaller segment of the work force than they did at their peak in the 1930s, and, even among their members, they appear to have less influence over the vote than they once did. With the spread of unionization beyond its blue-collar origins, the class homogeneity of the union movement has been strained as well. We concluded earlier that unions are the principal politicized secondary organization today, and this has probably been the case for years. Consequently, a declining intermediation role for them alters considerably the political influence of secondary organizations.

A plethora of single-interest or single-issue organizations that link their ersatz "members" through fund-raising letters and phone calls has appeared, however, as unions have declined. Several characteristics distinguish these organizations from the labor union. Requiring literacy and some amount of discretionary income from their members, they seem to focus more on the middle class than on the working class. They are more centralized, top-down organizations than the typical American union. And, without the bond of personal interactions at the local level between leaders and followers or even among followers with a common purpose, they are more impersonal. At this early stage of research on this new style of organization, it is hard to estimate its political consequences. Yet it hardly seems excessive to expect that the changing composition in the organizational life of the individual citizen has had considerable influence on the political information people receive and that such change has influenced their political behavior.

Finally, changes in American family life and structure have affected the political intermediation process as well. The family occupies a central position in the personal network within which things of importance, sometimes even including politics, are discussed. For most people, the family is a source of opinion reinforcement and support, as families typically are homogeneous in their political beliefs and dispositions. In the prototypical traditional American family, it was only the husband/father who ventured far outside the protective cocoon of this homogeneous family environment to encounter people with different viewpoints in the workplace and beyond. The traditional wife/mother restricted her personal interactions to other family members and friends with the same social background, and usually the same political beliefs (Fuchs, 1955).

However applicable this prototype may have been to an earlier age, it is undeniable that it requires substantial alteration today. The high level of geographical mobility within the American population and the increased proportions of single-adult households have combined to diminish familial interactions and consequently intrafamily political discussions. More important, the surge of women into the workplace in recent decades has exposed them to a broader array of political viewpoints. The joint effect of these trends has surely been to increase the heterogeneity of the network of political discussants for the American population overall.

Exposure to a broader circle of political discussants increases the probability that political viewpoints will be subtly or even directly challenged. As Mark Granovetter (1973) has argued, the personal contacts with whom one has the weakest ties may have the greatest influence on one's own attitudes—precisely because they are most likely to provide different information and viewpoints. As the effective personal discussion networks of the American population expand, then, so too should the political heterogeneity of personal intermediation environments.

Even with all this change, though, data from the 1988 Ohio study show that the traditional role of the family in political discussion remains strong. Spouses and relatives were named as the most important discussant where politics was concerned—a much higher percentage than that attained by friends, co-workers, or neighbors. As expected, women were more likely than men to name relatives, particularly spouses, as their main discussants. A parallel tendency for husbands to take the lead in political interactions was reported in the 1984 South Bend study (Brickell, Huckfeldt, and Sprague, 1988).

Although confirmation of our speculations awaits the results of the systematic empirical investigation we are undertaking on the 1992 campaign (and in other studies), we think that recent changes in the intermediation environments of Americans are having profound effects on their political behavior. The decline of the partisan mass media, the reduction in the number of daily newspapers with diverse political viewpoints, the rise of political neutrality as a professional norm among media analysts, and the reduced influence of politicized secondary organizations have all exposed Americans to a mix of intermediaries that provides substantially less guidance in the exercise of citizenship. The result may be a public that is weakly anchored and less partisan in its political convictions, increasingly dependent on social discourse for alternative political viewpoints, and perhaps more vulnerable to influence from momentary political forces and events.

The dynamics of American politics, in short, are substantially affected by changes in the environments of political intermediation. Some years ago, William Kornhauser (1959) theorized that the decay of traditional social anchors was creating an unattached, anomic mass society that constituted a threat to political democracy. Some Americans may resemble Kornhauser's anomic individual, but we do not, in general, share this view. Our own less pessimistic position is that most modern American citizens are not anomic; rather, they are firmly anchored within particular environments—environments that have important consequences for their responses to politics. But these environments are changing in important ways, and only by returning the American voter to a personal sociopolitical setting can we begin to comprehend the consequences of these changes.

NOTES

1. We are currently working with Russell Dalton of the University of California at Irvine on such a comprehensive study, focused on the 1992 presidential election. Analysis of personal, organizational, and media influence in 40 sites across the United States and, more intensively, in one urban county, should shed substantial light on the intermediation process in the United States. Comparison of the American case to companion studies in Germany, Britain, Spain, and Japan using the same design should advance our study even further.

2. The percentage of organizational members who belong to more than one organization is probably higher. The GSS figures understate associational ties because they ignore funding support and multiple memberships within a particular category (Baumgartner and Walker, 1988).

3. This neighborhood measure is obtained by aggregating the approximately 95 survey responses within each neighborhood.

4. Among the exceptions are Lazarsfeld, Berelson, and Gaudet (1948), Berelson, Lazarsfeld, and McPhee (1954), and Katz and Lazarsfeld (1955)—work conducted well over four decades ago!—and some limited analysis in Patterson (1980) and Beck and Crone (1990).

5. Other democratic nations appear to be headed in this direction as well, but most of them still have powerful newspapers with national readerships which play more or less partisan roles in politics.

12

Group Politics Reexamined:
From Pluralism to Political Economy

CLARENCE N. STONE

Once regarded as the centerpiece of American political science, the study of group politics has been accorded a more modest position in recent years. Researchers now equate groups with organized interests and see them as relatively weak participants in the governmental process (Bauer, Pool, and Dexter, 1963; Scholzman and Tierney, 1986). What I want to suggest in this essay is that the group basis of politics refers to something broader and deeper than the activity of organized interest groups. As Philip Selznick says, all societies face the same basic problem, "the same need for an accommodative balance between fragmentary group interests and the aims of the whole" (1957:9; cf. Lowi, 1979; Schwartz, 1988). Selznick's point is not that politics is only about group conflict. Quite the contrary, his message is, among other things, about how political freedom and group conflict accommodate one another. I will return to this important theme later.

For now I want to lay some foundation stones for the discussion. First, the group basis of politics involves more than how individuals tactically aggregate themselves in the pursuit of personal aims. It is about group identities and social purposes; it is also about a *tendency* for individuals to define themselves, their goals, and therefore their interests by making connections that are direct and immediate rather than inclusive.

Second, "interests" are not dictated by positions in a network of social and economic roles. We should not reduce politics to a form of social determinism. Instead, we should see group politics and the nation's institutional arrangements as reciprocally related (cf. Schlozman and Tierney, 1986:390–391). Institutions, however, include more than those of the formal governmental system; the political economy is the appropriate context for considering group-institution interactions.

David Truman defines an interest group as "any group that, on the basis of one or more shared attitudes" makes policy claims (1951:33). I propose a somewhat different approach—to substitute "preferences" for "attitudes," and treat them as open-ended rather than fixed. This understanding highlights the part played by institutions in shaping group identity as policymakers face the challenge of organizing political support and contending with political opposition.

The third foundation stone is an understanding of politics as concerned with forming, maintaining, and changing preferences. Political activity, James Wilson points out, involves "efforts to change wants by arguments, persuasion, threats, bluffs, and education" (1980:363). Overt efforts, however, are only part of the picture. They occur within a context—hence the need to take into account the characteristics of the American political economy. Attention needs to be given to interactions *with and within* a larger environment—interactions that enable some kinds of policy preferences to take shape and survive while others, even if they surface, are discouraged. Preferences do not simply take shape in a free-form fashion, nor are they atomistic "givens." They are molded, as Aaron Wildavsky argues, by the "organization of social relations," and they emerge through a "social filter," particularly institutional arrangements (Wildavsky, 1987:4; see also Elkin, 1985; Kelman, 1987; Mansbridge, 1992).

I propose to look at three aspects of group politics—the three faces of group politics, as it were. The first aspect involves the political implications of differences among groups in intensity of preference, which is the major concern of Truman and other classic pluralists. The second aspect involves differences among groups in their capacity to act on their preferences. This issue is brought to the forefront by Mancur Olson's (1965) *The Logic of Collective Action*, and is a focus of Jack Walker's (1983)examination of the role of patrons in mobilizing groups. The third aspect involves the impact of the American political economy on the formation and sustenance of preferences. It is the most difficult to pin down, but we need to consider why some types of policy preferences take hold more readily than others and what the implications of those differences are.

PREFERENCE INTENSITY AND PLURALIST POLITICS

Despite its title, Truman's (1951) classic work, *The Governmental Process*, is society-centered. Group political behavior emanates from an ongoing process of modernization, a process marked by heightening social differentiation and a proliferation of groups that reflect increasing role specialization in both economy and society. Within this context, Truman sees the trigger of group activity as disturbance in the environment, to which affected groups respond with political activity and demands for governmental action. Their demands, in turn, disturb the environment of still other groups, and they seek counteractions to restore circumstances to their earlier place.

With limited resources and highly specialized interests, groups tend to spawn narrow-gauge conflicts. Were any one group to seek change on a broad scale, it would find itself at odds with a wide-ranging coalition; it is better, then, to attend to a few issues of immediate concern unless provoked by the intrusive actions of others.

In classic pluralism, motivation can overcome disadvantages of status and wealth. In *Who Governs?*, Robert Dahl (1961) argues that, where voting lines are fluid and there are many groups, even a relatively small bloc may occupy a strategic place in the pursuit of majority support by elected officials. These officials therefore have an incentive to be responsive to all groups, lest their unresponsiveness give their competitors an advantage. Hence, socioeconomically disadvantaged groups can use their strategic leverage to open up opportunities.

What is lacking in Dahl's 1961 analysis (though present in his later work) is a political economy perspective—an appreciation of how the formal, public equality of citizens is modified by private inequalities in wealth (investment capital, in particular) and in organizational capacity. Classic pluralism is mainly about the political consequences of differences in intensity of preference (see, especially, Dahl, 1956). Combined with social complexity, differences in intensity of preference work in Madisonian fashion to prevent domination by a single faction. Hence conflict typically occurs between highly particular interests and is confined to narrow issue areas. Any large change requires substantial coalition building, and pluralists view large coalitions as too fragile to be instruments of domination (Polsby, 1980:137).

What might occur, however, is monopoly control over a narrow issue area.[1] Those with the greatest stake in a policy question might provide strong and durable political support to their allies in the legislative and executive branches to form an "iron triangle." The indifference of the larger public leaves it uninformed and unmobilized so that groups with a special interest can sometimes "capture" a narrow policy area so long as the costs of their monopoly are dispersed rather than concentrated. Some policy issues simply fail to produce competing groups with stakes large enough to sustain counterbalancing activity. Unequal stakes in an issue area produce unequal intensities in preference, and those with the most intense preferences prevail.

MOBILIZATION
AND THE COLLECTIVE ACTION PROBLEM

Truman's pluralism is society-centered in the sense that group activity stems from its position in a complex socioeconomic order. Raymond Bauer, Ithiel de Sola Pool, and Lewis Dexter (1963) signal a shift from society to state by questioning the role of organized groups in policy formation. And in a seminal review essay of their book, Theodore Lowi (1964) reverses the conventional understanding of the relationship between interest groups and policy formation. Lowi argues that groups respond to, rather than shape, the character of public policies—policy determines politics. As the impact of a policy broadens, so does the incentive to organize and respond accordingly (cf. Wilson, 1973:327–337).

Mancur Olson's (1965) analysis raises a different set of issues. Applying the economist's concept of a "public good" to the question of organizational membership, Olson argues that a rational individual might well choose to be a free rider and leave active organizational support up to others. Hence a shared interest does not generate an organized response even when government has enacted a significant policy. Having a preference and being conscious of that preference does not result in the capacity to act as a collectivity.

Structurally some groups are better able to organize than others. Groups with a large membership face an acute disparity between individual rationality and collective action. And the difference that individual effort can make is minute enough to encourage free-rider behavior. By contrast, small groups in close communication can wield social sanctions to encourage organizational participation (Hardin, 1982; but see Douglas, 1986). Perhaps more to the point, a corporate enterprise with a huge stake in public policy can make a substantial difference and also easily afford to contribute to organizational action. As Robert Salisbury (1984:68) points out, in contrast with mass-member groups, institutions have enormous discretionary resources that they can devote to interest representation.

According to the logic of collective action, viable groups require selective material incentives—something they can award to participants and withhold from nonparticipants. Without such an incentive, rational individuals will not engage in collective action. Even mass membership groups based on material incentives are less likely than institutions to enjoy durable and persistent representation in policymaking (Salisbury, 1984:75). After all, if membership is based on selective incentives, and not on a collective purpose, organizational support is likely to concentrate on the selective incentives, not on the group's collective goal (Schlozman and Tierney, 1986:131).

To put the matter in proper perspective, it should be added that there is ample empirical evidence showing that participation in group politics is not based exclusively on selective material benefits (Moe, 1980; Muller and Opp, 1986; Knoke, 1990). Motivation includes purposeful action (Wilson, 1973). However, organizational and strategic strength, even when purposeful motivation is tapped, can be considerably enhanced by the presence of selective incentives (Moe, 1980; Mansbridge, 1986).

The kinds and quantities of resources available thus have much to do with whether a group can be formed, maintained, and mobilized for political action. A feeling of being wronged is not enough to produce a collective response, that is, "a sense of injustice is too pervasive and rebellion too rare, for one to be a sufficient explanation of the other" (Tilly, 1981:16). Even if members are drawn to collective action by a sense of purpose rather than by selective material incentives, resources are needed to sustain an organization and its lines of communication.

How, then, does a group get started? Where are the resources for an initial effort? Jack Walker (1991) finds that patrons—often foundations, government agencies, or, for peak economic associations, large firms—play a crucial role in the initiation of group organizations or in providing resources to maintain an organization. In some cases, legislation precedes the organization of client groups, and government may be the creator of an organizational role as well as the provider of tangible resources for group activity (Culhane, 1981; Browne, 1988). In other cases, government plays no *direct* role in the formation of organizations, but may still have had a part in creating the climate within which organized groups form and gain strength. For example, the creation of the Commission on the Status of Women may have helped provide a favorable environment for feminist organizations (Walker, 1991:31).

Public officeholders have wide discretion about the issues they promote and the resources they deploy. They can, Walker observes, reinforce the organizational advantages business enjoys in political mobilization, or they can promote the countervailing influence of the nonprofit sector. In either case, officials are reshaping the political society in which they operate. However, once established, organized interest groups possess an autonomous capacity to pursue alternative bases of support. Their fate is not tied irrevocably to their original patrons, and they can use ideological and other purposeful appeals to garner membership support. For this reason, the Reagan administration was largely unsuccessful in its efforts to "defund the left" (Walker, 1991:141–156). Much, of course, depends on the nature of a group's membership and the resources it possesses.

COMPARING TRUMAN AND WALKER

Forty years separate the publication of David Truman's (1951) *The Governmental Process* from Jack Walker's (1991) *Mobilizing Interest Groups in America*. Walker's state-centered work contrasts sharply with Truman's more society-centered analysis. To be sure, Truman sees that governmental actions can contribute to new disturbances and further demands. But Truman's conception of government is one of reactiveness, and it contrasts sharply with Walker's view of politics-centered leadership.

The contrast between Truman and Walker is more than a matter of emphasis; they display different understandings of how the world operates. Truman assumes that human actions are embedded in and guided by predictable social forces—modernization especially. Government is a stable structure of access points to society-based demands.

Walker's world is more contingent; it evolves according to no preset pattern. As he sees it, American politics underwent profound changes in the 1960s. The nonprofit sector gained a greater voice, but not simply as an expansion of what had existed. A body of political actors inside and outside government made resources available to support a variety of citizen-based organizations and welfare-oriented associations. In doing so, they altered the previous balance between profit and nonprofit sectors of the society, strengthening the latter. This move, in interaction with the " Reagan revolution," polarized interest representation, and ideological differentiation became more pronounced. Thus the proliferation of organized groups in recent years is no mere extension of a modernization process of greater and greater role specialization. Proliferation occurred, not through an inevitable working out of a pattern of development, but because important political leaders chose to pursue ideologically based forms of mobilization.

For Walker, group politics is intertwined with a world of particular, historical actions. *None* of the processes that shape the American system "are products of natural forces beyond our leaders' controls" (Walker, 1991:viii). If the preferences of some groups are not advocated, that is not a circumstance beyond remedy—who is represented, and who is not, is politically determined. In Walker's view, this appears to be mainly a matter of the mobilization and maintenance of organized interest groups. Even in considering the enactment of programs, he treats such enactments as potential sources of organizational advantages, for example, the advantage of putting into place policy professionals who can provide leadership and patronage for political action. Thus Walker's emphasis on the contingent character of American politics and his dismissal of the notion that there is a preset pattern of development are needed correctives to Truman's classic work.

Walker shows that the 1960s ushered in a significant period of *political* change: The growth of the educated middle class combined with technologies of mass communication and direct mail have contributed to expanded group activity, as has new legislation and an increase in governmental programs. There are more voices; nonbusiness groups in particular have multiplied. Many previously closed subsystems have opened up, and conflict is more common. But, following Walker's lead, if one thinks of American politics as an ongoing struggle between a business sector and a nonprofit and government-based services sector, then it hardly seems that the 1960s altered the power balance in any fundamental way to leave business less influential or to make the government more social-minded. Walker's approach emphasizes the mobilization of groups and suggests that political struggle in America is a question of the capacity of the nonprofit and services sector to wield countervailing power against corporate business. Significant as the mobilization question is, it is only part of the overall picture. We need to turn to the "third face" of group politics, the ecology of preference formation.[2]

THE POLITICAL ECONOMY CONTEXT:
AN ECOLOGY OF POLICY PREFERENCES

In shifting attention to the issue of which and how many groups are mobilized, Walker neglects to question the *scope* of the interest represented by these groups, though he does remind us that the interest-group universe is not predetermined—that political choice is part of the picture. Classic pluralism, however, has something to offer on this score. It suggests that it is easier to organize around narrow and specialized interests. This issue brings us to the "third face" of group politics. Do our political and economic institutions reinforce a tendency to organize political support around narrow and specialized interests thereby giving them the means of expression? Or do our institutions serve, as James Madison hoped they would, to enlarge the vision that guides policymaking and informs political consent? To answer this question, we need to look beyond the mobilization of groups to the interaction between group identities and the larger political economy setting.

This interaction gives rise to an ecology of policy preferences and invites us to ask what thrives and what does not. Aside from organized backing, why are some policy preferences more likely than others to be acted on? Even among preferences that seem equal in intrinsic appeal, some fit in while others do not. What kinds of preferences can attract and maintain support *because they appear especially viable within the context of the American political economy*? The classic pluralist position was that it "is the claims of small, intense minorities that are usually attended to" (Polsby, 1980:118). Immediacy of the stake in the matter leads to intensity of preference and a likelihood that such minorities will prevail over those with more remote concerns and a less intense preference.

I want to transform this proposition. We need to be free of any assumption that "stake" has fixed boundaries attached to a particular position. Yet, *immediacy is an important factor*, as I shall maintain below, because human cognition is narrow. But narrow cognition is not to be equated with static understanding. Cognition is dynamic, and it can be reshaped to alter understanding of what is at stake (Baumgartner and Jones, 1991, 1993).

Put another way, though what is proximate is most readily understood, preferences and the intensity with which people hold them are socially and politically constructed (cf. Berger and Luckmann, 1967; Darnton, 1989).

Policy preference is greatly influenced by perceived feasibility. The larger environment makes some goals easier; they seem more fitting. Fittingness to a larger environment thus influences attachment to a policy preference because some preferences come to be seen as more viable than others *in that setting*. The ecological perspective enables us to ask what makes some preferences more viable than others. Walker's attention to political mobilization is only one step toward answering that question—a wider look is needed.

There is no single work that applies the ecological perspective systematically to group politics, but Aaron Wildavsky sets the stage with his reminder that preferences emerge through a "social filter," and that the filtering is a piecemeal process, based in concrete relationships (1987:9). The institutional relationships we need to focus on are those that bear directly on the shaping of political consent—on the building of support and the managing of conflict. Classic pluralism tells us that the basic building blocks have to do with immediacy of interest. The question then becomes one of whether the institutions of the political economy work to enlarge public understanding of what is at stake or whether these institutions serve mainly to reinforce a narrow and immediate understanding.

What is the basic character of the American institutional "filter" and how does it affect the group basis of politics? The political economy is one in which formal authority is highly fragmented, and political organization *reinforces* rather than mitigates that *fragmentation*. Despite increased ideological polarization, political parties have little programmatic coherence. Ideology, after all, is no guarantee of unity—splintering is as much a possibility as cohesion (Mansbridge, 1986). Outside the party system, fragmentation also reigns. In contrast with several European countries, major sectors of the American economy are not politically organized for corporatist participation. Peak business associations are relatively anemic compared to their counterparts in Europe, and they serve mainly as advocates of the class interest of business instead of as representatives of the business class in the deliberations of the nation. Thus neither law nor informal association does much to imbue business interests with a sense of social responsibility, even though corporate business is a major element in the actual governing of the nation. Corporations thus are not endowed collectively with a major public responsibility and face few constraints in pursuing their various and particular private interests.

The Tendency Toward Business Partnerships

To appreciate the role of business, it is helpful to rethink the language of group politics. "Pressure," "access," and "mobilization" are terms suggesting a scenario in which organized groups make demands that the government act or not act in a given way. This scenario assumes that groups attempt to impose their fixed preferences on governmental actors, who are especially concerned about being able to continue in office. This makes the electoral connection central.

But consider a different scenario. If one sees governance as an activity that typically involves the *cooperation* of governmental and nongovernmental actors whose policy preferences depend on the opportunities they see as realizable, then the process is no longer simply one of mobilizing to put pressure on, bargain with, or gain access to public officials. Instead of one actor with a fixed preference trying to dominate another or bargain with another, the situation is one where actors with open-ended preferences search for ways (or matches) that enable them to satisfy a need to be purposive with the means at hand.

As public officials form their own preferences, they are mindful of the *nongovernmental* actors who can further or impede actions, not only by political mobilization but also by the simple fact of cooperation or noncooperation. Hence the political economy context is enormously important; private control of investment activity gives business a privileged position (Lindblom, 1977; see also Domhoff, 1986; and Galambos and Pratt, 1988). Because the level of economic activity depends on the actions of corporate decisionmakers, public officials have a strong incentive to create a favorable business climate.

The business-government relationship is complex, however. Public officials are drawn to business by more than a general need for investment activity. They, also, are interested in active forms of cooperation to advance particular policy aims. Significantly, business executives control an important body of expertise in areas such as redevelopment, and they have networks, organizational capacities, and slack resources that can be devoted to civic causes (Stone, 1989). Hence public officials display a strong tendency to seek business cooperation, and they shape their preferences accordingly.

Therefore we need to think more carefully about the government-business relationship and the nature of the mutual (but not necessarily symmetrical) dependence in that relationship. If public officials want to launch a successful and visible action and want to do so sooner rather than later, cooperation with business is often attractive; slum clearance and enterprise zones make good examples. Policymaking is not simply a matter of enactment of a goal. Even when the official aim is social, business is often an essential partner. Redevelopment success depends on private activity. Cooperation with business can thus be attractive to goal-oriented actors, and business influence is by no means confined to campaign finance and related assistance.

Even when the policy objective is regulation of business activities, business cooperation is a significant factor. The finding that much lobbying activity consists of providing information is surprising only if one thinks about political relationships as a struggle over domination, resistance, and bargaining leverage. Often the business-government relationship is one in which, given the heavily privatized nature of the American political economy, government is dependent on business provision of necessary services. For example, Bruce Vladeck's (1980) account of the nursing-home industry shows that regulation is largely ineffective because there are so few alternatives for the dependent elderly. The threat to close a home leaves public authorities with the problem of where to house those in need of care. Similarly the imposition of health and safety codes in the workplace runs the risk of closing down sources of employment. Business advantage is thus neither universal nor unchallenged, as these examples show. The point of the above discussion is simply to suggest that business cooperation is attractive to officials in ways that other groups have difficulty matching. This has partly to do with usefulness as a policy partner, not with political mobilization as that term is usually understood; and it has to do in part with the essential nature of much business activity. So even when legislation specifies regulatory standards, administrators are reluctant to impose sanctions that would close a business.

To assert that business has a structural advantage through its position in the economy is not to deny variations in the force of that advantage (Quirk, 1981). And it is not to deny that mobilization has significance. Indeed, mobilization can play an important contributory part in regulatory policy, providing a counterbalance to producer groups, enhancing the oversight capacity of officials, and broadening what is at issue (Culhane, 1981). Particularly with modern means of communication and increasing levels of education, the middle class has a substantial capacity for mobilization, and the growth of that class may well have contributed to the emergence of a more vigorous citizen politics in the 1960s (Walker, 1991).

Further, dominance is not the issue. The role of business depends on the nature of the issue. Governance is a complex process—or, more accurately, a set of processes. Deliberating publicly and mobilizing to influence such deliberations are only a *part* of what is involved. Once a public goal is agreed to, resources must be brought to bear on the necessary tasks. In addition, behavior that is embedded in a network of private roles must often be altered. Moreover, enactments are only statements of intention. Resources must still be produced to bring about change, and business often has the resources needed for various policy objectives.

The Tendency Toward Distributional Policies

A need for cooperation from nongovernmental actors directs attention to the varying nature of policy goals and what it takes to accomplish them. Many policies are *relatively* simple, involving subsidizing or stimulating a particular action. Many regulatory activities are also *somewhat* simple, even if highly technical in content, and they entail monitoring fairly narrow and specific activities. Other proposed policies are broader and more complex, requiring mixtures of stimulating and regulating activities and coordinating the behaviors of a wide range of actors. As the goal broadens, the coordination task increases. These compound policies call for more far-reaching governmental efforts, and these are the efforts that the American system is poorly equipped to undertake.

As we think about a range of policy preferences—preferences that involve relatively narrow bases of activity versus those that involve the coordination of very wide bases of activity—we can see that those with lesser coordination requirements attached to them are more likely to be encouraged and reinforced than are their opposites. Hence, cooperation with specific producer groups is workable. Regulation of particular activities is workable, too, especially where there is an organized and active ally to help monitor what is going on. But broad policies that integrate production, regulation, and service-provision do not thrive (Vladeck, 1980). For example, agriculture policy is based on commodity groups, not on comprehensive economic planning; nor, as William Browne observes, is it based "on attention to the food-and-fiber related social problems of the world or the nation" (1988:215). Even when groups emerge that raise broad issues of a "farm crisis," policymakers have difficulty converting these concerns into concrete and workable programs. As one participant concluded, "It's just easier to set commodity policy than it is farm policy" (Browne, 1988:190).

Stated as a proposition, narrow-gauge preferences (e.g., commodity-price supports) that can simply be aggregated are more likely to be responded to than are broad-gauge preferences (e.g., a policy of promoting viable family-farm life). More is involved here than just a matter of which groups are organized and politically mobilized. Groups with broad-gauge and intensely felt preferences come into play and mobilize, but they find it hard to engage the policymaking apparatus (Browne, 1990), though the problems that triggered their activity may be unresolved.

That narrow-gauge preferences flourish in the American system does not preclude broad policy thrusts. It means only that policy directions are often *not* the intended consequences of planned actions (cf. Hardin,

1982:221). They involve a heavy admixture of inadvertence. It is, rather, a question of what building blocks are available and readily used.

Consider first a small and ideologically innocent example—one of bass fishing versus pike and trout fishing.[3] The Army Corps of Engineers, pursuing its central function, built dams and created a number of lakes. Because these lakes contain warm water and mud bottoms, they are a more suitable habitat for largemouth bass than for the trout or pike that had populated the undammed streams. The lakes provided development opportunities for land dealers, and a market for the boat industry. With bass-fishing opportunities in great abundance, conditions were right for formation of a Bass Anglers Sportsman Society, with the predictable acronym of BASS. Once formed, its members became politically active and sought posts such as appointments to state game and fish commissions.

Several features of this case are noteworthy. One is that government action (building dams) preceded the foundation of the interest group. Another is that no major political campaign revolved around bass fishing versus pike and trout fishing. Instead, particular and narrow benefits aggregated into a body of durable support, consisting of such diverse elements as the Army Corps of Engineers, developers, the boat industry, BASS, and state fish and game commissions. A similar situation, though with a larger-scale pattern, and with more far-reaching implications, is evident in the development of the American Southwest (Reisner, 1987). And even more far-reaching is the set of policies that reflect the military-industrial complex (a phenomenon rarely mentioned in studies of interest-group politics).

Summary

The limited ability of the United States to develop reasoned and coherent policies is not a mystery. *Policy reflects political arrangements;* these arrangements filter out broad-gauge preferences and retain those narrow in gauge, that is, they nurture preferences that correspond to a highly fragmented base of political support (see also Steinmo, chap. 5, this volume). This fragmentation tends to encourage distributive policies and enhance the role of business in public policy, not because business is in control, but because business is often a useful policy partner under conditions of diffuse authority. Businesses adapt well to distributive policy opportunities, though, of course, they can be, and on occasion are, defeated in this arena.

ECOLOGY VERSUS MOBILIZATION

To talk about an ecology of preference formation is to embrace Wildavsky's view that institutions filter some preferences out while enabling others to endure. But what about broad efforts to mobilize support for social reform, as happened in the 1960s? Does such a movement alter the ecology or does the ecology alter the movement? What happens in American politics when social ferment, big ideas, and political mobilization interact with the basic institutions of the American political economy? The answer suggested by the aftereffects of the 1960s is that the policy preferences that flourish are (despite the broad political mobilization) business-connected and (despite the social ferment and big ideas) distributional. What accounts for this pattern?

First of all, we can rule out ideological hegemony as a factor (Abercrombie, Hill, and Turner, 1980). As Walker argues, the 1960s saw conventional beliefs come under attack, and alternative ideas entered the public arena (1991:36). Second, Walker also points out that new groups were mobilized, especially groups in the nonbusiness sectors of society. An organizational foundation for social-minded change was established. Yet, the movement for social reform was itself never a coherent force. As advocacy groups proliferated, their tactics led them to develop narrow bases of support. Direct mail, for example, is a form of targeting—market differentiation, one might say. And often it sharpens differences rather than building broad coalitions.   ·

Despite widespread group mobilization, the 1960s were followed by a tripling of the national debt; a finance-industry collapse and costly bailout; the absence of a national policy for energy or health; and a program of environmental protection that loses shape and integrity as one looks beneath the legislative veneer to administrative reality. Further problems included inattention to problems of economic restructuring, employment, and urban revitalization; a program of foreign aid based heavily on satisfying sundry domestic constituencies; and military expenditures out of line with the state of international affairs.

Social movements can widen awareness, but appropriate institutional arrangements are needed to convert that awareness into broad and sustained policy efforts. Otherwise political turbulence may generate only narrow and essentially distributive policy responses. Why, for example, did the civil rights movement in the United States narrow its aims mostly to affirmative action in employment and contracts, whereas an earlier movement for welfare reform in Europe led to forms of universal coverage? Part of the answer rests in the institutional context. The creation of the welfare state in Western Europe suggests that lasting and broad-based reform, even when universal in form, is most likely when based on successful coalition-building among particular groups while reaching the broad, general public (Baldwin, 1990). European political economies facilitate the necessary coalition-building. By contrast, in the United States facilitating conditions were lacking. Big-city mayors, as principal inheritors of the civil rights torch, found themselves operating within a system of dispersed authority, a fragmented and highly personalized political structure, and a heavily privatized economy. They lacked the resources and the incentives to do more than focus on a few achievable aims at hand. So their actions and the preferences of their constituents gravitated to the narrow task of affirmative action, as infeasibility made a broad-scale attack on poverty unappealing.

The 1960s teach us that political mobilization is not enough. It has as its purpose countervailing power—that is, altering the balance of social control so that new policies can be enacted and sustained. But the notion of countervailing power suggests that political struggle is mainly a matter of direction—toward a different balance point between the corporate-business sector and the nonprofit and services sector. In American politics, the divide between profit and nonprofit sectors is real, but it does not contain all that is important about group conflict. Running through American politics is also the issue of the *scope* of the interests represented. While talk about broad and unifying social aims is sometimes a cover for perpetuating the status quo, the lesson of the 1960s is that conflict and a proliferation of advocacy groups by themselves are insufficient to bring about fundamental social reform.

Bernard Crick put the matter this way: "Ideally politics draws all ... groups into each other so that they each and together can make a positive contribution towards the general business of government" (1982:18). As we confront the group basis of politics, the challenge is one of creating institutions that enlarge vision by drawing groups "into each other."

Some will object that groups are an inappropriate focus; only individual interests are real. Others will object that only class struggle is real. But I am willing to argue, first, that the group basis of politics corresponds to something fundamental in human nature, and, second, that institution-building and reform need to start from that foundation.

HUMAN NATURE
AND THE FOUNDATIONS OF GROUP POLITICS

If individually defined interests were the sole foundation of political behavior, there would be little point in talking about the group basis of politics. Yet groups are a reality. Collective action does occur, and it cannot be explained in individualistic terms (Douglas, 1986). But, if individuals are socially minded, why are there so many competing groups? What about groups devoted to the public interest? Why do they often have a narrow agenda (McFarland, 1984)?

Complex Motivation—with Moral Agency

In brief, my argument is that the basic political condition is one in which people mainly identify with and have moral responsibility to small and proximate groups. Generally people concern themselves with their family, their work, and their friends and neighbors (variously defined). So strong is the sense of moral responsibility to others that in most circles, extensive preoccupation with the self is deemed pathological behavior,[4] and there is no surer way for leaders or officials to undermine their authority than by acting in regard to self at the expense of their followings or institutions (Chong, 1991).

While rational-choice analysts have come to accept the position that behavior is complex, they display a tendency to deal with complexity by dividing actors into categories by principal form of motivation, thereby providing their analyses with a supply of altruists to account for what cannot be explained by rational egoism. A more useful approach might be to credit all people with complex motivation, including a need to be social and purposive. While it is the case that society-wide norms often seem to be weak (Hechter, 1987; Elster, 1989), those who see humankind as moral do not rest their case on the efficacy of such norms. Nor do they deny self-regarding behavior. They do, however, believe some actions are best explained as obligatory, that is, based on a sense of obligation determined by the individual's sense of identity and what is appropriate to that identity (March and Olsen, 1989:23; Monroe et al., 1990). Put another way, human beings see themselves as moral creatures and embrace moral codes (Barnard, 1968; Selznick, 1957; Burns, 1978; Muir, 1977).

Chester Barnard is worth quoting at some length on this point, because his observations indicate that purposiveness and moral codes typically run in circles more confined than those of society-wide norms. Barnard questions whether publicly professed codes are the dominant ones and offers a characterization of a hypothetical pump-station machinist, whose "codes" are rank ordered as follows: the support and protection of his children, his obligations to the water system where he works, his code as a skilled artisan, his obligations to his parents, his religious code, and his role as a citizen. Barnard elaborates:

> For his children he will steal, cheat the government, rob the church, leave the water plant at a critical time, botch a job by hurrying. If his children are not directly at stake, he will sacrifice money, health, time, comfort, convenience, jury duty, church obligations, in order to keep the water plant running; except for his children and the water plant, he cannot be induced to do a botch mechanical job—steal, or do anything else contrary to his code as a citizen or his religious code; if his government legally orders him to violate his religious code, he will go to jail first. He is, however, a very responsible man. It not only takes extraordinary pressure to make him violate any of his codes, but when faced with such pressure he makes great effort to find some solution that is compatible with all of them; and because he makes that effort and is capable he has in the past succeeded. Since he is a very responsible man,

knowing his codes you can be fairly sure of what he will do under a rather
. wide range of conditions. (1968:267–268)

Barnard's hypothetical machinist is one for whom societywide obligations are *relatively* weak, but for whom proximate purposes and identities
are strong. If we take these proximate purposes and identities as the bed-
rock of group politics, then group politics and moral agency are compatible. Instead of amoral egoism, we have a tendency for human beings to
identify with and take responsibility for purposes and affiliations that are
concrete and immediate parts of their everyday lives (cf. Burns, 1978:
45–46).

Narrow Cognition

While motivations are complex, the moral agency of humankind is substantially conditioned by narrow cognition (March and Simon, 1958).
Consider the famous Milgram experiments on the willingness of individuals to follow orders that called for administering electric shocks to
others. One variation of those experiments had to do with the physical
proximity of the "victim"—the individual receiving the presumed electric
shocks. Milgram found that as the "victim" became more proximate, subjects were less willing to administer high levels of shock in obedience to
the commands of those in charge of the experiment. By contrast, the "Remote condition" allowed victims to be "put out of mind." One subject
said, "It's funny how you really begin to forget that there's a guy out
there, even though you can hear him. For a long time I just concentrated
on pressing the switches and reading the words" (Milgram, 1974:38). Narrow cognition suggests that the foundation for group politics is a *tendency*
to identify with others in one's immediate orbit of contacts and activities.

Narrow cognition has other implications. Preferences are *not fixed* by an
individual's position in a set of roles and statuses. Instead, as one's cognition is redirected and perhaps occasionally expanded by new activities or
dramatic events, preferences alter. Because perceptions are always incomplete, trade-offs are inadequately understood and common identities in-
completely developed. We are never delivered from a *state* of narrow cognition, but particular limitations can be transcended or at least replaced—
opening up the possibility of enlarged or different preferences holding
sway. Barnard's machinist will embrace a solution that makes his proximate responsibilities compatible with his larger obligations.

Narrow Cognition and Power

Though the notion of narrow cognition is itself "old hat," its implications
are far-reaching and generally underestimated. In particular, once we pro-

ceed from narrow cognition to open-ended preferences, then the standard view of power as a contest of wills no longer holds. The Weberian conception—A gets B to do what B would otherwise not do—applies only under conditions of stable preferences. One actor deploys resources to induce another to act in a different way than would have occurred if these resources had never been deployed.

In the Weberian conception, power is intentional (Wrong, 1980; see also Dahl, 1984; Nagel, 1975; Debnam, 1984).[5] Because A must in some sense intend for B to comply with A's wishes, B must in some sense intend to resist, unless the cost becomes too great. Weberian power involves actors with set preferences, actors who engage in struggle when their preferences clash. Outcomes depend on the resources controlled by the seeker of compliance and the depth of the resister's determination.

If we start with an assumption of open-ended preferences based on a narrow cognition and changing opportunities and relationships, power becomes a different phenomenon to examine. If intentions are not set, the crucial question is not one of whose preferences prevail. Instead, it is a question of how preferences come to be embraced in the first place (Cohen and March, 1986:219–223). What experiences and opportunities shape them? What kinds of preferences tend to emerge and why?

The assumptions of narrow cognition and purposive motivation suggest a partial answer. If people are purposeful, but have a limited capacity to see and act on the full range of possibilities, then the possibilities that are most immediate and concrete have an advantage, and these often are the most feasible as well. The ability to act and achieve something is attractive (cf. Skocpol, 1985:16). But, of course, what seems feasible to one actor is very much a matter of what other actors appear willing to support—hence the attraction to purpose is greatly influenced by the social, political, and institutional context.

A strong caution is in order. The question of feasibility does not *control* the direction of purposiveness. Perceived ease of achievement is a constraint rather than a full determinant. As a constraint, feasibility directly influences the *scope* of purpose to which people attach themselves and give their political support. It also influences the pattern of coalition formation and can thereby indirectly influence policy direction. Partners with ample resources and a ready capacity to act are especially attractive, and that is not a policy-neutral fact. Taking a coalition partner is not a simple matter of gaining assistance in the pursuit of a predetermined set of goals. Coalition relationships alter what is both salient and feasible. As Hannah Arendt observes, politics is transacted within a "framework of ties and bonds" (1961:164).

Politics thus is not about aggregating relatively fixed preferences. It is about establishing relationships out of which preferences emerge and modify. I have emphasized narrow cognition because, even when people are purposive and socially minded, they are often short-sighted in what they identify with and take into account. As James Madison observed in *Federalist No. 10*, people are not very good at "taking into view indirect and remote considerations" (Madison, Hamilton, and Jay, 1937). Still, what may be called group provincialism is not a fixed condition. Under the right condition, groups can, as Crick says, be drawn "into one another" (1982:18). Identification can and should be enlarged (Muir, 1977; Burns, 1978). Clearly, however, there are strong forces at work to perpetuate group provincialism, and the American political economy as presently constituted does little to overcome that provincialism.

Summary

Assumptions we make about human nature shape our understanding of what political analysis is about. I have offered the following assumptions as a foundation for examining group politics and the problem of political change: (1) that individuals are moral agents, but that their capacity to act on social obligations is limited by narrow cognition and a *tendency* to identify with groups and purposes that are proximate in everyday life, (2) that, because of narrow cognition, the preferences of individuals are open-ended, not fixed; that they are shaped by concrete experiences, including institutional arrangements, (3) that preferences are open-ended means that power cannot be treated only as a process involving the aggregation of conflicting preferences; that the concept of power must include the process through which preferences are shaped, (4) that preferences can differ in scope as well as direction, and that the character of political change is influenced by how policy and political-economic arrangements affect the scope of preferences.

CONCLUSION

Legally, the individual citizen is the fundamental unit of democratic politics. In practice, groups are central. Since the existence of groups poses the problem of diverse wants and common rule, the issue is one of how that diversity will be treated in the act of governance. One response to the problem might be to say, Why worry? Fragmentation, it could be contended, is a healthy sign of freedom—the large number of single-interest groups assures lively debate. That position, however, represents a limited understanding of freedom. Hannah Arendt offers a larger understanding. She describes politics as an activity in which people are engaged in deliberating and acting together in order to alter what would otherwise be an expected course of events. For her, that is political freedom; it expands what can be done. Interest fragmentation, by contrast, decreases freedom by lessening the viable policy alternatives available to society. It is for this reason that I have discussed the ecology of preference formation and have suggested that narrow alternatives, especially those with distributional benefits, tend to thrive—perhaps even more so in implementation than in legislation (Shepsle and Weingast, 1981; Mazmanian and Sabatier, 1983).

Encouraged by narrow cognition, the tendency toward fragmentation is natural and therefore hard to overcome. However, as interdependence and complexity increase, the consequences of fragmentation have become more grave (Heclo, 1978). As Madison predicted, taking indirect and remote considerations into view rarely prevails. It is ironic that the Madisonian structure of government may be a contributor to the weakness of "indirect and remote considerations." To Madison, the constitutional task was one of constructing institutional arrangements that would prevent dominance by a single faction, particularly one with a popular base. Divided authority, he believed, would preserve representative government, encourage deliberation, and work against domination by a cohesive majority faction. Fragmentation of authority, Madison argued, would encourage coalition-building by refining and enlarging "the public views" of the members of a majority coalition. Contemporary practice is more nearly the opposite.

Once we see that preferences are neither matters of individual taste nor "interests" attached to particular positions, then we can see that politics is not about aggregating a given set of wants. In a very real sense, politics is about what set of preferences we should encourage. This means that the most profound political deliberations do not focus on whose policy preferences to adopt, but instead, as Arendt says, they concern the creation of a set of bonds and relationships within which to act (1961:164). We want to be able to look beyond our proximate situation to broader and longer-term considerations, even though the natural tendency is to concentrate on the immediate. Coming to terms with larger considerations, Arendt argues, increases our freedom. Proliferating single-interest organizations does not.

Let me say a parting word about a state- versus society-centered focus and why a political economy perspective is preferable to both. The state is not a separate universe, but is one of a set of interrelated institutions (Mitchell, 1991, Skocpol, 1985:20; Katzenstein, 1978). Group "bonds and relationships" and a capacity to take a larger view depend on a range of considerations. For example, rearranging the formal structure of authority matters little if political organization continues to be so heavily candidate-centered. An enlarged and refined view of public affairs is unlikely to gain much of a hearing so long as social science treats the political economy as a set of separated institutions responding to the atomized wants of private "customers." The corporate economy warrants special attention. Legally, the business corporation is a device for limiting liabilities, but that should not include shirking social responsibilities. Business is heavily involved in the act of governance, and many of its actions impose substantial public costs. Hence we need to devise ways, formal and informal, to draw corporate decisionmakers into broad coalitions of problem solvers.

The group basis of politics teaches us that each segment of society tends to be preoccupied with what is proximate. The challenge is how to overcome that tendency and thereby expand our freedom to act on the large problems that beset us. An integrated political economy perspective should facilitate this broader view of the group basis of American politics and its relation to the capacity to govern.

NOTES

I wish to thank the General Research Board of the University of Maryland for support in the writing of this chapter.

1. For a critique of this line of argument, offering the alternative concept of an issue network, see Heclo (1978). See also Berry (1989), Walker, 1991, and Baumgartner and Jones (1991).

2. On "ecology," see Long (1958), and Crenson (1971).

3. This case is based on Loomis and Cigler (1983:16–17).

4. I am indebted to Meredith Ramsay for this point. Significant works outside political science include those by Hunt (1990), Kohn (1990), and Tyler (1990). See also Dawes, van de Kraft, and Orbell (1990).

5. A contrasting conception of power may be found in Pitkin (1972), Isaac (1987), Clegg (1989), and Stone (1989).

PART IV

Linkage Processes

13

Politics as Persuasion

JANE J. MANSBRIDGE

Political ends can be achieved by three means: persuasion, threats, and force. Since World War II, however, political scientists who study Congress, interest groups, and various other institutions of government have focused mainly on threats and force, which I will group together under the rubric of "power." Persuasion—the appeal to reason and emotion to change others' opinions, including their conceptions of their interests—has been largely neglected.[1] This essay lays out the case for redressing that imbalance.

POWER AND PERSUASION
IN COLLECTIVE ACTION

One great purpose of politics is to solve collective action problems. In the last fifty years, the development of game theory has allowed political scientists to model and understand more clearly the reciprocal interactions in collective action. The "prisoner's dilemma" in particular codifies a problem of social cooperation to which political organization is a solution. In a prisoner's dilemma, or in other "collective action problems" with structures much like the prisoner's dilemma, actions that are in each individual's rational self-interest produce aggregated outcomes that are not in those individuals' interests. For example, when a good is such that once it is made available to one person it is available to all (e.g., national defense or a local park), it is in the narrow self-interest of each individual to "free ride" on others' contributions in producing the good. But if each follows this logic, the good will never be produced. A similar logic generates the "tragedy of the commons," in which it is in each individual's self-interest to set another cow on the commons, but if everyone does this, the commons will be overgrazed (Axelrod, 1984; G. Hardin, 1968; R. Hardin, 1982).

Early game-theoretic "solutions" to the prisoner's dilemma and other collective action problems involved the use of power. All concerned in the dilemma might unanimously agree to institute sufficient coercion to change individual payoffs in such a way that they themselves, as well as the other players, would then have sufficient incentive to "cooperate" in producing the collective good rather than to "defect" by making the choice otherwise dictated by self-interest. In the seventeenth century, Thomas Hobbes pointed out that any sovereign, however chosen, could produce the necessary coercion, so long as the sovereign had sufficient legitimacy to govern effectively. This logic produces the core argument for government as legitimate coercion, making the state the author of the civil and criminal penalties that change the payoffs in the dilemma.

Several other solutions to the prisoner's dilemma (collateral, selective incentives, tit for tat in repeated interactions, and withdrawal in voluntary repeated interactions) all rely on no more than narrow self-interest. But non-self-interested motivations also produce effective solutions to collective action problems. If I make your individual good my own through empathy, I will be less likely to defect when the consequence is lowering your payoff. If I make the collective good my own (e.g., "love of nation"), I will be more likely to forgo my larger individual benefit for that good. If I am committed to a principle that for one reason or another prescribes cooperation, I will be more likely to forgo defection for reasons of duty. Of the two generic forms of altruism, one—variously called "love," "empathy," "sympathy," and "we-feeling"—connotes an emotional attachment to another individual or collective through which the actor makes the other's good his or her own. The other—variously called "duty," "commitment," "principle," and "conscience"—connotes a rational commitment to a principle or set of principles.[2]

In experiments with American college students in the late 1980s, as many as 35 percent of the participants in a "social dilemma" (a several-person dilemma structured like a prisoner's dilemma) made the cooperative choice under conditions of single-play anonymity with $5 to $15 payoffs when the dilemma was constructed so that the noncooperative choice was in each individual's self-interest. Asked why they made this choice against their own interests, the students often said they did so because the cooperative choice was "right." When the group facing the dilemma was allowed to discuss the situation together for ten minutes, promising one another to cooperate, another 50 percent made the cooperative choice, bringing the total cooperating to 85 percent. When the experimental conditions were changed so that, having promised one another to cooperate, the members of a group ended up playing with people other than those they had promised, the percentage of cooperators returned to about 35 percent (Dawes et al., 1990). Conscience (or duty) and some sense of "we-feeling" (or love) both seem to have played an important role in increasing non-self-interested cooperation. By doing some violence to the ordinary meaning of these concepts, one could say that love and duty change the individual's payoff matrix by generating extra "rewards" in two forms of nonmaterial satisfaction.

Solving collective action problems through love and duty, as opposed to material sanctions, has certain costs. These motivations can be evoked only in certain situations. They are often fragile, and may be unraveled by observing consistently rewarded defection. They are also at times less susceptible to compromise and negotiation than the motivation to gain material benefit. On the other hand, solutions based on love and duty are also usually cheaper, require less monitoring, and are more adaptable than solutions based only on material sanctions. When participants in a system develop an emotional attachment or moral commitment to a cooperative goal, they will tend to develop whatever policies they think will promote that goal, adapting themselves to situational changes rather than requiring a fixed schedule of regulations and sanctions. In the many cases where great adaptability is needed, where effective monitoring is not possible, or where the cost of effective sanctions is too high, "public spirited" solutions, based on love and duty, are the only feasible solutions to collective action problems.

Most existing forms of social organization rely on mixtures of sanctions and some combination of love and duty. Research on regulation and compliance, to which we will return later, indicates that in many cases systems that produce the most cooperation stress public-spirited values in conjunction with a backup system of incrementally graded, relatively certain sanctions. In such systems, public-spirited values produce most of the cooperation, while the backup sanctions keep potential defectors from making suckers of the cooperators. Because of the relative efficiencies of public-spirited solutions, systems that use public-spirited motivations efficiently to produce mutual cooperation in collective action problems will, when all else is equal, produce more of the goods they desire both absolutely and in comparison to others than will systems that rely heavily or entirely on self-interested material incentives.

Political systems help solve collective action problems in three ways. First, the state acts as an important source of legitimate force and threats of sanction, changing individual payoffs so that potential defectors will be induced to cooperate. Second, the state acts as an important cognitive and emotional locus for the collective feelings that lead individuals to put "we" ahead of "I" in their preferences and their understanding of themselves. Finally, the state serves as an important arena in which representatives of the individuals involved in collective organization engage in mutual acts of power and persuasion about the deployment of legitimate violence, the legitimacy of sanctions and force, and the means, ends, and constitution of their collective organization.

Understanding the interaction of power and persuasion is crucial both for the normative task of legitimating democratic politics and for the empirical task of understanding those politics. When political philosophers focus solely on persuasion (e.g., Rawls, 1971; Walzer, 1983), they miss the critical role of legitimate power in producing cooperative collective action. When political scientists focus solely on power, they miss the critical role of persuasion in both producing and legitimating political outcomes. The following sections provide examples of how investigating the processes of persuasion—in Congress, in the system of interest representation, and in governmental regulation—helps illuminate the workings of each set of institutions.

CONGRESS

In the 1970s, a "rational choice" strand in the study of Congress purified and incorporated into formal models the earlier pluralist focus on power. Rational choice models made the general simplifying assumption that political actors act on narrow self-interest; studies of Congress assumed that legislators act as if they sought only reelection. The self-interest assumption helped generate formal models with some predictive and much heuristic use, showing, for example, how parties in a two-party system would be led to try to capture the median voter and how individual legislators would try to be the decisive members of a coalition. Power, in the form of threats of sanction aimed at individual self-interest, played a large role in these new models. Except in the form of access to information, persuasion played no role at all.

Responding to the focus on power within the rational choice approach, Martha Derthick and Paul Quirk (1985) designed their study of deregulation to demonstrate the effect of persuasion as well as power on legislative behavior. Throughout the 1970s and 1980s, the regulated industries and their unions were almost all opposed to deregulation. An analysis based solely on power would predict that when unions, which can give or withhold the votes of their members, and great corporations, which can give or withhold their contributions to legislators' electoral coffers, unite against a bill, and when only diffuse unorganized interests such as consumers favor it, the bill will fail. That was precisely what political scientists had predicted about deregulation. But deregulation did not fail. Derthick and Quirk argue that certain members of Congress made up their minds about deregulation not by deciding which side could reward them with the most campaign funds or votes, but by deciding which side had the best arguments about what would be best for consumers and the nation as a whole. Empirical studies showing that deregulated airlines did not stop serving small cities, for example, helped reduce opposition to deregulation. Academic experts also greatly affected the outcome of the deliberations. Legislators who were least exposed to power, in the form of immediate voter retribution, were most open to arguments favoring deregulation. So were representatives whose positions gave them an increased sense of responsibility for this particular policy area.

Deregulation was not an isolated case. Survey research showing that the elderly were no more vulnerable to crime than other parts of the population had a major effect in reducing Congressional attempts to protect the elderly against crime. After this survey, advocates for the elderly could no longer appeal to the injustice of their clients' greater vulnerability (Cook and Skogan, 1990). Along with new information that changes perceptions of justice and injustice, various other factors, such as efficiency and inefficiency, or appeals to collective conscience, patriotism, humanitarian impulses, and images of "the other" as enemy can also affect what policies citizens and their representatives prefer, and how they order their priorities. During the 1980s and into the early 1990s, a growing empirical literature documented the role of persuasion in altering legislative behavior (Bessette, 1982, 1993; Muir, 1982; Maass, 1983; Vogler and Waldman, 1985; Mansbridge, 1988, 1990c, 1992; Derthick and Quirk, 1985; Kelman, 1987; Quirk, 1988, 1989; Reich, 1988; Kingdon, 1993).

In practice, however, it can often be impossible to distinguish persuasion from power. "Ideas"—which include cognitive conceptions of how the world works as well as moral and emotional commitments—are often impossible to distinguish in practice from "interests" (Kingdon, 1993). Constituents and interest groups often elect legislators with many of the same ideas and interests as their own, and then need often make no further effort to affect the legislator's behavior, either through power or persuasion. If a legislator's ideals (e.g., a belief in the efficiency of free trade) and interests are congruent, as is often the case, even the legislator may not know which motive, in which proportions, is driving any given political action.

Legislators voting for a bill because they believe it is "in the public interest" may also vote this way in part because they would face informal sanctions for voting otherwise. They may want, for example, to keep the respect of others they value. To the degree that legislators pursue respect rather than just reelection, even academics can threaten them with informal sanctions, especially if, like the economists in the deregulation proceedings, they act with near unanimity. Few people can distinguish clearly between doing something they think is good because otherwise they will lose the respect of others (an external sanction) and doing it because otherwise they would think less of themselves (an internal sanction). These motivations are mixed inside us, along with material self-interest.

Much persuasion has nothing to do with "the public interest." Rather than threatening B, A may simply try to convince B that a given course of action is not, in fact, in B's self-interest, as B had previously believed. In doing so, A will usually be motivated by a belief that the course of action B will choose on reflection is in A's interest. That is, A will believe that A and B have common interests on the particular point on which A exercises persuasion. But neither may be concerned with the larger public good.

At the moment the profession of political science has no consensus on normative models of how power "ought" to work in democratic legislatures such as the U.S. Congress. Nor do we have a great deal of evidence on how power actually does work in such settings. Similarly, although we have some relatively unhelpful slogans about what constitutes good deliberation (for example, that it should be "rational," in a way that seems to exclude emotion), we have no good normative models of how persuasion ought to work in democratic legislatures, nor much empirical evidence on how it actually does work.

INTEREST REPRESENTATION

Among all the democratic institutions, it should be hardest to make the case for the effects of persuasion rather than power in what has often been described, using terms of pure power, as "the pressure system." Yet interest groups manifestly function not only to pressure but to persuade. Recognizing the persuasive functions of interest groups reveals more fully how interest groups actually work. Normatively, it suggests a simple guide for reform: Maximize the deliberative benefits; minimize the rent-seeking costs.

To take normative issues first, if democracy means one person/one vote, it cannot easily be reconciled with interest groups whose primary purpose is to make the preferences of some count more than those of others. The best argument for interest groups is that they produce important information that is not otherwise available. This justification recognizes the importance of persuasion as well as power in the policy process. Interest groups spend much of their time and energy generating information about particular policies so that both their own members and legislators can understand better how such policies will affect them and the rest of the country. Interest groups also create arenas for deliberation between elites from different interest groups and between the elites and rank and file of any one interest group. That deliberation can identify areas of common interest and clarify areas of conflict. The normative argument is that the resulting gains in information and understanding outweigh the costs in exacerbating inequality.

Much deliberation between and within interest groups involves "negotiation," a mix of power and persuasion. In negotiation, the parties involved maneuver for advantageous positions, just as they do in conflict, while also trying to understand what the other really wants, in order to devise the cheapest way of giving the other side as much satisfaction as possible. The quest for understanding requires asking, listening, decoding the other's language, putting oneself in the other's place, making suggestions that the other may not have thought of, and learning both from acceptance and refusal. Negotiations between and within interest groups use the understanding so gained to change one another's preferences. As deliberation helps each side to discover what it really wants, the parties acquire new preferences that better reflect their deeper needs or values, and even help develop new values.

Thinking of interest groups in terms of power alone certainly captures the primary goal of many actual interest groups, which are organized to act as "rent-seekers." Groups use the power they derive from their organization and funding to wrest from the public treasury, or from individual citizens via state power, benefits ("rent") for their officers, staff, and members.[3] In these instances the interest groups use only threats of sanction instead of persuasion. The rent-seeking model of interest group activity is a zero-sum model, in which whatever I get must be taken from you, rather than a productive model, in which our joint productivity generates extra gains. The politics of persuasion, in contrast, often produces possibilities for joint gain. The information and internal deliberation that interest groups provide informs others and themselves about how different policies will affect them and the country as a whole. The deliberation helps group members decide what they really want. That deliberation, both inside and outside the group, may even encourage moral and emotional commitments to cooperative collective action. A well-designed system of interest representation should produce as many such joint gains as possible, through deliberation, with as few rent-seeking costs.

When particular interests can gain control of a legislative area, they are in an excellent position to extract "rent," or nonproductive benefits, for themselves and their members. Reforms seek to counter rent-seeking in several ways, but primarily through legislative oversight. I will look here at two less frequently discussed methods: the cultivation of elite concern for the public interest, and the balancing of interests in various neo-corporatist arrangements.

In Europe, socialization for public service in the different national cultures and civil services has more or less met with success. In the United States, with a less aristocratic culture than Great Britain and a less Lutheran culture than Sweden, socialization to public service is haphazard, and greatly influenced by local cultures. Hugh Heclo (1978:87-124), for example, reports on what he believes to be the recent noticeable effect on United States national policy of "issue networks," or "shared-knowledge" groups concerned with some aspect of public policy. The members of these issue networks, who often disagree with one another on policy matters, usually affect one another through persuasion rather than power. They are often motivated more by intellectual or emotional commitment than by direct material interest. Although "public interest" groups play a large role in these issue networks, interest groups nominally concerned only with the material good of their own members are also represented. Self-selection or socialization in the issue networks sometimes leads the leaders of these interest groups to pursue goals larger than those of their members. In addition, those elites often find, through negotiation among representatives of competing groups, ways of advancing the material interests of their members that have fewer costs both for other groups and for the public (see Fisher and Ury, 1981 for the roles of principle and community good in negotiation).

In international relations, "epistemic communities" of technocrats interested in a given issue work much the same way; through mutual persuasion they evolve policies and personal commitments to policies perceived as in the good of the whole, often conceived in broader than national terms (Haas, 1989).

In European corporatist arrangements, elite representatives from different functional interests negotiate among themselves on aspects of public policies that affect those interests. Observers of those negotiations suggest that bringing the negotiations under the aegis of the state can activate the public spirit of interest group elites to create outcomes that benefit the public as well as satisfy the material interests of the represented groups (Cohen and Rogers, 1992). These elites, of course, often conceive of the public good in ways that benefit themselves and the groups they represent (what's good for General Motors is good for the country). Nevertheless, building in an explicit concern for the public interest, both formally and informally, probably gives considerations affecting the public at large somewhat greater weight in the outcome. Hard evidence on this point is scarce.

A second kind of reform limits inequalities in power in order to create more room for the effects of uncoerced persuasion. European neo-corporatist arrangements explicitly try to equalize power among, say, labor, management, and consumers, to balance power against power, with the hope of reducing the possibility that any group can use force or the threat of sanctions to cause the others to act. In the last two decades in the United States, administrative agencies in the executive branch have often been required, either by their own codes or by the courts, to admit representatives of conflicting interests into the deliberative process. The new requirements, which have transformed the way American administrative law treats interest representation (Stewart, 1975), seem "proto-corporatist" in their intent. They often specifically include traditionally less well-represented groups and they sometimes take account of the difficulty of organizing small, diffuse interests (see also Petracca, 1986; Meidinger, 1987).

Moving from the external deliberative functions of interest groups to their internal ones, interest groups give information to their members, help distill and order individual preferences, and even help change their members' values and their conceptions of their identities. Interest groups encourage their members to think about, talk about, and bring to the point of individual decision considerations on various sides of an issue. When an interest group has democratic internal processes (not the usual case), distilling and ordering can come about through "voice"—mutual persuasion and voting on policies or leadership. In a direct mail interest group, the process works primarily through "exit"—constituents joining or sending money to the organization that makes the most persuasive appeal. These internal processes of distilling and ordering make external negotiation and legislation more fruitful, as the interest group takes on the burden of letting the other parties know what its constituency, in its present state of consciousness, wants most.

Richard Freeman and James Medoff (1984) demonstrate that even American unions, hardly models of a developed deliberative ideal, provide a forum in which collective voice can instruct employers on workers' needs more efficiently than can worker exit, the traditional market mechanism. Quitting the job is often more costly for both worker and employer than collective voice would be. Moreover, the processes of voice, including mutual persuasion, can often produce more complete information and more creative solutions than can autonomous management decision-making. Concluding from their quantitative research that in the United States "unions are associated with greater efficiency in most settings" Freeman and Medoff attribute that result primarily to deliberative efficiencies associated with the processes of internal mutual persuasion.

The processes of mutual persuasion are not aptly described as "collecting information" (Freeman and Medoff, 1984:13, table 1-1), or even "distilling and ordering" preferences. Mutual persuasion is "dialogic" (Offe and Wiesenthal, 1980), and can draw on or create commitments to a common good. Mutual persuasion can lead a union membership, on hearing and discussing the plea for help of a sister union, to forgo its own benefits to join a common boycott, or lead the same membership to break a traditional solidarity by giving its present material interests precedence. Through mutual persuasion business leaders from sectors that would benefit from protection become convinced that free trade is best for the country, and leaders who benefit materially from free trade become convinced that their colleagues need protection (Bauer, Pool, and Dexter, 1972). Mutual persuasion within interest groups can help change their members' values and even their understanding of themselves (Streek and Schmitter, 1985).

A fully developed empirical model of interest group behavior would thus describe not only how interest groups use power but also how the processes of persuasion both between and within interest groups inform and change preferences, sometimes changing the participants' conceptions of their identities. Such a model would indicate how interest group elites influence one another, how (if at all) rank and file members influence one another within their groups, and how (if at all) the members and the elites who represent them in negotiations with other groups engage in mutual influence.[4]

GOVERNMENTAL REGULATION

Basing their recommendations on their studies of regulatory compliance in the nursing home, pharmaceutical, and mining industries, Ian Ayres and John Braithwaite (1992) argue that regulation is more effective the more material sanctions can be kept in the background and regulation transacted through "moral suasion." In their analysis, successful regulation requires being able to use a combination of big sanctions, a hierarchy of lesser sanctions, and persuasion addressed to public-spirited motives. The regulatory strategy must be mixed, because the motives of the regulated are mixed. A strategy based totally on moral suasion will be exploited when actors are motivated by material self-interest, but a strategy based mostly on material sanctions will undermine the good will of actors when they are motivated by a sense of responsibility. In Ayres and Braithwaite's experience, the corporate actors in these three industries are, along with being value maximizers, often concerned to do what is right, to be faithful to their identities as law-abiding citizens, and to sustain self-concepts of social responsibility. These motives provide the node of common interest between regulated and regulator on which persuasion can be exercised. Whenever possible, an efficient strategy stresses moral suasion, because "punishment is expensive; persuasion is cheap."

Ayres and Braithwaite's observations lead them to conclude that a regulatory policy based mostly on material sanctions fosters "an organized business subculture of resistance to regulation," and a game of "regulatory cat-and-mouse" in which firms defy the spirit of the law by exploiting loopholes and the state writes more specific rules to cover the loopholes. The result is often an incoherent accretion of rules, a "barren legalism concentrating on specific, simple, visible violations to the neglect of underlying systemic problems" and a system unable to adapt to new technologies and environments. They find more effective a tit-for-tat regulatory strategy that begins with cooperation, prompting and expecting a cooperative (public-interested) response, and punishes a noncooperative response with small sanctions, keeping a graded hierarchy of bigger sanctions in the wings. This structure puts moral suasion in the foreground, in order to avoid the well-documented phenomenon of extrinsic incentives driving out intrinsic ones (Deci, 1971, 1972; Deci et al., 1981). But it allows the regulators to punish defectors in order to keep the cooperators from being "suckered."

With a similar stress on mixed motivation, Margaret Levi (1988) characterizes as "quasi-voluntary compliance" the behavior of taxpayers in efficient systems where most taxpayers comply. Taxpayers seem to comply in a contingent fashion, when they perceive both that the collective objective for which they have tacitly agreed to be taxed is achieved (that is, that those who control the revenue from taxes will use it effectively for public ends) and that others also comply. Much of the desired compliance derives from persuasion addressed to non-self-interested motivation, but power is an essential condition for achieving the second goal, which assures those who contribute that they will not be suckers.

The criminal justice system may have a similar structure, in which most compliance derives from moral suasion, but is supported by a graded set of sanctions. In each of these cases it seems critical to develop an extensive system of moral incentives based on persuasion addressed to public-spirited motivation and to keep the exercise of power in the background, lest the more extrinsic punishments begin to dominate, driving out the more intrinsic rewards.

CONCLUSION:
POLITICS AS POWER AND PERSUASION

The observation of effective political systems and the game-theoretic analysis of the structure of mutual cooperation in collective action problems leads to the same conclusion. In most cases, coordinating mutual cooperation requires some combination of power and persuasion. The appropriate mixture of power and persuasion varies by the context, in most cases with more than one appropriate mixture for any given context. Modern political systems, designed to promote cooperation among strangers, will typically require both complex systems of power, using force and the threat of sanction, and equally complex systems of persuasion, using appeals to material self-interest, to emotional relations of love and hatred, and to principles such as equality, liberty, or racial superiority.

Normative analysis is thus integrally built into any understanding of politics. To judge a political system, we need to ask not only how power or persuasion is used but whether it is being used legitimately. To make such a judgment, political science needs both close empirical observation and a philosophical probing of ideals. Recognizing the role of normative judgment, political science alone among the social sciences has nourished its apparatus for investigating normative ideals as well as its apparatus for investigating empirical data.

In the philosophical arena, the most influential recent investigations have tended to see politics as concerned only with legitimate persuasion and not with legitimate power. In the empirical arena, the most influential modern investigations have until recently tended to see politics as concerned only with power and not with persuasion. For the future, an integrated investigation of both normative ideals and the empirical workings of government requires the two branches of research to widen their scope to include the study of both power and persuasion.

NOTES

Portions of this chapter were adapted from "A Deliberate Theory of Interest Representation" in *The Politics of Interests: Interest Groups Transformed*, edited by Mark P. Petracca (Westview, 1992).

1. I define "power" as A's preferences causing B to do something that B would otherwise not do, through A's use of force or threat of sanction. I define "persuasion" as A causing B to do something B would otherwise not do, through A's arguments aimed at furthering B's own goals, broadly defined. Such arguments appeal to reason, emotion, and to conceptions of self that may not exist in the consciousness of the persuaded before the appeal. In deriving these definitions I draw loosely from Dahl (1957) as revised by Nagel (1975), and Bachrach and Baratz (1963) as revised by Lukes (1974). The concept of persuasion has not received as much attention as the concept of power. (See Mansbridge, 1992, for the roles of both reason and emotion in persuasion.)

Ordinary language does not produce an airtight distinction between "power" and "persuasion." A broad conception of power, as A getting B to do something that B would not otherwise do through any means, includes persuasion. Moreover, in practice it is hard to distinguish between A threatening B with an external social sanction, which under my definition would count as "power," and A activating within B an internal sanction (e.g., B's own feeling of guilt), which under my definition would count as "persuasion." Although these concepts shade into one another in ordinary usage and in practice, normative political judgments and long-term predictions of behavior rest on the distinction between the two.

2. See Mansbridge, 1990c. Some social scientists interpret all motives as "self-interested." Indeed, tautologically, if an action were not in some sense in one's interest, one would not do it. This collapsing of distinctions, however, does more harm than good. Much analytic and moral reasoning requires a distinction between self-

and other-regarding actions. If we define all motives as self-interested, we must then distinguish between "selfish" self-interest and "unselfish" self-interest. Interpreting all behavior as "self-interested" without distinguishing between "selfish" and "unselfish" self-interest reduces the number of models of "unselfishness" in discourse and cognition. The problem is that because seeing unselfishness modeled by others tends to produce unselfish behavior in those who observe the model, reducing the number of models of unselfishness in discourse and cognition is itself likely to reduce the amount of unselfish behavior that would otherwise be inspired by these models.

3. The concept of "rent-seeking" is often used to discredit any departure from pure laissez-faire. This appellation is justified, in my view, only insofar as the departure from laissez-faire does not have a public purpose, such as producing justice, repairing past wrongs, or creating a community that reflects the larger national diversity. Because much rent-seeking behavior pretends to have a public purpose, citizens and policymakers must always ask both whether they think the purpose is a genuinely public one, that is, whether it might reasonably be thought to benefit the polity as a whole in reasonable proportion to its costs, and also whether the policy in question is likely to further that public purpose.

4. The literature on negotiators' relations with their constituencies (e.g., Wall, 1975; Klimoski and Breaugh, 1977) begins to model the actual and potential reciprocal relationships between members and the elites who represent them.

14

Beyond the Iconography of Order: Notes for a "New Institutionalism"

KAREN ORREN
STEPHEN SKOWRONEK

A leading student of interest group politics writes: "In the 1990s, we are all 'neo-institutionalists'" (McFarland, 1991:262). Indeed, the claim that "institutions matter" can be heard today in every corner of political science. Unfortunately, as the cutting edge of a critical departure in the study of politics, this claim leaves much to be desired.

In the first place, the assertion that "institutions matter" fails to distinguish clearly current disciplinary interests from more traditional ones. Political science blossomed in the late nineteenth century as a study of the institutions of government, as a "science of the state." The so-called "revolt against formalism," which gathered steam in the 1920s, broadened the scope of inquiry considerably, but scholars never really lost sight of institutions. It is hardly any wonder that some of the leading lights of behavioral political science have found their "rediscovery" amusing and the critical thrust of the "new institutionialism" wide of the mark (Almond, 1988; Easton, 1981; Binder, 1986). The attention showered on the informal processes of politics and the social bases of power by the behavioralists was not so much an alternative to a study of institutions as it was an exploration of their connections to the larger social and economic system. The renewed emphasis on institutions in political study may elaborate these larger relationships in important ways, but new institutionalists cannot afford to disregard them.

The confusion goes deeper than that, however. The claim that institutions matter not only falls short of being an effective critique of past concerns, it fails to distinguish among currently contending intellectual currents. "New institutionalism" is a label associated with many different scholarly agendas. Although its pursuit appears to be a concerted movement, having gained momentum in the wake of the discipline's recent disenchantment with behavioralism, its adherents vie over what is at the heart of political study: Should we turn to economics and formal modeling for our new institutionalism? To sociology and organization theory? To history and comparative case studies?[1] All are pursued under the same rubric. The proposition that there is such a thing as *a* new institutionalism bespeaks a false consensus on the most basic disciplinary concerns.

It is not our intention to build a consensus. We recognize that a variety of approaches is appropriate, and we welcome the debates that variety engenders. In this essay we seek to clarify the case for historically oriented study and indicate the challenge it poses to diverse treatments of institutions found in both political science and history. Of all the various permutations of the "new institutionalism," the historical may seem easiest to dismiss. If the general assertion that "institutions matter" falls flat as the pronouncement of a new scholarly agenda, the insistence that "history is important" does so even more. We believe, however, that the distinctive thrust of a historically oriented institutional study is more incisive than either of these statements would suggest. We argue that this work is new because it brings questions of timing and temporality in politics to the center of the analysis of how institutions matter. The approach is historical because the analysis seeks to recast the basic premise of temporal order that has been the centerpiece of the study of American institutions in all of its incarnations past and present.

We begin with a review of the various conceptions of order that have been fundamental to political analysis over the course of our discipline's history. The intent of this historical sketch is to trace these conceptions to the point where we can—as we should—supersede them. We then go on to suggest how the study of institutions can generate a better, more penetrating conception of the relationship between order and time, the overall effect of which is to provide the foundation for an institutionalism genuinely worthy of the appellation "new."

POLITICAL SCIENCE AND INSTITUTIONAL ORDER

Political scientists have always agreed far more than they have disagreed about how institutions matter. Institutions have been approached variously as normative entelechies, as system balancers, and as game forms. But in each, institutions are seen as the pillars of order in politics, as the structures that lend the polity its integrity, facilitate its routine operation, and produce continuity in the face of potentially destabilizing forces. Institutional politics is "politics as usual," "normal politics," or, a politics "in equilibrium."

In the field of American politics (with which we will be primarily concerned in this essay) the study of institutions has advanced through successive reformulations that consider how this ordering function operates. Each formulation has generated a different and more sophisticated explanation concerning how institutions hold together a far-flung, loosely knit polity. But because the fundamental premise about what institutions do has remained pretty much the same, what political scientists have produced is an increasingly elaborate iconography of order. Over the years study of institutions by political scientists has yielded a succession of guiding images or "models"—the Constitution, the political system, the rational actor—from which the principles of order are deduced. The rationale of each successive "institutionalism" is that it has penetrated more deeply into the fundamentals of political order than the one before.

The "old institutionalism," which dominated the discipline's initial half-century (approximately between 1880 and 1930), found the pillars of order principally in the formal arrangements of the Constitution. As the United States Constitution provided the framework for political life, so it provided the framework for political study. In this view the formal constitutional arrangements were fundamental not only because they were, historically, foundational but because they were seen as the concrete expression of the political culture's most basic value commitments. Once its norms were deduced, the Constitution became a standard for critical inquiry.

Many practitioners of the old formalism, for example, John W. Burgess, W. W. Willoughby, and Edward Corwin, were specialists in public law, and their work elucidated the immutable principles of American constitutionalism that had guided the polity's evolution. At the climax of Corwin's study of the presidency (1940), for instance, we find a stunning indictment of Franklin Roosevelt for trampling on the separation of powers and threatening all that the constitutional system had theretofore guaranteed.[2] But formalism was not inherently antithetical to reform. On the contrary, in the early days of the discipline, reform was an important impetus to the study of politics. In the field of public administration, for example, political scientists like Woodrow Wilson and Frank Goodnow sought to help the operatives of the constitutional order accommodate to changing conditions while preserving distinctive constitutional ideals. They examined European models of "what to do" to figure out an American "how to do it" (Wilson, 1885). Alternatively, political science could be used to expose discrepancies between the constitutional formalities and real-life practice. In Wilson's scorching study of Congress, the formalities themselves became the driving wedge of a reform critique (Wilson, 1885).

The behavioral revolution of the 1950s and 1960s radically reoriented the study of politics and, with it, the study of institutions. The "soul stuff" of the old formalism about which Arthur Bentley had complained as early as 1908 gave way to more rigorous empirical investigation of how American government actually worked, addressing such issues as why, in fact, the American system was one of the few that did work during the 1930s and 1940s. If the old presumptions about how it should work did not fit the facts, the naiveté of these presumptions would have to be exposed and replaced with a more realistic account of current operations. Under this scrutiny, boundaries between government and politics, and between state and society, quickly broke down. Government became a "process," its institutions part of the larger political "system," and public elites just another set of "interests" with behavior of their own. By the time David Easton published his definitive work, *A Systems Analysis of Political Life* (1965), the new icons of order—system and equilibrium—had fully eclipsed the old images of state and constitution.

The pillars of order in the behavioralized political system were the conditions that stabilized the process. These were at once more abstract and more context-specific than the concrete and fixed institutions of government. They were arrangements within a set time frame: "rules of the game," observed and enforced by elites in and out of government; "conditions of polyarchy," including the overlapping memberships in voluntary organizations that served as balance wheels of otherwise freewheeling sociopolitical action. More fluid than the older constitutional forms, these institutions were also understood to be less dependable. The reforming impulse of the formalists was replaced by a recognition of the system's essential precariousness. It was an anxious David Truman, for example, who in the late 1950s observed the failure of elites to enforce the rules of the game by silencing Joseph McCarthy (Truman, 1951).

The behavioralists were by no means antagonistic to institutional or historical analysis. Truman's *The Governmental Process* (1951) located government institutions within the larger system of political action, and he analyzed the dynamics of system change through the organization and impact of social interests across American history. Richard Neustadt's (1960) study of the presidency queried how "mid-century" incumbents could operate effectively in a political or institutional system radically altered by the New Deal and World War II. Observe that the behavioralists' analysis of institutions—of both institutional order and change—was essentially homeostatic; that is, disruptions were exogenous to the system and were resolved into new and stable equilibria. Thus, in Truman's history, labor-management relations were disturbed periodically by changes in technology, and equilibrium was restored through new forms of association. Neustadt defined "politics as usual" in terms of a historically bounded governing environment, "mid-century," in which presidents had to act; incumbents were endogenous, working within this system rather than upon it; change came from outside (Neustadt, 1960).

The third and current phase of the study of order is the new institutionalism of rational choice. Attention to institutions entered rational choice theory as a resolution of a theoretical dilemma. Order, conceived here as equilibrium, is the central premise of all rational choice theorizing. The enterprise turns on the explication of historically abstracted and analytically formal covering laws that predict stability in the resolution of issues collectively contested by individuals who act on their own preferences. The problem, as rational choice theorists have been showing for years, is that such equilibria are inherently elusive. "Politics is the dismal science," William Riker has declared in the phrase coined for economics, "because there are no stable equilibria to predict." This instability might have provided an alternative premise for the study of politics, adjusting the conception of science accordingly. But rational choice theorists have instead turned to institutions to sustain the initial program of explaining law-governed regularities, and now they work backwards retrospectively, from decisions made to the underlying conditions of choice. "The outcome of the search for equilibria of tastes," Riker concludes, "is the discovery that, failing such equilibria, there must be some institutional element in the regularities observed" (Riker, 1982c:19).

The "positive theory of institutions" (PTI) has built on economists' postulates about the difficulties individuals have making collective choices, adding to them an understanding of "how institutional structure and procedure combine with agent preferences to determine equilibria" (Shepsle, 1989:145). Institutions solve problems of collective action by altering the strategic context in which individuals calculate their self-interest. When everyone agrees to follow a set of rules and to act under institutionally prescribed conditions, equilibrium may be induced in a way that is impossible without this structure. Note that the introduction of concrete institutions historicizes the rules of political action and therefore also historicizes the covering laws of the theory that can be derived from them. At present, however, the rational choice program is less concerned with the question of institutional origins than with determining how (and how well) a given set of institutional arrangements will perform by applying relatively timeless covering laws to particular situations. In "robust" institutions like the United States Congress, internal structures and procedures are seen to become incorporated into the preferences and strategic behaviors of those who act within them.

The point to underscore in this brief history of the discipline's conceptions of order is the essential complementarity of rational choice or PTI with the older forms of institutional analysis it intends to supersede. Kenneth Shepsle describes PTI's contributions to political science in precisely these terms, as an effort to reclaim and deepen the essential insights of both the old formalism and behavioralism. "From the philosophical, it has rescued a concern with [formal] institutions as the 'glue' that holds otherwise atomistic and self-interested individuals together in organized society. From the behavioral, it has taken a concern with empirical regularities, both as constraints on theory and as matters to be explained" (Shepsle, 1989:145). The metaphor for institutions as the "glue" of politics, holding various political actors together and making them cohere, is an apt summary of the historical continuities of institutional study in all of its phases. What the formal theorists have done, Shepsle claims, is to take "idiosyncratic," "time-bound," "descriptive minutiae" derived from the empirical study of how institutions actually work and translate them into the "specific details of a game form" (Shepsle, 1989:135). As this formulation itself suggests, there is really very little at issue in the translation proposed. Received presumptions about what institutions do in politics are merely transposed to a higher level of theoretical abstraction. The object of studying institutions is still, as before, to figure out the regularities, to make sense of institutional politics as a more or less stable game in play. The behavioralists took the rules of the game out of formal institutional arrangements; the formal theorists put them back in, showing how institutional rules, devised by individuals to better satisfy their goals, reproduce order. The result is not only a new institutionalism that formalizes the strategic behavior of individuals, it is also a "new behavioralism" in which self-interested individuals are led by institutional arrangements toward "structure-induced equilibria."

ORDER AND CHANGE

The persistence with which institutional study in political science has devoted itself to unveiling the secrets of order is yet to be appreciated for its implications. Most important, this understanding of institutions lies at the heart of otherwise very different treatments of political change offered by political scientists and historians alike. In each disciplinary phase described above, institutional politics appears as "normal," as politics as usual, explicitly or implicitly opposed to an extraordinary politics, in which equilibria are upset, norms break down, and new institutions are generated. If the association of institutions with "order" has been all but instinctive in the study of American politics, so too is the understanding of political change as a transition between institutionalized orders, and of transition periods themselves as resolving disorder through new institutional settlements.

Consider in this regard a recent award-winning history by Martin Sklar (1988), *The Corporate Reconstruction of American Capitalism*. Sklar's description of the systemic disruptions produced by the rise of corporate capitalism at the turn of the twentieth century, and of the complex of social, economic, political, and cultural factors accommodated in the readjustment, is a quantum leap beyond prior understandings of the institutional changes negotiated in the Progressive Era. For our purposes, however, Sklar's account is revealing for its familiar conception of institutions as evoked at the story's climax. Corporate consolidation prompts an intense, systemwide search for order; the search centers on the construction of new institutions and institutional relationships; and finally, a new institution (the Federal Trade Commission) is created, which redefines the rules for all the players.

> In restoring the common law construction of the Sherman Act, in its Rule of Reason decisions of 1911, the Supreme Court laid the juridical basis of what may be called the corporate liberal solution of the trust question, that is, of a non-statist accommodation of the law to the corporate reorganization of capitalism. … It was a solution capped by the legislation of 1914. Historians have long puzzled over the suddenness with which the trust question thereafter receded from the center of national politics, if not disappearing altogether. Some have thought that the American people grew tired of the issue or that the legislation of 1914 lulled them into complacency. With the Rule of Reason decisions of 1911 and the legislation of 1914, however, the American people (or the major American political forces) had not become tired with, or complacent about the issue; they had settled it. It was a settlement, that is, sufficiently satisfactory to the major concerns and interests among them, however unsatisfactory it may have been to the concerns and interests of historians. (Sklar, 1989:173)

Setting aside the uncomfortable history just beyond Sklar's periodization of trust regulation—the shattering of the 1914 settlement during World War I and the persistent turmoil over antitrust legislation until after World War II (Sanders, 1986)—Sklar's story of the establishment of the Federal Trade Commission (FTC) as the "solution" or "settlement" to a problem that produced decades of systemic dislocation, conforms to the successive versions of how institutions "matter" as told by political scientists. The FTC established a new game—a new set of rules—that could compromise the interests of politically significant actors and restore order.

Indeed, the grandest of all expositions of order are the overarching broad syntheses of American political history, the mutual efforts of political scientists and historians to periodize institutional order and political change in America at the macro level. For each stage in political science's study of institutions there is a corresponding historiographic synthesis. Corresponding to the "old" institutionalism in political science was a "presidential synthesis" in American historiography. This presidential synthesis took the constitutional frame itself as a periodizing scheme for politics and organized the study of American history around constitutionally mandated presidential elections (Cochran, 1948). Political history *was* presidential history, and presidential history was the story of individual incumbents, who tested themselves at the bar of the system of checks and balances.

Rejecting the excessive formality of the presidential scheme, a later generation of behaviorally oriented political scientists and historians joined in elaborating the "realignment synthesis," where periods of politics as usual are more clearly distinguished from moments of significant change. Here we find five or six distinct political regimes, or "party systems," defined by their contending coalitions vying for power and by the institutions that keep their policy agendas at the forefront of national attention (McCormick, 1982). Once established, the peculiarities of the American constitutional system make these orders difficult to dislodge; they persist until pent-up frustration is mobilized, and in a "critical election" (or a more extended "realigning period") the old regime is displaced and a new one takes shape.

Efforts to supersede the realignment synthesis, which are based on finding too much variance among transitional episodes and argue the irrelevance of electorally driven change in a bureaucratized polity, have centered on an "organizational synthesis." The organizational synthesis is less attuned to coalitional structures and policy agendas than to the characteristic institutional modalities that integrate state and society over extended periods of time (Galambos, 1970, 1983; McCormick, 1979; Balogh, 1991). While the realignment theorists claim the Civil War era and the New Deal as major period breaks, the organizational theorists collapse the first into a long "party period" beginning in the 1820s and the second into a "bureaucratic period" beginning near the turn of the twentieth century. Whereas realignment historians, like behaviorists, emphasize the role of the voters in catalyzing political-institutional change, organizational historians, like formal theorists, see the motor force of politics in elite managers and institution-builders, public and private.

We conclude this review with a final complementarity—found between political historians, who synthesize a "seamless flow of events" around one or another ordering principle, and formal theorists, who translate "time-bound" "descriptive minutiae" into "a game form." With history ordered by historians, formal theorists have a gold mine of material with which to elaborate the games people play. These explorations have centered in earnest on congressional politics where, for example, Barry Weingast has applied rational choice analysis to the Congress of the 1850s to explain the disintegration of the second party system and the rise of the

Republican coalition (Weingast, 1991b); John Hansen has done so with the Congress of the 1920s to explain the decline of partisan agricultural politics in favor of bureaucratic forms of influence (Hansen, 1987); and Morris Fiorina has used rational choice to explain Congress' repeated choice of regulatory forms (Fiorina, 1982:35, 1986:48).

Another historical application of rational choice is offered by Terry Moe (1987). Moe's critique is in many ways similar to our own. He criticizes PTI for having been too quick to identify Congress as the "keystone" of the system, too narrow in its designation of other institutions as "exogenous," and, ultimately, too intent on a timeless display of the "comparative statics" of institutional politics. In his view, PTI's potential power lies in its capacity to make the entire constitutional system "endogenous" and to model rule formation, equilibrium adjustments, and institutional breakdown systemwide. To this end, he outlines the politics of the National Labor Relations Board (NLRB), placing the Congress, the president, business, labor, and bureaucracy on an equal theoretical footing. He then periodizes the history of the agency in three stages: (1) the 1930s and 1940s, an unstable, conflict-ridden phase of rule formation, (2) the 1950s and 1960s, a phase of normal politics in which each interest subordinates its particular pursuits to the enforcement of agreed-upon rules, and (3) the 1970s and 1980s, a phase of institutional breakdown when "the stars line up" in favor of one contending interest (business) with the rules abandoned at the expense of another (labor).

Moe's critique of PTI pushes the exercise of modeling beyond "comparative statics" toward whole-system dynamics, and his sequence of creation, stability, and disruption comes tantalizingly close to being an explicit exploration of the institutional construction of temporality in politics. But upon inspection, his depiction of the stable system established under the auspices of the NLRB mirrors the post–New Deal order or what others have called the "fifth party system." At his most ambitious, Moe challenges rational choice theorists to show how the pieces fit together into a coherent whole. At the farthest reaches of his search for underlying principles of change he offers an interpolation—the distinction between a constitutional system of separate powers and a parliamentary system (Moe, 1990). When all is said and done, Moe's institutional analysis brings us back to the same old insights into system processes and the institutional forms of political stability.

Moe wants to challenge the boundary between formal theory and the system's view of order. We want to challenge the boundary between order and time. According to Moe, what stands in the way of formal theorists better explaining what the historians have richly described are the technical problems involved in modeling the entire institutional system. We hold that technical mastery will not substitute for a fundamental rethink-

ing of the relationship between institutions and history posited by the notion of a system itself. Fascination with how the pieces fit into a coherent
whole has reached a point of diminishing returns. New approaches to institutional study do not write history afresh but merely translate received
understandings of order and time into a new terminology. If the aim is to
learn something more about what institutions do in and to politics, the
discussion must proceed beyond both the homeostatics of behavioralism
and the comparative statics of positive theory. A different view of the subject will get us beyond descriptions of the ways the stars line up, and turn
inquiry to the movement of the stars themselves.

A NEW INSTITUTIONALISM

The assumption that institutions are systemically ordering mechanisms
underlies a powerful boast to disciplinary authority. Those who search for
master programs of order in time, or regularity over time, claim to be doing science; others are said to be doing something less. The leading propo-
nent of the realignment synthesis has suggested that political science will
either choose among various ordering constructs or be left to "assert with
full radicalness that everything flows, everything is change, or in short
that history is just one damn thing after another" (Burnham, 1986:265).
Spokesmen for rational choice theory urge us to move beyond "time-
bound descriptive minutiae" toward the explanation of transhistorical
regularities, arguing that those who "continue to assert that it all depends
on some critical incident or personality" will have to answer when others
"continue to ask what political science has to say" (Fiorina, 1982:35).

We reject these alternatives and argue that the search for master programs of order and regularity has obscured a good deal of what is characteristic about institutions in politics and what they have to teach us about
political change. The choice between analysis that will systematically ex-
aggerate the significance of order in politics and no analysis at all is, we
believe, as unnecessary as it is unacceptable. Ours is a genuinely "new"
institutionalism precisely because it cultivates analytic ground between
the seamless flow of events and period synthesis, and between time-
bound descriptive minutiae and purportedly timeless covering laws.

This reorientation proceeds on the observation that at any given time,
institutions, both individually and collectively, juxtapose different logics
of political order, each with their own temporal underpinnings. Separate
institutions and institutional arrangements, operating according to distinctive ordering principles, structure the passage of time—the sequences
and cycles, the changes and lulls—at varying rates. In this sense, the ordering propensities of institutions are about so many points of access to a
politics that is essentially open-ended and inherently unsettled. As institu-

tions congeal time, so to speak, within their spheres, they decrease the probability that politics will coalesce into neatly ordered periods, if only because the institutions that constitute the polity at that time will abrade against each other and, in the process, drive further change.

Institutional analysis harbors a simple but radical alternative to the overriding preoccupation with political order in periods: Discard it, and focus instead on the incongruities that political institutions routinely produce. Against the background of institutional frictions that drive and shape political change, pictures of ordered space in bounded time fade away, and with them the boundary that has separated order from change. What is revealed is neither chaos nor a seamless flow of events, but rather the institutional construction of temporality that occurs as one institutional ordering impinges on another (Elchardus, 1982).

The single presumption abandoned is that institutions are synchronized in their operations or synthetic in their effects; the more basic idea, that institutions structure change in time, is retained. But this strategy reverses the direction of analysis, which now moves no longer from history to order, but from orders (plural) back to history. The historical study of institutions remains no less dedicated than its predecessors to finding empirical patterns and structures and to formulating concepts with which to explore them. It is quite open to building upon the historical work of others in this respect, however, not at the expense of simplifying the temporality of institutional politics. A concern for the institutional construction of change in time makes our approach less random than the "garbage-can" models of James March and others, for it argues that the sequences and conjunctures can be understood in terms of how change along one time line affects order along the others (Cohen, March, and Olsen, 1972; Kingdon, 1984). It proposes that political scientists investigate, head on, the contingent temporal alignments and simultaneous movement of relatively independent institutional orderings that riddle political action.

Research of scholars engaged in the historical study of politics has already been moving in this direction, and it may be drawn on briefly for examples of what this perspective comprises. That political institutions, both singly and in their interactions, characteristically manifest ordering patterns that are conflicting and contradictory, is amply borne out in the recent work, for example, on Jacksonian America. In the area of institutional procedures, state judiciaries have been shown to have regulated commerce through the application of rules out of phase with the practices of a burgeoning industrial capitalism (Miller, 1971; Horowitz, 1992). Looking at structures, scholars have described the conflict between the articulation of a decentralized federalism and the increasing nationalism of the economy, (Scheiber, 1975:57; Dunlavy, 1991:1) and they have noted the hierarchical ordering of personal relations in the family in tandem with the flourishing of voluntary organization elsewhere in civil society (Baker, 1984:85). Insofar as institutions embody culture, the reigning perspective of "the liberal tradition" has been seen to incorporate several meanings, each with its own implications for political action, that explain the pattern of northern political coalitions on the subject of slavery (Greenstone, 1986). In contrast, divergent patterns of government among southern states have been shown to have promoted competing ideologies of slaveholding (Ellis, 1991b; Norton, 1986).

For other periods, research demonstrates similar themes of dissonance, asymmetry, incongruity. Study of the "New Deal order" has identified divergent capacities among administrative agencies within the same electoral regime—the success of the Agricultural Adjustment Act and the failure of the National Recovery Administration tied respectively to distinctive trajectories of reform in agriculture and industrial relations (Skocpol and Feingold, 1982). Institutions have been shown to collide along opportunity structures, meaning the pattern by which the operations of one institution interfere with the achievement of the goals of another. Thus, nineteenth-century workers, organized primarily around industrial issues, were impeded in their political efficacy by a party system organized primarily around regional and ethnic issues (Oestreicher, 1989). Furthermore, contrasting worker ideologies were differently obstructed by separate constitutional structures (Hattam, 1990). Other asynchronic elements have been identified, for instance, between allegedly formative ideas and their tardy implementation (if ever) within institutions. One study has found that the mutual outlook and career exchanges between government administrators and professionals in private life, often seen as fueling the growth of American bureaucracy throughout the twentieth century, did not occur on any significant scale outside the field of agriculture until World War II (Balough, 1991).

None of these incongruities is especially startling; our claim is that what is in plain view, analytically speaking, has not yet been appreciated for its theoretical significance. These incongruities are not based on a distinction between the normal and extraordinary, or between the stable and the transformative; it is their routine status that recommends incongruities as the central concern of a new analysis of how institutions "matter." Are we saying the stars never line up right, institutionally speaking, for truly extraordinary changes? We are not. But more often than not, we expect to find that continuities along one dimension of order and time will be folded into, and formative of, the extraordinary changes we are observing along another. The task is to sort out the elements, attend to their temporal alignments, and explain the institutional dynamics that push and pull the stars into their various configurations.

That such asymmetries, layerings, and intersections are characteristic of politics has been remarked upon by contemporary theorists who are concerned, as we are, with the reformulation of questions about time (or "time-space") in social analysis. In discussing the "only teleology involved in social systems," Anthony Giddens says: "Such teleology [comprised within the conduct of social actors] always operates within bounded conditions of the rationalization of action. All social reproduction occurs in the context of 'mixes' of intended and unintended consequences of action; every feature of whatever continuity a society has over time derives from such 'mixes,' against the backdrop of bounded conditions of rationalization of conduct" (Giddens, 1979:112). Elsewhere Giddens criticizes both Marxist and Weberian theories of class domination in an approach to institutional analysis "generically," institutions being constituted and reconstituted in the "tie between the durée of the passing moment and the longue durée of deeply sedimented time-space relations":

the totality/moment relation is compatible with a variety of different 'layers' … of relations of autonomy and dependence between collectivities. The significance of such a stress is that it enables us to avoid difficulties that have always been associated with functionalist views of the whole, or more broadly, those views in which the whole is a "present" combination of parts. Such approaches have only been able to deal with the participation of the part in the whole by assuming that the one share certain of the features of the other: that there is an homology between them. (Giddens, 1979:110)

ELEMENTS OF A NEW INSTITUTIONALISM

Why should these contrasts and incongruities appear? The assertion that institutions are characterized by conflicts and intersections of rules and that these are frequently rooted in history, is still a good way from explaining specifically how "mixes" occur and what their substance is in any particular institutional case. To elucidate those processes is the major task of a historically oriented reseach agenda for political science. Still, it is possible to tentatively identify certain intrinsic features of political institutions that account for their impinging, interactive, and contingent character.

Let us add to the standard definition of institutions as rules ("congealed tastes" and so forth persisting through time) the fact that political institutions have been created or instituted, at disparate points in the past. It is ironic that the neglect of this nonsimultaneity of institutional origins is most evident in political studies that would seem to be directly concerned with historical events or dependent on historical propositions. The field of public law, the most systematically historical subfield in the discipline, devotes little attention to continuities with institutional forms imported from England. Reconstructions of American political order as diverse as Robert Dahl's *A Preface to Democratic Theory* (1956), Louis Hartz's *The Liberal Tradition in America* (1955), and Samuel Huntington's *American Politics: The Promise of Disharmony* (1981), rest on the premise, though not the demonstration, of the absence of a feudal past. The assumption of historical synchronicity is pervasive, evident in such notions as "market society," "industrialism," and "the party period."

The nonsimultaneity of institutional origins may be illustrated in the case of research involving disparities so structured that they lasted a century and more. A first example comes out of the historiological debates over whether American institutions in the eighteenth and nineteenth centuries may be best understood in their spirit and organization as "republican" or "liberal." One recent analysis argues that the liberal and voluntary activities, mainly conducted by men, in economic and political institutions, was made possible by the hierarchical and republican strictures imposed in the family and the military, and on women and boys (Kann, 1990). In a related vein, American women, legally cut off from the democratic political institutions of white men, have been shown to have strategically extended their "separate sphere" to welfare state protection for mothers and their children, at a time when identical protections were denied men precisely through the limitations of the electoral system (Skocpol and Ritter, 1991). Or in another example of nonsimultaneity, a common perspective on the relations of government and the economy has been the concurrent development of democratic political institutions and the growth and intensification of capitalism. Study of the labor sector in the nineteenth century, however, reveals that it was governed by the judiciary according to the common law of a predemocratic and precapitalist age, based on prescriptive rather than voluntary principles, enforced as nonpolitical, and immune from legislative change (Orren, 1991).

Republicanism, family organization, judicial regulation—each has origins older than liberalism, party organization, and legislative regulation; none of these distinctions would be captured within a "synthesis" view. Since these examples refer to the interfaces among institutions, let us round out this point by observing discontinuities in a single institution, the American presidency, which has, in fact, been the focal point of several such syntheses. We have already referred to the periodization of political history around successive presidents' progress through the avenues and potholes of the Constitution, and this synthesis has already been challenged by others. Another type of synthesis, also associated with the "search for order," emphasizes the organization of politics by parties in the nineteenth century and by bureaucracies in the twentieth; still another is based on electoral realignments, with different party systems structuring presidential action. Each of these perspectives is itself a reflection of different origins and purposes built into the office: the first derived from the historical experience of kingship; the second, a response to the unruliness of Congress (in its party manifestations) and the unruliness of markets (in its bureaucratic phase); the third focuses on the changing political fragments, participation, and "tastes" in a democratic electorate. In the approach proposed here, these "syntheses" are most useful neither as alternative schemes of analysis nor as descriptions of the president's disparate "roles," but rather in terms of how these contrasting rules intersect and thereby structure the leadership dilemma of any particular administration. As with the other examples mentioned, they signal that segmented lines of development must be superimposed to bring the political moment into view. Consider the following mixes: Abraham Lincoln fought a Civil War and realized a "Second American Revolution" without changing the patronage-based, partisan organization of governmental operations; Theodore Roosevelt imposed new bureaucratic forms and displaced much of the old partisan mode of governmental operations, but he did so to preserve "politics as usual" vis-à-vis the basic governing commitments of the established Republican coalition; Franklin Roosevelt, like Lincoln, made extraordinary changes in the nation's basic commitments of ideology and interest, but he did so by invoking bureaucratic formulas for governing that had been made familiar by Theodore Roosevelt, Woodrow Wilson, and Herbert Hoover. Once we disaggregate the different ordering principles and sort through the different time lines of change, we can analyze each leadership experience along its several dimensions and by comparing them, show how the political impact of institutional action is reshaped at each unique conjuncture (Skowronek, 1986).

A second feature we see as fundamental is that *political institutions control (or attempt to control) the behavior of persons or institutions other than themselves.* Within political institutions there are, clearly, rules designed to control behavior of operatives and participants; characteristically, however, political institutions reach outward. It is the fact that institutional rules are intended to control outsiders that distinguishes political from purely social institutions, whose rules are characteristically self-referential. This is not to say that social institutions may never have political aspects or impacts or be usefully thought of as political institutions. The point is, rather, that this quality of "otherness" in the activity of institutions is what lends them political signficance.

The other-directedness of political institutions is reflected in the concepts used in all eras to describe them—authority, sovereignty, representation, legitimacy, public opinion, delegation. It is also suggested in the distinctions we draw between institutions of rule and the subject population—democracy, monarchy, polyarchy. The institution of American federalism, the distribution of powers between national and state government, is of more than descriptive interest only as it organizes the governance of various social activities outside itself. Thus, for example, it raises the abiding historical question of federalism's effects on an increasingly centralized system of commerce. The common law is interesting politically because it governed social behavior outside the institution of the judiciary. The interface of institutions with outsiders is so characteristic that any set of examples risks trivialization. Its importance is pervasive, engaging the diverse objectives and methods of operation entailed in various "mixes," and going far towards explaining persistence and change of political institutions as well as the behavior of those who act within them.

There may seem to be a paradox here, in that the concept of "institutionalization" is associated with the differentiation of roles within an organization rather than those outside it, and with the development of internal specializations and procedures. In our perspective, it is the interaction with other institutions that will be seen to drive the institutionalization process. This proposition would find support, for example, in the history of the U.S. Congress, where, quite apart from housekeeping and career benefits for insiders, such changes have historically been connected to relations with other constitutional branches and with the efficacy of the policymaking function, including its perception by the electorate. Once we discover the independent persistence of roles and norms within the boundaries of a single institution, the work of analysis has just begun; the political significance of their "relative autonomy" is not in its description but in its interaction with other persistent patterns.

This brings us to a third feature of political institutions that undermines systems perspectives and confronts the analyst with contingent mixes. *Institutions are purposive or intentional.* They are purposive in that the rules that compose them are constructed and reconstructed with reference to specific goals, thereby distinguishing the rules of political institutions from the more spontaneous regularities associated with political culture. Purposes may change or be entirely subverted; but the fact that rules are aimed at the achievement of particular ends evokes cued responses from within the institution and outside, and sets up the processes of monitoring and strategic readjustment of rules characteristic of institutional activity. Purposes are also the basis upon which actors within institutions may be required to explain their actions and establish their legitimacy. Notice that the question of legitimacy, again, derives from the environment, the "otherness" within which any institution operates and by which it may be called to account.

Insofar as they are operated by individual actors, institutions are also intentional in the further sense that they partake of the actors' personal motives and ambitions. These may be more or less coincidental with the purposes structured into the institution's rules upon its design. Institutions vary in the discretion they allow those who take up positions within them, and in how permeated decisions are by outside influences. It is here that the question of "structure" is important, for a crucial element of political-institutional analysis concerns the extent to which an institution is "structured" or "voluntary" with respect to actors' behavior. This question will be seen to be separate from whether the institution is "robust," in the sense of its being resilient. The U.S. Congress is more structured here than the presidency, and both of these are less structured than the federal court system, whereas all have proven themselves equally "robust." The regulatory system in the 1970s was highly structured, though not, as it turned out, "robust."

The notion of purposes includes connections immediately engaged by goal-directed actions but which are outside of actors' perceptions, secreted, so to speak, within the rules and contingencies entailed in any set of institutional purposes (Ferejohn, 1991). Consider in this regard two models of presidential leadership: "responsible party leadership" implicit in the notion of a party system and independent statesmanship implicit in the oath to "faithfully execute the office of President of the United States." Andrew Jackson built a new party and transformed the powers of the presidency by directing his energies against the political regime he came to power to displace. James Polk fractured the party of Jackson, the party he came to office to represent, and he did so by exercising the powers bequeathed to him by Jackson. Polk did not see any contradiction between his election as an "orthodox, whole hog" Jackson Democrat and his determination to exercise the full powers of his office in his own right. He penned the line "I intend to be myself President of the U.S." in the course of committing his administration to do "equal and exact justice" to every faction of the Democratic party."Nonetheless, the inherently disruptive effects entailed in that exercise transformed his political nickname from "Orthodox Polk" to "Polk the Mendacious" (Skowronek, forthcoming).

The successful pursuit of both goals—party leadership and constitutional independence—has historically depended on opportunities presented by secular conditions of electoral realignment over which presidents may have little awareness or control. Yet to analyze the "rules" of the presidency abstracted from this connection would provide a formal, but on the whole, empty description. Another example of "secretions" in institutional rules can be found in early industrial regulation. Congress scrupulously, that is, purposively, separated administrative setting of rates and policing fair competition from the "labor question," assigning the latter to other agencies based on distinctive principles and procedures. In industry, however, rates and competitive methods were tied not only to labor costs but also to the ease with which regulated industries could adjust them downward. This connection was acknowledged occasionally by regulatory actors, but was usually eclipsed by assumptions (already outdated) about managerial authority built into the regulatory scheme. Indeed, it is possible to tell the story of the rise and fall of American regulatory agencies as a gradual coming to terms with labor organization, beginning with the agency's recognition of labor in new procedures and leading to agency disfavor and regulatory decline (Orren, 1991).

All of these examples point to a fourth and final characteristic. *Political institutions are typically created by other political institutions.* As such, they carry forward incongruities and asymmetries already structured into the status quo. Even in so-called founding and revolutionary periods, where institutions are (arguably) not created by other institutions, they will be constructed against the background of their predecessors. This was true of the United States Constitution, for example, designed in conscious opposition to the "mixed" constitution of eighteenth-century Great Britain. Viewing institutions in terms of their relations to other institutions not only reveals active interfaces with the institutions they seek to control, but with those that, as a prior political event, have sought to control them. This sequencing dissolves not only the boundary of space, the "whole" into which "the pieces fit together," but also the boundary of time. That is to say, presuming there is no "whole," the movements of the pieces through history will themselves define the intersections that comprise any specific moment of institutional action.

The connections and intersections discussed here are not "functional" or indicative of "order." Indeed, although we have consciously eschewed the notion of chaos, what is produced is nonetheless a kind of patterned anarchy. True, the constant monitoring of results by institutional actors might bring about institutional learning and adaptive changes in the rules. At any given historical juncture, however, measures aimed at alleviating strain will as likely exacerbate as not. Thus, the attempt by the early Interstate Commerce Commission to ease competition through the establishment of regional rate-setting by railroads encouraged regional railroad labor organization, resulting in increased pressures on costs (Orren, 1991). President Lyndon Johnson intended the War on Poverty to shore up his party's relations with urban blacks; instead, it mobilized black communities against the old Democratic machines and further fragmented the governing coalition. In retrospect, that these pieces hung together—regional rates and labor costs, blacks and the old machines—is apparent. But the intricacies of control were hidden from actors who did not anticipate the systemically disruptive consequences of their ordering pursuits.

On the other hand, these same examples would seem to argue for "the uses of disorder," the degree to which successful functioning of institutions (their "robustness") may in certain cases depend precisely on the mix and ferment rather than the consistency of their principles and procedures. Congress' regulatory goal of imposing fixed rates depended on the responsiveness of an all-but-automatic system for coercing the labor force; when labor organized and asserted its own intentions, costs were passed through to a nonresistant consumer base; when consumers joined the contest and organized effectively, the original regulatory scheme, or at least leading parts of it, was abandoned by Congress. The model of the responsible party leader implies either voluntaristic performance on the part of the president, accompanied by party cohorts willing to stem their own voluntaristic interests and follow, or a president willing to sacrifice his personal ambitions when these clash with the intentions of leaders of his party. As institutions aim to control the behavior of others, their success will depend on the resistance or malleability of those so targeted, and thus upon the layers of discipline that exist at any given time.

CONCLUSION

There is no escaping a description of "the times" in the study of institutions. The outstanding question is how time is to be described. Indeed, if the priority of time over order in institutional study is evident anywhere, it is in the unreflected premise of simultaneous origins upon which overarching conceptions of order have been built. Once we discard this premise on the solid ground of empirical observation we will have to regain our historical bearings without it. Gone is the distinction between extraordinary politics (rulemaking) and politics as usual (game playing); gone is the icon of equilibrium readjustments, gone is the "system" that congeals time between reconstructions. Instead the field consists of relatively independent layers of institutional actions and is conceptually, if not analytically, boundless. It makes no more sense to describe all factors as endogenous than it does to describe them all as exogenous. The important questions are questions of timing.

In light of political science's historic preoccupation with order in the study of institutions, there is much to be gained from a general rethinking of the essential historicity of the subject matter. So long as the claim that "institutions matter" rides piggyback on old presumptions about how things change, to wit, between periods of order, the range of potential new insights will be narrow. We have argued here that the upshot of a new institutionalism should be a substantially different understanding of historical processes—a departure from those already available. Terry Moe is right to caution us against PTI's ahistoricism, and to call us back from a search for timeless covering laws. But there is no need to retreat from there to the illusion of systemic "fit." To advance we need to break with presumptions of system coherence and alter our basic conception of temporality in a way that accounts for the *patterned disorder* that institutions routinely create.

To fix on questions of timing in institutional politics requires using history in ways that historians themselves seldom do. In our view, time is not the medium through which the story of this or that institution will unfold; it is itself the central problem. The discovery of patterns—provisionally, even of orders—is an indispensable step. This may entail uncovering several layers of institutional politics that compose a single moment, or reaching across historical periods to identify a repeated sequence or configuration. The idea is not to detach the analysis from time-bound descriptive minutiae, but to explicate the timing of such details, and to explain institutionally the shifts and developments that are constantly changing the political landscape. There are no "time lags" in this perspective, no institutional delays where older arrangements "catch up" with new; pieces held over from earlier patterns are part and parcel of the institutional composition and of the institutional construction of temporality itself.[3]

Institutions make history by the routine engagement of the tensions and contradictions among their various ordering principles and by their bending and reshaping of each other into patterns of change in time. Layers, not systems; dissonance, not fit; conjunctures, not regularities: These are the points of entry to a genuinely "new" institutionalism.

NOTES

Colleagues who were kind enough to offer comments on this essay were Joyce Appleby, Paul DiMaggio, Morris Fiorina, Jeff Frieden, David Mayhew, David Plotke, Ian Shapiro, and Alex Wendt.

1. We deal with rational choice and historical alternatives in this chapter but give no attention to the new institutionalism in sociology. For a review, see DiMaggio and Powell (1991). For a stimulating discussion of work in sociology also see Elchardus (1982).

2. Edward Corwin (1940) notes, "The implication [of Roosevelt's assumptions of power in World War II] seemed to be that the President owed the transcendent powers he was claiming to some peculiar relationship between himself and the people—a doctrine with a strong family resemblance to the leadership principle against which the war was supposedly being fought."

3. "Thus, in the Progressive Era, it is not the decline of localistic, partisan forms of governance and the rise of nationalistic bureaucratic forms that calls for our attention; it is rather the stubborn persistence of the localistic forms—and of the pre-partisan Constitutional frame itself—as these refracted and recast the designs of those who would build the new bureaucratic forms" (Skowronek, 1982).

15

Political Learning and Political Change: Understanding Development Across Time

LAWRENCE C. DODD

A new political science is needed for a world itself quite new.
—Alexis de Tocqueville, *Democracy in America*[1]

We live in a time of great systemic change in the world. Political reality as we have known it during our lifetime is being restructured in fundamental ways, illustrated most dramatically by the collapse of the Soviet state and the demise of the Cold War. Such periods of change are sobering, and force us to consider why it is that reality, which seems so permanent, can collapse so unexpectedly. Such periods also pose for us what is perhaps the most difficult issue in political inquiry—how it is that societies confronted with systemic change reconstruct their understanding of reality and develop governing arrangements appropriate to a new world (Munitz, 1990).

These issues are of pressing concern today to scholars of comparative politics and international relations, confronting as they do extraordinary alterations in global politics that only a decade ago would have seemed inconceivable (Rosenau, 1991; Ferguson and Mansbach, 1991). The issues are no less important, however, to students of American politics.

When one looks back across American history, one sees periods of upheaval and change that altered American political reality just as dramatically as contemporary international upheavals are altering world politics today (Ackerman, 1991; Burnham, 1970; Dodd, 1981; Greenberg, 1985; Huntington, 1981; Jillson, chap. 2, this vol.). Thus American history brought us the founding period, when the apparent permanence of colonial status gave way to revolution and national independence. There was the Civil War and Reconstruction, when the preeminence of a plantation oligarchy collapsed and the nation embraced capitalist democracy. And there was the Depression and World War II when the activist state abandoned laissez-faire politics and international isolationism and acknowledged its domestic and international responsibilities.

These axial shifts in history pose three overarching questions to students of American politics. First, why is it that long periods of perceived constancy in our politics are followed by unexpected upheavals and political reconstructions? Second, why do upheavals and reconstructive processes differ across historical eras and political systems, generating an exceptional tendency towards transformational politics in the American experience, whereas other societies gravitate more towards gradualist or revolutionary change? In other words, why does American politics tend to experience dramatic and extensive alterations in politics that nevertheless leave the broad outlines of our institutional arrangements, participatory processes, and geopolitical identity intact? And third, why is it, in the midst of extraordinary upheaval and disorder, that a viable new pattern of governance can emerge? Answering these questions requires a theory of political development across time—a theory that can simultaneously explain the long-term sense of stasis, the dramatic short-term upheavals, the regenerative capacities, and the reconstructive alterations in our politics.

My purpose in this essay is to construct a theory of political development that can address these three critical questions.[2] In doing so I draw on a variety of cross-disciplinary works,[3] particularly on the cybernetic learning theory of anthropologist Gregory Bateson.[4] Bateson argues that individuals, groups, and societies learn by responding to changes in their environment in ways that are analogous to cybernetic systems. In other words, participants in a society hold to a strategy of political action until informational stimuli pass a critical threshold of change, whereupon societal participants engage in an experimental search for a new strategy of action. The extensiveness and effectiveness of participants' search for a new and viable strategy of action is then shaped by their structural and environmental context and by their capacity for pattern recognition. I build on Bateson because he offers an elegantly simple and yet empirically compelling model of change. He allows us both to acknowledge the open, contingent, and creative nature of societal development and to grasp the patterned interconnectedness of the micro, macro, and middle-range processes that shape developmental learning across time.

In this essay I argue that, in seeing politics as a process of learning, we come to understand the general characteristics of American political development. Thus, in the first section I propose that "metarational" learning at the *micro level* generates the long-term cyclical or cybernetic patterning of politics. In the second section I argue that *macro context* confronts societies with distinctive learning tasks and learning conditions and thereby generates the broad tendencies of nation-states toward gradualist, transformational, or revolutionary politics. In the third section I argue that political learning occurs as societal participants recognize new patterns of social reality and encapsulate such understandings in appropriate and widely shared metaphors that give a sense of order and meaning to politics; these shared metaphors then shape the *middle-range politics* of everyday life. In the final section I argue that insofar as we come to see politics as a process of learning across time, we can build *a developmental science of politics*; such a science would help us both to foresee the axial shifts of history and to understand history's reconstructive and governing processes. To this end, let us construct a theory of political learning, starting with a discussion of microlevel politics.

EXPLAINING THE CYCLES OF CHANGE:
THE MICRO DYNAMICS OF LEARNING AND RESISTANCE

I start with micro dynamics because the cyclical reconstruction of politics is a product of individual and group patterns of learning within society. To understand why societies experience long periods of constancy in their dominant patterns of politics, followed by short-term upheavals and reconstruction, we must understand the nature of such learning processes. The model of societal learning I construct below builds on the work of Gregory Bateson and is useful as a basis for interpreting the broad developmental outlines of American political history. In building on Bateson, I follow his particular empirical usage of two concepts, *epistemology as world view* and *ontology as objective reality*, and I do so to maintain consistency with the body of empirical theory derived from his work. Utilized in this manner, these two concepts are keys to understanding why societies experience long periods of order and stability, dissolve into crisis and reconstructive struggles, and then learn new strategies for orderly governance.

The Logic of Societal Learning: A Batesonian Perspective

In *Steps to an Ecology of Mind*, Bateson (1972) argues that social and political participants relate to one another in terms of a shared core understanding of how the world operates, with a broad and diffuse agreement along moral and empirical dimensions, as well as on collective responsibilities and individual interests (Bateson, 1972:279–337; Deutsch, 1963; Geertz, 1964). This shared understanding constitutes a collective epistemology of the political world—in a sense a shared imagining of the world (Anderson, 1983; Jung, 1963) that only approximates the ontology (or reality) of the world. The difference between perception and reality forces political participants to become accustomed to some ineffectiveness in their understanding of the world and their action in it. Nevertheless, they hold to their collective understanding for security and order, using it to operate within and exercise power over their world.

The content of collective epistemologies varies across historical eras in response to economic, technological, ecological, social, and moral possibilities. Before a collective epistemology can ensure collective survival, however, social and political actors must recognize that they live in an interdependent world. A viable epistemology will thus entail precepts, structures, and procedures that foster interdependent cooperation and mutuality appropriate to and possible in a historical time and place. At the heart of a viable collective epistemology, then, lies an ecological vision of political and social life, a "public-spirited" sense of the way in which political actors, groups, institutions and processes fit together in a particular time and place to ensure mutual enhancement and survival (Bateson, 1972:469–505; Anderson, 1994; Mansbridge, 1980, 1990a).

The success of a collective epistemology in creating a sense of order generates a paradoxical tension within societies. The survival of society requires adherence to collective governing processes; yet the success of such processes leads political actors to take them for granted, to lose much of their public-spirited support of collective institutions and processes, and to focus on short-term self-interests instead. The pursuit of short-term interests moves societies from political cooperation to competition in ways that erode the structure, norms, and processes that provide for interdependent and mutual interests (Dodd, 1977; Fiorina, 1977, 1980; Lichbach, forthcoming; Olson, 1982). The resultant breakdown in social order produces social and political crises, renewed attention to collective structures and processes of governance, and a return to epistemological orthodoxy. *Epistemological crises* are thus inherent in political life. Political participants seek to resolve such crises through *epistemological rationality* (that is, through the return to the precepts of their orthodox world view and attempts to pursue interests anew in a manner consistent with that world view).

If the ontology of the world remained constant, the explanation of political dynamics would be a relatively straightforward enterprise. Political actors would agree upon collective governing rules and structures, erode the collective governing processes as they increasingly pursued private interests, generate epistemological crises, and then return to epistemological orthodoxy (including particularly an adherence to collective rules and procedures) to resolve political and social crises (Huntington, 1981). But because the ontology of the world is not constant, we are led to a more complicated conception of political change.

According to Bateson, the great dilemma of human behavior is that the ontology of the world—the way it really is and really operates—can change extensively over time, while the epistemology that dominates human action—collective beliefs about the way the world operates—remain relatively unchanged. Individuals and groups hold onto traditional beliefs because of the sense of order and security that they provide, even as ontological change undermines the utility of such beliefs and generates a growing sense of political powerlessness. Societies thus allow great gaps to develop between their governing epistemologies and the ontology of the world.

Individuals and groups within societies will hold to the extant world view until crises are so great (and the ineffectiveness of epistemological restoration so clear) that they can significantly reduce their sense of powerlessness only by discarding the old world view and developing a new one (Dodd, 1981, 1991). I refer to such circumstances as *metacrises:* behavioral dilemmas unresponsive to resolution through the operation of existing epistemological principles, structures, and procedures. When the recognition of metacrises comes—when political participants experience sufficient frustration and powerlessness to let go of old assumptions and seek to experience the world more directly and experimentally—*epistemological reconstruction* can begin.

Epistemological reconstruction occurs through experiential rationality, that is, through participants' experimentation with beliefs, goals, preferences, structures, and procedures until a more efficacious epistemology of action emerges. In circumstances where participants rapidly recognize the growing gap between epistemology and ontology, and move to construct a new governing world view before a debilitating sense of powerlessness sets in, epistemological reconstruction may be a relatively straightforward process: Ontological change, in fact, may be experienced as creating new opportunities for political creativity and an increased sense of collective empowerment. By contrast, when the gap between an old epistemology and a new ontology grows relatively large, epistemological reconstruction may be long and difficult. In such circumstances, individuals and groups may experience feelings of deep powerlessness and insecurity that arouse irrational fears and unconscious behaviors, thus requiring extensive social catharsis before experimentation and epistemological reconstruction can proceed effectively. In extreme cases, fears and insecurities may be so great, and catharsis so difficult, that participants sabotage experimentation and induce political self-destruction (see Bateson, reprinted in Donaldson, 1991:93–110, 127–131; Arendt, 1966; Fromm, 1941; Hofstadter, 1965; Laing, 1967; Lasswell, 1930).

Epistemological reconstruction is thus not assured for a society. It involves trial-and-error experimentation, as political participants seek to create mutually enhancing beliefs and collective governing structures appropriate to a new world, with no guarantee of successful solution. It also can involve extensive resistance as individuals and groups cling to old beliefs and interests, with such resistance reinforced by rules and structures designed to serve such beliefs and interests (Dodd, 1986, 1993). Yet as individuals, groups, and societies experiment with new ideas and beliefs, they have the opportunity to construct an epistemology more appropriate to their world, a new epistemology that can empower them to operate in the world as it more truly is.[5] Central to such social learning is a process I call *metarationality*—the ultimate capacity of individuals, separately and collectively, to recognize that adherence to an inappropriate understanding of the world engenders a powerlessness and insecurity that is greater in cost than the difficulties involved in creating a new and more appropriate understanding.[6]

The Cycles of American Political Development

A metarational approach suggests a vision of society characterized by the periodic re-creation of political life. In this approach, political participants hold a shared and seemingly immutable core understanding of politics that gives a perceived order to their historical era. As long as the core understanding persists, politics is characterized by short-term cycles of political adjustment and reform within the reigning world view. These reform cycles are characterized by a variety of behavioral dynamics, including ideological mood swings between collective cooperation and group competitiveness (Schlesinger, 1986; Stimson, 1991), organizational shifts between centralization and decentralization (Dodd, 1977, 1986; Moe, 1985; Rockman, 1984; Sundquist, 1981), realignments in the groups and parties that win policy struggles within an era (Key, 1955; Brady, 1988; Burnham, 1970; Carmines and Stimson, 1989; Clubb, Flanigan, and Zingale, 1980; Sundquist, 1973), leadership shifts from creative policy assertiveness to managing and salvaging policy agendas (Skowronek, 1984, 1986), and the like.

Some learning and epistemological adaptation undoubtedly occurs during such reform cycles within an historical era, with such learning focused on secondary beliefs and structures within the dominant epistemology. Such adaptive learning may focus, in particular, on efforts to salvage the central principles of a governing epistemology by expanding the number of citizens who participate extensively in its central decision processes, and who most benefit from its central policy commitments. But as long as participants hold to the central beliefs of the dominant world view, societal change will outpace the ability of governments to respond to societal problems effectively. Problems will mount and crises will fester to the point that extensive epistemological reconstruction, and considerable political restructuring, will be necessary for crisis resolution and system survival.

In the long run, in other words, the persistence of an increasingly out-moded collective epistemology precipitates metacrises that can only be resolved by reconstructing critical central tenets of the collective episte-mology. Such metacrises are often evident in revolution; in civil war; in extensive social, moral, and economic dislocation; and in military defeat. Emergence from such societal crises requires the recreation of a shared in-terpretation of the world that enables participants to understand how to operate effectively in light of their new historical conditions. Seeing his-tory in this manner suggests that we can think of political life not just in terms of short-term "reform cycles" but in terms of long-term "meta-cycles" characterized by the creation, rigidification, breakdown, and reconstruction of the collective epistemology that dominates a society (Rockman, 1984; Goldstein, 1988). This perspective, I suggest, makes con-siderable sense out of the long-term pattern of American political devel-opment, as the nation has moved from an agrarian to a post-agrarian, and thence to an industrial society.

During the Revolutionary War and its aftermath, for example, political participants sought a workable form of representative self-government appropriate for an agrarian society (Foner, 1980; Jillson, 1988; Jillson and Wilson, 1994; Wood, 1969, 1992; Young, 1966). They produced an agrarian epistemology centered on a constrained national government dominated by regional and state elites, a mixed economy balancing the interests at-tached to slavery and free labor, and an isolated nationalism. This under-standing of government fit the agrarian and cultural conditions of the late eighteenth century and first decade or so of the nineteenth century, but by the 1820s the actual agrarian underpinnings of society were yielding to the industrial revolution, territorial expansion, and expanded interna-tional trade. These developments began to erode the viability of the slav-ery compromise, states' rights, and the isolationist ideology. For another forty years political actors adhered to the central tenets of this agrarian epistemology, seeking to maximize their sectional, economic, and partisan interests within its worldview. During this period the Jacksonian up-heaval represented a mild "learning episode" that adjusted the dominant epistemology, for example, by broadening mass political participation among white males (Silbey, 1991a). Yet in the verdict of history the long-term adherence to the antiquated agrarian understanding of society and politics, and rational short-term pursuits within it, was the defining and ultimately irrational characteristic of the era. The result was a metacrisis of severe proportions—a civil war—before participants could begin to recognize the limits of the antebellum worldview and restructure their understanding of society and politics.

Similar, though less dramatic, metacycles characterize the American experience following the Civil War (Gourevitch, 1986; Hofstadter, 1955, 1965; Lowi, 1969, 1979; Skowronek, 1984). Out of Reconstruction, for example, emerged a post-agrarian epistemology that envisioned an almost unbridled alliance between capitalism and an expansionary government that would fund and fuel laissez-faire capitalism. This post-agrarian worldview energized society after the Civil War and fueled the nation's adaptation to an industrial world. Like the agrarian worldview, however, the post-agrarian epistemology took hold in a deep and ultimately destructive manner. Thus as the nation's work force moved to the city and entered the factory, unregulated capitalist competition generated cycles of economic boom and bust that had an increasingly devastating effect on the social and economic security of a population made vulnerable by the decline of tight-knit extended families and self-sufficient farms. With the progressive movement the nation experienced a short-term learning episode, analogous to the Jacksonian upheaval, in which participants sought to reform and constrain the worst effects of the post-agrarian epistemology by expanding political participation and addressing some of the worst effects of corporate greed (Cronin, 1989; McDonagh and Price, 1985). But the Progressive Era left intact the nation's core commitment to laissez-faire capitalism. The eventual result was a great depression and global war in response to which the nation eventually embraced a proactive epistemology characterized by social and economic regulation at home and by an internationalist policy abroad.

For almost sixty years now, the United States has pursued the activist epistemology of the industrial era. In essence, the activist policies set in motion by Franklin Roosevelt "saved" capitalist democracy by closer attentiveness on the part of government to its social and economic responsibilities and through the solidification of an extraordinary cold war alliance between capitalism and the military. The industrial era experienced a notable learning episode in the 1960s and 1970s, with activists expanding political participation to include eighteen-year-olds and all ethnic and racial minorities, broadening the social and political rights of women, expanding the benefits and the beneficiaries of the service state, and adapting its institutions to the expanded participatory and service agenda (Costain, 1992; Huntington, 1981; Harris and Milkis, 1989). Yet the persistence of the activist epistemology, particularly the reliance on government bureaucracy to deliver social and economic benefits to citizens, seems increasingly at odds with the fiscal limits and expanding service needs of society. A growing gap between epistemology and ontology seems to demand yet a new restructuring of our understanding of society and politics (Dodd, 1993).

Metarationality and Political Understanding: Qualifications and Limits

This, then, is how I would assess the story of American political development: long periods during which political participants hold strongly to a dominant epistemological understanding of political life, even as the circumstances that gave rise to that understanding change; then deep crises resolved only by a modernization of the governing worldview. I illustrate this developmental pattern with a highly simplified analysis of complex dynamics—a kind of metarational parable on American politics.

One may disagree with my historical time frames and simplifications (See Jillson, chap. 2, and Orren and Skowronek, chap. 14, this vol.) A closer analysis, in fact, would stress overlapping layers of epistemological belief and conflict across history; it would stress the incremental way in which epistemological shifts are actually translated into political behavior; it would emphasize the disarray and confusion amidst the broad sense of shared understanding; and it would highlight more extensively the multiple phases of learning that occur within, as well as across, epistemological eras and that thereby lay the foundations for general epistemological shifts. Despite such necessary qualifications, I believe that seeing American political development through a metarational lens provides an interpretive coherence—and yet a creative openness—that approximates the real processes of history. As we grasp the creative openness of history, we then see that individuals, groups, and societies have the capacity to act responsibly and creatively in the face of severe metacrises by engaging in experimental and improvisational efforts to understand the emerging world and by translating that understanding into a new and viable governing epistemology.

A metarational perspective is thus essential to our understanding of American political development and to explaining the cyclical and reconstructive pattern of development across time. At the same time, a metarational perspective, and microlevel perspectives in general, are inherently limited understandings of politics (Cooper, 1988; Cooper and Brady, 1981; Eulau, 1969; Greenberg and Page, 1988). Such microlevel analysis can clarify why and how cycles of reconstruction occur. Yet it does not in itself clarify why reconstructive cycles differ in severity across time and space, ranging from gradual epistemological adjustments to deep crises and system transformation, to state revolution and system destruction. To some extent, of course, a metarational perspective suggests that such outcomes may be simply a product of "random" differences in human creativity or experimental success, perhaps analogous to the random mutation processes of species across evolutionary time.[7] Yet it is also the case that tendencies toward deep crises, and the capacity for crisis resolution, may be shaped in significant though not deterministic ways by the broad context within which individuals, groups, and societies find themselves (Farr, 1985), with some contexts facilitating metarational learning and others undermining it. Understanding the differential paths of societal development thus requires that we explore macro context.

UNDERSTANDING DEVELOPMENTAL PATHS: THE MACRO CONTEXT OF LEARNING

Macro context refers to the governing rules and structures of a society, its broad cultural and economic conditions, and its geopolitical circumstances. Change in macro context erodes the viability of an extant epistemology and thereby fuels movement toward metacrisis. Yet the broad and deeply ingrained historical contours of societal context also confront individuals, groups, and society with an extensive set of constraints, tensions, and opportunities that influence their capacity for developmental learning. As a result, while the *process* of epistemological reconstruction may be analogous in abstract ways across societies the *character* and *prospective success* of the process is significantly shaped by macro context and thus varies in distinctive ways across societies (Donaldson, 1991:133–145). This section clarifies how macro context shapes the character of developmental experience and why the American experience tends towards transformational politics.

The Contours of Macro Context: Crisis Magnification and Process Facilitation

Macro context influences societal response to ontological change in two primary ways. First, macro context may magnify or minimize the *learning tasks* of a society. In other words, while the development of metacrises is inherent in the nature of human learning (that is, in the tendency of individuals, groups, and societies to hold to old beliefs until ontological change and crises force them to reassess beliefs), the severity of the metacrisis experience can be magnified or minimized by the nature of the societal context. Thus in societies whose economic and social problems are mild, and whose decision processes are relatively responsive, metacrises may be recognized quite straightforwardly as products of outmoded belief systems; in such societies, the learning tasks of participants (as they seek to adjust old beliefs to new realities) will be relatively minimal. By contrast, in societies whose inherent economic and social problems are severe and whose decision processes are cumbersome and unresponsive, prolonged epistemological rigidification may interact with existing societal problems to produce system-threatening crises; in such societies, the learning tasks of societal participants are magnified by the severity of the society's environmental context (Barber, 1984; Dahl, 1971; Habermas, 1975, 1984, 1987; Rae and Taylor, 1970).

Second, macro context can create facilitative or inhibitory learning conditions. Context shapes the learning conditions of society, in particular, by influencing the opportunity of participants to engage in empathetic and collective deliberation (Mansbridge, 1980). For example, in societies with considerable geopolitical security, natural wealth, cultural affinities among citizens, and inclusive and authoritative decisionmaking structures, the process of collective learning can proceed in a relatively unencumbered way; participants faced with metacrises can deliberate and experiment extensively in their search for new and commonly acceptable understandings. Such societies may even face highly magnified metacrises and be able to resolve them. By contrast, societies lacking such favorable circumstances will have great difficulty in finding the time and opportunity to experiment, deliberate, and reconstruct their worldviews, so that even when confronting mild metacrises they may fail to resolve the crises (Berger, 1976; Dahl, 1982; Evans, Rueschemeyer, and Skocpol, 1985).

The ability of a nation to respond to metacrises and develop more appropriate governing arrangements will be heavily shaped by the combined impact that macro context has on the learning tasks and conditions that confront societal participants. Context does not determine the outcome of societal crises: Political development is an inherently open process that can succeed or fail in any environment as a result of creative learning, or the resistance to learning, among that society's citizens. But context structures the developmental tasks a nation faces, creates broad tendencies toward crisis magnification and collective learning that characterizes its political processes, and thereby affects the prospects of developmental success.

Figure 15.1 specifies four broad and distinctive types of developmental experience associated with the interactive nature of the learning tasks and learning conditions that confront a society. We can think, first, of self-correcting or gradualist politics as existing in societies characterized by limited learning tasks and facilitative learning conditions. Such situations, generally characterized by mild metacrises, may exist, for example, in small, culturally homogeneous, secure, and democratic nation-states (Dahl and Tufte, 1973). A second pattern, social revolution, would seem to arise in the opposite setting, produced by magnified learning tasks and inhibitory learning conditions. Russia in the early twentiethth century or France in the late eighteenth century are examples of the destructive revolutionary outcomes of such settings (Moore, 1966; Skocpol, 1979); modern

FIGURE 15.1
The Paths of Political Development

Learning Conditions

Learning Tasks	Facilitative	Inhibitive
Minimized	Gradualist politics	Problematic politics
Magnified	Transformational politics	Revolutionary politics

India illustrates the potential, despite extraordinary conflict and system upheaval, for some degree of common problem-solving even in such difficult settings (Erikson, 1969). A third pattern, that of problematic politics, is likely in societies characterized not only by limited learning tasks but also by inhibitory learning conditions. Such may be the experience of many traditional Third World societies (Berger, 1976).

Finally, we can identify societal conditions that generate strong tendencies toward transformational politics. Such societies exist in contexts that both magnify participants' learning tasks and facilitate their learning processes. These societies could be characterized, for example, by inherently difficult social and economic problems that divide citizens into highly contentious factions and by cumbersome decision processes that slow societal response to crises; yet such societies could also evidence historical affinities and inclusive decisionmaking structures that ultimately allow citizens to find new commonalities in the midst of change and upheaval. Societies such as these would be prone, as a result, to deep metacrises characterized by extensive conflicts and serious threats to the maintenance of the nation-state; yet they would also possess the capacity for the extensive processes of catharsis, experimentation, and deliberation that can allow citizens to come to new and mutually acceptable understandings of the world. Because such societies confront their metacrises so slowly and conflictually, large gaps develop between the ontology of the emerging world and the extant epistemology and governing procedures, thus requiring extensive transformations in worldviews and governing arrangements. Yet because of the capacity for empathetic and deliberative resolution of metacrises, society can maintain a sense of cultural and political continuity and sustain the integrity of the nation-state. I suggest that American politics has existed historically in precisely such a paradoxical context.

Macro Context: The Paradox of American Politics

My argument is that American politics has been prone to extensive cycles of political transformation because it exists in a macro context that both magnifies the metacrises inherent in political life and yet ultimately facilitates the process of social learning and crisis resolution. In presenting this argument, I see transformational politics as a tendency, not a deterministic process. Societal conditions can pose extraordinary problems, and can support or inhibit the experimentation and catharsis essential to problem resolution, but the transformational experience itself is subject to reflective and creative processes so complex and open that we can only discuss probabilities of success. With this caveat, consider the broad implications that the American context has had for political development.

With respect to crisis magnification, American politics has operated in a setting that, while varying in degree, has always been prone toward significant to extreme amplification of metacrises. First, throughout its history the nation has experienced inherently difficult social and economic problems, illustrated by the conflict over slavery and westward expansion during the agrarian era, class conflict and economic instability during the industrial transformation, and the struggle for social equality and international security during the industrial era (Dahl, 1981). These problems presented daunting tasks to the nation and any one of them could have overwhelmed its governing capacities. Second, ethnic and racial (Hero, 1993), regional (Bensel, 1984), and class (Manley, 1993; Orren, 1991) differences among citizens have created a conflictual heterogeneity that complicates policy dialogue and slows the nation's response to new societal problems; there has also been a significant vein of social intolerance within our culture (Hofstadter, 1965; Hanson, chap. 6, this vol.). Third, a broad propensity to bridge societal differences by a cultural emphasis on the founding heritage often fosters a resistance to recognizing new and complicating conditions, to experimenting with and embracing new values and political strategies, and thus to learning new and more appropriate approaches to governance (Ackerman, 1991). Finally, and perhaps most widely acknowledged, a constitutional system of fragmented power has created numerous veto points and cumbersome decision processes that factions in society can exploit to block policy change which is supported by a national majority but which the minority faction opposes (Burns, 1963). The combination of these attributes of macro context has crippled the nation's ability to respond to societal change, perhaps more so than in any other contemporary Western democracy (Dahl, 1981; Lipset, 1977; Lowi, 1984; Schattschneider, 1960); and it has oriented us to a reactionary politics of disorder (Lowi, 1971).

The real issue is how and why the American political system has survived and flourished despite a macro context that engenders deep metacrises. How is it that transformative reconstruction could have occurred in such difficult circumstances? To some extent, as I have stressed previously, the answer lies in the creative potential of societal participants beyond the determinacies of culture, procedural rules, and institutional structures. But the macro context also plays a role in facilitating crisis resolution, in ways often not fully appreciated.

American politics tends to experience crisis resolution rather than system destruction, I suggest, because its macro context facilitates the process of political learning *as citizens become concerned with collective survival in the face of severe and system-threatening crises.*[8] In other words, as societal crises deepen and conflict begins to broadly undermine security and well-being, societal participants will begin to look beyond segmented interests, as perceived through old mind-sets, to the issue of personal survival. As participants become concerned with survival, they become increasingly willing to learn new understandings of the world that will foster survival, even when such new understanding requires them to recognize mutualities and common interests with individuals and groups whom they previously opposed (Stone, 1989). The macro context of American politics, having helped engender deep metacrises, then can play a surprising role in the search for common ground.

First, consider the exceptional environmental context of American politics (Shafer, 1991b). Whatever the problems induced by its environment, including the economic and racial issues, the United States has lacked the deep cultural animosities engendered by the prolonged feudal experiences of many European nations (Boorstin, 1953; Hartz, 1955). This was the case particularly among the dominant Anglo majority. The absence of deep cultural animosities allowed the nation to avoid the depth of interpersonal class conflict present in many European societies. Moreover, while it lacked the worst legacies of feudal conflict, it benefited from a significant degree of shared cultural referents derived from a European heritage among most citizens. The nation also benefited from the existence, across cleavage lines, of a shared "new world" experience—the collective unifying experience involved in creating a new social and political world on a new continent. In addition, the greatest cultural and social barrier, that between blacks and whites, has been bridged to some extent by common religious referents (Niebuhr, 1975). As a result of these varied factors, even in the midst of system-threatening conflict there is the chance for empathy and for a recognition of mutuality across the heterogeneous factions of American society.

Second, the geopolitical context of American society has facilitated the resolution of deep metacrises. The oceans have protected the nation from easy invasion and thus allowed its internal struggles to proceed without intervention by foreign powers. Extensive internal resources have allowed the nation to fulfill the basic needs of its citizens, even in the midst of metacrises, so that they could survive political paralysis and search for mutual understandings and interests that would resolve the paralysis (Potter, 1954). The existence and exploration of a vast continent helped induce an openness to new worldviews and an experimental pragmatism in addressing new problems. And the existence of a western frontier provided a safety valve whereby deeply disgruntled groups could disengage from political conflict and seek a new political world as part of epistemological reconstruction, thereby defusing deep societal conflicts (Turner, 1920).

Third, a tradition of open discourse has supported a broad and constructive societal involvement in epistemological reconstruction. At a formal constitutional level open discourse is guaranteed by the freedoms of speech, of the press, and of religion, and by free elections; it is further protected by a judicial system sworn to uphold such constitutional rights (Kammen, 1987). On a more general societal level such discourse is supported by a public education system, by an independent and competitive press, and by an extensive community of artists, scholars, and political activists. It is also supported by cultural diversity across regions and groups that helps generate support for political and policy pluralism (Elazar, 1984; Erikson, Wright and McIver, 1993) and by popular commitment to a spirit of individualism, combined with a profound appreciation of community (Bellah et al., 1985; Tocqueville, 1946; Wildavsky, 1991b). The meaning and public manifestation of open discourse has varied across history, with each generation of Americans forced to grapple with the recreation of an atmosphere of tolerance and inclusion. But the historic vision of an open society, the evolving constitutional precepts of openness, and the societal supports for openness have all created a general presumption in favor of wide-ranging public dialogue.

Finally, there are ways in which American institutional arrangements facilitate the reconstructive process in the midst of system-threatening crises (Dahl, 1981; Kammen, 1987). First, our representational and deliberative arrangements provide an avenue whereby public discourse over policy problems can enter governmental debate in a formal manner and offer mechanisms whereby the concerns of the public can be assessed and translated into collective and authoritative public policy (Dodd, 1993; Erikson, Wright, and McIver, 1993; Mansbridge, 1980; Stone, 1990). Second, the complexity and cumbersomeness of our representational and deliberative procedures, particularly when combined with our adjudicatory systems, provide citizens with such a multiplicity of decision points that most groups can find ways to engage in the political process; in other words, institutional fragmentation not only creates numerous veto points *within* the system but a plethora of access points *into* the system. Third, the multiplicity of policy processes, evidenced not just in the national government but in the extraordinary number of reasonably autonomous state and local governments as well, creates a vast opportunity for policy experimentation and improvisation; this multiplicity of experimental and improvisational processes aids the discovery of viable epistemological solutions to societal crises (Gray, 1993; Osborne, 1988; Polsby, 1984). Fourth, the broad dispersion of institutional power, particularly the separation of power among the branches within state and national governments, means that the nation is forced to find a broadly consensual understanding of the world before comprehensive and legitimate reconstruction is possible; the nation thus avoids the imposition of simple majoritarian solutions that might so threaten large and excluded groups that they would envision system destruction as preferable to acquiescence. Finally, the deeply ingrained nature of our representational, deliberative, and adjudicatory arrangements means that in the depth of severe conflict, such as a civil war, when participants face the choice between fighting to the dire end or exploring conciliation and rapprochement, they can envision the possibility of reinclusion into civil discourse and a prospective role in political reconstruction.

In a paradoxical manner, then, the participatory processes and fragmented institutional arrangements that *initially* help magnify metacrises can also facilitate crisis resolution *as system destruction approaches*. Such arrangements do so by providing access points and deliberative processes through which citizens on the verge or in the midst of system destruction can reach out to one another if they are so inclined, step back from the precipice, and seek new common ground. In addition, these arrangements provide a vast range of experimental processes that support the search for common ground. Participants are likely to use these experimental and deliberative processes because they fear system destruction, because institutional arrangements force broadly consensual agreement that helps groups protect their most basic interests, and because citizens ultimately share deep cultural and historical affinities that lead them to believe that common ground and a new governing epistemology can be found.

American Politics: The Promise of Transformation

Deeply embedded within the context of American politics then, is a propensity toward system-threatening crisis, as evidenced in our Civil War, the Great Depression and perhaps today in increasingly severe ecological and economic crises; but there is also the promise of a resilient and transformational politics that enhances the long-term self-governing capacity of system participants. In presenting this interpretation, I do not suggest that the developmental transformations in our politics have been an easy, painless, or automatic process, a perfect process, or one that generates results that later generations always see as the morally correct or enlightened choices (as, for example, in the nation's treatment of the native Americans). It is, in fact, a very chancy politics, one that takes the nation into severe conflict, even to the verge of destruction, and then trusts to collective metarationality and the discovery of a deep mutuality in order for participants to use institutional arrangements for collective good. Along the way there are long periods of policy unresponsiveness and considerable suffering on the part of the disadvantaged. Ideally one would hope that the nation could find ways to lessen its tendency to magnify metacrises and move towards a more self-regulating and gradualist model of political development.

On the other hand, the United States is a large and diverse nation-state confronting immense social, economic, ecological, and international problems and seeking to do so in ways that approximate some degree of autonomous and democratic self-government. It is doubtful that such a nation can expect an easy, painless, morally pure, or automatic process of crisis resolution and political development. Seen in this manner, the American experience has its up side as well—not only in its cultural affinities and geopolitical good fortune but in its institutional arrangements and deliberative processes. When such processes are successful in facilitating epistemological learning, they can generate a broad and deep consensual acceptance among participants of the political processes and policy commitments appropriate to the context of their times. Such agreement provides an inner cohesiveness to the political system that facilitates both its survival and the continued pursuit of collective and particularized group interests through deliberative decisionmaking.

The great remaining mystery is how participants actually do develop a shared understanding that brings a sense of order and empowerment to a new world. This is an intriguing issue, since conflict may appear so pervasive and permanent to participants in the midst of serious metacrisis that they come to doubt the very possibility of a civil and orderly politics. In what sense is it that the creation of a new and more appropriate political epistemology can produce sufficient resolution of metacrises that participants can find a common and acceptable understanding and reengage in civil discourse? How is it, in the midst of seemingly intractable disorder, that a new perception of order can emerge and permeate the broad "middle-range politics" of an age, reshaping the nation's policy agendas, participatory process, organizational procedures, and governing patterns? These questions require that we grapple more directly with clarifying the attributes that characterize epistemological reconstruction.

CREATING A NEW POLITICAL ORDER: THE POWER OF METAPHOR

As I have argued thus far, the resolution of metacrises occurs as political participants embrace a collective and mutually enhancing epistemology appropriate to the world as it is. This is all well and good, and we may intuitively sense the necessity of approximate congruence between interpretation and reality, but what constitutes such congruence? What does it mean to say that an epistemological interpretation approximates the broad contours of reality in a particular time and place and in a way that provides new common ground to political participants? To address this question let us consider what it is that constitutes epistemological knowledge and how such knowledge shapes the everyday politics of our society.

The Structure of Epistemological Knowledge

I use the phrase epistemology here, as Bateson does, to mean an understanding of reality, a worldview. Such epistemological interpretations are necessarily *multilayered* understandings of reality, which we can think of as moving from core conceptions of reality (the idea of human nature, or of causality, for example) to intermediate concerns (the meaning of equality, collective empowerment, human well-being), and on to peripheral and transient concerns (the empirical impact of particular policy choices, for example). Such interpretations are *multifaceted*, encapsulating moral and value considerations, empirical perceptions, and causal interpretations. They are *systemically complex*, so that participants may share a collective understanding of the world, but that understanding may have very different implications among participants, owing to their distinctive social, economic, political, and regional interests. As a result, tensions and inequities are inherent in a collective epistemology. Finally, collective epistemologies, at heart, are relatively *simple* understandings of the world, simple enough to be inculcated by all societal participants; nonetheless, they are understandings with powerful and inclusive implications for behavior.

What form of understanding is it that can be multilayered, multifaceted, systemically complex, powerfully inclusive, and yet inherently simple? The answer, as Gregory Bateson and a growing number of theorists argue, is metaphorical reasoning.[9]

Metaphorical reasoning is the use of a simple system of interlocking metaphors to characterize the central essence of our world. Building on shared metaphorical foundations, individuals then develop common myths and stories, moral and empirical propositions, logical implications and admonitions, and principles of personal and political choice. We engage in metaphorical reasoning so completely that we cease to see the presence and power of the metaphor. We come to believe that our propositions about the world, and the logic we derive from them as well as the empirical proofs and stories we tell to validate them, are freestanding truths. In truth, they are an elaborated interpretation built on metaphor.

While we often fail to recognize the point, the movement in our discipline over the past several decades towards a rigorous formal science of politics has been fueled, at heart, by reliance on a set of interlocking and layered metaphors. Thus social choice theory is built around a central metaphorical allusion—politics as a game (Shubik, 1982; Arrow, 1963; Downs, 1957; Axelrod, 1984; Beer, 1986; Poundstone, 1991; Riker, 1962). Within this central metaphor we then have layers of metaphorical derivation—political choice as a prisoner's dilemma game, party competition as a spatial dimension game, international relations as a tic-tac-toe tournament—and so forth. Attached to these nested games we have stories and myths that provide a universal illustration of the political applicability of the metaphors, such as Axelrod's (1984) trench warfare story. And then we have an analogical leap in which it is asserted that the pattern of such games is the pattern of the world at large, thereby justifying an extended logical argument based on characteristics of games, derivations of empirical propositions, systematic empirical observations, and applications of the resulting conclusions to moral and political choice.

All human understanding parallels the metaphorical reasoning illustrated here by game theory, with science simply being a far more explicit, systematic, and formalized version of a universal metaphorical process (Bateson and Bateson, 1987:16–35; Bateson, reprinted in Donaldson, 1991:191–257). Because metaphors have extraordinary implications for meaning and action in the world, the critical issue in metaphorical reasoning is not the logic or even the heuristic capacity of the reasoning process to illuminate unforeseen aspects of the empirical world; logic and observation, after all, are often self-confirming enterprises (Kuhn, 1970). The critical issue is the analogical appropriateness of the general metaphor or model to the broad contours of the world under study (Bateson, 1972:478–487).

The effort of participants to truly understand the world thus requires what Bateson calls a *metalogue*: an experimental and experiential reassessment of the appropriateness of the metaphors and mythological narratives that underlie participants' understanding of the world.[10] Such reassessments necessarily require broad-ranging and creative dialogue among participants over the true nature of the world, as they seek new and more compelling understandings, but a metalogue is much more than an intellectual or dialogical discourse. A true metalogue also requires participants to experiment with behavioral applications of the metaphorical principles in order to assess whether real world experience with such understanding does in fact yield a sense of reempowerment and clarity in one's dealings in the world.

Appropriate metaphors and mythological narratives are thus validated when the act of seeing the world in new ways, and proceeding accordingly, generates a deeply felt and widely shared sense of renewed clarity and empowerment. Because no metaphor maps perfectly onto the ontology of the world, and because metaphorical shifts challenge participants' sense of the meaning of the world in ways that may be difficult and disruptive, such metalogical processes should proceed only insofar as is essential to a viable and reempowered understanding of the world. Successful epistemological reconstruction, even in the midst of deep metacrises, must necessarily leave many aspects of metaphorical understanding intact, lest efforts to reconceptualize the world engage participants in debilitative, obsessive, and unnecessary effort. On the other hand, precisely because metaphors and mythological narratives are so powerful in our construction of personal and political action, it is vital that we embrace appropriate metaphors as the foundations of our epistemological understanding, lest inappropriate conceptualizations and ideas about the world lead us into political pathologies and long-term disempowerment.

What this conception of epistemological reconstruction means for the political world is both quite simple and quite powerful: In the midst of deep metacrises, to survive and flourish, a polity must engage in a metalogical reassessment of its collective understanding of the world. Recognizing the metalogical nature of political reconstruction provides the central key to understanding how it is that American politics has resolved the paradoxical tensions inherent in its society and has developed viable political responses across two centuries of systemic change. The nation has done so through the creation of new metaphorical understandings of society and politics appropriate to new historical conditions and the translation of these new understandings into effective political action; such political action, from policy innovation to institutional reform to constitutional reconstruction, has used the deliberative procedures and authoritative decision structures of the American state to sustain a broadly inclusive and authentic political metalogue: to generate new and widely shared metaphorical understandings and then to implement them within the broad confines of an unfolding constitutional order.

American Political Development as Metalogue

The unfolding of the American metalogue can be demonstrated by examining the shifting metaphorical understandings that characterize our movement across historical eras (Hanson, 1985; Howe, 1988; McPherson, 1990; Ostrom, 1971; Reich, 1990; Wood, 1969, 1992; Young, 1966). In the founding era our revolutionary forefathers asserted the right of colonial children, having grown and matured, to seek independence from an increasingly oppressive mother country; in so doing they claimed an inherent right to the self-governance and equality of autonomous states that would band together only of their own free will. Among the numerous ways colonial development and late eighteenth century society could have been interpreted, this powerful rendition created a metaphorical narrative that was not only symbolically compelling but was reinforced by the demonstrated success of the colonies in waging an American War of Independence through the loosely cooperative self-governing arrangements.

In coping with the dilemma of independence they then continued their experimental metalogue. They saw that their move from colonial to confederated status had produced unforeseen problems whose management required a stronger national government; yet they were loath to create a strong centralized authority that would override state equality and popular self-governance. In addressing this dilemma they took one of the great metaphorical leaps of modern political theory; they shifted the predominant conception of society from an atomistic Hobbesian state of nature, which required an authoritarian Leviathan, to that of a collection of factions, which properly represented in government, would allow self-government through deliberative decisionmaking procedures. They shifted the predominant conception of governmental power from a holistic entity necessarily invested in one governing organ to a set of divisible processes that could be properly invested in separated organs checking and balancing one another within and between the state and national levels of government. And in experimenting with these arrangements they shortly discovered that the factions were too numerous, and the institutions too fragmented, to allow a government responsive to public cries for coherent policy change. In response they added yet a new metaphorical layer to their conception of government; they created the idea that political parties could unite societal factions and political institutions in the pursuit of a popularly supported policy agenda and thereby provide a democratic means for sustaining self-government amidst a factional and fragmented political system. Within twenty-five years of the Declaration of Independence they had reimagined and reinvented society and government through metaphorical leaps of faith that thereby legitimized a new form of constitutional democracy that would fit the historic needs of late eighteenth century America.

During the sectional crisis of the mid-nineteenth century, the nation experienced a second concentrated period of metalogical reconstruction. The opening of the western territories to settlement, and thus to the expansion of slavery, led the country to see itself as a house divided between the incompatible interests of slave and free labor; struggling to resolve this incompatibility, it came to a new conception of equality, one based not on the equal rights of states within a loose union but on the equal rights of individuals protected by a unified national government. The nation then came to believe that, within such a "house united," societal progress would come through a government that supported rugged individualism and survival of the fittest as the policy stance most appropriate to individual equality. This reconceptualization emerged over roughly twenty-five years, tested in the fires of electoral realignment, civil war, and reconstruction. It brought a fundamental alteration in the conception of the relationship between state and national government, a party system newly centered around Republican commitment to laissez-faire economics, and a new set of policy structures and institutional arrangements.

Finally, during the period of global depression and world war in the 1930s and 1940s, the nation experienced a third great transformative metalogue. As a result of the social and economic dislocations produced by advanced industrialization, and the subsequent threats presented by military imperialism among destabilized industrial nations, the United States came to see itself as an extended and communal family and began to view government as the ultimate provider and protector of familial well-being. The social problems and international vulnerabilities of the nation came to be seen as a result of governmental neglect of and isolation from its true social responsibilities and moral purpose. The solution came to be seen in providing a New Deal to the American people—committing their government to regulation of the economy, delivery of social entitlements, and containment of a hostile world. Out of this solution came the activist and bureaucratic state of the contemporary era.

At each of the deep metacrises of our history, then, and in lesser ways during critical transitional phases such as the Jacksonian uprising, the Progressive Era, or the movement politics of the 1960s, the resolution of societal crises required a reconceptualization and reconstruction of the political order. In such crisis periods, the central metaphors that came to epitomize the era were not primarily slogans but were, rather, essential elements of broad-based reasoning processes that enabled participants to revisualize and reinterpret politics and thus to act in new, more appropriate and effective ways. These processes served to reconceptualize and "modernize" the nation's understanding of its history, its contemporary context, and its future aspirations. In the process of developing and testing these reconceptualizations, participants restructured the nation's creedal precepts and constitutional principles, its policy commitments, and its consequent participatory and governing processes (Ackerman, 1991; Greenstone, 1986; Lowi, 1972; Wills, 1992).

Seeing the critical importance of metaphorical reconstruction in political development and change, then, puts a fundamentally new cast on our study of American politics.

1. The key to understanding the policy agendas, participatory processes, and governing arrangements of an historical era lies in exploring their relationship to the interlocked metaphors that dominated the collective epistemology of the era.
2. Understanding fundamental change lies in the study of the experimental alterations in participants' metaphorical understanding of the world.
3. Electoral contests and participatory control of government revolve, in their most central manifestations, around choice among metaphoric interpretations and visions of society, and secondarily around consideration of the logical application of particular metaphors to specific issue concerns; citizen knowledge of issues, facts, and candidates may be far less critical than is their grasp of the central metaphors at contest in a historical period.
4. Metaphorical alterations in our understanding of the world set in motion transformations in our dominant ideologies, policy agendas, partisan alignments, institutional rules, and constitutional interpretations.
5. Political leadership comes at its most fundamental level through metaphorical reasoning and reconstructive experiments that facilitate a reempowered understanding of politics; it comes secondarily through skillful application of such understandings.

Metaphors, Epistemologies, and Political Inquiry

From a metalogical conception of human understanding, metaphors create politics. Our efforts to understand and govern a world of change and crisis lead us to continuously reconstruct the metaphorical logic that dominates our politics. As we engage in an experimental reconstruction of our political metaphors, we embrace and institutionalize new understandings that then shape our consequent practice of politics and government. As we do so, we breathe renewed life into the body politic and set in motion a new season in our political existence.

Metaphors are, of course, only the broad foundations of our collective epistemologies. Epistemologies also include the narrative stories, logical arguments, and empirical observations that we build on our metaphorical allusions. They include the communicative, participatory, and deliberative processes that emerge from experimentation with new metaphorical understanding. And they include the policy prescriptions and institutional arrangements that flow from our metaphorical reasoning. Nevertheless, our metaphors are the essence of our understanding of political meaning and action; metaphorical reassessment must therefore be the primary focus of epistemological reconstruction when our understanding of meaning and appropriate action falters.

As we grasp the central role of metaphor, we can then understand how it is that societies learn and thereby develop new and more appropriate governing arrangements across time. Societies learn as citizens reassess and restructure the metaphors that give them a shared sense of meaning appropriate to the world in which they live. Societies develop new governing arrangements and new forms of politics through the experimental implementation of new metaphorical understandings. The discovery of a new and viable pattern of meaning amidst confusion and disarray then gives a renewed sense of order and direction to political life.

The metaphorical nature of political change provides us with the key to understanding why it is that the United States, confronting severe historical dilemmas and developmental tasks, could nevertheless survive and flourish for two hundred years. The answer lies in the capacity of the nation's citizenry to reimagine and restructure its politics in ways appropriate to the contexts and tasks of each historical era. This capacity is facilitated by cultural affinities, geopolitical security, and institutional pluralism. But the real foundations of political transformation lie in the citizenry's deeply felt metaphorical creativity and in its mastery of the deliberative political processes utilized to test and institutionalize that metaphorical understanding.

The genius of American politics, in other words, lies in the deep creative capacity of its citizens to engage in collective and sustained processes of political learning. I do not mean to suggest that this capacity is unique to our nation's citizens, or particularly distinctive among them. The capacity for political learning is a universal one, rooted in the human capacity to create shared meaning through metaphorical reasoning. The American experience is a testament, however, to the power of political learning; the capacity of individuals and societies to learn is so great—so powerful—that a citizenry can even survive and flourish amidst deep-seated conflicts and tensions that at face value would appear lethal to continued self-government. At the same time, the American experience (particularly the coming of the American Civil War) also provides a cautionary warning on how seductive and destructive static mind-sets and political orthodoxies can become, even when broad cultural, geopolitical, and institutional conditions exist that would seem to facilitate political learning. Political learning is thus not an automatic process but rather requires constant attentiveness to the appropriateness of our understanding of the world at hand, and vigilant reassessment of those beliefs and institutional structures that might lead us to resist the dominant realities of our age.

CONCLUSION: POLITICAL LEARNING AND POLITICAL SCIENCE— EMBRACING A DEVELOPMENTAL PARADIGM

These, then, are some thoughts on the study and interpretation of American politics and political change. I propose that we see American politics as a process of learning—and resistance—in which political participants create, implement, rigidify, dissolve, and recreate a collective epistemology appropriate to a changing world. The nature of the learning process is shaped by the distinctive learning tasks and learning conditions of an historical era. Societal success in learning new and appropriate governing strategies is dependent on the appropriateness of the metaphorical understanding that citizens develop of their historical era. This understanding may falter even in the most favorable circumstances or flourish in dire circumstances, depending on the experimental creativity of the nation's citizenry.

Seeing politics as a learning process, I suggest, allows us to understand American political development more fully and coherently than we would otherwise, and most particularly to address the three critical questions posed at the outset of this essay. Again, why are long periods of constancy in politics followed by sudden upheavals and political reconstruction? The answer lies in the propensity of citizens, having learned a way of understanding and governing society that enables them to redress critical policy problems, to then hold to the strategy until its inappropriateness for new societal conditions induces crises that force the citizenry to engage in a new learning process. Why do societies tend to vary in the severity of such learning episodes, and thus in the nature of their developmental paths? They do so because their learning tasks and learning conditions differ, with the United States being prone toward transformational politics as a result of learning tasks that induce prolonged and severe metacrises and learning conditions that facilitate crisis resolution. Finally, why is it that a new sense of order and meaning can arise out of deep metacrises? The re-creation of order and meaning occurs as citizens develop a metaphorical understanding of society and politics appropriate to their historical time and place.

Insofar as we see politics as a process of learning, we acknowledge the potential resilience of our political system and the central responsibility of political participants in fostering that resilience. In other words, we come to understand that politics is not primarily a clash of opposing and short-sighted interests that must necessarily induce societal destruction unless forestalled by authoritarian rules and rulers, as would seem to be implied by theorists from Thomas Hobbes (1986) to Garrett Hardin (1968) to Mancur Olson (1982). Nor is politics simply a rediscovery and reaffirmation by each generation of an unchanging set of values or creeds, as Huntington would suggest. It is, rather, a process of learning across time in which participants, confronted by potentially catastrophic crises induced by their obsession with outmoded beliefs, orthodox institutions, and shortsighted interests, can develop new and more appropriate understandings of politics made possible by societal change. Such understandings must build on and yet extend beyond the prescriptions of the past and, in so doing, yield a set of political ideals, institutional and societal arrangements, and personal interests informed by past experience and yet distinctly appropriate to present conditions. Seen as learning, in other words, politics is an open and creative process best facilitated by institutional rules and cultural mores that foster societal learning; it is best nurtured by a willingness to subject preestablished mind-sets to a respectful but probing challenge that assesses their true appropriateness to contemporary conditions. As participants engage in an open, creative, and appropriate reconstruction of political understanding, they defuse catastrophic crises and enable themselves to govern their society in a more responsible and constructive manner.

The perspective developed here can be characterized as a process of evolutionary social learning (Bateson, 1979; Campbell, 1988; Gould, 1989b; Heclo, chap. 16, this vol.). From this perspective, politics is a process of social learning and development because it centers around the social construction and reconstruction of a collective understanding of society and politics. It is, in other words, an ideational enterprise concerned with the development and transmission of knowledge (Kingdon, 1993). Politics is an evolutionary process because our social learning builds on "understanding" from the past and yet adjusts, adapts, expands, and reconstructs that understanding to fit the unique characteristics of the present, thereby evolving the ideational foundations for distinctly new— though historically continuous—forms of governing (Axelrod, 1984; Carmines and Stimson, 1989; Ostrom, 1990; Riker, 1982a). As evolutionary learning occurs across time, political participants empower themselves to operate in the present as fully and effectively as possible. By operating effectively and fully in the present they gain the capacity to shape and reshape society and politics in response to their deepest shared values and aspirations. Operating fully in the present thereby provides participants with the opportunity to play a conscious and constructive role in the shaping of human history and the progressive development of human understanding (Chambers, 1993).

Seeing politics as evolutionary learning requires, of course, that we assess politics across long stretches of time and consider how it is that patterns of governance develop and change. Political learning is thus a historical process that may take several generations to come to full fruition, so that analysts focused on any one historical period can easily find proof of the static and resistant nature of political mind-sets and the short-sighted and destructive capacities of political participants. Moreover, political learning can be a difficult and often a violent process, so that the "discourse" and "deliberation" that occurs among participants across time is not simply, or even primarily, a dispassionate and harmonious enterprise; it can also be an impassioned struggle in which new understandings arise on the brink or in the midst of mutually destructive engagements. Similarly, while political learning may induce some degree of mutual understanding and collective recognition of shared interests among participants, it does not necessarily involve an end to opposing values, distinctive interests, or adversarial relations (Stone, 1989).Therefore, analysts must not confuse an emphasis on political learning with the tranquil resolution of societal problems or with the creation of a homogeneous and contented citizenry. Learning is seen, rather, in the recognition and pursuit of common interests and understandings that were previously ignored or overridden, even when such recognition comes despite the continuance of conflicting values and interests.

Most critically, as we examine politics across time we come to see it as an open-ended and creative process. This process may momentarily take on the character of a well-ordered game, with fixed preferences and rules, as participants arrive at a shared metaphorical understanding of the politics of their era; one can thus isolate particular political decisions and behavioral patterns within historical periods and assess them in terms of being a rational choice among sets of simple interests and constant preferences. Across time, though, shared understandings break down, preferences cease to have a simple and obvious ordering, confusion as to the consequences of rational action mounts, and an improvisational search occurs for a new understanding of the character of the political game. Across history, then, politics is less a recurring game of choice among fixed preferences and more nearly an evolving game of experimentation, learning, and game adaptation to new historical conditions and concerns. Successful learning and adaptation yields a momentary sense of orderliness to politics as participants see a new and empowering metaphorical connection across the vast array of interests, rules, structures, and mores that have emerged and survived during historical and contemporaneous experimentations and political usage. Such connections give a sense of meaning and purpose to contemporary politics that enables participants to address the pressing concerns of their day. Yet with the passage of time such metaphorical connections lose their relevance and potency, a sense of disorder reemerges, and the political game begins to depend for its survival and renewed character on its experimental reconstruction by game participants. Seen in this manner, politics and political learning is a problematic and contingent process rather than a deterministic one. Game participants can induce self-destruction through resistance to experimentation and learning, through experimental failure in learning, or through pathological patterns of learning, just as they can experience renewal through evolutionary learning.

Insofar as we are willing to assess politics across time, and to accept its problematic and open-ended nature, we can acknowledge and embrace the insights of evolutionary learning and better understand the true nature of politics. Our understanding of politics thereby takes on a clarity and completeness that helps us to recognize the broad range of processes and factors that shape political learning and to appreciate the blending of theoretical approaches and interpretive strategies that is necessary to an adequate understanding of political development. We are thus led to a broadly focused and balanced strategy of political inquiry across the micro, macro, and middle-range levels of analysis and to an integrated conception of a science of politics.

At the micro level, a focus on evolutionary learning requires us to acknowledge the multiplicity of individual and group processes that constitute learning across time, as well as the variety of theoretical approaches to political behavior that are required to understand politics. This range of approaches must necessarily include social choice theory (designed to explain the rational calculation of short-term behavior in light of the personal preferences created by a pattern of societal interests), political and organizational sociology (designed to explain the origin, management, and maintenance of group and institutional cohesiveness in pursuit of shared preferences), and cultural anthropology (designed to explain the processes of individual and group recognition of new societal patterns and interests, particularly in periods of political reconstruction). It also must include social psychology (designed to explain the nature and resolution of political psychopathologies), and personal and clinical psychology (designed to explain individual behavior and thus the distinctive actions and experimental discoveries of individual political actors and leaders). Each of these microlevel approaches helps us understand a critical aspect of learning across time and is essential to a science of politics; on other hand, no one approach can provide a full understanding of political learning, thus no single approach can dominant our strategy of inquiry as a discipline. The challenge for a science of politics at a micro level is to acknowledge, clarify, and blend the contributions of these and related approaches in order to develop a full-scale microlevel theory of societal learning and resistance.

With respect to macroanalysis, a focus on evolutionary learning requires that we emphasize the interplay of institutional and societal factors as they together shape the learning experiences of a society. Thus scholars of politics, and particularly students of American politics, tend to divide into those who stress institutional arrangements (March and Olsen, 1989), and those who stress cultural patterns within society (King, 1973a, 1973b). They also divide into those who stress the conflictual and immobilizing character of American politics (particularly as a result of its institutional arrangements, Burns, 1963) and those who stress its consensual and survivalist aspects (particularly as a result of societal culture Hartz, 1955; Huntington, 1981). Seeing politics as evolutionary learning, by contrast, stresses the blended contribution that institutional and societal factors make to the existence of immobilizing conflict *and* to the consensual resolution of conflict: Both societal and institutional factors can—and do—magnify the learning tasks that give rise to deep societal crisis in American history; yet both societal and institutional factors can—and do—serve to facilitate the discovery of common ground among adversaries. From an evolutionary learning perspective, then, neither a societal nor an institutional perspective would seem inherently predominant in our macrolevel analysis of politics across time, or inherently virtuous or villainous in its consequence for politics. Both institutional and societal factors can serve to facilitate or inhibit learning so that the role of both, and their interaction, must be understood across time (see also Steinmo, chap. 5, and Hanson, chap. 6, this vol.)

At the middle-range level of analysis, a focus on evolutionary learning leads to an "ideational" conception of politics and thus to a broadly inclusive understanding of the influence of societal participants on political action (Baumgartner and Jones, 1993; Kingdon, 1993; Hanson, 1985; Weber, 1976). The distinctive character of the politics that emerges within an historical context depends on the ideas at play in that era, particularly on the deep and interlocked metaphors that undergird and integrate participants' collective understanding of the world. Because such metaphorical understanding is grounded in and driven by the multitude of experiences and creative discoveries that occur among citizens throughout a society, political learning across time must be seen as participant-driven rather than as elite-controlled; and because the survival of such metaphorical understandings depends on their true contextual appropriateness, politics across time is shaped far more by the historical truth and broad understanding of ideas than by strategies of power and manipulation. Within time, that is, within circumscribed moments of political action, elites may rule, power may predominate, and manipulation may work. But across time, truth trumps power, deep-felt understanding outlasts momentary manipulations, and—for good or for ill—the people rule.[11]

Finally, and most critically for the profession of political science, an emphasis on evolutionary learning provides scholars with an integrated way of thinking about the nature of political inquiry itself. Currently systematic political inquiry tends to be divided into two broad and opposing camps (Almond, 1990; Diesing, 1971; Hirschman, 1970; Riker, 1982b, 1982c; von Wright, 1971): formalists, who emphasize the search for general laws that identify and predict the regularities of politics, and interpretivists, who emphasize the unique and open-ended nature of politics across distinctive contexts and historical eras. A focus on evolutionary learning suggests that both of these schools have important contributions to make to a synthesized approach to inquiry. On the one hand, there may be an abstract process of political learning (or, the tendency to hold to beliefs until forced to reassess them by metacrises) that is a universal experience across societies and historical eras, rooted in human nature; it may thereby be possible for political science to discover general law-like principles of development and change that inform political analysis. On the other hand, the substantive nature of political learning is creative, open-ended, and distinctive to contexts, so that its content, patterning, and outcome will be specific to particular societies and historical eras; understanding the politics of any particular society or set of societies thus will require close attention to distinctive experiences of learning and resistance, and respect for the open-ended and creative nature of developmental processes.

Evolutionary learning thus suggests the need for a synthesized approach to political inquiry that I call formal interpretivism. In this approach, the central focus is the identification of law-like principles of political learning and resistance, and the utilization of such principles in deciphering and understanding the political development of distinctive societies. In the move to a synthesized approach, both formalists and interpretivists would be forced to sacrifice some cherished assumptions. In accepting the centrality of learning, formalists must necessarily forgo their emphasis on predictive laws, since learning involves a creativity that itself will be unpredictable; they also must abandon their vision of politics as a recurring and ordered game since the process of learning can involve prolonged periods of confusion and disarray. For their part, interpretivists must forgo the insistence on the unique and unordered nature of politics: The process of learning, if not its content, may follow general principles whose discovery can usefully illuminate the politics of any society in any historical era; among these principles, moreover, is the possibility that amidst the political disarray of an era participants may see a metaphorical connectedness from which they derive a meaningful sense of political order and strategic purpose. In letting go of these separate emphases, both formalists and interpretivists can embrace the metaphor of evolutionary learning and thereby join in a collective effort to clarify the learning processes of societies across time.

In providing a basis for synthesizing formal and interpretive modes of inquiry, an emphasis on evolutionary learning makes possible a developmental science of politics. As such, political science would necessarily focus on understanding the political development of societies—both through the construction of a core body of abstract theory about developmental process and through the creation of context-specific empirical theories of politics in particular historical settings. A science of politics would also be developmental in a different sense, however. Its core body of theory would be subject to developmental reconstruction across time should the principles of societal learning themselves change in response to new contexts; such change might particularly occur should the capacity of societies to learn from theories of learning thereby alter the learning process itself. Likewise, political science would have to reconstruct its empirical theories across time as historical contexts change, so that its empirical knowledge would be subject to continued development and reassessment. Through explicit attentiveness to the continued development of its context-specific theories, political science could then maintain a contemporaneous relevance that would enable it to clarify the dilemmas, constraints, and opportunities of each historical era.

The creation of a developmental science of politics holds out the prospect for conscious awareness of the nature of political learning on the part of future societies. As societies become more aware of the capacity to learn across time, the great systemic shifts in politics may come more expectedly, less traumatically, and with greater informed attention to the reconstruction of governing arrangements across time. A science of politics thereby can become a major contributor to the learning capacities of societies. Rather than building a body of deterministic theory that masks the creative learning capacities of society, and thereby increases resistance to learning, political science would construct a body of developmental theory designed to clarify and illuminate the learning processes and possibilities across societies and eras. Likewise, rather than an emphasis on uniqueness and disarray that obscures our commonalities and shared understandings, political science would seek to learn from the distinctive experiences of societies those principles of learning that foster political renewal amidst the complexities and disjunctures of history. Motivated by the failure of political science to foresee the great systemic reconstructions of contemporary politics, both formalists and interpretivists could, in this way, reconceptualize their understandings of the nature and study of politics and embrace a collective and developmental paradigm; together they could then construct a new science of politics more appropriate to understanding the new worlds which human learning creates across time.[12] The need for a new science of politics will become particularly evident should the broad systemic changes of the late twentieth century activate a fundamental restructuring in American politics—and thereby challenge the empirical and epistemological truths that dominate contemporary political science (Heclo, 1989; Maisel, 1990:307–323; Petracca, 1992:345–361; Rose, 1991).

NOTES

I wish to thank those who provided critiques of earlier drafts of this chapter, including Leslie Anderson, Douglas Ashford, Frank Beer, Ron Brunner, Walter Dean Burnham, Simone Chambers, Murray Edelman, Richard Fenno, Joan Fiore, Edward Greenberg, Richard Harris, Hugh Heclo, Ronald Inglehart, Bryan Jones, Cal Jillson, Peter Katzenstein, Sean Kelley, Jeffrey Kopstein, Mark Lichbach, Robert Lopez, Vince McGuire, John McIver, Sid Milkis, Carolyn Mohr-Hennefeld, T. J. Pempel, Paul Quirk, James Rosenau, Catherine Rudder, James Scott, Teodor Shanin, Michael Strine, James Thurber, and David Van Mill. I am also grateful to the graduate students in my seminar on scope and methods and in my American politics core seminar at the University of Colorado, Boulder.

1. See Alexis de Tocqueville (1945:12).

2. This effort reflects over a decade of attention on my part to building a theory of American political change; most of that work centered on the Congress. For a discussion of this theory-building process, see Dodd (1987, 1991). My initial theoretical effort came as a response to David Mayhew's arguments in *Congress: The Electoral Connection* (1974).

3. These cross-disciplinary theorists include Carl Jung (1963), Michael Lerner (1986), Thomas Kuhn (1970), and W. R. Ashby (1952). My numerous debts to fellow political scientists are evident in the citations throughout this essay.

4. Considered one of the leading scientific theorists of the twentieth century, though far better known in biology, ecological science, anthropology, psychiatry, and the philosophy of science than in political science, Bateson was one of the pioneers in the creation and social application of cybernetics and systems theory, game theory, and communications theory. It was out of the combination of these fields that he created modern cybernetic learning theory, which he then applied across a wide variety of phenomena, from the study of schizophrenia and family dynamics to work on dolphins and biological communication to large-scale social and ecological systems. See Bateson (1971, 1972, 1979), Bateson and Bateson (1987), and Donaldson (1991). The best overview of Bateson's life and work is contained in Lipset (1980). Bateson died in 1980 at the age of seventy-six.

5. Useful examples of political learning and resistance at an individual and group level can be found in Fenno (1991, 1992) and Fenno (1973), pp. 281–291; see

also the discussion in Dodd (1992). For examples of community learning and resistance, see Anderson (1994, particularly chapter 7, and (1991). Discussions of societal and governmental learning are contained in Inglehart (1989), particularly chaps. 1 and 2, and in Breslauer and Tetlock (1991).

6. As Lincoln put it early in the Civil War: "The dogmas of the quiet past are inadequate to the stormy present. The occasion is piled high with difficulty, and we must think anew, and act anew. We must disenthrall ourselves and then we shall save our country" (quoted in Greenstone, 1986:40).

7. My own view is that individuals within society grapple in their own lives with personal issues that reflect the epistemological conflicts of the age. Political "creativity" and "charismatic" leadership occur as individuals and leaders develop personal strategies that speak to the broader epistemological concerns of the era (Erikson, 1964, 1969; Greenstone, 1986:36–49).

8. My argument is somewhat foreshadowed by the German philosopher, Karl Jaspers (1958:320), in *The Future of Mankind*. Assessing the gloomy future that the atomic bomb had created, and the consequent need for exceptional leadership on the world stage, Jaspers writes: "In America—today the area of decision in the world of political reality—I hope for the old, pious, morally radical forces. There, where men have suddenly come to change and reflect before, the world situation may make everyone feel the unprecedented responsibility for the course of mankind—the breath of history and the unique task within it. A great transforming impulse might jolt the Americans out of superficial optimism, out of moral pharisaism, out of the rationalism of know-how, and awaken them to their own selves. A nation that constituted its government wisely and successfully, that produced great statesmen, poets, and theologians, the nation of Emerson and James, a Western nation, yet more open-minded than the rest because of its emigrant roots and ingenuous beginnings—such a nation may yet do the extraordinary which the life or death of mankind now depends upon." Jaspers appears to be pointing here to the distinctive transformative capacities of American society and politics, even in the midst of extraordinary crisis.

For my part I do not mean to suggest that the tendency towards transformational politics is unique to our nation. Other societies, particularly those whose contexts create magnified learning tasks and facilitative learning conditions, may experience patterns of political learning and change analogous to our own (with deep metacrises followed by transformative reconstructions that leave the broad governing arrangements and geopolitical identity of the nation-state intact). I do suggest that the American experience is a relatively distinctive one among large and complex nation-states in the contemporary world.

9. See particularly *Our Own Metaphor*, edited by Mary Catherine Bateson (1972). This is a report of the Wenner-Gren Conference on the Effects of Conscious Purpose on Human Adaptation, held July 17–24, 1968, at Burg Wartenstein, Austria, and chaired by Gregory Bateson. See also Geertz (1964), Lasswell and Kaplan (1950), McCloskey (1985), and Ortony (1979). A vivid illustration of the use of metaphorical reasoning in American politics is found in McPherson (1990), chapter 5, "How Lincoln Won the War with Metaphors."

10. This is a somewhat expanded use of metalogue, but one that I believe is consistent with Bateson's work. See Bateson (1972:1–58).

11. An illustration of this argument is provided by Wood's (1992) discussion of the ways in which popular learning and change during the early nineteenth century led to alterations in the nature of American society and politics that engulfed and overwhelmed the governing elite and set in motion the great transformations of the mid-nineteenth century. See also Young (1966) and Tocqueville (1946).

12. A comparison with other fields of inquiry may clarify this goal. Evolutionary theorists in biology give a systematic accounting of how evolution occurs, with its heavy doses of randomness and chance; they can also help us foresee the mutation and evolution of species and the conditions that facilitate or hinder such developments; but they are unable to predict the precise character of the species that will evolve, when it will do so, or whether it will survive. Psychologists identify the processes whereby individuation and personal growth occur and outline the attendant struggles, choices, and constraints, though they cannot predict how (or if) each individual will resolve life crises and create a new life structure. Political scientists likewise may be able to identify the processes of choice, experimentation, struggle, and learning through which societies reconstruct and conduct their politics over time, although they are unable to predict specific political structures, policies, and behavior patterns that will emerge. By clarifying and theorizing about such processes, scholars bring to the political world not a prediction of its long-term future course, and not just a description of its past, but an awareness of its creative processes, dilemmas, and possibilities. See Mayr, 1984; Gould, 1989b; Erikson, 1964; and Habermas, 1973.

PART V

Conclusion

16

Ideas, Interests, and Institutions

HUGH HECLO

How are we to understand the changing shape of American politics? What approach or approaches hold out the greatest hope of yielding genuine understanding of change? And because change has to be identified by reference to what has not changed, or changed less, the question also requires us to consider stability and continuity. The simplest-seeming political questions are the ones that can embarrass a political "scientist" most: How do things happen? What makes things happen?

The more seriously we take such elemental questions, the more it seems that humility is the appropriate posture. Political events swirling around us may be a recurring tide. But again, they may be some deeper current taking us in a particular direction. Or they may just be a passing ripple in our particular eddy of place and time. The vividness of personally living in the here and now—our inescapable presentism—is a standing invitation to mistake the ripple for the currents or the tide.

As if this were not enough, we are asking about ways to understand not simply the interplay of change and continuity but the dynamics that underlie such transformations. The term "dynamics" comes from the Greek word for power or force. To study the dynamics of American politics means to try to understand the inner workings of change, to seek to figure out "what makes things happen" (Schattschneider, 1960:vii).[1] Do we then verge on the preposterous arrogance of hoping to explain how history works?

The approaches discussed in this book do not presume to explain how history works. At most they offer successive and provisional approximations to partial knowledge. It is honest, perhaps liberating, to admit that our capacities to perceive and understand might not be up to the task of fully accounting for transformations in American politics. Humility involves accepting that likelihood, while still trying to advance our knowledge and understanding.

Unfortunately, as "learning" has become institutionalized in universities and other bureaucratic settings over the past 100 years, many pressures have developed that seem to hinder rather than promote broad-gauged understanding. The familiar problem of disciplinary specialization—knowing more and more about less and less in mutually isolated communities of discourse—is only one of those pressures. In the social sciences, particular approaches often seem to be developed and maintained, not for the contribution they make to further understanding but as vehicles for career advancement, ideological proselytizing, intellectual one-upsmanship and other benighted purposes. Moreover, since publication résumés grow on dissension, academics often develop a vested interest in not agreeing or in dwelling on minor differences contained within the larger body of unspoken, non-career-enhancing agreement. Then too, the most promising idea or approach may never be further explored or disseminated among graduate students unless its founder exhibits a good deal of overstatement and immodest advocacy. As if these time-honored traditions were not enough, in recent years we have witnessed the growth of some academic subcultures that dismiss any aspirations for objective understanding or accumulation of knowledge in social and political affairs. This is not a critical approach, which might ask, for example, if appearances are what they seem; it is a cynical approach that assumes appearances are never what they seem, what is said or written is never what is meant, and the only real agendas are hidden agendas. In this atmosphere the rhetoric of negation is the surest route to intellectual reputation whereas affirmation can only put one at risk (Kohn, 1990).

The preceding chapters have grown out of a conversation that has tried to be open-minded and affirmative in its attempt to talk across the normal academic boundaries, which too often resemble barricades. The conference that precipitated these chapters operated on the premise that mutual persuasion is possible and should be welcomed. And reading these chapters does suggest that a certain amount of persuasion occurred. It did so not by convincing people to substitute one approach for another but by revealing areas of convergent thinking (see Swift and Brady, chap. 4, this vol.).

At least that is the argument of this chapter. In what follows I will try to summarize three areas of convergence. These are in no sense an answer to the puzzle of political dynamics; instead, the convergences I will discuss focus on how to think about the question of political change in America. I will discuss the three areas in what is probably a descending order of agreement among the authors. What follows is certainly not a research program, which only the most desperate of graduate students would ever pay attention to in any event. The aim is simply to highlight central tendencies that seemed to emerge as several dozen thoughtful people tried to take this difficult subject seriously.

WHAT KIND OF KNOWLEDGE ARE WE LOOKING FOR?

The first common area of concern, and I think convergence, is epistemological. The authors of the preceding chapters have struggled over the basic question of what kind of knowledge we should expect to acquire about American political development. Are we trying to extract regularities, build general theories, make and test predictions? Or are we trying to flesh out more accurate descriptions, understand context, and anchor accounts of political development in the historical contingencies of time and place?

In struggling with these questions we are revisiting a more than century-old debate in the social sciences as well as an even more ancient battleground in the philosophy of history. The contesting positions have been vigorously demarcated in the past, and they often remain no less so today. Students of American politics should be aware of this intellectual landscape, for it is possible to drift into very stark and unproductive confrontations.

According to one line of thought, the social sciences should be modeled on the example of the natural sciences. The knowledge we are striving for should be as context-free as possible, with explanations that are applicable across time and space. Application of the scientific method in social and historical studies should lead to theories that are general in scope, that are cumulative, and capable of being confirmed or disproved through empirical, preferably quantitative, findings (Hempel, 1942:35). This view, usually labeled positivism, has taken various forms in the 150 years since Comte first expounded the ideal of a unified science that would reveal fundamental regularities in nature and society. But the essential positivist goals remain an animating force throughout much of contemporary social science (Deutsch, Markovits, and Platt, 1986).

A contrary school contends that the aims and methods of the natural sciences are not applicable to social and historical studies (Winch, 1958). In human affairs, knowledge is ultimately dependent on context, with any generalizations inevitably restricted to phenomena situated in a particular historical time and unique institutional setting. There are no invariable regularities or general laws of human activity to be discovered by the formal rationality and standardized operations of "science." Nor is there any privileged, objective position for the observer (Nagel, 1986). Subjectivity is the inevitable characteristic of a realm permeated by human values, emotions, and meanings. Thus knowledge acquired through the social disciplines is pluralistic and relative and is not a cumulative process based on the predictions and discoveries growing out of general theories (Smelser and Gernstein, 1986).

These differences reflect important and diverging intellectual histories; in the Anglo-American tradition the social and physical sciences were distinguished from the humanities, whereas the continental European tradition grouped social science with the humanities (human sciences, or *Geisteswissenschaften*) in contrast to the natural sciences. The contest between positivism and contextualism has racked the social sciences for over one hundred years (Dray, 1957; Ross, 1991). If anything, the clash has become more extreme in recent years, with deconstructionist, antifoundationalist movements emerging in literature, American studies, history, and philosophy. In one observer's words:

> It is a debate of method permeating most disciplines whereby positivist empirical methods are contrasted with qualitative, interpretive, hermeneutic and phenomenological methods. It is a debate of meta-theory whereby a progressive, cumulative science is contrasted with dialectical ... revolutionary ... or even anarchical theories of scientific change. It is a debate of philosophy whereby objectivism is contrasted with relativism, and absolutism is contrasted with nihilism. (Overman, 1988:x).

In political science today there are overlapping debates between what some call rationalist or microfoundational theories and what others variously term reflectivist, ideational, or normativist approaches (Keohane, 1988:379–396; Wilson, 1990; Almond, 1990). On both sides it is possible to strike extreme positions—possible but not necessary. The authors of this book have tended to agree that it is unconstructive to do so. Implicitly at least, they suggest it is unrealistic to think that good theory and adequate causal explanations must be of a universal form where historical date and provincial location are disregarded. But neither do the authors of these chapters contend that the political world is so particular in form—so complex, contingent, and irreversible—that everything interesting happens only once in its meaningful details" (Gould, 1989b:21). Complete situational uniqueness destroys any basis for shared understanding, much less for theory. If environmental context is everything, anything we might say is a "socially constructed author function" and politics and history become essentially unknowable.

It is not enough to say that here the knowledge being sought about political dynamics is of a "middle-range" type, somewhere between the positivist's universal laws and the contextualist's thick description of the particular. We can say more. The preceding chapters converge on a kind of knowing that deals with the substantive logic or patterns enfolded in historically concrete situations. The regularities and explanations being sought, without exception, are not absolute. Since "everything is known as a figure in a ground or not at all" (Davenport, 1987), generalizations are fully expected to be relative to certain contexts (a state of technology, a class of situations, a set of prevailing institutional practices, and so on.) Contrariwise, the inevitable exceptions and variations are expected to be variations in *something*, to be differences that are structured in some characteristic way. In talking about structured variation, relative generalization, or the characteristic logic of substantive situations, we are saying nothing particularly new, and indeed, we hearken back to ideas enunciated by Karl Popper and Max Weber. It is squarely in the Weberian spirit to stake out an intermediate epistemological position where we expect accounts and explanations to be relative to context but leave ourselves ample room for exposing more general processes and historical types. Just as a social scientist is rarely interested in explaining a single, particular event unconnected with anything else, so too there is little to be gained from a formulaic system of social science laws with absolutely general validity. As Weber notes, even if the latter were possible it would not contribute to an understanding of the varying patterns of historical and political reality that most people regard as worth knowing about. Followers of rational choice, or more historical, behavioral, or institutional approaches need not be at each other's throats. Our studies suggest how much we are approaching common ground from different directions. For example in this volume we can see how rational choice and microfoundational approaches are developing what historians have long employed as less formal "rational explanations"—or as William Dray put it thirty-five years ago—"reconstruction of the agent's calculation of means to be adopted toward his chosen end in the light of the circumstances in which he found himself" (Kedourie, 1992:112–120). Where rational choice and more behavioral accounts may differ is not on the matter of purposive rationality but in the emphasis on the degree to which the individual is independent of the environment. This difference in the extent of voters' social entanglements might well, for example, distinguish Aldrich's rational choice approach to voter choice from Huckfeldt and Beck's more behavioralist orientation in this volume. But the reverse can also occur! Richer rational choice models can elaborate voters' contextual parameters whereas, as Huckfeldt and Beck point out, it was the "behavioralist" Michigan voter studies that tended to rip individuals out of the social contexts that were so important in the earlier Columbia voter studies. To put the point more broadly, there seems little doubt that if a historical law of human behavior exists, it is something to the effect that: "When men are confronted with important decisions where they are obliged to choose between their own, or their group's, interests and those of others, they nearly always choose the former" (Lenski, 1966:3). But this of course tells us nothing about what attachments to a group or groups will exist or how inclusively and permeably the boundaries will be drawn with respect to "the other."

By the same token it is clear from themes in chapters by Stone, Mansbridge, and others that accounts of political dynamics must be concerned with not only the rational pursuit of purpose but also the development of purpose. Through an interplay of actions, context, and deliberation, the expression of rationality itself can become a variable. This is true when, for example, the pursuit of old purposes can lead to the discovery of new ends, values, and emotional commitments. The more novel such "moments" (or, in rational choice language, the looser the constraints of the system on the agent as attempts are made to shift from one equilibrium path to another) are, the more likely it is we may have to resort to "imaginative reenactment" in order to try and understand the meaning of the situation for the participants (Beer, 1963:1, 6–29). And in trying to re-experience the world as someone else saw it we are certainly drawing more upon historical arts than historical science.

Thus the relative generalizations and theories being sought are intended to be useful in explaining a class of events, not unique events, by using a common mechanism. This does not mean unique events (an assassination, the personality of a political leader) should be excluded from accounts of political change, but it does mean that our generalizations should have to be tested across instances, places, time, and the like. The fewer the exceptions that arise as we try to explain data from different sources, the more confidence we can have in our hypothesis or relative generalization. Our convergent approaches do not see this as second-best theory, shamed as compared to always-applicable models with a few timeless causes—the elegant pure theory political scientists sometimes pine for but cannot seem to achieve (Wilson, 1989:xi).[2] We believe there is nothing inelegant or ugly about nonpredictive general statements with a validity limited to certain contexts, such contexts being analytically and comparatively understood as classes of events and situations. And this approach certainly has more to offer our understanding than does a contextual determinism that tries to explain events by exhausting the concreteness of a particular historical situation.

While historical materials are clearly of great importance, the approaches in this volume reject what might be called history-rummaging. Understanding is not enhanced if one begins by asking, What theory or methodological schema do I have and how can it be applied here and there to historical situations? (It is even worse to sift history to assemble supportive evidence for a preexisting theory.) Instead, one should begin by asking, What interesting question do I want to answer and what are the most appropriate ways to try to answer it? From this starting point some

form of theory will still—inevitably—be important in defining and selecting categories of historical information to examine. But it will be a more
honest use of history and theory. In the view of this volume's authors, history is important as history, not as a repository of stylized facts and examples for theoretical models. As portrayed in these chapters, history as history matters in at least two ways. First, it is important in defining the
"situatedness" of the factors under examination. We should not presume
that present-day concepts (including means-end thinking itself) are applicable in all other times and places. Political institutions, for example, are
inherently historical. They exist in a context more than they incorporate a
context, carrying time-specific elements that are a function of when they
were formed (Orren and Skowronek, chap. 14, this vol.). Second, history
embodies the sequences through which one move implicates subsequent
possibilities, and outcomes are predicated on what came before. Or in the
language of rational choice approaches, outcomes are path-dependent in a
political world that normally has multiple equilibria. We will return to
this theme later.

Thus the kind of knowledge being sought tries to build context into its
explanations, rather than calling in context on an ad hoc basis in order to
rescue a theory that does not account for particular variations. If there are
constants or universal laws of political dynamics, we will probably only
obtain some notion of them as the absence of variation. That remains to be
seen.

So far we have considered what might be called the "reach" of the
knowledge being sought—namely, a hybrid (rather than second-best) version that lies between purely contextual and absolutely universal explanations. There is a second dimension of thinking about American political
development that needs to be addressed. The "level" of our accounts may
be pitched at the micro perspective of what has come to be called methodological individualism. It may also be scaled to macrolevel phenomena
where the massive and impersonal forces of an economic, technological,
demographic, and cultural nature sweep away any individual calculations of self-interest. Are we then caught up in another all-or-nothing
choice, this one between microlevel and macrolevel perspectives? Again
our conversation across approaches has shown an important convergence
regarding this level-of-analysis problem.

The central point of agreement is that any adequate approach should
seek to tie the two levels together. Accounts of political development from
the microlevel perspective need to elaborate parameters of larger compo-
sitional structure; they should not draw conclusions about aggregate outcomes simply by inflating the importance of the behavior of any single
representative individual (Langlois, 1989:241). Likewise accounts from
the macrolevel perspective need to be articulated into plausible render-

ings of individual level behavior; they should not produce aggregate-level explanations that cannot be meaningfully related to a realm of individuals making choices to pursue their goals. We need to show that there is a way of getting from "here to there" between bulky historical "forces" and the micro world of human actions. To take a common example, if we find a strong relationship between changes in economic conditions and certain kinds of election outcomes, it is not very informative to construct accounts of political development as if there were a self-contained world of macro-economic and political relations peopled only by aggregate variables. (This is perhaps the major reason for the intellectually disappointing results of so many of the aggregate correlation studies in economics and politics.) We need to recognize that what is at work is an articulated relationship extending from macroeconomic conditions, through intermediary bodies, and down to individuals responding to the resulting incentives in such a way as to produce the forecasted aggregate outcomes. By the same token, it is much too cramped a view to consider aggregate level behavior of the democratic state as a simple version writ large of individual voter preferences for high benefits and low taxes. (This is perhaps the major reason for the intellectually disappointing results from the rational-choice-inspired literature popular in the 1970s on the seemingly inevitable fiscal breakdown of democracy.) The same caution holds true for analogical leaps of faith in which game-theoretic patterns among individuals are simply transposed onto collectivities in the world at large (Dodd, chap. 15, this vol.).

Thus in terms of both the reach and the level of analysis, what we are looking for is not quite the same thing as the often-endorsed idea of "middle-range theory" (Merton, 1957; Steinmo, Thelen, and Longstreth, 1992). What we are looking for is theory that can work by moving and integrating across "ranges," not settle for a midpoint between micro and macro, or between the particular and the general.

Figure 16.1 offers a schematic view of what has been argued in this section. It takes the familiar form of a fourfold table, which counterposes the two dimensions we have discussed. The figure suggests the compartmentalized enclaves within which so many of the arguments about the kinds of knowledge we are looking for take place. At the micro level, compartment 1 offers thick descriptions of situations facing key individuals and the actions taken by them—the dramatic contingencies of political history that cannot be rewound and played again.

Compartment 2 takes us to the realm of pure methodological individualism, applicable in all places and times. Unlike compartment 1, here we are not looking at the experiences individuals have lived through but rather at the individual as a theoretical construct. Outcomes are produced

FIGURE 16.1   Level of the Account

Reach of the Account	Micro	Macro
Contextual	Key Actor Accounts/ Thick Description 1	Tolstoyan History 3
Universal	2 Elemental Rational Choice Accounts	4 Laws of Sociohistorical Development

by the summation and deducible consequences of individual choices made under the presumably universal law of self-interest.

Switching to the macro level finds us in compartment 3, where anything that might be said about individuals is drowned out in a roar of impersonal forces in unique combinations. In this Tolstoyan world, the towering individuals of the first quadrant are merely celebrated puppets, caught up in a collective motion produced by the incalculable interactions of nameless multitudes.

The final compartment is occupied by the grand theories of historical causation. While the notions of Hegel, Marx, Spengler, or Toynbee are surely out of fashion, one can still catch a whiff of the old yearning for regularity and direction in historical processes. It emerges, for example, in the literature on stages of economic, social, and political development, or in the way cycles of public activism and private withdrawal are thought to recur (Schlesinger, 1986; Hirschman, 1977; Phillips, 1969). The venerable theme of American exceptionalism is itself a backhanded way of thinking in this mode about a country that has stepped outside normal historical laws.

The emergent view suggested in this book is that all four of these cells are poor choices. The knowledge being sought here is of the kind that tries to navigate along the axial cross hairs, not the kind that comes to rest in one of the compartments. This is easy to say. How might this be done?

THREE COMMON BUILDING BLOCKS

The conversation among approaches in this volume has been directed toward the problem of change and dynamic relationships. But change in what? And relationships among what? In reading these chapters one senses a substantial convergence in views on the basic elements that are regarded as absolutely central. Whatever the preferred political science approach, the three common building blocks are ideas, interests, and institutions. Admittedly this is not a novel view. A good case could be made that many, if not most, of the classic studies of American politics use precisely these three categories as their guiding framework (Herring, 1940).[3]

There is no space here to enter into the extended discussion, including issues of definition, that these concepts deserve. The best we can do is sketch some of the important points that have emerged from the encounters on the previous pages.

It is certainly not news that different schools of thought develop proprietary interests in certain kinds of variables. To put it crudely, this often produces claims to the effect that "institutions matter," referring generally to those enduring rules, procedures, and organizations that tend to structure individual conduct. Or, intellectual historians will claim that "ideas matter," again meaning, roughly, that mental constructions play a crucial part in shaping what happens. Then too, few people with a realistic appreciation of politics doubt that "interests matter," which is usually interpreted to refer to the self-interested and purposive pursuit of material goals.

At this point any number of quagmires must be circumvented. For example, if interests are not self-defining and institutional norms must be internalized, do ideational factors not demand priority? Or is it that ideas are used merely to rationalize interests, with institutions likewise shaped to fit the latter's calculations of advantage? But then aren't institutions the embodiment of ideas and the shaping framework within which interests are created?

Our discussions generally acknowledged that self-interest probably explains more of the variance in political affairs than any other single factor, but this does not mean it explains very much. A recurring theme in the preceding chapters is the notion that understanding is best advanced, not by giving priority to one or another type of variable, but by concentrating on the interrelationships of ideas, interests, and institutions. The "action," so to speak, is at the intersection, where the influences among the three elements are reciprocal. Trying to understand the reciprocity is likely to be more useful than looking for the primacy of any one factor as a source of alternative explanations. This becomes clear when we consider particular themes in the preceding chapters.

While it is important to make analytic distinctions, the theme of American exceptionalism cannot be realistically rendered as a matter of choice between either institutions or cultural ideas. The cultural tradition of populism and the institutionalized system of primary elections is a cluster. In

Chapter 5, Steinmo, for example, enters the subject of American exceptionalism through institutional analysis and in Chapter 6 Hanson does so
primarily through cultural values. But having entered through different
doors, both writers converge on an analysis of institutions and cultural
values in interaction. And certainly neither approach denies that powerful
interests were involved in decisionmaking about taxes or liberal domestic
reforms.

The reciprocal interactions among ideas, interests, and institutions
have been vividly demonstrated in our group's discussions of political deliberation and choice. We might begin with a simple view of rational
choice and "methodological individualism." From this perspective political change is said to occur through the interaction of individuals whose
behavior is explainable in terms of choices, calculated in light of prevailing circumstances, to satisfy preexisting desires. No doubt this is one of
the purest formulations of the position that "interests" matter. Our discussions showed a succession of perspectives that can be added to produce a richer and more realistic picture of political life. What follows is
only one possible sequence that can add institutional and ideational tex-
ture.

First, as Aldrich points out in Chapter 9, the interaction of rational
choosers can easily produce familiar paradoxes of voting and collective
action. These problems lead one to consider rules and other constraints
that make it possible to discover elusive equilibrium conditions. In this
framework, institutional arrangements are then themselves choices to be
made by rational self-interested individuals pursuing their own ends.

A second perspective emphasizes that, quite apart from conscious construction of institutions, individual choices are embedded in institutional
settings that privilege some options and delete others. For example, this
can occur as institutional operations shape decisionmakers' perceptions of
what is doable (Steinmo, chap. 5, this vol.) or as institutional structures
give disproportional influence to some policy interests and values over
others (Hanson, chap. 6, this vol.). Then too, even with the same options,
the conclusions of one's reasoning may vary depending on how institutions frame those options and the procedures for eliciting the choices to be
made (Tversky, 1990). For example, only recently has it become clear that
the U.S. institutional system of dispersed power has not so much blocked
action in the construction of an American welfare state (the conventional
view) as it has shaped action to the benefit of groups that can fit in with its
particular institutional design (Skocpol, chap. 8, this vol.).

So far, we have complicated the original picture of rationally choosing
individuals by adding fairly standard observations about acts of choice in
institutional settings. A third line of thought invites us to suspend attention to the choosing activities of politics in order to consider activities that

precede choice. Perhaps the most familiar tactic here is to ask where the preferences that individuals act on in politics come from. Cultural theory, recently in vogue in political science, has sought to respond by identifying four socially constructed ways of life, or cultural predispositions that are based on how extensively one shares in a group life with others and how intensively the social prescriptions of others impinge on the individual (Thompson, Ellis, and Wildavsky, 1990). Preferences are said to be worked out in the social interactions through which individuals seek to support their given way of life. Although such an approach is helpful in showing that there can be more than a single, uniform type of rationality, one should be wary. We will not get very far in accounting for preferences if we simply substitute socially determined ways of life that exist outside historical processes for the preformed, autonomous preferences assumed by rational choice (Laitin, 1988; Friedman, 1991). Here too, attention to institutions as historical constructions may help us go deeper in thinking about interests, in this case as they shape not what to choose but what to want. By moving in this direction we are also clearly entering realms of intellectual history where "ideas matter" too.

It has been said that institutions are supposed to be things that stay around, fostering continuity and a long-term view of affairs (Rosenau, 1988). This tempts one to the view that when it comes to political change and continuity, institutions are simply sets of rules persisting through time to create order and stability—equilibrium points in the rational choice perspective, or "politics as usual" in the field of historical-institutional studies. However, this is seeing only the most obvious part of the picture. Particular actions—including individuated acts of choosing—exist in two dimensions of context: one is the actor's or chooser's own history and the other is the history of the setting to which those actions belong.

"Setting" is a rather anemic term for the meaning-endowed, socially embedded practices that orient actions and choices. Practices are endowed with meaning through historically transmitted social understandings, and this is the essential work done by institutions. To put it another way, political life can be seen as being made up of not only "options"—the choices which people have open to them—but also the inherited sociohistorical "ligatures" that give those choices meaning (Dahrendorf, 1979). Any reasoning, as such, takes place in the context of some inherited modes of understanding through which we appreciate—give meaning and value to—actions and practices, whether these are consciously chosen or not. We call these our preferences, tempted by the conceit that we have thought them up all on our own. Institutions are the bearers of such traditions of practice and meaning. It seems fair to say that most of the time people don't choose their institutions; their institutions choose them. Institutions serve as our point of departure, whether our "preference" is to affirm, amend, or repudiate that legacy. Attachments to such institutional traditions, far from being the opposite of reason, are the ways we format our reasoning, so to speak (Buchanan, 1992).[4] These attachments need not be seen simply as a source of stability and unchanging consensus. Following Alasdair MacIntyre, we can say that institutions express traditions of practice composed in part, of historically ongoing arguments about what any common life is and should be (MacIntyre, 1984). Living traditions and institutions carry forward continuities of conflict rather than immutable answers.

It was, for example, by exploring these connections that Tocqueville transcended the typical foreigner's travelogue on America. In the nation's rich institutional arrangements of self-government he found both an expression of and a powerful shaper of Americans' democratic understandings, or mores. These traditions of practice in turn gave rise to a distinctive form of reasoning—dubbed "individualism"—which yielded not so much settled answers as an ongoing, intensifying tension between a mass society of egoists and a functioning community of equal citizens. Or to take another example, when we speak of the party era in nineteenth century American politics we are referring not simply to a set of political organizations or rules. We are speaking of a time when parties embodied traditions of practice giving meaning to a shared, if conflictual, political life. These were socially and institutionally constructed understandings whereby being an "Independent" was simply not a thinkable preference for many people. Ultimately, I think, it is the parties' inability to carry forward meaning-endowed practices that makes us feel our own era is one of dying party institutions (however well-funded and technologically sophisticated the party national committees may have become!). This may be why it has been so easy for contemporary political science to dismiss social ligatures in its preoccupation with individual voting decisions (Huckfeldt and Beck, chap. 11, this vol.).

Paradoxically then, the more we take account of external environmental factors, such as socioeconomic or technological changes and their impact on the material "interests" of groups, the more important it is to pay attention to this institutional-ideational nexus. For the fact is, this environmental material does not come with an instruction sheet and self-interest is not self-defining. To comprehend what is happening we need to pay attention to appreciative settings that are receptacles for such external material.

Adding a fourth perspective takes us even further into the conjuncture of institutions and ideas with interests. Institutions may go beyond helping individuals signal and coordinate preferences more effectively, beyond privileging or deleting options, and beyond even the historical construction of understandings that bequeath meaning to our options and practices. Political institutions can also provide the means for changing ideas about our interests and preferences. As the authors are aware (Stone, chap. 12, and Mansbridge, chap. 13, this vol.), emphasizing the deliberative process and its transformative potential is hardly a new notion. It is a prominent theme, for example, in James Harrington (government by legislative discussion would achieve a unity not inherent in people's immediate wishes but capable of being elicited by rational debate and persuasion), James Madison (Constitutional arrangements would refine out factional claims so as to produce a larger view of the common good), and Tocqueville (participatory institutions promoted calculations of "self-interest rightly understood").

As noted earlier, deliberations under institutional auspices are not a free-form exercise, where all potential interests, meanings, and values are created or treated as equals. But deliberation understood broadly—as the large canvas of intercourse represented in democratic political institutions—is something more than simply a biased way of arraying and registering impervious preferences among self-contained individuals. Deliberation entails the distinctly human interactions of communication. In this process, warrants for historical understandings are contested, traditions are reexamined, views of what to prefer and what construction to assign to events are interrogated rather than taken as given. Preexisting conceptions of interests may be changed. Notions of how to get one's bearings on the issues at hand, or even to get a sense of what the issues are, may be subtly altered through interactions. This potentially reconstructive process is something rather different from the preference-signaling of a rational choice perspective, or the socially determined "ways of life" of cultural theory. It suggests a more open-ended, transformational capacity in the politics of democratic institutions.

At this point one begins to sense the liberating effect of seeing interests, institutions, and ideas not as the proprietary battleground among different social science "approaches" but as the shared patrimony of human materials for getting a better view of the world. The interrelationships are complicated, to be sure, but not every complication is a contradiction. We can recognize that interests, ideas, and institutions all "matter" in a very fundamental sense without forcing ourselves to choose which type of factor is analytically precedent (and therefore, which academic school is more worthy of esteem).

Consider for example the role of ideas, a subject that has tended to emerge in the borderlands of our discussions connecting interests and institutions. The temptation is to consider ideas as abstract, and as motives. It is often thought that, if ideas are to matter, actors must be seen to be behaving on the basis of articulated beliefs about the nature of the world, that is, they must have ideologies prompting their actions to change the world in line with their ideals. For example a prominent recent study self-consciously begins with the puzzle of relating ideas and institutions, and goes on to find the key dynamic of American political history in a recurring rediscovery of the dissonance between ideals of the American creed and actual performance of the society's institutions (Huntington, 1981:vii). This is no doubt a refinement on Louis Hartz's earlier interpretation that nothing every really changes due to the dominance of "liberal" ideas in America, but these and many studies are alike in eliciting the importance of ideas as abstract, motivational forces (Hartz, 1955).

Among other things, this stance toward the role of ideas raises problems of evidence (many people do not seem to have consistent ideologies, and how can we demonstrate these were the motivating impulses today, much less in the past?) and immediately sinks us in a hapless debate on the role of immaterial versus material forces in history. It loses sight of the fact that the ideologies in which "ideas matter" may be more the product than the cause or rationale for any political engagements and struggles. Perhaps worst of all, it is a perspective on ideas that distracts us from a realm of ideational importance where we can find historical evidence— the substratum of ideas that make up the states of mind people *do* bring to political events and actions. In this sense, the role of ideas is unavoidable. To engage in political activity and to enter the practices of the world is to stand in relation to theory, for although we may not have the ideological answers, we live some answer all the time. As noted earlier, our discussions have converged on the view that these patterns of discourse and frames of thought have to be understood in historical time. Frameworks of thought for interpreting the meaning of experience are historical rather than eternal and universal. In saying that it is useless to study ideas apart from their historical-institutional setting, we are not denying the value of efforts to find larger patterns (i.e., reaching beyond descriptions of immediate context). But as intellectual historians now tend to agree, it does mean we should try as best we can to understand ideas as they were thought and in terms of the meanings available at given times and places (Bernstein, 1983; Diggins, 1984; Hollinger, 1985).

The historical situatedness of ideas reinforces an awareness of the codependency among ideas, institutions, and interests (understood here as material interests taking form under concrete socioeconomic circumstances). In trying to account for change and continuity, these are categories that need each other, and it is largely arbitrary at which point we cut into the chain. Elision of one perverts the analytic reach of the other two. Thus, to be fair, it is not Hartz's work itself but superficial recyclers of Hartz who have ascribed monocausal historical force to an American value consensus on liberalism. Hartz's (1955) deeper point was to argue how configurations of socioeconomic interests facilitate or hinder certain oppositions from developing; lack of a feudal legacy shapes institutions and deliberations in the political conversation, enabling them to cast off certain values and meanings and not others. And as we have noted, this in turn can impact on conceptions of interest and preferences that are applied to the changing material conditions of society. The intellectual task we have broached in this volume is not how to cut the knot or pick out the single golden analytic strand: It is how to follow the strands of ideas, interests, and institutions as they intertwine and enfold in dynamic processes.

From our discussions there seem to be two senses—neither deserving priority—in which the codependency of ideas, interests, and institutions can be identified. One is instrumental, oriented but not inherently bounded by rational choice predispositions; the other is substantive, oriented but not inherently confined to what are today often labeled as historical-institutional studies.

Instrumental codependency arises in a familiar, politically foundational context, when: a group of more or less independent actors who, first, can plausibly believe (or at least hope to discover) that there is something in each's own interest to be gained from cooperation with the others, but, second, do not know how to go about achieving that happy outcome. This surely states the seminal problem during the founding of the American republic, as well as throughout the political world today.

Enter the interactive force of ideas and institutions. They acquire their importance not by virtue of anything intrinsic, but rather from their utility in helping actors achieve desired ends under prevailing constraints. Hence the instrumental nature of this codependency among interests, ideas, and institutions. Where decentralized, self-interested behavior alone cannot produce and sustain cooperation, ideas may combine with institutions to produce "positive constraints." By coordinating the expectations necessary for cooperation, the interaction of ideas and institutions can make results possible that could not be achieved otherwise. In this regard, for example, there are considerable similarities in the emergence of the American constitutional system and the modern day construction of international regimes. Ideas embodying notions of a common interest, where gains are to be had from exchange, have to be translated into institutional mechanisms that can then identify and punish defection, as well as give guidance on how to behave amid the inevitable uncertainties of the future. In doing this work institutions can in turn enhance shared beliefs and ideas about what constitutes defection, cooperation, and plausible paths of action (Garrett and Weingast, 1991; see also Schotter, 1981; Sugden, 1986). Seen in this light, institutions appear as more than a negative, status quo drag on leadership (Rockman, 1993). And ideas, rather than being spooky motivational abstractions, appear as working devices selected by real-world political actors and translated into social mechanisms called institutions. In identifying and responding to good and bad behavior, institutions build and reinforce common meanings and understandings in an ideational realm.

Notice that so far we have observed that things have happened, the form of interaction has changed, but little of substance has changed about the participants themselves. Substantive codependency among ideas, interests, and institutions emphasizes the intrinsic historical content and transformative capacity of these relationships. It takes us into the earlier-mentioned dimension where human reasoning is seen as inherently normative and acculturated. People, institutions, and political societies learn "what to want as well as how to get, what to be as well as what to do," although the two kinds of adaptation are clearly associated (Vickers, 1987).

In trying to get our bearings in a political world awash with change and continuity, we naturally seek to periodize, to identify eras when a particular combination of ideas, interests, and institutions have come together to form a distinctive "order,"(Burnham, chap. 3, this vol.) and indeed overlapping layers of orders (Jillson, chap.2, this vol.). But we also recognize these are artifacts alive with tensions as ideas, interests, and institutions move with the rhythm of their own logics and often in dissonance with each other (Orren and Skowronek, chap. 14, this vol.). The results of these tensions can be transformative in the sense that they affect the substance of our self-understanding, including ideas of what politics ought to be about. For example, the particular interests and institutions associated with Jacksonian democracy also embodied ideas whose effect was to shove aside the Republican idea of civic virtue. Leadership appeals to citizens' moral sensibilities could gradually yield ground to more narrow conceptions of self-interest in politics (Ketcham, 1984). Then too, as presumptions for a more inclusive political community grew, the meaning of property was redefined; it had been seen as the means to allow a person to participate more responsibly and disinterestedly in public affairs but became a source of private autonomy and self-indulgence. In short the moving combinations of ideas, interests, and institutions have made it impossible to have a single meaning or tradition of liberalism in America (McCoy, 1980; Appleby, 1984).

Institutions are central to the substantive codependency we have been discussing, for they are the bearers of standards outside our own desires or wishes. Such standards can as easily disrupt as maintain the political order, especially when the institutions of public life and private life impinge on each other. Thus even taking interests and preferences as given, our analytic schemes need to leave room for political behavior that consults standards that are regarded as standing in independent judgment of individual desires, tastes and choices. Interests involve a claim as to "what I want." This can of course be challenged by other interests, but it can also be challenged by the holder of the interest: Is this what I should want? At least in some places and times, people in politics give consideration to "ideas" about good and bad, and better and worse, that are not seen as validated simply by our own desires and choices.[5] When shared experiences or other circumstances lead many people to do that, the result can be transformative, with political upheavals and changes in social understandings that seem inexplicable solely in terms of interests (McLoughlin, 1978).

Methodological individualism gets an important part of the story right. Collectivities do not act; ideas do not act—only individual people do. But this should not tempt us to impoverish political analysis by abstracting individuals from the institutionally constructed influences that are also acting within people (Wildavsky, 1991b). We should always expect individuals' interests, particularly their personal material interests, to bear causal weight until shown otherwise. Yet that is not all we should expect. Much more could be said, but, stripped to formulaic essentials, what we can reasonably expect seems to come down to this. Interests tell institutions what to do; institutions tell ideas how to survive; ideas tell interests what to mean.

POLITICAL LEARNING
AND EVOLUTIONARY NARRATIVE

By now we have reached, or possibly surpassed, the boundaries of convergent conversation represented in this volume. To push on risks straining both the patience and goodwill of those involved. And yet it also seems that there is a convergent dissatisfaction with our own work. Therein may lie the intimations of a shared intellectual vector, however wanting we may be in terms of a precise research program. The periodization of nested ideas, interests, and institutions in a succession of political orders is, as I read our conversation, far less interesting than the dynamics of motion that create and recreate what we perceive as orders. And so we recircle the question: As we practice politics, what is happening when things happen? The periodization of political orders and realignments draws a pretty landscape, but we want to know ecology not just geography; beyond the still life, we want the movie version.

Let us—at last, the reader will justifiably say—look at some specifics, doing so in no particular order.

- Uneven socioeconomic changes and modernization continuously produce political problems, but the response of governing institutions is typically episodic and "sticky." As control by the majority party ages, new issues arise giving the opposition party an opportunity to exploit the changing agenda. There is also a generational decay in the political consciousness formed during the crisis that brought the majority party to power and at the same time each period breeds its own contradictions (public activism breeds exhaustion and a turn to the private). Buildup of these pressures leads to the bursts of change that characterize party realignments and demarcate the periods of political history. While this seems to be what happened with a crisis of interest group liberalism from the late 1960s onward, politicians have learned to use the modern technology of opinion polling to possibly change the traditional dynamics of such pressures (Burnham, chap. 3, this vol.; Jillson, chap. 2, this vol.).

- Parties are characterized by an ongoing process of accretion and loss of people, a process that extends from candidates to activists to voters. While party managers have incentives mainly to preserve the status quo, candidates competing for nominations are important as risk-takers. The outcome of their competitions within parties says much concerning what the conflict between the parties will be about. Depending on the candidates, different groups of political activists are attracted or repelled. This in turn sets the stage for how the party will frame choices attracting or repelling different members of the voting public. There is a recurring tension between the party's legacy invested in the status quo and the imperfect socialization of the next generation of activists to established party views. The growth of racial liberalism in the postwar Democratic party is an example of such eventual reshuffling of voters in the 1960s. Thus the competitive interactions of political elites affect the capacity of voters to use parties to make choices and of parties to interact with government institutions. (Carmines, 1993; Shefter, 1993).

- Changes in the economy register political effects by altering the agenda of issues and redistributing material resources for political participation. At the same time, policy responses at Time 1 can alter the capacities of government for action and change political groups' strategic positions and capacities, creating new preconditions for policy choices at Time 2 (Skocpol, chap. 8, and Greenberg, chap. 7, this vol.). Thus the economic disturbances and liberal policies associated with the Democrats opened up new opportunities for Reagan policymakers in the 1980s. Although not necessarily created on purpose, the federal deficit offered Reagan officials good strategic reasons (i.e., crippling big government activism and the liberal agenda) to tolerate deficit growth. But by the 1990s in turn, this growth contributed to persistent economic weakness, which, in the changing competitive context of the international economy, created the potential for a political backlash favorable to the Democrats and a new round of government activism.

- From the multiple realities that political language can construct, leaders search for and select constructions they expect will manufacture fears and hopes favorable to their cause. At the same time, changes, mass media, personal discussion networks, and secondary organizations have produced an environment increasingly favorable to messages of symbolic nature and disconnected from stable socioinstitutional frameworks. This may strengthen the electoral impact of momentary political events. It may also produce a public more adept at reading behind these messages and more resentful of symbolic manipulation. (Edelman, chap. 10, this vol.; Huckfeldt and Beck, chap. 11, this vol.).

As extracted from our discussions, do such vignettes have anything in common? At least to me it seems they do. In general terms, the movement of politics takes the form of a successive unfolding of imminent consequences, but with nothing foreordained. The "prose" one can suddenly discover we have been speaking all along has to do with processes of political learning embedded in evolutionary mechanisms of variation and selection. In speaking of evolution in the political realm, I am not simply trying to draw a clever, though vague, analogy with biological evolution. I am suggesting that the concept of evolutionary process captures the actual real-world mechanisms of political movement constituting change and continuity. Evolutionary learning is exactly what is happening when things happen. Particular codependencies of action among ideas, interests, and institutions are selected, due to demonstration of their adaptability to a changing environment, which is itself conditioned partly by the prior choices participants made and by the characteristics they have acquired.

This general perspective is most explicit in Chapter 15 by Dodd and Chapter 14 by Orren and Skowronek. Dodd, for example, views political participants as engaged in a cyclical process of constructing, having beliefs rigidify, encountering crises when faced with a changing context, and undergoing "metarational" transformations more suited to the new environment. Political participants are not engaged in a fixed, timeless game, but are continuously creating and recreating the game they play. Orren and Skowronek introduce us to an ecology of diverse institutions with incongrous ordering principles. Among the instructions, reflective bending and reshaping to the experience of each other's distinctive time line routinely produces, not routines and order, but a clumpy flow of mutual disturbances. However, it seems to me that, throughout this volume, varied evolutionary learning processes are the leitmotif for explicating political dynamics. Environmentally selected perpetuation—that is, election losses or victories—of a particular political party, politician, or political strategy is the most rudimentary form of what is being suggested here.

But before going further, the obvious objection has to be confronted: What has learning and evolution to do with the central driving force of politics, which consists of power relations and their attendant conflicts? Whatever one might say about a changing environment, those who have the power decide what the political agenda and outcome will be. Political dynamics is a question of who has the power. Since this is the dominant view in any claim to political realism, it needs to be taken seriously. The discussion that follows in no way denies that questions of power are crucial. The ability to dominate, ambition, and the will to power are central to what actually goes on. Power makes politics. Let us call it Politics I.

However, there is the no less realistic fact that politics is also created by the lack of power: Politics II, so to speak. It is a commonplace, especially in American politics, but also in generic problems of collective action throughout human life, that no one has the power to dominate and impose solutions. The inability of participants to control each other in any fully decisive way is another pervasive part of political reality. Moreover, even in situations where overwhelming dominance of some over others does exist, there is no human capacity to control all the consequences of one's actions or the play of chance in the larger world. "Look on my works, ye Mighty, and despair!" proclaimed the tumbled ruins of Ozymandias. Politics II takes Politics I seriously, but encompasses it in a larger view.

Seeing political dynamics in terms of evolution does not mean claiming there is a single, master evolutionary process at work. The general theme of variation and environmental selection allows for many different evolutionary processes to be operating in different corners of politics, from the comings and goings of today's politicians to the major historical transformations through which we periodize politics. In biology, species evolve. In politics what evolves through lines of descent are particular interrelations among ideas, interests, and institutions. For any evolutionary perspective, the twin essentials are means for generating variation, and mechanisms for selecting among and perpetuating certain of those variations.

In politics the variants might be thought of as so many different kinds of bids. What we immediately think of are conventional "bids for power" by politicians, parties, and interest groups. But depending on the subject matter in question, evolutionary bids can also take the form of efforts to promote an institutional innovation, a new policy idea, a particular strategy of persuasion, and the like. Bids occur for the same reason that quests for scientific and other knowledge do: A problem has arisen because some expectation has not been met or an opportunity is perceived that wasn't there before. Bids are the action-equivalent of conjectures, but they are also producers of parameters. Political environments are constantly throwing up bid-producing problems but they are also constantly restricting the initial responses that can be entertained. This is one reason we should not cling to any simple analogies between political evolution and Darwinian concepts. The latter requires variation through random mutations created independently of the natural selection process. Political life certainly demonstrates many instances where the generation of bids is separate from selecting processes; for instance, this is the way we usually describe the relationships between political elites that generate options and the mass of voters who choose among them (although even here the phenomenon of anticipated reactions undermines any clear separation). But politics is also rich in circumstances that combine the generating and selecting operations of evolutionary processes. We have emphasized how institutions provide an ongoing environment that in effect links the creation and selection of political bids. What makes an institution an institution is not the possession of this or that trait; rather, in terms of ideas and interests, it is a "community of descent" known by shared, derived characteristics. Institutions have a kind of restricted flexibility making possible some bids that would not have occurred otherwise and preventing others from ever occurring or eventually killing them off. Since the characteristics selected for tend to be different in different institutional spheres, institutional forms grate against each other as Orren and Skowronek argue, producing continuous disturbances that are themselves selecting mechanisms.

In thinking about the selective advantages and disadvantages of particular structures and behavior, we should try to clarify what tests have to be survived in demonstrating adaptive fitness. Certainly institutions' framing effects are likely to be important, as is the ability to pass power tests against competing interests. Rational foresight and calculated choice of the most adaptive bid or option can also be included in the realm of political dynamics, but the implications of an evolutionary perspective are clear. Although particular actors may demonstrate a capacity to avoid trial and error experiences by making calculated choices of the best-adapted behavior, this is unlikely to account for the course of any large, long-term political developments. Where many people are involved in many sequential steps of behavior, adaptiveness is likely to be a residual outcome of events rather than a direct choice that anyone has calculated or willed. Adaptiveness is shown by functional qualities in passing the tests of selection, not by the formal qualities of any given choice or set of choices.

At this point we risk recreating problems that beset older structural-functional theories—that is, structures survive because they perform important functions; we know they perform such functions because they survive. In natural science circles concerned with evolution, these are known as "Just-So Stories." One finds a trait and then tells a story explaining how just this trait performed an adaptive function for survival in a particular environment. An evolutionary narrative of political dynamics need not tell just-so stories if we recognize that there are other processes at work besides the adapting of political ideas, interests, and institutions to the selecting tests of the environment. Chance events form part of the picture (Kaufman, 1991). So too do constraints placed on the possibilities of evolutionary change by preexisting developmental pathways. We have urged that institutional analysis is largely an exploration of such pathways leading out of the past. Studying policy legacies—how chosen courses of action set off a downstream flow of experiences that shape what can later be learned and not learned—is another way of trying to understand how developmental pathways become "preexisting."

Thus selection in political evolution occurs through the editorship of an environment that, at least in part, we give to ourselves and constantly revise. Selection criteria are themselves the result of prior selection and learning processes. Sometimes through conscious "deliberation" (but mostly I suspect through inadvertence) we evolve tests with new or amended selection criteria. (The familiar crack that Abraham Lincoln probably could not be elected today is saying something of general importance about political evolution.) In making these observations we are also identifying a second and related divergence between political evolution and natural science versions. Not only are generative and selective mechanisms enfolded within each other. In political evolution the inheritance of acquired characteristics is the norm rather than a Lamarckian heresy. This follows from what we have already said about institutions, deliberation, the acculturated context of individual preferences and choice, policy legacies, and occasional references to learning.

But what does political learning mean in evolutionary narratives? The bids that form the material of political evolution might be said to arise from learning represented in the perception of a disappointed expectation or new opportunity. However, for present purposes such pattern recognition by political participants might be more usefully distinguished from other political learning by the terms discovery, conjecture, or bid-prompts. As used here, political learning means simply the process of acquiring characteristics that are bequeathed to inform subsequent behavior. In the practice of politics, it is a process made possible by the distinctly human capacity to use language to communicate the mutual influence of action and reflection on each other. It is this that creates "preexisting developmental pathways" in political evolution and allows our political and social institutions to take on, figuratively, a life of their own (Frank, 1988; Masters, 1989).

Political learning means that political evolution does not wait for repetitions to show adaptedness. People in politics not only make conjectures, invent strategies, and otherwise seize bid opportunities; they also operate vicariously and engage in one-trial learning, cueing behavior, imitation, and selective borrowing—or, to paraphrase Tacitus, people learn wisdom from the fortune of others. Thus political evolution exhibits a developmental opportunism whereby any perceived breakthrough stimulates a rushing in of adaptive mimicry. Pack movements in election campaign issues or media coverage are only the most obvious examples.

Political learning should *not* be taken to connote "getting smarter," or dominating the selective struggle, or even becoming able to perform particularly effectively. It merely means surviving well enough for some characteristic(s) to be acquired through historical transmission. But it is certainly possible to learn the "wrong" lessons. For example, as Dodd points out, Congress seems to have institutionally adapted so well to an industrial era agenda that it is ill-equipped to deal with contemporary postindustrial politics (Dodd, 1993). Likewise Presidents Eisenhower and Kennedy, together with their top advisors, seem to have adapted so well to their own respective experiences of the Cold War environment that neither could communicate effectively, even in well-meaning, face-to-face meetings, on a crucial issue like Vietnam (Greenstein, 1992:568–587). Indeed, the melancholy fact seems to be that political learning is likely to be a sign of adaptive success—carrying the seeds of its own potential failure. Leave aside the pernicious play of chance or unforeseen and perhaps unforeseeable consequences of power-wielders' actions. Surviving political forms (structures and practices) are the outcome of the environmental editing that occurred to get *to* now, not beyond. Since conditions then and there can never be quite the same as in the here and now (much less experientially suited to an as yet unexperienced future), there is an inescapable likelihood for flawed performance. This is a prime reason why power, the acquired ability to dominate others, is a poor guarantor of success in political evolution.

This is a melancholy fact indeed, but not one lost in the processes of political learning and evolution. We should pause to take stock. By mixing generative and selective mechanisms and by celebrating the inheritance of acquired characteristics, the concept of political evolution quickly diverges from theories of evolution in the natural sciences, and does so rather sharply. But there seems to be a good deal in common between sociological understandings of the evolution of "scientific knowledge" on the one hand—variant surprises and conjectural discoveries, testing and selection through evidentiary experience, convergent understandings and developmental opportunism (Campbell, 1988)—and political evolution on the other. All this holds true up to a point, and here we reach the point. At least in most instances, scientists are expected to internalize norms for policing their own conjectural "bids." By contrast we have the antimonies of people practicing politics and scientists pushing to refute their own epistomological claims. Political activity typically involves doing everything possible to affirm one's own bid and to suppress countervailing information. This is the essential truth contained in another catchphrase: Power corrupts and absolute power corrupts absolutely.

Political evolution therefore has a special tendency, compared with other evolutionary regimes, to be both highly and internally adaptive (through vicarious learning, path-dependency, and so on) as well as highly error-prone (by exercising power to repress falsification). In this environment the selective advantage for perpetuation may lie with those combinations of ideas, institutions, and interests geared to making bids testable and exposing error. To say this is to revisit the classic historic argument for democratically representative government itself: that it would vigorously expose to continual falsification the grandest of all political bids—the claim to be acting in the interests of the governed.

Assuming that the common vector in our thinking has been toward an evolutionary narrative of political learning, we can feel liberated from quests for equilibrium conditions, whether punctuated or not. There is only movement. Homeostatic, self-equilibrating structures or processes may exist, but that does not account for how such mechanisms come to be, may be transformed, or disappear. As Orren and Skowronek robustly argue, maintaining equilibrium is no answer for how to account for change. Even to explore how institutions defend themselves in their present forms is an exercise about change rather than one about normalcy and order. Thus it was not the rise of science but defensive adaptations within religious institutions themselves that opened the way for godlessness to become a viable approach in our public affairs (Turner, 1985). But that is another story.

AFTERWORD

There have been important gaps in our conversation. We have had little to say about the place of irrationality in politics. Beyond the questions of material or immaterial interests, there are also "passions" in politics where actions are based on impulse and emotion, not on the rationality of means-end calculations. Perhaps this gap exists because we have not been particularly self-aware of our own situatedness, nor have we tried to historicize our conversation about political dynamics. We have skirted the question of audience—whether we should be addressing a largely closed professional community, or whether we have an obligation to a larger public that is deeply worried about what is happening to this country and its politics.

If nothing else, our conversation has had the negative merit of not trying to erect a "system," a kind of "sacred grating behind which each novice is commanded to kneel in order that he may never see the real world, save though its interstices" (Overman, 1988:495). There is an intrinsic complexity to interlocking historical processes that the yearning for a tidy intellectual solution too often distorts. If we are to kneel with respect, it should be before the complexity, not the scholar's system—for there is much we may never understand. In the early 1980s, while policy experts, Sovietologists, and other political scientists plied their trade in Cold War theories and no one wrote about the coming breakup of communism, the Polish poet Artur Miedzyrzecki wrote a piece entitled "What Does the Political Scientist Know?" It is a fitting place to end.

What does the political scientist know?
The political scientist knows the latest trends
The current states of affairs
The history of doctrines

What does the political scientist not know?
The political scientist doesn't know about desperation
He doesn't know the game that consists
In renouncing the game

It doesn't occur to him
That no one knows when
Irrevocable changes may appear
Like an ice-floe's sudden cracks

And that our natural resources
Include knowledge of venerated laws
The capacity for wonder
And a sense of humor[6]

NOTES

1. "The great problem in American politics is: What makes things happen? We might understand the dynamics of American politics if we knew what is going on when things are happening. What is the process of change?" (Schattschneider, 1960:vii).

2. Here is a recent example from perhaps the leading writer on bureaucracy: "I wish that this book could be set forth in a way that proved, or at least illustrated, a simple, elegant, comprehensive theory of bureaucratic behavior. ... After all these decades of wrestling with the subject, I have come to have grave doubts that anything worth calling 'organization theory' will ever exist. ... Interesting explanations will exist, some even supported with facts, but these will be partial, place and time-bound insights" (Wilson, 1989).

3. Although Pendleton Herring's *The Politics of Democracy* is most explicit in this regard, the interplay of the same three factors can be found in accounts of U.S. political development by Tocqueville, Herbert Croly, Woodrow Wilson, and Henry Jones Ford. Indeed, James Madison's famous exposition of the American constitutional system was an extraordinarily elegant blending of ideational, institutional, and rational choice analysis—an achievement probably made possible by Madison's want of a modern social science education. Thus, *Federalist No. 10* and *No. 51* combine a rational-choice-sympathetic analysis of self-interested calculation ("If men were angels ..."), a vivid portrayal of the institutional structuring of incentives ("The interest of the man must be connected with the constitutional rights of the place. ... Extend the sphere ... you make it less probable that a majority of the whole will have a common motive to invade the rights of other citizens.") and a realistic appreciation of the motivating power of ideational values ("Justice is the end of government. ... It ever has been, and ever will be pursued, until it be obtained, or until liberty be lost in its pursuit") (Madison, Hamilton, and Jay, *Nos. 10* and *51*).

4. Thus is it not surprising that the founding of a rational choice approach to public affairs does not grow out of rational choice but out of a combination of "tradition, family, chance, and scholarship" (Buchanan, 1992). Likewise it is hardly frivolous to suggest that the overwhelming attention to individual "choice" in rational choice approaches and to social coordinates infringing on "individual autonomy" in cultural theory is well-fitted to the modern American context. Both tap the optimism of a culture that wants to see individuals as free to choose without being weighed down by history. Both fit what has now become the founding narrative of a people who have made calculated choices to come to a new land, choices in designing institutions of self-government, choices to go as they please and take what they want. And both fit a time when the moralizing authority of institutions is increasingly suspect.

5. It is worth repeating that the term "ideas" is not being used here as a motivational abstraction but rather as a description of states of mind and constructions superimposed on the world in the context of certain institutional affiliations, particularly religious, or others of a moralizing nature.

6. Quoted from "What Does the Political Scientist Know?" in *Polish Poetry of the Last Two Decades of Communist Rule*, Stanislaw Baranczak and Clare Cavanaugh (eds.) (Evanston, Ill.: Northwestern University Press, 1991), pp. 59–60.

References

Abbott, Grace. 1933. *Mothers' Aid, 1931.* U.S. Children's Bureau Publication no. 220. Washington, D.C.

———. 1935. "Mothers' Aid." *Social Work Yearbook* 282–285.

Abercrombie, Nicholas, Stephen Hill, and Bryan S. Turner. 1980. *The Dominant Ideology Thesis.* London: George Allen and Unwin.

Abramowitz, Alan I. 1989. "Viability, Electability, and Candidate Choice in a Presidential Primary Election: A Test of Competing Models." 51 *Journal of Politics* 977.

Abramson, Paul R., John H. Aldrich, and David W. Rohde. 1983. *Change and Continuity in the 1980 Elections.* Rev. ed. Washington, D.C.: Congressional Quarterly.

Abramson, Paul R., John H. Aldrich, Phil Paolino, and David W. Rohde. 1992. "'Sophisticated' Voting in the 1988 Presidential Primaries." 86 *American Political Science Review* 55.

Achen, Christopher H. 1989. "Prospective Voting and the Theory of Party Identification." Unpublished paper, University of Chicago, August.

Ackerman, Bruce. 1984. "The Storrs Lectures: Discovering the Constitution." 93 *Yale Law Journal* 1013.

———. 1989. "Constitutional Politics/Constitutional Law." 99 *Yale Law Journal* 453.

———. 1991. *We the People: Foundations.* Cambridge: Harvard University Press, Belknap.

Adair, Douglass. 1957. "That Politics May Be Reduced to a Science." 20 *Huntington Library Quarterly* 343.

Adams, John. 1856. *The Works of John Adams.* Boston: Little, Brown.

Aglietta, Michel. 1979. *A Theory of Capitalist Regulation.* London: Verso.

Agnew, John. 1987. *The United States in the Regional Economy: A Regional Geography.* New York: Cambridge University Press.

Aldrich, John H. 1987. "The Rise of the Republican Party, 1854–1860." Paper presented at the annual meeting of the Midwest Political Science Association, Chicago.

———. 1990a. "Presidential Selection." Paper presented at the Conference on Research on the American Presidency, November 12–14, University of Pittsburgh.

———. 1990b. "An Institutional Theory of a Legislature with Two Parties and a Committee System." *Duke Working Papers in American Politics, no.* 111.

———. 1993. "Turnout and Rational Choice." 37 *American Journal of Political Science* 246.

———. 1994. *Why Parties?* Chicago: University of Chicago Press.

Aldrich, John H., and William T. Bianco. 1992. "A Game-Theoretic Model of Party Affiliation of Candidates and Office Holders." 16 *Mathematical and Computer Modelling* 103.

Aldrich, John H., and Richard G. Niemi. 1990. "The Sixth American Party System: The 1960s Realignment and the Candidate-Centered Parties." Unpublished ms. Political Science Department, Duke University.

Aldrich, John H., John L. Sullivan, and Eugene Borgida. 1989. "Foreign Affairs and Issue Voting: Do Presidential Candidates 'Waltz Before a Blind Audience?'" 83 *American Political Science Review* 123.

Alford, John R., and David W. Brady. 1989. "Personal and Partisan Advantage in U.S. Congressional Elections, 1846–1986." In Lawrence C. Dodd and Bruce I. Oppenheimer, eds., *Congress Reconsidered*. 4th ed. Washington, D.C.: Congressional Quarterly.

Alford, Robert, and Roger Friedland. 1985. *The Powers of Theory.* New York: Cambridge University Press.

Almond, Gabriel A. 1988. "The Return of the State." 82 *American Political Science Review* 853.

_____. 1990. *A Discipline Divided.* Newbury Park, Calif.: Sage.

Althusser, Louis. 1969. *For Marx.* London: New Left Books.

Amenta, Edwin, and Theda Skocpol. 1988. "Redefining the New Deal: World War II and the Development of Social Provision in the United States." In Margaret Weir, Ann Shola Orloff, and Theda Skocpol, eds., *The Politics of Social Policy in the United States.* Princeton: Princeton University Press.

Amenta, Edwin, and Yvonne Zylan. 1991. "It Happened Here: Political Opportunity, the New Institutionalism, and the Townsend Movement." 56 *American Sociological Review* 250.

Anderson, Benedict. 1983. *Imagined Communities.* London: Routledge, Chapman and Hall.

Anderson, Kristi. 1979. *The Creation of a Democratic Majority, 1928–1936.* Chicago: University of Chicago Press.

Anderson, Leslie. 1991. "Mixed Blessings: Disruption and Organization Among Peasant Unions in Costa Rica." 26 *Latin American Research Review* 1.

_____. 1994. *The Political Ecology of the Modern Peasant: Calculation and Community.* Baltimore, Md.: Johns Hopkins University Press.

Anderson, William. 1975. *The Wild Man from Sugar Creek: The Political Career of Eugene Talmadge.* Baton Rouge: Louisiana State University Press.

Anton, Thomas, Claes Linde, and Anders Mellbourn. 1973. "Bureaucrats in Politics: A Profile of the Swedish Administrative Elite." 16 *Canadian Public Administration* 4.

Appleby, Joyce. 1984. *Capitalism and the New Social Order.* New York: New York University Press.

Arendt, Hannah. 1961. *Between Past and Future.* Cleveland: World.

_____. 1966. *The Origins of Totalitarianism.* New York: Harcourt, Brace, and World.

Arnold, R. Douglas. 1981. "The Local Roots of Domestic Policy." In Thomas Mann and Norman Ornstein, eds., *The New Congress.* Washington, D.C.: American Enterprise Institute.

Arrow, Kenneth J. [1951] 1963. *Social Choice and Individual Values*. Rev. ed. New York: John Wiley.

Ashby, W. R. 1952. *Design for a Brain*. New York: John Wiley.

Asher, Robert. 1969. "Business and Workers' Welfare in the Progressive Era: Workmen's Compensation Reform in Massachusetts, 1880–1911." 43 *Business History Review* 452.

Ashford, Douglas. 1986. *The Emergence of the Welfare State*. Oxford: Blackwell.

Axelrod, Robert. 1984. *The Evolution of Cooperation*. New York: Basic Books.

Ayres, Ian, and John Braithwaite. 1992. *Responsive Regulation: Transforming the Regulation Debate*. Oxford: Oxford University Press.

Bachrach, Peter, and Morton Baratz. 1963. "Decisions and Non-Decisions: An Analytical Framework." 57 *American Political Science Review* 632.

Bagehot, Walter. 1897. *The English Constitution and Other Political Essays*. New York: Appleton.

Bailyn, Bernard. 1973. "The Central Themes of the American Revolution: An Interpretation." In Stephen G. Kurtz and James H. Hutson, eds., *Essays on the American Revolution*. New York: W. W. Norton.

Baker, Paula. 1984. "The Domestication of Politics: Women and American Political Society, 1780–1920." 85 *American Historical Review* 620.

Baldwin, Peter. 1990. *The Politics of Social Solidarity*. New York: Cambridge University Press.

Balogh, Brian. 1991. "Reorganizing the Organizational Synthesis: Federal-Professional Relations in Modern America." In Karen Orren and Stephen Skowronek, eds., *Studies in American Political Development*, vol. 5. New York: Cambridge University Press.

Banks, Jeffrey S., and D. Roderick Kiewiet. 1989. "Explaining Patterns of Candidate Competition in Congressional Elections." 33 *American Journal of Political Science* 997.

Barber, Benjamin. 1984. *Strong Democracy*. Berkeley: University of California Press.

Barnard, Chester I. 1968. *The Functions of the Executive*. Cambridge: Harvard University Press.

Barron v. Baltimore, 7 Pet. 243 (1883).

Barry, Brian. 1970. *Sociologists, Economists, and Democracy*. London: Collier-Macmillan.

Bates, Robert H. 1981. *Markets and States in Tropical Africa*. Berkeley: University of California Press.

Bateson, Gregory. 1971. "The Cybernetics of 'Self'." 34 *Psychiatry* 1.

———. 1972. *Steps to an Ecology of Mind*. New York: Ballantine Books.

———. 1979. *Mind and Nature*. New York: Bantam.

Bateson, Gregory, and Mary Catherine Bateson. 1987. *Angels Fear*. New York: Bantam.

Bateson, Mary Catherine. 1972. *Our Own Metaphor*. New York: Knopf.

Baudrillard, Jean. 1983. *In the Shadow of the Silent Majorities*. New York: Semiotext.

Bauer, Raymond A., Ithiel de Sola Pool, and Lewis Anthony Dexter. 1963. *American Business and Public Policy*. New York: Atherton.

———. 1972. *American Business and Public Policy: The Politics of Foreign Trade*. Chicago: Aldine-Atherton.

Baum, Dale. 1984. *The Civil War Party System*. Chapel Hill: University of North Carolina Press.

Baumgartner, Frank R., and Bryan D. Jones. 1991. "Agenda Dynamics and Policy Subsystems." 53 *Journal of Politics* 1044.

_____. 1993. *Agendas and Instability in American Politics*. Chicago: University of Chicago Press.

Baumgartner, Frank R., and Jack L. Walker. 1988. "Survey Research and Membership in Voluntary Organizations." 32 *American Journal of Political Science* 908.

Bean, Clive, and Anthony Mughan. 1989. "Leadership Effects in Parliamentary Elections in Australia and Britain." 83 *American Political Science Review* 1164.

Beard, Charles. 1913. *An Economic Interpretation of the Constitution*. New York: Macmillan.

Beck, Paul Allen. 1974a. "A Socialization Theory of Partisan Realignment." In Richard Niemi, ed., *The Politics of Future Citizens*. San Francisco: Jossey-Bass.

_____. 1974b. "Environment and Party: The Impact of Political and Demographic County Characteristics on Party Behavior." 68 *American Political Science Review* 1229.

_____. 1979. "The Electoral Cycle and the Patterns of American Politics." 9 *British Journal of Political Science* 129.

_____. 1991. "Voters' Intermediation Environments in the 1988 Presidential Contest." 55 *Public Opinion Quarterly* 371.

Beck, Paul Allen, and Martha Ellis Crone. 1990. "Varieties of Political Intermediation: Intermediaries and Voting Behavior in the 1988 Presidential Election." Paper presented at the annual meeting of the American Political Science Association, San Francisco.

Beck, Paul Allen, and Bradley R. Richardson. 1989. "Personal, Organizational, and Media Intermediaries in the 1988 Presidential Contest." Paper presented at the annual meeting of the American Political Science Association, Atlanta.

Beer, Francis A. 1986. "Games and Metaphors." 30 *Journal of Conflict Resolution* 171.

Beer, Samuel H. 1963. "Causal Explanation and Imaginative Re-enactment." 3(1) *History and Theory* 6.

_____. 1969. *British Politics in the Collectivist Age*. New York: Vintage Books.

Bell, Daniel. 1967. *Marxian Socialism in the United States*. Princeton: Princeton University Press.

_____. 1989. "'American Exceptionalism' Revisited: The Role of Civil Society." 95 *Public Interest* 38.

Bellah, Robert, et al. 1985. *Habits of the Heart*. Berkeley: University of California Press.

Bendix, Reinhard. 1964. *Nation-Building and Citizenship*. Berkeley: University of California Press.

Bennett, W. Lance. 1980. *Public Opinion in American Politics*. New York: Harcourt Brace Jovanovich.

Bensel, Richard F. 1984. *Sectionalism and American Political Development, 1880–1980*. Madison: University of Wisconsin Press.

_____. 1990. *Yankee Leviathan: The Origins of Central State Authority in America, 1859–1877*. New York: Cambridge University Press.

Bentley, Arthur. 1935. *The Process of Government*. Evanston, Ill.: Principia.

Berelson, Bernard, Paul Lazarsfeld, and William McPhee. 1954. *Voting*. Chicago: University of Chicago Press.

Berger, Peter L. 1976. *Pyramids of Sacrifice*. New York: Doubleday.

Berger, Peter L., and Thomas Luckmann. 1967. *The Social Construction of Reality*. Garden City, N.Y.: Doubleday.

Bernstein, Richard J. 1983. *Beyond Objectivism and Relativism*. Philadelphia: University of Pennsylvania Press.

Berry, Brian. 1991. *Long Wave, Rhythms in Economic Development and Political Behavior*. Baltimore: Johns Hopkins University Press.

Berry, Jeffrey M. 1989. *The Interest Group Society*, 2nd ed. Glenview, Ill.: Scott, Foresman; Little, Brown.

Bessette, Joseph M. 1979. "Deliberation in Congress." Paper delivered at the annual meeting of the American Political Science Association, Washington, D.C.

———. 1982. "Is Congress a Deliberative Body?" In Dennis Hale, ed., *The United States Congress: Proceedings of the Thomas P. O'Neill Symposium*. Chestnut Hill, Mass.: Boston College.

———. 1993. *The Mild Voice of Reason*. Chicago: University of Chicago Press.

Bickerton, Derek. 1990. *Language and Species*. Chicago: University of Chicago Press.

Binder, Leonard. 1986. "The Natural History of Development Theory." 28 *Comparative Studies in Society and History* 3.

Birnbaum, Jeff, and Alan Murray. 1987. *Showdown at Gucci Gulch: Law Makers, Lobbyists and the Unlikely Triumph of Tax Reform*. New York: Random House.

Black, Duncan. 1958. *The Theory of Committees and Elections*. New York: Cambridge University Press.

Black, Gordon. 1972. "A Theory of Political Ambition: Career Choices and the Role of Structural Incentives." 66 *American Political Science Review* 144.

Black, Jerome H. 1978. "The Multicandidate Calculus of Voting: Application to Canadian Federal Elections." 22 *American Journal of Political Science* 609.

Block, Fred. 1977. "The Ruling Class Does Not Rule." 7 *Socialist Revolution* 6.

———. 1987. *Revising State Theory: Essays in Politics and Postindustrialism*. Philadelphia: Temple University Press.

Blumell, Bruce D. 1973. "The Development of Public Assistance in the State of Washington During the Great Depression." Ph.D. diss., University of Washington.

Boorstin, Daniel. 1953. *The Genius of American Politics*. Chicago: University of Chicago Press.

Boudon, Raymond. 1974. *Education, Opportunity and Social Inequality*. New York: John Wiley.

Bowles, Samuel, and Herbert Gintis. 1976. *Schooling in Capitalist America*. New York: Basic Books.

Boyer, Robert. 1979. "Wage Formation in Historical Perspective." 3 *Cambridge Journal of Economics* 99.

Brady, David W., and Mark A. Morgan. 1987. "Reforming the Structure of the House Appropriations Process: The Effects of the 1885 and 1919–20 Reforms on Money Decisions." In Mathew D. McCubbins and Terry Sullivan, eds., *Congress: Structure and Policy*. New York: Cambridge University Press.

Brady, David W. 1988. *Critical Elections and Congressional Policy-Making*. Stanford, Calif.: Stanford University Press.

Brady, David W., with Joseph Stewart. 1982. "Congressional Party Realignment and Transformations of Public Policy in Three Realignment Eras." 26 *American Journal of Political Science* 333.

Brady, Henry E., and Stephen Ansolabehere. 1989. "The Nature of Utility Functions in Mass Publics." 83 *American Political Science Review* 143.

Breslauer, George W. and Philip E. Tetlock. 1991. *Learning in U.S. and Soviet Foreign Policy*. Boulder: Westview Press.

Brickell, Bettina, Robert Huckfeldt, and John Sprague. 1988. "Gender Effects on Political Discussion: The Political Networks of Men and Women." Paper presented at the annual meeting of the Midwest Political Science Association, Chicago.

Broder, David S. 1980. *Changing of the Guard: Power and Leadership in America*. New York: Simon and Schuster.

Brown, Richard. 1979. *Rockefeller Medicine Men: Medicine and Capital*. Berkeley: University of California Press.

Browne, William P. 1988. *Private Interest, Public Policy, and American Agriculture*. Lawrence: University Press of Kansas.

———. 1990. "Organized Interests and Their Issue Niches." 52 *Journal of Politics* 477.

Bruner, Jerome. 1986. *Actual Minds, Possible Worlds*. Cambridge: Harvard University Press.

Buchanan, James. 1992. *Better Than Plowing and Other Personal Essays*. Chicago: University of Chicago Press.

Buchanan, James, and Gordon Tullock. 1962. *The Calculus of Consent*. Ann Arbor: University of Michigan Press.

Bucklin, Dorothy R., and John Lynch. 1939. "Public Aid for the Care of Dependent Children in Their Own Homes, 1932–38." 2(3) *Social Security Bulletin* 24. Bueno de Mesquita, Bruce. 1981. *The War Trap*. New Haven: Yale University Press.

Burnham, Walter Dean. 1965. "The Changing Shape of the American Political Universe." 59 *American Political Science Review* 7.

———. 1970. *Critical Elections and the Mainsprings of American Politics*. New York: W. W. Norton.

———. 1974. "Theory and Voting Research: Some Reflections on Converse's 'Change in the American Electorate.'" 68 *American Political Science Review* 1002.

———. 1981. "The 1980 Earthquake: Realignment, Reaction, or What?" In Thomas Ferguson and Joel Rogers, eds., *The Hidden Election*. New York: Pantheon.

———. 1981. "Social Stress and Political Response: Religion and the 1980 Election." In Thomas Ferguson and Joel Rogers, eds., *The Hidden Election*. New York: Pantheon.

———. 1986. "Periodization Schemes and Party Systems: The 'System of 1896' as a Case in Point." 10 *Social Science History* 263.

———. 1987. "Elections as Democratic Institutions." In Kay Lehman Schlosman, ed., *Elections in America*. Boston: Allen and Unwin.

———. 1991. "Critical Realignment: Dead or Alive?" In Byron E. Shafer, ed., *The End of Realignment? Interpreting American Electoral Eras*. Madison: University of Wisconsin Press.

Burns, Eveline M. 1942. *Security, Work and Relief Policies.* New York: Da Capo.

Burns, James MacGregor. 1963. *The Deadlock of Democracy.* Englewood Cliffs, N.J.: Prentice-Hall.

———. 1978. *Leadership.* New York: Harper and Row.

Butler, David, and Donald E. Stokes. 1969. *Political Change in Britain.* New York: St. Martin's.

Cain, Bruce E. 1978. "Strategic Voting in Britain." 22 *American Journal of Political Science* 639.

Campbell, Angus, Philip E. Converse, Warren E. Miller, and Donald E. Stokes. 1960. *The American Voter.* New York: John Wiley.

———. 1964. *Elections and the Political Order.* New York: John Wiley.

Campbell, Donald T. 1988. "Evolutionary Epistemology." In E. Samuel Overman, ed., *Methodology and Epistemology for Social Science.* Chicago: University of Chicago Press.

Carmines, Edward G. 1993. "Issue Evolution and Party Alignments." In Lawrence C. Dodd and Calvin Jillson, eds., *New Perspectives on American Politics.* Washington, D.C.: Congressional Quarterly.

Carmines, Edward G., and James H. Kuklinski. 1990. "Incentives, Opportunities, and the Logic of Public Opinion in American Political Representation." In John A. Ferejohn and James H. Kuklinski, eds., *Information and Democratic Processes.* Urbana: University of Illinois Press.

Carmines, Edward G., and James A. Stimson. 1981. "Issue Evolution, Population Replacement, and Normal Partisan Change." 74 *American Political Science Review,* 107.

———. 1989. *Issue Evolution: Race and the Transformation of American Politics.* Princeton: Princeton University Press.

Carnoy, Martin. 1984. *The State and Political Theory.* Princeton: Princeton University Press.

Carstairs, Andrew McLaren. 1980. *A Short History of Electoral Systems in Western Europe.* London: George Allen and Unwin.

Cash, Wilbur J. 1941. *The Mind of the South.* New York: Doubleday, Anchor Books.

Castles, Francis. 1978. *The Social Democratic Image of Society.* London: Routledge.

———. 1982. "The Impact of Parties on Public Expenditure." In *The Impact of Parties: Politics and Policies in Democratic Capitalist States.* Beverly Hills, Calif.: Sage.

Cates, Jerry R. 1983. *Insuring Inequality: Administrative Leadership in Social Security, 1935–54.* Ann Arbor: University of Michigan Press.

Chaffee, Steven H. 1982. "Mass Media and Interpersonal Channels: Competitive, Convergent, or Complementary?" In Gary Gumpert and Robert Cathcart, eds., *Inter/Media: Interpersonal Communication in a Media World.* New York: Oxford University Press.

Chambers, Simone. 1993. "Talking About Rights: Discourse Ethics and the Protection of Rights." 1 *Journal of Political Philosophy* 45.

Chicago, Burlington and Quincy Railroad v. Chicago, 166 U.S. 226 (1897).

Chicago Daily News Almanac for 1894. Editor's "Preface," reverse of title page.

Chicago Daily News Almanac for 1895. Editor's "Preface," reverse of title page.

Chicago Daily News Almanac for 1896. Editor's "Preface," reverse of title page.

Chicago Daily News Almanac for 1897. Editor's "Preface," reverse of title page.

Chong, Dennis. 1991. *Collective Action and the Civil Rights Movement.* Chicago: University of Chicago Press.

Chubb, John E. 1985. "Federalism and the Bias for Centralization." In John E. Chubb and Paul E. Peterson, eds., *New Directions in American Politics.* Washington, D.C.: Brookings Institution.

Cicero, Marcus Tullius. 1929. *On the Commonwealth.* New York: Liberal Arts.

Citrin, Jack. 1979. "Do People Want Something for Nothing: Public Opinion on Taxes and Government Spending." 32 *National Tax Journal* 113.

Clegg, Stewart R. 1989. *Frameworks of Power.* London: Sage.

Clubb, Jerome, William H. Flanigan, and Nancy Zingale. 1980. *Partisan Realignment.* Beverly Hills, Calif.: Sage.

Coats, A. W. 1981. "Britain: The Rise of the Specialist." 13 *History of Political Economy* 3.

Cochran, Thomas C. 1948. "The 'Presidential Synthesis' in Amercan History." 53 *American Historical Review* 748.

Cogan, John, Timothy J. Muris, and Allen Schick. 1993. *The Great Budget Puzzle: Understanding Federal Spending.* Stanford: Stanford University Press.

Cohen, Gerald A. 1978. *Karl Marx's Theory of History: A Defense.* Princeton: Princeton University Press.

Cohen, Joshua, and Joel Rogers. 1983. *On Democracy.* New York: Penguin.

————. 1992. "Secondary Associations and Democratic Governance." 20 *Politics and Society* 393.

Cohen, Michael D., and James G. March. 1986. *Leadership and Ambiguity.* 2nd ed. Boston: Harvard Business School Press.

Cohen, Michael D., James G. March, and Johan P. Olsen. 1972. "A Garbage-Can Model of Organizational Choice." 17 *Administrative Science Quarterly* 1–25.

Converse, Philip E. 1972. "Change in the American Electorate." In Angus Campbell and Philip Converse, eds., *The Human Meaning of Social Change.* New York: Russell Sage.

Cook, Fay Lomax. 1988. "Congress and the Public: Convergent and Divergent Opinions on Social Security." In Henry Aaron, ed., *Social Security and the Budget.* Lanham, Md.: University Press of America.

Cook, Fay Lomax, and Wesley G. Skogan. 1990. "Agenda Setting and the Rise and Fall of Policy Issues: The Case of Criminal Victimization of the Elderly." 8 *Government and Policy* 395.

Cooper, Joseph. 1988. "Comparing Micro and Macro Approaches to Institutional Analysis." 12 *Legislative Studies Section Newsletter* 115.

Cooper, Joseph, and David W. Brady. 1981. "Toward a Diachronic Analysis of Congress." 75 *American Political Science Review* 988.

Corwin, Edward. 1940. *The President: Office and Powers.* New York: New York University Press.

Costain, Anne. 1992. *Inviting Women's Rebellion: A Political Process Interpretation of the Women's Movement.* Baltimore: Johns Hopkins University Press.

Coughlin, Richard. 1980. *Ideology, Public Opinion, Welfare Policy: Attitudes Toward Taxing and Spending in Industrial Societies.* Berkeley: Institute of International Studies.

————. 1982. "Payroll Taxes for Social Security in the U.S.: The Future of Fiscal and Social Policy Illusions." 2 *Journal of Economic Psychology* 165.

Cox, Gary, and Mathew D. McCubbins. 1993. *Legislative Leviathan: Party Government in the House*. Berkeley: University of California Press.

Cox, Robert W. 1987. *Production, Power, and World Order*. New York: Columbia University Press.

Crenson, Matthew A. 1971. *The Un-Politics of Air Pollution*. Baltimore: Johns Hopkins University Press.

Crick, Bernard. 1982. *In Defense of Politics*. New York: Penguin.

Crocker, Royce. 1981. "Federal Government Spending and Public Opinion." Autumn 1 *Public Budgeting and Finance*.

Cronin, Thomas E. 1989. *Direct Democracy*. Cambridge: Harvard University Press.

Crotty, William J. 1971. "Party Effort and Its Impact on the Vote." 65 *American Political Science Review* 439.

Cuff, Robert D. 1973. *The War Industries Board: Business-Government Relations During World War I*. Baltimore: Johns Hopkins University Press.

Culhane, Paul J. 1981. *Public Lands Politics*. Baltimore: Johns Hopkins University Press.

Current, Richard N. 1955. *Daniel Webster and the Rise of National Conservatism*. Boston: Little, Brown.

Cutler, Lloyd. 1980. "To Form a Government." 59 *Foreign Affairs* 126.

Cutright, Phillips, and Peter Rossi. 1958. "Grass Roots Politicians and the Vote." 23 *American Sociological Review* 171.

Dahl, Robert A. 1956. *A Preface to Democratic Theory*. Chicago: University of Chicago Press.

————. 1957. "The Concept of Power." 2 *Behavioral Science* 201.

————. 1961. *Who Governs?* New Haven: Yale University Press.

————. 1971. *Polyarchy*. New Haven: Yale University Press.

————. 1981. *Democracy in the United States*. Boston: Houghton Mifflin.

————. 1982. *Dilemmas of Pluralist Democracy*. New Haven: Yale University Press.

————. 1984. *Modern Political Analysis*. 4th ed. Englewood Cliffs, N.J.: Prentice-Hall.

————. 1989. *Democracy and Its Critics*. New Haven: Yale University Press.

Dahl, Robert A., and Charles Lindblom. 1953. *Politics, Economics, and Welfare*. New York: Harper and Row.

Dahl, Robert A., and Edward Tufte. 1973. *Size and Democracy*. Stanford, Calif.: Stanford University Press.

Dahrendorf, Ralf. 1979. *Life Changes*. Chicago: University of Chicago Press.

Darnton, Robert. 1989. "What Was Revolutionary about the French Revolution?" *New York Review of Books*, 19 January, 3.

Davenport, Guy. 1987. "Pyrrhon of Elis." In *The Jules Verne Steam Balloon*. San Francisco: North Point.

Davis, Otto A., Melvin Hinich, and Peter C. Ordeshook. 1970. "An Expository Development of a Mathematical Model of the Electoral Process." 64 *American Political Science Review* 426.

Dawes, Robyn M., Alphons J. C. van de Kraft, and John M. Orbell. 1990. "Cooperation for the Benefit of Us—Not Me or My Conscience." In Jane J. Mansbridge, ed., *Beyond Self-Interest*. Chicago: University of Chicago Press.

Debnam, Geoffrey. 1984. *The Analysis of Power*. New York: St. Martin's.

Deci, Edward L. 1971. "Effects of Externally Mediated Awards on Intrinsic Motivation." 18 *Journal of Personality and Social Psychology* 105.

————. 1972. "Intrinsic Motivation, Extrinsic Reinforcement, and Inequity." 22 *Journal of Personality and Social Psychology* 113.

————, et al. 1981. "When Trying to Win: Competition and Intrinsic Motivation." 7 *Personality and Social Psychology Bulletin* 79.

Derthick, Martha. 1979. *Making Policy for Social Security*. Washington, D.C.: Brookings Institution.

Derthick, Martha, and Paul J. Quirk. 1985. *The Politics of Deregulation*. Washington, D.C.: Brookings Institution.

Deutsch, Karl W. 1963. *The Nerves of Government*. New York: Free Press.

Deutsch, Karl W., Andrei S. Markovits, and John Platt. 1986. *Advances in the Social Sciences, 1900–1980*. Lanham, Md.: University Press of America.

Diamond, Martin. 1981. *The Founding of the Democratic Republic*. Itasca, Ill.: F. E. Peacock.

Diesing, Paul. 1971. *Patterns of Discovery in the Social Sciences*. New York: Aldine.

Diggins, John Patrick. 1984. *The Lost Soul of American Politics*. New York: Basic Books.

DiMaggio, Paul, and Walter W. Powell. 1991. *The New Institutionalism and Organization Theory*. Chicago: University of Chicago Press.

Dodd, Lawrence C. 1977. "Congress and the Quest for Power." In Lawrence C. Dodd and Bruce I. Oppenheimer, eds., *Congress Reconsidered*. 1st ed. New York: Praeger.

————. 1981. "Congress, the Constitution and the Crisis of Legitimation." In Lawrence C. Dodd and Bruce I. Oppenheimer, eds., *Congress Reconsidered*. 2nd ed. Washington, D.C.: Congressional Quarterly.

————. 1986. "A Theory of Congressional Cycles." In Gerald Wright, Leroy Rieselbach, and Lawrence C. Dodd, eds., *Congress and Policy Change*. New York: Agathon.

————. 1987. "Woodrow Wilson's Congressional Government and the Modern Congress: The 'Universal Principle' of Change." 14 *Congress and the Presidency* 33.

————. 1991. "Congress, the Presidency, and the American Experience." In James A. Thurber, ed., *Divided Democracy*. Washington, D.C.: Congressional Quarterly.

————. 1992. "Learning to Learn: The Political Mastery of U. S. Senators." 16 *Legislative Studies Section Newsletter* 7.

————. 1993. "Congress and the Politics of Renewal." In Lawrence C. Dodd and Bruce I. Oppenheimer, eds., *Congress Reconsidered*. 5th ed. Washington, D.C.: Congressional Quarterly.

Dodd, Lawrence C., and Richard Schott. 1979. *Congress and the Administrative State*. New York: John Wiley.

Domhoff, G. William. 1971. *The Higher Circles: The Governing Class in America*. New York: Random House.

————. 1986. "State Autonomy and the Privileged Position of Business." 14 *Journal of Political and Military Sociology* 149.

Donaldson, Rodney E., ed. 1991. *A Sacred Unity: Further Steps to an Ecology of Mind.* New York: Harper Collins.

Douglas, Mary. 1986. *How Institutions Think.* Syracuse: Syracuse University Press.

Downs, Anthony. 1957. *An Economic Theory of Democracy.* New York: Harper and Row.

———. 1960. "Why Government's Budget Is Too Small in a Democracy." 12 *World Politics* 541.

Dray, William. 1957. *Laws and Explanation in History.* London: Oxford University Press.

Dred Scott v. Sandford, 60 U.S. 393 (1857).

DuBoff, Richard B. 1989. *Accumulation and Power.* Armonk, N.Y.: M. E. Sharpe.

Dunlavy, Coleen A. 1991. "Mirror Images: Political Structure and Early Railroad Policy in the United States and Prussia." In Karen Orren and Stephen Skowronek, eds., *Studies in American Political Development,* vol. 5. New Haven: Yale University Press.

Eagleton, Terry. 1984. *Literary Theory: An Introduction.* Minneapolis: University of Minnesota Press.

Easton, David. 1965. *A Systems Analysis of Political Life.* New York: John Wiley.

Easton, David. 1981. "The Political System Besieged by the State." 9 *Political Theory* 303.

Edelman, Murray. 1964. *The Symbolic Uses of Politics.* Urbana: University of Illinois Press.

———. 1988. *Constructing the Political Spectacle.* Chicago: University of Chicago Press.

Edsall, Thomas Byrne. 1984. *The New Politics of Inequality.* New York: W. W. Norton.

Edsall, Thomas Byrne, with Mary D. Edsall. 1992. *Chain Reaction: The Impact of Race, Rights, and Taxes on American Politics.* New York: W. W. Norton.

Eismeier, Theodore J. 1982. "Public Preferences About Government Spending: Partisan, Social and Attitudinal Sources of Policy Differences." 4 *Political Behavior* 133.

Ekstein, Harry. 1988. "A Culturalist Theory of Political Change." 82 *American Political Science Review* 789.

Elazar, Daniel J. 1970. *Cities of the Prairie: The Metropolitan Frontier and American Politics.* New York: Basic Books.

———. 1976. "The Generational Rhythm of American Politics." Temple University, Center for the Study of Federalism, *Working Paper* no. 13.

———. 1984. *American Federalism: A View from the States.* 3rd ed. New York: Harper and Row.

Elazar, Daniel J., Rozann Rothman, Stephen L. Schechter, Maren Allen Stein, and Joseph Zikmund II. 1986. *Cities of the Prairie Revisited: The Closing of the Metropolitan Frontier.* Lincoln: University of Nebraska Press.

Elchardus, Mark. 1982. "The Rediscovery of Chronos: The New Role of Time in Sociological Theory." 3 *International Sociology* 35.

Elkin, Stephen L. 1985. "Economics and Political Rationality." 18 *Polity* 253.

Elkins, David, and Richard Simeon. 1979. "A Cause in Search of Its Effects: Or What Does Political Culture Explain?" 11 *Comparative Politics* 127.

Elkins, Stanley M., and Eric McKitrick. 1961. "The Founding Fathers: Young Men of the Revolution." 76 *Political Science Quarterly* 181.

Ellis, Richard. 1991a. "American Political Cultures." Unpublished ms., Willamette University, Salem, Ore.

———. 1991b. "Legitimating Slavery in the Old South: The Effect of Political Institutions on Ideology." In Karen Orren and Stephen Skowronek, eds., *Studies in American Political Development*, vol. 5. New York: Cambridge University Press.

———. 1992. "Radical Lockeanism in American Political Culture." 45 *Western Political Quarterly* 825.

Ellsberg, Daniel. 1971. "The Quagmire Myth and the Stalemate Machine." 19 *Public Policy* 217.

Elster, Jon, ed. 1986. "Introduction." In *Rational Choice*. Oxford: Basil Blackwell.

Elster, Jon. 1989. *The Cement of Society*. New York: Cambridge University Press.

Enelow, James M., and Melvin J. Hinich. 1984. *The Spatial Theory of Voting: An Introduction*. New York: Cambridge University Press.

England, Paula. 1989. "A Feminist Critique of Rational-Choice Theories: Implications for Sociology." 20 *American Sociologist* 14.

Erbring, Lutz, Edie Goldenberg, and Arthur Miller. 1980. "Front-Page News and Real-World Cues: A New Look at Agenda-Setting by the Media." 24 *American Journal of Political Science* 16.

Erikson, Eric. 1964. *Childhood and Society*. New York: Norton.

———. 1969. *Gandhi's Truth*. New York: Norton.

Erikson, Robert, Gerald Wright, and John P. McIver. 1993. *Statehouse Democracy*. New York: Cambridge University Press.

Esping-Andersen, Gosta. 1985. *Politics Against Markets*. Princeton: Princeton University Press.

———. 1987. "The Comparison of Policy Regimes." In Martin Rein, Gosta Esping-Andersen, and Lee Rainwater, eds., *Stagnation and Renewal in Social Policy: The Rise and Fall of Policy Regimes*. Armonk, N.Y.: M. E. Sharpe.

Esping-Andersen, Gosta, and Walter Korpi. 1984. "Social Policy as Class Politics in Post-War Capitalism: Scandinavia, Austria and Germany." In John Gold Thorpe, ed., *Order and Conflict in Contemporary Capitalism*. Oxford: Clarendon.

Eulau, Heinz. 1969. *Micro-Macro Political Analysis: Accents of Inquiry*. Chicago: Aldine.

Evans, Peter, Dietrich Rueschemeyer, and Theda Skocpol, eds. 1985. *Bringing the State Back In*. New York: Cambridge University Press.

Farr, James. 1985. "Situational Analysis: Explanation in Political Science." 47 *Journal of Politics* 1085.

Farrand, Max. 1937. *The Records of the Federal Convention of 1787*. 4 vols. New Haven: Yale University Press.

Fenno, Richard F., Jr. 1973. *Congressmen in Committees*. Boston: Little, Brown.

———. 1978. *Home Style*. Boston: Little, Brown.

———. 1991. *The Emergence of a Senate Leader: Pete Domenici and the Reagan Budget*. Washington, D.C.: Congressional Quarterly.

———. 1992. *When Incumbency Fails: The Senate Career of Mark Andrews*. Washington, D.C.: Congressional Quarterly.

Ferejohn, John A. 1991. "Rationality and Interpretation: Parliamentary Elections in Early Stuart England." In Kristen Monroe, ed., *The Economic Approach to Politics: A Critical Reassessment of the Theory of Rational Action.* New York: Harper Collins.

Ferejohn, John A., and Morris P. Fiorina. 1974. "The Paradox of Not Voting: A Decision Theoretic Analysis." 68 *American Political Science Review* 525.

————. 1975. "Closeness Counts Only in Horseshoes and Dancing." 69 *American Political Science Review* 920.

Ferguson, Thomas, and Joel Rogers, eds. 1981. *The Hidden Election.* New York: Pantheon.

Ferguson, Yale H., and Richard W. Mansbach. 1991. "Between Celebration and Despair: Constructive Suggestions for Future International Theory." 35 *International Studies Quarterly* 363.

Festinger, Leon. 1964. *Conflict, Decision and Dissonance.* Stanford: Stanford University Press.

Fiorina, Morris P. 1976. "The Voting Decision: Instrumental and Expressive Aspects." 38 *Journal of Politics* 390.

————. 1977. *Congress: Keystone of the Washington Establishment.* New Haven: Yale University Press.

————. 1980. "On the Decline of Collective Responsibility in American Politics." 109(3) *Daedalus* 25.

————. 1981. *Retrospective Voting in American National Elections.* New Haven: Yale University Press.

————. 1982. "Legislative Choice of Regulatory Forms: Legal Process or Administrative Process." 39 *Public Choice* 33.

————. 1986. "Legislative Uncertainty, Legislative Control, and the Delegation of Legislative Power." 2 *Journal of Law, Economics and Organization* 33.

Fisher, Roger, and William Ury. 1981. *Getting to Yes.* New York: Penguin.

Fiske, Susan T. 1990. "The Motivated Tactician: Cognition and Motivation in Research on the Presidency." Paper presented at the Conference on Research on the American Presidency, November 12–14, University of Pittsburgh.

Flora, Peter, and Jens Alber. 1977. "The Development of Welfare States in North America." In Peter Flora and Arnold Heidenheimer, eds., *Modernization, Democratization, and the Development of Welfare States in Western Europe.* New Brunswick, N.J.: Transaction Books.

Flora, Peter, and Arnold Heidenheimer. 1977. *The Development of Welfare States in Europe and America.* New Brunswick, N.J.: Transaction Books.

Foner, Eric. 1980. *Politics and Ideology in the Age of the Civil War.* New York: Oxford University Press.

Forbath, William E. 1991. *Law and the Shaping of the American Labor Movement.* Cambridge: Harvard University Press.

Formisano, Ronald. 1974. "Deferential-Participant Politics: The Early Republic's Political Culture, 1789–1840." 68 *American Political Science Review* 473.

Fossett, Roy E. 1960. "The Impact of the New Deal on Georgia Politics, 1933–1941." Ph.D. diss., University of Florida.

Foucault, Michel. 1971. *The Order of Things.* New York: Pantheon.

————. 1976. *The Archeology of Knowledge.* New York: Harper and Row.

Frank, Robert. 1988. *Passions Within Reason*. New York: W. W. Norton.

Fraser, Derek. 1973. *The Evolution of the British Welfare State*. London: Macmillan.

Free, Lloyd, and Hadley Cantril. 1967. *The Political Beliefs of Americans*. New Brunswick, N.J.: Rutgers University Press.

Freeman, Richard B., and James L. Medoff. 1984. *What Unions Do*. New York: Basic Books.

Friedman, Jeffrey. 1991. "Cultural Theory vs. Cultural History." 3 *Critical Review*.

Friedman, Milton. 1953. "The Methodology of Positive Economics." In *Essays in Positive Economics*. Chicago: University of Chicago Press.

Fromm, Erich. 1941. *Escape from Freedom*. New York: Farrar and Rinehart.

Fuchs, Lawrence H. 1955. "American Jews and the Presidential Vote." 49 *American Political Science Review* 385.

Fudenberg, Drew, and Jean Tirole. 1991. *Game Theory*. Cambridge: MIT Press.

Galambos, Louis. 1970. "The Emerging Organizational Synthesis in Modern American History." 44 *Business History Review* 279.

———. 1983. "Technology, Political Economy, and Professionalism: Central Themes of the Organizational Synthesis." 57 *Business History Review* 471.

Galambos, Louis, and Joseph Pratt. 1988. *The Rise of the Corporate Commonwealth*. New York: Basic Books.

Galbraith, John Kenneth. 1952. *American Capitalism*. Boston: Houghton Mifflin.

———. 1968. *The New Industrial State*. New York: Houghton Mifflin.

Garrett, Geoffrey, and Barry R. Weingast. 1991. "Ideas, Interests and Institutions: Constructing the EC's Internal Market." Stanford University. Photocopy.

Geertz, Clifford. 1964. "Ideology as a Cultural System." In David E. Apter, ed., *Ideology and Discontent*. New York: Free.

———. 1973. "Thick Description: Toward an Interpretative Theory of Culture." In *The Interpretation of Cultures*. New York: Basic Books.

Georgia State Department of Public Welfare. 1939. *Official Report, for the Fiscal Year July 1, 19xx to June 30, 19yy*. Atlanta, Ga.

Gibbons v. Ogden, 9 Wheat. 1 (1824).

Gibson, James L., Cornelius P. Cotter, John F. Bibby, and Robert J. Huckshorn. 1983. "Assessing Party Organizational Strength." 27 *American Journal of Political Science* 193.

Giddens, Anthony. 1979. *Central Problems in Social Theory: Action, Structure and Contradiction in Social Analysis*. Berkeley: University of California Press.

Gienapp, William E. 1987. *The Origins of the Republican Party, 1852–1856*. New York: Oxford University Press.

Gilbert, Jess, and Carolyn Howe. 1991. "Beyond 'State vs. Society': Theories of the State and New Deal Agricultural Policies." 56 *American Sociological Review* 204.

Gilligan, Thomas, and Keith Krehbiel. 1987. "Collective Decision-Making and Standing Committees: An Informational Rationale for Restrictive Amendment Procedures." 3 *Journal of Law, Economics and Organization* 287.

Gilpin, Robert. 1987. *The Political Economy of International Relations*. Princeton: Princeton University Press.

Goldstein, Joshua S. 1988. *Long Cycles: Prosperity and War in the Modern Age*. New Haven: Yale University Press.

Goodman, Nelson. 1978. *Ways of Worldmaking*. Indianapolis: Hacker.

———. 1984. *Of Mind and Other Matters*. Cambridge: Harvard University Press.

Gordon, David, Richard Edwards, and Michael Reich. 1982. *Segmented Work, Divided Workers*. New York: Cambridge University Press.

Gottschalk, Louis. 1963. "Categories of Historiographical Generalization." In Louis

Gottschalk, ed., *Generalization in the Writing of History*. Chicago: University of Chicago Press.

Gould, Stephen Jay. 1981. *The Mismeasure of Man*. New York: W. W. Norton.

———. 1989a. Quoted in *New York Review of Books*, 1 June, 21.

———. 1989b. *Wonderful Life: The Burgess Shale and the Nature of History*. New York: W. W. Norton.

Gourevitch, Peter A. 1986. *Politics in Hard Times: Comparative Responses to International Economic Crises*. Ithaca: Cornell University Press.

Graber, Doris A. 1989. *Mass Media and American Politics*. Washington, D.C.: Congressional Quarterly.

Graebner, William. 1977. "Federalism in the Progressive Era: A Structural Interpretation of Reform." 64 *Journal of American History* 331.

Granovetter, Mark S. 1973. "The Strength of Weak Ties." 78 *American Journal of Sociology* 1360.

Gray, Virginia. 1993. "Innovation and Diffusion in the American States." In Lawrence C. Dodd and Calvin Jillson, eds., *New Perspectives on American Politics*. Washington, D.C.: Congressional Quarterly.

Greenberg, Edward S. 1985. *Capitalism and the American Political Ideal*. Armonk, N.Y.: M. E. Sharpe.

———. 1990a. "Reaganism as Corporate Liberalism." 10 *Policy Studies Review* 103.

———. 1990b. "State Change: Approaches and Concepts." In Edward S. Greenberg and Thomas F. Mayer, eds., *Changes in the State*. Newbury Park, Calif.: Sage.

Greenberg, Edward S., and Benjamin I. Page. 1988. "Why the State Does What It Does: Towards a Synthetic Model." Paper presented at Conference on State Change, University of Colorado, Boulder. Mimeo.

Greenstein, Fred I. 1992. "What did Eisenhower Tell Kennedy about Indochina? The Politics of Misperception." 79 *Journal of American History* 568.

Greenstone, David, 1969. *Labor in American Politics*. New York: Knopf.

———. 1986. "Political Culture and Political Development: Liberty, Union and the Liberal Bi-Polarity." In Karen Orren and Stephen Skowronek, eds., *Studies in American Political Development*, vol. 1. New Haven: Yale University Press.

Grodzins, Morton. 1960. "American Political Parties and the American System." 13 *Western Political Quarterly* 974.

Gurin, Patricia, Shirley Hatchett, and James S. Jackson. 1989. *Hope and Independence*. New York: Russell Sage.

Gurr, Ted Robert. 1970. *Why Men Rebel*. Princeton: Princeton University Press.

Gusfield, Joseph. 1963. *Symbolic Crusade*. Urbana: University of Illinois Press.

Haas, Peter M. 1989. "Do Regimes Matter? Epistemic Communities and Mediterranean Pollution Control." 43 *International Organization* 377.

Habermas, Jergen. 1973. *Theory and Practice*. Trans. John Viertel. Boston: Beacon Press.

———. 1975. *Legitimation Crisis*. Boston: Beacon.

———. 1984; 1987. *The Theory of Communicative Action*. vols. 1 and 2. Translated by Thomas McCarthy. Boston: Beacon.

Hadenius, Axel. 1985. "Citizens Strike a Balance: Discontent with Taxes, Content with Spending." 5 *Journal of Public Policy* 349.

———. 1986. *A Crisis of the Welfare State? Opinions About Taxes and Public Expenditure in Sweden*. Stockholm: MiniMedia AB.

Hall, Stuart. 1984. "The Rise of the Representative/Interventionist State 1880s–1920s." In Gregor McLennan, David Held, and Stuart Hall, *State and Society in Contemporary Britain*. New York: Polity.

Hamilton, Alexander, James Madison, and John Jay. 1961. *The Federalist Papers*. New York: New American Library.

Hansen, John M. 1987. "Choosing Sides: The Creation of an Agricultural Policy Network in Congress, 1919–1932." In Karen Orren and Stephen Skowronek, eds., *Studies in American Political Development*, vol. 2. New Haven: Yale University Press.

Hanson, Russell L. 1985. *The Democratic Imagination in America*. Princeton: Princeton University Press.

Hanson, Russell L., and John Hartman. 1988. "Mean Seasons and Warm Business Climates in the American States." Paper presented at the annual meeting of the American Political Science Association, Washington, D.C.

Hardin, Garrett. 1968. "The Tragedy of the Commons." 162 *Science* 1234.

Hardin, Russell. 1982. *Collective Action*. Baltimore: Johns Hopkins University Press.

Hardin, Russell, and Brian Barry, eds. 1982. *Rational Man and Irrational Society?* Beverly Hills, Calif.: Sage.

Harrington, Michael. 1972. *Socialism*. New York: Saturday Review.

Harris, Richard A., and Sidney M. Milkis. 1989. *Remaking American Politics*. Boulder, Co.: Westview Press.

Hartz, Louis. 1955. *The Liberal Tradition in America*. New York: Harcourt, Brace.

Hattam, Victoria. 1990. "Economic Visions and Political Strategies: American Labor and the State, 1865–96." In Karen Orren and Stephen Skowronek, eds., *Studies in American Political Development*, vol. 4. New Haven: Yale University Press.

———. 1992. "Institutions and Political Change: Working-Class Formation in England and the United States, 1820–1896." In Sven Steinmo, Kathleen Thelen, and Frank Longstreth, eds., *Structuring Politics: Historical Institutionalism in Historical Perspective*. New York: Cambridge University Press.

———. 1993. *Labor Visions and State Power: The Origins of Business Unionism in the United States*. Princeton: Princeton University Press.

Hays, Samuel. 1957. *The Response to Industrialism, 1885–1914*. Chicago: University of Chicago Press.

———. 1965. "The Social Analysis of American Political History: 1880–1920." 80 *Political Science Quarterly* 373.

———. 1975. "Political Parties and the Community-Society Continuum." In William Chambers and Walter Dean Burnham, eds., *The American Political System: Stages of Development*. 2nd ed. New York: Oxford University Press.

Headey, Bruce. 1978. *Housing Policy in the Developed Economy*. London: Croom Helm.

Hechter, Michael. 1987. *Principles of Group Solidarity*. Berkeley: University of California Press.

Heclo, Hugh. 1974. *Modern Social Politics in Britain and Sweden*. New Haven: Yale University Press.

————. 1978. "Issue Networks and the Executive Establishment." In Anthony King, ed., *The New American Political System*. Washington, D.C.: American Enterprise Institute for Public Policy Research.

————. 1989. "The Emerging Regime." In Richard Harris and Sidney Milkis, eds., *Remaking American Politics*. Boulder, Co.: Westview.

Heilbroner, Robert. 1980. *Marxism: For and Against*. New York: W. W. Norton.

————. 1985. *The Nature and Logic of Capitalism*. New York: W. W. Norton.

Heller, Walter. 1966. *The Godkin Lectures*. Cambridge: Harvard University Press.

Hempel, Carl G. 1942. "The Function of General Laws in History." 39 *Journal of Philosophy* 35.

Hero, Rodney. 1993. "Two-Tiered Pluralism: The Impact of Race and Ethnicity on American Politics." In Lawrence C. Dodd and Calvin Jillson, eds., *New Perspectives on American Politics*. Washington, D.C.: Congressional Quarterly.

Herring, Pendleton. 1940. *The Politics of Democracy*. New York: Norton.

Hirschman, Albert O. 1970. "The Search for Paradigms as a Hindrance to Understanding." 22 *World Politics* 329.

————. 1977. *Passions and Interests*. Princeton: Princeton University Press.

Hobbes, Thomas. 1986. *The Leviathan*. Harmondsworth, Eng.: Penguin.

Hochschild, Jennifer. 1981. *What's Fair: American Beliefs About Distributive Justice*. Cambridge: Harvard University Press.

Hofstadter, Richard. [1954] 1974. *The American Political Tradition*. New York: Vintage Books.

————. 1955. *The Age of Reform*. New York: Random House.

————. 1963. *The Progressive Movement, 1900–1915*. Englewood Cliffs, N.J.: Prentice-Hall.

————. 1965. *The Paranoid Style in American Politics*. New York: Knopf.

————. 1969. *The Idea of a Party System*. Berkeley: University of California Press.

Hollinger, David. 1985. *In the American Province*. Bloomington: Indiana University Press.

Hollingsworth, J. Rogers. 1963. *The Whirligig of Politics: The Democracy of Cleveland and Bryan*. Chicago: University of Chicago Press.

————. 1978. "The United States." In Raymond Grew, ed., *Crises in Political Development in Europe and the United States*. Princeton: Princeton University Press.

Holmes, Michael S. 1975. *The New Deal in Georgia: An Administrative History*. Westport, Conn.: Greenwood.

Hooks, Gregory. 1990. "From an Autonomous to a Captured State Agency: The Decline of the New Deal in Agriculture." 55 *American Sociological Review* 29.

Horowitz, Morton. 1992. *The Transformation of American Law*. New York: Oxford University Press.

Howe, Daniel Walker. 1988. "The Language of Faculty Psychology in 'The Federalist Papers'." In Terry Ball and J.G.A. Pocock, eds., *Conceptual Change and the Constitution*. Lawrence: University Press of Kansas.

Huckabee, David C. 1989. "Reelection Rates of House Incumbents: 1790–1988." Washington, D.C.: Congressional Research Service, Library of Congress.

Huckfeldt, Robert, and Carol Weitzel Kohfeld. 1989. *Race and the Decline of Class in American Politics*. Urbana: University of Illinois Press.

Huckfeldt, Robert, and John Sprague. 1987. "Networks in Context: The Social Flow of Political Information." 81 *American Political Science Review* 1197.

_____. 1991. "Discussant Effects on Vote Choice: Intimacy, Structure, and Interdependence." 53 *Journal of Politics* 122.

_____. 1992. "Political Parties and Electoral Mobilization: Political Structure, Social Structure, and the Party Canvass." 86 *American Political Science Review* 70.

Hume, David. 1955. *An Inquiry Concerning Human Understanding*. New York: Bobbs-Merrill.

_____. 1970. *Hume's Moral and Political Philosophy*. Darien, Conn.: Hafner.

Hunt, Morton. 1990. *The Compassionate Beast*. New York: Morrow.

Huntington, Samuel P. 1968. "Political Modernization: America Versus Europe." Chap. 2 in *Political Order in Changing Societies*. New Haven: Yale University Press.

_____. 1973. "Congressional Responses to the Twentieth Century." In David B. Truman, ed., *The Congress and America's Future*. 2nd ed. Englewood Cliffs, N.J.: Prentice-Hall.

_____. 1981. *American Politics: The Promise of Disharmony*. Cambridge: Harvard University Press.

_____. 1982. "American Ideals versus American Institutions." 97(1) *Political Science Quarterly* 1.

Hurley, Patricia A. 1991. "Partisan Representation, Realignment, and the Senate in the 1980s." 53 *Journal of Politics* 3.

Immergut, Ellen. 1992. "The Rules of the Game: The Logic of Health Policy-Making in France, Switzerland, and Sweden." In Sven Steinmo, Kathleen Thelen, and Frank Longstreth, eds., *Structuring Politics: Historical Institutionalism in Comparative Analysis*. New York: Cambridge University Press.

Indiana Welfare Investigation Commission. 1944. *Official Report*. Indianapolis, Ind.

Inglehart, Ronald. 1989. *Culture Shift in Advanced Industrial Societies*. Princeton: Princeton University Press.

Isaac, Jeffrey C. 1987. *Power and Marxist Theory*. Ithaca: Cornell University Press.

Iyengar, Shanto. 1991. *Is Anyone Responsible?* Chicago: University of Chicago Press.

Iyengar, Shanto, and Donald Kinder. 1987. *News That Matters*. Chicago: University of Chicago Press.

Jackson, John E., ed. 1990. *Institutions in American Society*. Ann Arbor: University of Michigan Press.

Jacobson, Gary C. 1992. *The Politics of Congressional Elections*. 3rd ed. Pacific Grove, Calif.: Brooks, Cole.

Jacobson, Gary C., and Samuel Kernell. 1983. *Strategy and Choice in Congressional Elections*. 2nd ed. New Haven: Yale University Press.

Jaffa, Harry V. 1959. *The Crisis of the House Divided: The Lincoln-Douglas Debates of 1858*. New York: Doubleday.

Jahnige, Thomas. 1971. "Critical Elections and Social Change." 4 *Polity* 465.

James, Patterson. 1967. *Congressional Conservatism and the New Deal*. Lexington: University of Kentucky Press.

Janis, Irving. 1982. *Stress, Attitudes, and Decisions*. New York: Praeger.

Jaspers, Karl. 1958. The *Future of Mankind*. Trans. by E. B. Ashton. Chicago: University of Chicago Press.

Jefferson, Thomas. 1955. *Political Writings: Representative Selections*. Indianapolis, Ind.: Bobbs-Merrill.

Jennings, Edward T. 1979. "Competition, Constituencies, and Welfare Policies in American States." 73 *American Political Science Review* 414.

Jensen, Richard. 1971. *The Winning of the Midwest*. Chicago: University of Chicago Press.

Jillson, Calvin C. 1988. *Constitution Making: Conflict and Consensus in the Federal Convention of 1787*. New York: Agathon.

Jillson, Calvin C., and Rick K. Wilson. 1994. *Congressional Dynamics: Structure, Coordination, and Choice in the First American Congress, 1774–1789*. Stanford: Stanford University Press.

Johnson, Paul Edwards. 1987. "Foresight and Myopia in Organizational Membership." 49 *Journal of Politics* 679.

Jung, Carl. 1963. *Memories, Dreams, Reflections*. Recorded and edited by Aniela Jaffe. New York: Pantheon.

Jung, Hwa Yol. 1971. "The Political Relevance of Existential Phenomenology." 33 *Review of Politics* 538.

Kahneman, Daniel, Paul Slovic, and Amos Tversky, eds. 1982. *Judgment Under Uncertainty: Heuristics and Biases*. New York: Cambridge University Press.

Kammen, Michael. 1987. *A Machine That Would Go of Itself: The Constitution in American Culture*. New York: Vintage.

Kann, Mark. 1990. "Individualism, Civic Virtue and Gender in America." In Karen Orren and Stephen Skowronek, eds., *Studies in American Political Development*, vol. 4. New Haven: Yale University Press.

Karl, Barry. 1983. *The Uneasy State*. Chicago: University of Chicago Press.

Katz, Daniel, and Samuel Eldersveld. 1961. "The Impact of Local Party Activity upon the Electorate." 25 *Public Opinion Quarterly* 1.

Katz, Elihu. 1957. "The Two-Step Flow of Communication: An Up-to-Date Report on a Hypothesis." 21 *Public Opinion Quarterly* 67.

Katz, Elihu, and Paul Lazarsfeld. 1955. *Political Influence*. Glencoe, Ill.: Free.

Katzenstein, Peter, ed. 1978. *Between Power and Plenty*. Madison: University of Wisconsin Press.

Katznelson, Ira. 1981. *City Trenches: Urban Politics and the Patterning of Class in the United States*. New York: Pantheon.

———. 1985. "Working Class Formation and the State." In Peter B. Evans, Dietrich Rueschemeyer, and Theda Skocpol, eds. *Bringing the State Back In*. New York: Cambridge University Press.

Katznelson, Ira, and Bruce Pietrykowski. 1991. "Rebuilding the American State:

Evidence from the 1940s." In Karen Orren and Stephen Skowronek, eds., *Studies in American Political Development*, vol. 5. New York: Cambridge University Press.

Kaufman, Herbert. 1991. *Time, Chance, and Organizations*. Chatham, N.J.: Chatham House.

Kedourie, Elie. 1992. "Why Brutus Stabbed Caesar." 16(4) *Wilson Quarterly* 112.

Keller, William. 1990. *The Liberals and J. Edgar Hoover*. Princeton: Princeton University Press.

Kelley, Robert. 1977. "Ideology and Political Culture from Jefferson to Nixon." 82 *American Historical Review* 531.

Kelman, Stephen. 1987. *Making Public Policy*. New York: Basic Books.

———. 1990. "Congress and Public Spirit." In Jane Mansbridge, ed., *Beyond Self-Interest*. Chicago: University of Chicago Press.

Kennedy, Paul. 1987. *The Rise and Fall of the Great Powers*. New York: Random House.

Keohane, Robert. 1988. "International Institutions: Two Approaches." 32 *International Studies Quarterly* 379.

Kernell, Samuel. 1977. "Toward Understanding 19th Century Congressional Careers: Ambition, Competition, and Rotation." 21 *American Journal of Political Science* 669.

Ketcham, Ralph. 1984. *Presidents Above Party: The First American Presidency, 1789–1829*. Chapel Hill: University of North Carolina Press.

Key, V. O., Jr., with the assistance of Alexander Heard. 1949. *Southern Politics in State and Nation*. New York: Knopf.

———. 1952. "The Future of the Democratic Party." 28 *Virginia Quarterly Review* 161.

———. 1955. "A Theory of Critical Elections." 17 *Journal of Politics* 3.

———. 1966. *The Responsible Electorate: Rationality in Presidential Voting, 1936–60*. Cambridge: Harvard University Press.

Key, V. O., Jr., and Frank Munger. 1959. "Social Determinism and Electoral Decision: The Case of Indiana." In Eugene Burdick and Arthur J. Brodbeck, eds. *American Voting Behavior*. Glencoe, Ill.: Free.

Kincaid, John, ed., 1982. "Introduction." In *Political Culture, Public Policy and the American States*. Philadelphia, Pa.: Institute for the Study of Human Issues.

Kinder, Donald R. 1986. "Presidential Character Revisited." In Richard R. Lau and David O. Sears, eds., *Political Cognition*. Hillsdale, N.J.: Lawrence Erlbaum Associates.

Kinder, Donald R., and Susan T. Fiske. 1986. "Presidents in the Public Mind." In Margaret G. Hermann, *Political Psychology*. San Francisco: Jossey-Bass.

Kinder, Donald R., and David O. Sears. 1985. "Public Opinion and Political Behavior." In Gardner Lindzey and Elliot Aronson, eds. *Handbook of Social Psychology*, vol. 2. New York: Random House.

King, Anthony. 1973a. "Ideas, Institutions and the Policies of Governments: A Comparative Analysis, Parts I and II." 3 *British Journal of Political Science* 291.

———. 1973b. "Ideas, Institutions and the Policies of Governments: A Comparative Analysis, Part III." 3 *British Journal of Political Science* 409.

King, Michael, and Lester Seligman. 1976. "Critical Elections, Congressional Recruitment and Public Policy." In Heinz Eulau and Moshe Czudnowski, eds., *Elite Recruitment in Democratic Politics: Comparative Studies Across Nations*. New York: Halstead.

Kingdon, John. 1984. *Agendas, Alternatives and Public Policies*. Boston. Little Brown.

————. 1993. "Agendas, Ideas, and Policy Change." In Lawrence C. Dodd and Calvin Jillson, eds., *New Perspectives on American Politics*. Washington, D.C.: Congressional Quarterly.

Klass, Gary M. 1985. "Explaining America and the Welfare State: An Alternative Theory." 15 *British Journal of Political Science* 427.

Kleppner, Paul. 1979. *The Third Electoral System*. Chapel Hill: University of North Carolina Press.

————. 1987. *Continuity and Change in Electoral Politics, 1893–1928*. Westport, Conn.: Greenwood.

Klimoski, Richard J., and James A. Breaugh. 1977. "When Performance Doesn't Count: A Constituency Looks at Its Spokesman." 20 *Organizational Behavior and Human Performance* 301–311.

Knoke, David. 1990. *Organizing for Collective Action*. New York: Aldine de Gruyter.

Kohn, Alfie. 1990. *The Brighter Side of Human Nature: Altruism and Empathy in Everyday Life*. New York: Basic Books.

Kolko, Gabriel. 1965. *Railroads and Regulation*. Princeton: Princeton University Press.

Kornhauser, William. 1959. *The Politics of Mass Society*. Glencoe, Ill.: FreePress.

Korpi, Walter. 1983. *The Democratic Class Struggle*. London: Routledge and Kegan Paul.

Korpi, Walter, and Micheal Shalev. 1979. "Strikes, Industrial Relations, and Class Conflict in Capitalist Societies." 30 *British Journal of Society* 164.

Koven, Seth, and Sonya Michel. 1990. "Womanly Duties: Maternalist Politics and the Origins of Welfare States in France, Germany, Great Britain, and the United States, 1880–1920." 95 *American Historical Review* 1076.

Kramer, Gerald. 1971. "The Effects of Precinct-Level Canvassing on Voter Behavior." 34 *Public Opinion Quarterly* 560.

Krasner, Stephen. 1978. *Defending the National Interest*. Princeton: Princeton University Press.

————. 1988. "Sovereignty: An Institutional Perspective." 21 *Comparative Political Studies* 66.

Krebs, Dennis L. 1970. "Altruism: An Examination of the Concept." 73 *Psychological Bulletin* 258.

Krehbiel, Keith. 1991. *Information and Legislative Organization*. Ann Arbor: University of Michigan Press.

Kuhn, Thomas. 1970. *The Structure of Scientific Revolutions*. Chicago: University of Chicago Press.

Kuznets, Simon. 1953. *Economic Change*. New York: W. W. Norton.

Ladd, Everett Carl, Jr., Marilyn Potter, Linda Basilick, Sally Daniels, and Dana Suszliw. 1979. "The Polls: Taxing and Spending." 43 *Public Opinion Quarterly* 126.

Ladd-Taylor, Molly. 1986. *Raising a Baby the Government Way: Mothers' Letters to the Children's Bureau, 1915–1932*. New Brunswick, N.J.: Rutgers University Press.

Laing, R. D. 1967. *The Politics of Experience.* New York: Pantheon.

Laitin, David. 1988. "Political Culture and Political Preferences." 82 *American Political Science Review* 589.

Lancaster, Lane W. 1937. *Government in Rural America.* New York: D. Van Nostrand.

Langer, Suzanne. 1970. *Philosophy in a New Key.* Cambridge: Harvard University Press.

Langlois, Richard, ed. 1989. *Economics as a Process.* New York: Cambridge University Press.

Larson, Magali Sarfatti. 1977. *The Rise of Professionalism: A Sociological Analysis.* Berkeley: University of California Press.

Lasswell, Harold. 1930. *Psychopathology and Politics.* Chicago: University of Chicago Press.

Lasswell, Harold, and Abraham Kaplan. 1950. *Power and Society.* New Haven: Yale University Press.

Lazarsfeld, Paul, Bernard Berelson, and Hazel Gaudet. 1948. *The People's Choice.* New York: Columbia University Press.

Leege, David, and Wayne Francis. 1974. *Political Research: Design, Measurement and Analysis.* New York: Basic Books.

Leman, Christopher. 1977. "Patterns of Policy Development: Social Security in the United States and Canada." 25 *Public Policy* 261.

Lemmon, Sara McCulloh. 1954. "The Ideology of Eugene Talmadge." 38 *Georgia Historical Quarterly* 226.

Lenski, Gerhard. 1966. *Power and Privilege.* New York: McGraw-Hill.

Lerner, Michael. 1986. *Surplus Powerlessness.* Oakland, Calif.: Institute for Labor and Mental Health.

Levi, Margaret. 1981. "The Predatory Theory of Rule." 10 *Politics and Markets* 431.

———. 1988. *Of Rule and Revenue.* Berkeley: University of California Press.

Lichbach, Mark I. Forthcoming. "Rethinking Rationality and Rebellion: Theories of Collective Action and Problems of Collective Dissent." *Rationality and Society.*

Lichtman, Allan J. 1976. "Critical Election Theory and the Reality of American Presidential Politics, 1916–1940." 81 *American Historical Review* 317–350.

———. 1982. "The End of Realignment Theory? Toward a New Research Program for American Political History." 15 *Historical Methods* 170–188.

Lichtman, Allan J., and Ken DeCell. 1990. *Thirteen Keys to the Presidency: Prediction Without Polls.* New York: Madison Books.

Light, Paul. 1985. *The Artful Work.* New York: Random House.

Lindblom, Charles. 1977. *Politics and Markets.* New York: Basic Books.

———. 1990. *Inquiry and Change: The Troubled Attempt to Understand and Shape Society.* New Haven: Yale University Press.

Lipset, David. 1980. *Gregory Bateson: The Legacy of a Scientist.* Englewood Cliffs, N.J.: Prentice-Hall.

Lipset, Seymour Martin. 1963. *The First New Nation.* New York: Basic Books.

———. 1968. *Revolution and Counterrevolution.* New York: Basic Books.

———. 1976. "Radicalism in North America: A Comparative View of the Party

Systems in Canada and the United States." 4 *Transactions of the Royal Society of Canada* 19.

———. 1977. "Why No Socialism in the United States?" In Seweryn Bialer and Sophia Sluzar, eds., *Radicalism in the Contemporary Age*. Boulder, Co.: Westview.

———. 1980. *Gregory Bateson: The Legacy of a Scientist*. Englewood Cliffs, N.J.: Prentice-Hall.

———. 1991. "American Exceptionalism Reaffirmed." In Byron E. Shafer, ed., *Is America Different? A New Look at American Exceptionalism*. New York: Oxford University Press.

Lipset, Seymour Martin, and Stein Rokkan, eds. 1967. *Party Systems and Voter Alignments*. New York: Free.

Lipset, Seymour Martin, and William Schneider. 1983. *The Confidence Gap*. New York: Free.

Litwack, Leon. 1962. *The American Labor Movement*. Englewood Cliffs, N.J.: Prentice-Hall.

Lockhart, Charles. 1984. "Explaining Social Policy Differences Among Advanced Industrial Societies." 16 *Comparative Politics* 335.

———. 1991. "American Exceptionalism and Social Security: Complementary Cultural and Structural Contributions to Social Program Development." 53 *Review of Politics* 510.

Lodge, Milton, and Ruth Hamill. 1986. "A Partisan Schema for Political Information Processing." 80 *American Political Science Review* 505.

Lodge, Milton, Kathleen M. McGraw, and Patrick Stroh. 1989. "An Impression-Driven Model of Candidate Evaluation." 83 *American Political Science Review* 399.

Long, Norton E. 1958. "The Local Community as an Ecology of Games." 64 *American Journal of Sociology* 251.

Longstreth, Frank H., and Desmond S. King. 1990. "The New Institutionalism." University of Colorado. Mimeo.

Loomis, Burdett A., and Allan J. Cigler. 1983. "Introduction: The Changing Nature of Interest Group Politics." In Allan J. Cigler and Burdett A. Loomis, eds., *Interest Group Politics*. Washington, D.C.: Congressional Quarterly.

Lowery, Charles D. 1984. *James Barbour, A Jeffersonian Republican*. University, Ala.: University of Alabama Press.

Lowi, Theodore J. 1964. "American Business, Public Policy, Case Studies and Political Theory." 16 *World Politics* 677.

———. 1967. "The Public Philosophy: Interest-Group Liberalism." 61 *American Political Science Review* 5.

———. 1969. *The End of Liberalism*. New York: W. W. Norton.

———. 1971. *The Politics of Disorder*. New York: Basic Books.

———. 1972. "Four Systems of Policy, Politics, and Change." 32 *Public Administration Review* 298.

———. 1979. *The End of Liberalism*. 2nd ed. New York: W. W. Norton.

———. 1984. "Why There Is No Socialism in the United States: A Federal Analysis." In Robert T. Golembiewski and Aaron Wildavsky, eds., *The Cost of Federalism*. New Brunswick, N.J.: Transaction Books.

_____. 1985. *The Personal President*. Ithaca: Cornell University Press.

_____. 1992. "The State in Political Science: How We Became What We Study." 86 *American Political Science Review* 1–7.

Lubell, Samuel. 1951. *The Future of American Politics*. New York: Harper and Brothers.

Lubove, Roy. [1968] 1986. *The Struggle for Social Security, 1900–1935*. 2nd ed. Pittsburgh: University of Pittsburgh Press.

Luce, R. Duncan, and Howard Raiffa. 1957. *Games and Decisions*. New York: John Wiley.

Lukes, Stephen. 1974. *Power: A Radical View*. London: Macmillan.

Lustig, Jeffrey R. 1982. *Corporate Liberalism: The Origins of Modern America*. Berkeley: University of California Press.

Maass, Arthur. 1983. *Congress and the Common Good*. New York: Basic Books.

MacIntyre, Alasdair. 1984. *After Virtue*. Notre Dame, Ind.: University of Notre Dame Press.

MacKuen, Michael. 1990. "Speaking of Politics: Individual Conversational Choice, Public Opinion, and the Prospects for Deliberative Democracy." In John A. Ferejohn and James H. Kuklinski, eds., *Information and Democratic Processes*. Urbana: University of Illinois Press.

MacNeill, William. 1992. Review of *The End of History and the Last Man*, by Francis Fukuyama. *New York Times Book Review*, 26 January.

Madison, James. 1900. *The Writings of James Madison*. New York: G. P. Putnam's Sons.

Madison, James, Alexander Hamilton, and John Jay. 1937. *The Federalist Papers*. New York: Modern College Library Editions.

Madison, James H. 1982. *Indiana Through Tradition and Changes: A History of the Hoosier State and Its People, 1920–1945*. Indianapolis: Indiana Historical Society.

Magaziner, Ira, and Robert Reich. 1982. *Minding America's Business: The Decline and Rise of the American Economy*. New York: Harcourt Brace Jovanovich.

Main, Jackson Turner. 1962. *The Anti-Federalists: Critics of the Constitution*. Williamsburg: University of North Carolina Press.

Maisel, L. Sandy, ed. 1990. *The Parties Respond: Changes in the American Party System*. Boulder, Co.: Westview.

Mandel, Ernst. 1975. *Late Capitalism*. London: New Left Books.

Manheim, Jarol B., and Richard C. Rich. 1991. *Empirical Political Analysis*. 3rd ed. New York: Longman.

Manley, John. 1970. *The Politics of Finance*. Boston: Little, Brown.

_____. 1993. "The Significance of Class Politics in American History and Politics." In Lawrence C. Dodd and Calvin Jillson, eds., *New Perspectives on American Politics*. Washington, D.C.: Congressional Quarterly.

Mannheim, Karl. 1936. *Ideology and Utopia*. New York: Harcourt, Brace.

Mansbridge, Jane J. 1980. *Beyond Adversary Democracy*. Chicago: University of Chicago Press.

_____. 1986. *Why We Lost the ERA*. Chicago: University of Chicago Press.

_____. 1988. "Motivating Deliberation in Congress." In Sarah Baumgartner Thurow, ed., *Constitutionalism in America*, vol. 2. New York: University Press of America.

———. ed. 1990a. *Beyond Self-Interest.* Chicago: University of Chicago Press.

———. 1990b. "The Rise and Fall of Self-Interest." In Jane J. Mansbridge, ed., *Beyond Self-Interest.* Chicago: University of Chicago Press.

———. 1990c. "On the Relationship of Altruism and Self-Interest." In Jane J. Mansbridge, ed., *Beyond Self-Interest.* Chicago: University of Chicago Press.

———. 1992. "A Deliberative Theory of Interest Representation." In Mark P. Petracca, ed., *The Politics of Interests.* Boulder, Co.: Westview.

March, James G., ed. 1965. "Introduction." In *Handbook of Organizations.* Chicago: Rand McNally.

———. 1989. *Rediscovering Institutions: The Organizational Basis of Politics.* New York: Free.

March, James G., and Johan P. Olsen. 1984. "The New Institutionalism: Organizational Factors in Political Life." 78 *American Political Science Review* 734.

———. 1989. *Rediscovering Institutions.* New York: Free.

March, James G., and Herbert A. Simon. 1958. *Organizations.* New York: John Wiley.

Marmor, Theodore. 1970. *The Politics of Medicine.* London: Routledge.

Marquette, Jesse. 1974. "Social Change and Political Mobilization in the United States, 1870–1960." 68 *American Political Science Review* 1058.

Martin, James Kirby. 1973. *Men In Rebellion.* New Brunswick, N.J.: Rutgers University Press.

Masters, Roger D. 1989. *The Nature of Politics.* New Haven: Yale University Press.

Mather, Lynn. 1990. "Dispute Processing and a Longitudinal Approach to Trial Courts." 24 *Law and Society Review* 357.

Mayhew, David R. 1968. "Party Systems in American History." 1 *Polity* 139.

———. 1974. *Congress: The Electoral Connection.* New Haven: Yale University Press.

———. 1986. *Placing Parties in American Politics.* Princeton: Princeton University Press.

———. 1991. *Divided We Govern: Party Control, Lawmaking, and Investigation, 1946–1990.* New Haven: Yale University Press.

Mayr, Ernst. 1984. *The Growth of Biological Thought.* Cambridge: Harvard University Press.

Mazmanian, Daniel A., and Paul A. Sabatier. 1983. *Implementation and Public Policy.* Glenview, Ill.: Scott, Foresman.

McAdams, Doug. 1982. *Political Process and the Development of Black Insurgency.* Chicago: University of Chicago Press.

McCloskey, Donald N. 1985. *The Rhetoric of Economics.* Madison: University of Wisconsin Press.

McCloskey, Robert G. 1960. *The American Supreme Court.* Chicago: University of Chicago Press.

McClosky, Herbert, and John Zaller. 1984. *The American Ethos.* Cambridge: Harvard University Press.

McClure, Richard D. 1969. "The Recurring Sequence in American Politics: A Longitudinal Theory of Two-Party Democracy." Ph.D. diss. Indiana University.

McConnell, Grant. 1966. *Private Power and American Democracy.* New York: Knopf.

McCormick, Richard L. 1982. "The Realignment Synthesis in American History." 13 *Journal of Interdisciplinary History* 85.

McCormick, Richard P. 1960. "New Perspectives on Jacksonian Politics," 65 *American Historical Review* 288.

———. 1966. *The Second American Party System: Party Formation in the Jacksonian Era.* New York: W. W. Norton.

———. 1979. "The Party Period and Public Policy: An Exploratory Hypothesis." 66 *Journal of American History* 279.

———. 1981. "The Discovery That Business Corrupts Politics: A Reappraisal of the Origins of Progressivism." 86 *American Historical Review* 247.

McCoy, Drew R. 1980. *The Elusive Republic: Political Economy in Jeffersonian America.* New York: W. W. Norton.

McCulloch v. Maryland, 4 Wheat. 316 (1819).

McDonagh, Eileen Lorenzi. 1990. "Policy Innovation in the Progressive Era: Bringing the 'Legislature Back In' to a Study of State Building." Paper presented at the annual meeting of the American Political Science Association, San Francisco.

McDonagh, Eileen Lorenzi, and H. Douglas Price. 1985. "Woman Suffrage in the Progressive Era." 79 *American Political Science Review* 415.

McFarland, Andrew S. 1984. *Common Cause: Lobbying in the Public Interest.* Chatham, N.J.: Chatham House.

———. 1991. "Interest Groups and Political Time: Cycles in America." 21 *British Journal of Political Science* 257.

McKelvey, Richard D. 1976. "Intransitivities in Multi-Dimensional Voting Models and Some Implications for Agenda Control." 12 *Journal of Economic Theory* 472.

McKelvey, Richard D., and Peter C. Ordeshook. 1986. "Information, Electoral Equilibria, and the Democratic Ideal." 48 *Journal of Politics* 909.

McLoughlin, William G. 1978. *Revivals, Awakenings and Reform.* Chicago: University of Chicago Press.

McMurry, Donald M. 1922. "The Political Significance of the Pension Question, 1885–1897." 9 *Mississippi Valley Historical Review* 19.

McPhee, William N., with Robert B. Smith, and Jack Ferguson. 1963. "A Theory of Informal Social Influence." In William N. McPhee, *Formal Theories of Mass Behavior.* New York: Free.

McPherson, James M. 1990. *Abraham Lincoln and the Second American Revolution.* New York: Oxford University Press.

McQuaid, Kim. 1982. *Big Business and Presidential Power.* New York: William Morrow.

McSeveney, Samuel. 1972. *The Politics of Depression: Political Behavior in the Northeast, 1893–1896.* Cambridge, Mass.: Oxford University Press.

Mead, George Herbert. 1934. *Mind, Self, and Society.* Chicago: University of Chicago Press.

Meade, Howard N. 1981. "Russell vs. Talmadge: Southern Politics and the New Deal." 65 *Georgia Historical Quarterly* 28.

Meidinger, Errol. 1987. "Regulatory Culture: A Theoretical Outline." 9 *Law and Policy* 355.

Meijer, Hans. 1969. "Bureaucracy and Policy Formation." 4 *Scandinavian Political Studies* 103.

Merelman, Richard M. 1991. *Partial Visions: Culture and Politics in Britain, Canada, and the United States.* Madison: University of Wisconsin Press.

Merton, Robert K. 1957. *Social Theory and Social Structure.* Glencoe, Ill.: Free.

Middlekauff, Robert. 1987. "The Assumptions of the Founders in 1787." 68 *Social Science Quarterly* 656.

Milgram, Stanley. 1974. *Obedience to Authority.* New York: Harper and Row.

Miliband, Ralph. 1969. *The State in Capitalist Society.* New York: Basic Books.

―――. 1983. "State Power and Class Interests." 138 *New Left Review* 57.

Miller, George H. 1971. *Railroads and the Granger Laws.* Madison: University of Wisconsin Press.

Miller, Warren. 1956. "One-Party Politics and the Voter." 50 *American Political Science Review* 707.

Mills, C. Wright. 1959. "Uses of History." In *The Sociological Imagination.* New York: Grove.

Mitchell, Timothy. 1991. "The Limits of the State: Beyond Statist Approaches and Their Critics." 85 *American Political Science Review* 77.

Moe, Terry M. 1980. *The Organization of Interests.* Chicago: University of Chicago Press.

―――. 1984. "The New Economics of Organization." 28 *American Journal of Political Science* 739.

―――. 1985. "The Politicized Presidency." In John E. Chubb and Paul E. Peterson, eds., *The New Direction in American Politics.* Washington, D. C.: Brookings Institution.

―――. 1987. "Interests, Institutions, and Positive Theory: The Politics of the NLRB." In Karen Orren and Stephen Skowronek, eds., *Studies in American Political Development*, vol. 2. New Haven: Yale University Press.

―――. 1990. "Political Institutions: The Neglected Side of the Story." 6 *Journal of Law, Economics and Organization* 213.

―――. 1991. "The Political Institutions: The Neglected Side of the Story." Unpublished manuscript, Stanford University.

Mollenkopf, John. 1983. *The Contested City.* Princeton, N.J.: Princeton University Press.

Monroe, Kristen R. et al. 1990. "Altruism and the Theory of Rational Action." 101 *Ethics* 103.

Moore, Barrington, Jr. 1966. *Social Origins of Dictatorship and Democracy.* Boston, Mass.: Beacon.

Morone, James A. 1990. *The Democratic Wish: Popular Participation and the Limits of American Government.* New York: Basic Books.

Morris, Richard. 1967. *The American Revolution Reconsidered.* New York: Harper and Row.

Muir, William K. 1977. *Police: Streetcorner Politicians.* Chicago: University of Chicago Press.

―――. 1982. *Legislature: California's School for Politics.* Chicago: University of Chicago Press.

Muller, Edward N., and Karl-Dieter Opp. 1986. "Rational Choice and Rebellious Collective Action." 80 *American Political Science Review* 471.

Munitz, Milton Karl. 1990. *The Question of Reality*. Princeton: Princeton University Press.

Nagel, Jack H. 1975. *The Descriptive Analysis of Power*. New Haven: Yale University Press.

Nagel, Thomas. 1986. *The View from Nowhere*. New York: Oxford University Press.

Namenwirth, J. Zvi, and Philip Weber. 1987. *Dynamics of Culture*. Boston: Allen and Unwin.

Natanson, Maurice, ed. 1962. *Collected Papers of Alfred Schutz*. Vol. 1. The Hague: Nijhoff. National Archives. 1935–1940. Records of the Executive Director of the Social Security Board, 1935–1940. "Confidential Reports of Regional Directors." Box 212, binder.

————. 1938a. Records of the Executive Director of the Social Security Board, 1935–1940. "Report of the Bureau of Public Assistance on Assistance to States in Personnel Training Programs, April 30, 1938." Box 278, file 631.34.

————. 1938b. Records of the Executive Director of the Social Security Board, 1935–1940. "Summary Analysis of Confidential Reports of Regional Directors, November 1, 1938." Box 291, file 322.

Neustadt, Richard. 1960. *Presidential Power: The Politics of Leadership*. New York: John Wiley.

Nettl, J. P. 1968. "The State as Conceptual Variable." 20 *World Politics* 559.

Newcomb, Theodore. 1957. *Personality and Social Change: Attitude Formation in a Student Community*. New York: Dryden.

Nie, Norman H., Sidney Verba, and John R. Petrocik. 1979. *The Changing American Voter*. Cambridge: Harvard University Press.

Niebuhr, Richard. 1975. *Social Sources of Denominationalism*. New York: New American Library.

Nordhaus, William D. 1974. "The Falling Share of Profit." In Arthur Okum and G. Perry, eds., *Brookings Papers on Economic Activity*. Vol. 1. Washington, D.C.: Brookings Institution.

Nordlinger, Eric. 1981. *On the Autonomy of the Democratic State*. Cambridge: Harvard University Press.

Norton, Ann. 1986. *Alternative Americas*. Chicago: University of Chicago Press.

Oakley, Imogen B. 1912. "The More Civic Work, the Less Need of Philanthropy." 6 *American City* 805.

O'Connor, James. 1973. *The Fiscal Crisis of the State*. New York: St. Martin's.

Oestreicher, Richard. 1989. "Urban Working-Class Political Behavior and Theories of American Electoral Politics, 1870–1940." 74 *Journal of American History* 1257.

Offe, Claus. 1975. "The Theory of the Capitalist State. In Leon Lindberg et al., eds., *Stress and Contradiction in Modern Capitalism*. Lexington, Mass.: Lexington Books.

Offe, Claus, and Helmut Wiesenthal. 1980. "Two Logics of Collective Action: Theoretical Notes on Social Class and Organizational Form." In Maurice Zeitlin, ed., *Political Power and Social Theory*, vol. 1. Greenwich, Conn.: JAI Press.

Olson, Mancur, Jr. 1965. *The Logic of Collective Action*. Cambridge: Harvard University Press.

————. 1982. *The Rise and Decline of Nations*. New Haven: Yale University Press.

Ordeshook, Peter C. 1986. *Game Theory and Political Theory: An Introduction.* New York: Cambridge University Press.

Ori, Kan. 1961. "Basic Ideas in Federal-State Relations: The Indiana 'Revolt' of 1951." Ph.D. diss., Indiana University.

Orloff, Ann Shola. 1988. "The Political Origins of America's Belated Welfare State." In Margaret Weir, Ann Shola Orloff, and Theda Skocpol, *The Politics of Social Policy in the United States.* Princeton: Princeton University Press.

Orloff, Ann Shola, and Theda Skocpol. 1984. "Why Not Equal Protection? Explaining the Politics of Public Spending in Britain, 1900–1911 and the United States, 1880s–1920." 46 *American Sociological Review* 726.

Orren, Karen. 1991. *Belated Feudalism: Labor, the Law, and Liberal Development in the United States.* New York: Cambridge University Press.

Ortony, Andrew. 1979. *Metaphor and Thought.* New York: Cambridge University Press.

Osborne, David. 1988. *Laboratories of Democracy.* Cambridge: Harvard Business School Press.

Osgood, Charles, Percy Tannenbaum, and George Suci. 1957. *The Measurement of Meaning.* Urbana: University of Illinois Press.

Ostrom, Elinor. 1990. *Governing the Commons: The Evolution of Institutions for Collective Action.* New York: Cambridge University Press.

Ostrom, Vincent. 1971. *The Theory of a Compound Republic.* Blacksburg, Va.: Public Choice.

Overman, E. Samuel, ed. 1988. *Methodology and Epistemology for Social Science.* Chicago: University of Chicago Press.

Page, Benjamin I., Robert Y. Shapiro, and Glenn R. Dempsey. 1987. "What Moves Public Opinion?" 81 *American Political Science Review* 23.

Palfrey, Thomas, and Howard Rosenthal. 1985. "Voter Participation and Strategic Uncertainty." 79 *American Political Science Review* 62.

Patterson, James T. 1969. *The New Deal and the States: Federalism in Transition.* Princeton: Princeton University Press.

Patterson, Thomas. 1980. *The Mass Media Election.* New York: Praeger.

Patterson, Thomas, and Robert McClure. 1976. *The Unseeing Eye.* New York: Putnam's Sons.

Peacock, Alan, and Jack Wiseman. 1961. *The Growth of Public Expenditure in the United Kingdom.* Princeton: Princeton University Press.

Perkins, Ellen J. 1951. "Old-Age Assistance and Aid to Dependent Children, 1940–50." 14 *Social Security Bulletin* 11.

Peterson, Paul. 1981. *City Limits.* Chicago: University of Chicago Press.

Peterson, Paul, and Mark Rom. 1990. *Welfare Magnets: A New Case for National Standards.* Washington, D.C.: Brookings Institution.

Petracca, Mark. 1986. "Federal Advisory Committees, Interest Groups, and the Administrative State." 13 *Congress and the Presidency* 83.

———, ed. 1992. *The Politics of Interest.* Boulder, Co.: Westview.

Phillips, Kevin. 1969. *The Emerging Republican Majority.* New Rochelle, N.Y.: Arlington House.

Pitkin, Hanna F. 1972. *Wittgenstein and Justice.* Berkeley: University of California Press.

Piven, Frances Fox, and Richard A. Cloward. 1971. *Regulating the Poor: The Functions of Public Welfare*. New York: Pantheon Books.

———. 1981. *The New Class War*. New York: Basic Books.

———. 1991. "Race and the Democrats." 253 *Nation* 737.

Pocock, John. 1975. *The Machiavellian Moment*. Princeton: Princeton University Press.

Poen, Monte. 1979. *Harry Truman versus the Medical Lobby*. Columbia: University of Missouri Press.

Polanyi, Karl. 1957. *The Great Transformation: The Political and Economic Origins of Our Time*. Boston: Beacon.

Polsby, Nelson W. 1968. "The Institutionalization of the U.S. House of Representatives." 62 *American Political Science Review* 144–168.

———. 1980. *Community Power and Political Theory: A Further Look at Problems of Evidence and Inference*. New Haven: Yale University Press.

———. 1982. "Contemporary Transformations of American Politics." 96 *Political Science Quarterly* 551–570.

———. 1984. *Political Innovation in America*. New Haven: Yale University Press.

Polsby, Nelson W., Miriam Gallagher, and Barry Rundquist. 1969. "The Growth of the Seniority System in the House of Representatives." 63 *American Political Science Review* 787.

Pomper, Gerald. 1968. *Elections in America*. New York: Dodd, Mead.

Popkin, Samuel. 1979. *The Rational Peasant*. Berkeley: University of California Press.

———. 1991. *The Reasoning Voter: Communication and Persuasion in Presidential Campaigns*. Chicago: University of Chicago Press.

Potter, David M. 1954. *People of Plenty: Economic Abundance and the American Character*. Chicago: University of Chicago Press.

———. 1969. "C. Vann Woodward and the Uses of History." Reprinted in Don E. Fehrenbacher, ed., *Essays of David M. Potter*. New York: Oxford University Press.

———. 1973. "Explicit Data and Implicit Assumptions in Historical Study." In Don E. Fehrenbacher, ed., *History and American Society: Essays of David M. Potter*. New York: Oxford University Press.

Poulantzas, Nicos. 1973. *Political Power and Social Classes*. London: New Left Books.

———. 1976. "The Capitalist State: A Reply to Miliband and Laclau." 95 *New Left Review* 63.

Poundstone, William. 1991. *Prisoner's Dilemma*. New York: Doubleday.

Price, H. Douglas. 1971. "The Congressional Career—Then and Now." In Nelson W. Polsby, ed., *Congressional Behavior*. New York: Random House.

———. 1975. "Congress and the Evolution of Legislative 'Professionalism.' " In Norman Ornstein, ed., *Congress in Change*. New York: Praeger.

Przeworski, Adam. 1985. *Capitalism and Social Democracy*. Cambridge: Cambridge University Press.

Przeworski, Adam, and John Sprague. 1986. *Paper Stones: A History of Electoral Socialism*. Chicago: University of Chicago Press.

Putnam, Robert. 1966. "Political Attitudes and the Local Community," 60 *American Political Science Review* 640.

Quadagno, Jill S. 1984. "Welfare Capitalism and the Social Security Act of 1935." 49 *American Sociological Review* 632.

———. 1985. "Two Models of Welfare State Development: Reply to Skocpol and Amenta." 50 *American Sociological Review* 575.

———. 1988. *The Transformation of Old Age Security.* Chicago: University of Chicago Press.

Quirk, Paul J. 1981. *Industry Influence in Federal Regulatory Agencies.* Princeton: Princeton University Press.

———. 1988. "In Defense of the Politics of Ideas." 50 *Journal of Politics* 31.

———. 1989. "The Cooperative Resolution of Policy Conflicts." 83 *American Political Science Review* 905.

Rae, Douglas W., and Michael Taylor. 1970. *The Analysis of Political Cleavages.* New Haven: Yale University Press.

Rahn, Wendy M. 1990. *Perception and Evaluation of Political Candidates: A Social-Cognitive Perspective.* Ph.D. diss., University of Minnesota.

Rahn, Wendy M., John H. Aldrich, Eugene Borgida, and John L. Sullivan. 1990. "A Social-Cognitive Model of Candidate Appraisal." In John F. Ferejohn and James Kuklinski, eds., *Information and Democratic Processes.* Urbana: University of Illinois Press.

Randall, J. G., and David Donald. 1961. *The Civil War and Reconstruction.* 2nd ed. Boston, Mass.: D. C. Heath.

Rawls, John. 1971. *A Theory of Justice.* Cambridge: Harvard University Press.

Reich, Robert, ed. 1988. *The Power of Public Ideas.* Cambridge, Mass.: Ballinger.

———. 1990. *Tales of a New America.* New York: Random House.

Reisner, Marc. 1987. *Cadillac Desert: The American West and Its Disappearing Water.* New York: Penguin. *Report of the National Advisory Commission on Civil Disorders.* 1968. New York: Bantam Books.

Richards, Alan, and John Waterbury. 1990. *The Political Economy of the Middle East.* Boulder, Co.: Westview.

Riker, William H. 1962. *The Theory of Political Coalitions.* New Haven: Yale University Press.

———. 1977. "The Future of a Science of Politics." 21 *American Behavioral Scientist* 11.

———. 1980. "Implications from the Disequilibrium of Majority Rule for the Study of Institutions." 74 *American Political Science Review* 432.

———. 1982a. *Liberalism Against Populism: A Confrontation Between the Theory of Democracy and the Theory of Social Choice.* San Francisco: W. H. Freeman.

———. 1982b. "The Two-Party System and Duverger's Law: An Essay on the History of Political Science," 62 *American Political Science Review* 25.

———. 1982c. "Implications from the Disequilibrium of Majority Rule for the Study of Institutions." In Peter Ordeshook and Kenneth Shepsle, eds., *Political Equilibrium.* Boston: Kluwer-Nijhoff.

———. 1984. "The Heresthetics of Constitution-Making: The Presidency of 1787, with Comments on Determination and Rational Review." 78 *American Political Science Review* 1.

———. 1986. *The Art of Political Manipulation.* New Haven: Yale University Press.

Riker, William H., and Peter C. Ordeshook. 1968. "A Theory of the Calculus of Voting." 62 *American Political Science Review* 25.

———. 1973. *An Introduction to Positive Political Theory*. Englewood Cliffs, N.J.: Prentice-Hall.

Rimlinger, Gaston. 1971. *Welfare Policy and Industrialization in Europe, America, and Russia*. New York: John Wiley.

Robertson, David Brian. 1989. "The Bias of American Federalism: The Limits of Welfare-State Development in the Progressive Era." 1 *Journal of Policy History* 261.

———. 1993. "The Return to History and the New Institutionalism in American Political Science." 17 *Social Science History*. Forthcoming.

Robertson, G. H. 1912. "The State's Duty to Fatherless Children." 6 *Child-Welfare Magazine* 156.

Robinson, Michael J. 1977. "Television and American Politics, 1956–1976." 48 *Public Interest* 3.

Robinson, Michael J., and Margaret A. Sheehan. 1983. *Over the Wire and on TV: CBS and UPI in Campaign '80*. New York: Russell Sage.

Robinson, W. S. 1950. "Ecological Correlations and the Behavior of Individuals." 15 *American Sociological Review* 351.

Rockman, Bert. 1984. *The Leadership Question: The Presidency and the American System*. New York: Praeger.

———. 1993. "The New Institutionalism and the Old Institutions." In Lawrence C. Dodd and Calvin Jillson, eds., *New Perspectives on American Politics*. Washington, D.C.: Congressional Quarterly.

Rogowski, Ronald. 1974. *Rational Legitimacy*. Princeton: Princeton University Press.

Rohde, David W. 1979. "Risk-Bearing and Progressive Ambition: The Case of Members of the United States House of Representatives." 23 *American Journal of Political Science* 1.

Rohde, David W., and Kenneth A. Shepsle. 1978. "Thinking About Legislative Reform." In Leroy N. Rieselbach, ed., *Legislative Reform: The Policy Impact*. Lexington, Mass.: Lexington Books.

Rorty, Richard. 1979. *Philosophy and the Mirror of Nature*. Princeton: Princeton University Press.

Rose, Richard. 1984. *Understanding Big Government: The Programme Approach*. London: Sage.

———. 1991. *The Postmodern President*. Chatham: Chatham House.

Rose, Richard, and Terrance Karran. 1983. "Inertia or Incrementalism? A Long-term View of the Growth of Government." In *Comparative Resource Allocation*. London: Sage.

Rose, Richard and Derek Urwin. 1969. "Social Cohesion, Political Parties, and Strains in Regimes." 2 *Comparative Political Studies* 7.

Rosenau, James N. 1988. "The State in an Era of Cascading Politics." 21 *Comparative Political Studies* 13.

———. 1991. *Turbulence in World Politics: A Theory of Change and Continuity*. Princeton: Princeton University Press.

Rosenberg, Morris. 1968. *The Logic of Survey Analysis*. New York: Basic Books.

Ross, Dorothy. 1991. *The Origins of American Social Science*. New York: Cambridge University Press.

Ross, Robert, and Kent C. Trachte. 1990. *Global Capitalism: The New Leviathan*. Albany: State University of New York Press.

Rothstein, Bo. 1992. "Labor Market Institutions and Working Class Strength." In Sven Steinmo, Kathleen Thelen, and Frank Longstreth, eds., *Structuring Politics: Historical Institutionalism in Comparative Analysis*. New York: Cambridge University Press.

Rubin, Richard L. 1981. *Press, Party and Presidency*. New York: W. W. Norton.

Rueschemeyer, Dietrich, Evelyn Stephens, and John Stephens. 1992. *Capitalist Development and Democracy*. Chicago: University of Chicago Press.

Rusk, Jerrold G. 1974. "Comment" on Walter Dean Burnham, "Theory and Voting Research: Some Reflections on Converse's 'Change in the American Electorate'." 68 *American Political Science Review* 1028.

Salisbury, Robert H. 1969. "An Exchange Theory of Interest Groups." 13 *Midwest Journal of Political Science* 1.

———. 1984. "Interest Representation: The Dominance of Institutions." 78 *American Political Science Review* 64.

Samuelson, Paul A. 1954. "The Pure Theory of Public Expenditure." 36 *Review of Economics and Statistics* 386.

Sanders, Elizabeth. 1986. "Industrial Concentration, Sectional Competition and Anti-Trust Politics in America 1880–1980." In Karen Orren and Stephen Skowronek, eds., *Studies in American Political Development*, vol. 1. New Haven: Yale University Press.

Santa Clara County v. Southern Pacific Railroad, 118 U.S. 394 (1886).

Sartori, Giovanni. 1969. "The Sociology of Politics: A Critical View." In Otto Stammer, ed., *Party Systems, Party Organizations, and the Politics of the New Masses*. Berlin: Institute for Political Research, Free University of Berlin.

Schattschneider, Elmer E. 1942. *Party Government*. New York: Holt, Rinehart.

———. 1960. *The Semi-Sovereign People*. New York: Holt, Rinehart, and Winston.

Scheiber, Harry. 1975. "Federalism and the American Economic Order, 1789–1910." 10 *Law and Society Review* 57.

Schiesl, Martin. 1977. *The Politics of Efficiency: Municipal Administration and Reform in America: 1880–1920*. Berkeley: University of California Press.

Schlesinger, Arthur, Jr. 1945. *The Age of Jackson*. Boston: Little, Brown.

———. 1986. *The Cycles of American History*. Boston: Houghton, Mifflin.

Schlesinger, Arthur, Sr. 1949. *Paths to the Present*. New York: Macmillan.

Schlesinger, Joseph A. 1966. *Ambitions and Politics: Political Careers in the United States*. Chicago, Ill.: Rand McNally.

Schlozman, Kay Lehman, and John T. Tierney. 1986. *Organized Interests and American Democracy*. New York: Harper and Row.

Schofield, Norman. 1978. "Instability of Simple Dynamic Games." 7 *Review of Economic Studies* 183.

Schotter, Andrew. 1981. *The Economic Theory of Social Institutions*. New York: Cambridge University Press.

Schumpeter, Joseph. 1942. *Capitalism, Socialism, and Democracy*. New York: Harper.

Schutz, Alfred. 1962. *Collected Papers*. Edited and introduced by Maurice Natanson. The Hague: M. Nijhoff.

Schwartz, Nancy L. 1988. *The Blue Guitar: Political Representation and Community*. Chicago: University of Chicago Press.

Segal, Leon. 1973. *Reporters and Officials*. Lexington: D. C. Heath.

Selznick, Philip. 1957. *Leadership in Administration*. New York: Harper and Row.

Shackelford, Lynn B. 1939. "Interpretation Takes to the Road." 10 *Public Welfare News* 2.

Shafer, Byron E., ed. 1991a. *The End of Realignment? Interpreting American Electoral Eras*. Madison: University of Wisconsin Press.

Shafer, Byron E., ed. 1991b. *Is America Different?* Oxford: Clarendon.

Shapiro, Michael, ed. 1981. *Language and Politics*. New York: New York University Press.

Sharkansky, Ira. 1969. "The Utility of Elazar's Political Culture: A Research Note." 2 *Polity* 66.

Shaw, Donald, and Maxwell E. McCombs. 1977. *The Emergence of American Political Issues: The Agenda-Setting Function of the Press*. St. Paul, Minn.: West.

Shefter, Martin. 1977. "Party and Patronage: Germany, England, and Italy." 7 *Politics and Society* 403.

———. 1978. "Party, Bureaucracy, and Political Change in the United States." In Louis Maisel and Joseph Cooper, eds., *Political Parties: Development and Decay*. Beverly Hills, Calif.: Sage.

———. 1983. "Regional Receptivity to Reform: The Legacy of the Progressive Era." 98 *Political Science Quarterly* 459.

———. 1993. "International Influences on American Politics." In Lawrence C. Dodd and Calvin Jillson, eds., *New Perspectives on American Politics*. Washington, D.C.: Congressional Quarterly.

Shepsle, Kenneth A. 1979. "Institutional Arrangements and Equilibrium in Multidimensional Voting Models." 23 *American Journal of Political Science* 27.

———. 1981. "Structure and Strategy: The Two Faces of Agenda Power." Paper presented at the annual meeting of the American Political Science Association, New York.

———. 1986. "Institutional Equilibrium and Equilibrium Institutions." In Herbert F. Weisberg, ed., *Political Science: The Science of Politics*. New York: Agathon.

———. 1989. "Studying Institutions: Some Lessons from the Rational Choice Approach." 1 *Journal of Theoretical Politics* 131.

Shepsle, Kenneth A., and Michael Laver. 1991. "Subgame-Perfect Portfolio Allocations in Parliamentary Government Formation." Paper delivered at the Duke University Political Economic Workshop.

Shepsle, Kenneth A., and Barry R. Weingast. 1981. "Political Preferences for the Pork Barrel." 25 *American Journal of Political Science* 96.

———. 1987. "The Institutional Foundations of Committee Power." 81 *American Political Science Review* 85.

Shubik, Martin. 1982. *Game Theory in the Social Sciences*. Cambridge: MIT Press.

Silbey, Joel H. 1977. *A Respectable Minority: The Democratic Party in the Civil War Era, 1860–1868*. New York: Norton.

_____. 1991a. *The American Political Nation, 1838–1893*. Stanford: Stanford University Press.

_____. 1991b. "Beyond Realignment and Realignment Theory: American Political Eras, 1789–1989. In Byron E. Shafer, ed., *The End of Realignment? Interpreting American Electoral Eras*. Madison: University of Wisconsin Press.

Simon, Herbert A. 1985. "Human Nature in Politics: The Dialogue of Psychology with Political Science." 79 *American Political Science Review* 293.

Sinclair, Barbara. 1977. "Party Realignment and the Transformation of the Political Agenda: The House of Representatives, 1925–1938." 71 *American Political Science Review* 940.

Sklar, Kathryn Kish. 1986. "Florence Kelley and the Integration of 'the Women's Sphere' into American Politics, 1890–1921." Paper presented at the Organization of American Historians, New York.

Sklar, Martin. 1988. *The Corporate Reconstruction of American Capitalism, 1890–1916*. New York: Cambridge University Press.

_____. 1991. "Periodization and Historiography: Studying American Political Development in the Progressive Era, 1890s–1916." In Karen Orren and Stephen Skowronek, eds., *Studies in American Political Development*, vol. 5. New York: Cambridge University Press.

Skocpol, Theda. 1979. *States and Social Revolution*. Cambridge, Mass.: Cambridge University Press.

_____. 1980. "Political Response to Capitalist Crisis: Neo-Marxist Theories of the State and the Case of the New Deal." 10 *Politics and Society* 155.

_____. 1983. "The Legacies of New Deal Liberalism." In Douglas MacLean and Claudia Mills, eds., *Liberalism Reconsidered*. Totowa, N.J.: Roman and Allanheld.

_____. 1985. "Bringing the State Back In." In Peter B. Evans, Dietrich Rueschemeyer, and Theda Skocpol, eds. *Bringing the State Back In*. New York: Cambridge University Press.

_____. 1992. *Protecting Soldiers and Mothers: The Political Origins of Social Policy in the United States*. Cambridge: Harvard University, Belknap.

Skocpol, Theda, and Edwin Amenta. 1985. "Did Capitalists Shape Social Security?" 50 *American Sociological Review* 572.

_____. 1986. "States and Social Policies." 12 *Annual Review of Sociology* 131.

Skocpol, Theda, and Kenneth Feingold. 1982. "State Capacity and Economic Intervention in the Early New Deal." 97 *Political Science Quarterly* 255.

Skocpol, Theda, and John Ikenberry. 1983. "The Political Formation of the American Welfare State in Historical and Comparative Perspective." 6 *Comparative Social Research* 87.

Skocpol, Theda, and Gretchen Ritter. 1991. "Gender and the Origins of Modern Social Policies in Britain and the United States." In Karen Orren and Stephen Skowronek, eds., *Studies in American Political Development*, vol. 5. New York: Cambridge University Press.

Skowronek, Stephen. 1982. *Building a New American State: The Expansion of National Administrative Capacities, 1880–1920*. Cambridge, Mass.: Cambridge University Press.

_____. 1984. "Presidential Leadership in Political Time." In Michael Nelson, ed.,

The Presidency and the Political System. Washington D.C.: Congressional Quarterly.

_____. 1986. "Notes on the Presidency in the Political Order." In Karen Orren and Stephen Skowronek, eds., *Studies in American Political Development,* vol. 1. New Haven: Yale University Press.

_____. Forthcoming. *The Politics Presidents Make: Persistent, Emergent, and Recurrent Patterns from John Adams to George Bush.*

Skowronek, Stephen, and Karen Orren, eds. 1986. *Studies in American Political Development.* Vol. 1. New Haven: Yale University Press.

Smelser, Neil. 1962. *Theory of Collective Behavior.* New York: Free.

Smelser, Neil, and Dean Gernstein, eds. 1986. *Behavioral and Social Sciences: Fifty Years of Discovery.* Washington, D.C.: National Academy.

Smith, Adam. [1776] 1965. *The Wealth of Nations,* ed., Edwin Cannan. New York: Modern Library.

Smith, J. Allen. 1965. *The Spirit of American Government.* Cambridge: Harvard University Press.

Sombart, Werner. 1905. "Study of the Historical Development and Evolution of the American Proletariat." B *International Socialist Review.*

State Survey of Public Assistance in Indiana. 1938. *Past Development in Care of Dependent Children in Indiana.* March.

Steiner, Gilbert Y. 1966. *Social Insecurity: The Politics of Welfare.* Chicago, Ill.: Rand McNally.

Steinmo, Sven. 1988. "Social Democracy vs. Socialism: Goal Adaptation in Social Democratic Sweden." 16 *Politics and Society* 403.

_____. 1989. "Political Institutions and Tax Policy in the United States, Sweden and Britain." 41 World Politics.

_____. 1993. *Taxation and Democracy: Swedish, British, and American Approaches to Financing the Modern State.* New Haven: Yale University Press.

Steinmo, Sven, Kathleen Thelen, and Frank Longstreth, eds. 1992. *Structuring Politics.* New York: Cambridge University Press.

Stepan, Alfred. 1978. *The State and Society.* Princeton: Princeton University Press.

Stephens, John D. 1979. *The Transition from Capitalism to Socialism.* New York: Macmillan.

Stewart, Charles H. III. 1989. *Budget Reform Politics: The Design of the Appropriations Process in the House of Representatives, 1865–1921.* New York: Cambridge University Press.

Stewart, Charles H. III, and Barry R. Weingast. 1991. "Stacking the Senate, Changing the Nation: Republican Rotten Boroughs and American Political Development." Paper presented at the annual meeting of the American Political Science Association, Washington, D.C.

Stewart, Richard B. 1975. "The Reformation of American Administrative Law." 88 *Harvard Law Review* 1669.

Stimson, James. 1991. *Public Opinion in America: Moods, Cycles and Swings.* Boulder, Co.: Westview.

Stone, Clarence N. 1989. *Regime Politics: Governing Atlanta, 1946–1988.* Lawrence: University Press of Kansas.

Stone, Walter J. 1990. *Republic at Risk*. Pacific Grove, Calif.: Brooks; Cole.

———. 1993. "Asymmetries in the Electoral Bases of Representation." In Lawrence C. Dodd and Calvin Jillson, eds., *New Perspectives on American Politics*. Washington, D.C.: Congressional Quarterly.

Streek, Wolfgang, and Philippe Schmitter, eds. 1985. *Private Interest Government*. Beverly Hills, Calif.: Sage.

Sugden, Robert. 1986. *The Economics of Rights, Cooperation and Welfare*. Oxford: Blackwell.

Sundquist, James. 1973. *The Dynamics of the Party System*. Washington, D.C.: Brookings Institution.

———. 1981. *The Decline and Resurgence of Congress*. Washington, D. C.: Brookings Institution.

———. 1983. *Dynamics of the Party System: Alignment and Realignment of Political Parties in the United States*. 2nd ed. Washington, D.C.: Brookings Institution.

Swift, Elaine K. 1988. "The Electoral Connection Meets the Past: Lessons from Congressional History, 1789–1899." 102 *Political Science Quarterly* 625.

———. 1989. "Reconstitutive Change in the U.S. Congress: The Early Senate, 1789–1841." 14 *Legislative Studies Quarterly* 175.

Swift, Elaine K., and David W. Brady. 1991. "Out of the Past: Theoretical and Methodological Contributions of Congressional History." 24 *PS* 61.

Taylor, Michael. 1976. *Anarchy and Cooperation*. New York: John Wiley.

Thompson, Michael, Richard Ellis, and Aaron Wildavsky. 1990. *Cultural Theory*. Boulder, Co.: Westview Press.

Thurow, Lester. 1980. *The Zero-Sum Society*. New York: Basic Books.

Tilly, Charles. 1975. *The Formation of National States in Western Europe*. Princeton: Princeton University Press.

———. 1978. *From Mobilization to Revolution*. Reading, Mass.: Addison-Wesley.

———. 1981. *Introduction to Class Conflict and Collective Action*. Beverly Hills, Calif.: Sage.

———. 1984. *Big Structures, Large Processes, Huge Comparisons*. New York: Russell Sage.

Tingsten, Herbert. 1963. *Political Behavior: Studies in Election Statistics*. Totowa, N.J.: Bedminster.

Titmuss, Richard. 1978. "War and Social Policy." In *Essays on the Welfare State*. London: Allen and Unwin.

Tocqueville, Alexis de. 1946. *Democracy in America*. New York: Knopf.

Trimberger, Ellen Kay. 1978. *Revolution From Above*. New Brunswick, N.J.: Transaction Books.

Truman, David. 1951. *The Governmental Process*. New York: Knopf.

Turner, Frederick Jackson. 1920. *The Frontier in American History*. New York: Holt, Rinehart, and Winston.

Turner, James. 1985. *Without God, Without Creed: The Origins of Unbelief in America*. Baltimore: Johns Hopkins University Press.

Tversky, Amos. 1990. "The Causes of Preference Reversal." 80 *American Economic Review*.

Tyler, Tom R. 1990. *Why People Obey the Law*. New Haven: Yale University Press.

van den Berg, Axel. 1988. *The Immanent Utopia: From Marxism on the State to the State of Marxism*. Princeton: Princeton University Press.

Vatter, Harold G. 1985. *The U.S. Economy in World War II*. New York: Columbia University Press.

Verba, Sidney, and Norman H. Nie. 1972. *Participation in America*. New York: Harper and Row.

Vickers, Sir Jeffrey. 1987. "Policymaking and Social Change." In Guy B. Adams, John Forester, and Bayard L. Catron, eds., *Policymaking, Communication, and Social Learning*. New Brunswick: Transaction Books.

Vladeck, Bruce C. 1980. *Unloving Care: The Nursing Home Tragedy*. New York: Basic Books.

Vogel, David. 1978. "Why Businessmen Distrust Their State: The Political Consciousness of American Corporate Executives." 8 *British Journal of Political Science* 45.

———. 1989. *Fluctuating Fortunes: The Political Power of Business in America*. New York: Basic Books.

Vogler, David J., and Sidney R. Waldman. 1985. *Congress and Democracy*. Washington, D.C.: Congressional Quarterly.

von Neumann, John, and Oscar Morganstern. 1945. *The Theory of Games and Economic Behavior*. Princeton: Princeton University Press.

von Wright, Georg Henrik. 1971. *Explanation and Understanding*. Ithaca, N.Y.: Cornell University Press.

Vygotsky, Lev. 1962. *Thought and Language*. Cambridge: Harvard University Press.

Wald, Kenneth D., Dennis E. Owen, and Samuel S. Hill, Jr. 1988. "Churches as Political Communities." 82 *American Political Science Review* 531.

Walker, Jack. 1983. "The Origins and Maintenance of Interest Groups in America." 77 *American Political Science Review* 390.

———. 1991. *Mobilizing Interest Groups in America*. Ann Arbor: University of Michigan Press.

Wall, James A. 1975. "The Effects of Constituent Trust and Representative Bargaining Visibility on Intergroup Bargaining," 17 *Organizational Behavior and Human Performance* 244–256.

Walzer, Michael. 1983. *Spheres of Justice: A Defense of Pluralism and Equality*. New York: Basic Books.

Ward, Hugh. 1989. "Evolution and Regulation: A Defense of 'Weak Economism'." University of Essex, *Essex Papers in Politics and Government*. Mimeo.

Washington State Department of Public Welfare. 1937. *Biennial Report of the State Department of Public Welfare, April 1, 1935–March 31, 1937*. Olympia, Wash.

Watson, Harry L. 1990. *Liberty and Power: The Politics of Jacksonian America*. New York: Hill and Wang.

Weatherford, M. Stephen. 1982a. "Measurement Problems in Contextual Analysis: On Statistical Assumptions and Social Processes." 8 *Political Methodology* 61.

———. 1982b. "Interpersonal Networks and Political Behavior." 26 *American Journal of Political Science* 117.

Weber, Max. 1976. *The Protestant Ethic and the Spirit of Capitalism*. New York: Scribner's.

Weingast, Barry R. 1991a. "Institutions and Political Commitment: A New Political Economy of the American Civil War Era." Unpublished manuscript, Hoover Institution, Stanford University.

_____. 1991b. "The Political Economy of Slavery: Credible Commitments and the Preservation of the Union, 1800–1860." Paper presented at the annual meeting of the American Political Science Association.

Weinstein, James. 1968. *The Corporate Ideal in the Liberal State*. Boston: Beacon.

Weir, Margaret. 1992. *Politics and Jobs: The Boundaries of Employment Policies in the United States*. Princeton: Princeton University Press.

Weir, Margaret, Ann Shola Orloff, and Theda Skocpol. 1988. "Understanding American Social Policy." In *The Politics of Social Policy in the United States*. Princeton: Princeton University Press.

White, R. Clyde. 1936. "Recent Public Welfare and Social Security Legislation in Indiana." 2 *Social Service Review* 206.

Wiebe, Robert H. 1967. *The Search for Order: 1877–1920*. New York: Hill and Wang.

Wildavsky, Aaron. 1987. "Choosing Preferences by Constructing Institutions." 81 *American Political Science Review* 3.

_____. 1990. "A World of Difference—The Public Philosophies and Political Behaviors of Rival American Cultures." In Anthony King, ed., *The New American Political System*, 2nd version. Washington, D.C.: American Enterprise Institute.

_____. 1991a. "Myths of Rational Choice." 5 *Critical Review*.

_____. 1991b. "Resolved, That Individualism and Egalitarianism Be Made Compatible in America: Political-Cultural Roots of Exceptionalism." In Byron R. Shafer, ed., *Is America Different?* Oxford: Clarendon.

_____. 1975. *The Welfare State and Equity: Structural and Ideological Roots of Public Expenditures*. Berkeley: University of California Press.

Wilensky, Harold. 1975. *The Welfare State and Equity: Structural and Ideological Roots of Public Expenditures*. Berkeley: University of California Press.

Wilensky, Harold, and Charles N. Lebeaux. 1958. *Industrial Society and Social Welfare*. New York: Russell Sage.

Williams, Raymond. 1976. *Keywords*. New York: Oxford University Press.

Wills, Garry. 1992. *Lincoln at Gettysburg: The Words that Remade America*. New York: Simon and Schuster.

Wilson, James Q. 1973. *Political Organizations*. New York: Basic Books.

_____. 1980. *The Politics of Regulation*. New York: Basic Books.

_____. 1989. *Bureaucracy*. New York: Basic Books.

_____. 1990. "Interests and Deliberation in the American Republic." Lexington, Mass.: D. C. Heath. Reproduced.

Wilson, Rick K. 1986. "What Was It Worth to Be on a Committee in the U.S. House, 1889–1913?" 11 *Legislative Studies Quarterly* 47.

Wilson, Woodrow. 1885. *Congressional Government: A Study in American Politics*. New York: Houghton Mifflin.

_____. 1887. "The Study of Administration." 2 *Political Science Quarterly* 197.

Winch, Peter. 1958. *The Idea of a Social Science and Its Relation to Philosophy*. London: Routledge and Kegan Paul.

Wirt, Frederick M. 1991. "'Soft' Concepts and 'Hard' Data: A Research Review of Elazar's Political Culture." 21 *Publius: The Journal of Federalism* 1.

Witte, John F. 1985. *The Politics and Development of the Federal Income Tax*. Madison: University of Wisconsin Press.

Wood, Gordon S. 1969. *The Creation of the American Republic, 1776–1787*. Chapel Hill: University of North Carolina Press.

———. 1992. *The Radicalism of the American Revolution*. New York: Knopf.

Woodward, C. Vann. 1966. *Reunion and Reaction: The Compromise of 1877 and the End of Reconstruction*. New York: Oxford University Press.

Wright, Erik Olin. 1979. *Class, Crisis, and the State*. London: Verso.

Wrong, Dennis H. 1980. *Power: Its Forms, Bases and Uses*. New York: Harper and Row.

Young, James Sterling. 1966. *The Washington Community, 1800–1828*. New York: Columbia University Press.

Zinn, Howard. 1980. *A People's History of the United States*. New York: Harper and Row.

About the Book and Editors

This book offers a comprehensive assessment of the major theoretical approaches to the study of American politics. Written by leading scholars in the field, the book's essays focus particularly on the contributions that competing macro- and microanalytic approaches make to our understanding of political change in America.

The essays include systematic overviews of the patterns of constancy and change that characterize American political history as well as comparative discussions of theoretical traditions in the study of American political change. The volume concludes with four provocative essays proposing new and integrated interpretations of American politics.

This is a path-breaking book that all scholars concerned with American politics will want to read and that all serious students of American politics will need to study. *The Dynamics of American Politics* is appropriate for graduate core seminars on American politics, undergraduate capstone courses on American politics, courses on political theory and approaches to political analysis, and rigorous lower-division courses on American politics.

Lawrence C. Dodd is professor of political science and director of the Center for the Study of American Politics at the University of Colorado, Boulder. He is the author of *Coalitions in Parliamentary Government* (1976), the coauthor of *Congress and the Administrative State* (1979), and coeditor of *Congress and Policy Change* (1986). He has served as president of the Southwestern Political Science Association, as a Congressional Fellow, and as a Hoover National Fellow. **Calvin C. Jillson** is associate professor of political science and director of the Keller Center for the Study of the First Amendment at the University of Colorado, Boulder. He is the author of *Constitution-Making: Conflict and Consensus in the Federal Convention of 1787* (1988) and coauthor of *Congressional Dynamics: Structure, Coordination, and Choice in the First American Congress, 1774–1789* (1994). He has served as chair of the political science department at the University of Colorado, Boulder, and as president of the Southwestern Political Science Association.

About the Contributors

JOHN ALDRICH is professor and chair of the Department of Political Science at Duke University. His teaching and research interests focus on American politics, formal theory, and methodology. His most recent book, with Paul Abramson and David Rohde, entitled *Change and Continuity in the 1988 Elections,* was published by Congressional Quarterly Press.

PAUL ALLEN BECK is chairman of the Department of Political Science at Ohio State University. His research on American political parties, voting behavior, political socialization, and electoral change has been published in leading political science journals; he is coauthor of *Party Politics in America* (1992) and coeditor of *Electoral Change in Advanced Industrial Democracies* (1984), among other books.

DAVID W. BRADY is the Bowen H. and Janice Arthur McCoy Professor of Political Science, Business, and the Environment in the Graduate School of Business as well as professor in the Political Science Department at Stanford University. His most recent book, *Critical Elections and Congressional Policy Making* (1988) won the 1989 Richard F. Fenno Prize as the best book published in the area of legislative studies.

WALTER DEAN BURNHAM holds the Frank C. Erwin, Jr., Centennial Chair in Government at the University of Texas, Austin. He has made numerous contributions in the field of American electoral politics and political history, including *Critical Elections and the Mainsprings of American Politics* (1982), along with dozens of journal articles. He is probably best known for his work on critical realignment as a defining change process in American politics.

MURRAY EDELMAN is WARF Senior Distinguished Research Professor of Political Science Emeritus, University of Wisconsin, Madison. His books include *The Symbolic Uses of Politics* (1964) and *Constructing the Political Spectacle* (1988).

EDWARD S. GREENBERG is professor of political science and director of the research program on political and economic change in the Institute of Behavioral Science at the University of Colorado, Boulder. He is the author of *The Struggle for Democracy* (1993), *Workplace Democracy* (1986), and *The American Political System* (1985) and is editor of several anthologies, including *Changes in the State* (1991). He is presently engaged in a NIH-funded research project that examines the impact of job routines and workplace authority relations on political participation and alienation.

RUSSELL L. HANSON is associate professor of political science at Indiana University, Bloomington. He is the author of *The Democratic Imagination in America: Conversations with Our Past* (1985)and coeditor of *Political Innovation and Conceptual Change* (1989) and *Reconsidering the Democratic Public* (1993). He is currently examining the impact of efforts to promote economic growth on states' willingness and ability to provide social welfare benefits.

HUGH HECLO is Clarence J. Robinson Professor at George Mason University and former professor of government at Harvard University. He is author of *Modern Social Politics* (1974), *Comparative Public Policy* (1976, coauthored with Arnold Heidenbaum and Carolyn Adams), and *A Government of Strangers* (1978). He served as chairman of the Ford Foundation's research committee on "Social Welfare and the American Future" and as a member of the Advisory Board for the American studies program at the Smithsonian Institution's Woodrow Wilson Center for Scholars.

ROBERT HUCKFELDT is professor of political science at Indiana University. His areas of interest are urban and electoral politics. He is author or coauthor of *Dynamic Modeling* (1982), *Politics in Context* (1986), *Race and the Decline of Class in American Politics* (1989), and *Citizens, Politics, and Social Communication* (forthcoming).

THEODORE J. LOWI has been the John L. Senior Professor of American Institutions at Cornell University since 1972. He has contributed to the study of American politics in a variety of areas, including political theory, public policy analysis, and American political behavior. He is the author or editor of a dozen books, including *The End of Liberalism* (2nd., 1979) and *The Personal President* (1985).

JANE J. MANSBRIDGE is Jane W. Long Professor of the Arts and Sciences in the Department of Political Science at Northwestern University and is a Faculty Fellow of the Center for Urban Affairs and Policy Research. She is author of *Beyond Adversary Democracy* (1983) and *Why We Lost the ERA* (1986) and editor of *Beyond Self-Interest* (1990). She is currently working on *Becoming a Feminist,* an analysis of the effects of social movements on nonactivists, based on interviews with working-class women.

KAREN ORREN is a professor in the Department of Political Science at UCLA. Her most recent book is *Belated Feudalism: Labor, the Law, and Liberal Development in the United States* (1991).

THEDA SKOCPOL is professor of sociology at Harvard University; she was previously professor of sociology and political science at the University of Chicago. Her first book, *States and Social Revolutions: A Comparative Analysis of France,*

Russia, and China (1979), won the 1979 C. Wright Mills Award and the 1980 American Sociological Association Award for a Distinguished Contribution to Scholarship. She was a founding member and the 1991–1992 president of the History and Politics Section of the American Political Science Association. Her most recent book, entitled *Protecting Soldiers and Mothers: The Political Origins of Social Policy in the United States* (1992), won the 1993 Woodrow Wilson Foundation Award.

STEPHEN SKOWRONEK is professor of Political Science at Yale University. He is the author of *Building a New American State: The Expansion of National Administrative Capacities, 1877–1920* (1982) and is the Founder and Managing Editor of *Studies in American Political Development: An Annual* (1986–).

CLARENCE N. STONE is professor of government and politics at the University of Maryland, College Park. He is a past recipient of the university's Distinguished Faculty Research Fellowship. Stone's most recent book, *Regime Politics: Governing Atlanta, 1946–1988*, won the American Political Science Association's Ralph Bunche Award and the Best Book Award of the APSA's Urban Politics Section. His current research interests include urban education, city politics, and political leadership.

SVEN H. STEINMO teaches comparative politics and American government at the University of Colorado, Boulder. He is coeditor of *Structuring Politics: Historical Institutionalism in Comparative Politics* (1992) and author of *Taxation and Democracy* (1993), a comparative analysis of the politics and development of taxation in Britain, Sweden, and the United States.

ELAINE K. SWIFT is assistant professor of Political Science at Dartmouth College. Her teaching and research interests focus on the development of American national institutions, particularly the U.S. Congress.

Index